Edited by

John J. Macionis
Kenyon College

Nijole V. Benokraitis
University of Baltimore

Bruce Ravelli
Mount Royal College

Seeing
Ourselves

Classic, Contemporary, and Cross-Cultural Readings in Sociology

Second Canadian Edition

PEARSON

Prentice
Hall

Toronto

To my siblings, Sharon, Lorraine, and Ross, and to my mother, Shirley.

—BR

Library and Archives Canada Cataloguing in Publication

Seeing ourselves : classic, contemporary, and cross-cultural readings in sociology / [edited by] John J. Macionis, Nijole V. Benokraitis, Bruce Ravelli.—2nd Canadian ed.

ISBN 0-13-197828-4

1. Sociology—Textbooks. 2. Sociology—Cross-cultural studies. I. Macionis, John J.
II. Benokraitis, Nijole V. (Nijole Vaicaitis) III. Ravelli, Bruce Douglas, 1963–

HM586.S44 2007   301   C2005-906476-5

Vice-President, Editorial Director: Michael J. Young
Senior Acquisitions Editor: Ky Pruesse
Sponsoring Editor: Carolin Sweig
Executive Marketing Manager: Judith Allen
Senior Developmental Editor: John Polanszky
Production Editor: Charlotte Morrison-Reed
Copy Editor: Reena Krindler
Proofreader: Anne Holloway
Production Coordinator: Janis Raisen
Composition: Laserwords Private Limited
Art Director: Julia Hall
Cover Design: Anthony Leung
Cover Image: Jon Feingersh/Masterfile

1 2 3 4 5   11 10 09 08 07

Printed and bound in the United States of America.

Contents

Preface

I remember reading C.W. Mills' article, *The promise of sociology*, for the first time while teaching anthropology at a small college in British Columbia. I was surprised by the impact that the article had on me and how Mills' perspective on society changed the way I viewed the social world. In fact, I was so inspired by this new perspective that the following year I left a tenured teaching position (in anthropology) and returned to school to complete my Ph.D. in sociology. For me, Mills' approach defines the very best of sociology and what it can offer those who study it— learning the ability to systematically reflect on the dynamic relationship between the individual and the social. For Mills, people exposed to what he termed the *sociological imagination* would be able to see more clearly the social landscape in which we all travel. *Seeing Ourselves*, Second Canadian Edition, continues our commitment to providing students with a unique opportunity to discover their sociological imagination through the exploration of sociology from personal, national and global perspectives.

Seeing Ourselves presents the very best of sociological thought, from the work of the discipline's pioneers to the men and women who are doing today's leading-edge research. The articles in this anthology explore Canadian and American social issues as well as the global trends influencing us all. This reader provides excellent material for a wide range of courses, including introductory sociology, social problems, cultural anthropology, social theory, social stratification, Canadian and American studies, women's studies, and marriage and the family.

This edition of *Seeing Ourselves* is completely revised and updated with forty percent more Canadian articles written by Canadian sociologists. The organization is also completely new and intended to facilitate a more logical flow through the material, while at the same time providing instructors and students with a versatile collection of readings that can be used to complement and enhance a variety of course structures. Further, this new edition is also slightly shorter than the first Canadian edition with 67 articles rather than the original 72, and therefore more manageable for a broad range of curricula. These modifications reflect feedback from both students and teachers and make *Seeing Ourselves*, Second Canadian Edition an even more inspiring resource than the first edition.

THE THREE C'S: CLASSIC, CONTEMPORARY, AND CROSS-CULTURAL

Since its introduction over a decade ago, the American edition of *Seeing Ourselves* has been a popular reader in the discipline. The second Canadian edition offers a diverse cross-section of the discipline and those areas of interest to sociologists. *Seeing Ourselves*, Second Canadian

Edition is not only the most extensive anthology currently available, it is the only one that systematically weaves together three themes into its selections. For each topic typically covered in a sociology course, three types of articles are offered: *classic, contemporary*, and *cross-cultural*.

Classic articles, (22 in all), are sociological statements of recognized importance and lasting significance. Included here are the ideas of sociology's founders and supporters – including Emile Durkheim, Karl Marx, Max Weber, W.E. Du Bois, Georg Simmel, as well as Margaret Mead, George Herbert Mead and Thomas Robert Malthus. Also found in the classic sections are more recent contributions by Alfred Kinsey, Samuel Bowles and Herbert Gintis, Jessie Bernard, John Porter, Erving Goffman, Peter Berger, C. Wright Mills, Lee Guemple, Talcott Parsons, and Jo Freeman.

Contemporary selections (23 in all and 21 of which are Canadian) focus on current sociological issues, controversies, and applications. These articles show sociologists at work and demonstrate the importance of investigating our social environment and the forces influencing it. Each article offer stimulating reading and thought-provoking insights about ourselves and the world around us. Among the contemporary selections some of the topics covered include: squeegee kids in Toronto, intensive hog farming, the defining features of Canadian sociology, the differences between Canadian and American values, adolescent girls' impressions of their bodies, Canadian children's socialization, life inside a Canadian biker gang, lesbians' use of "gaydar," how parents reconstruct their sons' earlier lives after finding out they are gay, female athletes' experiences with sexual harassment, the role ethnicity plays in Canadian society, how Native Canadians' identity has been defined by historical factors as well as the residential school system, the training of medical doctors in Canada, and how environmentalism and globalization influence our collective futures. All these articles demonstrate how the sociological

imagination can be used to achieve a deeper understanding of contemporary society.

The 22 *cross-cultural* selections offer sociological insights about cultural diversity around the world. Included are well-known works such as "Body Ritual among the Nacirema" by Horace Miner, "The Amish: A Small Society" by John Hostetler, J.M. Carrier's "Homosexual Behavior in Cross-Cultural Perspective," and Alan Thein Durning's "Supporting Indigenous Peoples". Other articles explore issues and problems including Japanese mothering practices, ethnically heterogamous marriages, domestic violence across cultures, prostitution as a world-wide business of sexual exploitation, female genital mutilation, the staggering burden of African poverty, Islam's view of women, and the rising global population. Cross-cultural selections stimulate critical thinking about social diversity across North America as well as broaden students' understanding of, and appreciation for, other cultures.

ORGANIZATION OF THE READER

The chapter sequences for *Seeing Ourselves*, Second Canadian Edition is completely new and better reflects the sequence of topics common to many textbooks used in introductory sociology. Now, instructors can more easily and effectively use these articles in a host of other courses, as well as assign articles in any order they wish. For each of the twenty-one general topics, a cluster of three or four articles is presented, each cluster including at least one classic, one contemporary, and one cross-cultural selection. The expansive coverage of these sixty-seven articles ensures that instructors can choose readings well suited to their own classes, preferences and course outcomes.

A NOTE ON LANGUAGE

All readings are presented in their original form but some may have been edited for length. Readers should be aware that some of the older selections—especially the *classic* selections—use male pronouns rather than more contemporary gender-neutral terminology.

TEACHING FEATURES

This reader has two features that enhance the learning of students. First, a brief introduction preceding each selection presents the essential argument and highlights important issues to keep in mind while completing the reading. Second, each article is followed by three or four "Critical-Thinking Questions" that develop the significance of the reading, help students evaluate their own learning, and stimulate class discussion.

SUPPLEMENTS

Instructors using *Seeing Ourselves*, Second Canadian Edition can take advantage of an Instructor's Manual and Test Item File. These supplements can be downloaded from a password-protected location on Pearson Education Canada's online catalogue (**vig.pearsoned.ca**). Simply search for the text, and then click on "Instructor" under "Resources" in the left hand menu. You can also contact your local sales representative for further information.

The new Instructor's Manual features a guide with suggestions for using the readings in *Seeing Ourselves*, Second Canadian Edition in conjunction with specific chapters typically found in an introductory sociology textbook. The Instructor's Manual also provides brief descriptions and summaries for each of the 67 readings in the text.

The Test Item File offers 6 multiple-choice and 4 essay questions for all 67 readings in *Seeing Ourselves*, Second Canadian Edition.

ACKNOWLEDGMENTS

I am grateful to many people for their help in preparing this reader. First, I would like to thank my colleagues at Mount Royal College who are a constant source of inspiration, as well as my colleagues from across Canada who provided helpful feedback on the development of this new edition. In particular I would like to thank Gerald Booth, University of Windsor; Dr. Raymond Foui, University of Manitoba; Bernie Hammond, King's University College; Cyndy Parker, New Brunswick Community College; Sian Reid, Carleton University; Dr. Sandra Rollings-Magnusson, Grant MacEwan College; Reuben N. Roth, Laurentian University; John Steckley, Humber Institute of Technology and Advanced Learning; and Laura Suski, Dalhousie University. Second, the efforts of the acquisition and editorial staff at Pearson Education have been invaluable. Patty Riediger, Acquisitions Editor, Carolin Sweig, Sponsoring Editor, Charlotte Morrison-Reed, Production Editor, and John Polanszky, Senior Developmental Editor were all a pleasure to work with. Third, I would like to thank all of my students (past, present and future) for their enthusiasm and their desire to learn more about the world – all of you inspire me to become a better teacher and sociologist. And finally, I would like to thank my family and friends for their confidence in me and their love, and in particular, my wonderful wife Sacha.

I welcome all faculty and students to share their thoughts and reactions to this reader with me in whatever form they find most convenient. You can write to me at: Bruce Ravelli, Department of Behavioural Sciences, Mount Royal College, 4825 Mount Royal Gate, S.W. Calgary, Alberta T3E 6K6. You can also send me an email at: bravelli@mtroyal.ca.

1

The Sociological Imagination

The Sociological Perspective

CLASSIC

CONTEMPORARY

CROSS-CULTURAL

C. Wright Mills

To C. Wright Mills, the sociological imagination *is a special way to engage with the world. To think sociologically is to realize that what we experience as personal problems are often widely shared by others similar to ourselves. Thus, many personal problems are actually social issues. For Mills, as one of sociology's most outspoken activists, the sociological imagination encouraged collective action that would change the world.*

Nowadays men often feel that their private lives are a series of traps. They sense that within their everyday worlds, they cannot overcome their troubles, and in this feeling, they are often quite correct: What ordinary men are directly aware of and what they try to do are bounded by the private orbits in which they live; their visions and their powers are limited to the close-up scenes of job, family, neighborhood; in other milieux, they move vicariously and remain spectators. And the more aware they become, however vaguely, of ambitions and of threats which transcend their immediate locales, the more trapped they seem to feel.

Alex Colville (1920–), *To Prince Edward Island*, 1965, acrylic emulsion on masonite, 61.9 x 92.5 cm. National Gallery of Canada, Ottawa. © NGC/MBAC.

Source: From *The Sociological Imagination* by C. Wright Mills. Copyright © 1959 by Oxford University Press, Inc. Renewed 1987 by Yaraslava Mills. Used by permission of Oxford University Press, Inc.

Underlying this sense of being trapped are seemingly impersonal changes in the very structure of continent-wide societies. The facts of contemporary history are also facts about the success and the failure of individual men and women. When a society is industrialized, a peasant becomes a worker; a feudal lord is liquidated or becomes a businessman. When classes rise or fall, a man is employed or unemployed; when the rate of investment goes up or down, a man takes new heart or goes broke. When wars happen, an insurance salesman becomes a rocket launcher; a store clerk, a radar man; a wife lives alone; a child grows up without a father. Neither the life of an individual nor the history of a society can be understood without understanding both.

Yet men do not usually define the troubles they endure

1

in terms of historical change and institutional contradiction. The well-being they enjoy, they do not usually impute to the big ups and downs of the societies in which they live. Seldom aware of the intricate connection between the patterns of their own lives and the course of world history, ordinary men do not usually know what this connection means for the kinds of men they are becoming and for the kinds of history-making in which they might take part. They do not possess the quality of mind essential to grasp the interplay of man and society, of biography and history, of self and world. They cannot cope with their personal troubles in such ways as to control the structural transformations that usually lie behind them.

Surely it is no wonder. In what period have so many men been so totally exposed at so fast a pace to such earthquakes of change? That Americans have not known such catastrophic changes as have the men and women of other societies is due to historical facts that are now quickly becoming "merely history." The history that now affects every man is world history. Within this scene and this period, in the course of a single generation, one-sixth of mankind is transformed from all that is feudal and backward into all that is modern, advanced, and fearful. Political colonies are freed; new and less visible forms of imperialism installed. Revolutions occur; men feel the intimate grip of new kinds of authority. Totalitarian societies rise, and are smashed to bits—or succeed fabulously. After two centuries of ascendancy, capitalism is shown up as only one way to make society into an industrial apparatus. After two centuries of hope, even formal democracy is restricted to a quite small portion of mankind. Everywhere in the underdeveloped world, ancient ways of life are broken up and vague expectations become urgent demands. Everywhere in the overdeveloped world, the means of authority and of violence become total in scope and bureaucratic in form. Humanity itself now lies before us, the super-nation at either pole concentrating its

most coordinated and massive efforts upon the preparation of World War III.

The very shaping of history now outpaces the ability of men to orient themselves in accordance with cherished values. And which values? Even when they do not panic, men often sense that older ways of feeling and thinking have collapsed and that newer beginnings are ambiguous to the point of moral stasis. Is it any wonder that ordinary men feel they cannot cope with the larger worlds with which they are so suddenly confronted? That they cannot understand the meaning of their epoch for their own lives? That—in defense of selfhood—they become morally insensible, trying to remain altogether private men? Is it any wonder that they come to be possessed by a sense of the trap?

It is not only information that they need—in this Age of Fact, information often dominates their attention and overwhelms their capacities to assimilate it. It is not only the skills of reason that they need—although their struggles to acquire these often exhaust their limited moral energy.

What they need, and what they feel they need, is a quality of mind that will help them to use information and to develop reason in order to achieve lucid summations of what is going on in the world and of what may be happening within themselves. It is this quality, I am going to contend, that journalists and scholars, artists and publics, scientists and editors are coming to expect of what may be called the sociological imagination.

The sociological imagination enables its possessor to understand the larger historical scene in terms of its meaning for the inner life and the external career of a variety of individuals. It enables him to take into account how individuals, in the welter of their daily experience, often become falsely conscious of their social positions. Within that welter, the framework of modern society is sought, and within that framework the psychologies of a variety of men and women are formulated. By such means the personal uneasiness of individuals is focused upon explicit troubles and the indifference of publics is transformed into involvement with public issues.

The first fruit of this imagination—and the first lesson of the social science that embodies it—is the idea that the individual can understand his own experience and gauge his own fate only by locating himself within his period, that he can know his own chances in life by becoming aware of those of all individuals in his circumstances. In many ways it is a terrible lesson; in many ways [it is] a magnificent one. We do not know the limits of man's capacities for supreme effort or willing degradation, for agony or glee, for pleasurable brutality or the sweetness of reason. But in our time we have come to know that the limits of "human nature" are frighteningly broad. We have come to know that every individual lives, from one generation to the next, in some society, that he lives out a biography, and that he lives it out within some historical sequence. By the fact of his living he contributes, however minutely, to the shaping of this society and to the course of its history, even as he is made by society and by its historical push and shove.

The sociological imagination enables us to grasp history and biography and the relations between the two within society. That is its task and its promise. To recognize this task and this promise is the mark of the classic social analyst. It is characteristic of Herbert Spencer—turgid, polysyllabic, comprehensive; of E. A. Ross—graceful, muckraking, upright; of Auguste Comte and Emile Durkheim; of the intricate and subtle Karl Mannheim. It is the quality of all that is intellectually excellent in Karl Marx; it is the clue to Thorstein Veblen's brilliant and ironic insight, to Joseph Schumpeter's many-sided constructions of reality; it is the basis of the psychological sweep of W. E. H. Lecky no less than of the profundity and clarity of Max Weber. And it is the signal of what is best in contemporary studies of man and society.

No social study that does not come back to the problems of biography, of history, and of their

intersections within a society has completed its intellectual journey. Whatever the specific problems of the classic social analysts, however limited or however broad the features of social reality they have examined, those who have been imaginatively aware of the promise of their work have consistently asked three sorts of questions:

1. What is the structure of this particular society as a whole? What are its essential components, and how are they related to one another? How does it differ from other varieties of social order? Within it, what is the meaning of any particular feature for its continuance and for its change?

2. Where does this society stand in human history? What are the mechanics by which it is changing? What is its place within and its meaning for the development of humanity as a whole? How does any particular feature we are examining affect, and how is it affected by, the historical period in which it moves? And this period—what are its essential features? How does it differ from other periods? What are its characteristic ways of history-making?

3. What varieties of men and women now prevail in this society and in this period? And what varieties are coming to prevail? In what ways are they selected and formed, liberated and repressed, made sensitive and blunted? What kinds of "human nature" are revealed in the conduct and character we observe in this society in this period? And what is the meaning for "human nature" of each and every feature of the society we are examining?

Whether the point of interest is a great power state or a minor literary mood, a family, a prison, a creed—these are the kinds of questions the best social analysts have asked. They are the intellectual pivots of classic studies of man in society—and they are the questions inevitably raised by any mind possessing the sociological imagination. For that imagination is the capacity to shift from one perspective to another—from the political to the psychological; from examination of a single family to comparative assessment of the national budgets of the world; from the theological school to the military establishment; from considerations of an oil industry to studies of contemporary poetry. It is the capacity to range from the most impersonal and remote transformations to the most intimate features of the human self—and to see the relations between the two. [At the b]ack of its use there is always the urge to know the social and historical meaning of the individual in the society and in the period in which he has his quality and his being.

That, in brief, is why it is by means of the sociological imagination that men now hope to grasp what is going on in the world, and to understand what is happening in themselves as minute points of the intersections of biography and history within society. In large part, contemporary man's self-conscious view of himself as at least an outsider, if not a permanent stranger, rests upon an absorbed realization of social relativity and of the transformative power of history. The sociological imagination is the most fruitful form of this self-consciousness. By its use men whose mentalities have swept only a series of limited orbits often come to feel as if [they have] suddenly awakened in a house with which they had only supposed themselves to be familiar. Correctly or incorrectly, they often come to feel that they can now provide themselves with adequate summations, cohesive assessments, comprehensive orientations. Older decisions that once appeared sound now seem to them products of a mind unaccountably dense. Their capacity for astonishment is made lively again. They acquire a new way of thinking, they experience a transvaluation of values: In a word, by their reflection and by their sensibility, they realize the cultural meaning of the social sciences.

Perhaps the most fruitful distinction with which the sociological imagination works is between "the personal troubles of milieu" and "the public issues of social structure." This distinction is an essential tool of the sociological imagination and a feature of all classic work in social science.

Troubles occur within the character of the individual and within the range of his immediate relations with others; they have to do with his self and with those limited areas of social life of which he is directly and personally aware. Accordingly, the statement and the resolution of troubles properly lie within the individual as a biographical entity and within the scope of his immediate milieu—the social setting that is directly open to his personal experience and to some extent his willful activity. A trouble is a private matter: Values cherished by an individual are felt by him to be threatened.

Issues have to do with matters that transcend these local environments of the individual and the range of his inner life. They have to do with the organization of many such milieux into the institutions of an historical society as a whole, with the ways in which various milieux overlap and interpenetrate to form the larger structure of social and historical life. An issue is a public matter: Some value cherished by publics is felt to be threatened. Often there is a debate about what that value really is and about what it is that really threatens it. This debate is often without focus if only because it is the very nature of an issue, unlike even widespread trouble, that it cannot very well be defined in terms of the immediate and everyday environments of ordinary men. An issue, in fact, often involves a crisis in institutional arrangements, and often too it involves what Marxists call "contradictions" or "antagonisms."

In these terms, consider unemployment. When, in a city of 100,000, only one man is unemployed, that is his personal trouble, and for its relief we properly look to the character of the man, his skills, and his immediate opportunities. But when in a nation of 50 million employees, 15 million men are unemployed, that is an issue, and we may not hope to find its solution within the range of opportunities open to any one individual. The very structure of opportunities has collapsed. Both the correct statement of the problem and the range of possible solutions require us to consider the economic and political institutions of the society and not merely the personal situation and character of a scatter of individuals.

Consider war. The personal problem of war, when it occurs, may be how to survive it or how to die in it with honor; how to make money out of it; how to climb into the higher safety of the military apparatus; or how to contribute to the war's termination. In short, according to one's values, to find a set of milieux and within it to survive the war or make one's death in it meaningful. But the structural issues of war have to do with its causes; with what types of men it throws up into command; with its effects upon economic and political, family and religious institutions, with the unorganized irresponsibility of a world of nation-states.

Consider marriage. Inside a marriage a man and a woman may experience personal troubles, but when the divorce rate during the first four years of marriage is 250 out of every 1,000 attempts, this is an indication of a structural issue having to do with the institutions of marriage and the family and other institutions that bear upon them.

Or consider the metropolis—the horrible, beautiful, ugly, magnificent sprawl of the great city. For many upper-class people, the personal solution to "the problem of the city" is to have an apartment with private garage under it in the heart of the city and, forty miles out, a house by Henry Hill, garden by Garrett Eckbo, on a hundred acres of private land. In these two controlled environments—with a small staff at each end and a private helicopter connection—most people could solve many of the problems of personal milieux caused by the facts of the city. But all this, however splendid, does not solve the public issues that the structural fact of the city poses. What should be done with this wonderful monstrosity? Break it up into scattered units, combining residence and work? Refurbish it as it stands? Or, after evacuation, dynamite it and build new cities according to new plans in new places? What should those plans be? And who is to decide and to accomplish whatever choice is made? These are structural issues; to confront them and to solve them requires us to consider political and economic issues that affect innumerable milieux.

Insofar as an economy is so arranged that slumps occur, the problem of unemployment becomes incapable of personal solution. Insofar as war is inherent in the nation-state system and in the uneven industrialization of the world, the ordinary individual in his restricted milieu will be powerless—with or without psychiatric aid—to solve the troubles this system or lack of system imposes upon him. Insofar as the family as an institution turns women into darling little slaves and men into their chief providers and unweaned dependents, the problem of a satisfactory marriage remains incapable of purely private solution. Insofar as the overdeveloped megalopolis and the overdeveloped automobile are built-in features of the overdeveloped society, the issues of urban living will not be solved by personal ingenuity and private wealth.

What we experience in various and specific milieux, I have noted, is often caused by structural changes. Accordingly, to understand the changes of many personal milieux, we are required to look beyond them. And the number and variety of such structural changes increase as the institutions within which we live become more embracing and more intricately connected with one another. To be aware of the idea of social structure and to use it with sensibility is to be capable of tracing such linkages among a great variety of milieux. To be able to do that is to possess the sociological imagination....

CRITICAL THINKING QUESTIONS

1. Why do people tend to think of the operation of society in personal terms?
2. What are the practical benefits of the sociological perspective? Are there liabilities?
3. What does Mills have in mind when he suggests that by developing the sociological imagination, we learn to assemble facts into social analysis?

The Sociological Perspective		**2**
CLASSIC		
CONTEMPORARY		Invitation to Sociology
CROSS-CULTURAL		*Peter L. Berger*

Using the sociological perspective changes how we perceive the surrounding world and ourselves. Peter Berger compares thinking sociologically with entering a new and unfamiliar society—one in which "things are no longer what they seem." This article should cause you to rethink your social world and become aware of issues you may have never before considered.

…It can be said that the first wisdom of sociology is this—things are not what they seem. This too is a deceptively simple statement. It ceases to be simple after a while. Social reality turns out to have many layers of meaning. The discovery of each new layer changes the perception of the whole.

Anthropologists use the term "culture shock" to describe the impact of a totally new culture upon a newcomer. In an extreme instance such shock will be experienced by the Western explorer who is told, halfway through dinner, that he is eating the nice old lady he had been chatting with the previous day—a shock with predictable physiological if not moral consequences. Most explorers no longer encounter cannibalism in their travels today. However, the first encounters

with polygamy or with puberty rites or even with the way some nations drive their automobiles can be quite a shock to an American visitor. With the shock may go not only disapproval or disgust but a sense of excitement that things can *really* be that different from what they are at home. To some extent, at least, this is the excitement of any first travel abroad. The experience of sociological discovery could be described as "culture shock" minus geographical displacement. In other words, the sociologist travels at home—with shocking results. He is unlikely to find that he is eating a nice old lady for dinner. But the discovery, for instance, that his own church has considerable money invested in the missile industry or that a few blocks from his home there are people who engage in cultic orgies may not be drastically different in emotional impact. Yet we would not want to imply that sociological discoveries are always or even usually outrageous to moral sentiment. Not at all. What they have in common with exploration in distant lands, however, is the

Source: From *Invitation to Sociology* by Peter L. Berger. Copyright © 1963 by Peter L. Berger, Bantam, Doubleday Dell Publishing Group, Inc. Reprinted with permission of Bantam, Doubleday Dell Publishing Group, Inc.

sudden illumination of new and unsuspected facets of human existence in society. This is the excitement and, as we shall try to show later, the humanistic justification of sociology.

People who like to avoid shocking discoveries, who prefer to believe that society is just what they were taught in Sunday school, who like the safety of the rules and the maxims of what Alfred Schuetz has called the "world-taken-for-granted," should stay away from sociology. People who feel no temptation before closed doors, who have no curiosity about human beings, who are content to admire scenery without wondering about the people who live in those houses on the other side of that river, should probably also stay away from sociology. They will find it unpleasant or, at any rate, unrewarding. People who are interested in human beings only if they can change, convert, or reform them should also be warned, for they will find sociology much less useful than they hoped. And people whose interest is mainly in their own conceptual constructions will do just as well to turn to the study of little white mice. Sociology will be satisfying, in the long run, only to those who can think of nothing more entrancing than to watch men and to understand things human....

To ask sociological questions, then, presupposes that one is interested in looking some distance beyond the commonly accepted or officially defined goals of human actions. It presupposes a certain awareness that human events have different levels of meaning, some of which are hidden from the consciousness of everyday life. It may even presuppose a measure of suspicion about the way in which human events are officially interpreted by the authorities, be they political, juridical, or religious in character. If one is willing to go as far as that, it would seem evident that not all historical circumstances are equally favorable for the development of sociological perspective.

It would appear plausible, in consequence, that sociological thought would have the best chance to develop in historical circumstances marked by severe jolts to the self-conception, especially the official and authoritative and generally accepted self-conception, of a culture. It is only in such circumstances that perceptive men are likely to be motivated to think beyond the assertions of this self-conception and, as a result, question the authorities....

Sociological perspective can then be understood in terms of such phrases as "seeing through," "looking behind," very much as such phrases would be employed in common speech—"seeing through his game," "looking behind the scenes"—in other words, "being up on all the tricks."

...We could think of this in terms of a common experience of people living in large cities. One of the fascinations of a large city is the immense variety of human activities taking place behind the seemingly anonymous and endlessly undifferentiated rows of houses. A person who lives in such a city will time and again experience surprise or even shock as he discovers the strange pursuits that some men engage in quite unobtrusively in houses that, from the outside, look like all the others on a certain street. Having had this experience once or twice, one will repeatedly find oneself walking down a street, perhaps late in the evening, and wondering what may be going on under the bright lights showing through a line of drawn curtains. An ordinary family engaged in pleasant talk with guests? A scene of desperation amid illness or death? Or a scene of debauched pleasures? Perhaps a strange cult or a dangerous conspiracy? The facades of the houses cannot tell us, proclaiming nothing but an architectural conformity to the tastes of some group or class that may not even inhabit the street any longer. The social mysteries lie behind the facades. The wish to penetrate these mysteries is an analogon to sociological curiosity. In some cities that are suddenly struck by calamity this wish may be abruptly realized. Those who have experienced wartime bombings know of the sudden encounters with unsuspected (and sometimes unimaginable) fellow tenants in the air-raid shelter of one's apartment building. Or they can recollect the startling morning sight of a house hit by a bomb during the night, neatly sliced in half, the facade torn away and the previously hidden interior mercilessly revealed in the daylight. But in most cities that one may normally live in, the facades must be penetrated by one's own inquisitive intrusions. Similarly, there are historical situations in which the facades of society are violently torn apart and all but the most incurious are forced to see that there was a reality behind the facades all along. Usually this does not happen, and the facades continue to confront us with seemingly rocklike permanence. The perception of the reality behind the facades then demands a considerable intellectual effort.

A few examples of the way in which sociology "looks behind" the facades of social structures might serve to make our argument clearer. Take, for instance, the political organization of a community. If one wants to find out how a modern American city is governed, it is very easy to get the official information about this subject. The city will have a charter, operating under the laws of the state. With some advice from informed individuals, one may look up various statutes that define the constitution of the city. Thus one may find out that this particular community has a city-manager form of administration, or that party affiliations do not appear on the ballot in municipal elections, or that the city government participates in a regional water district. In similar fashion, with the help of some newspaper reading, one may find out the officially recognized political problems of the community. One may read that the city plans to annex a certain suburban area, or that there has been a change in the zoning ordinances to facilitate industrial development in another area, or even that one of the members of the city council has been accused of using his office for personal gain. All such matters still occur on the, as it were, visible, official, or public level of political life. However, it would be an exceedingly naive

person who would believe that this kind of information gives him a rounded picture of the political reality of that community. The sociologist will want to know above all the constituency of the "informal power structure" (as it has been called by Floyd Hunter, an American sociologist interested in such studies), which is a configuration of men and their power that cannot be found in any statutes, and probably cannot be read about in the newspapers. The political scientist or the legal expert might find it very interesting to compare the city charter with the constitutions of other similar communities. The sociologist will be far more concerned with discovering the way in which powerful vested interests influence or even control the actions of officials elected under the charter. These vested interests will not be found in city hall, but rather in the executive suites of corporations that may not even be located in that community, in the private mansions of a handful of powerful men, perhaps in the offices of certain labor unions, or even, in some instances, in the headquarters of criminal organizations. When the sociologist concerns himself with power, he will "look behind" the official mechanisms that are supposed to regulate power in the community. This does not necessarily mean that he will regard the official mechanisms as totally ineffective or their legal definition as totally illusionary. But at the very least he will insist that there is another level of reality to be investigated in the particular system of power. In some cases he might conclude that to look for real power in the publicly recognized places is quite delusional....

Let us take one further example. In Western countries, and especially in America, it is assumed that men and women marry because they are in love. There is a broadly based popular mythology about the character of love as a violent, irresistible emotion that strikes where it will, a mystery that is the goal of most young people and often of the not-so-young as well. As soon as one investigates, however, which people actually marry each other, one finds that the lightning-shaft of Cupid seems to be guided rather strongly within very definite channels of class, income, education, [and] racial and religious background. If one then investigates a little further into the behavior that is engaged in prior to marriage under the rather misleading euphemism of "courtship," one finds channels of interaction that are often rigid to the point of ritual. The suspicion begins to dawn on one that, most of the time, it is not so much the emotion of love that creates a certain kind of relationship, but that carefully predefined and often planned relationships eventually generate the desired emotion. In other words, when certain conditions are met or have been constructed, one allows oneself "to fall in love." The sociologist investigating our patterns of "courtship" and marriage soon discovers a complex web of motives related in many ways to the entire institutional structure within which an individual lives his life—class, career, economic ambition, aspirations of power and prestige. The miracle of love now begins to look somewhat synthetic. Again, this need not mean in any given instance that the sociologist will declare the romantic interpretation to be an illusion. But, once more, he will look beyond the immediately given and publicly approved interpretations....

We would contend, then, that there is a debunking motif inherent in sociological consciousness. The sociologist will be driven time and again, by the very logic of his discipline, to debunk the social systems he is studying. This unmasking tendency need not necessarily be due to the sociologist's temperament or inclinations. Indeed, it may happen that the sociologist, who as an individual may be of a conciliatory disposition and quite disinclined to disturb the comfortable assumptions on which he rests his own social existence, is nevertheless compelled by what he is doing to fly in the face of what those around him take for granted. In other words, we would contend that the roots of the debunking motif in sociology are not psychological but methodological. The sociological frame of reference, with its built-in procedure of looking for levels of reality other than those given in the official interpretations of society, carries with it a logical imperative to unmask the pretensions and the propaganda by which men cloak their actions with each other. This unmasking imperative is one of the characteristics of sociology particularly at home in the temper of the modern era....

CRITICAL THINKING QUESTIONS

1. How can we explain the fact that people within any society tend to take their own way of life for granted?
2. What does Berger think is the justification for studying sociology?
3. What is involved in sociological "debunking"? How are others likely to respond to sociological insights?

3

Women and the Birth of Sociology

Patricia Madoo Lengermann and Jill Niebrugge-Brantley

Most beginning students of sociology know about Karl Marx, Max Weber, and Emile Durkheim; but Harriet Martineau, Ida Wells-Barnett, Anna Julia Cooper, Charlotte Perkins Gilman, and other women were also important founders of the discipline.

The history of sociology's theories is conventionally told as a history of white male agency—an account of the theoretical contributions of a "founding" generation of men: Auguste Comte, Herbert Spencer, and Karl Marx, writing in the middle of the nineteenth century; expanded by a second, "classic" generation of men: Emile Durkheim, Max Weber, Georg Simmel, George Herbert Mead, and Robert E. Park, who wrote between 1890 and 1930. This history is presented as an account of the natural way things occurred, a chronicle beyond the powers of human tellers to change. In contrast, we portray this history as a social construction arising out of the discipline's power arrangements, and like all histories, reflecting an ongoing conflict between exclusionary and inclusionary values and practices (Becker, 1971; Lemert, 1995; D. Smith, 1987).

The claim that a group has been "written out" of history is different from the claim that a group has been "invisible." "Invisibility" suggests not being seen, that is, never having one's presence

acknowledged as significant—a concept applied by many African Americans to their experience of marginalization (e.g., Collins, 1990; Cooper, 1892; DuBois, 1903; Ellison, 1952; Lorde, 1984; Rollins, 1985). "Being written out" suggests having once been seen as a presence in a community and then having been erased from its record. For several reasons, the case of the fifteen women sociologists treated in this volume is an instance of erasure rather than invisibility. First, almost all these women were well-known public figures in their lifetime, larger than the fledgling discipline of sociology they helped create; like the work of Marx, Max Weber, or Durkheim, their work has relevance for all the social sciences. Second, they created social theory and did sociology in the same times and places as the male founders (see 3.1). Third, they were widely recognized by their contemporaries, including male sociologists, as significant social analysts. Fourth, they all acted as members of a sociological community, meeting at least one of the following criteria: employment as a sociologist, membership in a national sociological association, publication framed by an explicit concern with sociological principles, self-identification as a sociologist and recognition by

Source: From *The Women Founders: Sociology and Social Theory, 1830–1930,* eds. Patricia Madoo Lengermann and Jill Niebrugge-Brantley. Copyright © 1998 McGraw-Hill.

FIGURE 3.1   Lifelines of Women and Men Founders of Sociology

1790	1800	1810	1820	1830	1840	1850	1860	1870	1880	1890	1900	1910	1920	1930	1940	1950	1960

```
        Auguste Comte 1798–1857 _ _ _ _ _ _ _ _
      Harriet Martineau 1802–1876 _ _ _ _ _ _ _ _ _ _ _ _ _
          Karl Marx 1818–1883 _ _ _ _ _ _ _ _ _ _ _ _ _ _ _
        Herbert Spencer 1820–1903 _ _ _ _ _ _ _ _ _ _ _ _ _ _ _ _ _ _
                          Anna Julia Cooper 1858–1964 _ _ _ _ _ _ _ _ _ _ _ _ _ _ _ _ _ _ _ _ _ _ _ _ _
                           Emile Durkheim 1858–1917 _ _ _ _ _ _ _ _ _
                              Julia Lathrop 1858–1932 _ _ _ _ _ _ _ _ _ _ _ _ _ _ _ _
                             Georg Simmel 1858–1918 _ _ _ _ _ _ _ _ _ _
                             Marion Talbot 1858–1947 _ _ _ _ _ _ _ _ _ _ _ _ _ _ _ _ _ _ _ _
                        Beatrice Potter Webb 1858–1943 _ _ _ _ _ _ _ _ _ _ _ _ _ _ _ _ _
                           Florence Kelley 1859–1932 _ _ _ _ _ _ _ _ _ _ _ _ _ _ _ _
                              Jane Addams 1860–1935 _ _ _ _ _ _ _ _ _ _ _ _ _ _ _ _
                  Charlotte Perkins Gilman 1860–1935 _ _ _ _ _ _ _ _ _ _ _ _ _
                           Ida B. Wells-Barnett 1862–1931 _ _ _ _ _ _ _ _ _ _ _
                       George Herbert Mead 1863–1931 _ _ _ _ _ _ _ _ _ _
                             W. I. Thomas 1863–1947 _ _ _ _ _ _ _ _ _ _ _ _ _ _ _ _ _ _ _ _ _
                             Robert E. Park 1864–1944 _ _ _ _ _ _ _ _ _ _ _ _ _ _ _ _ _ _
                              Max Weber 1864–1920 _ _ _ _ _ _ _ _ _ _
                  Sophonisba Breckinridge 1866–1948 _ _ _ _ _ _ _ _ _ _ _ _ _
                    Annie Marion MacLean ca. 1870–1934 _ _ _ _ _ _
                         Marianne Weber 1870–1954 _ _ _ _ _ _ _ _ _ _ _ _ _ _ _ _ _ _ _ _ _
                         Frances Kellor 1873–1952 _ _ _ _ _ _ _ _ _ _ _ _ _ _ _ _ _ _ _
                             Edith Abbott 1876–1957 _ _ _ _ _ _ _ _ _ _ _ _ _ _ _ _ _ _ _ _ _
                            Grace Abbott 1878–1939 _ _ _ _ _ _ _ _ _ _ _
```

contemporaries as a sociologist (Käsler, 1981; Deegan, 1991).

Martineau—whose *Illustrations of Political Economy* (1832–1834) outsold even Charles Dickens (Hoecker-Drysdale 1992)—was Britain's preeminent woman of letters until her death, writing social analysis, journalism, history, novels, children's stories, and travel books. Long identified in the history of sociology for her 1853 translation and abridgement of Comte, she was herself writing sociology as early as 1834, drafting what would become the first major statement of method, *How to Observe Morals and Manners* (1838b) and testing her methodology in her classic study *Society in America* (1836). Addams was the founder of Hull-House, the famous Chicago social settlement; a major spokesperson for Progressive reform on behalf of immigrants, trade unions, women, children, working-class people, and African Americans; and consistently named in public opinion polls as one of the most admired Americans (Davis, 1973; Daniel Levine, 1971).

At Hull-House, she administered a major research institution, drawing on her experiences there to formulate a social theory in eight major books and some 200 articles. She self-identified as a sociologist; taught sociology; was a member of the American Sociological Society (ASS)—until 1959 the name of the American Sociological Association (ASA); published in the *American Journal of Sociology (AJS);* and had significant relationships with Mead, Park, W. I. Thomas, Albion Small, and Ernest Burgess (Deegan, 1988). Gilman was widely regarded as the leading feminist intellectual of her day. Her *Women and Economics* (1898) went through nine printings by 1920, was translated into seven languages, and was the bible of many women's college student bodies (Ceplair, 1991). Besides the classic feminist novella *The Yellow Wallpaper* (1892) and some 2,000 pieces of journalism, poetry, and prose, she wrote six significant works of formal social theory, including *Women and Economics, Human Work* (1904), and *The Man-Made World*

(1911). She also published in the *AJS,* was a member of the ASS, and maintained intellectual relationships with Lester Ward and E. A. Ross.

Wells-Barnett spearheaded national and international anti-lynching campaigns, writing major analyses of lynching—*Southern Horrors* (1892) and *A Red Record* (1895)—and carrying the battle to Britain, where she often spoke to crowds in the thousands. She was an active organizer for African American civil rights, helping to found the National Association for the Advancement of Colored People (NAACP). Cooper's major book *A Voice from the South* (1892) received superlative reviews from black and white publications alike, establishing her as a prominent intellectual and spokesperson for African American women; she was one of two women to address the world's first Pan-African Conference in London in 1900. Cooper and Wells-Barnett created a genuine American non-Marxian conflict theory, in which they spoke of the sociological framing of their argument; but American racism made tentative any relationship between them and white professional sociology, although both knew and worked with black sociologist W. E. B. DuBois. Marianne Weber lived at the center of German sociological circles and debated the ideas of both Simmel and her husband Max in her own writings. She was a leading figure in the German feminist movement, the first woman to be elected to a German parliament, and the author of nine books of social analysis and sociology, including her monumental work on the legal position of women, *Ehefrau und Mutter in der Rechtsentwicklung (Marriage, Motherhood, and the Law)* (1907), and her collected essays, *Frauenfragen und Frauengedanken (Reflections on Women and Women's Issues)* (1919). She secured Max's position within sociology after his death by editing and publishing ten volumes of his work and writing her important interpretive biography of him.

Webb was tutored by Spencer, self-identified as a sociologist, taught sociology, worked as a social investigator on the major empirical study of her age (Charles Booth's *Life and Labour of the People of London*), and did her own independent investigations, leading to the socialist reform classic *The Co-operative Movement in Great Britain* (1891). With her husband Sidney, she researched and co-authored eleven voluminous works of empirical sociology that formed the blueprint for the British welfare state. All the members of the Chicago Women's School of Sociology (hereafter referred to as the Chicago Women's School or the Chicago Women) wrote prolifically as social analysts, all publishing in the *AJS*. Many were prominent public figures: Kelley headed the National Consumers League (1899–1932); Lathrop (1912–20)—and then Grace Abbott (1920–34)— served as chief of the Children's Bureau, the highest-ranking woman in the federal government at that time; Edith Abbott and Breckinridge founded the University of Chicago's School of Social Service Administration (1922); Talbot was dean of women at the University of Chicago (1893–1925); Kellor was a founder and executive officer of the American Arbitration League (1926–53); Kelley knew Friedrich Engels, maintained a correspondence with him until his death, and did the first English translation of *The Condition of the Working Class in England in 1844*; MacLean studied with Small, Mead, and Charles Henderson; Keller also studied with Henderson; Edith Abbott, Grace Abbott, and Breckinridge are all referenced in Park and Burgess's *Introduction to the Science of Sociology;* Talbot served as an associate editor of the *AJS* from its founding by Small to her retirement in 1925.

These women knew each other or each other's work. Gilman, Webb, Weber, and Wells-Barnett all visited Hull-House, which was, of course, the working base for Addams and most of the Chicago Women. Many of them read Gilman's *Women and Economics*——Webb, Weber, Addams, Kelley, Lathrop, and Talbot. Addams published with Wells-Barnett on lynching on at least two occasions, one of which was in a remarkable issue of *Survey* in February of 1913 in which Addams, Wells-Barnett, Breckinridge, and DuBois all analyze the problem of race. Addams, Wells-Barnett, Kelley, and Breckinridge participated in the founding of the NAACP. Hull-House residents, including Addams,

Lathrop, and Kelley, used Webb's *The Co-operative Movement in Great Britain* in preparation for their own venture into cooperative housing for working women. The persons most outside this network are Martineau, a full generation earlier than the rest of the women, and Cooper, whose life course rarely took her to Chicago. Yet Edith Abbott knew and responded to Martineau's work on women's employment in America, and Gilman refers to Martineau's struggle to overcome gender barriers to her career as a social analyst. And Cooper spoke in Chicago in 1893 at the white feminist Women's Congress, was active, as was Wells-Barnett, in the National Federation of Colored Women's Clubs and the African American settlement house movement, and wrote a sympathetic response to Gilman's suicide.

These women knew that they were part of a larger movement to create a science of society and had their own sense of what that science should be: a project of social critique in which research and theory had as a morally necessary focus the description, analysis, and correction of social inequality. The women vary in terms of the particular inequality focused on—gender, class, race, ethnicity, age, or combinations thereof; the relative balance between research and theory, and the choice of research strategy and theoretical method. Working out this commitment to critical social theory, these women engaged with sociology and the sociological community at the moment in which the discipline was itself emerging. Their varying relationships to that community thus reflect both the instability of sociology's emerging identity and the effects of gender, class, and race on access to what would become a formal academic enterprise, the province of educated white men. But at the moment these women were writing, sociology was as much their intellectual project as the men's; it is only in the retelling that they have disappeared.

CRITICAL THINKING QUESTIONS

1. What does it mean to say that women have been "written out" of sociology's history? Why did this happen?
2. What issues or ideas did sociology's women founders have in common?
3. What is the importance today of recognizing the contributions of sociology's women founders?

The Sociological Perspective

CLASSIC

CONTEMPORARY

CROSS-CULTURAL

4

Body Ritual Among the Nacirema

Horace Miner

Most people take their lives for granted; when they think about society at all, they usually view it as both natural and good. To help us step back from our society, anthropologist Horace Miner describes the Nacirema, a peculiar people living in North America (whose lives should seem familiar). Miner's intellectual sleight of hand illustrates how the sociological perspective involves detachment, so that everyday life becomes something new and unusual.

The anthropologist has become so familiar with the diversity of ways in which different peoples behave in similar situations that he is not apt to be surprised by even the most exotic customs. In fact, if all of the logically possible combinations of behavior have not been found somewhere in the world, he is apt to suspect that they must be present in some yet undescribed tribe. This point has, in fact, been expressed with respect to clan organization by Murdock (1949: 71). In this light, the magical beliefs and practices of the Nacirema present such unusual aspects that it seems desirable to describe them as an example of the extremes to which human behavior can go.

Professor Linton first brought the ritual of the Nacirema to the attention of anthropologists twenty years ago (1936: 326), but the culture of this people is still very poorly understood. They are a North American group living in the territory between the Canadian Cree, the Yaqui and Tarahumare of Mexico, and the Carib and

Source: "Body Ritual among the Nacirema" by Horace Miner. Reproduced by permission of the American Anthropological Association from *American Anthropologist*, vol. 58, no. 3, June, 1956. Not for further reproduction.

Arawak of the Antilles. Little is known of their origin, although tradition states that they came from the east. According to Nacirema mythology, their nation was originated by a culture hero, Notgnihsaw, who is otherwise known for two great feats of strength—the throwing of a piece of wampum across the river Pa-To-Mac and the chopping down of a cherry tree in which the Spirit of Truth resided.

Nacirema culture is characterized by a highly developed market economy which has evolved in a rich natural habitat. While much of the people's time is devoted to economic pursuits, a large part of the fruits of these labors and a considerable portion of the day are spent in ritual activity. The focus of this activity is the human body, the appearance and health of which loom as a dominant concern in the ethos of the people. While such concern is certainly not unusual, its ceremonial aspects and associated philosophy are unique.

The fundamental belief underlying the whole system appears to be that the human body is ugly and that its natural tendency is to debility and disease. Incarcerated in such a body, man's only hope is to avert these characteristics through the use of the powerful influences of ritual and ceremony. Every household has one or more shrines devoted to this purpose. The more powerful individuals in this society have several shrines in their houses, and, in fact, the opulence of a house is often referred to in terms of the number of such ritual centers it possesses. Most houses are of wattle and daub construction, but the shrine rooms of the more wealthy are walled with stone. Poorer families imitate the rich by applying pottery plaques to their shrine walls.

While each family has at least one such shrine, the rituals associated with it are not family ceremonies but are private and secret. The rites are normally only discussed with children, and then only during the period when they are being initiated into these mysteries. I was able, however, to establish sufficient rapport with the natives to examine these shrines and to have the rituals described to me.

The focal point of the shrine is a box or chest which is built into the wall. In this chest are kept the many charms and magical potions without which no native believes he could live. These preparations are secured from a variety of specialized practitioners. The most powerful of these are the medicine men, whose assistance must be rewarded with substantial gifts. However, the medicine men do not provide the curative potions for their clients, but [they] decide what the ingredients should be and then write them down in an ancient and secret language. This writing is understood only by the medicine men and by the herbalists who, for another gift, provide the required charm.

The charm is not disposed of after it has served its purpose, but is placed in the charm-box of the household shrine. As these magical materials are specific for certain ills, and the real or imagined maladies of the people are many, the charm-box is usually full to overflowing. The magical packets are so numerous that people forget what their purposes were and fear to use them again. While the natives are very vague on this point, we can only assume that the idea in retaining all the old magical materials is that their

presence in the charm-box, before which the body rituals are conducted, will in some way protect the worshipper.

Beneath the charm-box is a small font. Each day every member of the family, in succession, enters the shrine room, bows his head before the charm-box, mingles different sorts of holy water in the font, and proceeds with a brief rite of ablution. The holy waters are secured from the Water Temple of the community, where the priests conduct elaborate ceremonies to make the liquid ritually pure.

In the hierarchy of magical practitioners, and below the medicine men in prestige, are specialists whose designation is best translated "holy-mouth-men." The Nacirema have an almost pathological horror of and fascination with the mouth, the condition of which is believed to have a supernatural influence on all social relationships. Were it not for the rituals of the mouth, they believe that their teeth would fall out, their gums bleed, their jaws shrink, their friends desert them, and their lovers reject them. They also believe that a strong relationship exists between oral and moral characteristics. For example, there is a ritual ablution of the mouth for children which is supposed to improve their moral fiber.

The daily body ritual performed by everyone includes a mouth-rite. Despite the fact that these people are so punctilious about care of the mouth, this rite involves a practice which strikes the uninitiated stranger as revolting. It was reported to me that the ritual consists of inserting a small bundle of hog hairs into the mouth, along with certain magical powders, and then moving the bundle in a highly formalized series of gestures.

In addition to the private mouth-rite, the people seek out a holy-mouth-man once or twice a year. These practitioners have an impressive set of paraphernalia, consisting of a variety of augers, awls, probes, and prods. The use of these objects in the exorcism of the evils of the mouth involves almost unbelievable ritual torture of the client. The holy-mouth-man opens the client's mouth and, using the above-mentioned tools, enlarges any holes which decay may have created in the teeth. Magical materials are put into these holes. If there are no naturally occurring holes in the teeth, large sections of one or more teeth are gouged out so that the supernatural substance can be applied. In the client's view, the purpose of these ministrations is to arrest decay and to draw friends. The extremely sacred and traditional character of the rite is evident in the fact that the natives return to the holy-mouth-man year after year, despite the fact that their teeth continue to decay.

It is to be hoped that, when a thorough study of the Nacirema is made, there will be careful inquiry into the personality structure of these people. One has but to watch the gleam in the eye of a holy-mouth-man, as he jabs an awl into an exposed nerve, to suspect that a certain amount of sadism is involved. If this can be established, a very interesting pattern emerges, for most of the population shows definite masochistic tendencies. It was to these that Professor Linton referred in discussing a distinctive part of the daily body ritual which is performed only by men. This part of the rite involves scraping and lacerating the surface of the face with a sharp instrument. Special women's rites are performed only four times during each lunar month, but what they lack in frequency is made up in barbarity. As part of this ceremony, women bake their heads in small ovens for about an hour. The theoretically interesting point is that what seems to be a preponderantly masochistic people have developed sadistic specialists.

The medicine men have an imposing temple, or *latipso*, in every community of any size. The more elaborate ceremonies required to treat very sick patients can only be performed at this temple. These ceremonies involve not only the thaumaturge but a permanent group of vestal maidens who move sedately about the temple chambers in distinctive costume and headdress.

The *latipso* ceremonies are so harsh that it is phenomenal that a fair proportion of the really

sick natives who enter the temple ever recover. Small children whose indoctrination is still incomplete have been known to resist attempts to take them to the temple because "that is where you go to die." Despite this fact, sick adults are not only willing but eager to undergo the protracted ritual purification, if they can afford to do so. No matter how ill the supplicant or how grave the emergency, the guardians of many temples will not admit a client if he cannot give a rich gift to the custodian. Even after one has gained admission and survived the ceremonies, the guardians will not permit the neophyte to leave until he makes still another gift.

The supplicant entering the temple is first stripped of all his or her clothes. In everyday life the Nacirema avoids exposure of his body and its natural functions. Bathing and excretory acts are performed only in the secrecy of the household shrine, where they are ritualized as part of the body-rites. Psychological shock results from the fact that body secrecy is suddenly lost upon entry into the *latipso*. A man, whose own wife has never seen him in an excretory act, suddenly finds himself naked and assisted by a vestal maiden while he performs his natural functions into a sacred vessel. This sort of ceremonial treatment is necessitated by the fact that the excreta are used by a diviner to ascertain the course and nature of the client's sickness. Female clients, on the other hand, find their naked bodies are subjected to the scrutiny, manipulation, and prodding of the medicine men.

Few supplicants in the temple are well enough to do anything but lie on their hard beds. The daily ceremonies, like the rites of the holy-mouth-men, involve discomfort and torture. With ritual precision, the vestals awaken their miserable charges each dawn and roll them about on their beds of pain while performing ablutions, in the formal movements of which the maidens are highly trained. At other times they insert magic wands in the supplicant's mouth or force him to eat substances which are supposed to be healing.

From time to time the medicine men come to their clients and jab magically treated needles into their flesh. The fact that these temple ceremonies may not cure, and may even kill, the neophyte, in no way decreases the people's faith in the medicine men.

There remains one other kind of practitioner, known as a "listener." This witch-doctor has the power to exorcise the devils that lodge in the heads of people who have been bewitched. The Nacirema believe that parents bewitch their own children. Mothers are particularly suspected of putting a curse on children while teaching them the secret body rituals. The counter-magic of the witch-doctor is unusual in its lack of ritual. The patient simply tells the "listener" all his troubles and fears, beginning with the earliest difficulties he can remember. The memory displayed by the Nacirema in these exorcism sessions is truly remarkable. It is not uncommon for the patient to bemoan the rejection he felt upon being weaned as a babe, and a few individuals even see their troubles going back to the traumatic effects of their own birth.

In conclusion, mention must be made of certain practices which have their base in native esthetics but which depend upon the pervasive aversion to the natural body and its functions. There are ritual fasts to make fat people thin and ceremonial feasts to make thin people fat. Still other rites are used to make women's breasts larger if they are small, and smaller if they are large. General dissatisfaction with breast shape is symbolized in the fact that the ideal form is virtually outside the range of human variation. A few women afflicted with almost inhuman hyper-mammary development are so idolized that they make a handsome living by simply going from village to village and permitting the natives to stare at them for a fee.

Reference has already been made to the fact that excretory functions are ritualized, routinized, and relegated to secrecy. Natural reproductive functions are similarly distorted. Intercourse is taboo as a topic and scheduled as an act. Efforts are made to avoid pregnancy by the use of magical materials or by limiting intercourse to certain phases of the moon. Conception is actually very infrequent. When pregnant, women dress so as to hide their condition. Parturition takes place in secret, without friends or relatives to assist, and the majority of women do not nurse their infants.

Our review of the ritual life of the Nacirema has certainly shown them to be a magic-ridden people. It is hard to understand how they have managed to exist so long under the burdens which they have imposed upon themselves. But even such exotic customs as these take on real meaning when they are viewed with the insight provided by Malinowski when he wrote (1948: 70):

> Looking from far and above, from our high places of safety in the developed civilization, it is easy to see all the crudity and irrelevance of magic. But without its power and guidance early man could not have mastered his practical difficulties as he has done, nor could man have advanced to the higher stages of civilization.

CRITICAL THINKING QUESTIONS

1. When did you realize (if you did) that Miner is describing the "American"—Nacirema spelled backwards? Why do we not recognize this right away?
2. Using Miner's approach, describe a baseball game, an auction, shoppers in a supermarket, or a university classroom.
3. What do we gain from being able to step back from our way of life as Miner has done here?

REFERENCES

Linton, R. 1936. *The study of man*. New York: Appleton-Century.

Malinowski, B. 1948. *Magic, science and religion*. Glencoe, Ill.: Free Press.

Murdock, G. P. 1949. *Social structure*. New York: Macmillan.

5

The Case for Value-Free Sociology

Max Weber

The following is part of a lecture given in 1918 at Germany's Munich University by Max Weber, one of sociology's pioneers. Weber lived in politically turbulent times, in which the government and other organizations were demanding that university faculty teach the "right" ideas. Weber responded to these pressures by encouraging everyone to be politically involved as citizens, while maintaining that teachers and scholars should prize dispassionate analysis rather than political advocacy. This selection stimulates critical thinking about the mix of facts and values that is found in all sociological research.

Let us consider the disciplines close to me: sociology, history, economics, political science, and those types of cultural philosophy that make it their task to interpret the sciences. It is said, and I agree, that politics is out of place in the lecture-room. It does not belong there on the part of the students.... Neither does [it] belong in the lecture-room on the part of the [instructors], and when the [instructor] is scientifically concerned with politics, it belongs there least of all.

Source: Excerpts from From *Max Weber: Essays in Sociology by Max Weber*, edited by H. H. Gerth and C. Wright Mills. Translation copyright © 1946, 1958 by H. H. Gerth and C. Wright Mills. Used by permission of Oxford University Press, Inc.

To take a practical stand is one thing, and to analyze political structures and party positions is another. When speaking in a political meeting about democracy, one does not hide one's personal standpoint; indeed, to come out clearly and take a stand is one's damned duty. The words one uses in such a meeting are not means of scientific analysis but means of canvassing votes and winning over others. They are not plowshares to loosen the soil of contemplative thought; they are swords against the enemies: Such words are weapons. It would be an outrage, however, to use words in this fashion in a lecture or in the lecture-room. If, for in stance, "democracy" is under discussion, one considers its various forms, analyzes them in the way they function, determines what results for the conditions of life the one form has as compared with the other. Then one confronts the forms of democracy with nondemocratic forms of political order and endeavors to come to a position where the student may find the point from which, in terms of his ultimate ideals, he can take a stand. But the true teacher will beware of imposing from the platform any political position upon the student, whether it is expressed or suggested. "To let the facts speak for themselves" is the most unfair way of putting over a political position to the student.

Why should we abstain from doing this? I state in advance that some highly esteemed colleagues are of the opinion that it is not possible to carry through this self-restraint and that, even if it were possible, it would be a whim to avoid declaring oneself. Now one cannot demonstrate scientifically what the duty of an academic teacher is. One can only demand of the teacher that he have the intellectual integrity to see that it is one thing to state facts, to determine mathematical or logical relations or the internal structure of cultural values, while it is another thing to answer questions of the value of culture and its individual contents and the question of how one should act in the cultural community and in political associations. These are quite heterogeneous problems. If he asks further why he should not deal with both types of problems in the lecture-room, the answer is: because the prophet and the demagogue do not belong on the academic platform.

To the prophet and the demagogue, it is said: "Go your ways out into the streets and speak openly to the world," that is, speak where criticism is possible. In the lecture-room we stand opposite our audience, and it has to remain silent. I deem it irresponsible to exploit the circumstance that for the sake of their career the students have to attend a teacher's course while there is nobody present to oppose him with criticism. The task of the teacher is to serve the students with his knowledge and

scientific experience and not to imprint upon them his personal political views. It is certainly possible that the individual teacher will not entirely succeed in eliminating his personal sympathies. He is then exposed to the sharpest criticism in the forum of his own conscience. And this deficiency does not prove anything; other errors are also possible, for instance, erroneous statements of fact, and yet they prove nothing against the duty of searching for the truth. I also reject this in the very interest of science. I am ready to prove from the works of our historians that whenever the man of science introduces his personal value judgment, a full understanding of the facts ceases....

The primary task of a useful teacher is to teach his students to recognize "inconvenient" facts—I mean facts that are inconvenient for their party opinions. And for every party opinion there are facts that are extremely inconvenient, for my own opinion no less than for others. I believe the teacher accomplishes more than a mere intellectual task if he compels his audience to accustom itself to the existence of such facts. I would be so immodest as even to apply the expression "moral achievement," though perhaps this may sound too grandiose for something that should go without saying.

CRITICAL THINKING QUESTIONS

1. Why does Weber seek to set the campus apart from society as an "ivory tower"?
2. How is the classroom a distinctive setting in terms of political neutrality? If instructors cannot be entirely free from value positions, why should they strive to point out "inconvenient facts" to their students?
3. Do you see arguments *for* instructors presenting passionate advocacy of issues that are of great political and moral significance?

Sociological Research

CLASSIC

CONTEMPORARY

CROSS-CULTURAL

6

Defining Features of Canadian Sociology

Bruce Ravelli

In this brief review, Bruce Ravelli looks at some of the defining features of Canadian sociology. This article should inspire you to think about Canadian society and whether you believe it is reflected in Canadian sociology.

Canadian sociology often mirrors the nature of Canada itself: a diverse landscape where Canadians struggle to find their unique voice within a chorus dominated by Americans. In fact, some analysts suggest that Canadian sociology is a product of its experiences with, and at times its resistance to, the larger and more dominant American sociological tradition (see Brym & Saint-Pierre, 1997; Hiller, 2001; Hiller & Di Luzio, 2001). The dominance of the American sociological tradition in Canada is largely due to its longer history[1] and its sheer size.[2] However, at least four elements influence the presence of a distinctly Canadian sociology:

1. Canada's physical geography, defined by its vast and often challenging physical environment, and its regionalism, evidenced in the important role Quebec plays in Canadian sociology's intellectual development
2. Canadian sociology's focus on the political economy
3. The Canadianization movement of the 1960s and 1970s in response to the number of American faculty in our postsecondary institutions
4. The radical nature of Canadian sociology

CANADA'S GEOGRAPHY AND REGIONALISM

Canada, the world's second-largest country—in terms of total area, not population (Countries of the World, 2002)—is blessed with rich natural resources and a beautiful and diverse landscape. As we will see, these environmental factors have influenced Canadian sociology. According to Hiller (2001), Canadian sociology is not simply a culmination of the varieties of sociology practised in Canada; it is instead the product of Canadian sociologists' efforts to understand the Canadian experience. For Hiller (2001), one of Canadian sociology's defining pursuits has been the attempt to understand a changing national society. Everett Hughes asserted in 1959 that Canadian sociology should be grounded in its own societal context: as society changes, so too should its sociology (cited in Hiller, 2001). Sociology "should reflect both the unique aspects of the society's character as well as the evolution of that society" (Hiller, 2001: 262).

External and internal forces help to shape and define a Canadian sociology. The particular nature of the relationship between Canada's physical landscape and Canadian sociology is seen clearly in Brym and Saint-Pierre (1997). They suggest that one defining characteristic of Canadian sociology is its survivalism (1997: 543) and propose that a core theme of Canadian sociology is the development and maintenance of a community in the face of hostile elements (e.g., geographically, socially) and outside forces (i.e., political and intellectual pressures from the United States and American sociologists). One inside force defining Canadian sociology is the role that regionalism plays in our country's development (e.g., west versus east) and, in particular, Quebec's influence. Quebec has a unique linguistic and cultural influence on Canadian society generally and on Canadian sociology specifically.

The teaching of Canadian francophone sociology began in 1943, when the Faculty of Social Sciences was established at Laval University in Quebec City. Although francophone sociology is comparatively young, it experienced explosive growth from the 1960s to the 1980s, as demonstrated by rising student enrolment and the wealth of research produced by francophone sociologists (Brym & Saint-Pierre, 1997: 544). During the 1960s, a social movement in Quebec called the Quiet Revolution saw the influence of the Catholic Church diminish, replaced by an expanded provincial bureaucracy and, ultimately, a resurgence in nationalistic sentiments (seen in the rising popularity of the separatist movement and the growing influence of the Parti Québécois and its then-leader, René Lévesque).

The Quiet Revolution not only inspired changes in Quebec society and politics, but it also influenced sociologists to focus on issues of social class and social policy (see Brym & Saint-Pierre, 1997; Hiller, 2001). In fact, some Quebec sociologists have played leadership roles in the transformation of francophone society as senior advisors and civil servants for the provincial government (Brym & Saint-Pierre, 1997: 544). This is consistent with Southcott's (1999: 459) position that francophone sociologists are more likely to see themselves as "agents of change" than are their anglophone colleagues. Again, we see that the society in which sociologists work affects their approach to the discipline. One of those approaches involves an interest in the political economy.

CANADIAN FOCUS ON THE POLITICAL ECONOMY

Wallace Clement (2001), a leading figure in Canadian sociology, believes that one of the defining elements of Canadian sociology is its interest in the political economy. The political economy encompasses politics, government, and governing, as well as the social and cultural constitution of markets, institutions, and actors (Clement, 2001: 406). For Clement, this intellectual pursuit is characterized by the attempt to uncover tensions and contradictions within society and use them as the bases for social change.

Arguably, the first Canadian sociologist to investigate Canada's political economy was Harold A. Innis in *The Fur Trade in Canada* (1970/1930) and *The Cod Fisheries* (1954/1940). In these works, Innis develops what has been termed the *staples thesis*, which contends that Canada's development was based on the exploitation of raw materials sent back to European countries to satisfy their industrial thirsts. Innis suggests that each staple (e.g., commercial: cod, fur, timber; industrial: pulp and paper, minerals) had its own characteristics that imposed a particular logic on its individual development (Clement, 2001: 407). As Canada grew and these economic developments continued, these raw materials were sent abroad, refined into more valuable commodities (e.g., furniture, automobiles), and returned to Canada at vastly inflated prices. Innis suggests that since Canada's economic position was subordinate to Britain and to the United States, Canadians were seen as "hewers of wood, drawers of water"—people who performed menial tasks. Certainly, the historical development of Canada's natural resources suggests that Canadian society has been, at least in part, defined by the realization that Canada is not one of the world's major economic or social forces. This underdog mentality was evident in the attempt by Canadian universities in the 1960s and 1970s to Canadianize our postsecondary education system.

THE CANADIANIZATION MOVEMENT

The development of Canadian anglophone sociology was influenced by American sociology as practised at the University of Chicago (see Brym & Saint-Pierre, 1997; Eichler, 2001; Hiller, 2001; Hiller & Di Luzio, 2001; Langlois, 2000; McKay, 1998).

Founded in 1892 by Albion Small, the department of sociology at the University of Chicago defined the American sociological tradition for much of the early twentieth century. The Chicago School of sociology was dominated by the symbolic-interactionist approach, focusing on social reform and collective social responsibility. The Chicago School's influence was most profound on early francophone sociology in Quebec, particularly at Canada's founding department of sociology, McGill. In fact, many influential sociologists in Canada trained at the University of Chicago (such as C. A. Dawson, Everett Hughes, Harold Innis, A. C. McCrimmon, and Roderick D. McKenzie). The Chicago School was instrumental in defining Canadian sociology, but in the 1950s and 1960s, a movement to increase the number of Canadian faculty teaching at Canadian universities began.

During the late 1960s, Connors and Curtis (1970, cited in Hiller & Di Luzio, 2001: 494) found that more than 60 percent of sociologists in Canada had received their highest degree from a foreign institution. Even in 1971, Hedley and Warburton (1973: 305, cited in Hiller & Di Luzio, 2001: 494) found that in large Canadian sociology departments (those with more than twenty faculty members), more than 50 percent of instructors were American, 20 percent were from other countries, and 30 percent were Canadian. These finding were important as they emphasized the need to hire and train more Canadian sociologists if we ever hoped to investigate and understand Canadian society.

The discipline's Canadianization movement was also prompted by the explosion in the number of university enrolments in Canada beginning in the 1950s. In 1962–63, full-time university enrolment in Canada was 132 681, while only 10 years later (1972–73) it had more than doubled to 284 897. Ten years later (1982–83) the number had reached 640 000 (Hiller & Di Luzio, 2001: 491), and at the end of 1999, the number of full-time Canadian university enrolments hovered around 580 000 (Statistics Canada, 1999). Clearly, the need for Canadian-trained sociologists to teach students about Canadian society was a pressing one. This sentiment was clearly expressed when the Association of Universities and Colleges of Canada appointed a Commission on Canadian Studies in 1972, which resulted in The Symons Report (1975).

The report called on the Canadian academic community to increase its efforts to contribute to the knowledge of their own society. The reaction to this report came in an increase in the number of Canadian society courses taught by sociologists across the country, as well as in an increased focus on publishing sociological materials for Canadian sociology students. The assertion that these measures have worked has some support in the number of part- and full-time students who are undergraduate majors in sociology: the figure rose from 13 638 in 1982–83 to 21 028 in 1996–97 (Hiller & Di Luzio, 2001: 493). These students are making a sociological analysis of their own society, and they are also learning about the comparatively radical nature of Canadian sociology.

THE RADICAL NATURE OF CANADIAN SOCIOLOGY

Brym and Saint-Pierre (1997) suggest that one of the defining features of English-Canadian sociology is its radical nature, seen in its focus on the political economy and feminist ideas and perspectives. The important distinction these authors add, however, is how little of this radicalism is seen by the public (1997: 546). Certainly, Quebec sociologists are more focused on the policy ramifications of their endeavours, but Brym and Saint-Pierre recognize that many leading English-Canadian sociologists (such as Margrit Eichler, Graham Lowe, and Susan McDaniel) are mindful of the impact their ideas have on the larger society (1997: 546). Their investigations into the political economy were instrumental in showing that Canadian sociology was not afraid to uncover the hidden power structures that influence and guide society. Canadian feminist sociologists continue this tradition by looking at how gender acts as a locus of oppression and domination.

Margrit Eichler (2001) suggests that the simultaneous emergence of the Canadianization movement and the feminist movement led to a politics of knowledge that proved helpful to both groups. By expanding university departments by adding Canadian academics during the 1960s and 1970s, the feminist movement found a new voice on university campuses. In Eichler's paper *Women Pioneers in Canadian Sociology: The Effects of a Politics of Gender and a Politics of Knowledge* (2001), she attempts to reverse the politics of erasure that she argues effectively allowed the historical contributions of female sociologists in Canada to be written out of the literature. Eichler undertakes the project by conducting interviews with ten of the leading

female sociologists born before 1930. Through the interviews, Eichler utilizes a life-history approach, allowing the women to tell their own stories about being female sociologists during a period of rapid growth within the university system in general, and sociology departments in particular, as well as in a period when feminist issues first entered the sociological discourse.

One important finding from Eichler's investigation into these women's lives is the fact that they never had problems finding jobs in academe (2001: 393). The expanding university system, as well as the emerging recognition of feminist issues, allowed these women to begin full-time careers with little effort. Although they all faced sexism in some form during their careers, they were able to initiate significant institutional change by their mere presence on campus (e.g., pay equity measures, sexual harassment policies). Their ability to be a critical social presence within the academic community was an important factor in advancing feminist issues on university campuses and in the larger society as the feminist movement gained momentum in Canada.

That impetus led to the establishment of the Royal Commission on the Status of Women in 1967 to "inquire into and report upon the status of women in Canada, and to recommend what steps might be taken by the Federal Government to ensure for women equal opportunities with men in all aspects of Canadian society" (Cross, 2000). The final report was released in 1970 with 167 recommendations and "became the blueprint for mainstream feminist activism" (Womenspace, 2002). The feminist movement inspired women to reflect differently on their social surroundings and reinforced the need to question social convention. The influence on early female sociology pioneers was equally important, as it encouraged them to critique their own intellectual foundations generally and sociology specifically. As Dorothy Smith notes about this time, "Because we were free to take up issues for women, we didn't feel committed to reproducing the discipline,…it had the effect…of really liberating the discipline in general in Canada, so that you now have an orientation where people feel absolutely comfortable in raising current issues, in addressing what's going on in Canada" (cited in Eichler, 2001: 394). The Royal Commission report opened the debate on women's positions in Canadian society and resulted in the formation of the women's caucus at the Canadian Sociology and Anthropology Association, which still exists today. The feminist movement, and sociology's role within it, is just one example of Canadian sociology's critical foundation and how Canada continues to influence the discipline today.

CONCLUSION

Canadian sociology is defined by its geography, focus on the political economy, the Canadianization movement, and its radical approach to social issues. This brief review should give you some appreciation for the flavour of Canadian sociology and how it represents a unique approach to the discipline and to our understanding of what it means to be Canadian.

CRITICAL THINKING QUESTIONS

1. Do you believe that social forces influence how academics in a given country see the world? Support your answer.
2. Provide examples of how Canadian winters influence the way Canadians think about themselves. Can similar examples be found for how Canadian summers influence our national identity?
3. In your opinion, was the Canadianization movement at universities and colleges necessary? Why or why not?

NOTES

1. The University of Chicago established the first American department of sociology in 1892 and McGill University established the first Canadian one in 1924.
2. The American postsecondary system serves more than 14 800 000 students and the Canadian system around 827 000 (NCES, 2002; Statistics Canada, 1999). In 1999 more than 2400 departments of sociology existed in the United States (ASA, 2002). Canada had around 45 university departments of sociology—including joint sociology/anthropology departments—(McMaster, 2002) and approximately 150 colleges, the majority of which offered at least introductory sociology (ACCC, 2002).

REFERENCES

ACCC (Association of Canadian Community Colleges). 2002. Membership list. [Online]: Available: **http://www.accc.ca/english/colleges/ membership_list.cfm**. Accessed October 27, 2002.

ASA (American Sociological Association). 2002. Departmental listings for 1999. [Online]. Available: **http://www.asanet.org/pubs/dod.html**. Accessed October 27, 2002.

Brym, R., and C. Saint-Pierre. 1997. Canadian sociology. *Contemporary Sociology*, 26(5): 543–46.

Clement, W. 2001. Canadian political economy's legacy for sociology. *Canadian Journal of Sociology*, 26(3): 405–20.

Connor, D. M., and E. Curtis. 1970. *Sociology and anthropology in Canada: Some characteristics of the disciplines and their current university programs*. Montreal: Canadian Sociology and Anthropology Association.

Countries of the World. 2002. Country statistics at a glance. [Online]. Available: **http://www.infoplease.com/ipa/ A0762380.html**. Accessed July 17, 2002.

Cross, P. 2000. Report of the Royal Commission on the Status of Women: Where are we after thirty years? [Online]. Available: **http://www.owjn.org/issues/equality/thirty.htm**. Accessed January 31, 2003.

Eichler, M. 2001. Women pioneers in Canadian sociology: The effects of a politics of gender and a politics of knowledge. *Canadian Journal of Sociology*, 26(3): 375–403.

Hedley, R. A., and R. T. Warburton. 1973. The role of national courses in the teaching and development of sociology: The Canadian case. *Sociological Review*, 21(2): 299–319.

Hiller, H. H. 2001. Legacy for a new millennium: Canadian sociology in the twentieth century as seen through its publications. *Canadian Journal of Sociology*, 26(3): 257–63.

Hiller, H. H., and L. Di Luzio. 2001. Text and context: Another "chapter" in the evolution of sociology in Canada. *Canadian Journal of Sociology*, 26(3): 487–512.

Innis, H. A. 1954. *The cod fisheries: The history of an international economy.* University of Toronto Press (original work published 1940).

———. 1970. *The fur trade in Canada.* Toronto: University of Toronto Press (original work published 1930).

Langlois, S. 2000. A productive decade in the tradition of Canadian sociology. *Canadian Journal of Sociology,* 25(3): 391–97.

McKay, I. 1998. Changing the subject(s) of the "History of Canadian sociology": The case of Colin McKay and Spencerian Marxism, 1890–1940." *Canadian Journal of Sociology,* 23(4): 389–426.

McMaster University. 2002. Sociology institutions—departments. [Online]. Available: **http://www.mcmaster.ca/socscidocs/w3virtsoclib/cansoc.htm**. Retrieved October 27, 2002.

NCES (National Center for Education Statistics). 2002. Digest of education statistics, 2001—Chapter 3: Postsecondary education. [Online]. Available: **http://nces.ed.gov//pubs2002/digest2001/ch3.asp#1**. Accessed January 31, 2003.

Southcott, C. 1999. The study of regional inequality in Quebec and English Canada: A comparative analysis of perspectives. *Canadian Journal of Sociology,* 24(4): 457–84.

Statistics Canada. 1999. University enrolment, full-time and part-time, by sex. [Online]. Available: **http://www.statcan.ca/english/Pgdb/educ03a.htm**. Accessed October 27, 2002.

Womenspace. 2002. Since the Royal Commission on the Status of Women. [Online]. Available: **http://herstory.womenspace.ca/ RCSW.html**. Retrieved October 23.

Sociological Research

CLASSIC

CONTEMPORARY

CROSS-CULTURAL

7

Arab Women in the Field

Soraya Altorki

Social scientists often rely on ethnography—*the study of people using observation or interviews—to provide detailed descriptions of groups, organizations, and communities. Such fieldwork, like other data collection methods, has both strengths and limitations. As Soraya Altorki shows, a major advantage of studying one's own culture is a familiarity with the people and the environment; however, the researcher also encounters several problems. One of Altorki's challenges, for example, was resocializing herself into her culture, having been abroad for many years. She also had to overcome the subjects' reluctance to address sensitive questions about their religious practices and family life to an "outsider."*

AT HOME IN THE FIELD

Having been socialized many years in Egypt and identifying with its people, I had regarded it, on one level, to be my home. On another level, however, I had been brought up in a Saudi Arabian family committed in great measure to that country's cultural heritage and the observance of its cultural norms, even while selectively observing certain Egyptian values and practices. Throughout my college days, I had been reminded that I could not do what my Egyptian girlfriends could do, because "our" traditions were different and for "us" such behavior was unacceptable.

Source: "At Home in the Field," by Soraya Altorki, in *Arab Women in the Field: Studying Your Own Society*, eds. Soraya Altorki and Camillia Fawzi El-Solh, pp. 51–9. New York: Syracuse University Press, 1988. Reprinted by permission.

Besides, it was not only the constraining elements of Saudi Arabian culture that molded my growing-up experiences in Egypt, but also the rich rewards that I reaped from kinship support and shared cultural knowledge. These provided for me the security of a closure that was not attainable in Egypt. Thus, Saudi Arabia was home for me on a more fundamental level.

Arriving in Jiddah [Saudi Arabia], my native city, I knew I wanted to study urban life. Although the entire northern portion of the Arabian Peninsula was virtually unknown to social scientists,...early travelers and even scholars avoided its study in favor of the nomad and the camel. Barring Hürgrouje and Burton, almost nothing was known about urban life. In retrospect, I believe that my choice to focus on urban society was partly a reaction to the stereotypical view of Saudi Arabia as a society of nomads and oil wells.

There were also social constraints to my choice. I knew that, as an unmarried woman, I could neither travel alone in the country nor wander around with the nomads. Living alone, anywhere in the country, was out of the question. Thus, for many considerations, an urban-based study seemed most appropriate, and the city of Jiddah the most convenient.

The realities of being an unmarried woman in many ways dictated my field of research, although it did not determine my choice of research topic within that field (Altorki, 1986). This essentially meant that I could work with women and that I had limited access to men. Within these bounds, my choice was absolutely free....

INSIDER/OUTSIDER

Being literally at home in Jiddah, I was spared having to worry about the problems of settling in that most anthropologists face when entering the field. Furthermore, I needed no research permit (or if I did, I never bothered to find out) and no letters of guarantee. Neither was I required to make commitments to local authorities and research institutes concerning the conduct of my work and the use and distribution of my data.

The people I studied saw me as one of themselves. Some of them had ties of kinship and friendship to my family. Others knew my family members by name. This state of affairs provided me with significant advantages. Others, working in their own society, have observed similar benefits in knowing the culture and consequently being able to select their research agenda in consonance with what is most expedient for the research task and what is most feasible within the limits of what will be allowed by the subjects under investigation (see Stephenson & Greer, 1981: 126).

However, some facets of my life concerned my informants. Why, for example, was I not a married woman with children, like all my peers? And why was I still living abroad rather than residing in Jiddah, awaiting marriage? My unmarried status at the age of twenty-two made

me somewhat of an anomaly. More distressing to the older women among whom I worked was the conclusion that I was more interested in following my studies than in settling down to married life. Although the role of an educated woman had come to be accepted by the community at large and the elite in particular, the problem was in the priorities this role took over what was perceived to be the more important aspect of gender role, namely the status that marriage and motherhood bring. According to both men and women, it is these dimensions of womanhood that are primary. In fact, given the segregation of Saudi Arabian women from men, and their isolation from public life, marriage and motherhood become a woman's avenues to maturity, security, and greater prestige. Being a member of the society, I anticipated this and was well prepared to deal with its consequences.

Although women come of age with marriage, and prestige for them is attained by motherhood, my status within the community had to rest on other things: It relied greatly on my education. Lacking husband and child, I predicated my adulthood on education and depended on the community's acceptance of it as a legitimate goal for women to attain. Men and women alike respected this, although never failing to remind me of the fundamentals of my role as a woman. As one older woman put it to me: "Education is good, but women are weak. No matter how much money they have, no matter their education, they cannot manage without men. May Allah save your father and your brother. But you have to start your own family." That statement accurately reflects the dependence of women on men, a dependence that also correlates with their segregation in Saudi Arabian society. But my role as a Saudi Arabian woman, educated abroad, permitted me more flexibility and autonomy. For one thing, my interaction with men who were not my relatives was tolerated.

My long absence abroad was an additional factor leading to more mobility. While abroad, I had been immersed in a different way of life, and hence women and men alike did not expect me to conform totally to the cultural norms governing the relationship of men and women in Saudi Arabian society. My absence had a complex effect on my reentry into my own community. On the one hand, it allowed more maneuverability in my role as an unmarried woman, and, on the other hand, it made conformity especially expedient in strengthening my ties to my informants.

Repeatedly, men and women expressed their surprise and approval when my behavior showed conformity to Saudi Arabian culture. They were, for example, delighted that my many years in Egypt had not changed my accent to Egyptian. Whenever I showed observance of norms that young people my age had begun to modify, members of the older generation were astonished and particularly delighted. Those of the younger generation, however, saw such conformity as awkward and continued to remind me that times had changed: "Nobody is observing such things these days."

For example, norms of deference to older siblings necessitate that they be addressed in specific terms. To an older brother and kinsmen his age the term is *sidi*, which means "my master." My use of these terms of address was welcomed by all, barring girls of my age who by then were seeking to substitute as equivalent for the term *sidi* those of *akhuya* (my brother) and the sobriquet *abu flan* (father of). In doing this, I took my cues from young men who had obtained their college education abroad, sometimes through graduate school, and who continued to use traditional terms of reference in addressing older female siblings and other kinswomen in their age group.

It was in the same spirit that I observed some norms of modesty, particularly those related to veiling. Such practices were changing at the time of my fieldwork, so that the families I studied showed the whole spectrum of veiling practices, from those who had considerably modified its use to leave the face bare, to those who still observed the traditional practice of covering the face as well. While visiting the homes of the latter, I made sure to conform and to cover my face carefully. This gesture of respect did not go unnoticed: Women and men alike commented that my many years abroad had not made me behave like a "foreigner."

The years abroad had been spent as a student, and now I had come back as a researcher with the intention of recording a way of life that had not previously been studied. Everyone understood that role. Female education was not a novelty. Girls were sent to *faqihas* (informal traditional schools) as far back as older informants could remember; and formal girls' schools were opened by the government in 1960. By the time I went to the field, the first women's university had already opened in Jiddah. College education was thoroughly acceptable for women; indeed, it had become greatly valued.

Thus, I had no problem in defining part of my role to the subjects of my research. I wanted to study social life, family organization, rituals, beliefs, and customs, and to document how these have changed for the younger people in the study. In another way, my role was more ascribed. My return to Jiddah meant taking my place in a family and getting involved in the various ramifications of family life. It also meant belonging to a class with the task of conforming to the behavior of that class. I was aware that I could in fact not conform to that behavior, but I had little choice with regard to involvement in family life.

The ascribed aspects of my role, i.e., gender, age, and kinship, were more fundamental in people's perception of me, which may be unavoidable in doing research among one's own people. My education was important in allowing me to explore areas of social life (e.g., more access to the world of men) that other women could not undertake. Despite my research objective, known and accepted to all the families, I remained primarily a Saudi Arabian woman. As such, I was known to some as the daughter or a sister of a friend, while to others as a member of a lineage they knew from other mutual friends. These considerations were always present in my interaction with others.

While criteria centering on the individual are not without relevance in structuring relations, the world of these elite families was in the first instance structured by consanguineous and marital ties, and in the second place by friendship and business networks.

Within this world an individual—whether man or woman—is deeply embedded in the *'aila* (family). One's status is, to a considerable degree, ascribed by the status of the *'aila*. Individual achievement is an avenue to mobility, but clearly it is the achievement of men and not of women that is associated with family prestige. Recent changes in the wider society have introduced more emphasis on individuality and an increase of distance from the *'aila*. This is evidenced in neolocal residence patterns, more individual involvement in marriage choice, relative reduction of parental authority, independent career choices for men, and less observance of traditional obligations to kinsmen (Altorki, 1986).

On the whole, I experienced no problems in establishing rapport—that quality in the relationship between the ethnographer and the host community that the introductions to ethnographic monographs rarely fail to mention, but which probably involves the most enigmatic aspect of our methodological trademark: participant observation. I spoke the language, and the trademark itself had no special meaning for me, although, as I will explain, it had very special implications in my case.

In short, I found practical advantages in my particular field situation: Unencumbered by bureaucratic impediments, comfortably set up in my family's home, fluent in the vernacular, and personally known in some of the households I was to study, I could begin my research under very auspicious circumstances—or so it seemed until I realized the implications of being an indigenous anthropologist. I discovered that almost every one of the advantages had its negative side.

In a very real sense, my fieldwork experience was a process of resocialization into my own

society. Although I was raised in a Saudi Arabian family, my long years of residence abroad had established considerable distance between me and my society. The advantages were that much of the culture was not so familiar that it could easily escape my notice. This problem in the collection of data has been observed by other ethnographers working under similar conditions (cf. Spradley & McCurdy, 1972; Ablon, 1977; Stephenson & Greer, 1981), but it is one that can be overcome by rigorous training. The researcher can counteract familiarity by close observation, meticulous recording of ethnographic scenes, and detailed probing to uncover the "taken-for-granted" world he or she may share with members of the community being studied.

Living at home meant that I had to assume the role expected of a family member in my position within the household group. The ordinary field situation reversed itself in my case. I became what may best be described as an observant participant. My primary duty was to participate. To observe became an incidental privilege.

My status did not afford me immunity from observing all the taboos and attending to all the obligations my culture prescribed for me—an immunity usually granted to foreign anthropologists. I had to accept severe restrictions on my movements and on my interaction with other people. For example, I had no freedom to move in public on my own, and challenging any norms of conduct would have jeopardized my relationships with the families I had decided to study. Had I not conformed, I would have risked ostracism and termination of my research. Persistently, if slowly, I achieved a precarious balance of roles that allowed me mobility and freedom to do my research as well as to be accepted and taken seriously. I became a conscious witness to my own resocialization as an Arab woman in my society and thus learned and comprehended many aspects of this role in the best possible manner.

This, perhaps, is one of the hidden advantages of being an insider. For example, veiling norms can be observed and described by an outsider, and one can also learn about the meaning of veiling by soliciting relevant information from informants. Yet the participant charged with the task of abiding by the norms experiences the constraints, to be sure, but also the rewards of these norms on a more basic level. In that sense, my resocialization generated data on an experiential level different from that to which an outsider could bear witness. This point has also been observed as a merit of indigenous research elsewhere. Aguilar, for example, summarizing the pros and cons of this kind of research, mentions that its advocates insist "that the covert culture of the insider has the heuristic value of lending psychological reality (or cultural reality) to ethnographic analyses" (1981: 16).

My status affected my research in another way. Restricted possibilities for movement outside the house and pervasive segregation of men and women in public confined the research predominantly to the world of women. These realities affected the choice of topic for investigation. I could not study market or political relations, for example. Neither could I investigate any other subject in which men, rather than women, are the dominant actors. Family organization seemed the most accessible for a female researcher, and elites became my focus. Within that, my emphasis was on how ideology and practice affect and are influenced by one another. But, as noted elsewhere, elites are the least accessible to inquiry, especially through the technique of prolonged participant observation. The families I elected to study formed closed groups, and although the observation of and participation in their daily lives was possible for me as a member of the group, even I could gain their confidence only through patient approaches along the lines of friendship.

Although generous hospitality is highly valued behavior, there remain degrees of formality that the families must always maintain vis-à-vis the whole community. Only with considerable caution can a nonmember see their lives as they live them, as opposed to how they want the rest of the community to perceive them. For example, it takes a long time, coupled with intensive interaction, before people allow a friend to move within their home free of the façade of formality exhibited to outsiders. Indeed, it took between six and eight months before I could develop the friendships that made close observation of their daily lives possible to the degree that my presence was more or less ignored. Being an insider has even more serious consequences for research. Information may be withheld when it relates to behavior that must be concealed from public knowledge. If one is outside the system, one's awareness of goings-on may not be problematical. But as a participant, the researcher constitutes a threat of exposure and judgment. Lewis (1973: 588) explains this situation very well:

> There is a growing fear that the information collected by an outsider, someone not constrained by group values and interests, will expose the group to outside manipulation and control.... The insider, on the other hand, is accountable; s/he must remain in the community and take responsibility for her/his actions. Thus, s/he is forced through self-interest to exercise discretion.

This was one of the hardest areas to overcome in doing research among one's own people. For example, family solidarity and cohesion are greatly valued. Verbally, men and women endorse the ideal of love and support between siblings; respect and obedience in filial relations; and honoring family duties of financial support to the needy and maintenance of elderly parents. In practice, the older generations approximated many of these ideals (Altorki, 1986).

But family conflict does occur, and younger generation members have begun to modify family obligations in general. Differences over inheritance constitute the most serious threat to family solidarity—a threat that mounts as the stakes become higher and people's wealth increases. The ideal remains that such differences must be kept out of the public eye and should be reconciled between family members without recourse to the courts. So important is this family ideal that information about conflict, especially that considered to be serious, was at first not revealed to me. I learned about such conflicts indirectly from domestic servants working in these homes who, by coincidence, happened to be related to women working in my family's household. On other occasions, I obtained relevant information from women with whom I had established such strong ties of friendship that we had come to be considered "sisters." This family idiom symbolized our enclosure in the same kinship group and, by implication, showed our interest in protecting that group and shielding it from public criticism.

On one point, my learning about family conflicts was fortuitous. Is it conceivable that I would have returned from the field with the belief that the ideal of family solidarity was the reality? By being an insider, and from my own kinship network, I "experienced" the fact that reality was different and that disagreement can escalate to conflicts between family members. The problem, however, was in collecting data about conflict from the other families to uncover patterns in its expression and management. What, for example, were the patterns for the expression of intrafamily conflict? How was it managed, and what are the patterns for its resolution?

In this respect, my status as an insider prevented people from divulging such information for fear of having it exposed to the wider community. Obviously, disseminating information about intrafamilial conflict to the community also implies that the disseminator, i.e., the indigenous anthropologist, has judged it negatively and is now taking an active role in censoring the behavior it bespeaks. While the question of exposure to the public can be bridged by trust and confidence in the researcher, the threat of judgment is harder to overcome. Being a participating family member implies, of course, subscribing to the cultural norms and values of the group and to the sanctions that follow a breach of valued behavior.

These considerations are different for a foreign anthropologist. As an outsider investigating family organization and interfamilial conflict,

she or he must gain the confidence of the people and be trusted not to expose family differences to the community. But outsider status does not imply shared cultural knowledge, and thus protects the outsider from applying the same moral judgments. The nonindigenous researcher is outside the system, and for this very reason people may not conceal family differences to the same degree as they would from a member of their own group. In collecting relevant data, the indigenous researcher is twice bound and must be able to overcome barriers to confidence and to potential value judgment.

Other social scientists have made similar observations. Aguilar, for example, highlights the constraints indigenous status may place on access to data (1981: 21), although, as he points out, other anthropologists claim the opposite (1981: 18). However, the Saudi Arabian case indicates that while confidence can be established, a morally neutral judgment is harder to demonstrate. An effective strategy is to be drawn into the same closure that allows sharing of such delicate information. In my case, the idiom of kinship and the ties of close friendships provided such a closure.

My general familiarity with these families had another irksome drawback. My informants presumed that I knew my own culture, and for a long time they either misinterpreted my questions as implying an unbecoming skepticism or failed to appreciate that I truly did not know what I had asked them to explain. This was especially true for knowledge of religious beliefs and rituals, which for me was a difficult area to explore. Such knowledge is essential to an adult Muslim, and any queries about it reveal a lapse in religious duties. Fed up with my questions, an older woman put it to me this way: "Are you not ashamed that you do not know how to pray at your age? What then did they teach you abroad?"

This revealed to me the cultural givens of the community and the cultural repertoire indispensable to membership in it. The best research strategy to circumvent this role was to openly admit my ignorance and to blame it all on my long absence abroad. Women and men patiently explained matters to me in a desire to resocialize me as a Muslim Arab woman. In fact, it was especially pleasing to the older women, often illiterate, to instruct me despite my higher formal education.

These considerations have been well described by Stephenson and Greer. They note that while familiarity with the culture under study can be a bonus, prior knowledge of the people studied provides no guaranteed advantage. The expectations people may have of the investigator could make it more difficult for her or him to break out of fixed patterns and thus serve to restrict the work at hand (1981: 129). The role that the community attributes to the researcher may inhibit other relationships and bias the researcher's thoughts. Moreover, the role ascribed by kinship to the indigenous anthropologist may forcefully draw that person into factionalism within the community and thereby limit the work that can be accomplished. Sometimes, such problems can be circumvented by conscious strategy. As Stephenson and Greer observe, "the researcher can mitigate the effects of already established roles by emphasizing some over others" 1981: 127)....

CRITICAL THINKING QUESTIONS

1. How did Altorki's sex and background influence her decisions about where and how to conduct her research on Arab society?
2. Field researchers must often balance the advantages and disadvantages of playing "insider" and "outsider" roles. How did being an insider both benefit and limit Altorki's research? What barriers did she have to overcome?
3. What strengths and weaknesses did Altorki have as an outsider? Is it possible for researchers who are outsiders to offer information about and valid insights into the societies they study? Explain your answer.

REFERENCES

Ablon, J. 1977. Field methods in working with middle class Americans: New issues of values, personality and reciprocity. *Human Organization,* 36(1): 69–72.

Aguilar, J. 1981. Insider research: An ethnography of a debate. In *Anthropologists at home in North America: Methods and issues in the study of one's own society,* ed. D. A. Messerschmidt. Cambridge: Cambridge University Press.

Altorki, S. 1986. *Women in Saudi Arabia: Ideology and behavior among the elite.* New York: Columbia University Press.

Lewis, D. 1973. Anthropology and colonialism. *Current Anthropology,* 14(12): 581–602.

Spradley, J. P., and D. W. McCurdy. 1972. *The cultural experience.* Chicago: Science Research Association.

Stephenson, J. B., and L. S. Greer. 1981. Ethnographers in their own cultures: Two Appalachian cases. *Human Organization,* 40(2): 123–30.

8

Symbol: The Basic Element of Culture

Leslie A. White

Leslie A. White, a noted anthropologist, argues in this selection that the key to human existence is the ability to use symbols. Although all animals are capable of complex behaviour, only humans depend on symbolic activity. This special power underlies our autonomy as the only creatures who live according to meanings we set for ourselves. Thus, symbols convert our animal species into humanity, in the process transforming social behaviour into true civilization.

…All human behavior originates in the use of symbols. It was the symbol which transformed our anthropoid ancestors into men and made them human. All civilizations have been generated, and are perpetuated, only by the use of symbols. It is the symbol which transforms an infant of *Homo sapiens* into a human being; deaf mutes who grow up without the use of symbols are not human beings. All human behavior consists of, or is dependent upon, the use of symbols. Human behavior is symbolic behavior; symbolic behavior is human behavior. The symbol is the universe of humanity.…

Source: From "The symbol: The origin and the basis of human behavior," in *The Science of Culture: A Study of Man and Civilization* by Leslie White. Copyright © 1949 Leslie White. Copyright renewed 1976 by Crocker National Bank. Reprinted by permission of Farrar, Straus & Giroux, LLC.

That there are numerous and impressive similarities between the behavior of man and that of ape is fairly obvious; it is quite possible that chimpanzees and gorillas in zoos have noted and appreciated them. Fairly apparent, too, are man's behavioral similarities to many other kinds of animals. Almost as obvious, but not easy to define, is a difference in behavior which distinguishes man from all other living creatures. I say "obvious" because it is quite apparent to the common man that the nonhuman animals with which he is familiar do not and cannot enter, and participate in, the world in which he, as a human being, lives. It is impossible for a dog, horse, bird, or even an ape, to have *any* understanding of the meaning of the sign of the cross to a Christian, or of the fact that black (white among the Chinese) is the color of mourning. No chimpanzee or laboratory rat can appreciate the difference between Holy water and distilled water, or grasp the meaning of *Tuesday*, *3*, or *sin*. No animal save man can distinguish a cousin from an uncle, or a cross cousin from a parallel cousin. Only man can commit the crime of incest or adultery; only he can remember the Sabbath and keep it Holy. It is not, as we well know, that the lower animals can do these things but to a lesser degree than ourselves; they cannot perform these acts of appreciation and distinction at all. It is, as Descartes said long ago, "not only that the brutes have less Reason than man, but that they have none at all."...

A symbol may be defined as a thing the value or meaning of which is bestowed upon it by those who use it. I say "thing" because a symbol may have any kind of physical form; it may have the form of a material object, a color, a sound, an odor, a motion of an object, a taste.

The meaning, or value, of a symbol is in no instance derived from or determined by properties intrinsic in its physical form: The color appropriate to mourning may be yellow, green, or any other color; purple need not be the color of royalty; among the Manchu rulers of China it was yellow.... The meaning of symbols is derived from and determined by the organisms who use them; meaning is bestowed by human organisms upon physical things or events which thereupon become symbols. Symbols "have their signification," to use John Locke's phrase, "from the arbitrary imposition of men."

All symbols must have a physical form otherwise they could not enter our experience.... But the meaning of a symbol cannot be discovered by mere sensory examination of its physical form. One cannot tell by looking at an *x* in an algebraic equation what it stands for; one cannot ascertain with the ears alone the symbolic value of the phonetic compound *si*; one cannot tell merely by weighing a pig how much gold he will exchange for; one cannot tell from the wave length of a color whether it stands for courage or cowardice, "stop" or "go"; nor can one discover the spirit in a fetish by any amount of physical or chemical

examination. The meaning of a symbol can be grasped only by nonsensory, symbolic means....

Thus Darwin says: "That which distinguishes man from the lower animals is not the understanding of articulate sounds, for as everyone knows, dogs understand many words and sentences."[1]...

The man differs from the dog—and all other creatures—in that *he can and does play an active role in determining what value the vocal stimulus is to have, and the dog cannot*. The dog does not and cannot play an active part in determining the value of the vocal stimulus. Whether he is to roll over or go fetch at a given stimulus, or whether the stimulus for roll over be one combination of sounds or another is a matter in which the dog has nothing whatever to "say." He plays a purely passive role and can do nothing else. He learns the meaning of a vocal command just as his salivary glands may learn to respond to the sound of a bell. But man plays an active role and thus becomes a creator: Let *x* equal three pounds of coal and it does equal three pounds of coal; let removal of the hat in a house of worship indicate respect and it becomes so. This creative faculty, that of freely, actively, and arbitrarily bestowing value upon things, is one of the most commonplace as well as *the* most important characteristic of man. Children employ it freely in their play: "Let's pretend that this rock is a wolf."...

All culture (civilization) depends upon the symbol. It was the exercise of the symbolic faculty that brought culture into existence, and it is the use of symbols that makes the perpetuation of culture possible. Without the symbol there would be no culture, and man would be merely an animal, not a human being.

Articulate speech is the most important form of symbolic expression. Remove speech from culture and what would remain? Let us see.

Without articulate speech we would have no *human* social organization. Families we might have, but this form of organization is not peculiar to man; it is not *per se*, human. But we would have no prohibitions of incest, no rules prescribing exogamy and endogamy, polygamy, monogamy.

How could marriage with a cross cousin be prescribed, marriage with a parallel cousin proscribed, without articulate speech? How could rules which prohibit plural mates possessed simultaneously but permit them if possessed one at a time, exist without speech?

Without speech we would have no political, economic, ecclesiastic, or military organization; no codes of etiquette or ethics; no laws; no science, theology, or literature; no games or music, except on an ape level. Rituals and ceremonial paraphernalia would be meaningless without articulate speech. Indeed, without articulate speech we would be all but toolless: We would have only the occasional and insignificant use of the tool such as we find today among the higher apes, for it was articulate speech that transformed the nonprogressive tool-using of the ape into the progressive, cumulative tool-using of man, the human being.

In short, without symbolic communication in some form, we would have no culture. "In the Word was the beginning" of culture—and its perpetuation also.

To be sure, with all his culture man is still an animal and strives for the same ends that all other living creatures strive for: the preservation of the individual and the perpetuation of the [species]. In concrete terms these ends are food, shelter from the elements, defense from enemies, health, and offspring. The fact that man strives for these ends just as all other animals do has, no doubt, led many to declare that there is "no fundamental difference between the behavior of man and of other creatures." But man does differ, not in *ends* but in *means*. Man's means are cultural means: Culture is simply the human animal's way of living. And, since these means, culture, are dependent upon a faculty possessed by man alone, the ability to use symbols, the difference between the behavior of man and of all other creatures is not merely great, but basic and fundamental.

The behavior of man is of two distinct kinds: symbolic and nonsymbolic. Man yawns, stretches, coughs, scratches himself, cries out in pain, shrinks with fear, "bristles" with anger, and so on. Nonsymbolic behavior of this sort is not peculiar to man; he shares it not only with the other primates but with many other animal species as well. But man communicates with his fellows with articulate speech, uses amulets, confesses sins, makes laws, observes codes of etiquette, explains his dreams, classifies his relatives in designated categories, and so on. This kind of behavior is unique; only man is capable of it; it is peculiar to man because it consists of, or is dependent upon, the use of symbols. The nonsymbolic behavior of *Homo sapiens* is the behavior of man the animal; the symbolic behavior is that of man the human being. It is the symbol which has transformed man from a mere animal to a human animal....

The infant of the species *Homo sapiens* becomes human only when and as he exercises his symbol faculty. Only through articulate speech—not necessarily vocal—can he enter the world of human beings and take part in their affairs. The questions asked earlier may be repeated now. How could a growing child know and appreciate such things as social organization, ethics, etiquette, ritual, science, religion, art, and games without symbolic communication? The answer is of course that he could know nothing of these things and have no appreciation of them at all....

Children who have been cut off from human intercourse for years by blindness and deafness but who have eventually effected communication with their fellows on a symbolic level are exceedingly illuminating. The case of Helen Keller is exceptionally instructive....

Helen Keller was rendered blind and deaf at an early age by illness. She grew up as a child without symbolic contact with anyone. Descriptions of her at the age of seven, the time at which her teacher, Miss Sullivan, came to her home, disclosed no *human* attributes of Helen's behavior at all. She was a headstrong, undisciplined, and unruly little animal.

Within a day or so after her arrival at the Keller home, Miss Sullivan taught Helen her first word, spelling it into her hand. But this word was merely a sign, not a symbol. A week later Helen knew several words but, as Miss Sullivan reports, she had "no idea how to use them or that everything has a name." Within three weeks Helen knew eighteen nouns and three verbs. But she was still on the level of signs; she still had no notion "that everything has a name."

Helen confused the word signs for "mug" and "water" because, apparently, both were associated with drinking. Miss Sullivan made a few attempts to clear up this confusion but without success. One morning, however, about a month after Miss Sullivan's arrival, the two went out to the pump in the garden. What happened then is best told in their own words:

I made Helen hold her mug under the spout while I pumped. As the cold water gushed forth, filling the mug, I spelled "w-a-t-e-r" into Helen's free hand. The word coming so close upon the sensation of cold water rushing over her hand seemed to startle her. She dropped the mug and stood as one transfixed. A new light came into her face. She spelled "water" several times. Then she dropped on the ground and asked for its name and pointed to the pump and the trellis, and suddenly turning round she asked for my name.... *In a few hours she had added thirty new words to her vocabulary.*

But these words were now more than mere signs as they are to a dog and as they had been to Helen up to then. They were *symbols*. Helen had at last grasped and turned the key that admitted her for the first time to a new universe: the world of human beings. Helen describes this marvelous experience herself:

We walked down the path to the well-house, attracted by the fragrance of the honeysuckle with which it was covered. Someone was drawing water and my teacher placed my hand under the spout. As the cool stream gushed over one hand she spelled into the other the word *water*, first slowly, then rapidly. I stood still, my whole attention fixed upon the motion of her fingers. Suddenly I felt a misty consciousness as of something forgotten—a thrill of returning thought; and *somehow the mystery of language was revealed to me.* I knew then that "w-a-t-e-r" meant the

wonderful cool something that was flowing over my hand. That living word awakened my soul, gave it light, hope, joy, set it free!

Helen was transformed on the instant by this experience. Miss Sullivan had managed to touch Helen's symbol mechanism and set it in motion. Helen, on her part, grasped the external world with this mechanism that had lain dormant and inert all these years, sealed in dark and silent isolation by eyes that could not see and ears that heard not. But now she had crossed the boundary and entered a new land. Henceforth the progress would be rapid.

"I left the well-house," Helen reports, "eager to learn. Everything had a name, and each name gave birth to a new thought. As we returned to the house every object which I touched seemed to quiver with life. That was because I saw everything with the strange new sight that had come to me."

Helen became humanized rapidly. "I see an improvement in Helen from day to day," Miss Sullivan wrote in her diary, "*almost from hour to hour.* Everything must have a name now.... She drops the signs and pantomime she used before as soon as she has words to supply their place.... We notice her face grows more expressive each day...."

A more eloquent and convincing account of the significance of symbols and of the great gulf between the human mind and that of minds without symbols could hardly be imagined.

The natural processes of biologic evolution brought into existence in man, and man alone, a new and distinctive ability: the ability to use symbols. The most important form of symbolic expression is articulate speech. Articulate speech means communication of ideas; communication means preservation—tradition—and preservation means accumulation and progress. The emergence of the faculty of symboling has resulted in the genesis of a new order of phenomena: an extra-somatic, cultural order. All civilizations are born of, and are perpetuated by, the use of symbols. A culture, or civilization, is but a particular kind of form which the biologic, life-perpetuating activities of a particular animal, man, assume.

Human behavior is symbolic behavior; if it is not symbolic, it is not human. The infant of the genus *Homo* becomes a human being only as he is introduced into and participates in that order of phenomena which is culture. And the key to this world and the means of participation in it is—the symbol.

CRITICAL THINKING QUESTIONS

1. Why does White argue that a someone who is deaf and mute and unable to communicate symbolically is not fully human? What opposing argument might be made? What position would White take in the pro-choice versus pro-life abortion controversy?
2. Because the reality we experience is based on a particular system of symbols, how do we tend to view members of other cultures? What special efforts are needed to overcome the tendency to treat people of other cultures as less worthy than we are?
3. How did gaining the capacity to use symbols transform Helen Keller? How did this ability alter her capacity for further learning?

NOTE

1. Charles Darwin, *The Descent of Man*, chap. 3, 1871.

9

Investigating Canadian and American Value Differences Through an Analysis of Media Portrayals of Native Issues

Bruce Ravelli

In this article, Bruce Ravelli tests Seymour Martin Lipset's predictions, as outlined in the next article, about the differences between Canadian and American values by analyzing each country's print media presentations of Native issues. The analysis fails to find support for many of Lipset's arguments but does reveal some interesting differences between media portrayals. Keep these findings in mind when you read Lipset's piece.

CULTURE

One of sociology's defining interests is the study of the relationship between the individual and society (Brym with Fox, 1989: 4). A critical component of this investigation is the attempt to understand the role culture plays in defining people's perception of their social environment.

The first section of this article reviews the defining characteristics of culture and many of the concepts that sociologists use to analyze and study it. The second section investigates Canadian and American cultural values, to determine whether they are different. The purpose of this article then is twofold: the first is to acquaint you with the sociological analyses of culture, and the second is to compare and contrast Canadian and American cultures in the hope of helping you appreciate what it means to be Canadian.

DEFINING ELEMENTS OF CANADIAN CULTURE

Before we begin our analysis, it is important to define what sociologists mean when they refer to a society's *culture* and *values*.[1] *Culture* is defined as a broad spectrum of beliefs, values, and material objects that help people define their way of life. For example, Canadians' appreciation of multiculturalism and support for universal health care are two defining attributes of what it means to be Canadian. *Values* are defined in more general terms and involve standards, principles, and broad guidelines as to how people should try to live their lives. For example, a Canadian value might be the belief that it is better to compete fairly and lose than to cheat and win. As we will see, Canadian culture and values are shaped by an intricate and diverse set of physical and social circumstances.

Physically, Canada is the second-largest country in the world (Countries of the World, 2002). Although it boasts a rich and diverse supply of natural resources, it also endures challenging, cold winters. Noted Canadian writer Margaret Atwood believes that Canada's adaptation to its harsh physical environment defines Canadian culture and, to some extent, what it means to be Canadian (Atwood, 1970: 33, cited in Lipset, 1986: 124). Socially, Canadian culture has been defined by the coexistence of, and at times conflict between, the English and the French (Hiller, 1996). The fact that 87 percent of the people living in Quebec identify French as their mother tongue suggests that on this criterion at least, Quebec is certainly *distinct* from the rest of the country (Statistics Canada, 2002). However, Quebec's distinctiveness does not rest solely on language; it also rests on its people's shared history, symbols, ideas, and perceptions of reality (McGuigan, 1997: 52). Clearly, Canada's physical and social environments have influenced its culture, but arguably, they have also influenced its values as well.

Canadian values were of primary interest to a 1991 federal commission called the Citizens' Forum on Canada's Future, or the Spicer Commission (CFCF, 1991: 35–45). In its report, the commission identified seven primary cultural values:

1. *Equality and fairness in a democratic society:* Canadians believe in treating all citizens equally (e.g., people with disabilities).
2. *Consultation and dialogue:* Canadians try to settle differences peacefully through discussion and collective problem solving (e.g., Aboriginal self-government initiatives).
3. *Importance of accommodation and tolerance:* Canadians attempt to accommodate the traditions and customs of various ethnic populations (e.g., Aboriginal peoples and the French in Quebec).
4. *Appreciation for diversity:* Canadians support diversity (e.g., regional, ethnic, linguistic, or cultural differences).
5. *Compassion and generosity:* Canadians value their social safety net as an attempt to provide a fair and accessible society for all (e.g., universal health care, pension plans, economic development programs, openness to refugees, and commitment to reducing regional disparities).
6. *Attachment to Canada's natural beauty:* Canadians believe they have a close connection to the natural environment and feel that governments should do more to protect it from pollution and other forms of industrialization (e.g., environmental protection legislation).
7. *Commitment to freedom, peace, and nonviolent change:* Canadians see themselves as peaceful people who maintain an active role in international peacekeeping (e.g., Canada's support for UN-sponsored peacekeeping initiatives)

(Macionis, Jansson, & Benoit, 2002: 36).

Clearly, Canadian culture and values are a culmination of many physical and social forces, and studying Canadian–American differences fascinates Canadians (Lipset, 1999: 124; 1990: 53; 1986: 123) and Canadian sociologists in particular (Arnold & Tigert, 1974; Brym & Saint-Pierre, 1997; Clark, 1942; Clement, 1975; Hull, 1998: 4; Porter, 1965; Ravelli, 1994; Reitz & Breton, 1994). Seymour Martin Lipset (an American) has based his career on the study of what makes Canadians and Americans different (Tiryakian, 1991: 1040; Waller, 1990: 380). Lipset's book *Continental Divide* (1990) summarizes and consolidates his almost forty-five years of research on Canadian–American differences; in it he justifies his research, arguing that

> Knowledge of Canada or the United States is the best way to gain insight into the other North American country. Nations can only be understood in comparative perspective. And the more similar the units being compared, the more possible it should be to isolate the factors responsible for differences between them. Looking intensively at Canada and the United States sheds light on both of them. (1990: xiii)

Canadians, historically at least, defined themselves by what they were not—Americans (Lipset: 1990: 53; 1986: 123). For Lipset, the primordial event that generated the different founding ideologies of Canada and the United States was the American Revolution (Lipset, 1990: 8; 1986: 114; 1985: 160; 1963: 239). The United States emerged from the Revolution as a manifestation of the classic liberal state, rejecting all ties to the throne, ascriptive elitism, noblesse oblige, and communitarianism (1986: 114). English Canada, however, fought to maintain its imperial ties through the explicit rejection of liberal revolutions (Lipset, 1986: 115). Canadian identity was not defined by a successful revolution, but instead a successful counterrevolution (Lipset, 1993: 161; 1990: 42). America, conversely, was defined by a rigid and stable ideology Lipset called Americanism (1950: 181).[2]

Lipset offers evidence that Canadian and American founding ideologies are present in each country's literature (1986: 123). For example, American literature concentrates on themes of winning, opportunism, and confidence, while Canadian writing focuses on defeat, difficult physical circumstances, and abandonment by Britain (Lipset, 1990: 1; 1986: 123). Lipset cites well-known Canadian novelist Margaret Atwood, who suggests that national symbols reveal a great deal about the cultural values a nation embraces. For Atwood, the defining symbol for America was "the frontier," which inspired images of vitality and unrealized potential, while the symbol of "survival" summed up Canada's national character: "Canadians are forever taking the national pulse like doctors at a sickbed; the aim is not to see whether the patient will live well but simply whether he will live at all" (Atwood, 1970: 33, cited in Lipset, 1986: 124). Lipset suggests that the symbols, attitudes, and values of a people do not exist in a vacuum; rather, social and political institutions embody and reinforce them (Lipset, 1990: xiv; 225; 1986: 114, 119; Baer, Grabb, & Johnston, 1990a: 693). For Lipset, values are the basis on which society builds its social and political structures, and different value systems manifest themselves in all social realms, not just literature (Lipset, 1990: xiv).

Lipset argues that social structures reflect a society's values and beliefs (Baer, Grabb, & Johnston, 1990a: 693; Grabb & Curtis, 1988: 129, 137; Lipset, 1963: 210). To understand the importance of culture in determining a society's social structure, Lipset incorporated Talcott Parsons' (1952) pattern variables typology into his research (Lipset, 1963: 210). Parsons' pattern variables provide researchers with a method for classifying social values that is more sensitive to cultural variation than the older polar concepts of sociology, such as core–periphery, folk–urban, mechanical–organic, and primary–secondary.

Lipset's thesis of cross-national value differences suggests that Canadians are more elitist and ascriptive; appreciate racial and ethnic variation; and are more community-oriented than Americans. Although Lipset is a dominant figure in North American sociology,[3] his Canadian–American research has been the subject of much interest and debate. Various researchers (see Baer, Grabb, & Johnston, 1990a, 1990b, 1990c, 1993; Curtis, Grabb, & Baer, 1992; Grabb & Curtis, 1988) have attempted to test Lipset's thesis but have faced several difficulties, the most challenging being the following:

- Lipset's research is based on subjective data that are difficult, if not impossible, to test systematically.
- Lipset's pattern variables are at times contradictory and often suggest Canadian–American differences that are opposite to what his thesis would predict.
- Lipset fails to recognize how contemporary social change may influence Canadian and American values.
- Lipset's approach ignores regional variations.
- Lipset fails to offer alternative explanations for Canadian and American value differences.

In spite of such pointed criticism, sociologists generally agree that Lipset's fundamental proposition that Canadian and American cultural values are different, is sound (see Brym with Fox, 1989: 16–8; Clark, 1975: 26; Baer, Grabb, & Johnston, 1990a: 708; 1990c: 276; McGuigan, 1990: 127; Ogmundson & Fisher, 1994: 196).

One area of investigation that may shed a contemporary light on Canadian–American differences is an analysis of each country's media, looking for evidence of national value differences.[4]

THE MEDIA'S INFLUENCE ON DEFINING CULTURE

In *Inventing Reality* (1993), Michael Parenti argues that although the media may not mould our every opinion, they do mould *opinion visibility* (Parenti, 1993: 23; see also Gamson & Modigliani, 1989: 3). In effect, journalists, reporters, and news anchors set our *perceptual agenda* (a view shared by Adams, 1978: 30; and Smith, 1992: 210). Parenti states, "The media may not always be able to tell us what to think, but they are strikingly successful in telling us what to think about" (1993: 23; see also Smith, 1992: 210). It is not so much that the media construct opinion; it is enough that they give legitimacy to certain views and illegitimacy to others (Parenti, 1993: 24). This ability has important implications for how the media define and reflect our perceptions and guide our interactions with the social world by effectively constructing news that reflects dominant values (Parenti, 1993: 69). Edward Herman and Noam Chomsky explore this issue in *Manufacturing Consent* (1988).

Herman and Chomsky suggest that the media intentionally create a social environment favourable to the dominant classes by *manufacturing consent* through the filtering of stories (Herman & Chomsky, 1988: xi, 2). This filtering takes two forms: (1) deciding not to cover a story and (2) presenting a story in such a way as to diffuse or bias its objective content. This filtering influences how people see and interpret the social world because it defines their reality. Herman and Chomsky suggest that the primary role of mainstream media is to ensure popular support for the economic, social, and political agenda of the privileged classes (1988: 298). Their *propaganda* model reveals many of the techniques media use to manufacture consent.

One way to find evidence for Canadian and American cultural differences would be to study a single social phenomenon common to both countries, such as how the media present a common and familiar issue. This brief review of how the media reflect and define a society's values reinforces the selection of media as one avenue by which to investigate Lipset's thesis of cross-national value differences in more detail. As argued by many, the media are becoming *the* conduit through which much of the world defines and reflects its cultural values (see Adams, 1978: 30; Campbell, 1999; Gamson & Modigliani, 1989: 3; Gitlin, 1980; Herman & Chomsky, 1988: 2; Parenti, 1993: 23; Smith, 1992: 210; Tetzlaff, 1992). My approach uses Native issues as a social phenomenon for study since both Canada and the United States have a long history of Native–White contact (see Berelson & Salter, 1946; Grenier, 1993; Singer, 1982; Skea, 1993).[5]

To test Lipset's thesis, I employed a fifty-year longitudinal study of Canadian and American media and how they presented Native issues. The medium I chose for the comparison was newsmagazines, in particular, *Maclean's* in Canada and *Newsweek* in the United States.[6] These newsmagazines were selected because they are regarded as journalistic leaders (see Roy, 1990: 510; van Driel & Richardson, 1988: 38) and attract national audiences. Thus, they should present national values to the extent that they exist. To test Lipset's theory, I formulated seven hypotheses flowing directly out of his four pattern variables (see Table 9.1).

My sampling frame included all articles referring to Natives in *Maclean's* and *Newsweek* from 1943 to 1993.[7] After locating the articles, I conducted a content analysis to determine whether there were systematic differences between each magazine's coverage of Native issues.

My analysis of *Maclean's* and *Newsweek* incorporated two complementary perspectives, the first a quantitative examination testing whether Lipset's value differences were evident (see Appendix A), and the second a qualitative exploration to detect themes speaking to Lipset's thesis (see Appendix B). The quantitative analysis provides a rudimentary statistical assessment of Lipset's thesis, while the qualitative has greater sensitivity to themes appearing in the articles pertaining to cultural differences. By coding the articles from both quantitative and qualitative perspectives, I hoped to gain a more complete appreciation of their portrayals of Native issues than would be possible by using either approach independently.

Results suggest little quantitative or qualitative support for Lipset's thesis of Canadian–American value differences (see Table 9.2).

TABLE 9.1: Testing Lipset's Thesis

Lipset's Pattern Variable	Hypothesis
Elitism–Egalitarianism	1a: Canadians will view political leaders more positively than Americans. 1b: Canadians will view minority leaders more critically than Americans.
Ascription–Achievement	2a: Canadians will support government-sponsored redistribution programs more than Americans. 2b: Canadians will criticize lawlessness more than Americans.
Particularism–Universalism	3: Canadians will support the mosaic perspective more than Americans.
Diffuseness–Specificity	4a: Canadians will support the collectivist perspective more than Americans. 4b: Canadians will criticize minority challenges to the collective more than Americans.

TABLE 9.2: Qualitative/Quantitative Results Summary

Pattern Variable	Hypothesis	Quantitative Results	Qualitative Results
Elitism versus Egalitarianism	1a: Political Leadership 1b: Native Leadership	Reject Reject	Reject Reject
Ascription versus Achievement	2a: Redistribution Programs 2b: Native Lawlessness	Reject Reject	Support Reject
Particularism versus Universalism	3: Mosaic Perspective	Support	Support
Diffuseness versus Specificity	4a: Collectivist Perspective 4b: Native Challenge to the Collective	Reject Reject	Support Reject

Table 9.2 illustrates that six of the seven quantitative results fail to support Lipset's thesis. Statistical differences existed between *Maclean's* and *Newsweek* and their presentation of Native issues, but the differences were often in the opposite direction of what Lipset's thesis would predict. Qualitative results were similar to the quantitative in that four of the seven hypotheses rejected Lipset's thesis.

1. Elitism versus Egalitarianism is **not supported** as all four tests reject Lipset's hypothesis.
2. Ascription versus Achievement is **not supported** as three of the four tests refute Lipset's hypothesis.
3. Particularism versus Universalism is **supported** as both tests support Lipset's hypothesis.
4. Diffuseness versus Specificity is **not supported** as three of the four tests reject Lipset's hypothesis.

My findings suggest that Canadian and American cultural values do vary, but not in a manner consistent with Lipset's pattern variable thesis. The only pattern variable to be supported was *Particularism versus Universalism*, which suggests that Canadians do recognize and encourage racial and ethnic diversity more than Americans. Although my research found little support for the three remaining pattern variables, it did find evidence to support the common experience that Canadian and American cultures differ (see Reitz & Breton, 1994).

CONCLUSION

After reading almost 400 magazine articles, on at least three separate occasions, I was struck by how often *Maclean's* presented Native issues with emotion and passion and how rarely any empathy was shown for the plight of American Natives in *Newsweek*. For me, this suggests one of the defining differences between Canadians and Americans—the belief in, and support for, multiculturalism. Granted, Canada's record of dealing with Native populations has often been strained and difficult; however, the dialogue between the parties has played a central and defining role in constructing our national value systems. This level of public debate and discussion between American Natives and the larger American society has not yet occurred. Canadians, however, must appreciate that just saying that Canada is a multicultural society is not enough. All people in Canada need to know, and be shown, that for Canadians, multiculturalism is not just an abstract philosophy; it is one of the defining elements of who we are as a people—multiculturalism means nothing if we don't practise what we preach.

APPENDIX A

My quantitative coding tested Lipset's overall thesis of cross-national value differences by comparing how each article portrayed issues that were relevant to Lipset's pattern variables. For example, when an article discussed political leaders (pertinent to hypothesis 1a), I noted every reference to political leaders as positive, negative, or indeterminate in the margins of the article. Positive statements about political leaders were coded as PL+, negative as PL–, and indeterminate as PL? When I completed the coding, I added the number of positive, negative, and indeterminate references and determined an overall coding for that article. That is, if the article had 15 positive statements about the political leader, 3 negative, and 0 indeterminate, I concluded that the article presented a supportive portrayal of political leaders. The statistical analyses were based on these comparisons. An obvious concern at this point is how confident I am that my coding of the articles was reliable.

Research is deemed reliable when the particular research technique, applied repeatedly to the same phenomenon, yields the same results (Babbie, 1995: 124). I am confident that my coding was reliable for two reasons. First, totals for the three possible codings (i.e., PL+, PL–, PL?) were never within 10 percent of each other. This indicates that the article's editorial bias (or lack of one) was readily apparent. Second, even though I was the only person coding the articles, I re-coded a 10 percent random sample of the articles (30 articles from *Maclean's*, 10 from *Newsweek*) six months after I completed my initial coding. The coefficient of reliability between the codings was 72 percent (coefficient of reliability = number of units in identical category/total number of units). Since coefficient values higher than 60 percent are deemed reliable (Jackson, 1995: 72), I am confident that my coding reliably reflects the articles' (and by extension, the newsmagazines') editorial bias.

APPENDIX B

Content analysis is a set of procedures used to study text (Weber, 1990: 9) and is appropriate for most forms of communication (Babbie, 1995: 307). Using content analysis I was able to investigate themes in media content that went beyond those explicitly stated. Robert Weber (1990: 9) suggests that content analysis of media can reveal international differences and uncover the cultural patterns of groups, institutions, or societies. The ability to look beyond the text makes content analysis well suited for a cross-national analysis of culture differences in media (Babbie, 1995: 315).

CRITICAL THINKING QUESTIONS

1. What are pattern variables? Do you feel they are useful concepts when investigating national value differences? Why?
2. Mass media play an important role in our lives today. What are some ways in which mass media influence your world view that was not possible in your parents' generation?
3. An ongoing debate for researchers is whether media actively *define* our reality or alternatively, simply *reflect* it. Which do you feel is the more convincing position? Why?

NOTES

1. The majority of the following analysis is a consolidation of my doctoral dissertation, "Canadian–American Value Differences: Media Portrayals of Native Issues" (1997), unpublished manuscript, Department of Sociology, University of Victoria.
2. An ideology is a system of beliefs, common ideas, perceptions, and values held in common by members of a collective (Parsons, 1952: 349). Ideology can be thought of as the filter through which we interpret our social world.
3. As demonstrated, in part, by his election as president of the American Sociological Association for 1993–94.
4. My working assumption behind this analysis is the belief that media content will reflect national values to secure the widest audience possible and, by extension, the greatest financial benefit for its shareholders.
5. The term "Native" is used to describe the indigenous populations of North America. This terminology was selected over others (e.g., Aboriginal, First Nations, Amerindian, Indian) as it is the standard in contemporary literature (see Francis, 1992: 9).
6. Electronic media are too recent to study and print media lend themselves to better contextual analysis (see Neumann, Just, & Crigler, 1992: 58–9; Vipond, 1992: 27, 78, 128).
7. To locate the articles, I first consulted the Library of Congress subject heading Indians of North America. I then manually searched the *Reader's Guide to Periodical Literature* (Reader's Guide) and the *Canadian Periodical Index* (CPI) for references to the subject title. This strategy located 296 articles in *Maclean's* and 96 in *Newsweek*.

REFERENCES

Adams, W. C. 1978. Network news research in perspective: A bibliographic essay. In *Television network news: Issues in content research*. Washington, DC: George Washington University Press.

Arnold, S. J., and D. J. Tigert. 1974. Canadians and Americans: A comparative analysis. *International Journal of Comparative Sociology*, 15: 68–83.

Atwood, M. 1970. *The journals of Susanna Moodie: Poems*. Toronto: Oxford University Press.

Babbie, E. 1995. *The practice of social research*, 7th ed. Belmont, Calif.: Wadsworth Publishing Company.

Baer, D., E. Grabb, and W. A. Johnston. 1990a. *The values of Canadians and Americans: A critical analysis and reassessment*. Social Forces, 68(3): 693–713.

———. 1990b. Reassessing differences in Canadian and American values. In *Images of Canada: The sociological tradition*, eds. J. Curtis, and L. Tepperman, 86–97. Scarborough, Ont.: Prentice-Hall Canada.

———. 1990c. The values of Canadians and Americans: A rejoinder. *Social Forces*, 69(1): 273–77.

———. 1993. National character, regional culture, and the values of Canadians and Americans. *Canadian Review of Sociology and Anthropology*, 30(1): 13–36.

Berelson, B., and P. J. Salter. 1946. Majority and minority Americans: An analysis of magazine fiction. *Public Opinion Quarterly*, 10.

Brym, R. J., with B. J. Fox. 1989. *From culture to power: The sociology of English Canada*. Toronto: Oxford University Press.

Brym, R., and C. Saint-Pierre. 1997. Canada: Canadian sociology. *Contemporary Sociology*, 26(5): 543–46.

Campbell, K. 1999. Why we must protect Canadian culture from the U.S. juggernaut. In *Canadian communications: Issues in contemporary media culture*, eds. B. Szuchewycz, and J. Sloniowski, 214–18. Scarborough, Ont.: Prentice Hall/Allyn and Bacon Canada.

CFCF (Citizen's Forum on Canada's Future). 1991. *Report to the People and Government of Canada*. Ottawa: Supply and Services Canada.

Clark, S. D. 1942. *The social development of Canada: An introductory study with select documents*. Toronto: University of Toronto Press.

———. 1975. The post–Second World War Canadian society. *Canadian Review of Sociology and Anthropology*, 12(1).

Clement, W. 1975. *The Canadian corporate elite: An analysis of economic power*. Toronto: McClelland and Stewart.

Countries of the World. 2002. Country statistics at a glance. [Online]. Available: **http://www.infoplease.com/ipa/A0762380.html**. Accessed July 17, 2002.

Curtis, J. E., E. G. Grabb, and D. E. Baer. 1992. Voluntary association membership in fifteen countries: A comparative analysis." *American Sociological Review*, 57(April): 139–52.

Francis, D. 1992. *The imaginary Indian: The image of the Indian in Canadian culture*. Vancouver: Arsenal Pulp Press.

Gamson, W. A., and A. Modigliani. 1989. Media discourse and public opinion on nuclear power: A constructionist approach." *American Journal of Sociology*, 95(1) : 1–37.

Gitlin, T. 1980. *The whole world is watching*. Berkeley: University of California Press.

Grabb, E. G., and J. E. Curtis. 1988. English Canadian–American differences in orientation toward social control and individual rights. *Sociological Focus*, 21(2): 127–40.

Grenier, M. 1993. Native Indians in the English-Canadian press: The case of the Oka Crisis. *Media, Culture and Society*, 16 (April): 313–36.

Herman, E. S., and N. Chomsky. 1988. *Manufacturing consent: The political economy of the mass media*. New York: Pantheon Books.

Hiller, H. 1996. *Canadian society: A macro analysis*, 3rd ed. Scarborough, Ont.: Prentice Hall Canada.

Hull, J. P. 1998. From many, two: A bibliographic history of Canadian–American relations. *American Studies International*, 36(2): 4–22.

Jackson, W. 1995. *Methods: Doing social research*. Scarborough, Ont.: Prentice Hall Canada.

Lipset, S. M. 1950. *Agrarian socialism: The Cooperative Commonwealth Federation in Saskatchewan*. Berkeley and Los Angeles: University of California Press.

———. 1963. *The first new nation: The United States in historical and comparative perspective*. New York: Basic Books.

———. 1985. Canada and the United States: The cultural dimension. *In Canada and the United States*, eds. C. F. Doran, and J. H. Sigler, 109–160. Englewood Cliffs, N.J.: Prentice Hall.

———. 1986. Historical traditions and national characteristics: A comparative analysis of Canada and the United States. *Canadian Journal of Sociology* 11(2): 113–55.

———. 1990. Continental divide: The values and institutions of the United States and Canada. New York: Routledge.

———. 1993. Revolution and counterrevolution: The United States and Canada. In *A passion for identity: An introduction to Canadian studies*, eds. D. Taras, B. Rasporich, and E. Mandel, 150–61. Scarborough, Ont.: Nelson Canada.

———. 1999. American union density in comparative perspective. *Contemporary Sociology*, 27(2): 123–25.

Macionis, J. J., S. M. Jansson, and C. M. Benoit. 2002. *Society: The basics*, 2nd Cdn ed. Toronto: Pearson Education Canada.

McGuigan, B. 1990. *The comparative sociology of Seymour Martin Lipset: An analysis and critique*. Unpublished master's thesis. University of Calgary.

———. 1997. Issues in Canadian culture. In *Issues in Canadian sociology*, 2nd ed., eds. M. Kanwar, and D. Swenson, 35–60. Dubuque, Iowa: Kendall/Hunt Publishing.

Neumann, R. W., M. R. Just, and A. N. Crigler. 1992. *Common knowledge: News and the construction of political meaning*. Chicago: University of Chicago Press.

Ogmundson, R. L., and L. Fisher. 1994. Beyond Lipset and his critics: An initial reformulation. *Canadian Review of Sociology and Anthropology*, 31(2): 196–99.

Parenti, M. 1993. *Inventing the politics of news media reality*, 2nd ed. New York: St. Martin's Press.

Parsons, T. 1952. *The social system*. London: Tavistock Publications Ltd.

Porter, J. 1965. *The vertical mosaic: An analysis of social class and power in Canada*. Toronto: University of Toronto Press.

Ravelli, B. 1994. Health care in the United States and Canada. In *The sociological outlook: A text with readings*, 4th ed., ed. R. Luhman, 467–68. San Diego: Collegiate Press.

Reitz, J. G., and R. Breton. 1994. *The illusion of difference: Realities of ethnicity in Canada and the United States*. Toronto: C.D. Howe Institute.

Roy, D. 1990. The U.S. print media and the conventional military balance in Europe. *Armed Forces & Society*, 16(4): 509–28.

Singer, B. D. 1982. Minorities in the media: A content analysis of Native Canadians in the daily press. *Canadian Review of Sociology and Anthropology*, 19(3): 348–59.

Skea, W. H. 1993. The Canadian newspaper industry's portrayal of the Oka Crisis. *Native Studies Review*, 9(1): 15–31.

Smith, R. L. 1992. Media networking: Toward a model for the global management of sociocultural change. In *Mass media effects across cultures*, eds. F. Korzenny et al., 201–28. Newbury Park, Calif.: Sage.

Statistics Canada. 2002. Population by home language, 2001 Census. [Online]. Available: **http://www.statcan.ca/english/Pgdb/demo29b.htm**. Accessed July 16, 2002.

Tetzlaff, D. 1992. Popular culture and social control in late capitalism. In *Culture and power: A media, culture and society reader*, eds. P. Scannell, P. Schlesinger, and C. Sparks, 48–72. London: Sage.

Tiryakian, E. A. 1991. Book review of *Continental divide: The values and institutions of the United States and Canada* by S. M. Lipset. *American Journal of Sociology*, 96(4): 1040–42.

Van Driel, B., and Richardson, J. T. 1988. Print media coverage of new religious movements: A longitudinal study. *Journal of Communication*, 38(3): 37–61.

Vipond, M. 1992. *The mass media in Canada*. Toronto: James Lorimer & Company.

Waller, H. M. 1990. Book review of *Continental divide: The values and institutions of the United States and Canada* by S. M. Lipset. *Canadian Journal of Political Science*, 23: 380–81.

Weber, R. P. 1990. *Basic content analysis*, 2nd ed. Newbury Park, Calif.: Sage Publications.

10

Canada and the United States: A Comparative View

Seymour Martin Lipset

Lipset suggests that Canadian and American values are fundamentally different and result from each nation's response to the American Revolution. For Lipset, this historical event continues to define each society's values along predictable and observable lines.

The 23 independent states plus the assorted colonies and autonomous commonwealths of North and South America provide a magnificent laboratory for comparative analysis, of which relatively few social scientists have taken advantage. The obvious advantage for such an analysis of common cultural and linguistic origin among twenty of those societies, the Latin-American republics and Puerto Rico, has not encouraged many systematic efforts to account for their differences. The Caribbean nations offer the diversity of being former colonies of six foreign powers and the similarity of having preponderantly Negro populations of slave descent, providing an interesting and as yet relatively untapped arena for comparative research. English-speaking Canada and the United States have long presented unused opportunities to analyse the variations in institutional arrangements in highly similar cultural contexts.

As an illustration of the value of such comparative analysis within the Americas, I would like to deal briefly with the two northernmost nations. There is little question that a comprehensive analysis of institutional patterns and groups in the United States and Canada would be enormously fruitful for sociologists. These two nations share a British legacy, frontier areas, immigrants of comparable origin from the same historic epoch, and comparable ecological conditions. Both have attained a high level of economic development and stable democratic political institutions.

Although the United States and English-speaking Canada probably resemble each other as much as any two nations on earth, the fact remains that various observers have noted a consistent pattern of differences between them. To analyse

Source: S. M. Lipset. (1964). Canada and the United States: A Comparative View. *Canadian Review of Sociology and Anthropology*, 1, 173–185. Reprinted by permission of the Canadian Sociology and Anthropology Association.

the factors which underlie the perpetuation of small differences among nations is one of the more intriguing and difficult tasks in comparative study. What makes the Canadian more law-abiding? Why is there a much lower divorce rate in Canada? Why do fewer Canadians than Americans or Filipinos or Puerto Ricans attend universities? Why is the Canadian "quieter" in many of his behaviour traits than his American neighbour? Many of our assumptions about sources of national differences can be tested in this North American laboratory.

To a considerable extent comparative macroscopic sociology deals with polarity concepts when it seeks to compare core aspects of societies—gemeinschaft-gesellschaft, organic solidarity–mechanical solidarity, inner-directed versus other-directed, diffuseness-specificity, achievement-ascription, traditional-modern, and so forth. As I have attempted to demonstrate elsewhere, one particularly effective set of polarities for systematically classifying the central values of social systems is the pattern variables as originally set forth by Talcott Parsons.[1] Pattern variables are dichotomous categories of interaction in different structures. Those distinctions which seem particularly suitable for the analysis of Canada and the United States are achievement-ascription, universalism-particularism, self-orientation–collectivity-orientation, and equalitarianism-elitism. (The latter is not one of Parsons' distinctions, but one added here.) A society's value system may emphasize that a person in his orientation to others treats them in terms of their abilities and performances or in terms of inherited qualities (achievement-ascription); applies a general standard or responds to some personal attribute or relationship (universalism-particularism); perceives the separate needs of others or subordinates the individual's needs to the defined interests of the larger group (self-orientation–collectivity-orientation); and stresses that all persons must be respected because they are human beings or emphasizes the general superiority of those who hold elite positions (equalitarianism-elitism).[2]

The great mass of literature on these two democracies suggests the United States to be more achievement-oriented, universalistic, equalitarian, and self-oriented than Canada. Because the value differences of Canada and the United States are not great, the test of the utility of the comparative approach to the two North American societies depends upon specifying the special differences that *do* exist and identifying the historic issues and problems which sustain the near differences between them.

Though many factors in the history of these nations account for the variations between them, the following factors may be singled out: varying origins in their political systems and national identities, varying religious traditions, and varying frontier experiences. In general terms, the value orientations of Canada stem from a counter-revolutionary past, a need to differentiate itself from the United States, the influence of monarchical institutions, a dominant Anglican religious tradition, and a less individualistic and more governmentally controlled expansion of the Canadian than of the American frontier.

HOW DIFFERENT, HOW SIMILAR?

Both nations are largely urbanized, heavily industrialized, and politically stabilized. They share many of the same ecological and demographic conditions, approximately the same level of economic development, similar rates of upward and downward social mobility. To a very great extent Canada and the United States share the same values but, as Kaspar Naegele has pointed out, in Canada these values are held much more tentatively.[3] Both are new peoples and new states, but Canada's relationship to Britain has helped perpetuate in a North American nation the elements of a set of values having Old World origins and a conservative character. Thus, while equality and achievement, for example, are values emphasized in both American societies, in Canada the emphasis is somewhat less and therefore the contrast between the nations remains one of degree.

Perhaps no other value emphases are as paramount in American life as the twin values of equalitarianism and achievement. Both have been strongest in the school system where the principles of the "common school," and "equal opportunity for success" remain viable educational ideals. By contrast, in Canada education has held a more elitist and ascriptive import. These value differences are quantitatively indicated by a comparison of college enrolment figures. If we relate the number enrolled in institutions of higher learning to the size of the age cohort 20 to 24, we find that 30.2 per cent in the United States were attending universities in 1960, compared with 9.2 per cent in Canada.[4]

It has been suggested that elitist tendencies among the Canadians account for the education of a limited few at the college level. Some Canadian writers have pointed out that until very recently education in their country was designed to train an ecclesiastical and political *élite* much in the British tradition.[5] Canadian educators, unlike American, have shown resistance to the introduction into higher education of purely vocational training. Technical training has been viewed as corrupting the "aristocracy of intellect," those being educated for political and social leadership.

Status distinctions, which exist in the United States as in all nations, do not have as much legitimacy as in Canada. For example, the greater strength of elitist and ascriptive value emphases in Canada would seem to be reflected comparatively in the paternalistic organization of the family, in the reverence paid to the clergy by the laity, in the diffuse deference granted the old by the young, men by women, teachers by students, and politicians by the electorate.[6] From James Bryce to S. D. Clark, sociological observers have stressed the greater respect in Canada for political leaders than in the United States. The democratic ethos with its stress on populist values derivative from equalitarian emphases in the United States also "leads to certain impatience with legal process and, occasionally, to outright disrespect for the law."[7]

There are several indicators of the differences in Canadian and American respect for public authority. Where diffuse respect for public authority exists, we should expect to find greater reliance on informal social controls based on traditional obligations. One indicator of the relative strength of the informal normative mechanisms of social control as compared with the restrictive emphases of legal sanctions may be the extent to which a nation requires police protection. The data in Table 10.1 indicate that the ratio of police to population is more than one-third greater in the United States than in Canada. In 1961 only one police officer in Canada was killed by criminal action while on duty, compared to 37 police officers killed in the United States. By 1963, the latter figure had risen to 55 police officers in a single year while the former remained at one.[8] (The United States has about ten times the population of Canada.) The proportionately fewer lawyers in private practice in Canada (one for 1,630 people) as compared to the United States (one for 868) suggests the lesser propensity of Canadians to rely on the law even for civil matters.[9]

TABLE 10.1: Number and Rates of Police Protection in Canada and the United States

Country	Number of Police Personnel	Ratio per 100,000 Population
Canada (1961)	26,189	143.2
United States (1962)	360,000	193.8

Source: Canada: Dominion Bureau of Statistics, *Police Administration Statistics*, 1961, 18; United States: United States Department of Commerce, Bureau of the Census, *Statistical Abstracts of the United States*, 1963, 436.

The greater obedience paid to the law by Canadians may be reflected also in the rates of charges for criminal offences in the two countries. Though data on crime rates are far from amenable to accurate cross-national comparisons, both countries offer the same definition and report statistics for several major criminal offences. The data in Table 10.2 indicate that crime rates for particular offences are substantially higher in the United States than in Canada.

The greater respect for the law in Canada, as compared to the United States, may underlie the greater freedom of political dissent, and the lesser corruption.[10] In English-speaking Canada it is not at all unexpected that one writer has remarked that "Canadians are today perhaps more aware of the differences in their attitudes toward the law than anything else distinguishing them from Americans."[11]

The variation in the strength of the achievement and self-orientations in the United States and Canada may account for another political difference, the fact that "free enterprise" ideology, though accepted in Canada, has never been the source of as violent political conflicts there as in the United States. The greater respect for

government and political leaders, derived in part from elitism and in part from the need dictated by special historic circumstances (see below) requiring that the central government intervene repeatedly in economic and local political matters to assure national survival, has inhibited the development of strong economic individualism as a dominant political virtue. Canada has been much more collectivity-oriented than the United States: proposals for medicare, support for large families, government intervention in the economy, and public ownership of major enterprises have encountered much less opposition north of the border than south of it. "The extreme economic individualism expressed by such slogans as 'the best government is the one that governs least' does not have such deep roots in Canada" as it has in the United States.[12] As one English writer notes:

One of the strange contradictions of Canada is that although it has never had anything resembling a Socialist Government in Ottawa, the list of its "nationalized" industries is almost as imposing as Britain's: more than half the railways; the principal airline; most of radio and television; the Atomic Energy Corporation and one of the biggest uranium producers; a big plastics industry; many of the power utilities [and telephone and telegraph]; and the entire liquor retailing business.[13]

TABLE 10.2: Adults Charged on Selected Indictable Offences, by Class of Offence, 1960, for Canada and the United States

	Canada Rate per 100,000		United States* Rate per 100,000	
	Number	Population	Number	Population
Burglary	8,267	46.4	137,800	126.7
Criminal homicide	207	1.16	7,956	7.3
Forgery and counterfeiting	1,158	6.4	25,244	23.2
Fraud and embezzlement	2,414	13.5	42,189	38.8
Theft-larceny	15,545	87.2	237,193	218.1

Source: Canada: Dominion Bureau of Statistics, *Canada Year Book*, 1962, 356; United States: United States Bureau of the Census, *Statistical Abstracts of the United States*, 1962, 152.

*The rate for the United States was computed from a total population base of 108,779,000; for Canada's rates, the population base used was 17,814,000. The weaker authority over local policing of the American federal government as compared to the Canadian makes it more difficult for the former to collect reliable crime statistics; hence the discrepancy in the proportion of the total population for whom data exist.

And as a Canadian points out, "it is interesting to note that at a time when the *laissez-faire* philosophy was prevailing in the rest of the Western World, there was no protest in Canada against government intervention and interference, not even from business circles."[14] Far from turning to McCarthyism or Goldwaterism, Canadian conservatives responded to years of political defeat by renaming their party the *Progressive* Conservatives.

The lower divorce rate in Canada, compared to that in the United States, presented in Table 10.3, may be viewed as another reflection of the strength of collectivity-orientation in the North. The semi-Establishment status of churches in Canada has lent strong support to traditional morality. It is more difficult to obtain a divorce in all the Canadian provinces than in almost all of the American states. S. D. Clark argues that "the institution of the family [in Canada] has found support in much the same set of conservative forces which have upheld the institutions of law and order."[15]

TABLE 10.3: Divorce Rates per 1,000 Marriages for Specified Years in Canada and the United States

Year	Canada	United States
1891	less than 1	60.0
1911	less than 1	93.4
1941	29.3	168.5
1951	41.0	230.4
1956	45.2	233.0
1960	53.5	257.3

Source: Canada: Dominion Bureau of Statistics, *Canada Year Book*, 1962, 209, 211; United States: United States Department of Commerce, Bureau of the Census, *Statistical Abstracts of the United States*, 1962, 52, and United Nations, Demographic Yearbook, 1960 (New York), 607. See also Lincoln Day, "Patterns of Divorce in Australia and the United States," *American Sociological Review*, XXIX, 4, 1964, 509–22, n.b. Table II.

The weakness in Canada of the sort of rugged individualism (self-orientation) and emphasis on achievement so characteristic of its neighbour to the south may be reflected also in the reluctance of Canadians to be over-optimistic, assertive, or experimentally inclined. Alistair Horne points out that Canadian caution manifests itself in several ways: "one is that Canadians take out more insurance per capita than any other race in the world. Another is that they buy considerably less on hire-purchase [installment plan] than the Americans.... The average Canadian is also cautious about his savings, favoring Government bonds and savings banks. Whereas over the years the American big investor has tended to take a risk on the future of Canada and invest heavily in more speculative Canadian enterprises, the wealthy Canadian cautiously puts his money into Standard Oil of New Jersey."[16] It has been more difficult for the Horatio Alger model of success to take hold in Canadian society where there is strong resistance to economic aggressiveness, social informality, and unabashed materialism. A leading Canadian historian, Arthur Lower, has argued that "Henry Ford was a figure who could hardly have been other than American. Canada did not provide a stage for such as he. Yet this was not on account of lack of opportunities here [in Canada] for accumulating wealth, but rather because that process called for more betting on the sure thing than was necessary across the border."[17] The muted effect of the achievement pattern in Canada is also observed by an English commentator: "Canadian 'quietness' extends also to the worlds of both business and politics...the rat race exists, of course; the North American urge to get ahead, to keep up with the Jones's, is all there, but in Canada, it seems to be kept to a healthier mean."[18]

The emphasis on achievement in the United States is strongly linked to universalism. For instance, in the United States there is a proclaimed need to treat everyone according to the same standard. This universalistic objective underlies the concept of the "melting pot" which holds that no one should be disqualified from full participation on the grounds of ethnic origin or other social distinctions. The melting-pot concept is achievement orientation applied to entire ethnic groups.[19] In contradistinction to the melting pot of the United States, Canadians speak of their society as a "mosaic," a concept which embodies in theory the "right to sustained collective individuality."[20] Vincent Massey, a former Governor General, has expressed the Canadian stress on the presentation of particularistic values:

> We have been successful in our manner of adjusting the relations of the varied communities making Canada their home. About one out of three speaks French as his mother tongue. He is no minority assimilated within a common Canadianism, but rather a partner sharing equally in the joint project of Confederation. Then there are the "new Canadians" of whom two million from Great Britain and from Europe have reached our shores since 1945.... We try to fit in the newcomers much as they are, as pieces in the Canadian mosaic.[21]

Canadian particularism has been demonstrated also in the requirement, in existence until recently, that Canadian passports indicated ethnic origin, for example, a Canadian of German origin even though the German origin may go back more than a century. The Canadian Census not only records religious data gathered from each individual, but also reports the national origins of every Canadian, except for Jews. Jews, regardless of country of paternal ancestry, are classified as such under both religion and national origin.

Canada's political party system has witnessed the rise of a number of "particularistic" third parties, various French-Canadian nationalist or separatist movements, plus the Progressives, Social Credit, and the Co-operative Commonwealth Federation (CCF). The latter, a socialist party, has recently joined with the Canadian Labour Congress to form the New Democratic Party which, based on trade unions, is the largest contemporary "third" party. This pattern of Canadian politics—that is, the continued presence of strong particularistic third parties—is consistent with the assumption that Canada is more particularistic (group-attribute conscious) than the seemingly more universalistic United States.

THE ROOTS OF TWO DEMOCRACIES

Many writers seeking to account for value differences between the United States and Canada suggest that they stem in large part from the revolutionary origins of the United States and the counter-revolutionary history of Canada, from two disparate founding ethos. The Loyalist *émigrés* from the American Revolution and Canada's subsequent and repeated fears of encroachment by the United States fostered the institutionalization of a counter-revolutionary or conservative ethos.[22] By contrast the core values of the United States are linked to the idealistic ideology which emerged during the Revolution and were codified in the Declaration of Independence and elaborated in the principles successfully pressed by the Jeffersonian Democrats in the first formative post-Revolutionary decades.

In Canada's counter-revolutionary beginnings we find the clue to the continuance of British ascriptive and elitist value patterns. The Canadian historian, Arthur Lower, has pointed out that "in its new wilderness home and its new aspect of British North Americanism, colonial Toryism made its second attempt to erect on American soil a copy of the English social edifice. From one point of view this is the most significant thing about the Loyalist movement; it withdrew a class concept of life from the south, moved it up north and gave it a second chance."[23] The anti-revolutionary and anti-American character of Canada's political and social development helped strengthen ethnic particularism. The English rulers of French Canada opposed assimilation as a means of resisting Americanization. Falconer indicates that "as late as 1822 Lord Dalhousie favored the French Canadians of the lower province as a make-weight against Americanizing tendencies which he discerned in Upper Canada."[24] Similarly, the unification of the British North American colonies was procured by Empire-oriented Canadian Conservatives who feared expansion by the United States across the border. The decision to provide

Canada with a much stronger central government than that of the United States was based on anti-American feeling.[25]

In distinction to Canada, the United States is a result of a successful Revolution and prolonged War of Independence organized around an ideology which proclaimed the validity of a specific system of equalitarian and universalistic social relations. Populist beliefs were at the root of early demands from the citizenry that the franchise be extended to everyone. Such populist tendencies lead to the "conviction that government should reflect the will of the people.... [It] breeds a suspicion of strong leaders...."[26] The populist demands on American politicians to be competent and deliver rewards to the people were as natural in the Revolutionary era as they are today.

In addition to the norms directly derived from or linked to political concepts, American values have fostered strong positive orientations to hard work and economic development. The emphasis on equality and achievement reinforced the belief that one could and should get ahead by continuous hard work, frugality, self-discipline, and individual initiative. The absence of an aristocratic model in the nation as a whole after the Revolution left the United States free to develop a socially as well as economically dominant class of merchants and manufacturers whose desire for wealth was uninhibited by norms denigrating hard work and the accumulation of capital.

The special character of American religion has been of considerable significance in the development of the related values of equalitarianism and achievement. Much of the United States was heir to a Calvinistic Puritanism, supplanted by Arminian religious beliefs by the early nineteenth century. According to the Arminian doctrines of free will, free grace, and unlimited hope for the conversion of all men, a devout man was an ambitious man and righteousness was to be rewarded both in this life and in the next.[27] It has been argued that this change occurred because "in a period when special privileges of individuals were being called into question or being

destroyed, there would naturally be less favor for that form of theology which was dominated by the doctrine of special election of a part of mankind, a growing favor for forms which seemed more distinctly to be based upon the idea of the natural equality of all men."[28]

The abolition of religious establishment in the United States which followed on the Revolution and the political successes of the Democrats fostered a strong commitment to voluntarism. This commitment, together with the early dominance of the dissenting anti-statist Methodist and Baptist denomination, meant that religion not only contributed to the economic ethos of the country, but reinforced the egalitarian and democratic social ethic as well.

The ecclesiastical character of Canadian religions greatly inhibited the development of achievement and equalitarian values. Religion in Canada, being related to the state, has provided that country with a control hierarchical mechanism rooted in tradition, which is wholly lacking in the history of the United States. Because of the strong tie between church and state in Canada, religious development there, in contrast to religious movements in the United States, has been less prone to fundamentalism and experimentalism.[29]

Some of the flavour of the social distinctions between Canada and the United States which reflect the greater strength of traditionalist and more conservative values in Canada may be traced also to a Canadian frontier fashioned in a spirit of cautious defensiveness against American expansionist tendencies. Rarely did Canada leave its borders unprotected or its frontier communities autonomous. Law and order in the form of the centrally controlled North West Mounted Police moved into frontier settlements before and along with the settlers. Not only did this establish respect for institutions of law and order, but the special constabulary force which followed on the heels of the frontiersman in Canada also meant that the Mounted Police dominated the frontier scene.[30] In addition, the presence of national government controls on the Canadian frontier weakened the development of excessive individualism.

In the United States on the other hand, frontier agricultural, ranching, and mining areas, unrelated for long periods to any central government or policing system, provided uncontrolled opportunities and encouraged settlers to use their own resources as they saw fit. The cowboy, the frontiersman, and even the vigilante, not the uniformed Mountie, are the heroes of western settlement in the United States.

THE PROBLEM OF CANADIAN IDENTITY

It is not unusual for Americans to refer to Canada as if it had no special independent national character; in fact, Americans frequently think of Canada as a northern extension of their own country, a place for fishing in the summer, hunting in the fall, and skiing in the winter. This attitude towards Canada is aptly described by Douglas LePan, a former Canadian diplomat, who once called upon a United States Senator to discuss the building of a bridge across one of the rivers along the border only to find the Senator oblivious to the need for a boundary at all. He reports that he was rather taken aback when the Senator blithely stated: "You know, I have never been able to see why there should be a border between us at all, our two countries so much alike." LePan, remarking on his feelings, reports that "the Senator, for all his generous good nature, seemed quite unaware that if the boundary were obliterated, the result in the case of a country of some 19 million people living alongside a much richer and more powerful country of almost 190 million people would not be some kind of union; it would be simply absorption."[31] The United States views Canada through a myopia of ethnocentrism in which "in a large country…people find it hard to understand that a much smaller country [in terms of population] is just as mature, viable, well-established, and distinct as the larger. Add to this the relatively

small overt differences of culture and language, and one gets a situation in which the larger is inclined to assume that the smaller is an accident which will soon fade away. English Canadians seem to assume that French Canada will go away, that it won't always be French. Americans seem to imply, by many words and deeds, that Canada will not always be Canada."[32]

The existing Canadian national identity is in large part a reaction against a long-term supposed threat to its independence and traditions, against absorption into the American republic.[33] Loyalty to the British Crown has been one effective means of providing sentiment against American intervention and control. The social consequence of Canadian allegiance to a British monarch has been the acceptance of a national purpose based on the principle of "indivisibility of the Commonwealth." As Vincent Massey has put it:

> There are some people in Canada with strong nationalist feelings who think that their end could only be achieved through a republican reform of government. There are, happily, very few persons with such views, and they are profoundly misguided in labouring under the delusion that as a republic we could remain an independent nation. We could not. The Crown-in-Parliament is the supreme symbol of our nationhoood and our greatest defense against absorption into a continental state.[34]

There is at present extensive American capital investment in Canada, high consumption of American goods, and a wide audience for American communication media. Many have rebelled against this American penetration into Canadian life.[35] The Canadian nationalist points to such facts as proof of "domination" by the United States.[36]

Nationalism in English-speaking Canada has undergone some curious changes from the time when it represented a left-wing, often pro–United States protest against the Imperial connection, and the closed economic-political-ecclesiastical system sustained by this connection. Today it is often the left-winger who is most anti-American and pro-British. The more traditional form of Canadian nationalism would seem to continue in the French-Canadian protest movements with their anti-English and anti-Establishment over-tones directed at those within Canadian borders who represent English cultural, political, and economic domination. As English-speaking Canadians seek to isolate Canada from the United States, French Canadians look for means to assure the safety of their own culture, surrounded as it is by two hundred million English speakers. In a sense both English-speaking and French-speaking Canadians have similar objectives: to protect two minority cultures from being absorbed by more powerful neighbours.[37]

The problem of changing Canadian and American identities is clearly linked to the broad topic of this paper, the nature and sources of the differences in values and institutions of the two North American democracies. In the past decades the image of the United States has changed dras-tically. Relatively few in the rest of the world still see the United States as it sees itself, the cham-pion of democratic and egalitarian ideals. To the leaders of the underdeveloped nations and the Communist world, and of many others, including Canada, the United States is now the leading defender of conservative traditional social forms, and is governed from within by an oligarchy of power-*élite*. Many Canadians now seek to defend the integrity of Canada against the United States by defining their own country as more humane, more equalitarian, more democratic, and more anti-imperialist than the United States. Many Canadians now view their country as more "left-ist" or liberal in its institutions and international objectives than the United States. Whether this shift in the definition of the character of the United States, Canada's chief reference group, will also affect Canadian values remains to be seen. For anyone interested in Canada or in the general problem of how a nation maintains or changes its basic identity, the situation provides a fascinating question for observation and study.

CRITICAL THINKING QUESTIONS

1. Do you believe that Canadian and American values are different? What evidence do you have to support your position?

2. If Canadian and American values are differ-ent, do you feel they are becoming more or less alike over time?

3. Are the concepts of "mosaic" and "melting pot" still useful for defining national differ-ences in how Canadians and Americans treat minority groups? What examples can you offer to support your position?

4. Given recent terrorist events (e.g., the 11 September 2001, attacks) do you agree with Lipset's assertion that the United States is *revo-lutionary* and Canada *counter-revolutionary*? Why or why not?

NOTES

1. S. M. Lipset, *The First New Nation* (New York, 1963), n.b. 248–73.

2. Because of the absence of clear indicators and the overlap with the equalitarian-elitist dimension, the specificity-diffuseness pattern variable is not discussed in this paper. For reasons of parsimony, I ignore Parsons' other pattern variables—affectivity, affectivity-neutrality and instru-mental-consummatory distinctions. See Talcott Parsons, *The Social System* (Glencoe, Ill., 1951), 58–67. See also Parsons' recent elaboration of the pattern variables in "Pattern Variables Revisited," *American Sociological Review*, xxv, 4, 1960, 467–83.

3. Kaspar D. Naegele, "Canadian Society: Some Reflections," in Bernard Blishen, Frank Jones, Kaspar Naegele, and John Porter, eds., *Canadian Society* (Toronto, 1961), 27. This article is an excellent effort to summarize the general value system of Canada. Naegele argues convincingly that Canada on many matters lies "in the middle between America and England" and that it both accepts and rejects various aspects of the English and American models.

4. The educational data are calculated from materials in UNESCO, *Basic Facts and Figures*, 1960 (Paris, 1963); United Nations *Demographic Yearbook*, 1960 (New York, 1960); 2nd United Nations Compendium of Social Statistics (New York, 1963).

5. Dennis Wrong, *American and Canadian Viewpoints* (Washington, 1955), 20; Wilson Woodside, *The University Question* (Toronto, 1958), 21–2.

6. One of the more subtle signs of certain status distinctions was noted by A. R. M. Lower, *Canadians in the Making* (Toronto, 1958), 446, n. 11, who observed that, to his astonishment, in one midwestern university in the United States known to him, students and faculty actually share the same lavatory. Dennis Wrong points out that "with respect to the position of women, greater conservatism exists in Canada than in the United States…relatively fewer women have achieved prominence as public figures." *American and Canadian Viewpoints*, 11.

7. Wrong, *American and Canadian Viewpoints*, 36–7.

8. Canada: Dominion Bureau of Statistics, *Police Administration Statistics*, 1961, 19; United States: Federal Bureau of Investigation, *Uniform Crime Report*—1961, 20, 110, Table 36, and *Uniform Crime Report*—1963, 33–4. Dennis Wrong notes that "one finds less of the frequent American distrust of lawyers as 'shysters,' or as ambitious politicians, in English-speaking Canada and a greater sense of remoteness and majesty of the law." Wrong argues that the contrast between the popular-culture heroes of American and Canadian frontier expansion indicate the respect among Canadians for the law and the converse for Americans: "…in the United States it is the cowboy, a rugged individualist whose relationship to the forces of law and order was at least ambiguous, who has come to symbolize the frontier, while in Canada the 'mountie,' a policeman who clearly stands for law and order and traditional institutional authority, is the corresponding symbol of Canadian westward expansion." *Wrong, American and Canadian Viewpoints*, 38.

9. S. M. Lipset, *The First New Nation*, 264–65.

10. For example, S. D. Clark has pointed out that McCarthyism, a populist movement expressing political intolerance, is not likely to emerge in Canada. "In Canada it would be hard to conceive of a state of political freedom great enough to permit the kind of attacks upon responsible leaders of the government which have been carried out in the United States." S. D. Clark, "The Frontier and Democratic Theory," *Transactions of the Royal Society of Canada*, XLVIII, June 1954, 72. Regarding judiciary appointments, see Henry H. Bull, "The Career Prosecutor of Canada," *Journal of Criminal Law, Criminology, and Police Science*, LIII, 1962, 89–96.

11. Wrong, *American and Canadian Viewpoints*, 38.

12. Ibid., 29.

13. Alistair Horne, *Canada and the Canadians* (London, 1961), 248–49. It might be added that hotels are owned by the CNR, and now all provinces except Quebec have hospitalization insurance plans; Canada also has Family Allowances of $6 per month for every child under 10, and $8 for those between 10 and 15 (see Horne, 250).

14. Maurice Lamontagne, "The Role of Government," in G. P. Gilmour, ed., *Canada's Tomorrow* (Toronto, 1954), 125. See also James Byrce's discussion on Canada's resistance to the policy of *laissez-faire: Modern Democracies*, vol. I (London, 1921), 471.

15. S. D. Clark, "The Canadian Community," in G. Brown, ed., *Canada* (Berkeley, California, 1950), 386–87.

16. Horne, *Canada and the Canadians*, 245.

17. Lower, *Canadians in the Making*, 426. In Quebec, also, there has been notable Catholic resistance to aggressive business enterprise, due primarily to the strength of religious and traditionalist views. See Wrong, *American and Canadian Viewpoints*, 29–30.

18. A. Horne, *Canada and the Canadians*, 9.

19. "In the United States the Briton hastened to become a good American; in Canada he has been encouraged to remain a good Briton. Nor has any vigorous effort been made to assimilate continental European peoples in Canada, except through the public school; as with the French Canadians, the break of continental Europeans from their cultural past has tended to expose them to European influences." S. D. Clark, "The Canadian Community," 386–87.

20. Kaspar Naegele, "Canadian Society: Some Reflections," in Blishen et al., *Canadian Society*, 44.

21. Vincent Massey, *Canadians and Their Commonwealth* (Oxford, 1961), 5–6.

22. See J. M. S. Careless, *Canada: A Story of Challenge* (Cambridge, 1963), 111, 112, 113. Even since World War II, as Careless argues, Canada has remained more conservative than the United States: "In comparison with the rich and restless republic [the United States], Canada was a cautious and conservative country: cautious because her path was harder, more conservative because of her closer bonds with the Old World, and the stronger power of traditions brought from Britain and France" (p. 405).

23. Arthur Lower, *From Colony to Nation* (Toronto, 1946), 114.

24. Sir Robert Falconer, *The United States as a Neighbour* (Cambridge, 1925), 23.

25. W. L. Morton, "The Extension of the Franchise in Canada," *Report of the Canadian Historical Association* (Toronto, 1943), 76.

26. Wrong, *American and Canadian Viewpoints*, 31–2.

27. See Philip Schaff, *America: A Sketch of the Political, Social and Religious Character of the United States of North America* (New York, 1855), 259.

28. Franklin Jameson, *The American Revolution Considered as a Social Movement* (Princeton, 1926), 157.

29. S. D. Clark, *The Developing Canadian Community* (Toronto, 1962), 178. Clark remarks: "Political pressures have forced the community to come to the support of organized religion and such support has placed a definite limitation upon sectarian activity. With the collective weight of the community brought to bear upon them, the sects have been forced either to retreat behind a wall of isolation or build themselves into an integral part of the community, or else to seek denominational supports by aligning themselves with the state and with the traditional institutions of the community."

30. Clark, *The Developing Canadian Community*, 386–87.

31. Douglas V. LePan, "The Outlook for the Relationship," in John Sloan Dickey, ed., *The United States and Canada* (Englewood Cliffs, N.J., 1964), n.b. 155–56.

32. Everett C. Hughes, " A Sociologist's View," in John Sloan Dickey, *The United States and Canada*, 18.

33. "Canadian national life can almost be said to take its rise in the negative will to resist absorption in the American republic. It is largely about the United States as an object that the consciousness of Canadian national unity has grown up..." S. D. Clark, "The Importance of Anti-Americanism in Canadian National Feeling," in H. F. Angus, ed., *Canada and Her Great Neighbor* (Toronto, 1938), 243.

34. Vincent Massey, *Canadians and Their Commonwealth*, 19.

35. The concern of Canadians with the large amount of American investment is not merely based on the historical insecurity of Canada vis-à-vis its more powerful neighbour. It is interesting to note that Americans owned 44 per cent of Canadian manufacturing industry in 1959 and that the United States has more money invested in Canada than in any other area in the world. See Norman L. Nicholson, *Canada in the American* Community (Princeton, N.J., 1963), 119.

36. Harry G. Johnson, "Problems of Canadian Nationalism," *International Journal* (Summer, 1961), 238–49.

37. S. D. Clark, "Canada and Her Great Neighbour," paper presented at the meeting of the *American Sociological Association* (Montreal, Canada), September 3, 1964.

11

Manifesto of the Communist Party

Society

CLASSIC

CONTEMPORARY

CROSS-CULTURAL

Karl Marx and Friedrich Engels

Karl Marx, collaborating with Friedrich Engels, produced the "Manifesto" in 1848. This document is a well-known statement about the origin of social conflict in the process of material production. The ideas of Marx and Engels have been instrumental in shaping the political lives of more than one-fifth of the world's population, and, of course, they have been instrumental in the development of the social-conflict paradigm in sociology.

BOURGEOIS AND PROLETARIANS[1]

The history of all hitherto existing society[2] is the history of class struggles.

Freeman and slave, patrician and plebeian, lord and serf, guild-master[3] and journeyman, in a word, oppressor and oppressed, stood in constant opposition to one another, carried on an uninterrupted, now hidden, now open fight, a fight that each time ended, either in a revolutionary reconstitution of society at large, or in the common ruin of the contending classes.

In the earlier epochs of history, we find almost everywhere a complicated arrangement of society into various orders, a manifold gradation of social rank. In ancient Rome we have patricians, knights, plebeians, slaves; in the Middle Ages, feudal lords, vassals, guild-masters, journeymen, apprentices, serfs; in almost all of these classes, again, subordinate gradations.

The modern bourgeois society that has sprouted from the ruins of feudal society has not done away with class antagonisms. It has but established new classes, new conditions of oppression, new forms of struggle in place of the old ones.

Our epoch, the epoch of the bourgeoisie, possesses, however, this distinctive feature; it has simplified the class antagonisms. Society as a whole is more and more splitting up into two great hostile camps, into two great classes directly facing each other: Bourgeoisie and Proletariat.

From the serfs of the Middle Ages sprang the chartered burghers of the earliest towns.

Source: From *Manifesto of the Communist Party,* Part I, by Karl Marx and Friedrich Engels.

From these burgesses the first elements of the bourgeoisie were developed.

The discovery of America, the rounding of the Cape, opened up fresh ground for the rising bourgeoisie. The East Indian and Chinese markets, the [colonization] of America, trade with the colonies, the increase in the means of exchange, and in commodities generally, gave to commerce, to navigation, to industry, an impulse never before known, and thereby, to the revolutionary element in the tottering feudal society, a rapid development.

The feudal system of industry, under which industrial production was monopolized by close guilds, now no longer sufficed for the growing wants of the new markets. The manufacturing system took its place. The guild-masters were pushed on one side by the manufacturing middle class; division of labor between the different corporate guilds vanished in the face of division of labor in each single workshop.

Meantime the markets kept ever growing, the demand, ever rising. Even manufacture no longer sufficed. Thereupon, steam and machinery revolutionized industrial production. The place of manufacture was taken by the giant, Modern Industry, the place of the industrial middle class, by industrial millionaires, the leaders of whole industrial armies, the modern bourgeois.

Modern industry has established the world-market, for which the discovery of America paved the way. This market has given an immense development to commerce, to navigation, to communication by land. This development has, in its turn, reacted on the extension of industry; and in proportion as industry, commerce, navigation, railways extended, in the same proportion the bourgeoisie developed, increased its capital, and pushed into the background every class handed down from the Middle Ages.

We see, therefore, how the modern bourgeoisie is itself the product of a long course of development, of a series of revolutions in the modes of production and of exchange.

Each step in the development of the bourgeoisie was accompanied by a corresponding political advance of that class. An oppressed class under the sway of the feudal nobility, an armed and self-governing association in the mediæval commune,[4] here independent urban republic (as in Italy and Germany), there taxable "third estate" of the monarchy (as in France), afterwards, in the period of manufacture proper, serving either the semi-feudal or the absolute monarchy as a counterpoise against the nobility, and, in fact, cornerstone of the great monarchies in general, the bourgeoisie has at last, since the establishment of modern industry and of the world-market, conquered for itself, in the modern representative State, exclusive political sway. The executive of the modern State is but a committee for managing the common affairs of the whole bourgeoisie.

The bourgeoisie, historically, has played a most revolutionary part.

The bourgeoisie, wherever it has got the upper hand, has put an end to all feudal, patriarchal, idyllic relations. It has pitilessly torn asunder the motley feudal ties that bound man to his "natural superiors," and has left remaining no other nexus between man and man than naked self-interest, than callous "cash payment." It has drowned the most heavenly ecstasies of religious fervour, of chivalrous enthusiasm, of philistine sentimentalism, in the icy water of egotistical calculation. It has resolved personal worth into exchange value, and in place of the numberless indefeasible chartered freedoms, has set up that single, unconscionable freedom—Free Trade. In one word, for exploitation, veiled by religious and political illusions, it has substituted naked, shameless, direct, brutal exploitation.

The bourgeoisie has stripped of its halo every occupation hitherto honoured and looked up to with reverent awe. It has converted the physician, the lawyer, the priest, the poet, the man of science, into its paid [wage-laborers].

The bourgeoisie has torn away from the family its sentimental veil, and has reduced the family relation to a mere money relation.

The bourgeoisie has disclosed how it came to pass that the brutal display of vigour in the Middle Ages, which reactionists so much admire, found its fitting complement in the most slothful indolence. It has been the first to show what man's activity can bring about. It has accomplished wonders far surpassing Egyptian pyramids, Roman aqueducts, and Gothic cathedrals; it has conducted expeditions that put in the shade all former Exoduses of nations and crusades.

The bourgeoisie cannot exist without constantly revolutionizing the instruments of production, and thereby the relations of production, and with them the whole relations of society. Conservation of the old modes of production in unaltered form, was, on the contrary, the first condition of existence for all earlier industrial classes. Constant revolutionizing of production, uninterrupted disturbance of all social conditions, everlasting uncertainty and agitation distinguish the bourgeois epoch from all earlier ones. All fixed, fast-frozen relations, with their train of ancient and venerable prejudices and opinions, are swept away, all new-formed ones become antiquated before they can ossify. All that is solid melts into air, all that is holy is profaned, and man is at last compelled to face with sober senses, his real conditions of life, and his relations with his kind.

The need of a constantly expanding market for its products chases the bourgeoisie over the whole surface of the globe. It must nestle everywhere, settle everywhere, establish [connections] everywhere.

The bourgeoisie has through its exploitation of the world-market given a cosmopolitan character to production and consumption in every country. To the great chagrin of reactionists, it has drawn from under the feet of industry the national ground on which it stood. All old-established national industries have been destroyed or are daily being destroyed. They are dislodged by new industries, whose introduction becomes a life and death question for all civilised nations, by industries that no longer work up indigenous raw material, but raw material drawn from the remotest zones;

industries whose products are consumed, not only at home, but in every quarter of the globe. In place of the old wants, satisfied by the productions of the country, we find new wants, requiring for their satisfaction the products of distant lands and climes. In place of the old local and national seclusion and self-sufficiency, we have intercourse in every direction, universal interdependence of nations. And as in material, so also in intellectual production. The intellectual creations of individual nations become common property. National one-sidedness and narrow-mindedness become more and more impossible, and from the numerous national and local literatures there arises a world-literature.

The bourgeoisie, by the rapid improvement of all instruments of production, by the immensely facilitated means of communication, draws all, even the most barbarian, nations into civilization. The cheap prices of its commodities are the heavy artillery with which it batters down all Chinese walls, with which it forces the barbarians' intensely obstinate hatred of foreigners to capitulate. It compels all nations, on pain of extinction, to adopt the bourgeois mode of production; it compels them to introduce what it calls civilization into their midst, i.e., to become bourgeois themselves. In a word, it creates a world after its own image.

The bourgeoisie has subjected the country to the rule of the towns. It has created enormous cities, has greatly increased the urban population as compared with the rural, and has thus rescued a considerable part of the population from the idiocy of rural life. Just as it has made the country dependent on the towns, so it has made barbarian and semi-barbarian countries dependent on the civilised ones, nations of peasants on nations of bourgeois, the East on the West.

The bourgeoisie keeps more and more doing away with the scattered state of the population, of the means of production, and of property. It has agglomerated population, centralized means of production, and has concentrated property in a few hands. The necessary consequence of this was political centralization. Independent, or but loosely connected provinces, with separate interests, laws, governments and systems of taxation, became lumped together in one nation, with one government, one code of laws, one national class-interest, one frontier and one customs-tariff.

The bourgeoisie, during its rule of scarce one hundred years, has created more massive and more colossal productive forces than have all preceding generations together. Subjection of Nature's forces to man, machinery, application of chemistry to industry and agriculture, steam-navigation, railways, electric telegraphs, clearing of whole continents for cultivation, canalization of rivers, whole populations conjured out of the ground—what earlier century had even a present-iment that such productive forces slumbered in the lap of social labor?

We see then: The means of production and of exchange on whose foundation the bourgeoisie built itself up were generated in feudal society. At a certain stage in the development of these means of production and of exchange, the conditions under which feudal society produced and exchanged, the feudal organization of agriculture and manufacturing industry, in one word, the feudal relations of property became no longer compatible with the already developed productive forces; they became so many fetters. They had to burst asunder; they were burst asunder.

Into their places stepped free competition, accompanied by a social and political constitution adapted to it, and by the economical and political sway of the bourgeois class.

A similar movement is going on before our own eyes. Modern bourgeois society with its relations of production, of exchange and of property, a society that has conjured up such gigantic means of production and of exchange is like the sorcerer who is no longer able to control the powers of the nether world whom he has called up by his spells. For many a decade past the history of industry and commerce is but the history of the revolt of modern productive forces against modern conditions of production, against the property relations that are the conditions for the existence of the bourgeoisie and of its rule. It is enough to mention the commercial crises that by their periodical return put on its trial, each time more threateningly, the existence of the entire bourgeois society. In these crises a great part not only of the existing products, but also of the previously created productive forces, are periodically destroyed. In these crises there breaks out an epidemic that, in all earlier epochs, would have seemed an absurdity—the epidemic of over-production. Society suddenly finds itself put back into a state of momentary barbarism; it appears as if a famine, a universal war of devastation had cut off the supply of every means of subsistence; industry and commerce seem to be destroyed; and why? Because there is too much civilization, too much means of subsistence, too much industry, too much commerce. The productive forces at the disposal of society no longer tend to further the development of the conditions of bourgeois property; on the contrary, they have become too powerful for these conditions, by which they are fettered, and so [as] soon as they overcome these fetters, they bring disorder into the whole of bourgeois society, endanger the existence of bourgeois property. The conditions of bourgeois society are too narrow to comprise the wealth created by them. And how does the bourgeoisie get over these crises? On the one hand by enforced destruction of a mass of productive forces; on the other, by the conquest of new markets, and by the more thorough exploitation of the old ones. That is to say, by paving the way for more extensive and more destructive crises, and by diminishing the means whereby crises are prevented.

The weapons with which the bourgeoisie felled feudalism to the ground are now turned against the bourgeoisie itself.

But not only has the bourgeoisie forged the weapons that bring death to itself; it has also called into existence the men who are to wield those weapons—the modern working class—the proletarians.

In proportion as the bourgeoisie, i.e., capital, is developed, in the same proportion is the proletariat, the modern working class, developed, a class of laborers, who live only so long as they find work, and who find work only so long as their labor increases capital. These laborers, who must sell themselves piecemeal, are a commodity, like every other article of commerce, and are consequently exposed to all the vicissitudes of competition, to all the fluctuations of the market.

Owing to the extensive use of machinery and to division of labor, the work of the proletarians has lost all individual character, and, consequently, all charm for the workman. He becomes an appendage of the machine, and it is only the most simple, most monotonous and most easily acquired knack that is required of him. Hence, the cost of production of a workman is restricted, almost entirely, to the means of subsistence that he requires for his maintenance, and for the propagation of his race. But the price of a commodity, and also of labor, is equal to its cost of production. In proportion, therefore, as the repulsiveness of the work increases, the wage decreases. Nay more, in proportion as the use of machinery and division of labor increases, in the same proportion the burden of toil also increases, whether by prolongation of the working hours, by increase of the work enacted in a given time, or by increased speed of the machinery, etc.

Modern industry has converted the little workshop of the patriarchal master into the great factory of the industrial capitalist. Masses of laborers, crowded into the factory, are organized like soldiers. As privates of the industrial army they are placed under the command of a perfect hierarchy of officers and sergeants. Not only are they the slaves of the bourgeois class, and of the bourgeois State, they are daily and hourly enslaved by the machine, by the over-looker, and, above all, by the individual bourgeois manufacturer himself. The more openly this despotism proclaims gain to be its end and aim, the more petty, the more hateful and the more embittering it is.

The less the skill and exertion or strength implied in manual labor, in other words, the more modern industry becomes developed, the more is the labor of men superseded by that of women. Differences of age and sex have no longer any distinctive social validity for the working class. All are instruments of labor, more or less expensive to use, according to their age and sex.

No sooner is the exploitation of the laborer by the manufacturer, so far, at an end, that he receives his wages in cash, than he is set upon by the other portions of the bourgeoisie, the landlord, the shopkeeper, the pawnbroker, etc.

The lower strata of the middle class—the small tradespeople, shopkeepers, and retired tradesmen generally, the handicraftsmen and peasants—all these sink gradually into the proletariat, partly because their diminutive capital does not suffice for the scale on which Modern Industry is carried on, and is swamped in the competition with the large capitalists, partly because their specialised skill is rendered worthless by new methods of production. Thus the proletariat is recruited from all classes of the population.

The proletariat goes through various stages of development. With its birth begins its struggle with the bourgeoisie. At first the contest is carried on by individual laborers, then by the workpeople of a factory, then by the operatives of one trade, in one locality, against the individual bourgeois who directly exploits them. They direct their attacks not against the bourgeois conditions of production, but against the instruments of production themselves; they destroy imported wares that compete with their labor, they smash to pieces machinery, they set factories ablaze, they seek to restore by force the vanished status of the workman of the Middle Ages.

At this stage the laborers still form an incoherent mass scattered over the whole country, and broken up by their mutual competition. If anywhere they unite to form more compact bodies, this is not yet the consequence of their own active union, but of the union of the bourgeoisie, which class, in order to attain its own political ends, is compelled to set the whole proletariat in motion, and is moreover yet, for a time, able to do so. At this stage, therefore, the proletarians do not fight their enemies, but the enemies of their enemies, the remnants of absolute monarchy, the landowners, the non-industrial bourgeois, the petty bourgeoisie. Thus the whole historical movement is concentrated in the hands of the bourgeoisie; every victory so obtained is a victory for the bourgeoisie.

But with the development of industry the proletariat not only increases in number, it becomes concentrated in greater masses, its strength grows, and it feels that strength more. The various interests and conditions of life within the ranks of the proletariat are more and more equalized, in proportion as machinery obliterates all distinctions of labor, and nearly everywhere reduces wages to the same low level. The growing competition among the bourgeois, and the resulting commercial crises, make the wages of the workers ever more fluctuating. The unceasing improvement of machinery, ever more rapidly developing, makes their livelihood more and more precarious; the collisions between individual workmen and individual bourgeois take more and more the character of collisions between two classes. Thereupon the workers begin to form combinations (Trades' Unions) against the bourgeois; they club together in order to keep up the rate of wages; they found permanent associations in order to make provision beforehand for these occasional revolts. Here and there the contest breaks out into riots.

Now and then the workers are victorious, but only for a time. The real fruit of their battles lies, not in the immediate result, but in the ever expanding union of the workers. This union is helped on by the improved means of communication that are created by modern industry, and that place the workers of different localities in contact with one another. It was just this contact that was needed to centralize the numerous local struggles,

all of the same character, into one national struggle between classes. But every class struggle is a political struggle. And that union, to attain which the burghers of the Middle Ages, with their miserable highways, required centuries, the modern proletarians, thanks to railways, achieve in a few years.

This organization of the proletarians into a class, and consequently into a political party, is continually being upset again by the competition between the workers themselves. But it ever rises up again, stronger, firmer, mightier. It compels legislative recognition of particular interests of the workers, by taking advantage of the divisions among the bourgeoisie itself. Thus the ten-hours'-bill in England was carried.

Altogether collisions between the classes of the old society further, in many ways, the course of development of the proletariat. The bourgeoisie finds itself involved in a constant battle. At first with the aristocracy; later on, with those portions of the bourgeoisie itself, whose interests have become antagonistic to the progress of industry; at all times, with the bourgeoisie of foreign countries. In all these battles it sees itself compelled to appeal to the proletariat, to ask for its help, and thus, to drag it into the political arena. The bourgeoisie itself, therefore, supplies the proletariat with its own elements of political and general education, in other words, it furnishes the proletariat with weapons for fighting the bourgeoisie.

Further, as we have already seen, entire sections of the ruling classes are, by the advance of industry, precipitated into the proletariat, or are at least threatened in their conditions of existence. These also supply the proletariat with fresh elements of enlightenment and progress.

Finally, in times when the class-struggle nears the decisive hour, the process of dissolution going on within the ruling class, in fact within the whole range of old society, assumes such a violent, glaring character, that a small section of the ruling class cuts itself adrift, and joins the revolutionary class, the class that holds the future in its hands. Just as, therefore, at an earlier period, a section of the nobility went over to the bourgeoisie, so now a portion of the bourgeoisie goes over to the proletariat, and in particular, a portion of the bourgeois ideologists, who have raised themselves to the level of comprehending theoretically the historical movements as a whole.

Of all the classes that stand face to face with the bourgeoisie today, the proletariat alone is a really revolutionary class. The other classes decay and finally disappear in the face of modern industry; the proletariat is its special and essential product.

The lower-middle class, the small manufacturer, the shopkeeper, the artisan, the peasant, all these fight against the bourgeoisie, to save from extinction their existence as fractions of the middle class. They are therefore not revolutionary, but conservative. Nay more, they are reactionary, for they try to roll back the wheel of history. If by chance they are revolutionary, they are so, only in view of their impending transfer into the proletariat, they thus defend not their present, but their future interests, they desert their own standpoint to place themselves at that of the proletariat.

The "dangerous class," the social scum, that passively rotting mass thrown off by the lowest layers of old society, may, here and there, be swept into the movement by a proletarian revolution; its conditions of life, however, prepare it far more for the part of a bribed tool of reactionary intrigue.

In the conditions of the proletariat, those of old society at large are already virtually swamped. The proletarian is without property; his relation to his wife and children has no longer anything in common with the bourgeois family-relations; modern industrial labor, modern subjection to capital, the same in England as in France, in America as in Germany, has stripped him of every trace of national character. Law, morality, religion, are to him so many bourgeois prejudices, behind which lurk in ambush just as many bourgeois interests.

All the preceding classes that got the upper hand sought to fortify their already acquired status by subjecting at large to their conditions of appropriation. The proletarians cannot become masters of the productive forces of society, except by abolishing their own previous mode of appropriation, and thereby also every other previous mode of appropriation. They have nothing of their own to secure and to fortify; their mission is to destroy all previous securities for, and insurances of, individual property.

All previous historical movements were movements of minorities, or in the interest of minorities. The proletarian movement is the self-conscious, independent movement of the immense majority, in the interest of the immense majority. The proletariat, the lowest stratum of our present society, cannot stir, cannot raise itself up, without the whole superincumbent strata of official society being sprung into the air.

Though not in substance, yet in form, the struggle of the proletariat with the bourgeoisie is at first a national struggle. The proletariat of each country must, of course, first of all settle matters with its own bourgeoisie.

In depicting the most general phases of the development of the proletariat, we traced the more or less veiled civil war, raging within existing society, up to the point where that war breaks out into open revolution, and where the violent overthrow of the bourgeoisie, lays the foundation for the sway of the proletariat.

Hitherto, every form of society has been based, as we have already seen, on the antagonism of oppressing and oppressed classes. But in order to oppress a class, certain conditions must be assured to it under which it can, at least, continue its slavish existence. The serf, in the period of serfdom, raised himself to membership in the commune, just as the petty bourgeois, under the yoke of feudal absolutism, managed to develop into a bourgeois. The modern laborer, on the contrary, instead of rising with the progress of industry, sinks deeper and deeper below the conditions of existence of his own class. He becomes a pauper, and pauperism develops more rapidly than population and wealth. And here it becomes evident, that the bourgeoisie is unfit any longer to be the ruling class in society, and to impose its conditions of existence upon society as an overriding law. It is unfit to rule, because it is incompetent to assure an existence to its slave within his slavery, because it cannot help letting him sink into such a state, that it has to feed him, instead of being fed by him. Society can no longer live under this bourgeoisie, in other words, its existence is no longer compatible with society.

The essential condition for the existence, and for the sway of the bourgeois class, is the formation and augmentation of capital; the condition for capital is wage-labor. Wage-labor rests exclusively on competition between the laborers. The advance of industry, whose involuntary promoter is the bourgeoisie, replaces the isolation of the laborers, due to competition, by their involuntary combination, due to association. The development of modern industry, therefore, cuts from under its feet the very foundation on which the bourgeoisie produces and appropriates products. What the bourgeoisie therefore produces, above all, are its own grave-diggers. Its fall and the victory of the proletariat are equally inevitable.

CRITICAL THINKING QUESTIONS

1. What are the distinguishing factors of "class conflict"? How does class conflict differ from other kinds of conflict, as between individuals or nations?
2. Why do Marx and Engels argue that understanding society in the present requires investigating the society of the past?

3. On what grounds did Marx and Engels *praise* industrial capitalism? On what grounds did they *condemn* the system?

NOTES

1. By *bourgeoisie* is meant the class of modern capitalists, owners of the means of social production and employers of wage-labor. By *proletariat,* the class of modern wage-laborers who, having no means of production of their own, are reduced to selling their labor-power in order to live.

2. That is, all written history. In 1847, the prehistory of society, the social organization existing previous to recorded history, was all but unknown. Since then, Haxthausen discovered common ownership of land in Russia. Maurer proved it to be the social foundation from which all Teutonic races started in history, and by and by village communities were found to be, or to have been, the primitive form of society everywhere from India to Ireland. The inner organization of this primitive Communistic society was laid bare, in its typical form, by Morgan's crowning discovery of the true nature of the gens and its relation to the tribe. With the dissolution of these primæval communities society begins to be differentiated into separate and finally antagonistic classes. I have attempted to retrace this process of dissolution in "Der Ursprung der Familie, des Privateigenthums und des Staats," 2d ed. Stuttgart 1886.

3. Guild-master, that is, a full member of a guild, a master within, not a head of, a guild.

4. "Commune" was the name taken, in France, by the nascent towns even before they had conquered from their feudal lords and masters, local self-government and political rights as "the Third Estate." Generally speaking, for the economical development of the bourgeoisie, England is here taken as the typical country, [and] for its political development, France.

12

Disaster through Dirty Windshields: Law, Order, and Toronto's Squeegee Kids

Patrick Parnaby

Society

CLASSIC

CONTEMPORARY

CROSS-CULTURAL

Parnaby's article reviews the diverse social processes involved in constructing the image of "squeegee kids"—homeless youths who clean car windshields for money. The research reveals that framing squeegee kids as a menace to society creates the impression that these youth represent a social problem in need of resolution. Parnaby's research investigates media coverage of this issue and the impact of the implementation of the Safe Streets Act *in Toronto.*

Abstract: Over the past decade, anti-panhandling bylaws have been adopted in several Canadian cities, including Vancouver, Winnipeg, and Montreal. This article examines the rhetorical processes used to construct "squeegee kids"—homeless youths who clean car windshields for money—as a social problem requiring a law-and-order resolution in Toronto. Using materials gathered from newspapers, magazines, government documents, and official reports, it is argued that the implementation of the *Safe Streets Act* depended on anti-squeegee claimants' use of disaster rhetoric and the rhetorical disassociation of squeegee kids from the larger homeless population. These processes are further discussed in relation to emerging trends in neo-liberal forms of governance.

Source: P. Parnaby (2003). "Disaster through Dirty Windshields: Law, Order, and Toronto's Street Kids." *Canadian Journal of Sociology*, 28(3), 281–307. Used by permission.

INTRODUCTION

Between 1995 and 2000, on some of the busiest street corners in Toronto, Ontario, "squeegee kids" waited in small groups for traffic lights to turn red. With squeegees in hand, the youths would skillfully weave through the lines of stopped vehicles and wash windshields. Their technique was simple: use as few strokes as possible; keep an eye on the traffic lights; and always finish the job on the side of the vehicle closest to the curb so as to avoid being hit by impatient drivers. In one minute or less, some kids could wash two windshields and, if they were fortunate, receive some money in return. Indeed, squeegeeing had become essential to their socio-economic survival (O'Grady et. al., 1998; Boston, 1998, Gaetz et. al., 1999). By the summer of 1997, however, the squeegee-kid phenomenon had become a major source of social and political contention. According to many drivers, pedestrians, and merchants, squeegee kids were much more than a nuisance. They were symbolic of an overall decline in urban habitability. Despite considerable opposition on the part of those who argued that squeegeeing resulted from youth poverty, the Ontario provincial government passed the *Safe Streets Act* in December of 1999. Squeegeeing and other forms of "aggressive" panhandling were made illegal within the province of Ontario.

How did Toronto's homeless youth population eventually find itself unable to squeegee for money? Through an extensive use of "disaster" rhetoric (Cohen, 1972: 144–158; Goode and Ben-Yehuda, 1994: 29), anti-squeegee claimants were able to construct the condition as a social problem requiring a "law and order" resolution.[1] Squeegee kids' willful and deliberate participation in deviant conduct, they argued, was to be addressed *primarily* through punitive measures of social control backed by consonant legislation. Essential to the anti-squeegee position, however, was the rhetorical differentiation of squeegee kids from the larger homeless population. These "dividing practices" (Foucault 1982: 210) helped render anti-poverty rhetoric *less* applicable to the squeegee kid phenomenon, thereby minimizing a cross-fertilization of the two social problems' discourses and further legitimating the need for the youths' differential treatment through measures of social control.

Following a review of the relevant literature, I will provide a brief outline of the squeegee kid "problem," tracing its progression toward social problem status. I will then discuss the emergence of the squeegee kid typology, and undertake an analysis of how it was constructed as a problem requiring a law-and-order resolution through the use of disaster rhetoric. Although pro-squeegee claimants played an essential role in the problem's development and eventual resolution, I will pay particular attention to the ways in which anti-squeegee claimants and journalists differentiated squeegee kids from the larger homeless population. The intent is not to devalue the importance of pro-squeegee claims but, rather, to explore the criminalization and differentiation process as a unique claims-making activity in and of itself. I will conclude with further discussion of the aforementioned processes as they relate to larger social, political, and economic trends unfolding across Ontario and North America more generally.

HOMELESS YOUTHS AND CONSTUCTIONIST OPPORTUNITIES

Contemporary research often begins with the presupposition that youth homelessness is a social problem in need of socio-political intervention. To this end, many researchers have attempted to lay bare the lived experiences of young people who live on the street.[2] For example, looking closely at the relationship between employment and delinquent behaviour among street youths, researchers have argued that work experience provides the essential forms of social and human capital that homeless youths require in order to endure, if not entirely escape, life on the streets (Hagan and McCarthy, 1998: 232; O'Grady et. al., 1998: 317; Baron, 2001; also see Hagan, 1994).

Criminologists, too, have taken a special interest in the homeless condition, particularly the prevalence of delinquent and/or criminal conduct among street youths. Although only a small number of adolescents become homeless, those who do eventually account for a disproportionate amount of serious delinquent behaviour (Tanner, 1996: 151; Hagan and McCarthy, 1998). Building on theories of criminogenic situations, McCarthy and Hagan (1991; 1992) and Hagan and McCarthy (1998) have suggested that the socio-economic conditions unique to street life—rather than background variables such as gender, age, and family status—provide the fertile ground from which delinquent and criminal behaviour eventually emerge (McCarthy and Hagan, 1991: 398–407).

Before taking to the streets, however, many youths experience considerable turmoil at home, often enduring physical, sexual, and psychological abuse (Raychaba, 1989; Breakey and Fischer, 1990; Webber, 1991; Hagan and McCarthy, 1998; O'Grady et. al., 1998; Whitbeck and Hoyt, 1999;

Baron, 2001). With parents sometimes abusing drugs and/or alcohol, and with persistent difficulties in school, taking to the streets is often understood to be a source of refuge. Unfortunately, life on the streets seldom offers more than a temporary reprieve, as many eventually experience downward life trajectories characterized by narcotics use, prostitution, and interpersonal conflict (Webber, 1991; Fitzgerald, 1995; Hagan and McCarthy, 1998; Golden et. al., 1999; Whitbeck and Hoyt, 1999; Baron, 2001).

Although such research has generated invaluable data—with much of it being used to inform social policy—comparatively less attention has been paid to how homeless youths *in particular* have been socially constructed.[3] Applied to the study of street youths, constructionism offers a unique opportunity to explore the complex interrelationships between socio-political ideologies, claims-making activities, and the lived experiences of those on the street. How homeless youths are socially constructed at particular times and in particular places, therefore, is of the utmost importance if street life is to be fully understood within its larger socio-political framework.

Essential to the constructionist approach to social problems is the belief that "... whether a condition is physical, genetic, physiological, psychological, medical, or technological, the process by which it becomes the focus of attention and defined as a social problem is social" (Spector and Kitsuse, 1977: 47). Social problems are, therefore, understood to be processes and activities involving those who allege the existence of specific conditions and who define them as problematic (Blumer, 1970; Spector and Kitsuse, 1977; Best, 1989, 2001; Miller and Holstein, 1993; Loseke, 1999). The research agenda is shifted away from a study of conditions in and of themselves to a study of the rhetorical and idiomatic claims that are made with respect to the proposed existence, magnitude, causes, and solutions to "problematic" social phenomena (Best, 2001).

The constructionist approach to social problems has its roots in American symbolic interactionism. Its central focus is, therefore, "... to view the social problems process from "within" by examining how members do what they do, how they understand what they are doing, and how they connect these understandings to their diverse lines of action" (Kitsuse and Schneider, 1989: xiii). Primary emphasis is placed on the form and content of symbolic communication in and of itself. While this study borrows from both theoretical traditions, it remains more sympathetic, on both methodological and theoretical grounds, to American-style constructionism as it emerged in the wake of Spector and Kitsuse's (1977) *Constructing Social Problems*.

METHODOLOGY

The methodological approach used in this study is consistent with what Altheide has called "ethnographic content analysis" (ECA) (Altheide, 1987).

Using the Canadian Business and Current Affairs (CBCA) and Virtual News electronic indexes, newspaper and magazine articles that made specific reference to squeegee kids were obtained.[4] The articles began to emerge as early as 1995 and tapered off near the end of 2000. In total, over 200 articles were generated; the vast majority were found in Toronto's three major newspapers: *The Globe and Mail* (N=32), *The Toronto Sun* (N=95), and *The Toronto Star* (N=106).

Borrowing from Erickson et al. (1989), the aforementioned newspapers can be classified into three categories: "quality," "popular," and "mass" publications respectively. As a national paper with a history of catering to the nation's middle- and upper-class business communities, *The Globe and Mail* tends to be a more conservative newspaper, concerned with matters of national and international significance (Ramp, 2000: 32). In contrast, the right-leaning *Toronto Sun* is often seen as the city's tabloid press, its popularity being established through its closeness to "reality," highly opinionated columns, and readily consumable thematic and material content (Ericson et. al., 1989: 35; Ramp, 2000: 31; Hier, 2002: 39). Lastly, as a "mass" publication, *The Toronto Star* attempts to appeal to both ends of the market while generally espousing a more liberal point of view. With an estimated combined weekly circulation of over 6 million, these newspapers provide Toronto with the bulk of its daily print media.[5]

In addition to newspaper and magazine articles, I obtained and analysed government and agency reports as well as minutes from both Toronto City Council and provincial parliamentary debates. Such material provided considerable insight into how the problem was being constructed among those who played instrumental roles in the problem's eventual political and legal resolution.

A "PROBLEM" IN BRIEF

Toronto's squeegee kid "problem" emerged at a time when the provincial government was espousing a neo-liberal approach to social policy that emphasized economic restructuring, government downsizing through privatization, and a more aggressive approach to adult and youth crime.[6] In their *Blueprint for Justice and Community Safety in Ontario* (BJCS), the governing party promised a shift from "... criminals' rights to victims' rights; from increasing school violence to more respect for authority; and from rhetoric to a concrete plan of action" (*BJCS,* 1994: 2)—a "common sense" approach to crime control that was to include the use of "strict discipline facilities" for recidivist young offenders (*BJCS,* 1994: 22).

That the Conservative party made fighting crime an essential part of its electoral platform is not surprising. Indeed, "tough on crime" mandates continue to dominate electoral platforms across North America, often cutting across the entire political spectrum (Pratt and Valverde, 2002: 139; Ungar, 2001). What is important, however, is that homeless youths began cleaning car windshields in Toronto at a time when institutionalized political

sentiment was becoming increasingly weary, if not completely intolerant, of such forms of urban "incivility."

Although it is not altogether clear when youths *actually* began cleaning car windshields for money, they attracted media attention as early as 1995, when conservative social critic David Frum suggested that "squeegee men" were indicative of rising crime rates and the overall deterioration of urban living conditions (*The Financial Post,* 5/08/95: 16).

By the summer of 1998, anti-poverty claimants, as well as both provincial and city government critics, became more adamant in their struggle to rhetorically construct squeegeeing as if it were symptomatic of youth poverty; a much *larger* problem, they argued, that had everything to do with an unwillingness on the part of government officials to address issues relating to social inequality and a lack of affordable housing in the city of Toronto (*The Toronto Sun,* 27/07/98: 21). The squeegee kid problem was, therefore, being constructed along two rhetorical lines: on one hand, youths were constructed as willfully engaging in forms of delinquent and/or criminal behaviour that justified punitive intervention by the state (therefore, undeserving of state assistance). On the other hand, they were constructed as members of a larger homeless-youth population in need of immediate social assistance.

Although initially beset by logistical and sociolegal complications (see, for example *Emergency and Protective Services Committee* [EPSC], Report 8, Clause 1, July 29–31, 1999: 6), Toronto City Council, with financial assistance from the federal government, eventually approved, in November of 1998, the expenditure of $250,000 to develop and run a Squeegee Youth Working Mobilization project (SYWM) (City Council Legislative Documents, 2000: 2). This program was designed to meet the complex social and economic needs of those engaged in the squeegee trade. Before the program could be implemented, however, council members requested that the province of Ontario provide the necessary legislation to effectively prohibit all forms of aggressive panhandling. The legislative component of the plan was slow to emerge, however, and after the typical winter hiatus, Toronto endured another summer of broken windshields, intimidation, angry merchants, and police "crackdowns."

In the winter of 1999, the provincial government finally drafted the requested legislation and made the necessary amendments to the *Ontario Highway Traffic Act.* After debate in the provincial legislature, the *Safe Streets Act* was eventually granted royal assent and became law on December 4, 1999, with official implementation to take effect on January 31, 2000.[7] Although eventually challenged before the courts on the grounds that it violated Canada's *Charter of Rights and Freedoms, Safe Streets Act* was eventually upheld by a provincial court judge (*The Toronto Star,* 04/02/01: A10).

CREATING SQUEEGEE KIDS

In September,1995, a "squeegee kid" typology began to emerge in media discourse with a degree of particularity that was unparalleled. Although the youths had been mentioned one month earlier (see, for example, *The Financial Post,* 05/08/95: 16), definitions of who squeegee kids were, and what their behaviour entailed, remained largely unspecified. When, as a human interest story, the *Canadian Press Newswire* introduced its readers to two squeegee kids—16-year-old Stephanie and 19-year-old Drew— the squeegee kid typology began to take form. The ethnographic style of the article graphically illustrated the experience of squeegeeing:

> The unsuspecting driver is jolted out of his rush-hour daze as two street kids swoop in with squeegies dripping and vigorously start scrubbing what seems a clean windshield. As the seconds tick away before the light changes, Stephanie, 16, and Drew, 19, soak the windshield with warm soapy water, flipping the squeegies to wipe off the excess, ensuring they leave no streaks, before peering into the driver's front window for payment (*Canadian Press Newswire,* 28/09/95).

Less than one year later, and using a similar ethnographic approach, a *Toronto Life* magazine article described a day on the streets with Acid Boy, Turtle, Doob, Nathalie, and their friends Scruff and Beavis (all of whom used their street names). This added a new dimension to the emerging typology: a sense of lost innocence and missed opportunity juxtaposed on a backdrop of domestic turmoil and youth poverty:

> Why did he [Beavis] leave home? He shakes his head: "Really, really screwed-up situation." No one wants to talk about this. It is the topic that casts quick shadows across the giggling faces, that makes people stare out at traffic for a second. Only Beast will open up. "I left home, Muskoka, four days after my sixteenth birthday. I hadn't seen my father in thirteen years, so I met him and stayed with him in Scarborough. He's a severe alcoholic, and he's got a one-bedroom apartment and you open up our fridge and you might see a bottle of hot sauce and alcohol. That's about it. I basically ate when he was hungry" (*Toronto Life.* April 1996).

This rhetoric of loss (Ibarra and Kitsuse, 1993) was further accentuated by the disclosure of the youths' continuing struggles with drug and/or alcohol abuse. There was, apparently, more to squeegee life than simply washing car windshields. There was a depth to their existence, a series of ongoing trials and tribulations complemented by a sense of novelty and drama that made for a good human interest story. At the same time, the detail also served to refine the squeegee kid typology, giving it a sense of multi-dimensionality that would, ironically, fall victim to the simplicity of future claims-making activity. Nevertheless, acting as primary claims-makers, the media had positioned the typology within the lexicon of public and media discourse. The youths were no longer "those kids who washed windshields at stop lights," they were "squeegee kids," part of Toronto's urban cultural landscape.

Relying heavily on a rhetoric of disaster, squeegee kids were constructed as a symptom of impending social disorder and decline by virtue of their willful engagement in deviant and/or criminal social conduct. It is to a more focussed analysis of anti-squeegee rhetoric that we now turn.

CONSTRUCTIONS OF DISASTER

Between the summers of 1995 and 2000, both journalists and, in particular, anti-squeegee claimants implicitly and explicitly constructed the problem as if it were symptomatic of an impending state of disaster, devastation, and/or social decay. This disaster theme entailed three, somewhat overlapping, points of emphasis: the size of the social problem, the youths' unruly appearance and demeanor, and the public's subsequent fear of crime and urban disorder. In its entirety, the disaster theme set the rhetorical stage for the consonant "law and order" resolution that eventually followed.

GROUNDING THE PROBLEM: FROM "PLAGUES" TO "HEAVENS"

Although their estimates often conflicted, journalists and anti-squeegee claimants were preoccupied from the outset with determining how many squeegee kids there actually were in Toronto. Estimates ranged from a "handful" in 1995 to nearly 100 in the summer of 1996, and Toronto's print media seemed certain that the number of squeegee kids was growing.

A sense of disaster and disproportionality (Goode and Ben-Yehuda, 1994: 36–38) was more readily apparent in the idiomatic claims that accompanied the statistical estimates. As squeegee kids began "popping up all over" (*The Globe and Mail,* 11/06/97: A1), their presence was compared to the spread of dandelions (*Canadian Press Newswire,* 07/05/98), the arrival of Canada geese (*The Toronto Sun,* 26/04/99: 17), and even the spread of insects (*The Globe and Mail,* 29/07/99: A22). According to columnist

Margaret Wente: "Like the mosquitoes and the black flies, they hatch every spring with the onset of warm weather, and swarm the innocent motorists from the suburbs. Are squeegee people harmless pests, or harbingers of urban disorder and decay?" (*The Globe and Mail,* 29/07/99: A22). Similarly, paraphrasing Jim Brown, head of the Ontario Crime Control Commission, *The Toronto Star* wrote: "'I think Toronto is becoming the squeegee capital of the world,' said Brown. 'I think we're squeegee heaven. You are going to see more and more violence and they are certainly getting more and more aggressive'" (*The Toronto Star,* 23/07/98: C5). Journalists and anti-squeegee claimants alike constructed squeegee kids to be spreading uncontrollably throughout the city.

Anti-squeegee claimants also compared the number of squeegee kids to the spread of a deadly disease. After losing his windshield wipers, a Liberal MPP proclaimed that squeegee kids were a "plague" that required immediate intervention (*The Globe and Mail,* 20/07/96: A3: also see *The Toronto Sun,* 23/07/98: 15). Similarly, in July of 1998, during a subcommittee meeting of Toronto City Council, a spokesperson for a business improvement coalition argued: "We've had a *plague* of panhandlers, an *infestation* in our area. Where has this committee been for the last seven years? [italics mine]" (*The Globe and Mail,* 15/07198: A8). These idiomatic references to disease were implicitly apocalyptic and were likely meant to heighten the level of anxiety surrounding the putative condition, making it something insidious, impending, and larger than life.

Whether squeegee kids were characterized as a disease or a swarm of insects, anti-squeegee claimants understood them to be harbingers of impending disaster. As Toronto mayor Mel Lastman suggested: "This is a crisis, this is a problem, this is a major problem in the city.... This is a menace and there's a disaster waiting to happen on our streets. There's people being hurt, there's people who could be hurt, there's people who could be killed and you don't think that's a disaster?" (*The Toronto Star*, 30/07198: B3). Eventually proclaiming Toronto to be the "squeegee capital of the world" (*The Toronto Sun*, 22/07/98: 4; *The Toronto Star*, 03/08/99: B1), Lastman and Brown demanded forms of remedial legislation that would rid the city of the windshield-washing youths, a request that was eventually granted four months later.

Yet the objective here is not to evaluate the accuracy of the statistical or idiomatic claims that emerged (an undertaking that even some contextual constructionists might resist). Instead, of interest is why such claims emerged in the first place and why they were essential to the emerging social problem.

According to Best (1987), claims-makers often attempt to "ground" a social problem in order to convince or reassure the public that the putative condition is real, urgent, and in need of immediate intervention (Best, 1987). Whether it be the use of official statistics (Best. 1987: 108–110; Jenkins, 1994: 122) or other idiomatic references alleging the widespread nature of the condition, the process of grounding a social problem is essential to its construction. A social condition that is effectively constructed as being both problematic *and* widespread lends a degree of legitimacy to the level of concern inherent within such claims-making activity. Therefore, journalists and anti-squeegee claimants routinely sought to establish the size of the squeegee kid phenomenon so as to validate their own apparent interest and help garner additional support from others.

APPEARANCE

The youths' visual appearance proved politically useful for and-squeegee claimants and organizationally useful for Toronto's print media. Shaved heads, mohawks, pierced eyebrows, and fishnet stockings provided newspapers with a source of novel and dramatic content. This allowed anti-squeegee claimants to rhetorically associate the youths' appearance with all that was unruly about contemporary youth culture while simultaneously differentiating the youths from the homeless population.

In the early stages of the problem's construction, shortly before it became a social and political issue of significance, claims about the youths' appearance (and what it represented) were less derogatory and suggested a degree of concern. For example, in *Toronto Life* magazine, a group of young squeegee kids were described as being dishevelled and generally unhealthy:

Scruff is nineteen and Beavis is seventeen; their skin is the colour of paper glue, poked with scabs and acne. Even their Mohawks cackatoos, dyed yellow and purple, look wilted. Beavis's [sic] torn army pants are covered with ballpoint scribbles; Scruff wears canvas sneakers that are quickly soaked through with antifreeze (*Toronto Life*, April 1996).

An endless array of photographs accompanied articles in each of Toronto's major newspapers. In addition to being essential to a newspaper's overall sense of visual appeal (Gans, 1980; also see Altheide, 2002: 135), photographs play an important role in the construction of a social problem by creating a visual point of reference for readers who may find the condition unfamiliar and thus less worthy of their attention and concern. Although there were far too many photographs of squeegee kids to mention here, a few comments are in order.

With their torn clothing, pierced faces, and tattoos, squeegee kids provided claimants (journalists in particular) with an opportunity to capitalize on their unusual appearance. Most importantly, however, the youths were often photographed standing in the middle of an intersection, hunched over a windshield, or on a street corner with squeegees in hand (see, for example, *The Toronto Sun*, 29/07/98: 10). The media's imagery effectively decontextualized their lives by removing them from street life as a complex totality of lived experience and symbolically placing them within a conceptually limited frame of reference. They were portrayed to be in a perpetual state of confrontation with unsuspecting and innocent drivers who peered at them through the presumed safety of their windows. They were "squeegee kids," and what they did on a daily basis was occupy street corners (not shelters, abandoned buildings, or underpasses) and clean car windshields. With the exception of a special report printed in *The Toronto Star* in August of 1998 (*The Toronto Star,* 08/02/98: F1), photographs of squeegee kids doing something other than cleaning windshields rarely appeared, in spite of ample opportunity to acquire and present such material.

The defiant and decontextualized squeegee kid image, therefore, helped to disassociate the youths from contemporary homeless imagery. As portrayed by the media, the squeegee kid image did not resonate clearly with prevailing constructions of homeless people. They bore little resemblance to the media's homeless image of choice: the dishevelled middle aged man sleeping alone on a steaming subway grate wrapped in a sleeping bag. Squeegee kids acted differently, looked different, and appeared to have more in common with disgruntled teenage gangs—who generate fear and anxiety in the minds of the public—than with Toronto's down-and-out homeless population.

SQUEEGEE KIDS AND FEAR OF CRIME

Claims that acknowledge the existence of a pervasive fear of crime and disorder among an otherwise "reasonably" minded public can be highly effective in mobilizing support for law-and-order policy (see, for example, Altheide, 2002). Often capitalizing on the prospect of becoming saviours in a time of unrest, claims makers rhetorically align themselves with the voice of reason (the public), while giving credence to the belief that crime and disorder are ubiquitous, and legitimacy to fear as a prudent and commonsensical response.

Acknowledging the public's fear of squeegee kids and aggressive panhandlers became the rhetorical path of choice in the struggle to vilify and eliminate squeegee kids from the streets. Toronto newspapers quickly responded by looking abroad for more dramatic examples of squeegee-related disorder. *The Globe and Mail* contrasted Toronto's relatively mild situation with the "squeegee riots" that allegedly took place in Montreal in May of 1996, when approximately 250 youths vandalized businesses along the city's main street (*The Globe and Mail*, 20/07/96: A3). Similarly, *The Toronto Star* reminded its readers that New York City had a similar experience with squeegee kids, though apparently more severe by comparison (*The Toronto Star,* 08/08/96: G10)— the implication being that there was always the potential for escalating social disorder.

By the late spring of 1998, claims of broken car antennas, damaged windshield wipers, and intimidation gave way to claims that squeegee kids were actually "accosting" people on the streets and frightening women in particular. According to a local Toronto merchant: "There is accosting going on out there. It has to change or you're allowing the squeegee kids to dictate their own law... I mean, say you're a woman in a car, and you have someone with 52 nails stuck in their face coming at you waving a stick... what do you expect?" (*The Toronto Star,* 31/05198: A6). The rhetorical convergence of femininity with fear of crime recurred numerous times. For example, according to a "spokesperson" for the Ontario Attorney General's office: "It's a priority of the government and the ministry to allow Ontarians, *particularly women,* to feel safe and not to be harassed on the streets [italics mine]" (*The Toronto Star,* 25/07/98: A4). By conflating both fear and vulnerability with femininity, eliminating squeegee kids became not just a matter of crime control, but a matter of chivalrous obligation.

Squeegee kids had, therefore, challenged those who represented the very principles of order and civility, and, most importantly, appeared willing to use violence. Both dramatic and entertaining, these stories were recounted by Toronto journalists on numerous occasions—crime stories are entertaining and ultimately help to sell newspapers. For anti-squeegee claimants and journalists, the public, more than ever before, had good reason to be afraid. Squeegee kids had weapons, dogs, and, if reports were accurate, they were willing to accost and terrorize people. Crime-control commissioner Jim Brown even proclaimed squeegee kids to be similar to modern-day cultists (*The Toronto Sun,* 28/07/98: 7). With an entertaining victim/villain dynamic emerging, Premier Harris promised to rid the city of squeegee kids entirely. He requested that the Ontario Crime Control Commission (OCCC) meet to devise an effective solution to the squeegee problem, a problem that was assumed to be in the commission's area of expertise—that being the fight against crime and disorder, not the fight against poverty.

THE PRO-SQUEEGEE POSITION

I have emphasized the rhetorical and idiomatic themes that emerged within anti-squeegee claims in particular. In doing so, I have deliberately excluded a similar analysis of pro-squeegee rhetoric. This decision was not meant to imply that the pro-squeegee position was unimportant or that their claims-making activities were ineffective. Indeed, policy initiatives such as the SYWM were the result of persistent claims-making activities by anti-poverty activists, concerned city councillors, and journalists alike. A brief overview of pro-squeegee rhetoric is in order.

By rhetorically constructing the act of squeegeeing as being an inextricable response to youth poverty, pro-squeegee claimants engaged in a process of "domain expansion" (Loseke, 1999: 82) whereby the conceptual framework surrounding the larger problem of homelessness was rhetorically expanded so as to include the plight of Toronto's squeegee kids. For example, at a meeting of the Standing Committee on Justice

and Social Policy (SCJSP), an NDP member of provincial parliament suggested the following:

...my colleagues from my caucus and I today went out and squeegeed cars here in the Queen's Park parking lot at lunch time. We were white, male, middle age, unfortunately, and middle class. I'm wondering if you've thought about the fact that it isn't really conduct here that's being prohibited or targeted, be it in panhandling or indeed squeegeeing. Is it the conduct that's being targeted or is it certain classes of people that are in fact being targeted? (SCJSP minutes, 11/29/99)

Remedial legislation and/or police crackdowns were, therefore, equated with an "attack" on the homeless population (*The Globe and Mail,* 23/07/98: C5; *The Toronto Sun,* 16/11/99: 8). This process of domain expansion proved to be at the very heart of the pro-squeegee campaign, allowing claims-makers to champion the youths as yet another sign of the Ontario government's inability to effectively address the homeless "crisis."[8] That anti-squeegee rhetoric emerged *vis-a-vis* these pro-squeegee claims is without question. Indeed, both existed in a highly symbiotic relationship. What needs to be emphasized here is that my intent was to assess anti-squeegee rhetoric as a method of claims-making in and of itself; to extract particular themes, tactics, and processes that could be used as tools in future research that shares a similar interest in how particular individuals or groups become criminalized. Pro-squeegee claims *were* essential to how the squeegee kid problem unfolded in Toronto, yet they require a focussed analysis that is beyond what could have been *effectively* provided here.

DISCUSSION AND CONCLUSION

Anti-squeegee claimants introduced disaster rhetoric into the stages of identifying, grounding, and vilifying the social condition while simultaneously differentiating squeegee kids from the larger homeless population. In doing so, the politically volatile issues that typically surround the problem of homelessness were rendered less rhetorically applicable. This process of differentiation helped construct a relatively simplistic moral imperative. The fight against squeegee kids was to be a fight against crime and disorder where the victims were to be law-abiding members of the public and the villains unruly juveniles.

Yet, according to Pearson (1983), anxiety about youth deviance and/or crime is not new (Pearson, 1983; also see Tanner, 1996: 1–33). Successive generations have contrasted a largely mythical "golden age" of obedient youths with what is believed to be an unprecedented state of social disorder in the present. As Pearson (1983) demonstrates, the media has routinely played an essential role in creating such moral panic. These recurring cycles of "respectable fear," Pearson argues, demonstrate that the etiology of juvenile delinquency lies not in the easily rectified conditions of the present, but in the fundamental socio-economic relations that have defined modem capitalist societies for generations (Pearson, 1983: 236–242).

What, then, makes the attention garnered by Toronto's squeegee kids different from social problems involving other deviant youths in the past? The answer lies in how squeegee kids made use of what was, ostensibly, public space and how that usage affected the nature of claims-making activities. Unlike teenage gangs (Cohen, 1972; Pearson, 1983) or youths taking ecstacy [sic] at raves (Hier, 2002), squeegee kids were highly visible to literally thousands of commuters on a daily basis, many of whom were unable to efficiently navigate around them. Because the condition was experienced both widely and directly, pro-and anti-squeegee claims-making activities likely resonated with considerable clarity amongst their respective audiences.

In addition, the youths' exposure also rendered them readily available to members of the press for either photographs or interviews, neither of which were likely to have required the permission of a caregiver. With a steady stream of entertaining photos and provocative interviews, Toronto's print media were able to fuel the debate with content that was guaranteed to be both entertaining and relevant.

Lastly, squeegee kids' use of public space involved a simultaneous violation of what is generally assumed to be *private* space. Coming within inches of an unsuspecting driver, squeegee kids violated the symbolically demarcated sense of privacy that the automobile provides. Thus, they provided an unwanted bridge between the unruly city "out there" and the controlled, comfortable space within the automobile. Unlike social problems that are typically experienced by the public through claims-making activities (such as serial homicide [see, for example, Jenkins, 1994]), squeegee kids *directly* challenged perceptions of public and private space by routinely interacting with thousands of commuters in person.

Together, the aforementioned conditions helped catapult squeegee kids into social-problem status. Yet, as Cohen (1972) makes clear, the construction of moral panics and/or social problems takes place within a larger social and political framework that inevitably helps determine the nature of the claims-making activities that unfold (Cohen, 1972; Goode and Ben-Yehuda, 1994). It is therefore essential to expand the constructionist lens so as to take into consideration the macro-sociological context within which social problems emerge.

In this instance, the implementation of the *Safe Streets Act* reflects a recent trend in the rhetorical/political mandate of neo-liberal governance. With the advent of globalization, local and national governments are now being pressured to provide cheap labour, fewer social benefits, and a more inviting economic environment for (inter) national investment (Teeple, 1995; Stein, 2001). In addition to making "public" space virtually off-limits to those deemed undesirable (see, for example, Teeple, 1995; Mitchell, 1997; Hannigan, 1998; Parenti, 1999), these social, political, and economic transformations have contributed to the further erosion of the welfare state and a subsequent moralization of those who are in need of social assistance (Pratt and Valverde, 2002: 139;

see also Armitage, 1996). *Vis-a-vis* the presumably self-evident virtues of self-sufficiency, thrift, and economic efficiency, those in need of state assistance are often constructed as being morally inferior (see, for example Little, 1998) and sometimes even criminal.

Thus, the news, as well as all forms of claims-making, is about the social, political, economic, and cultural hierarchies that define contemporary society (Gans, 1980; Hackett, 1991). It is, indeed, from within these hierarchies, situated as they are in both time and space, that particular claims come forth. As this study has demonstrated, rhetorical and idiomatic themes often emerge which have considerable social and political currency. Sometimes becoming the proverbial "trump card," such themes help to displace alternative visions while traversing political boundaries under the rhetorical pretense of a moral imperative. Resonating clearly, and sometimes even emotionally, with broader cultural sensibilities, these themes provide us with a unique opportunity to examine not only the nature of larger cultural anxieties, but also the onset and/or further development of particular rhetorical processes that may, and often do, become the taken-for-granted *rationalities* of the future.

In the case of Toronto's squeegee kids, that taken-for-granted theme was one of disaster. More specifically, it was the synergy between two politically vibrant bodies of cultural imagery—one relating to the unruly nature of youth culture (see, for example Epstein, 1998; Lucas, 1998: 151) and the other to the now virtually axiomatic assumption that urban crime and disorder are spiralling out of control (see, for example Davis, 1992, 1998; Parenti, 1999; Altheide, 2002)—that gave the anti-squeegee position its rhetorical leverage. Although squeegee kids have apparently "disappeared" from Toronto's street corners, they are likely making ends meet in some other way. Should they take to the streets again in the future, the rhetorical framework (and thus the rationality) for future debate—not to mention the remedial legislation—will already be in place. The squeegee kid phenomenon will likely be understood, once again, as an issue of criminality "versus" poverty, but certainly not a complex mixture of both.

CRITICAL THINKING QUESTIONS

1. As a young sociologist, and with reference to the article, how would you explain the public's strong negative reaction toward squeegee kids?
2. Explain what the *constructionist approach* is and how it applies to squeegee kids. Can this approach be applied to any other social groups? If so, discuss your example; if not, describe why this approach only applies to squeegee kids.
3. Are there squeegee kids in your community? If there are, are they portrayed in a manner consistent with Parnaby's description? If there are not, how would you explain their absence?

NOTES

1. I have used the term "anti-squeegee claimants" here to refer to those individuals who demonstrated a clear desire to end squeegee activity in Toronto on the primary grounds that it represented an unwanted form of social disorder.
2. In the literature, "homeless youth" is a phrase used rather broadly to refer to those who are either runaways, who leave home without consent, or who are said to be "street kids"—those who have adapted to street life largely through illegal activities (see, for example, Breakey and Fischer, 1990).
3. There has been a great deal of interest in the social construction of juvenile delinquency in general (see, for example, Munice, 1984; Tanner. 1996: 1–33; Pearson, 1983).
4. The key words used while searching the databases included "squeegee kid," "squeegees," "cleaning windshields," "homelessness," and "homeless youths."
5. Circulation statistics were obtained from *The Campaign for Press and Broadcasting Freedom* organization. Available online at: www.presscampaign.org/circulation-data.html.
6. On the basis of this neo-liberal approach, Mike Harris's Progressive Conservative party won two successive provincial elections in 1995 and 1999.
7. According to the act, "No person shall, while on a roadway, solicit a person who is in or on a stopped, standing, or parked vehicle" (*Safe Streets Act*, 1999, ss. 3 (2) (f)). Similarly, amendments were also made to the *Ontario Highway Traffic Act.* In section 7, subsection 2: "No

person, while on the roadway, shall stop, attempt to stop or approach a motor vehicle for the purpose of offering, selling or providing any commodity or service to the driver or any other person in the motor vehicle" (*The Safe Streets Act,* 1999, ss. 7(2)). Squeegeeing car windshields, and other forms of aggressive panhandling, had become a provincial offence punishable by fine or, upon repeat conviction, incarceration (*The Safe Streets Act,* 1999. ss. 5(1)).

8. For a complete discussion of pro-squeegee rhetoric, see Parnaby (2000).

REFERENCES

Altheide, David L. 1987. Ethnographic content analysis. *Qualitative Sociology* 10(1): 65–77.

—2002. *Creating fear: News and the construction of crisis.* New York: Aldine de Gruyter.

Baron, Stephen W. 2001. Street youth labour market experiences and crime. *Canadian Review of Sociology and Anthropology* 38(2): 189–215.

Best, Joel. 1987. "Rhetoric in claims-making: Constructing the missing children problem. *Social Problems* 34(2):101–121.

—1989. *Images of issues: Typifying contemporary social problems.* New York: Aldine deGruyter.

—2001. *How claims spread: Cross-national diffusion of social problems.* New York: Aldine de Gruyter.

Blumer, Herbert. 1970. Social Problems As Collective Behaviour. *Social Problems* 18(1): 298–306.

Breakey, William R. and Pamela J. Fischer. 1990. "Homelessness: The Extent of the Problem." *Journal of Social Issues* 46(4): 31–47.

Cohen, Stanley. 1972. *Folk devils and moral panics.* London: MacGibbon & Kee.

Davis, Mike. 1992. *City of quartz: Excavating the future in Los Angeles.* New York: Vintage Books.

—1998. *Ecology of fear: Los Angeles and the imagination of disaster.* New York: Metropolitan Books.

Epstein, Jonathon S. 1998. *Youth culture in a postmodern world.* Massachusetts: Blackwell Publishers.

Erickson, Richard, Patricia Baranek, and Janet Chan. 1989. *Negotiating control: A study of news sources.* Toronto: University of Toronto Press

Fitzgerald, Michael D. 1995. Homeless youths and the child welfare system: Implications for policy and service. *Child Welfare* 74(3): 717–30.

Foucault, Michel. 1982. The subject and power. In *Michel Foucault: Beyond structuralism and hermeneutics,* eds. H. Dreyfus and P. Rabinow. Chicago: University of Chicago Press: 208–226.

Gaetz, Stephen, et al. 1999. *Making money: The Shout Clinic report on homeless youth and employment.* Toronto: Central Toronto Community Health Centres.

Gans, Herbert J. 1980. *Deciding what's news: A study of CBS Evening News, NBC Nightly News, Newsweek, and Time.* New York: Vintage Books.

Goode, Erich, and Nachman Ben-Yehuda. 1994. *Moral panics: The social construction of deviance.* Massachusetts: Blackwell Publishers.

Hackett, Robert A. 1991. *News and Dissent.* New Jersey: Alex Publishing Incorporated.

Hagan, John. 1994. *Crime and disrepute.* California: Pine Forge Press.

Hagan, John, and Bill McCarthy. 1998. *Mean streets: Youth crime and homelessness.* Cambridge: Cambridge University Press.

Heir, Sean. 2002. Raves, risks and the ecstacy panic: A case study in the subversive nature of moral regulation. *Canadian Journal of Sociology* 27(1): 33–57.

Ibarra, Peter R., and John I. Kitsuse. 1993. Vernacular constituents of moral discourse: An interactionist proposal for the study of social problems. In *Constructionist Controversies: Issues in Social Problems Theory,* eds. G. Miller and J.A. Holstein. New York: Aldine de Gruyter; 21–54.

Jenkins, Philip. 1994. *Using murder: The social construction of serial homicide.* New York: Aldine de Gruyter.

Kitsuse, John I. and Joseph W. Schneider. 1989. Preface in *Images of Issues,* 1st edition, Ed. J. Best New York: Aldine de Gruyter: x–xiv.

Loseke, Donileen. 1999. *Thinking about social problems: An introduction to constructionist perspectives.* New York: Aldine de Gruyter.

Lucas, Tim. 1998. Youth gangs and moral panics in Santa Cruz, California. In *Cool Places: Geographies of Youth Cultures,* eds. T. Skelton and G. Valentine. New York: Routledge:145–60.

McCarthy, Bill, and John Hagan. 1991. Homelessness: A criminogenic situation? *British Journal of Criminology* 31(4): 393–410.

—1992. Mean streets: The theoretical significance of situational delinquency among homeless youths. *American Journal of Sociology* 98(3): 597–627.

Miller, Gale and James A. Holstein. 1993. *Constructionist controversies: Issues in social problems theory.* New York: Aldine de Gruyter.

O'Grady. Bill, et al. 1998. Sub-employment and street youths: An analysis of the impact of squeegee cleaning on homeless youths. *Security Journal* 11: 315–23.

Parenti, Christian. 1999. *Lockdown America: Police and prisons in the age of crisis.* New York: Verso.

Parnaby, Patrick. 2000. Streets of pain and streets of gain: The social construction of squeegee kids in Toronto. Unpublished masters thesis, Department of Sociology, Queen's University, Kingston, Ontario.

Pearson, Geoffrey. 1983. *Hooligan: A history of respectable fears.* London: The Macmillan Press.

Pratt, Anna, and Mariana Valverde. 2002. From deserving victims to "Masters of Confusion". Redefining refugees in the 1990s. *Canadian Journal of Sociology* 27(1): 135–61.

Ramp, William. 2000. Moral spectacles: Norm and transgression in the news media. In *New Perspectives on Deviance: The Construction of Deviance in Everyday Life,* ed. L.G. Beaman. Scarborough: Prentice Hall Allyn Bacon Canada: 18–49.

Raychaba, Brian. 1989. Canadian youth in care: Leaving care to be on our own with no direction from home. *Children and Youth Services Review* 11: 61–73.

Spector, Malcolm, and John I. Kitsuse. 1977. *Constructing social problems.* California: Cummings Publishing Company.

Stein, Janice Gross. 2001. *The cult of efficiency.* Toronto: House of Anansi Press Limited.

Tanner, Julian. 1996. *Teenage troubles.* Scarborough: Nelson Canada.

Teeple, Gary. 1995. *Globalizing and the decline of social reform.* Toronto: Garamond Press.

Ungar, Sheldon. 2001. Moral panic versus risk society: The implications of the changing sites of social anxiety. *British Journal of Sociology* 52(2): 271–91.

Webber, Marlene. 1991. *Street kids: The tragedy of Canada's runaways.* Toronto: University of Toronto Press.

Whitbeck, Les B., and Dan R. Hoyt. 1999. *Nowhere to grow: Homeless and runway adolescents and their families.* New York: Aldine de Gruyter.

Government Documents and Reports

Boston, T. 1998 *Surviving the streets: Street youth and squeegeeing in Toronto.* Toronto: Community and Social Planning Council of Toronto.

City Council Legislative Documents

2000. Online source: **www.city.toronto.on.ca/legdocs/2000/agendas/council/cc/cc000201** (accessed: 03/12/2000)

13

CLASSIC

CONTEMPORARY

CROSS-CULTURAL

The Amish: A Small Society

John A. Hostetler

Some 100 000 Old Order Amish live in the rolling farmland of Pennsylvania, Ohio, Indiana, and southern Ontario. These descendants of sixteenth-century Germans, who fled persecution for their religious beliefs, constitute a distinctive "small society" that keeps the larger world at arm's length. This description of the Amish suggests the extent of cultural diversity within North America and raises questions about why some people would reject the "advantages" that many others take for granted.

Small communities, with their distinctive character—where life is stable and intensely human—are disappearing. Some have vanished from the face of the earth, others are dying slowly, but all have undergone changes as they have come into contact with an expanding machine civilization. The merging of diverse peoples into a common mass has produced tension among members of the minorities and the majority alike.

The Old Order Amish, who arrived on American shores in colonial times, have survived in the modern world in distinctive, viable, small communities. They have resisted the homogenization process more successfully than others. In planting and harvest time one can see their bearded men working the fields with horses and their women hanging out the laundry in neat rows to dry. Many American people have seen Amish families, with the men wearing broad-brimmed black hats and

the women in bonnets and long dresses, in railway depots or bus terminals. Although the Amish have lived with industrialized America for over two and a half centuries, they have moderated its influence on their personal lives, their families, communities, and their values.

The Amish are often perceived by other Americans to be relics of the past who live an austere, inflexible life dedicated to inconvenient and archaic customs. They are seen as renouncing both modern conveniences and the American dream of success and progress. But most people have no quarrel with the Amish for doing things the old-fashioned way. Their conscientious objection was tolerated in wartime, for after all, they are meticulous farmers who practice the virtues of work and thrift.

…The Amish are a church, a community, a spiritual union, a conservative branch of Christianity, a religion, a community whose members practice simple and austere living, a familistic entrepreneuring system, and an adaptive human community.…

Source: From *Amish Society,* 3rd ed., by John A. Hostetler (Baltimore: The Johns Hopkins University Press, 1980), pp. 3–12. Reprinted with permission.

The Amish are in some ways a little commonwealth, for their members claim to be ruled by the law of love and redemption. The bonds that unite them are many. Their beliefs, however, do not permit them solely to occupy and defend a particular territory. They are highly sensitive in caring for their own. They will move to other lands when circumstances force them to do so.

Commonwealth implies a place, a province, which means any part of a national domain that geographically and socially is sufficiently unified to have a true consciousness of its unity. Its inhabitants feel comfortable with their own ideas and customs, and the "place" possesses a sense of distinction from other parts of the country. Members of a commonwealth are not foot-loose. They have a sense of productivity and accountability in a province where "the general welfare" is accepted as a day-to-day reality. Commonwealth has come to have an archaic meaning in today's world, because when groups and institutions become too large, the sense of commonwealth or the common good is lost. Thus it is little wonder that the most recent dictionaries of the American English language render the meaning of commonwealth as "obsolescent." In reality, the Amish are in part a commonwealth. There is, however, no provision for outcasts.

It may be argued that the Amish have retained elements of wholesome provincialism, a saving power to which the world in the future will need more and more to appeal. Provincialism need not turn to ancient narrowness and ignorance, confines from which many have sought to escape. A sense of province or commonwealth, with its cherished love of people and self-conscious dignity, is a necessary basis for relating to the wider world community. Respect for locality, place, custom, and local idealism can go a long way toward checking the monstrous growth of consolidation in the nation and thus help to save human freedom and individual dignity.

...Anthropologists, who have compared societies all over the world, have tended to call semi-isolated peoples "folk societies," "primitives," or merely "simple societies." These societies constitute an altogether different type in contrast to the industrialized, or so-called civilized, societies.

The "folk society," as conceptualized by Robert Redfield,[1] is a small, isolated, traditional, simple, homogeneous society in which oral communication and conventionalized ways are important factors in integrating the whole life. In such an ideal-type society, shared practical knowledge is more important than science, custom is valued more than critical knowledge, and associations are personal and emotional rather than abstract and categoric.

Folk societies are uncomfortable with the idea of change. Young people do what the old people did when they were young. Members communicate intimately with one another, not only by word of mouth but also through custom and symbols that reflect a strong sense of belonging to one another. A folk society is *Gemeinschaft*-like; there is a strong sense of "we-ness." Leadership is personal rather than institutionalized. There are no gross economic inequalities. Mutual aid is characteristic of the society's members. The goals of life are never stated as matters of doctrine, but neither are they questioned. They are implied by the acts that constitute living in a small society. Custom tends to become sacred. Behavior is strongly patterned, and acts as well as cultural objects are given symbolic meaning that is often pervasively religious. Religion is diffuse and all-pervasive. In the typical folk society, planting and harvesting are as sacred in their own ways as singing and praying.

The folk model lends itself well to understanding the tradition-directed character of Amish society. The heavy weight of tradition can scarcely be explained in any other way. The Amish, for example, have retained many of the customs and small-scale technologies that were common in rural society in the nineteenth century. Through a process of syncretism, Amish religious values have been fused with an earlier period of simple country living when everyone farmed with horses and on a scale where family members could work together. The Amish exist as a folk or "little" community in a rural subculture within the modern state.... The outsider who drives through an Amish settlement cannot help but recognize them by their clothing, farm homes, furnishings, fields, and other material traits of culture. Although they speak perfect English with outsiders, they speak a dialect of German among themselves.

Amish life is distinctive in that religion and custom blend into a way of life. The two are inseparable. The core values of the community are religious beliefs. Not only do the members worship a deity they understand through the revelation of Jesus Christ and the Bible, but their patterned behavior [also] has a religious dimension. A distinctive way of life permeates daily life, agriculture, and the application of energy to economic ends. Their beliefs determine their conceptions of the self, the universe, and man's place in it. The Amish world view recognizes a certain spiritual worth and dignity in the universe in its natural form. Religious considerations determine hours of work and the daily, weekly, seasonal, and yearly rituals associated with life experience. Occupation, the means and destinations of travel, and choice of friends and mate are determined by religious considerations. Religious and work attitudes are not far distant from each other. The universe includes the divine, and Amish society itself is considered divine insofar as the Amish recognize themselves as "a chosen people of God." The Amish do not seek to master nature or to work against the elements, but try to work with them. The affinity between Amish society and nature in the form of land, terrain, and vegetation is expressed in various degrees of intensity.

Religion is highly patterned, so one may properly speak of the Amish as a tradition-directed group. Though allusions to the Bible play an important role in determining their outlook on the world, and on life after death, these beliefs have been fused with several centuries of struggling to survive in community. Out of intense religious experience, societal conflict, and intimate agrarian experience, a mentality has developed that prefers the old rather than the new. While the principle seems to apply especially to religion, it has also become a charter for social behavior. "The old is the best, and the new is of the devil" has become a prevalent mode of thought. By living in closed communities where custom and a strong sense of togetherness prevail, the Amish have formed an integrated way of life and a folklike culture. Continuity of conformity and custom is assured and the needs of the individual from birth to death are met within an integrated and shared system of meanings. Oral tradition, custom, and conventionality play an important part in maintaining the group as a functioning whole. To the participant, religion and custom are inseparable. Commitment and culture are combined to produce a stable human existence.

...A century ago, hardly anyone knew the Amish existed. A half-century ago they were viewed as an obscure sect living by ridiculous customs, as stubborn people who resisted education and exploited the labor of their children. Today the Amish are the unwilling objects of a thriving tourist industry on the eastern seaboard. They are revered as hard-working, thrifty people with enormous agrarian stamina, and by some, as islands of sanity in a culture gripped by commercialism and technology run wild.

CRITICAL THINKING QUESTIONS

1. In what ways does this description of the Amish way of life make you think about your own way of life differently?
2. Why would the Amish reject technological advances that most members of our society hold to be invaluable?
3. What might the majority of the North American population learn from the Amish?

NOTE

1. Robert Redfield, "The Folk Society," *American Journal of Sociology,* 52 (Jan. 1947), 293–308. See also his book *The Little Community* (Chicago: University of Chicago Press, 1955).

14

The Self

George Herbert Mead

The self is not the body but arises in social experience. Explaining this insight is perhaps George Herbert Mead's greatest contribution to sociology. Mead argues that the basic shape of our personalities is derived from the social groupings in which we live. Note, too, that even the qualities that distinguish each of us from others emerge only within a social community.

In our statement of the development of intelligence we have already suggested that the language process is essential for the development of the self. The self has a character which is different from that of the physiological organism proper. The self is something which has a development; it is not initially there, at birth, but arises in the process of social experience and activity, that is, develops in the given individual as a result of his relations to that process as a whole and to other individuals within that process....

Source: From *Mind, Self and Society: From the Standpoint of a Social Behaviorist* by George Herbert Mead (Chicago: University of Chicago Press, 1934), pp. 135–42, 144, 149–56, 158, 162–64. Copyright © 1934 by The University of Chicago Press. Reprinted with permission of the University of Chicago Press.

We can distinguish very definitely between the self and the body. The body can be there and can operate in a very intelligent fashion without there being a self involved in the experience. The self has the characteristic that it is an object to itself, and that characteristic distinguishes it from other objects and from the body. It is perfectly true that the eye can see the foot, but it does not see the body as a whole. We cannot see our backs; we can feel certain portions of them, if we are agile, but we cannot get an experience of our whole body. There are, of course, experiences which are somewhat vague and difficult of location, but the bodily experiences are for us organized about a self. The foot and hand belong to the self. We can see our feet, especially if we look at them from the wrong end of an opera glass, as strange things which we have difficulty in recognizing as our own. The parts of the body are quite distinguishable from the self. We can lose parts of the body without any serious invasion of the self. The mere ability to experience different parts of the body is not different from the experience of a table. The table presents a different feel from what the hand does when one hand feels another, but it is an experience of something with which we come definitely into contact. The body does not experience itself as a whole, in the sense in which the self in some way enters into the experience of the self.

It is the characteristic of the self as an object to itself that I want to bring out. This characteristic is represented in the word "self," which is a reflexive, and indicates that which can be both subject and object. This type of object is essentially different from other objects, and in the past it has been distinguished as conscious, a term which indicates an experience with, an experience of, one's self. It was assumed that consciousness in some way carried this capacity of being an object to itself. In giving a behavioristic statement of consciousness we have to look for some sort of experience in which the physical organism can become an object to itself.[1]

When one is running to get away from someone who is chasing him, he is entirely occupied in this action, and his experience may be swallowed up in the objects about him, so that he has, at the time being, no consciousness of self at all. We must be, of course, very completely occupied to have that take place, but we can, I think, recognize that sort of a possible experience in which the self does not enter. We can, perhaps, get some light on that situation through those experiences in which in very intense action there appear in the experience of the individual, back of this intense action, memories and anticipations. Tolstoi as an officer in the war gives an account of having pictures of his past experience in the midst of his most intense action. There are also the pictures that flash into a person's mind when he is drowning. In such instances there is a contrast between

an experience that is absolutely wound up in outside activity in which the self as an object does not enter, and an activity of memory and imagination in which the self is the principal object. The self is then entirely distinguishable from an organism that is surrounded by things and acts with reference to things, including parts of its own body. These latter may be objects like other objects, but they are just objects out there in the field, and they do not involve a self that is an object to the organism. This is, I think, frequently overlooked. It is that fact which makes our anthropomorphic reconstructions of animal life so fallacious. How can an individual get outside himself (experientially) in such a way as to become an object to himself? This is the essential psychological problem of selfhood or of self-consciousness; and its solution is to be found by referring to the process of social conduct or activity in which the given person or individual is implicated. The apparatus of reason would not be complete unless it swept itself into its own analysis of the field of experience; or unless the individual brought himself into the same experiential field as that of the other individual selves in relation to whom he acts in any given social situation. Reason cannot become impersonal unless it takes an objective, noneffective attitude toward itself; otherwise we have just consciousness, not *self*-consciousness. And it is necessary to rational conduct that the individual should thus take an objective, impersonal attitude toward himself, that he should become an object to himself. For the individual organism is obviously an essential and important fact or constituent element of the empirical situation in which it acts; and without taking objective account of itself as such, it cannot act intelligently, or rationally.

The individual experiences himself as such, not directly, but only indirectly, from the particular standpoints of other individual members of the same social group, or from the generalized standpoint of the social group as a whole to which he belongs. For he enters his own experience as a self or individual, not directly or immediately, not by becoming a subject to himself, but only insofar as he first becomes an object to himself just as other individuals are objects to him or in his experience; and he becomes an object to himself only by taking the attitudes of other individuals toward himself within a social environment or context of experience and behavior in which both he and they are involved.

The importance of what we term "communication" lies in the fact that it provides a form of behavior in which the organism or the individual may become an object to himself. It is that sort of communication which we have been discussing—not communication in the sense of the cluck of the hen to the chickens, or the bark of a wolf to the pack, or the lowing of a cow, but communication in the sense of significant symbols, communication which is directed not only to others but also to the individual himself. So far as that type of communication is a part of behavior it at least introduces a self. Of course, one may hear without listening; one may see things that he does not realize; do things that he is not really aware of. But it is where one does respond to that which he addresses to another and where that response of his own becomes a part of his conduct, where he not only hears himself but responds to himself, talks and replies to himself as truly as the other person replies to him, that we have behavior in which the individuals become objects to themselves.…

The self, as that which can be an object to itself, is essentially a social structure, and it arises in social experience. After a self has arisen, it in a certain sense provides for itself its social experiences, and so we can conceive of an absolutely solitary self. But it is impossible to conceive of a self arising outside of social experience. When it has arisen we can think of a person in solitary confinement for the rest of his life, but who still has himself as a companion, and is able to think and to converse with himself as he had communicated with others. That process to which I have just referred, of responding to one's self as another responds to it, taking part in one's own conversation with others, being

aware of what one is saying and using that awareness of what one is saying to determine what one is going to say thereafter—that is a process with which we are all familiar. We are continually following up our own address to other persons by an understanding of what we are saying, and using that understanding in the direction of our continued speech. We are finding out what we are going to say, what we are going to do, by saying and doing, and in the process we are continually controlling the process itself. In the conversation of gestures what we say calls out a certain response in another and that in turn changes our own action, so that we shift from what we started to do because of the reply the other makes. The conversation of gestures is the beginning of communication. The individual comes to carry on a conversation of gestures with himself. He says something, and that calls out a certain reply in himself which makes him change what he was going to say. One starts to say something, we will presume an unpleasant something, but when he starts to say it he realizes it is cruel. The effect on himself of what he is saying checks him; there is here a conversation of gestures between the individual and himself. We mean by significant speech that the action is one that affects the individual himself, and that the effect upon the individual himself is part of the intelligent carrying-out of the conversation with others. Now we, so to speak, amputate that social phase and dispense with it for the time being, so that one is talking to one's self as one would talk to another person.[2]

This process of abstraction cannot be carried on indefinitely. One inevitably seeks an audience, has to pour himself out to somebody. In reflective intelligence one thinks to act, and to act solely so that this action remains a part of a social process. Thinking becomes preparatory to social action. The very process of thinking is, of course, simply an inner conversation that goes on, but it is a conversation of gestures which in its completion implies the expression of that which one thinks to an audience. One separates the significance of what he is saying to others from the actual speech and gets it ready before saying it. He thinks it out, and perhaps writes it in the form of a book; but it is still a part of social intercourse in which one is addressing other persons and at the same time addressing one's self, and in which one controls the address to other persons by the response made to one's own gesture. That the person should be responding to himself is necessary to the self, and it is this sort of social conduct which provides behavior within which that self appears. I know of no other form of behavior than the linguistic in which the individual is an object to himself, and, so far as I can see, the individual is not a self in the reflexive sense unless he is an object to himself. It is this fact that gives a critical importance to communication, since this is a type of behavior in which the individual does so respond to himself.

We realize in everyday conduct and experience that an individual does not mean a great deal of what he is doing and saying. We frequently say that such an individual is not himself. We come away from an interview with a realization that we have left out important things, that there are parts of the self that did not get into what was said. What determines the amount of the self that gets into communication is the social experience itself. Of course, a good deal of the self does not need to get expression. We carry on a whole series of different relationships to different people. We are one thing to one man and another thing to another. There are parts of the self which exist only for the self in relationship to itself. We divide ourselves up in all sorts of different selves with reference to our acquaintances. We discuss politics with one and religion with another. There are all sorts of different selves answering to all sorts of different social reactions. It is the social process itself that is responsible for the appearance of the self; it is not there as a self apart from this type of experience.

A multiple personality is in a certain sense normal, as I have just pointed out....

The unity and structure of the complete self reflects the unity and structure of the social process as a whole; and each of the elementary selves of which it is composed reflects the unity and structure of one of the various aspects of that process in which the individual is implicated. In other words, the various elementary selves which constitute, or are organized into, a complete self are the various aspects of the structure of that complete self answering to the various aspects of the structure of the social process as a whole; the structure of the complete self is thus a reflection of the complete social process. The organization and unification of a social group is identical with the organization and unification of any one of the selves arising within the social process in which that group is engaged, or which it is carrying on.[3]

...Another set of background factors in the genesis of the self is represented in the activities of play and the game.... We find in children...imaginary companions which a good many children produce in their own experience. They organize in this way the responses which they call out in other persons and call out also in themselves. Of course, this playing with an imaginary companion is only a peculiarly interesting phase of ordinary play. Play in this sense, especially the stage which precedes the organized games, is a play at something. A child plays at being a mother, at being a teacher, at being a policeman; that is, it is taking different roles, as we say. We have something that suggests this in what we call the play of animals: A cat will play with her kittens, and dogs play with each other. Two dogs playing with each other will attack and defend, in a process which if carried through would amount to an actual fight. There is a combination of responses which checks the depth of the bite. But we do not have in such a situation the dogs taking a definite role in the sense that a child deliberately takes the role of another. This tendency on the part of children is what we are working with in the kindergarten where the roles which the children assume are made the basis for training. When a child does assume a role he has in himself the stimuli which call out that particular response or group of responses. He may, of course, run away when he is chased, as the dog does, or he may turn around and strike back just as the dog does in his play. But that is not the same as playing at something. Children get together to "play Indian." This means that the child has a certain set of stimuli that call out in itself the responses that they would call out in others, and which answer to an Indian. In the play period the child utilizes his own responses to these stimuli which he makes use of in building a self. The response which he has a tendency to make to these stimuli organizes them. He plays that he is, for instance, offering himself something, and he buys it; he gives a letter to himself and takes it away; he addresses himself as a parent, as a teacher; he arrests himself as a policeman. He has a set of stimuli which call out in himself the sort of responses they call out in others. He takes this group of responses and organizes them into a certain whole. Such is the simplest form of being another to one's self. It involves a temporal situation. The child says something in one character and responds in another character, and then his responding in another character is a stimulus to himself in the first character, and so the conversation goes on. A certain organized structure arises in him and in his other which replies to it, and these carry on the conversation of gestures between themselves.

If we contrast play with the situation in an organized game, we note the essential difference that the child who plays in a game must be ready to take the attitude of everyone else involved in that game, and that these different roles must have a definite relationship to each other. Taking a very simple game such as hide-and-seek, everyone with the exception of the one who is hiding is a person who is hunting. A child does not require more than the person who is hunted and the one who is hunting. If a child is playing in the first sense he just goes on playing, but there is no basic organization gained. In that early stage he passes from one to another just as a whim takes him. But in a game where a number of individuals are involved, then the child taking one role must be ready to take the role of everyone else. If

he gets in a ball game he must have the responses of each position involved in his own position. He must know what everyone else is going to do in order to carry out his own play. He has to take all of these roles. They do not all have to be present in consciousness at the same time, but at some moments he has to have three or four individuals present in his own attitude, such as the one who is going to throw the ball, the one who is going to catch it, and so on. These responses must be, in some degree, present in his own make-up. In the game, then, there is a set of responses of such others so organized that the attitude of one calls out the appropriate attitudes of the other.

This organization is put in the form of the rules of the game. Children take a great interest in rules. They make rules on the spot in order to help themselves out of difficulties. Part of the enjoyment of the game is to get these rules. Now, the rules are the set of responses which a particular attitude calls out. You can demand a certain response in others if you take a certain attitude. These responses are all in yourself as well. There you get an organized set of such responses as that to which I have referred, which is something more elaborate than the roles found in play. Here there is just a set of responses that follow on each other indefinitely. At such a stage we speak of a child as not yet having a fully developed self. The child responds in a fairly intelligent fashion to the immediate stimuli that come to him, but they are not organized. He does not organize his life as we would like to have him do, namely, as a whole. There is just a set of responses of the type of play. The child reacts to a certain stimulus, and the reaction is in himself that is called out in others, but he is not a whole self. In his game he has to have an organization of these roles; otherwise he cannot play the game. The game represents the passage in the life of the child from taking the role of others in play to the organized part that is essential to self-consciousness in the full sense of the term.

…The fundamental difference between the game and play is that in the former the child must have the attitude of all the others involved in that game. The attitudes of the other players which the participant assumes organize into a sort of unit, and it is that organization which controls the response of the individual. The illustration used was of a person playing baseball. Each one of his own acts is determined by his assumption of the action of the others who are playing the game. What he does is controlled by his being everyone else on that team, at least insofar as those attitudes affect his own particular response. We get then an "other" which is an organization of the attitudes of those involved in the same process.

The organized community or social group which gives to the individual his unity of self may be called "the generalized other." The attitude of the generalized other is the attitude of the whole community.[4] Thus, for example, in the case of such a social group as a ball team, the team is the generalized other insofar as it enters—as an organized process or social activity—into the experience of any one of the individual members of it.

If the given human individual is to develop a self in the fullest sense, it is not sufficient for him merely to take the attitudes of other human individuals toward himself and toward one another within the human social process, and to bring that social process as a whole into his individual experience merely in these terms: He must also, in the same way that he takes the attitudes of other individuals toward himself and toward one another, take their attitudes toward the various phases or aspects of the common social activity or set of social undertakings in which, as members of an organized society or social group, they are all engaged; and he must then, by generalizing these individual attitudes of that organized society or social group itself, as a whole, act toward different social projects which at any given time it is carrying out, or toward the various larger phases of the general social process which constitutes its life and of which these projects are specific manifestations. This getting of the broad activities of any given social whole or organized society as such within the experiential field of any one of the individuals involved or included in that whole is,

in other words, the essential basis and prerequisite of the fullest development of that individual's self: Only insofar as he takes the attitudes of the organized social group to which he belongs toward the organized, cooperative social activity or set of such activities in which that group as such is engaged, does he develop a complete self or possess the sort of complete self he has developed. And on the other hand, the complex cooperative processes and activities and institutional functionings of organized human society are also possible only insofar as every individual involved in them or belonging to that society can take the general attitudes of all other such individuals with reference to these processes and activities and institutional functionings, and to the organized social whole of experiential relations and interactions thereby constituted—and can direct his own behavior accordingly.

It is in the form of the generalized other that the social process influences the behavior of the individuals involved in it and carrying it on, i.e., that the community exercises control over the conduct of its individual members; for it is in this form that the social process or community enters as a determining factor into the individual's thinking. In abstract thought the individual takes the attitude of the generalized other[5] toward himself, without reference to its expression in any particular other individuals; and in concrete thought he takes that attitude insofar as it is expressed in the attitudes toward his behavior of those other individuals with whom he is involved in the given social situation or act. But only by taking the attitude of the generalized other toward himself, in one or another of these ways, can he think at all; for only thus can thinking—or the internalized conversation of gestures which constitutes thinking—occur. And only through the taking by individuals of the attitude or attitudes of the generalized other toward themselves is the existence of a universe of discourse, as that system of common or social meanings which thinking presupposes at its context, rendered possible.

...I have pointed out, then, that there are two general stages in the full development of the self. At the first of these stages, the individual's self is considered simply by an organization of the particular attitudes of other individuals toward himself and toward one another in the specific social acts in which he participates with them. But at the second stage in the full development of the individual's self that self is constituted not only by an organization of these particular individual attitudes, but also by an organization of the social attitudes of the generalized other or the social group as a whole to which he belongs.... So the self reaches its full development by organizing these individual attitudes of others into the organized social or group attitudes, and by thus becoming an individual reflection of the general systematic pattern of social or group behavior in which it and the others are all involved—a pattern which enters as a whole into the individual's experience in terms of these organized group attitudes which, through the mechanism of his central nervous system, he takes toward himself, just as he takes the individual attitudes of others.

...A person is a personality because he belongs to a community, because he takes over the institutions of that community into his own conduct. He takes its language as a medium by which he gets his personality, and then through a process of taking the different roles that all the others furnish he comes to get the attitude of the members of the community. Such, in a certain sense, is the structure of a man's personality. There are certain common responses which each individual has toward certain common things, and insofar as those common responses are awakened in the individual when he is affecting other persons he arouses his own self. The structure, then, on which the self is built is this response which is common to all, for one has to be a member of a community to be a self. Such responses are abstract attitudes, but they constitute just what we term a man's character. They give him what we term his principles, the acknowledged attitudes of all members of the community toward what are the values of that community. He is putting himself in the place of the generalized other, which represents the organized responses of all the members of the group. It is that which guides conduct controlled by principles, and a person who has such an organized group of responses is a man who we say has character, in the moral sense.

...I have so far emphasized what I have called the structures upon which the self is constructed, the framework of the self, as it were. Of course we are not only what is common to all: Each one of the selves is different from everyone else; but there has to be such a common structure as I have sketched in order that we may be members of a community at all. We cannot be ourselves unless we are also members in whom there is a community of attitudes which control the attitudes of all. We cannot have rights unless we have common attitudes. That which we have acquired as self-conscious persons makes us such members of society and gives us selves. Selves can only exist in definite relationships to other selves. No hard-and-fast line can be drawn between our own selves and the selves of others, since our own selves exist and enter as such into our experience only insofar as the selves of others exist and enter as such into our experience also. The individual possesses a self only in relation to the selves of the other members of his social group; and the structure of his self expresses or reflects the general behavior pattern of this social group to which he belongs, just as does the structure of the self of every other individual belonging to this social group.

CRITICAL THINKING QUESTIONS

1. How does Mead distinguish between the body and the self? What makes this a radically *social* view of the self?
2. How is the self both a subject and an object to itself? How is the ability to assume the role of the other vital to our humanity?

3. The idea that socialization produces conformity is easy to understand, but explain Mead's argument that individual distinctiveness is also a result of social experience.

NOTES

1. Man's behavior is such in his social group that he is able to become an object to himself, a fact which constitutes him a more advanced product of evolutionary development than are the lower animals. Fundamentally it is this social fact—and not his alleged possession of a soul or mind with which he, as an individual, has been mysteriously and supernaturally endowed, and with which the lower animals have not been endowed—that differentiates him from them.

2. It is generally recognized that the specifically social expressions of intelligence, or the exercise of what is often called "social intelligence," depend upon the given individual's ability to take the roles of, or "put himself in the place of," the other individuals implicated with him in given social situations; and upon his consequent sensitivity to their attitudes toward himself and toward one another. These specifically social expressions of intelligence, of course, acquire unique significance in terms of our view that the whole nature of intelligence is social to the very core—that this putting of one's self in the places of others, this taking by one's self of their roles or attitudes, is not merely one of the various aspects or expressions of intelligence or intelligent behavior, but is the very essence of its character. Spearman's "X factor" in intelligence—the unknown factor which, according to him, intelligence contains—is simply (if our social theory of intelligence is correct) this ability of the intelligent individual to take the attitude of the other, or the attitudes of others, thus realizing the significations or grasping the meanings of the symbols or gestures in terms of which thinking proceeds; and thus being able to carry on with himself the internal conversation with these symbols or gestures which thinking involves.

3. The unity of the mind is not identical with the unity of the self. The unity of the self is constituted by the unity of the entire relational pattern of social behavior and experience in which the individual is implicated, and which is reflected in the structure of the self; but many of the aspects or features of this entire pattern do not enter into consciousness, so that the unity of the mind is in a sense an abstraction from the more inclusive unity of the self.

4. It is possible for inanimate objects, no less than for other human organisms, to form parts of the generalized and organized—the completely socialized—other for any given human individual, insofar as he responds to such objects socially or in a social fashion (by means of the mechanism of thought, the internalized conversation of gestures). Any thing—any object or set of objects, whether animate or inanimate, human or animal, or merely physical—toward which he acts, or to which he responds, socially, is an element in what for him is the generalized other; by taking the attitudes of which toward himself he becomes conscious of himself as an object or individual, and thus develops a self or personality. Thus, for example, the cult, in its primitive form, is merely the social embodiment of the relation between the given social group or community and its physical environment—an organized social means, adopted by the individual members of that group or community, of entering into social relations with that environment, or (in a sense) of carrying on conversations with it; and in this way that environment becomes part of the total generalized other for each of the individual members of the given social group or community.

5. We have said that the internal conversation of the individual with himself in terms of words or significant gestures—the conversation which constitutes the process or activity of thinking—is carried on by the individual from the standpoint of the "generalized other." And the more abstract that conversation is, the more abstract thinking happens to be, the further removed is the generalized other from any connection with particular individuals. It is especially in abstract thinking, that is to say, that the conversation involved is carried on by the individual with the generalized other, rather than with any particular individuals. Thus it is, for example, that abstract concepts are concepts stated in terms of the attitudes of the entire social group or community; they are stated on the basis of the individual's consciousness of the attitudes of the generalized other toward them, as a result of his taking these attitudes of the generalized other and then responding to them. And thus it is also that abstract propositions are stated in a form which anyone—any other intelligent individual—will accept.

15

Socialization

CLASSIC
CONTEMPORARY
CROSS-CULTURAL

The Importance of the Family as an Agent of Socialization: Developmental Pathways and Crime Prevention

Michael C. Boyes, Nancy A. Ogden, and Joseph P. Hornick

After a brief review of the key elements of human socialization, Boyes, Ogden, and Hornick describe a new approach to helping to reduce human suffering by curtailing the development of criminal activity. As you read, think about your own assumptions about the program and its potential for further success.

We will discuss a specific program that operates at the level of the individual family in an attempt to reduce human suffering, both today and in the future, by curtailing the development of criminal activity, particularly violent criminal activity. Considerable evidence supports the existence of a relationship between child maltreatment and subsequent delinquency and criminality. Programs that provide children with healthier beginnings early in life endeavour to prevent such children from choosing the maladaptive pathways that commonly lead to criminality, substance abuse, or both. We'll begin by outlining the basic premises on which such assumptions are based, follow with a discussion about general programs, and conclude with a specific Canadian program and its early findings.

Source: Reprinted by permission of the authors, 2002.

INFLUENCES AT THE BEGINNING OF LIFE

Every human being is a product of their biology as well as their individual and sociocultural experiences. Our genetic blueprint, our heredity, provides us with the basic material for our development but does not absolutely determine our behaviour. Although the self has a strong biological element, most social scientists agree that social influence is critical for creating truly human individuals. In fact, few behaviours are not socially influenced. Sociologists use the term *socialization* to refer to lifelong social experiences through which individuals develop a self-identity and learn culture: the physical, mental, and social skills needed for the survival of both the individual and the society. Human beings create and maintain their own culture and transmit it from one generation to the next through socialization. Socialization serves as the fundamental connection between the individual and society and as such is essential for maintaining the stability of society. Therefore, to support and sustain the existing social structure, individual members of a society must be socialized.

How does society ensure that its newest members receive appropriate socialization? Teaching the infant and young child—and eventually the older child, adolescent, and adult—what they need to know to participate in society is the task of persons, groups, or institutions that are collectively called *agents of socialization*. These agents come in many forms: schools, media, peers, families, and so on. Fitting children into their sociocultural environment is an important responsibility for socialization agents. For most individuals the family is the first and most important agent of socialization and is the centre of the infant and young child's world. Parents are our earliest teachers, transmitting cultural and social values to us. The family provides infants with their first social interactions and is likely to be children's primary contact with the world during the early years. Moreover, the family context places children within society in terms of class, religion, race, and ethnicity. Individuals of various social classes demonstrate different expectations for their children's behaviours. For example, working class parents are more likely to demand obedience and conformity from their children than are middle-class parents.

This socialization process is most effective when individuals adhere to the accepted norms and values of society because they come to recognize the function and importance of those norms and values. Ideally, parents help their children learn to be caring and contributing members of society. "Successfully" socialized children grow into adults who act as their own socialization agents. They choose not to break the rules because to do so would be "wrong." This implies that very early in their lives, children develop a warm and trusting relationship with a parent and *want* to please that parent by doing the things the parent considers "right" or "good." How then does a parent establish such a relationship with a young infant?

The Importance of Early Relationships

The initial love and nurturing children receive from their families, usually their parents, are central to their cognitive, emotional, and physical development. If infants live in such an environment, they learn to trust their caregivers; this makes infants feel secure. Security is vitally important for children's sense of well-being. When infants feel safe, they explore the environment, using the caregiver as a secure base. This pattern is part of the normal development of infants and very young children and is essential for healthy growth and development. Most children are nurtured by their parents and live in secure, loving, trusting environments. But the sad truth is that not all infants and children feel safe. Large numbers of infants and children experience maltreatment at the hands of those whom they depend upon, those whom they cannot leave or reject. These children are insecure. Documented cases of child abuse and neglect indicate that human infants without adequate social interaction with other human beings are unable to fully develop healthy human characteristics.

Child maltreatment includes physical, emotional, and sexual abuse, as well as neglect. Research on the community, family, and individual causes of violence in the lives of children and youth emphasizes the importance of the family as an agent of socialization. Deprivation, poor parenting practices, and dysfunctional family interaction are associated with the development of antisocial and delinquent behaviour (Snyder & Patterson, 1987).

Perhaps you are thinking of someone you know who lived in a dysfunctional environment, yet is not abusing any substances and is not involved in any criminal activity. Perhaps this person is you. Not everyone from an abusive, dysfunctional, or violent home will experience these outcomes. The relationship among family violence, substance abuse, and criminal behaviour is not absolute; these consequences are not inevitable. To determine just who *is* at risk, researchers assess the presence or absence of two types of variables: risk factors and protective factors.

In infants' and children's lives, risk factors in their family, school, and community include variables such as discrimination, family violence and dysfunction, poverty, lack of supervision, violent neighbourhoods, and multiple moves. The presence of any of these risk factors significantly increases children's later risk for negative outcomes such as depression, mental illness, conduct problems, suicide, delinquency and criminality, substance abuse, and aggressive or violent behaviour. The greatest risk factor for the development of nearly all forms of behavioural problems is poverty. The number of children living in poverty continues to increase in most industrialized nations, including Canada (Canadian Council on Social Development, 1997). The National Longitudinal Survey of Children and Youth (in Canadian Council on Social Development, 1997) reports that poverty has a negative impact on family functioning and school performance. Family dysfunction and parental depression are significantly higher in families living below the poverty line.

The presence of four or more risk factors increases the risk of negative outcomes tenfold (Sameroff et al., 1987; Smith et al., 1995). The prevalence of serious delinquency and substance abuse is strongly associated with increased numbers of risk factors. Many risk factors are interrelated. For example, family breakdown is related to high levels of juvenile delinquency, high conflict, lowered income, and parent absence, which are in turn each related to juvenile delinquency (Garbarino, 1999). Thus, the factors involved in criminal offending are complex, cumulative, and can be explained through both individual and social history.

An excellent example of the interrelationship between individual and sociocultural influences is the relatively recent research documenting the destructive consequences of children's exposure to community violence (Bell & Jenkins, 1993;

Osofsky et al., 1993; Sheidow et al., 2001). Of course, substantial discrepancy exists in the degree and extent of exposure to violence among children and youth living in inner-city communities. Nevertheless, the Canadian Council on Social Development reports that one in four Canadian children lives in an area that is considered unsafe after dark (Canadian Council on Social Development, 1997). Characteristics of the neighbourhood (such as the percentages of families working or living below the poverty level and the stability of the neighbourhood) and family functioning are important influences on how children function within their local community environments. How important is the family as an agent of socialization in violent communities? Unfortunately, the importance of family functioning is not independent of neighbourhood characteristics; Sheidow et al. (2001) report that in inner-city communities without positive social processes, the risk of exposure to violence cannot be assuaged by family functioning. That is, for many children exposed to violence within their communities, it does not matter how their family is functioning; these children are at risk simply by living within their community. Children in functional families are at risk; children in dysfunctional families are *more* at risk. These observations underscore the importance of understanding the social ecology of development for identifying how risk factors relate to outcomes (Gorman-Smith, Tolan, & Henry, 1999; National Crime Prevention Council, 1995) and serve as an important reminder that the family is not the *only* agent of socialization affecting children.

The impact of violence on children differs with the type of violence, the pattern of violence, the presence of supportive adult caretakers and other support systems, and the age of the child (Perry, 1995). Children at risk at an early age are in greater jeopardy for multiple negative outcomes later in life. This is due in part to the fact that younger children have fewer defensive capabilities (Grizenko & Fisher, 1992; Perry, 1995).

Early Risk and Resilience

Children at risk for later negative outcomes can be identified through particular sets of risk factors. Are researchers equally adept at identifying those factors that will protect children from inferior environments? The answer is, in part, yes. Factors such as high intelligence, secure attachment, average to above average family income, educated parents, and so on, can serve as protection for children in destitute environments, causing them to be more resilient. In fact, most studies of protective factors (see, for example, Losel & Bliesener, 1990) suggest that under adverse circumstances, 80 percent of children will "bounce back" from developmental challenges. This assumption is proving to be overly optimistic (Garbarino, 2001; Perry, 1994). For instance, resilience is drastically diminished under conditions of extreme risk accumulation or if children receive inadequate care in the first two years. Garbarino (2001) suggests that these observations could be interpreted to mean that the children and youth best able to survive functionally are those who have the least to lose morally and psychologically. The data yielded by his conversations with youths incarcerated for murder and other acts of violent crime confirm his theory. He reports that the crimes were unaffected by moral compunction or emotional responsibility for others.

How can this be? The work of Perry and his colleagues (1994, 1995) documents the impact of early neglect and abuse on the development of the brain. This research contends that infant's and children's brains are more plastic (i.e., receptive to inputs from the environment) than more mature brains are: the infant or child is most vulnerable to disadvantaged environments during the first three or four years. These developmental experiences determine how the brain will be organized and therefore how it will function. Early trauma can produce inadequate development of the brain's cortex (the part of the brain that controls higher abilities such as abstract reasoning and impulse control) by stimulating a stress-related hormone—cortisol—that impedes brain growth.

These findings have implications for research, intervention, and prevention. For example, the earlier an intervention occurs, the more effective and preventative it is likely to be (Blair, Ramey, & Hardin, 1995; Kiser, Heston, & Millsap, 1991; McFarlane, 1987) and thus the more enduring its impact. Furthermore, insightful sociocultural and public policy implications should arise from understanding the critical role that early experience plays in socializing children as they mature and acculturate or identify as traumatized and maladapted, thereby affecting our society for ill or good. Perry forcefully argues that we must stop accepting the myth that children are resilient; evidence contradicts such assertions, and children are irrevocably affected by maltreatment. "Persistence of the pervasive [political acceptance of] maltreatment of children in the face of devastating global and national resources will lead, inevitably, to sociocultural devolution" (Perry, 1994: 12).

In Canada, where children and youth compose 23 percent of the population, nearly one-quarter of police-reported assaults are visited on children and youth (Statistics Canada, 1996). This statistic is disturbing enough; however, of greater concern is the belief of officials that many incidents of maltreatment are not documented because they are either not observed or reported, leading to an underestimate of the extent of the problem. Factors such as the secrecy surrounding the issue, the dependency of the victim on the abuser, and the lack of knowledge about potential sources for help also contribute to underreporting.

We can conclude that the ramifications of the maltreatment of children involve tremendous personal and sociocultural costs. The financial costs are also staggering. In its report *Preventing Crimes by Investing in Families* (1996), the National Crime Prevention Council conservatively estimates that the annual cost of crime in Canada is in the range of 46 *billion* dollars (of which approximately one-quarter may be attributed to youth crime). Family violence escalates social and economic costs to the health care system, affects the civil and criminal justice systems, and creates immeasurable human suffering. The prevention of crime translates into meaningful reductions in human anguish, community victimization, and money spent on services for young offenders and their families. Society must rethink its priorities with respect to dedicating adequate time, energy, and resources to every aspect of prevention. Programs that support families and parents of very young children can significantly reduce child abuse and juvenile crime.

Secure attachments have recently been used to ascertain levels of vulnerability for those at risk of serious criminal behaviour. Many young offenders have been abused or have witnessed abuse in their homes. As already discussed, family violence is a problem that creates lasting physical, psychological, or economic repercussions for children and for society. The impacts of child abuse are experienced throughout the individual's lifetime. For example, 50 percent of those who were abused as children reported also being abused as adults (McCauley et al., 1997).

A DEVELOPMENTAL APPROACH TO CRIME PREVENTION

Over the past few decades, the focus on crime prevention has shifted from treatment and punishment to preventative initiatives targeting the family and parenting skills, using a multi-systemic, developmental approach. It is essential to turn individuals from harmful pathways before maladaptive patterns of behaviour are well established. Thus, early prevention is the most effective strategy. Early intervention approaches involve various aspects of the family and those outside factors that influence family functioning. Willing participation in intensive, high-quality early intervention programs has been shown to be associated with improved developmental outcomes for high-risk children (Ramey & Ramey, 1994). For the first three years of children's lives, home-visiting programs are a successful way to reach high-risk children and their families and to promote resiliency (Luthar & Ziglar, 1991). Farrington (1994) summarizes research evidence attesting to the positive impact that early intervention programs have on deflecting criminal behaviour and other social problems. Interventions at crucial developmental transition points can have a major positive effect on at-risk families and their children, improving quality of life and potentially preventing criminal activity.

The saying "it takes a village to raise a child" does more than simply suggest that raising children requires a lot of work. What it points to is the essential importance of considering *both* the direct contacts that children have as they develop *and* the multiple contexts in which those contacts occur to properly see what facilitates or hampers optimal development. There have been several attempts to capture a broader perspective on development using ecological developmental models. Based on Bronfenbrenner's (1979) pioneering work, ecological models identify the familial and contextual influences that contribute to abuse. However, these influences are transactional; that is, the individual and the immediate and larger social contexts are viewed as actively influencing one another.

From this ecological developmental model perspective, opportunities for risk reduction must be considered in the contexts comprising the child and his or her immediate family, friends, neighbourhood, spiritual community, and school. Other influential contexts include aspects of social and physical geography such as weather, local and national laws, social conventions, and cultural and subcultural values and ideals. How all these contextual forces interact with the child's physical makeup determines the actual developmental course taken by an individual child (Garbarino, 1990).

Interventions for Reducing Risks and Bolstering Protective Factors: The Healthy Families Example

Creating specific programs aimed at reducing stress, enhancing family functioning, and promoting child development was the logical first step in implementing theoretical developmental models. The Healthy Start program in Hawaii was designed to improve family coping skills, as well as family functioning, and promoted positive parenting. The stated purpose of the Hawaii Healthy Start program was to reduce child abuse and neglect. The program identified families at high risk for abuse or neglect by screening newborns and their families in hospital and followed up with home visits from community-based family support services. Families were linked to family physicians or to nursing clinics and connected to a number of community services. Families were followed until the child was five years old. Evaluation of the program revealed that the high-risk families that participated in the program had half the state average for child maltreatment and abuse, whereas the rate of abuse for high-risk families that did not participate in the program was twice the state average.

Since their inception in 1992, Healthy Families America Inc. has modelled their programs on Hawaii's groundbreaking initiative, and has implemented nearly 200 programs throughout the United States. However, escalating health costs in a country without socialized medicine caused the Healthy Families America program interventions to became increasingly focused on helping low income, at-risk families to access state-funded health services. The Health Insurance Association of America (1999) estimates that by the year 2007, 53.5 million people in the United States will be uninsured, and more than one-third of these people will be children. This, coupled with the fact that at both the state and federal levels child and family services (i.e., Child Welfare) are less broadly organized in the American system, indicated that modifications to the Healthy Families initiative would be necessary if the program were to come to Canada. Canada has a system of socialized medicine that guarantees universal health care and is strongly supported through efficient community public health support. In fact, Canadian children at all income levels make the same average number of visits to doctors, whereas insured American children are eight times more likely to visit a doctor than are uninsured children (Canadian Council on Social Development, 1997). Moreover, Canada boasts more formally organized child and family ministries. These differences enabled Canadian researchers to redefine program objectives and allowed them to focus more intensely and more broadly on the other issues involved in assessing risk.

The Department of Justice Canada, through the National Crime Prevention Centre (NCPC), financed a Healthy Families demonstration project. The main goal of the investment is to establish effective programs for reducing delinquency and crime. Three programs were chosen to pilot the project: "Best Start" in Prince Edward Island, "Healthy Families" in Yukon, and "Success by 6 Healthy Families" in Alberta. Each program and the people they serve were chosen because they represent very different types of communities. The Prince Edward Island program is in a small urban centre with a large rural population, the Yukon program serves an Aboriginal community, and the Edmonton program serves a large urban community. In 1999, the Canadian Research Institute for Law and the Family (CRILF), located in Alberta, began a three-year project to complete process and outcome evaluations of these Healthy Families programs.

The Healthy Families program utilized trained paraprofessional visitors to provide home visitation services to families identified by the public health system as requiring assistance. Healthy Families programs administer initial and follow-up screenings and establish schedules for home visits. The model requires that the entire child-raising system be assessed. Evaluators from CRILF used existing measures and developed measures to assess for each child the risk and protective factors that could influence a less than optimal developmental trajectory, potentially influencing the child's vulnerability to delinquent and criminal behaviour.

The overall mandate of all Healthy Families Programs is to optimize the development of young at-risk children and their families and to increase the children's opportunities for later success through early screening, assessment, and intervention. The Canadian focus has been on the transition to parenting, enabling parents to become more effective caregivers. First, the program empowers parents and enables them to access a broad range of community programs and resources (e.g., community kitchens, library reading programs, parenting support groups). Second, the program has an intense focus on the interaction between the parent and the child, with an eye to identifying issues and facilitating positive parent–child interaction and healthy growth and development for both. Program personnel are trained to identify and address maladaptive parenting attitudes and behaviours.

A key issue underlying the Healthy Families project in Canada (and the United States) is whether early experience and intervention make a difference to later occurrence of delinquency or crime. The answer in a recent comprehensive longitudinal review of developmental and early intervention approaches conducted in Australia is unequivocally "yes" (National Crime Prevention, 1999). In Canada, this question will remain unanswered until the young children involved in the Healthy Families project reach adulthood, but initial data from the project are causing researchers to be cautiously optimistic.

Early outcome data from the Canadian project suggest that if at-risk families are involved in a Healthy Families program, they have a reduced likelihood of Child Welfare involvement (both contacts and apprehensions). For example, data from Prince Edward Island indicate Child Welfare involvement in less than 2 percent of the families involved in the program compared with more than 25 percent of families in a matched comparison group. This is of particular note given that the number of children apprehended by Child Welfare agencies across Canada has increased (Canadian Council on Social Development, 1997). Outcomes will not actually be known for another twenty years, but existing data on welfare apprehension and crime suggest that a reduction in apprehensions should lead to better developmental outcomes, which in turn should lower rates of violent crime and incarceration. In the short term, kindergarten teachers will assess every child associated with the Healthy Families program for school readiness, as this is considered a strong indicator of a young child's early developmental experiences, especially whether the child received the enrichment and support that they needed.

To summarize, the foundations for crime are laid early, within the broad social and economic early environment of the child. If society is determined to reduce crime and victimization, it must support families and provide, maintain, and enhance opportunities for children from the beginning of their lives. As Canadians, we need many more proactive strategies of intervention when children are at risk. We should enable child welfare services to be proactively engaged at the moment when children and families need them most. We need to emphasize prevention not punishment, because by the time society intervenes to punish, it is already too late. Programs that work to optimize the socialization of the next generation of Canadians hold the most promise for reducing rates of abuse and crime and brightening Canada's future. The greatest protection society can give itself is to ensure that every individual has access to basic necessities: health care, childcare, housing, education, job training, employment, and recreation.

CRITICAL THINKING QUESTIONS

1. What are the agents of socialization? Which do you feel is the most important for the healthy development of children? Support your answer.
2. With reference to the article, discuss the adage "It takes a village to raise a child."
3. As argued in the article, instead of placing our limited social wealth into punishing the perpetrators of crime, we should invest more effort and resources into prevention. Discuss this assertion with examples from your own community.

REFERENCES

Bell, C. C., & E. J. Jenkins. 1993. Community violence and children on Chicago's southside, *Psychiatry,* 56: 46–54.

Blair, C., C. T. Ramey, & J. M. Hardin. 1995. Early intervention for low birthweight, premature infants: Participation and intellectual development. *American Journal on Mental Retardation,* 99: 542–54.

Bronfenbrenner, U. 1979. *The ecology of human development: Experiments by nature and design.* Cambridge, Mass.: Harvard University Press.

Canadian Council on Social Development. 1997. *The progress of Canada's children,* Ottawa: SSCD Publications.

Farrington, D. P. 1994. Early developmental prevention of juvenile delinquency. *Child Behavior and Mental Health,* 4: 209–27.

Garbarino, J. 1990. The human ecology of early risk. In *Handbook of early childhood intervention,* eds. S. J. Meisels, and J. P. Shonkoff. New York: Cambridge University Press.

———. 2001. An ecological perspective on the effects of violence on children. *Journal of Community Psychology,* 29(3): 361–78.

Gorman-Smith, D., P. H. Tolan, & D. B. Henry. 1999. The relation of community and family to risk among urban poor adolescents. In *Where and when: Influence of historical time and place on aspects of psychopathology,* eds. P. Cohen, L. Robins, & C. Slomskoski. Hillsdale, N.J.: Erlbaum.

Grinzenko, N., & Fischer, C. 1992. Review of studies of risk and protective factors for psychopathology in children. *Canadian Journal of Psychiatry,* 37: 711–21.

Health Insurance Association of America. 1999. "Patient protection" bills give short shrift to the uninsured. [Online]. Available: **http://www.hiaa.org/search/content.cfm?ContentID=304**. Accessed July 10, 2002.

Kiser, L., J. Heston, & P. Millsap. 1991. Physical and sexual abuse in childhood: Relationship with post-traumatic stress disorder. *Journal of the American Academy of Child and Adolescent Psychiatry,* 30(2): 776–83.

Losel, F., & T. Bliesener. 1990. Resilience in adolescence: A study on the generalizability of protective factors. In *Health Hazards in Adolescence,* eds. K. Hurrelmann, & F. Losel. New York: Walter de Gruyter.

Luther, S. S., & E. Zigler. January 1991. Vulnerability and competence: A review of research on resilience in childhood. *American Journal of Orthopsychiatry,* 61: 6–22.

McCauley, J., D. Kern, K. Kolodner, L. Dill, A. F. Schroeder, H. K. DeChant, J. Ryden, L. R. Derogatis, and E. B. Bass. 1997. Clinical characteristics of women with a history of child abuse. *Journal of the American Medical Association,* 277(17): 1362–68.

McFarlane, A. C. 1987. Post-traumatic phenomena in a longitudinal study of children following a natural disaster. *Journal of American Academy of Child and Adolescent Psychiatry,* 26: 764–69.

National Crime Prevention Council of Canada (NCPC). 1996. Preventing crime by investing in families: An integrated approach to promote positive outcomes in children. [Online]. Available: **http://www.crime-prevention.org/english/publications/children/family/index.html**. Accessed July 10, 2002.

———. 1995. *Resiliency in young children.* Ottawa: NCPC/CNPC.

———. 1999. *Pathways to prevention: Developmental and early intervention approaches to crime in Australia.* Ottawa: National Crime Prevention, Attorney-General's Department, Canberra.

Ontario Association of Children's Aid Societies. 1998. Child protection: Pay now or pay later, *OACAS Journal,* 42(3): 14–5.

Osofsky, J. D., S. Wewers, D. M. Hann, & A. C. Fick. 1993. Chronic community violence: What is happening to our children? *Psychiatry,* 56: 36–45.

Perry, B. D. 1994. Neurobiological sequelae of childhood trauma: Post-traumatic stress disorders in children. In *Catecholamine function in posttraumatic stress disorder: Emerging concepts,* ed. M. Murburg. Washington: American Psychiatric Press.

———. 1995. Incubated in terror: Neurodevelopmental factors in the "cycle of violence." In *Children, youth, and violence: Searching for solutions,* ed. J. D. Osofsky. New York: Guilford Press.

Ramey, C. T., & S. L. Ramey. 1994. Which children benefit the most from early intervention? *Pediatrics,* 94: 1064–66.

Sameroff, A., R. Seifer, R. Barocas, M. Zax, & S. Greenspan. 1987. Intelligence quotient scores of 4-year-old children: Socio-environmental risk factors. *Pediatrics,* 79: 343–50.

Sheidow, A. J., D. Gorman-Smith, P. H. Tolan, & D. B. Henry. 2001. Family and community characteristics: Risk factors for violence exposure in inner-city youth, *Journal of Community Psychology,* 29(3): 345–60.

Smith, C., A. J. Lizotte, T. P. Thornberry, & M. D. Krohn. 1995. Resilient youth: Identifying factors that prevent high-risk youth from engaging in delinquency and drug use. In *Current perspectives on aging and the life cycle, Volume 4: Delinquency and disrepute in the life course,* eds. Z. S. Blau & J.Hagan, 217–47. London: JAI Press Inc.

Snyder, J., & G. Patterson. 1987. Family interaction and delinquent behaviour. In *Handbook of juvenile delinquency,* ed. H. C. Quay. New York: Wiley Publishing.

Statistics Canada. 1996. *Crime statistics.* [Online]. Available: **http://www.StatCan.ca.Daily.English/970730/d97/0730.htm**. Accessed July 10, 2002.

Socialization

CLASSIC

CONTEMPORARY

CROSS-CULTURAL

16

Parents' Socialization of Children in Global Perspective

D. Terri Heath

One of the most important functions of the family is the socialization of children. Although parents might receive help from others (such as relatives, neighbours, and professional caregivers), most communities expect parents themselves to raise their children to be productive and responsible adults. Across vastly different cultural environments, D. Terri Heath shows the universal importance of closeness with parents in children's "life satisfaction, psychological well-being, lack of substance use, and absence of delinquent behavior."

THE BENEFITS OF CLOSE PARENT–YOUTH RELATIONSHIPS IN ADOLESCENCE

This article…[describes] how a positive relationship between parents and children later enhances the life satisfaction and psychological well-being of older youths and protects them from juvenile delinquency and substance abuse. As the cross-cultural examples illustrate, youth who perceive a close relationship with their parents exhibit more positive outcomes in each of these four areas. Life satisfaction and psychological well-being are described first, followed by illustrative cross-cultural examples. Next is a description of the impact of close parent–child relationships and their protective value on the substance abuse and juvenile delinquency of adolescents.

Relevant, illustrative cross-cultural examples conclude this section.

Life satisfaction is a subjective measure of an individual's perception of his/her quality of life. Rather than objective measures of income, education, accumulation of wealth, and home ownership, life satisfaction is the level of individual satisfaction each person perceives in his/her own life: that which is privately known and privately evaluated. A multitude of factors influence life satisfaction, and because it is a personal evaluation, these factors differ for individuals. A study of life satisfaction among Hong Kong adolescents illustrates the profound effects peers and parents can exert on an adolescent's life satisfaction.

Psychological well-being is a measure of multiple submissions: self-esteem, locus of control, anxiety, loneliness, and sociability. Persons who exhibit high self-esteem, an internal locus of control, low anxiety and loneliness, and high sociability are considered to have strong psychological well-being. Just as with life satisfaction, many factors can influence psychological well-being, but

Source: From *Families in Multicultural Perspective,* eds. Bron B. Ingoldsby and Suzanna Smith, pp. 161–86. Copyright © 1995 Guilford Press, NY. Reprinted by permission of Guilford Press.

this section focuses specifically on the association between strong relationships with parents and positive outcomes for youth and young adults.

Hong Kong

Adolescence is a transitional period in the life cycle. Associations with family and peers are changing, and adolescents often feel increased pressure to succeed in social relationships outside their families. Their level of attachment, identification, and frequency of consultation with parents relative to that with peers influences the life satisfaction of adolescents in general and, specifically, their satisfaction with school, family, and others. Hong Kong, on the south coast of China, is heavily influenced by current political and economic changes in China. Chinese culture, with its emphasis on family and community over individual independence, continues to play a significant role in the culture of Hong Kong. Because the orientation of adolescents toward their peers and parents has important implications for their satisfaction with life, Hong Kong offers a unique look at this relationship in a rapidly developing society. In a study of 1,906 students, ages thirteen to sixteen, adolescents who were more oriented toward their parents, as well as those who were more oriented toward their peers, were equally satisfied with school, their acceptance by others, the government, and the media. However, those adolescents who are most oriented toward their parents were additionally satisfied with life in general, their families, and the environment (Man, 1991). Man (1991) concludes that "in a predominantly Chinese society like Hong Kong, the family remains a highly important determinant of the adolescents' life satisfaction" (p. 363).

Iran

Parents continue to influence the lives of their children as young adults through parental interactions, guidance, and shared history. When young adults are dissatisfied with their parents,

their adult psychological well-being appears to be negatively influenced. When Iranian students, ages seventeen to thirty-nine, studying at universities in Iran and the United States, were asked about their childhood dissatisfactions with their parents, an interesting pattern emerged. Those adults who perceived the most childhood dissatisfaction with parents were most likely to experience current loneliness, anxiety, external locus of control, misanthropy, neurosis, and psychosis when compared to adults who scored low on the dissatisfaction scale. They were also more likely to experience lower self-esteem and lower sociability, as well as decreased satisfaction with peer relationships, than were adults who had perceptions of childhood satisfaction with parents (Hojat, Borenstein, & Shapurian, 1990). There were no differences between the Iranian students studying at U.S. universities and those studying at Iranian institutions. The authors conclude that when a child's needs for closeness, attachment, and intimacy are not fulfilled to the child's satisfaction in early childhood, the result can be adult dissatisfactions with peer relationships and decreased psychological well-being in adulthood.

Puerto Rico

Can a child's need for closeness and intimacy be adequately fulfilled when the parents of the child are either alcohol dependent or mentally ill? By comparing three groups of children—those with an alcoholic parent, with a mentally ill parent, and with other parents without obvious diagnoses—researchers in Puerto Rico believe that children and adolescents, ages four to sixteen, with alcoholic or mentally ill parents are more likely than other children to be exposed to adverse family environments, such as stressful life events, marital discord, and family dysfunction. In addition, the children in these families were more maladjusted than were children in families without a diagnosed parent, according to reports by psychiatrists, parents, and the children themselves (Rubio-Stipec et al., 1991). (However, the teachers of these three groups of children were unable to detect differences in child behavior, probably because 43 percent of them rated their familiarity with the child as "not good.") It appears from this research that children of alcoholic or mentally ill parents suffer negative consequences during childhood, and these consequences are readily apparent to psychiatrists, their parents, and even the children themselves.

In many cultures, adolescence is a period of rapid psychological growth and a shift in orientation from parents to peers. Adolescents move through this period from childhood at the beginning to adulthood at the end. Most choose educational and career paths during this period. Many choose marriage partners. They move from residing with their parents to residing with peers, with spouses, or by themselves. Because this is a time of such change, some adolescents cope with the transitions by engaging in problematic behaviors (e.g., drug and alcohol abuse and juvenile delinquency). This section presents some of the factors that contribute to problematic behaviors for youth in Canada and three subcultures in the United States: Native American, white, and Hispanic.

Canada

Social control theorists contend that adolescent alcohol consumption is influenced by the degree to which youth are influenced by peers more than parents. A study of alcohol consumption by Canadian eleventh and twelfth graders demonstrates this relationship (Mitic, 1990). Students were divided into three groups: (1) those who drank only with their parents, (2) those who drank only with their peers, and (3) those who drank both with and without their parents. The consumption rates of this last group were further divided into the amount of drinking with and without parents. As might be expected, students who drank only with parents consumed the least amount of alcohol. Those who drank with both parents and peers consumed the most alcohol and drank more heavily when they were with peers. It appears that what

parents model for their children regarding alcohol consumption has only a small influence in the youths' consumption behaviors when the parents are not present.

Hispanics and Whites in the United States

Researchers found that Hispanic and white youth (ages nine to seventeen) in the United States are also significantly influenced in their drug and alcohol consumption by their relationships with friends and parents. For white and Hispanic adolescents who used either licit substances (e.g., cigarettes and alcohol), marijuana, or other illicit substances (e.g., cocaine, heroin, and prescription drugs used for recreational purposes), the single most important influence was the percentage of friends who used marijuana. Those youths who had higher percentages of friends who used marijuana were more likely to use each category of drug (licit, marijuana, and other illicit) than were youths who had fewer friends who used marijuana; this is equally true for both Hispanic and white youth. Although both users and abstainers were more affiliated with their parents than their peers, users were more strongly influenced by their peers; more likely to disregard parental objections to their friends; more likely to believe that their friends, rather than their parents, understand them best; and more likely to respect the ideas of their friends in difficult situations. The only cultural difference was that, in general, Hispanic youths respected their parents' views more than did white youths, regardless of whether they used or abstained from drugs and alcohol (Coombs, Paulson, & Richardson, 1991). Coombs et al. conclude that "youths having viable relationships with parents are less involved with drugs and drug-oriented peers" (p. 87).

Ojibway Native Americans

Delinquent behavior represents a dysfunctional response to stressors and strains in adolescence. On Native American reservations in the United

States, an orientation toward parents and tribal elders appears to protect some youth from these negative behaviors. High percentages of Native American Ojibway adolescents, ages twelve to eighteen, reported inappropriate or illegal activities, such as using alcohol (85 percent), stealing something (70 percent), skipping school (64 percent), smoking marijuana (53 percent), and intentional damage to property (45 percent). However, those who spent more time with their family in chores, recreation, family discussions, and meals were less involved in negative behaviors. As expected, those youth who spent more time in activities away from their families—such as listening alone to the radio, and partying with drugs and alcohol—were at greatest risk for delinquent behaviors and court adjudications (Zitzow, 1990). Ojibway youths who spent more time in activities with parents and tribal elders were less likely to engage in delinquent behaviors resulting in court adjudications.

Summary

This last section focuses on how close parent–youth relationships are associated with the life satisfaction, psychological well-being, lack of substance use, and absence of delinquent behavior in adolescents. Without exception, adolescents in all six studies benefit from increased involvement with healthy parents. Parental involvement enhanced life satisfaction among adolescents in Hong Kong and contributed to psychological well-being among Iranian college students and Puerto Rican youths. The presence of parents was associated with less alcohol consumption among Canadian adolescents, a strong bond with parents was associated with less drug consumption by Hispanic and white youth in the United States, and spending time with parents and tribal elders was associated with less involvement in delinquent behaviors for Native American adolescents in the United States.

CONCLUSION

In reviewing the literature on cross-cultural research on parent–child relations for this chapter, a clear trend became increasingly apparent. When parents are more involved and/or have greater expectations of their children's behavior, children demonstrate better outcomes. As is apparent from the illustrative examples, greater parental involvement is an active involvement, not a passive one. It is acquired not simply by the amount of time parents and children spend together but rather by how the time is spent. An involved parent is not one who spends the majority of the day near his/her child but rarely interacting with the child. It is, instead, the parent who uses opportunities to share activities such as teaching the child a local trade, reading together, or fostering a close, supportive relationship through companionship. This active, involved parent appears much more likely to rear a successful child. Illustrative cross-cultural examples...of high-quality interaction between parents and children, such as spending time reading together in Great Britain, establishing firm limits and offering support in China, and engaging adolescents in activities with parents and tribal elders in the United States, has been associated with better child outcomes. These patterns emerged even when examining parent–son versus parent–daughter relations, relationships among family members in developing versus developed countries, or parent–child relationships in families that resided in Western cultures versus Eastern ones....

CRITICAL THINKING QUESTIONS

1. According to Heath, are there greater differences or similarities across cultures in the relationship between parent–child closeness and adolescent behaviour?
2. What are some of the factors that contribute to the problematic behaviour of adolescents both cross-culturally and within Canada?

3. What does Heath mean by "parental involvement"? What other variables might have an impact on parent–child relationships that are not discussed in this section?

REFERENCES

Coombs, R. H., M. J. Paulson, and M. A. Richardson. 1991. Peer versus parental influence in substance use among Hispanic and Anglo children and adolescents. *Journal of Youth and Adolescence*, 20(1): 73–88.

Hojat, M., B. D. Borenstein, and R. Shapurian. 1990. Perception of childhood dissatisfaction with parents and selected personality traits in adulthood. *Journal of General Psychology*, 117(3): 241–53.

Man, P. 1991. The influence of peers and parents on youth life satisfaction in Hong Kong. *Social Indicators Research*, 24(4): 347–65.

Mitic, W. 1990. Parental versus peer influence on adolescents' alcohol consumption. *Psychological Reports*, 67: 1273–74.

Rubio-Stipec, M., H. Bird, G. Canino, and M. Alegria. 1991. Children of alcoholic parents in the community. *Journal of Studies on Alcohol*, 52(1): 78–88.

Zitzow, D. 1990. Ojibway adolescent time spent with parents/ elders as related to delinquency and court adjudication experiences. *American Indian and Alaska Native Mental Health Research*, 4(1): 53–63.

17

The Presentation of Self

Erving Goffman

Face-to-face interaction is a complex process by which people both convey and receive information about one another. In this selection, Erving Goffman presents basic observations about how everyone tries to influence how others perceive them. In addition, he suggests ways in which people can evaluate how honestly others present themselves.

When an individual enters the presence of others, they commonly seek to acquire information about him or to bring into play information about him already possessed. They will be interested in his general socioeconomic status, his conception of self, his attitude toward them, his competence, his trustworthiness, etc. Although some of this information seems to be sought almost as an end in itself, there are usually quite practical reasons for acquiring it. Information about the individual helps to define the situation, enabling others to know in advance what he will expect of them and what they may expect of him. Informed in these ways, the others will know how best to act in order to call forth a desired response from him.

For those present, many sources of information become accessible and many carriers (or "sign-vehicles") become available for conveying this information. If unacquainted with the individual, observers can glean clues from his conduct and appearance which allow them to apply their previous experience with individuals roughly similar to the one before them or, more important, to apply untested stereotypes to him. They can also assume from past experience that only individuals of a particular kind are likely to be found in a given social setting. They can rely on what the individual says about himself or on documentary evidence he provides as to who and what he is. If they know, or know of, the individual by virtue of experience prior to the interaction, they can rely on assumptions as to the persistence and generality of psychological traits as a means of predicting his present and future behavior.

However, during the period in which the individual is in the immediate presence of the others, few events may occur which directly provide the others with the conclusive information they will need if they are to direct wisely their own activity. Many crucial facts lie beyond the time and place of interaction or lie concealed within it. For example,

Source: From *The Presentation of Self in Everyday Life* by Erving Goffman, copyright © 1959 by Erving Goffman, Bantam Doubleday Dell Publishing Group, Inc. Reprinted with permission.

the "true" or "real" attitudes, beliefs, and emotions of the individual can be ascertained only indirectly, through his avowals or through what appears to be involuntary expressive behavior. Similarly, if the individual offers the others a product or service, they will often find that during the interaction there will be no time and place immediately available for eating the pudding that the proof can be found in. They will be forced to accept some events as conventional or natural signs of something not directly available to the senses. In Ichheiser's terms,[1] the individual will have to act so that he intentionally or unintentionally *expresses* himself, and the others will in turn have to be *impressed* in some way by him.

The expressiveness of the individual (and therefore his capacity to give impressions) appears to involve two radically different kinds of sign activity: the expression that he *gives,* and the expression that he *gives off.* The first involves verbal symbols or their substitutes which he uses admittedly and solely to convey the information that he and the others are known to attach to these symbols. This is communication in the traditional and narrow sense. The second involves a wide range of action that others can treat as symptomatic of the actor, the expectation being that the action was performed for reasons other than the information conveyed in this way. As we shall have to see, this distinction has an only initial validity. The individual does of course intentionally convey misinformation by means of both of these types of communication, the first involving deceit, the second feigning.

…Let us now turn from the others to the point of view of the individual who presents himself before them. He may wish them to think highly of him, or to think that he thinks highly of them, or to perceive how in fact he feels toward them, or to obtain no clear-cut impression; he may wish to ensure sufficient harmony so that the interaction can be sustained, or to defraud, get rid of, confuse, mislead, antagonize, or insult them. Regardless of the particular objective which the individual has in mind and of his motive for having this objective, it will be in his interests to control the conduct of the others, especially their responsive treatment of him. This control is achieved largely by influencing the definition of the situation which the others come to formulate, and he can influence this definition by expressing himself in such a way as to give them the kind of impression that will lead them to act voluntarily in accordance with his own plan. Thus, when an individual appears in the presence of others, there will usually be some reason for him to mobilize his activity so that it will convey an impression to others which it is in his interests to convey. Since a girl's dormitory mates will glean evidence of her popularity from the calls she receives on the phone, we can suspect that some girls will arrange for calls to be made, and Willard Waller's finding can be anticipated:

> It has been reported by many observers that a girl who is called to the telephone in the dormitories will often allow herself to be called several times, in order to give all the other girls ample opportunity to hear her paged.[2]

Of the two kinds of communication—expressions given and expressions given off—this report will be primarily concerned with the latter, with the more theatrical and contextual kind, the nonverbal, presumably unintentional kind, whether this communication be purposely engineered or not. As an example of what we must try to examine, I would like to cite at length a novelistic incident in which Preedy, a vacationing Englishman, makes his first appearance on the beach of his summer hotel in Spain:

> But in any case he took care to avoid catching anyone's eye. First of all, he had to make it clear to those potential companions of his holiday that they were of no concern to him whatsoever. He stared through them, round them, over them—eyes lost in space. The beach might have been empty. If by chance a ball was thrown his way, he looked surprised; then let a smile of amusement lighten his face (Kindly Preedy), looked round dazed to see that there *were* people on the beach, tossed it back with a smile to himself and not a smile *at* the people, and then resumed carelessly his nonchalant survey of space.

But it was time to institute a little parade, the parade of the Ideal Preedy. By devious handlings he gave any who wanted to look a chance to see the title of his book—a Spanish translation of Homer, classic thus, but not daring, cosmopolitan too—and then gathered together his beach-wrap and bag into a neat sand-resistant pile (Methodical and Sensible Preedy), rose slowly to stretch at ease his huge frame (Big-Cat Preedy), and tossed aside his sandals (Carefree Preedy, after all).

The marriage of Preedy and the sea! There were alternative rituals. The first involved the stroll that turns into a run and a dive straight into the water, thereafter smoothing into a strong splashless crawl towards the horizon. But of course not really to the horizon. Quite suddenly he would turn on to his back and thrash great white splashes with his legs, somehow thus showing that he could have swum further had he wanted to, and then would stand up a quarter out of water for all to see who it was.

The alternative course was simpler, it avoided the cold-water shock and it avoided the risk of appearing too high-spirited. The point was to appear to be so used to the sea, the Mediterranean, and this particular beach, that one might as well be in the sea as out of it. It involved a slow stroll down and into the edge of the water—not even noticing his toes were wet, land and water all the same to *him!*—with his eyes up at the sky gravely surveying portents, invisible to others, of the weather (Local Fisherman Preedy).[3]

The novelist means us to see that Preedy is improperly concerned with the extensive impressions he feels his sheer bodily action is giving off to those around him. We can malign Preedy further by assuming that he has acted merely in order to give a particular impression, that this is a false impression, and that the others present receive either no impression at all, or, worse still, the impression that Preedy is affectedly trying to cause them to receive this particular impression. But the important point for us here is that the kind of impression Preedy thinks he is making is in fact the kind of impression that others correctly and incorrectly glean from someone in their midst....

There is one aspect of the others' response that bears special comment here. Knowing that the individual is likely to present himself in a light that is favorable to him, the others may divide what they witness into two parts; a part that is relatively easy for the individual to manipulate at will, being chiefly his verbal assertions, and a part in regard to which he seems to have little concern or control, being chiefly derived from the expressions he gives off. The others may then use what are considered to be the ungovernable aspects of his expressive behavior as a check upon the validity of what is conveyed by the governable aspects. In this a fundamental asymmetry is demonstrated in the communication process, the individual presumably being aware of only one stream of his communication, the witnesses of this stream and one other. For example, in Shetland Isle one crofter's wife, in serving native dishes to a visitor from the mainland of Britain, would listen with a polite smile to his polite claims of liking what he was eating; at the same time she would take note of the rapidity with which the visitor lifted his fork or spoon to his mouth, the eagerness with which he passed food into his mouth, and the gusto expressed in chewing the food, using these signs as a check on the stated feelings of the eater. The same woman, in order to discover what one acquaintance (A) "actually" thought of another acquaintance (B), would wait until B was in the presence of A but engaged in conversation with still another person (C). She would then covertly examine the facial expressions of A as he regarded B in conversation with C. Not being in conversation with B, and not being directly observed by him, A would sometimes relax usual constraints and tactful deceptions, and freely express what he was "actually" feeling about B. This Shetlander, in short, would observe the unobserved observer.

Now given the fact that others are likely to check up on the more controllable aspects of behavior by means of the less controllable, one can expect that sometimes the individual will try to exploit this very possibility, guiding the impression he makes through behavior felt to be reliably informing.[4] For example, in gaining admission to a tight social circle, the participant observer may not only wear an accepting look while listening to an informant, but may also be careful to wear the same look when observing the informant talking to others; observers of the observer will then not as easily discover where he actually stands. A specific illustration may be cited from Shetland Isle. When a neighbor dropped in to have a cup of tea, he would ordinarily wear at least a hint of an expectant warm smile as he passed through the door into the cottage. Since lack of physical obstructions outside the cottage and lack of light within it usually made it possible to observe the visitor unobserved as he approached the house, islanders sometimes took pleasure in watching the visitor drop whatever expression he was manifesting and replace it with a sociable one just before reaching the door. However, some visitors, in appreciating that this examination was occurring, would blindly adopt a social face a long distance from the house, thus ensuring the projection of a constant image.

This kind of control upon the part of the individual reinstates the symmetry of the communication process, and sets the stage for a kind of information game—a potentially infinite cycle of concealment, discovery, false revelation, and rediscovery. It should be added that since the others are likely to be relatively unsuspicious of the presumably unguided aspects of the individual's conduct, he can gain much by controlling it. The others of course may sense that the individual is manipulating the presumably spontaneous aspects of his behavior, and seek in this very act of manipulation some shading of conduct that the individual has not managed to control. This again provides a check upon the individual's behavior, this time his presumably uncalculated behavior, thus re-establishing the asymmetry of the communication process. Here I would like only to add the suggestion that the arts of piercing an individual's effort at calculated unintentionality seem better developed than our capacity to manipulate our own behavior, so that regardless of how many steps have occurred in the information game, the witness is likely to have the advantage over the actor, and the initial asymmetry of the communication process is likely to be retained....

In everyday life, of course, there is a clear understanding that first impressions are important. Thus, the work adjustment of those in service occupations will often hinge upon a capacity to seize and hold the initiative in the service relation, a capacity that will require subtle aggressiveness on the part of the server when he is of lower socioeconomic status than his client. W. F. Whyte suggests the waitress as an example:

The first point that stands out is that the waitress who bears up under pressure does not simply respond to her customers. She acts with some skill to control their behavior. The first question to ask when we look at the customer relationship is, "Does the waitress get the jump on the customer, or does the customer get the jump on the waitress?" The skilled waitress realizes the crucial nature of this question....

The skilled waitress tackles the customer with confidence and without hesitation. For example, she may find that a new customer has seated himself before she could clear off the dirty dishes and change the cloth. He is now leaning on the table studying the menu. She greets him, says, "May I change the cover, please?" and, without waiting for an answer, takes his menu away from him so that he moves back from the table, and she goes about her work. The relationship is handled politely but firmly, and there is never any question as to who is in charge.[5]

When the interaction that is initiated by "first impressions" is itself merely the initial interaction in an extended series of interactions involving the same participants, we speak of "getting off on the right foot" and feel that it is crucial that we do so. Thus, one learns that some teachers take the following view:

You can't ever let them get the upper hand on you or you're through. So I start out tough. The first day I get a new class in, I let them know who's boss.... You've got to start off tough, then you can ease up as you go along. If you start out easy-going, when you try to get tough, they'll just look at you and laugh.[6]

...In stressing the fact that the initial definition of the situation projected by an individual tends to provide a plan for the cooperative activity that follows—in stressing this action point of view—we must not overlook the crucial fact that any projected definition of the situation also has a distinctive moral character. It is this moral character of projections that will chiefly concern us in this report. Society is organized on the principle that any individual who possesses certain social characteristics has a moral right to expect that others will value and treat him in an appropriate way. Connected with this principle is a second, namely that an individual who implicitly or explicitly signifies that he has certain social characteristics ought in fact to be what he claims he is. In consequence, when an individual projects a definition of the situation and thereby makes an implicit or explicit claim to be a person of a particular kind, he automatically exerts a moral demand upon the others, obliging them to value and treat him in the manner that persons of his kind have a right to expect. He also implicitly forgoes all claims to be things he does not appear to be[7] and hence forgoes the treatment that would be appropriate for such individuals. The others find, then, that the individual has informed them as to what is and as to what they *ought* to see as the "is."

One cannot judge the importance of definitional disruptions by the frequency with which they occur, for apparently they would occur more frequently were not constant precautions taken. We find that preventive practices are constantly employed to avoid these embarrassments and that corrective practices are constantly employed to compensate for discrediting occurrences that have not been successfully avoided. When the individual employs these strategies and tactics to protect his own projections, we may refer to them as "defensive practices"; when a participant employs them to save the definition of the situation projected by another, we speak of "protective practices" or "tact." Together, defensive and protective practices [compose] the techniques employed to safeguard the impression fostered by an individual during his presence before others. It should be added that while we may be ready to

see that no fostered impression would survive if defensive practices were not employed, we are less ready perhaps to see that few impressions could survive if those who received the impression did not exert tact in their reception of it.

In addition to the fact that precautions are taken to prevent disruption of projected definitions, we may also note that an intense interest in these disruptions comes to play a significant role in the social life of the group. Practical jokes and social games are played in which embarrassments which are to be taken unseriously are purposely engineered.[8] Fantasies are created in which devastating exposures occur. Anecdotes from the past—real, embroidered, or fictitious— are told and retold, detailing disruptions which occurred, almost occurred, or occurred and were admirably resolved. There seems to be no grouping which does not have a ready supply of these games, reveries, and cautionary tales, to be used as a source of humor, a catharsis for anxieties, and a sanction for inducing individuals to be modest in their claims and reasonable in their projected expectations. The individual may tell himself through dreams of getting into impossible positions. Families tell of the time a guest got his dates mixed and arrived when neither the house nor anyone in it was ready for him. Journalists tell of times when an all-too-meaningful misprint occurred, and the paper's assumption of objectivity or decorum was humorously discredited. Public servants tell of times a client ridiculously misunderstood form instructions, giving answers which implied an unanticipated and bizarre definition of the situation.[9] Seamen, whose home away from home is rigorously he-man, tell stories of coming back home and inadvertently asking mother to "pass the fucking butter."[10] Diplomats tell of the time a near-sighted queen asked a republican ambassador about the health of his king.[11]

To summarize, then, I assume that when an individual appears before others he will have many motives for trying to control the impression they receive of the situation.

CRITICAL THINKING QUESTIONS

1. How does the "presentation of self" contribute to a definition of a situation in the minds of participants? How does this definition change over time?
2. Apply Goffman's approach to the classroom. What are the typical elements of the instructor's presentation of self? a student's presentation of self?
3. Can we evaluate the validity of people's presentations? How?

NOTES

1. Gustav Ichheiser, "Misunderstandings in Human Relations," supplement to *The American Journal of Sociology* 55 (Sept., 1949), 6–7.
2. Willard Waller, "The Rating and Dating Complex," *American Sociological Review* 2, 730.
3. William Sansom, *A Contest of Ladies* (London: Hogarth, 1956), pp. 230–32.
4. The widely read and rather sound writings of Stephen Potter are concerned in part with signs that can be engineered to give a shrewd observer the apparently incidental cues he needs to discover concealed virtues the gamesman does not in fact possess.
5. W. F. Whyte, "When Workers and Customers Meet," chap. 7, *Industry and Society,* ed. W. F. Whyte (New York: McGraw-Hill, 1946), pp. 132–33.
6. Teacher interview quoted by Howard S. Becker, "Social Class Variations in the Teacher–Pupil Relationship," *Journal of Educational Sociology* 25, 459.
7. This role of the witness in limiting what it is the individual can be has been stressed by Existentialists, who see it as a basic threat to individual freedom. See Jean-Paul Sartre, *Being and Nothingness,* trans. Hazel E. Barnes (New York: Philosophical Library, 1956), pp. 365ff.
8. Goffman, op. cit., pp. 319–27.
9. Peter Blau, "Dynamics of Bureaucracy" (Ph.D. dissertation, Department of Sociology, Columbia University, forthcoming, University of Chicago Press), pp. 127–29.
10. Walter M. Beattie, Jr., "The Merchant Seaman" (unpublished M.A. Report, Department of Sociology, University of Chicago, 1950), p. 35.
11. Sir Frederick Ponsonby, *Recollections of Three Reigns* (New York: Dutton, 1952), p. 46.

18

The Body Beautiful: Adolescent Girls and Images of Beauty

Beverly J. Matthews

Social Interaction in Everyday Life

CLASSIC

CONTEMPORARY

CROSS-CULTURAL

Matthews investigates the social world of adolescent girls and the role it plays in defining their physical selves. Her interviews suggest that young women's self-perception is the result of complex interactions between diverse social influences.

INTRODUCTION

The tyranny of appearance norms have long been recognized in the lives of women (see Brownmiller, 1984; Greer, 1970; or Freedman, 1986, for example). Both academic literature and the popular media have examined factors which underlie the intense pressure women experience to adhere to a cultural ideal and the price they pay for either attempting to comply or failing to do so (see Chernin, 1981; Shute, 1992; Hesse-Biber, 1996; Bordo, 1993). While we are aware of the problem among older teenagers and adult women, recent studies indicate that even girls in early adolescence are prone to eating problems and a preoccupation with food (Pipher, 1996; Brumberg, 1997). Some of the literature in this

Source: "The Body Beautiful: Adolescent Girls and Images of Beauty," by Beverly J. Matthews. In Lori G. Beaman (Ed.), *New Perspectives on Deviance: The Construction of Deviance in Everyday Life* (pp. 208–19). Toronto: Prentice Hall, 2000. Reprinted by permission.

area focuses on media images and unhealthy portrayals of beauty and the ways in which women are influenced by such portrayals (Wolf, 1991). While this has been a fruitful line of inquiry, it is incomplete. It implies that women uncritically, or helplessly, follow a cultural ideal, simply because it is prescribed by society. The findings of this research study into the social world of adolescent girls reveal that straining to conform to the "ideal look" is not always an end in itself, that it is often a purposeful act designed to achieve social goals.

Young women are surrounded by images which define attractiveness as a very particular, thin, "perfect" ideal. While many strive to achieve this goal, they do not all do so out of blind conformity, or simply because they have negative images of themselves. The problem is more complex: many girls use appearance as a means for achieving social status and power; they conform to avoid the costs associated with deviating from the ideal. They experience the gender system in a unique way, because of their stage in life, which compounds the pressures all women experience around appearance; however, these girls are not all misguided individuals passively following a societal definition of beauty. Just like older women, adolescents are working to negotiate and achieve their individual goals within a micro and macro gender structure. They are actively finding their location within the peer arena and their relationships with food and appearance play a key role in this endeavor. In this research, in-depth interviews with adolescent women reveal much about the adolescent world and the importance of appearance norms within it.

EXAMINING THE MULTILEVEL GENDER SYSTEM AND THE SOCIAL WORLD OF ADOLESCENT GIRLS

When studying the social world it is essential to recognize the interplay between the individual and the social context. Although women have the freedom to make their own choices, these choices are constrained by the socially created structures which surround them. Sociologists have long recognized the existence of social structures and have worked to explain their relation to individuals: "social structures create social persons who (re)create social structures who create social persons who (re)create...ad infinitum" (Stryker, 1980: 53). They also recognize that such structures operate on two levels. "[W]e inhabit the *micro-world* of our immediate experience with others in face-to-face relations. Beyond that, with varying degrees of significance and continuity, we inhabit a *macro-world* consisting of much larger structures.... Both worlds are essential to our experience of society" (Berger & Berger, 1975: 8). Sociologists and feminists have studied the creation of the social person and the role that gender plays in that development. They have also examined the gendered dimensions of social structures and their impact upon

members of the society (see Risman & Schwartz, 1989; Smith, 1987; Bem, 1993).

Through my research into gender and social behaviour (Matthews & Beaujot, 1997; Matthews, 1997), it has become clear that the gender system can be more fully understood by acknowledging that it operates on several levels at one time. And that analyses are more complete when three levels are integrated into the explanatory framework. This tri-level model of the gender system includes the individual gender role orientation, a micro structure, and a macro structure. On the most basic level, men and women have individual gender role orientations, which they have developed through socialization and interaction over the course of their lives. These orientations consist of their beliefs about the appropriate roles for women and men and serve as guidelines for choices regarding presentation of self, relationships, and activities, as well as attitudes and values. However, these gender role orientations alone do not determine behaviour. Women's choices about how to behave, and how to present themselves, are also influenced by the micro level gender structure, where they encounter others in daily interaction and negotiate their roles. Conforming to expectations is an integral part of interaction; people play roles in order to facilitate communication and joint action. They are also influenced by the macro level gender structure: the societal context which provides a landscape within which people act out their choices. It is my contention that the combination of the three levels and the way in which they interact, sometimes complementary and sometimes contradictory, can advance our understanding of the gender system and of young women's actions concerning weight and appearance.

For women making decisions about weight, food, and dieting, it is apparent that all three levels of the gender system influence their choices and behaviour. The macro structure, which has evolved over time, emphasizes the importance of appearance for women. While women's accomplishments are many, they continue to be judged by their appearance. It provides media images of "perfect bodies" and advertising which constantly criticizes and undermines women with appearance "flaws" (i.e., extra pounds, "problem" skin, gray hair). On the micro level, appearance is also salient. Because slenderness is the norm, there is some pressure in daily interaction to achieve it. Friends and family often encourage, and occasionally coerce, women into dieting and following the cultural ideal. Choosing not to diet, not following the ideal, seems to imply either slovenliness— "she's really let herself go"—or a personal statement about her unwillingness to conform. It is rarely accepted as a woman choosing to be comfortable with herself as she is. Thus interaction with others is influenced by their interpretation of her appearance. At the individual level, women's understanding of themselves is filtered through the existing social structures. Women know that they may be afforded more attention and respect if they follow the ideal;[1] they may also have internalized the societal standards throughout their lives. Thus, not "measuring up" to the ideal may cause personal anguish.

Women's decisions to diet are bound up with several levels of gender and must be considered in this light. The three levels of gender may be complementary or contradictory. That is, while people all live in a social world that appears to appreciate and promote only one body type, individual micro structures or individual gender role orientations may be in agreement or at odds with this standard. Women may be surrounded by people who disregard the cultural ideal and thus feel less pressure to conform in their interactions. They may have developed a critical stance to the societal ideal and experience no internal misgivings about weight and appearance. Or they may experience pressure on all three levels to follow the ideal. Clearly, in order to understand women's relationships to food and diet it is insufficient to focus on only one level. Women's social contexts and their individual gender role orientations are unique and must be considered as such.

Adolescence compounds the imperatives of the gender system. While all people feel the effects of the gender systems in which they operate, adolescents face unique challenges; adolescence is (1) a time of identity construction and (2) a time to find one's own location in the social world. They must navigate their ways through the layers of gender, making their choices and moderating their behaviours based on the context in which they live. And because individuals in this age group do not necessarily have a strong gender role orientation guiding their choices and actions, they are more vulnerable to the influences of the micro and macro gender structures. Also, because they have moved into a new "adolescent world," they can no longer rely on the "borrowed identity" from their childhood or the social status of their families. They must construct a unique self and establish their own position within the social world. This new self will largely be based on measures of status determined by peer groups and the broader youth culture.

Scholars and clinicians have developed a body of literature which discusses adolescent experience in great detail. We can trace study in this area back to Erikson's theory of stages. He argued that adolescence is a time of identity construction (Erikson, 1956). Until adolescence, identity is acquired through the family; individuals are socialized to see themselves much as the family sees them. In childhood, attitudes, values, and definitions are accepted uncritically. During adolescence, the earlier "borrowed" identity is questioned. Individuals ask themselves whether they agree with what they have been told, what they have learned. While reconstructing themselves, adolescents rely less on families (who played an important role in defining their childhood selves) and, in an effort to become independent and autonomous, turn towards their peers and societal standards. Part of this identity construction is, of course, the gender role orientation. Not just "who am I?" but "who am I as a woman?" "What does this involve?" "How should I act? think?" By the time these girls become adults, most have developed a sense of who they are as women. Therefore, when they are confronted with external stressors—for example, pressure from conflicts among individual, micro, and macro levels of the gender system—they have an internal sense of self that provides direction, which is lacking during early adolescence.

During adolescence, peers play a critical role. They are all experiencing similar changes, though at varying paces. By observing each other, they gain a sense of what is considered desirable and appropriate. While they observe, they are painfully aware that they are also being observed. The "imaginary audience" hypothesis suggests that adolescents are so sensitive to the evaluation/judgement of others that they perceive an audience, and behave accordingly, even when they are not being observed (Elkind & Bowen, 1979). As each adolescent is looking at others she is gathering the "raw resources" to shape her "self." Seltzer calls this the "comparative act" (Seltzer, 1989). Through the evaluation and critique and assessment of peers as well as imitation and experimentation, an adolescent gains the materials necessary to construct her "self." The knowledge that one is both judging and being judged makes adolescents highly conscious of their social desirability. Seltzer describes the adolescent world as the "peer arena," the micro structure where identity is constructed.

A further aspect of adolescence is finding one's location; that is, answering the question "where do I fit in?" This clearly is associated with the "social desirability" mentioned above. Just as the adult society is stratified—around class, race, and gender, for example—and one gains social power through position based on resources, the adolescent world is also hierarchical and also involves social power. The young person must find his or her place in this social structure. The social class from which the adolescent has come is still prevalent, but it is not sufficient to define who has power in the peer arena, because it is based on the parent's resources and not on the adolescent's own characteristics. So the hierarchy

among adolescents is based largely on personal resources. Because a significant part of constructing the self at this point is coming to understand gender role orientation and sexuality, the adolescent hierarchy is based in large part on one's presentation of manhood or womanhood. That is to say, the more "manly" men, displaying evidence of the strength, courage, and competence stereotypically expected of males, are considered more desirable than others. And among women, appearance and desirability are key attributes.

The powerful effect of the peer arena determines where any individual will fit in the social world. And in this arena, status is linked to appearance. Do you look the part? Or, as important, are you "playing" the part by dieting and making appearance a key part of your conversations and social world? Drawing messages from the larger macro gender structure, peers set the rules for "fitting in." And the unstable aspect of individual adolescents' own sense of self and their incomplete individual gender role orientation makes withstanding the pressure to conform difficult. By later adolescence, the tendency to conform is reduced (Berndt, 1979); individuals are more sure of themselves, have established their identities and gender role orientations, and may be, therefore, less vulnerable to the pressures of the micro and macro structures.

THIS STUDY

We undertook a qualitative research project in the summer of 1997 in Southern Alberta entitled "Growing Up Female." Through 25 depth interviews and focus groups with 6 girls, we explored adolescents' own perceptions of the challenges they face and how they navigate through the peer arena. The analysis was based on the principles of grounded theory (Glaser & Strauss, 1967; Strauss, 1987). That is, rather than trying to verify a specific hypothesis, we attempted to see their world as adolescents see it and discover how the three levels of the sex/gender system interact in their lives. From listening to the girls, reviewing the tapes, and examining transcripts, patterns emerged. The patterns were then explored more fully in subsequent interviews. The goal was not to quantify, but rather to get a sense of the importance of conforming to appearance norms within the adolescent social hierarchy.

The study began with a "typical" sample of young women chosen to represent different ages, social classes, and family arrangements. We quickly came to recognize that one's location in the hierarchy—insider, outsider, popular, outcast, etc.—was a critical variable and that the sample needed to reflect this diversity as well. (The girls' location in the hierarchy was also seen to influence them in terms of vulnerability to outside pressure and suggestion, but not in the ways one might predict.) The girls interviewed were from junior high, high school (one of whom attended an all girl's high school), post-secondary institutions, and "drop outs" (many of whom had moved to alternative schools).

The importance of qualitative studies is that they can answer the question "why?" While quantitative studies can measure patterns to determine how many suffer from eating disorders and/or depression, and can assess the correlation [among] class, race, family and behaviour numerically, one must look deeper to understand the underlying causal connection between these behaviours and the social factors in the girls' lives. One must try to understand their social world as they define and live it. It is vital for the researchers to avoid directing the discussions so as not to artificially focus on "constraints." Question(s) about what boys do to them or what society does to them [deny] the agency of the young women. Instead, this study asked the girls what they did to get along in their world. What are the rules in their world? Where did the rules come from?

Once we had collected information from all of the respondents, we identified patterns and came to understand how fully social hierarchy, and therefore social power, influenced their lives and how salient appearance is within that hierarchy. The best way to convey these findings is through case studies. In the following section, I will present the cases of women located in each of the various positions in the adolescent hierarchy, allowing each to speak about where they fit and how they came to hold that position. (Obviously, names have been changed but other details are unaltered.)

FINDINGS

Not surprisingly, the study indicates that for adolescent girls, appearance is salient and notions about what is a desirable appearance are influenced by cultural norms: the macro structure provides powerful images and pressures. However, the girls made it clear that they were not all victims blindly following a goal set by the larger society without thought. And not all were dissatisfied with their appearances—not even all of those who spent a considerable amount of time and energy complaining about themselves and dieting. As they explained, appearance equals status. "Life would be easier if you looked like that [like the women on *Melrose Place*] because people give you an easier time if you are pretty. If more guys like you, the girls give you an easier time,…I don't think it should be that way, but I think society puts a lot of importance on your looks and size." And dieting and "fat" talk are also linked to status. The girls say they hate their bodies, or themselves, but when they discuss it more fully they often acknowledge that these statements are a means of fitting in.[2] They see that being part of the group means "obsessing" about their bodies, and group membership leads to success and social power. Those who fit the appearance criteria belong to the elite group, have power, know they have it, and enjoy wielding it. They reinforce their own position by deliberately making others feel inadequate. In fact, the power that they gain from their elite status is the power to exclude others. Their actions enhance their own positions while making appearance more salient for all girls (that is, making the micro structure extremely appearance-based).

The findings indicate that the most difficult time for young women was during junior high school, sooner than most people would like to believe is the case. Why should twelve-year-olds be caught up in issues about body and appearance? Are they trying to attract boys or men? Not really. They perceive other girls as both their audience and their harshest critics. Therefore, their preoccupation with weight and body is not about being desirable to the boys so much as gaining acceptance within the hierarchy. Boys can certainly exacerbate the pressure through name-calling and harassment, but this is only one part of the larger issue: finding your place in the social world is based on playing a role and looking the part. Even girls who attended "all girl schools" were subject to appearance pressures.

By later adolescence, women have already begun to develop a stronger sense of self and [have] grown less vulnerable to the group's definition of who they are. By the end of high school, most girls had worked through much of their confusion and vulnerability. While they continued to talk about dieting and eating, about shape and size, this was much less about really planning to change their physical appearance than about "playing the game." Those who wanted to fit into the social hierarchy recognized that playing by these rules was necessary. However, by this stage, many girls had found their own groups of friends and set their own goals and challenges; they felt freer express their own gender role orientations rather than following the group's definition of "woman."[3]

But in early adolescence, in junior high, most girls are just beginning the process of becoming independent and autonomous. There is a shift from living with the self-image that your parents and family defined for you to finding your "own" self with the assistance of peers. The peers' opinions count for a great deal because they form the social world in which this new self must establish

herself. This is for most girls the period of most intense pressure to be autonomous and independent, greatest confusion about self, and therefore greatest vulnerability. And in this setting, young adolescent girls are becoming themselves, adults, and "women."

As indicated, most of the girls had worked through and beyond this understanding that their self worth and status as women was tied to appearance by the time they reached the end of high school. But some girls did not get past this stage as easily as others. They continued to measure themselves by their appearance.

The Elite Group

The first group of those who had trouble moving beyond the adolescent definitions of desirability is made up of girls who were popular in junior high and high school; they were at the top of the social hierarchy. They seemed to be the winners who enjoyed the power that accompanied their status. They basked in the attention of all: other girls, boys, and most teachers. Two of the respondents talked about their experiences at the top of this hierarchy.

Jillian said that she is so good at being part of the group that she has no very clear sense of who she is. While in high school she knew exactly where she belonged. "I was definitely one of the popular ones." She said bluntly, "I consider myself to be pretty, that might have something to do with it [her popularity]. All my friends were popular." In fact, she revelled in the attention she received. She was teased by the boys about her looks ("I have big boobs") but found this flattering rather than intimidating or threatening. Being a part of the elite group was not a problem while in the insulated world of the high school, but she feels completely lost since leaving school. She found that the attributes that had given her power were no longer as valuable and she had no sense of direction. Jillian had allowed herself to be defined by the micro structure of her peer group and did not develop her own identity. She adopted the norms of the group without truly developing her own gender role orientation. Now that she has moved into a new environment, and without the guidance of her own individual gender role orientation, she feels aimless. "Where I stand now I'm not going anywhere. I'm not moving forward, I'm not moving backward, I'm just not going anywhere."

Reva was also very popular in high school, but [she] recognized even at the time that this popularity had no solid foundation. She tried to hang on to status and popularity via appearance but was constantly concerned about it. "I was insecure but I don't know if other people knew it." She was unsure of her "self" and her true desirability. She recognized that popularity in high school was all about "material things, the way things look, everything on the outside." And she knew that she and her friends maintained their position by belittling others: "I think we were back stabbers and snobby, pretty snobby." But at the time this seemed reasonable. Having a boyfriend was an affirmation of Reva's status and her desirability. When she and her boyfriend broke up, she believed that she need only lose weight to regain her social position. "Actually, there were a couple of us that wanted to like, starve ourselves, try to lose weight so we just wouldn't eat." As a result, she developed an eating disorder. Eventually, she went into counselling and slowly has come to recognize the damage that her bulimia caused. But at the time, being thin made sense and gaining a even a little bit of weight "really stressed me out."

Being in the elite group is no guarantee of success or well-being. While it worked for some in the short-term because they really did attain power—the power to exclude others—it did not bring long-term contentment. Upon graduation, the micro structure which had given girls power and a valued position was disbanded, leaving them directionless. Even within high school, all was not well. While this group appeared to dictate what was the appropriate appearance around the school, this was often a reflection of media images.

"Popular" respondents mentioned TV shows and magazines that influenced their "style." And maintaining their social position involved a constant effort to keep up with the cultural ideal. For some this seemed easy, but for others like Reva, it was both difficult and undermining.

The "Wannabes"

While this seems like a pejorative term, it's how these girls describe themselves. They believe they will be in the most popular group if they just make a few changes; as a result, they spend their adolescent years struggling to reach the top of the pyramid. Kim is a member of this group. She says she understands the hierarchy and knows how it works: "The pressure increases as you move towards the popular group. You always have to prove yourself—based on how you look." She also knows that she is very close to the top and believes she could get there if she could just play the game right. And despite acknowledging that being popular doesn't always allow you to be a good person—"Popular people are jerks, they don't care about others, are very competitive, and treat people badly"—this doesn't stop her from wanting to be one of them. She works hard to win favour, to accept the rules. She believes that she could be popular if she was just a bit thinner. People in her group tend to diet for real, thinking they are just ten pounds away from having social power. She said the whole group began smoking on the same day when one person found out that it suppressed appetite. "We always talked about weight and how to lose it—drink Slimfast®, take Dexatrim®." Expending so much energy on reaching the top of the social hierarchy means that Kim spends little time trying to find her own direction or "self." She just knows she isn't happy. She feels "insecure, always beating myself up" and says "trying to fit in is limiting." She does not have a strong sense of self and therefore accepts the peer arena as the ultimate arbiter. The unquestioning acceptance of the peer arena and of the validity of the social hierarchy leaves people in this group, like those in the group "above" them on the popularity scale, vulnerable to a gender system which focuses on appearance. Their gender role orientation reflects this desire to achieve the ideal appearance: being a woman means looking the part.

Life in the Middle

The girls on the next level "down" on the hierarchical scale are the least vulnerable. While girls in this group still cope with pressure in the peer arena, they know they will never be at the top. As a result, they tend to examine it more critically, asking whether increased popularity is worth achieving. The answer is usually no. These girls form their own rules, have outside interests, and define "self" by a standard other than that of the hierarchy. One result of this alternate definition of self is that appearance is less salient than ability.

The individuals in this group often have outside interests—music, sports, religion, or the guiding movement, for example—that seem to help them find a self worth regardless of their status at school. And at school they either are not picked on or don't let it bother them because they know that it isn't real. They construct their "self" based on what they are, not on what someone tells them they should be. Jana is never going to be at the top of the social hierarchy; she knows it and doesn't care. Her parents are of different races and she perceives that being biracial makes her "different." But it isn't a problem for her, she says, she just has to find her own way. When listening to Jana, she convinces you that this makes her stronger. She sees other "kids who try their hardest to be like another person and follow what they do" but distinguishes herself. She says unequivocally, "I am who I am." Racial slurs don't bother her, she makes a joke of it. When her best friend goes on and on about being fat, Jana believes "she does it just for attention." She isn't affected by media images either: "I'm not saying they're not beautiful but I'm saying that you don't know what's

under all that make-up, that's four hours of make-up put on. I could look like that too." In essence, Jana isn't caught up in the gender system because she is not trying to prove herself in the peer arena. She has a strong sense of self and does not accept the salience of appearance. However, she also notes that "I've never gotten fat so it has never been an issue for me." She can be truly comfortable with herself even when others in her world are striving to attain an ideal.

Una is also in this middle group. She is involved in both music and sports and spends much of her time with these activities. She says, "there's no pressure in my group. We don't have to spend time on make-up and hair." They don't want to be skinny partly because "the coach encourages us to stay fit." "I just don't have the time or the money to keep up." But she does acknowledge that it was harder to "be yourself" in junior high: "People were starting to form groups and you were left out if you didn't follow the group." But her close circle of friends didn't value the "popular" behaviours and didn't try to look the part.

Freedom from the tyranny of the gender system—which offers an almost impossible beauty standard—seems much more attainable for these young women. Because they do not have an opportunity to join the elite group, and because they have other qualities which make them strong, they are less vulnerable to its dictates. Not being part of the "in" crowd enables them to critique the hierarchy and its norms. In essence, these girls have developed gender role orientations which conflict with the macro structure and most of them have found a group of peers who also reject the salience of appearance.

On The Fringe

The next group—the "lowest" on the scale I have identified—is that of individuals who define themselves as "outsiders." They believe they are excluded because of their size and shape (though some of them have other characteristics which also contribute to their exclusion). These girls don't have the ability to break out of the outsider role into which they have been cast. For adolescents in this group, not fitting in really hurts; they feel rejected, ridiculed, isolated. Because they are so far from the norm—often very overweight or dealing with severe acne—they feel that they are suffering at the hands of their peers.

Some do come to hate themselves because they are treated so cruelly. Rachel describes one hurtful experience "I was trying to walk through the crowd when one guy said 'R, you don't belong in this crowd.' There was another girl who told me to f— off. I was watching them I guess. I was pretty shy too. But I think *it* made me shy" The "it" she refers to is being excluding for not looking the "right" way. She feels very alone, even though there are several other girls on the "outside." She now "rejects the image thing" because she knows she doesn't fit ("I'm big boned like my dad") but she tried really hard in junior high. She really hated herself, even though she believed she was good on the inside, because of the way she was treated, because her body was devalued. In fact, Rachel feels pressure from her family to try harder to fit in—her mom would like her to change her appearance but she says she "just gave up trying."

Terry was also on the outside because of her weight. She had a couple of close friends "but the rest just left me out." Unlike Rachel, though, she "successfully" lost weight and reaped the rewards of following the group standard. She wanted to be small no matter what and simply stopped eating. At first everyone was pleased. She got more attention at school. People noticed her and talked to her. Initially, Terry liked being popular. "I felt better for a while but then came to realize that my life still sucked. Even when I was skinny I wasn't happy." She came to hate being popular because she could see more clearly than most how artificial the distinction was. Terry believes being skinny actually made her feel worse because the "popular Terry" wasn't the "real Terry." Her peers only saw her outside and still didn't recognize her

true worth. Her family and few close friends became worried and did not support her dieting. And "I got tired of measuring every mouthful, having everyone watching and measuring every mouthful, so I started eating again." She gained the weight back and is now more comfortable with herself. "A whole new world opened up when I left school." Both Terry and Rachel understood how the social hierarchy worked. They knew how to gain power by following the mandate of the peer group. But they both chose not to. They lost status within the micro structure but grew more comfortable with themselves.

Karla was in a similar situation and it was terribly damaging. She started out in the popular group but " I found you had to stoop quite low to become popular. You had to be willing to be rude to all the other people." She wanted to be friendly to everyone and eventually the popular crowd turned their backs on her. They began to harass her and single her out; most of the insults were based on her appearance. "After a while, when so many people tell you something, you know you start to believe it's true, like you get it from enough people it starts to seem true, so I got enough people telling me I was ugly enough times, it kind of makes you believe it." Eventually she quit school because it became unbearable. She'd like to go back but "it's hard to get started up again if you live in the same place and you stay in the same place because everyone knows your past.... I can't start over again because the people who knew me, knew me as a geek, a freak." She feels better about herself now but doesn't want to face that kind of pressure again.

Examining the fringe group in terms of the three levels of gender, the "hell" for these girls was the micro gender structure of the peer arena; however, the values of the microsystem seemed to be reinforced—though not caused—by the larger macro structure. Our society is far more conscious of racism and sexism than of "lookism," especially as it is manifested in the adolescent world. Rachel and Karla internalized the negative messages directed at them by their peers. And they both came to hate themselves. Fortunately, they also both were able to overcome those feelings and recognize that their value was determined neither by their appearance nor by the critics in the peer arena.

IMPLICATIONS

Why is appearance so salient for adolescent girls? This study reinforces the understanding that at this period in her life, a girl has few measuring sticks and no long list of personal accomplishments. She must seek some means of reassuring herself that she is becoming an adult, a woman, an individual separate from her earlier, family-defined self. The larger macro gender structure of fashion magazines and advertisement sends messages that appearance is an important feature of power and desirability. This notion is adopted by adolescent girls in part because it is a field over which many feel they have some control (however illusory such a perception might be). They think that they can change their bodies, their clothing, their hairstyles. And they recognize that a specific kind of beauty is valued by the society at large. Thus appearance becomes a standard. This means that appearance actually does serve as a means of attaining social acceptability and power within the peer arena. As the study revealed, becoming a woman has less to do with the role one might play and more to do with the body. An interesting—perhaps startling—paradox emerged when we asked the respondents to define "woman." On the one hand, being a woman, they said, does not constrain career choices. They believe women can become anything they want. As available "sexual" roles grow, women are not defined by filling a specific role—for example, wife or mother. And as they perceive that more and more options are available in the work world, no particular job defines "woman." On the other hand, something distinguishes women from men. And that something is appearance. It is the girl's

body that makes her a woman. Therefore, being a woman means one should be preoccupied with one's body and making one's body fit the part. None of the girls we spoke to was trying to diet to avoid growing up into womanhood; indeed, they were dieting to *achieve* womanhood, which they have come to accept is characterized by a very particular physical stature.

Young women are not all passive recipients of society's messages about the body. They perceive that they are not victims, that they are not trying to achieve certain appearances because men or boys want them to. Instead, they see themselves as actively involved in struggles with other women. Their female peers are the harshest critics. Among these critics, appearance brings social power, even if it is only the power to exclude others. They want the right body in order to attain social power and to prove themselves as women. Having a "boyfriend" is important in part because it sends a message to the peer arena that one has successfully achieved the requisite look. This becomes part of the measuring stick.

When the three levels of the gender system—the individual, micro, and macro levels—all agree that appearance is salient, the girl who experiences this will strive to attain the beauty standard. She believes that achieving this look will bring her social acceptance and membership into the elite group. If she fails to measure up to the standard, she faces the painful realization that she will be devalued by those with power in the peer arena. However, if she also learns that the imperatives of the peer arena are not absolute, and she is able to develop her own gender role orientation, then appearance loses its salience, and the elite group loses its power over her. If the three levels do not all agree, if girls have developed gender role orientations which do not incorporate the societal beauty ideal, or they belong to micro structures (as adolescents, perhaps a group of friends, sports team, or social club apart from the school-based peer arena) which value ability rather than appearance, then they are less subject to the appearance standards.

While adolescent girls face an exaggerated version of the gender system, all women are subject to the same forces. We must find our way within a societal landscape that valorizes beauty often above ability. And frequently we must do so in micro structures (in the work place and in our homes) which adopt this standard and devalue our actions. Like these adolescent girls, we remain strong if we develop gender role orientations which do not centre around appearance, and if we foster relationships and micro structures which value women for their strength and skill rather than their outward appearance. The results of this study are suggestive—not yet detailed enough or broad enough to be conclusive—but give us some insight into girls' own perceptions of their world and perhaps into the roots of gender role uncertainty that continues for some women into adulthood.

CRITICAL THINKING QUESTIONS

1. What are some of the characteristics that define a "Wannabe"?
2. Why do you think the girls' social positions influenced their perceptions of their physical selves?
3. Given Matthews' findings, do you think that adolescent boys face similar social pressures concerning their appearance? What examples from your own experiences help support your opinion?
4. In your view, are the social pressures on young women's appearance becoming more or less powerful over time? Why do you think that is the case?

NOTES

1. Obviously, this is a generalization. An important point of this argument is that individual women—especially adult women—move in microstructures and have developed "selves" that allow them to function effectively in a way inconsistent with the "body beautiful" standards…society.
2. This is not to say that…[none of the] girls…experience[d] genuine pain and self-hatred—their situations will be explored more fully in subsequent sections. It does mean that many girls are not as negative about themselves as it might appear from listening to their conversations among their peers.
3. It is possible that for university women, living in dormitories, food, eating, and weight once again become salient as a new social hierarchy must be established. While this was not investigated in this study, we are currently interviewing women in residences to see if the pattern re-emerges.

REFERENCES

Bem, S. 1993. *The lenses of gender.* New Haven: Yale University Press.

Berger, P., and B. Berger. 1975. *Sociology: A biographical approach.* New York: Basic Books.

Berndt, T. 1979. Developmental changes in conformity to peers and parents." *Developmental Psychology,* 15: 606–16.

Bordo, S. 1993. *Unbearable weight: Feminism, western culture and the body.* Los Angeles: University of California Press.

Brownmiller, S. 1984. *Femininity.* New York: Linden Press.

Brumberg, J. 1997. *The body project: An intimate history of American girls.* New York: Random House.

Chernin, K. 1981. *The obsession: Reflections on the tyranny of slenderness.* New York: Harper and Row.

Elkind, D., and Bowen. 1979. Imaginary audience behaviour in children and adults. *Developmental Psychology,* 15: 33–44.

Erikson, E. 1956. The problem of ego identity. *Journal of the American Psychoanalytic Association,* 4: 56–121.

Freedman, R. 1986. *Beauty bound.* Lexington, Mass.: D.C. Heath and Company.

Glaser, B., and A. Strauss. 1967. *The discovery of Grounded Theory: Strategies for qualitative research.* Mill Valley: Sociology Press.

Greer, G. 1970. *The female eunuch.* London: MacGibbon & Kee.

Hesse-Biber, S. 1996. *Am I thin enough yet? The cult of thinness and the commercialization of identity.* New York: Oxford University Press.

Matthews, B. 1997. *The gender system and fertility: An examination of the hidden links.* Population Studies Centre: Working Paper.

Matthews, B., and R. Beaujot. 1997. Gender orientations and fertility strategies. *Canadian Review of Sociology and Anthropology,* 34(4): 415–28.

Pipher, M. 1996. *Reviving Ophelia: Saving the selves of adolescent girls.* New York: Ballantine Books.

Risman, B., and P. Schwartz. 1989. *Gender in intimate relationships: A microstructural approach.* Belmont: Wadsworth Publishing Co.

Seltzer, V. 1989. *The psychosocial worlds of the adolescent: Public and private.* New York: John Wiley and Sons.

Shute, J. 1992. *Life size.* New York: Avon Books.

Smith, D. 1987. *The everyday world as problematic: A feminist sociology*. Toronto: University of Toronto Press.

Strauss, A. 1987. *Qualitative analysis for social scientists*. New York: Cambridge University Press.

Stryker, S. 1980. *Symbolic interactionism: A social structural version*. Menlo Park: Benjamin Cummings Publishing.

Wolf, N. 1991. *The beauty myth*. New York: Morrow Books.

19

The Do's and Taboos of Body Language Around the World

Roger E. Axtell

Social Interaction in Everyday Life

CLASSIC

CONTEMPORARY

CROSS-CULTURAL

In a world that grows smaller every year, it is easy to offend others simply by being ourselves—gestures that we take as innocent may be seen by someone else as deeply insulting. This selection suggests the extent of the problem and, in an age of global business dealings, the need to cultivate cultural sensitivity.

THREE GREAT GAFFES OR ONE COUNTRY'S GOOD MANNERS, ANOTHER'S GRAND FAUX PAS

In Washington they call protocol "etiquette with a government expense account." But diplomacy isn't just for diplomats. How you behave in other people's countries reflects on more than you alone. It also brightens—or dims—the image of where you come from and whom you work for. The Ugly American about whom we used to read so much may be dead, but here and there the ghost still wobbles out of the closet.

Three well-traveled Americans tell how even an old pro can sometimes make the wrong move in the wrong place at the wrong time.

Source: From *Do's and Taboos around the World*, 3rd ed., by Roger Axtell. Copyright © 1993 Parker Pen Company. A Benjamin Book distributed by John Wiley & Sons, Inc. Reprinted by permission of John Wiley & Sons, Inc.

A Partner in One of New York's Leading Private Banking Firms

When the board chairman is Lo Win Hao, do you smile brightly and say, "How do you do, Mr. Hao?" or "Mr. Lo"? Or "Mr. Win"?

I traveled nine thousand miles to meet a client and arrived with my foot in my mouth. Determined to do things right, I'd memorized the names of the key men I was to see in Singapore. No easy job, inasmuch as the names all came in threes. So, of course, I couldn't resist showing off that I'd done my homework. I began by addressing top man Lo Win Hao with plenty of well placed Mr. Hao's—and sprinkled the rest of my remarks with a Mr. Chee this and a Mr. Woon that. Great show. Until a note was passed to me from one man I'd met before, in New York. Bad news. "Too friendly too soon, Mr. Long," it said. Where diffidence is next to godliness, there I was, calling a roomful of VIPs, in effect, Mr. Ed and Mr. Charlie. I'd remembered everybody's name—but forgotten that in Chinese the surname comes *first* and the given name *last*.

An Associate in Charge of Family Planning for an International Human Welfare Organization

The lady steps out in her dazzling new necklace and everybody dies laughing. (Or what not to wear to Togo on a Saturday night.)

From growing up in Cuba to joining the Peace Corps to my present work, I've spent most of my life in the Third World. So nobody should know better than I how to dress for it. Certainly one of the silliest mistakes an outsider can make is to dress up in "native" costume, whether it's a sari or a sombrero, unless you really know what you're doing. Yet, in Togo, when I found some of the most beautiful beads I'd ever seen, it never occurred to me not to wear them. While I was up-country, I seized the first grand occasion to flaunt my new find. What I didn't know is that locally the beads are worn not at the neck but at the waist—to hold up a sort of loincloth under the skirt. So, into the party I strutted, wearing around my neck what to every Togolese eye was part of a pair of underpants.

An Account Executive at an International Data Processing and Electronics Conglomerate

Even in a country run by generals, would you believe a runny nose could get you arrested?

A friend and I were coming into Colombia on business after a weekend in the Peruvian mountains touring Machu Picchu. What a sight that had been. And what a head cold the change in temperature had given my friend. As we proceeded through customs at the airport, he was wheezing and blowing into his handkerchief like an active volcano. Next thing I knew, two armed guards were lockstepping him through a door. I tried to intercede before the door slammed shut, but my spotty Spanish failed me completely. Inside a windowless room with the guards, so did his. He shouted in English. They shouted in Spanish. It was beginning to look like a bad day in Bogotá when a Colombian woman who had seen what happened burst into the room and finally achieved some bilingual understanding. It seems all that sniffling in the land of the infamous coca leaf had convinced the guards that my friend was waltzing through their airport snorting cocaine.

CUDDLY ETHNOCENTRICS

If only the world's customs inspectors could train their German shepherds to sniff out the invisible baggage we all manage to slip with us into foreign countries. They are like secret little land mines of the mind. Set to go off at the slightest quiver, they can sabotage a five-minute stroll down the Champs-Élysées or a $5 million tractor sale to Beijing. Three of our most popular national take-alongs:

Why Don't They Speak English? For the same reason we don't speak Catalan or Urdu. The wonder, in fact, is that so many people do speak so many languages. Seldom is a Continental European fluent in fewer than three, often more. Africans grow up with language of the nation that once colonized theirs plus half a dozen different tribal dialects. Japan has three distinct Japanese languages, which even the lowliest street sweeper can understand. Middle Eastern businesspeople shift effortlessly from their native tongue(s) to Oxford English to Quai d'Orsay French. Yet most of the English-speaking world remains as cheerfully monolingual as Queen Victoria's parakeet. If there are any complaints, then, it is clear they should not be coming from the American/English-speaking traveler.

Take Me to Your Burger King. In Peoria a Persian does not go looking for pot-au-feu. Alone among travelers, Americans seem to embark like astronauts—sealed inside a cozy life-support system from home. Scrambled eggs. Rent-a-cars. Showers. TV. Nothing wrong with any of it back home, but to the rest of the universe it looks sadly like somebody trying to read a book with the cover closed. Experiment! Try the local specialties.

American Know-How to the Rescue! Our brightest ideas have taken root all over the world—from assembling lines in Düsseldorf to silicone chips in Osaka to hybrid grains that are helping to nourish the Third World. Nonetheless, bigger, smarter, and faster do not inevitably add up to better. Indeed, the desire to take on shiny new American ways has been the downfall of nations whose cultures were already rich in art and technology when North America was still a glacier. As important as the idea itself is the way it is presented.

A U.S. doctor of public health recently back from West Africa offers an example of how to make the idea fit the ideology. "I don't just pop over and start handing out antimalarial pills on the corner," she says. "First I visit with the village chief. After he gives his blessing, I move in with the local witch doctor. After she shows me her techniques and I show her mine—and a few lives are saved—maybe then we can get the first native to swallow the first pill."

This is as true at the high-tech level as at the village dispensary. "What is all this drinking of green tea before the meeting with Mitsubishi?" The American way is to get right down to business. Yet if you look at Mitsubishi's bottom line, you have to wonder if green tea is such a bad idea after all.

It should come as no surprise that people surrounded by oceans rather than by other people end up ethnocentric. Even our biggest fans admit that America often strikes the rest of the world as a sweet-but-spoiled little darling, wanting desperately to please, but not paying too much attention to how it is done. Ever since the Marshall Plan, we seemed to believe that *our* games and *our* rules were the only ones in town. Any town. And that all else was the Heart of Darkness.

Take this scene in a Chinese cemetery. Watching a Chinese reverently placing fresh fruit on a grave, an American visitor asked, "When do you expect your ancestors to get up and eat the fruit?" The Chinese replied, "As soon as your ancestors get up and smell the flowers."

HANDS ACROSS THE ABYSS

Our bad old habits are giving way to a new when-in-Rome awareness. Some corporations take it so seriously that they put employees into a crash course of overseas cultural immersion. AT&T, for instance, encourages—and pays for—the whole family of an executive on the way to a foreign assignment to enroll in classes given by experts in the mores and manners of other lands.

Among the areas that cry out loudest for international understanding are how to say people's names, eat, dress, and talk. Get those four basics right and the rest is a piece of kuchen.

Basic Rule #1: What's in a Name?

…The first transaction between even ordinary citizens—and the first chance to make an impression for better or worse—is, of course, an exchange of names. In America there usually is not very much to get wrong. And even if you do, so what?

Not so elsewhere. Especially in the Eastern Hemisphere, where name frequently denotes social rank or family status, a mistake can be an outright insult. So can switching to a given name without the other person's permission, even when you think the situation calls for it.

"What would you like me to call you?" is always the opening line of one overseas deputy director for an international telecommunications corporation. "Better to ask several times," he advises, "than to get it wrong." Even then, "I err on the side of formality until asked to 'Call me Joe.'" Another frequent traveler insists his company provide him with a list of key people he will meet, country by country, surnames underlined, to be memorized on the flight over.

Don't Trust the Rules. Just when you think you have broken the international name code, they switch the rules on you. Take Latin America. Most people's names are a combination of the father's and mother's, with only the father's name used in conversation. In the Spanish-speaking countries the father's name comes first. Hence, Carlos Mendoza-Miller is called Mr. Mendoza. *But* in Portuguese-speaking Brazil it is the other way around, with the mother's name first.

In the Orient the Chinese system of surname first, given name last does not always apply. The Taiwanese, many of whom were educated in missionary schools, often have a Christian first name, which comes before any of the others—as in Tommy Ho Chin, who should be called Mr. Ho or, to his friends, Tommy Ho. Also, given names are often officially changed to initials, and a Y. Y. Lang is Y. Y.; never mind what it stands for. In Korea, which of a man's names takes a Mr. is determined by whether he is his father's first or second son. Although in Thailand names run backwards, Chinese style, the Mr. is put with the *given* name, and to a Thai it is just as important to be called by his given name as it is for a Japanese to be addressed by his surname. With the latter, incidentally, you can in a very friendly relationship respond to his using *your* first name by dropping the Mr. and adding *san* to his last name, as in Ishikawa-san.

Hello. Are you still there? Then get ready for the last installment of the name game, which is to disregard all of the above—sometimes. The reason is that many Easterners who deal regularly with the West are now changing the order of their names to un-confuse us. So, while to one another their names remain the same, to us the given name may come before the surname. Then again, it may not.

The safest course remains: Ask.

Basic Rule #2: Eat, Drink, and Be Wary

…[M]ealtime is no time for a thanks-but-no-thanks response. Acceptance of what is on your plate is tantamount to acceptance of host, country, and company. So, no matter how tough things may be to swallow, swallow. Or, as one veteran globe-girdler puts it, "Travel with a cast-iron stomach and eat everything everywhere."

Tastiness Is in the Eye of the Beholder. Often, what is offered constitutes your host country's proudest culinary achievements. What would we Americans think of a Frenchman who refused a bite of homemade apple pie or sizzling sirloin? Squeamishness comes not so much from the thing itself as from our unfamiliarity with it. After all, an oyster has remarkably the same look and consistency as a sheep's eye, and at first encounter a lobster would strike almost anybody as more a creature from science fiction than something you dip in melted butter and pop into your mouth.

Incidentally, in Saudi Arabia sheep's eyes are a delicacy, and in China it's bear's paw soup.

Perhaps the ultimate in exotic dining abroad befell a family planning expert on a trip for an international human welfare organization. It was a newly emerged African country where the national dish—in fact, the *only* dish eleven months of the year—is yam. The visitor's luck, however, was to be there the *other* month, when gorillas come in from the bush to steal the harvest. Being the only available protein, gorilla meat is as prized as sirloin is over here, and the village guest of honor was served a choice cut. Proudly, a platter of the usual mashed yams was placed before her—but with a roast gorilla hand thrusting artfully up from the center.

Is there any polite way out besides the back door?

Most experienced business travelers say no, at least not before taking at least a few bites. It helps, though, to slice whatever the item is very thin. This way, you minimize the texture—gristly, slimy, etc.—and the reminder of whence it came. Or, "Swallow it quickly," as one traveler recommends. "I still can't tell you what sheep's eyeballs taste like." As for dealing with taste, the old canard that "it tastes just like chicken" is often mercifully true. Even when the "it" is rodent, snake—or gorilla.

Another useful dodge is not knowing what you are eating. What's for dinner? Don't ask. Avoid poking around in the kitchen or looking at English-language menus. Your host will be flattered that you are following his lead, and who knows? Maybe it really is chicken in that stew.…

Bottoms Up—or Down? Some countries seem to do it deliberately, some inadvertently, except for Islam, where they don't do it at all. Either way, getting visitors as tipsy as possible as fast as possible stands as a universal sign of hospitality, and refusal to play your part equals rebuff. Wherever you go, toasts are as reciprocal as handshakes: If one does, all do. "I don't drink, thank you" rarely gets you off gracefully. Neither does protesting that you must get up early. (So must everyone else.)

"I try to wangle a glass of wine instead of the local firewater," one itinerant American says. "The only trouble is, the wine is usually stronger than the hard stuff." Mao-tai, Chinese wine made from sorghum, is notorious for leaving the unsuspecting thoroughly shanghaied. The Georgian wine so popular in Russia is no ladylike little Chablis either. In Nordic lands proper form for the toast is to raise the glass in a sweeping arc from belt buckle to lips while locking stares with your host. It takes very few akvavit-with-beer-chasers before you both start seeing northern lights.

In Africa, where all the new countries were once old European colonies, it is often taken for granted that if you are white you must have whiskey or gin or whatever the colonials used to like. A traveler to a former French possession describes the dilemma of being served a large gourdful of Johnnie Walker Red at nine in the morning. The host was simply remembering how the French had always loved their Scotch. *When* they drank it and *how much* were details he had never noticed. Yet there was no saying no without giving offense. A few sips had to be taken and a promise made to finish the rest later.

Basic Rule #3: Clothes Can Also *Un*make the Man

…Wherever you are, what you wear among strangers should not look strange to *them*. Which does not mean, "When in Morocco wear djellabas," etc. It means wear what you look natural in—and know how to wear—that also fits in with your surroundings.

For example, a woman dressed in a tailored suit, even with high heels and flowery blouse, looks startlingly masculine in a country full of diaphanous saris. More appropriate, then, is a silky, loose-fitting dress in a bright color—as opposed to blue serge or banker's gray.

In downtown Nairobi, a safari jacket looks as out of place as in London. With a few exceptions (where the weather is just too steamy for it), the general rule everywhere is that for business, for eating out, even for visiting people at home, you should be very buttoned up: conservative suit and tie for men, dress or skirt-suit for women. To be left in the closet until you go on an outdoor sight-seeing trek:

jeans, however haute couture
jogging shoes
tennis and T-shirts
tight-fitting sweaters (women)
open-to-the-navel shirts (men)
funny hats (both)

Where you *can* loosen up, it is best to do it the way the indigenes do. In the Philippines men wear the barong tagalog—a loose, frilly, usually white or cream-colored shirt with tails out, no jacket or tie. In tropical Latin American countries the counterpart to the barong is called a *guayabera* and, except for formal occasions, is acceptable business attire. In Indonesia they wear *Batiks*—brightly patterned shirts that go tieless and jacketless everywhere. In Thailand the same is true for the collarless Thai silk shirt. In Japan dress is at least as formal as in Europe (dark suit and tie for a man, business suit or tailored dress for a woman) except at country inns (called *ryokans*), where even big-city corporations sometimes hold meetings. Here you are expected to wear a kimono. Not to daytime meetings but to dinner, no matter how formal. (Don't worry—the inn always provides the kimono.)

One thing you notice wherever you go is that polyester is the mark of the tourist. The less drip-dry you are, the more you look as if you have come to do serious business, even if it means multiple dry-cleaning bills along the way.

Take It Off or Put It On—Depending. What you do or do not wear can be worse than bad taste—ranging from insulting to unhygienic to positively sinful. Shoes are among the biggest offenders in the East, even if you wear a 5AAA. They are forbidden within Muslim mosques and Buddhist temples. Never wear them into Japanese homes or restaurants unless the owner insists, and in Indian and Indonesian homes, if the host goes shoeless, do likewise. And wherever you take your shoes off, remember to place them neatly together facing the door you came in. This is particularly important in Japan....

In certain conservative Arab countries, the price for wearing the wrong thing can hurt more than feelings. Mullahs have been known to give a sharp whack with their walking sticks to any woman whom they consider immodestly dressed. Even at American-style hotels there, do not wear shorts, skirts above the knee, sleeveless blouses, or low necklines—much less a bikini at the pool....

CRITICAL THINKING QUESTIONS

1. Historically, people in North America have been rather indifferent to the dangers of inadvertently offending others. Why do you think this has been the case?
2. Have you ever offended others—or been offended—in the way depicted by Axtell? If so, how? How did you and others respond?
3. Can the type of cultural conflict Axtell describes occur here in Canada? How?

20

"His" and "Her" Marriage

Jessie Bernard

Family

CLASSIC

CONTEMPORARY

CROSS-CULTURAL

Social scientists have found that men and women are not joined at the hip by a wedding ceremony. Rather, their subsequent lives differ in terms of gender roles, power, and ways of communicating. Bernard was among the first sociologists to point out that marriage has a different meaning for women and men. As this selection shows, spouses rarely define reality in the same way, even with regard to simple routines such as sweeping the floor or mowing the lawn.

…[T]here is by now a very considerable body of well-authenticated research to show that there really are two marriages in every marital union, and that they do not always coincide.

"HIS" AND "HER" MARRIAGES

…[T]he differences in the marriages of husbands and wives have come under the careful scrutiny of a score of researchers. They have found that when they ask husbands and wives identical questions about the union, they often get quite different replies. There is usually agreement on the number of children

Source: From *The Future of Marriage* by Jessie Bernard. Copyright © 1972, World Publishing. Reprinted with permission.

Edward Hopper (1882–1967), *Room in New York*, 1932. Oil on Canvas, 29 x 36 in. UNL-Sheldon Memorial Art Gallery & Sculpture Garden. F.M. Hall Collection, 1932. H-166.

they have and a few other such verifiable items, although not, for example, on length of premarital acquaintance and of engagement, on age at marriage, and interval between marriage and birth of first child. Indeed, with respect to even such basic components of the marriage as frequency of sexual relations, social interaction, household tasks, and decision making, they seem to be reporting on different marriages. As, I think, they are.

In the area of sexual relations, for example, Kinsey and his associates found different responses in from one- to two-thirds of the couples they studied. Kinsey interpreted these differences in terms of selective perception. In the generation he was studying, husbands wanted sexual relations oftener than the wives did, thus "the females may be overestimating the actual frequencies" and "the husbands…are probably underestimating the frequencies." The differences might also have been vestiges of the probable situation earlier in the marriage when the desired frequency of sexual relations was about six to seven times greater among husbands than among wives. This difference may have become so impressed on the spouses that it remained in their minds even after the difference itself had disappeared or even been reversed. In a sample of happily married, middle-class couples a generation later, Harold Feldman found that both spouses attributed to their mates more influence in the area of sex than they did to themselves.

Companionship, as reflected in talking together, he found, was another area where differences showed up. Replies differed on three-fourths of all the items studied, including the topics talked about, the amount of time spent talking with each other, and which partner initiated conversation. Both partners claimed that whereas they talked more about topics of interest to their mates, their mates initiated conversations about topics primarily of interest to themselves. Harold Feldman concluded that projection in terms of needs was distorting even simple, everyday events, and lack of communication was permitting the distortions to continue. It seemed to him that "if these sex differences can occur so often among these generally well-satisfied couples, it would not be surprising to find even less consensus and more distortion in other less satisfied couples."

Although, by and large, husbands and wives tend to become more alike with age, in this study of middle-class couples, differences increased with length of marriage rather than decreased, as one might logically have expected. More couples in the later than in the earlier years, for example, had differing pictures in their heads about how often they laughed together, discussed together, exchanged ideas, or worked together on projects, and about how well things were going between them.

The special nature of sex and the amorphousness of social interaction help to explain why differences in response might occur. But household tasks? They are fairly objective and clear-cut and not all that emotion-laden. Yet even here there are his-and-her versions. Since the division of labor in the household is becoming increasingly an issue in marriage, the uncovering of differing replies in this area is especially relevant. Hard as it is to believe, Granbois and Willett tell us that more than half of the partners in one sample disagreed on who kept track of money and bills. On the question, who mows the lawn? more than a fourth disagreed. Even family income was not universally agreed on.

These differences about sexual relations, companionship, and domestic duties tell us a great deal about the two marriages. But power or decision making can cover all aspects of a relationship. The question of who makes decisions or who exercises power has therefore attracted a great deal of research attention. If we were interested in who really had the power or who really made the decisions, the research would be hopeless. Would it be possible to draw any conclusion from a situation in which both partners agree that the husband ordered the wife to make all the decisions? Still, an enormous literature documents the quest of researchers for answers to the question of marital power. The major contribution it has made has been to reveal the existence of differences in replies between husbands and wives.

The presence of such inconsistent replies did not at first cause much concern. The researchers apologized for them but interpreted them as due to methodological inadequacies; if only they could find a better way to approach the problem, the differences would disappear. Alternatively, the use of only the wife's responses, which were more easily available, was justified on the grounds that differences in one direction between the partners in one marriage compensated for differences in another direction between the partners in another marriage and thus canceled them out. As, indeed, they did. For when Granbois and Willett, two market researchers, analyzed the replies of husbands and wives separately, the overall picture was in fact the same for both wives and husbands. Such canceling out of differences in the total sample, however, concealed almost as much as it revealed about the individual couples who composed it. Granbois and Willett concluded, as Kinsey had earlier, that the "discrepancies…reflect differing perceptions on the part of responding partners." And this was the heart of the matter.

Differing reactions to common situations, it should be noted, are not at all uncommon. They are recognized in the folk wisdom embedded in the story of the blind men all giving different replies to questions on the nature of the elephant. One of the oldest experiments in juridical psychology demonstrates how different the statements of witnesses of the same act can be. Even in laboratory studies, it takes intensive training of raters to make it possible for them to arrive at agreement on the behavior they observe.

It has long been known that people with different backgrounds see things differently. We know, for example, that poor children perceive coins as larger than do children from more affluent homes. Boys and girls perceive differently. A good deal of the foundation for projective tests rests on the different ways in which individuals see identical stimuli. And this perception—or, as the sociologists put it, definition of the situation—is reality for them. In this sense, the realities of the husband's marriage are different from those of the wife's.

Finally, one of the most perceptive of the researchers, Constantina Safilios-Rothschild, asked the crucial question: Was what they were getting, even with the best research techniques, family sociology or wives' family sociology? She answered her own question: What the researchers who relied on wives' replies exclusively were reporting on was the wife's marriage. The husband's was not necessarily the same. There were, in fact, two marriages present:

One explanation of discrepancies between the responses of husbands and wives may be the possibility of two "realities," the husband's subjective reality and the wife's subjective reality—two perspectives which do not always coincide. Each spouse perceives "facts" and situations differently according to his own needs, values, attitudes, and beliefs. An "objective" reality could possibly exist only in the trained observer's evaluation, if it does exist at all.

Interpreting the different replies of husbands and wives in terms of selective perception, projection of needs, values, attitudes, and beliefs, or different definitions of the situation, by no means renders them trivial or incidental or justifies dismissing or ignoring them. They are, rather, fundamental for an understanding of the two marriages, his and hers, and we ignore them at the peril of serious misunderstanding of marriage, present as well as future.

IS THERE AN OBJECTIVE REALITY IN MARRIAGE?

Whether or not husbands and wives perceive differently or define situations differently, still sexual relations are taking place, companionship is or is not occurring, tasks about the house are being performed, and decisions are being made every day by someone. In this sense, some sort of "reality" does exist. David Olson went to the laboratory to see if he could uncover it.

He first asked young couples expecting babies such questions as these: Which one of them would decide whether to buy insurance for the newborn child? Which one would decide the husband's part in diaper changing? Which one would decide whether the new mother would return to work or to school? When there were differences in the answers each gave individually on the questionnaire, he set up a situation in which together they had to arrive at a decision in his laboratory. He could then compare the results of the questionnaire with the results in the simulated situation. He found neither spouse's questionnaire response any more accurate than the other's; that is, neither conformed better to the behavioral "reality" of the laboratory than the other did.

The most interesting thing, however, was that husbands, as shown on their questionnaire response, perceived themselves as having more power than they actually did have in the laboratory "reality," and wives perceived that they had less. Thus, whereas three-fourths (73 percent) of the husbands overestimated their power in decision making, 70 percent of the wives underestimated theirs. Turk and Bell found similar results in Canada. Both spouses tend to attribute decision-making power to the one who has the "right" to make the decision. Their replies, that is, conform to the model of marriage that has characterized civilized mankind for millennia. It is this model rather than their own actual behavior that husbands and wives tend to perceive.

We are now zeroing in on the basic reality. We can remove the quotation marks. For there is, in fact, an objective reality in marriage. It is a reality that resides in the cultural—legal, moral, and conventional—prescriptions and proscriptions and, hence, expectations that constitute marriage. It is the reality that is reflected in the minds of the spouses themselves. The differences between the marriages of husbands and of wives are structural realities, and it is these structural differences that constitute the basis for the different psychological realities.

THE AUTHORITY STRUCTURE OF MARRIAGE

Authority is an institutional phenomenon; it is strongly bound up with faith. It must be believed in; it cannot be enforced unless it also has power. Authority resides not in the person on whom it is conferred by the group or society, but in the recognition and acceptance it elicits in others. Power, on the other hand, may dispense with the prop of authority. It may take the form of the ability to coerce or to veto; it is often personal, charismatic, not institutional. This kind of personal power is self-enforcing. It does not require shoring up by access to force. In fact, it may even operate subversively. A woman with this kind of power may or may not know that she

possesses it. If she does know she has it, she will probably disguise her exercise of it.

In the West, the institutional structure of marriage has invested the husband with authority and backed it by the power of church and state. The marriages of wives have thus been officially dominated by the husband. Hebrew, Christian, and Islamic versions of deity were in complete accord on this matter. The laws, written or unwritten, religious or civil, which have defined the marital union have been based on male conceptions, and they have undergirded male authority.

Adam came first. Eve was created to supply him with companionship, not vice versa. And God himself had told her that Adam would rule over her; her wishes had to conform to his. The New Testament authors agreed. Women were created for men, not men for women; women were therefore commanded to be obedient. If they wanted to learn anything, let them ask their husbands in private, for it was shameful for them to talk in the church. They should submit themselves to their husbands, because husbands were superior to wives; and wives should be as subject to their husbands as the church was to Christ. Timothy wrapped it all up: "Let the woman learn in silence with all subjection. But I suffer not a woman to teach, nor to usurp authority over the man, but to be in silence." Male Jews continued for millennia to thank God three times a day that they were not women. And the Koran teaches women that men are naturally their superiors because God made them that way; naturally, their own status is one of subordination.

The state as well as the church had the same conception of marriage, assigning to the husband and father control over his dependents, including his wife. Sometimes this power was well-nigh absolute, as in the case of the Roman *patria potestas*—or the English common law, which flatly said, "The husband and wife are as one and that one is the husband." There are rules still lingering today with the same, though less extreme, slant. Diane B. Schulder has summarized the legal framework of the wife's marriage as laid down in the common law:

The legal responsibilities of a wife are to live in the home established by her husband; to perform the domestic chores (cleaning, cooking, washing, etc.) necessary to help maintain that home; to care for her husband and children.... A husband may force his wife to have sexual relations as long as his demands are reasonable and her health is not endangered.... The law allows a wife to take a job if she wishes. However, she must see that her domestic chores are completed, and, if there are children, that they receive proper care during her absence.

A wife is not entitled to payment for household work; and some jurisdictions in the United States expressly deny payment for it. In some states, the wife's earnings are under the control of her husband, and in four, special court approval and in some cases husband's consent are required if a wife wishes to start a business of her own.

The male counterpart to these obligations includes that of supporting his wife. He may not disinherit her. She has a third interest in property owned by him, even if it is held in his name only. Her name is required when he sells property.

Not only divine and civil law but also rules of etiquette have defined authority as a husband's prerogative. One of the first books published in England was a *Boke of Good Manners,* translated from the French of Jacques Le Grand in 1487, which included a chapter on "How Wymmen Ought to Be Gouerned." The thirty-third rule of Plutarch's *Rules for Husbands and Wives* was that women should obey their husbands; if they "try to rule over their husbands they make a worse mistake than the husbands do who let themselves be ruled." The husband's rule should not, of course, be brutal; he should not rule his wife "as a master does his chattel, but as the soul governs the body, by feeling with her and being linked to her by affection." Wives, according to Richard Baxter, a seventeenth-century English divine, had to obey even a wicked husband, the only exception being that a wife need not obey a husband if he ordered her to change her religion. But, again, like Plutarch, Baxter warned that the husband should love his wife; his authority should not be so coercive or so harsh as to destroy love. Among his twelve rules for carrying out the

duties of conjugal love, however, was one to the effect that love must not be so imprudent as to destroy authority.

As late as the nineteenth century, Tocqueville noted that in the United States the ideals of democracy did not apply between husbands and wives:

> Nor have the Americans ever supposed that one consequence of democratic principles is the subversion of marital power, or the confusion of the natural authorities in families. They hold that every association must have a head in order to accomplish its objective, and that the natural head of the conjugal association is man. They do not therefore deny him the right of directing his partner; and they maintain, that in the smaller association of husband and wife, as well as in the great social community, the object of democracy is to regulate and legalize the powers which are necessary, not to subvert all power.
>
> This opinion is not peculiar to men and contested by women; I never observed that the women of America consider conjugal authority as an unfortunate usurpation [by men] of their rights, nor that they thought themselves degraded by submitting to it. It appears to me, on the contrary, that they attach a sort of pride to the voluntary surrender of their own will, and make it their boast to bend themselves to the yoke, not to shake it off.

The point here is not to document once more the specific ways (religious, legal, moral, traditional) in which male authority has been built into the marital union—that has been done a great many times—but merely to illustrate how different (structurally or "objectively" as well as perceptually or "subjectively") the wife's marriage has actually been from the husband's throughout history.

THE SUBVERSIVENESS OF NATURE

The rationale for male authority rested not only on biblical grounds but also on nature or natural law, on the generally accepted natural superiority of men. For nothing could be more self-evident than that the patriarchal conception of marriage, in which the husband was unequivocally the boss, was natural, resting as it did on the unchallenged superiority of males.

Actually, nature, if not deity, is subversive. Power, or the ability to coerce or to veto, is widely distributed in both sexes, among women as well as among men. And whatever the theoretical or conceptual picture may have been, the actual, day-by-day relationships between husbands and wives have been determined by the men and women themselves. All that the institutional machinery could do was to confer authority; it could not create personal power, for such power cannot be conferred, and women can generate it as well as men.... Thus, keeping women in their place has been a universal problem, in spite of the fact that almost without exception institutional patterns give men positions of superiority over them.

If the sexes were, in fact, categorically distinct, with no overlapping, so that no man was inferior to any woman or any woman superior to any man, or vice versa, marriage would have been a great deal simpler. But there is no such sharp cleavage between the sexes except with respect to the presence or absence of certain organs. With all the other characteristics of each sex, there is greater or less overlapping, some men being more "feminine" than the average woman and some women more "masculine" than the average man. The structure of families and societies reflects the positions assigned to men and women. The bottom stratum includes children, slaves, servants, and outcasts of all kinds, males as well as females. As one ascends the structural hierarchy, the proportion of males increases, so that at the apex there are only males.

When societies fall back on the lazy expedient —as all societies everywhere have done—of allocating the rewards and punishments of life on the basis of sex, they are bound to create a host of anomalies, square pegs in round holes, societal misfits. Roles have been allocated on the basis of sex which did not fit a sizable number of both sexes—women, for example, who chafed at subordinate status and men who could not master

superordinate status. The history of the relations of the sexes is replete with examples of such misfits. Unless a modus vivendi is arrived at, unhappy marriages are the result.

There is, though, a difference between the exercise of power by husbands and by wives. When women exert power, they are not rewarded; they may even be punished. They are "deviant." Turk and Bell note that "wives who...have the greater influence in decision making may experience guilt over this fact." They must therefore dissemble to maintain the illusion, even to themselves, that they are subservient. They tend to feel less powerful than they are because they *ought* to be.

When men exert power, on the other hand, they are rewarded; it is the natural expression of authority. They feel no guilt about it. The prestige of authority goes to the husband whether or not he is actually the one who exercises it. It is not often even noticed when the wife does so. She sees to it that it is not.

There are two marriages, then, in every marital union, his and hers. And his...is better than hers. The questions, therefore, are these: In what direction will they change in the future? Will one change more than the other? Will they tend to converge or to diverge? Will the future continue to favor the husband's marriage? And if the wife's marriage is improved, will it cost the husband's anything, or will his benefit along with hers?

CRITICAL THINKING QUESTIONS

1. What evidence does Bernard offer to support her conclusion that there are "his" and "her" marriages rather than "our" marriage?
2. Does the traditional inequality of men and women support or undermine marital roles? How?
3. In your opinion, have marital roles in Canada changed since this article was written in 1972? How?

21

Housework in Canada: The National Picture*

M. R. Nakhaie

Family

CLASSIC

CONTEMPORARY

CROSS-CULTURAL

Researchers generally agree that women perform the majority of domestic work. Nakhaie looks at this assertion from a Canadian perspective and attempts to address the lack of research on domestic labour in Canada.

Recent survey research indicates that women are still overwhelmingly responsible for, and primarily carry out, the chief household chores (Coverman & Sheley, 1986; Berardo et al., 1987; Michelson, 1988). Most importantly, there appears to be little significant increase in the amount of domestic labour performed by men when their wives take on a second job (i.e., full-time paid work outside the home). Canadian local studies in Vancouver (Meissner et al., 1975), Halifax (Harvey Clarke, 1975), Toronto (Michelson,

*I gratefully acknowledge that the data presented here were drawn from Class Structure and Class Consciousness: Merged Multi-Nation File, the Canadian portion of which was conducted by Professor John Myles of Carleton University with funding from the Social Sciences and Humanities Research Council of Canada. I am indebted to Professors Robert Arnold, James Curtis and Roberta Hamilton, and anonymous reviewers for their helpful and critical comments.

Source: M. R. Nakhaie. (1995). "Housework in Canada". *Journal of Comparative Family Studies,* 26(3), 409–25. Reprinted with the permission of the Journal of Comparative Family Studies.

1985), Quebec (Bourdais et al., 1987), and Flin Flon (Luxton, 1980; Luxton & Rosenberg, 1986) support these conclusions.

There is, however, no national Canadian research to substantiate these findings. This is a surprising shortcoming, given the persistent conclusion among contributors to the domestic labour debate that there is a great need for empirical research (Fox, 1986: 188; Seccombe, 1986: 207; Armstrong & Armstrong, 1990: 33). In an attempt to contribute to the ongoing debate, this paper provides a multivariate analysis of housework and evaluates its major determinant in the Canadian national setting.

HYPOTHESES

Aside from the importance of capitalism and patriarchy in the institutionalization of gender specific task allocations (see Molyneux, 1979; Fox, 1980; Hamilton & Barrett, 1986; Armstrong & Armstrong, 1990), most theorists agree that the organization of domestic life is a negotiated process between household occupants.... There is, however, little agreement as to whether this process is power-based or a free choice.

The best-known sociological theory which is concerned with the conjugal power as an explanation of housework performance is that of Wolfe (1959), Blood and Wolfe (1960: 48, 73–4) and Spitze (1986: 691). This theory views power and resources such as income as instrumental in the family structure whereby those members with more income or power are better able to exercise their wills, or to achieve desired goals or outcomes. Davidoff (1976: 124), likewise, argues that the performance of housekeeping and housework are a means of maintaining order and predictability in the immediate environment thus making meaningful patterns of activity, people and material. Cleaning, for example, entails the separation of wanted from unwanted, desirable from undesirable, and is therefore a way of making the environment conform to cultural standards. Those who are powerful, however, can enforce and maintain this order by delegating it to the less powerful. Thus, the resource/power theory suggests that housework is generally undesirable and those with more resources confer power and negotiate or impose household tasks on the powerless. Empirical research has supported this hypothesis (see Bane, 1976; Clark et al., 1978; Nicols and Metzen, 1978; Ericksen et al., 1979; Vanek, 1980; Model, 1982; Bird et al., 1984; Spitze, 1986; Bourdais et al., 1987; but see, Farkas, 1976; Robinson, 1977; Herdesty & Bokemeir, 1989: 263). For example, Ericksen et al. (1979) show a negative relationship between men's income and their hours of housework performance. Similarly, Nicols and Metzen (1978) show that as wives' incomes increase, the number of hours they spend on housework decrease, and that the husbands' housework increases.

The New Home Economics, or Chicago School, builds on the resource/power theory but sees the household operation as based on free choice. It suggests that the household unit seeks to maximize the aggregate utility of the occupants'

labour power in the house and in the market by deciding which commodities to produce in the house and which to purchase from the market. Since women often earn less for the same work as men, this thesis argues that households can maximize utility by adopting a gendered division of labour. This places wives at home doing domestic work while their husbands are involved in the paid work force (Becker, 1974). The traditional sexual division of labour is thus seen as a rational decision made by households which wish to maximize utility (see also Becker, 1976, 1981).

More precisely, this theory is concerned with the "husband-wife earning ratio" as the determinant of home responsibility (Becker, 1974: 303). It suggests that the relative income contribution of spouses to the family signifies the worth of each partner's work in the market and thus is used as the determinant of housework performance. The earliest test of this thesis by Farkas (1976), based on the national U.S. Income Dynamic data, shows that the strength of the net effect of wage-ratio does not appear to warrant the conclusion that the value of human time is the main explanation for spousal contribution to housework. Model (1982), however, revealed that the level of contribution to housework is determined by income differentials between spouses. The latter, in fact, proves to be a better predictor of housework responsibilities than individual income. Similarly, Maret and Finlay's (1984) findings support the hypothesis that the wife's relative economic contribution to the household determines her domestic responsibilities (1984: 362; but see [the] Hardesty and Bokemeir study of rural Kentucky, 1989: 263).

Finally, the time availability hypothesis also sees housework allocation as a negotiated process but not so much based on power or utility maximization. This thesis suggests that husbands and wives perform housework in response to the availability of time after involvement in paid work. Blood and Wolfe (1960: 74), for example, argue that "more household tasks are humdrum and menial in nature," and the most important factor contributing to their performance is available time. Usually the person with the most time is the wife who is not working outside the home. But if she works for pay, the husband incurs a moral obligation to contribute to the housework. Thus, this thesis suggests that as more women work for pay, they have less time to perform housework. Consequently, their husbands have to contribute more to the housework because "the work must be done." Or, alternatively, the more husbands have available free time, because their jobs require fewer hours, the more they will contribute to domestic work.

Several studies point to women's participation in the labour force as the reason for a decrease in their housework and an increase in the home responsibilities of their partners. (Walker, 1970; Epstein, 1971; Holmstrom, 1973; Elliott et al., 1973; Vanek, 1974; Nicols and Metzen, 1978; Pleck, 1979; Sanik, 1981; Berk, 1985; Bourdais et al., 1987; Michelson, 1988; Luxton, 1980). For example, Spitze (1986) uses data from the National Longitudinal Surveys of Young and Mature Women and finds that, as women's hours of employment increases, their share of housework decreases slightly. Similarly, Barnett and Baruch (1987) reveal that women's employment outside the home prompts increased male acceptance of housework.

Despite the positive relationship in the above studies, the impact of wives' employment on husband's housework is also shown to be insignificant (Vanek, 1974; Sanik, 1981), quite small (Walker & Woods, 1976), or at best modest (Nicols & Metzen, 1978). Most importantly, there appears to be little significant increase in men's domestic labour as women take on paid work outside the home. For example, Meissner et al. (1975) studied a random sample of Vancouver couples on a week day and weekend day. They show that women's total workload, involving work both inside and outside the home, increases as they take on paid work, but husbands' does not. While men are reported to spend only a fraction of the time that women spend doing housework, it

is women who are found to adjust their schedules to the changing family situation. Based on a similar study in 1971–72 in Halifax, Harvey and Clarke (1975) also conclude that women, and not men, adjust their work efforts to changing family needs. Michelson's (1985) 1980 survey of Toronto families, based on time-budget data, also shows that full-time paid working women still do far more housework than men. Finally, another local study by Bourdais et al. (1987) in Quebec, reveals that women, on average, contribute three times as many hours as men to household chores. This proportion decreases to twice as much as men's when both partners have a paid job. However, even though a woman's employment decreases her work around the house by nine hours, it increases men's housework by only one hour (Bourdais et al., 1987).

In sum, American and Canadian local studies reveal that women who work for pay outside the home do not necessarily decrease and their husbands increase their share of housework. Moreover, while homemaking is the largest occupational category in this country (Luxton & Rosenberg, 1986), housework ranks as the most systematically under-researched (Hale, 1990). There have been several very informative studies of local samples, referred to above. The present study will show the generalizability to national data of several results from these earlier local studies. Furthermore, due, perhaps, to differences in research procedures (measures, samples, and the extent of controls), the previous American literature is inconsistent enough in its findings to require further tests. Most American studies rely on a ordinal level of measurement for housework—mostly husband, mostly wife, jointly (Stafford et al., 1977; Clarke et al., 1978; Ericksen et al., 1979; Marret and Finlay, 1984; Bird et al., 1984; Hardesty and Bokemeir, 1989). Other researchers ask respondents to estimate their contribution to housework in terms of the percentage of time or number of hours (Coverman, 1985; Barnett & Baruch, 1987; Berardo et al., 1987). Still other researchers obtain time-use data by a diary of activities kept by each respondent for about 24 hours or a week (Walker, 1970; Walker & Woods, 1976; Robinson et al., 1972; Robinson, 1977; Juster and Stafford, 1985; Coverman and Sheley, 1986). These American studies have also been limited in population coverage to white middle class families (Berardo et al., 1987; Barnet & Baruch, 1987), to women aged 30–44 (Marret & Finlay, 1984), to college students (Stafford et al., 1977), to college and university administrators (Bird et al., 1984), or to local samples (Clarke et al., 1978; Ericksen et al., 1979), although national samples have also been used, as discussed above.[1]

DATA SOURCE

Our data source is the Canadian portion of "The Class Structure and Class Consciousness: Merged Multi-Nation File" (CSCC) which involved in-home personal interviews with a national multi-stage stratified sample of Canadians. The interviews were conducted between November 1982 and April 1983. There were 2576 respondents, 1,810 of whom were married and/or cohabiting and 480 of which both partners worked more than 30 hours per week for pay. The latter subsample is selected to evaluate the findings by Maret and Finlay (1984) that women in dual-earner families continue to bear full responsibility for housework. The sample is weighted to make it representative of the population in terms of gender, age, household size, and community size within provinces.

Dependent Variables

Housework refers to all types of activities which are undertaken to maintain the household, both physically and socially, as well as the maintenance of the physical structure of the house (Clark & Stephenson, 1986: 75). The CSCC survey asked respondents to report how they handle various routine household chores by indicating what percentage of particular tasks is done by them.[2] These tasks, however, were limited to eight, including: looking after children and doing things with them, cooking meals, cleaning after meals, doing laundry, general housecleaning, grocery shopping, yardwork, and house maintenance.

Independent Variables

The measures of personal resource and power include two variables: (1) income scaled from 1 = none to 12 = over \$100,000; and (2) perceived power. Blood and Wolfe (1960), in their study of Detroit and Michigan, measured power in terms of an individual's ability to make decisions in critical areas of life (including income and expenditures) and showed that this measure was strongly related to various measures of inequality such as income and prestige. Likewise, the CSCC contained three questions which could measure conjugal power: (1) "who has the most say in making major financial decisions in [the respondent's] household, like a decision to take out a loan or buy a car"; (2) "who has most say about the overall family budget; that is, about how much of the family income goes for different general purposes such as running the house, recreation, new clothes, and so forth"; and (3) "who has the most say in deciding the specific neighborhood where you live now." If the respondents make the decision in any of these areas they receive a score of +1; if their partners make this decision the respondents receive a score of –1 and if both equally decide the respondents receive a score of zero (0). The power variable is created by summing the scores for these questions. Scores range from –3 to +3.

Relative income represents the respondent's relative contribution to the family income. Respondents are asked to report the percentage of annual family income resulting from their spouses' jobs. A score of zero (0) is assigned to those respondents who reported that their spouse does not have a paying job.

There are two measures of time availability. First, the survey asked the respondents to report the number of hours they work per week. This variable ranges from 8 to 97. The second measure evaluates the time availability of spouses. The survey asked the respondents to report their part-ner's number of hours of paid work per week. This variable ranges from 8 to 87.

In addition to the predictors of homework discussed above we were concerned about the extent to which the presence of children increases women's and men's share of housework (Berk & Berk, 1979; Meissner et al., 1975; Hamilton, 1981). We included the number of children and their ages (under 5, 6–12, 13 plus) to control for children's effect.

RESULTS

Among the total sample, male respondents have a higher mean level of income (about $20K) than females (about $7K) and work more per week (37.4 hours) than females (18.6 hours). Spouses of the male respondents spend 15.44 hours per week in the paid force and contribute 17.3% to the family income, while spouses of the female respondents spend 35.28 hours per week in the paid force and contribute 66.9% to the family income. On aver-age, males score higher in the power construct (.45) than females (–.20). As expected, the magnitude of these gaps declines, though not substantially, among full-time respondents when compared to the total sample. The main differences between males and females in the total and full-time paid working sample are in the income and time avail-ability areas. Among full-time paid working respondents, men's total income does not differ much from that reported by males in the full sample but females' total income increases from about $7K to $13K and their contribution to the family income increases from 17.2 percent to 40.6 percent. The total hours of paid employment for males does increase slightly (from 37.4 to 45.7), but that of females increases substantially (from 18.6 to 40.2). Similarly, when comparing the two groups, males report that their partners' total hours of paid work increase from 15.4 to 40.3 while

females report that their partners' total hours of paid work increases from 35.3 to 44.2.

Another expected difference between the two sub-samples is in the numbers of children. Although there is little difference in the number of children reported by either males or females in the total sample, full-time paid working females report fewer children than their male counterparts.

Finally, male respondents reported perform-ing about 33% of the housework, compared to 62% for the female respondents. A similarly large gap in performing housework emerged among full-time paid working respondents. Men increased their housework by about 4% and females decreased theirs by about 3% when compared to the total sample (see Table 21.1). Consistent with previous research, full-time paid work by women does not relieve them from most of the housework (Maret and Finlay, 1984; Meissner et al., 1975; Luxton, 1980)....

DISCUSSION AND CONCLUSIONS

The results of this study support previous find-ings that relative income, personal resources and time availability as well as the presence of chil-dren affect the division of housework. Among these, power, as measured by the ability to make decisions regarding the affairs of the house, receives the least support when compared to the time availability (Meissner et al., 1975: 425; Blood & Wolfe, 1960; Spitze, 1986; Walker, 1970; Epstein, 1971; Holmstrom, 1973; Pleck, 1979; Sanik, 1981; Berk, 1985; Bourdais et al., 1987), relative income (Farkas, 1976: 482; Model, 1982; Maret & Finlay, 1984), presence of children (Hamilton, 1981; Berk & Berk, 1979; Bourdais et al., 1987; Meissner, 1975) and income (Bane, 1976; Nicols & Metzen, 1978; Bourdais et al., 1987) variables. The power measure failed to show the expected effect, prob-ably because it is measured by asking respon-dents who makes what decisions and therefore indicates perceived authority rather than actual power (McDonald, 1980).

TABLE 21.1: Mean Scores for the Dependent and Independent Variables by Gender:
Total Sample and Full-Time Paid Working Respondents (Canada, 1983)

	Total Sample		Full-time	
	Males	*Females*	*Males*	*Females*
Power	.45	−.20	−.37	−.08
Income	6.93	3.90	6.81	5.54
Relative income	17.28	66.95	40.46	60.98
# Hours of paid work by spouse	15.44	35.28	40.39	44.23
# Hours of paid work by Resp.	37.40	18.62	45.74	40.24
# Children	1.24	1.25	1.13	1.02
Age of children	10.72	10.82	10.90	9.82
Share of Housework	33.30	62.30	37.50	59.30

Although the New Home Economic model is supported in our study, the impact of the husband-wife earning ratio on doing housework is stronger for males than females. This finding suggests that the economic model, by assuming that people make decisions based on free choice, has ignored power relationships involved in the household. As Coverman (1989) argued, the allocation of household chores is subject to difficult negotiation and conflict among household members. The outcome of these negotiations often depends, however, on the ability and power of the household occupants. Husbands seem to have a structural advantage in this process. Wives, however, have to develop a variety of tactics and strategies to increase their spouses' contributions to housework (Luxton, 1980; see also Hartmann, 1981; Hamilton, 1981).

The suggestion that housework is power-based is also borne out by findings on the relationships between the time availability measures and doing housework. As males increase their hours of paid work per week, they do less housework (particularly among double earner couples), while women do *more* of the housework as they increase their hours of paid work. Moreover, women are more responsive to the increases in their partners' hours of paid work than are men.

Two conclusions can be reached by these findings. First, among the total sample, females do more housework because gender stands as a proxy of a relatively fewer paid hours of work by women compared to men. Thus, among the full-time paid respondents, gender in itself does not have a significant impact on doing housework. Second, there are indications of a "superwomen" (Steinem, 1987: 57; Luxton, 1980) ethic among women who work for long hours in the paid work force and do an even larger share of housework than before. These findings, thus, support the studies in Vancouver (Meissner, 1975), Halifax (Harvey & Clarke, 1975), Flin Flon (Luxton, 1980) and in Quebec (Bourdais et al., 1987) which show that full-time paid working women still do most of the housework, perhaps at the expense of their own leisure and personal care. As these local studies conclude, women's involvement in the paid labour force simply adds to their housework in the family (Anderson, 1988: 165).

The differential impact of the hours of paid work for males and females, particularly among the full-time two income earners, may thus point to Eichler's (1990) argument that the value of time differs systematically in relation to one's power position. Since women as a group are less powerful than men, time spent performing paid work becomes less valuable and cannot easily help reduce their share of housework. This power seems to have been derived from husbands' economic advantage in the labour force, their greater cognitive power in the public domain and from women's cultural mandate, which places priority on the family (Mackie, 1991: 234–235; Luxton & Rosenberg, 1986: 11; Gaskell, 1988).

Finally, one of the persistent findings in this study (and of the previous research) is that gender/sex is the most significant force in accounting for the performance of housework, net of other variables. These consistent findings point to the structural and historical forces which have gradually helped institutionalize a "gender factory" in the house so that each generation of sons learned to do less housework and each generation of daughters continued to be trained in domestic activities. This gendered socialization of housework seems to have been sealed in the best social cement of all: the patterns of daily life and the relationship between parents and children (Cowan, 1983: 86; England & Farkas, 1986; Finley, 1989; Molyneux, 1979; Fox, 1980; Zaretsky, 1982; Hamilton & Barrett, 1986; Armstrong & Armstrong, 1990).

Moreover, the gendered division of labour is passed down to children in the family and schools and through media and religions which portray women as engaged in a narrow range of "female" occupations and household-related tasks (see Russell, 1986; Mackie, 1991). These forces have constructed sex-specific images and stereotypes and have enforced a "tendency for many women to accept as truth the social constraints and mental images which society has prescribed for them" (Pike & Zureik, 1975: 3). Thus, boys' and girls' involvement in housework in their early teens becomes readily distinguishable along gender lines (Benin & Edwards, 1990; White and Brinkerhoff, 1981). Not surprisingly, Gaskell's (1988) study of young girls in their last years of high school in a Vancouver working-class neighborhood revealed that they all assumed that eventually they would care for their children and do the housework. Young girls seem to have learned that "[c]ooking a nice meal, providing clean sheets or eliminating dull, yellow floor wax" are ways of expressing love (Luxton, 1980: 159). Boys, on the other hand, internalize the male breadwinner ideology as their fundamental gender consciousness (Livingstone & Luxton, 1989).

There are some indications of a shift in Canadian attitudes toward sharing housework. Canadians' support for husbands sharing housework has increased from 57% in 1976 to 81% in 1986 (Wilson, 1991: 56). However, these attitude changes are very slowly translated into changes in behaviour. Although the men of Flin Flon seem to have increased their contribution to housework by 8.3 hours per week between 1976–81, women of this town decreased their contribution to housework by only 4.3 hours per week (Luxton, 1986). Perhaps an equal contribution to housework is possible only if the power relationship between men and women in the wider society and in the house is altered. Simultaneously, gender consciousness should be transcended so that an ideology of breadwinning for males and family priority for females loses its gendered-significance. These, however, may not be easy tasks, given the powerful forces which have split the labour market and have segregated the household as a private domain.

CRITICAL THINKING QUESTIONS

1. Review the *conjugal power* explanation for who performs the majority of housework. Given your own experiences, does this explanation seem accurate?
2. Why do you think there has not been more research into domestic labour in Canada?
3. Do you believe that the gender factory continues to reinforce traditional male and female roles as they relate to domestic labour? If yes, how? If not, why?

NOTES

1. There are substantial differences among the American studies. It is difficult to know to what extent these differences in findings are due to small sample areas, measurement differences and/or differing interpretations of the results. It is plausible that since there is little variation in the amount of housework performed by men, every different analysis will likely conclude with the explanatory importance of different variables.

2. The exact question is: "Now we would like to ask you some questions about how you handle various routine household chores. For each of the following tasks, please tell me roughly what percentage of this task is done by you."

REFERENCES

Armstrong, P., and H. Armstrong. 1990. *Theorizing women's work.* Toronto: Network Basics Series.

Bane, M. J. 1976. *Here to stay: American families in the twentieth century.* New York: Basic Books.

Benin, M. H., and D. A. Edwards. 1990. Adolescents' chores: The difference between dual and single-earner families." *Journal of Marriage and the Family,* (52): 361–73.

Barnett, R. C., and G. K. Baruch. 1987. Determinants of father's participation in family work. *Journal of Marriage and the Family,* (49): 29–40.

Becker, G. S. 1974. A theory of marriage. In *Economics of the family*, ed. T. W. Schultz. Chicago: University of Chicago Press.

———. 1976. *The economic approach to human behavior.* Chicago: University of Chicago Press.

———. 1981. *A treatise on the family.* Harvard, Mass.: Harvard University Press.

Berk, R. 1980. The new home economics: An agenda for sociological research. In *Women and household labor*, ed. S. F. Berk, 113–48. Beverly Hills, Calif.: Sage.

Berk, R., and S. Berk. 1979. *Labour and leisure at home.* Beverly Hills: Sage.

Berk, S. 1985. *The gender factory: The apportionment of work in the American household,* New York: Plenum Press.

Berardo, D. H., C. L. Shehah, and G. R. Leslie. 1987. A residue of tradition: Jobs, careers, and spouses' time in house work. *Journal of Marriage and the Family,* 49: 381–90.

Bird, G. W, G. A. Bird, and M. Scruggs. 1984. Determinants of family task sharing: A study of husbands and wives. *Journal of Marriage and the Family,* 46(2): 345–55.

Blood, R. O., and D. M. Wolfe. 1960. *Husbands and wives: The dynamics of married living.* Glencoe, Ill.: Free Press.

Bourdais, C., P. J. Hamel, and R. Bernard. 1987. Le travail et l'ouvrage: Charge et portage des tâches domestiques chez les couples québécois. *Sociologie et Sociétés,* XIX(1: Avril): 37–55.

Clark, R. A., F. I. Nye, and V. Gecas. 1978. Work involvement and marital role performance. *Journal of Marriage and the Family*, 40: 9–22.

Clark S., and M. Stephenson. 1986. Housework as real work. In *Work in the Canadian context*, eds. K. L. P. Lundy, and B. Warme, 211–31. Markham, Ont.: Butterworths.

Coverman, S., and J. E. Sheley. 1986. Change in men's housework and child care time 1965–1975. *Journal of Marriage and the Family,* 48: 413–22.

Cowan, R. S. 1983. *More work for mothers: The ironies of household technology from the open hearth to the microwave.* New York: Basic Books.

Davidoff, L. 1976. The rationalization of housework. In *Dependence and exploitation in work and marriage*, eds. D. L. Barker, & S. Allen. London: Longman.

Eichler, M. 1991. Gender and the value of time. In *Images of Canada: The sociological tradition*, eds. J. Curtis, and L. Tepperman. Scarborough, Ont.: Prentice-Hall Canada Inc.

Elliott, D., A. S. Harvey, and D. Procos. 1973. *An overview of Halifax time-budget.* Halifax/Institute of Public Affairs, Dalhousie University.

England, P., and G. Farkas. 1986. *Households, employment, and gender: A social, economic, and demographic view.* New York: Aldine de Gruyter.

Ericksen, J., W. Yancey, and E. Ericksen. 1979. The division of family roles. *Journal of Marriage and the Family,* 41: 301–14.

Epstein, C. 1971. Law partners and marital partners: Strains and solutions in the dual-career family enterprise. *Human Relations*, 24 (December): 549–64.

Farkas, G. 1976. Education, wage rate and the division of labour between husband and wife. *Journal of Marriage and the Family,* 38: 473–84.

Finley, N. J. 1989. Theories of family labour as applied to gender differences in caregiving for elderly parents. *Journal of Marriage and the Family,* 51: 79–86.

Fox, B. 1980. *Hidden in the household: Women's domestic labour under capitalism.* Oshawa, ON: Women's Press.

Gaskell, J. 1988. The reproduction of family life: Perspectives of male and female adolescents. In *Gender and society: Creating a Canadian women's sociology*, ed. A. T. McLaren, 146–68. Toronto: Copp Clark Pitman.

Hale, S. M. 1990. *Controversies in sociology: A Canadian introduction.* Toronto: Copp Clark Pitman Ltd.

Hamilton, R. 1981. Working at home. *Atlantis*, 7(1): 114–26.

Hamilton, R., and M. Barrett. 1986. Introduction. In *The politics of diversity: Feminism, Marxism and nationalism*, eds. R. Hamilton and M. Barrett, 1–35. London: Verso.

Hardesty, C., and J. Bokemeir. 1989. Finding time and making do: Distribution of household labour in nonmetropolitan marriages. *Journal of Marriage and the Family,* 51: 253–67.

Hartmann, H. I. 1981. The family as the locus of gender, class, and political struggle: The example of housework. *Signs,* 6(3): 366–94.

Harvey, A. S., and S. Clarke. 1975. *Descriptive analysis of Halifax time-budget data.* Halifax: Institute of Public Affairs, Dalhousie University.

Holmstrom, L. L. 1973. *The two-career family.* Cambridge, Mass.: Schenkman.

Juster, F. T., and F. J. Stafford. 1985. *Time, goods and well-being.* Ann Arbor, Mich.: Survey Research Center, Institute for Social Research, University of Michigan.

Livingstone, D. W., and M. Luxton. 1988. Gender consciousness at work: Modification of the male breadwinner norm among steelworkers and their spouses. *Canadian Review of Sociology and Anthropology*, 26(2): 240–74.

Luxton, M. 1980. *More than a labour of love: Three generations of women's work at home.* Toronto: Women's Press.

Luxton, M., and H. Rosenberg. 1986. *Through the kitchen windows: The politics of home and family.* Toronto: Garamond Press.

Mackie, M. 1991. *Gender relations in Canada: Further explorations.* Markham, Ont.: Butterworths Canada Ltd.

Maret, E., and B. Finlay. 1984. The distribution of household labour among women in dual-earner families. *Journal of Marriage and the Family*, 46: 357–64.

McDonald, G. W. 1980. Family power: The assessment of a decade of theory and research, 1970–1979. *Journal of Marriage and the Family,* 42: 841–54.

Meissner, M., E. W. Humphrey, S. M. Meis, and W. J. Scheu. 1975. No exit for wives: Sexual division of labour and cumulation of household demands. *Canadian Review of Sociology and Anthropology,* 12: 424–39.

Michelson, W. 1985. *From sun to sun: Daily obligations and community structure in the lives of employed women and their families.* Tomwa, N.J.: Rowman & Allanheld Publishers.

———. 1988. The daily routines of employed spouses as a public affairs agenda. In *Readings in sociology: An introduction*, eds. L. Tepperman, and J. Curtis, 400–09. Toronto: McGraw-Hill Ryerson Limited.

Model, S. 1982. Housework by husbands: Determinants and implications. In *Two paychecks: Life in dual earner families*, ed. J. Aldous, 193, 206. Beverly Hills, Calif.: Sage Publications.

Molyneux, M. 1979. Beyond the domestic labour debate. *New Left Review,* 116: 3–27.

Nicols, S., and E. Metzen. 1978. Housework time of husband and wife. *Home Economics Research Journal,* 17: 85–97.

Pike, R., and E. Zuriek. 1975. *Socialization and values in Canadian society.* Toronto: McClelland and Stewart Limited.

Pleck, J. H. 1979. Men's family work: Three perspectives and some new data. *Family Coordinator*, 28: 481–88.

Robinson, J. 1977. *How Americans use time.* New York: Praeger.

Robinson, J., P. Converse, and A. Szali. 1972. Everyday life in the twelve countries. In *The use of time*, ed. A. Szalai. The Hague: Mouton.

Sanik, M. 1981. Division of household work: A decade of comparison, 1967–1977. *Home Economic Research Journal,* 10: 175–80.

Seccombe, W. 1986. Patriarchy stabilized: The construction of male breadwinner wage norm in nineteenth-century Britain. *Social History*, II (1).

Spitze, G. D. 1986. Division of home responsibilities. *Social Forces*, 64: 689–701.

Stafford, R., E. Backman, and R Dibona. 1977. The division of labour among cohabiting and married couples. *Journal of Marriage and the Family,* 39: 43–57.

Steinem, G. 1987. Looking to the future. *Ms.* (July/August): 55–7.

Vanek, J. 1974. Time spent in housework. *Scientific American* (November): 116–21.

Vanek, J. 1980. Household work, wage work and sexual equality. In *Women and household labor*, ed. S. F. Berk, 275–95. Beverly Hills, Calif.: Sage.

Walker, K. E. 1970. *Time-use patterns for household work related to homemaker's employment.* Washington, DC: U.S. Department of Agriculture.

Walker, K. E., and M. E. Woods. 1976. *Time use: A measure of household production of family goods and services.* Washington, DC: Center for the Family of the American Home Economic Association.

White, L. K., and D. B. Brinkerhoff. 1981. Children's work in the family: Its significance and meaning. *Journal of Marriage and the Family*, 81: 789–98.

Wilson, S. J. 1991. *Women, families, and work,* 3rd ed. Toronto: McGraw-Hill Ryerson Limited.

Wolfe,. D. 1959. Power and authority in the family. In *Studies in social power*, ed. D. Cartwright. Ann Arbor, Mich.: University of Michigan Press.

Zaretsky, E. 1982. *Capitalism, the family and personal life.* London: Pluto Press.

22

Mate Selection and Marriage Around the World

Bron B. Ingoldsby

The institution of marriage is very popular throughout the world, but how mates are chosen varies considerably from one culture to another. As Bron B. Ingoldsby shows, free-choice mate selection—common in Western countries—is not how couples have been paired with their prospective spouses in most other societies.

MATE SELECTION PROCEDURES

Historically, there have been three general approaches to choosing one's mate: marriage by capture, marriage by arrangement, and free-choice mate selection. I examine each of them in turn.

Marriage by Capture

Although it has probably never been the usual method of obtaining a wife, men have taken women by force in many times and places. This typically occurred in patriarchal societies in which women were often considered property. Often women were seized as part of the spoils of war, and other times a specific woman was forced into marriage because the man wanted her and

could not afford the brideprice or obtain the permission of her parents. The capture and marriage of a woman was legal in England until the reign of Henry VII, who made it a crime to abduct an heiress (Fielding, 1942).

The ancient Hebrews would seize wives under certain circumstances. A dramatic example is recounted in the Old Testament (Judges, chapter 21), where it was arranged for young women to be kidnapped from two different areas to serve as wives so that the tribe of Benjamin would not die out after a war that they had lost.

There was also a formal procedure for dealing with wives captured in warfare:

> When thou goest forth to war against thine enemies, and the Lord thy God hath delivered them into thine hands, and thou has taken them captive, And seest among the captives a beautiful woman, and hast a desire unto her, that thou wouldest have her to thy wife; Then thou shalt bring her home to thine house; and she shall shave her head, and pare her nails; And she shall put the raiment of her captivity from off her, and shall

Source: "Mate Selection and Marriage," by Bron B. Ingoldsby, in *Families in Multicultural Perspective,* eds. Bron B. Ingoldsby and Suzanna Smith, pp. 143–57. Copyright © 1995 Guilford Press, NY. Reprinted by permission of Guilford Press.

remain in thine house, and bewail her father and her mother a full month: and after that thou shalt go in unto her, and be her husband, and she shall be thy wife. And it shall be, if thou have no delight in her, then thou shalt let her go whither she will; but thou shalt not sell her at all for money, thou shalt not make merchandise of her, because thou has humbled her. (Deuteronomy 21: 10–14)

At least she was given time to get used to the idea and never sold into slavery! Fielding (1942) cites a number of different cultures, including the Australian aborigines, who frequently resorted to marriage by capture in the recent past. The Yanomamö of Venezuela (an Amazonian tribe) are reported (Peters, 1987) to use capture as one of their mate selection options. One village is often raided by another for the specific purpose of finding wives. If a man captures a young, attractive female, he must be careful as other men from his own village will try to steal her from him.

In the popular musical *Seven Brides for Seven Brothers,* the concept of marriage by capture is acted out, and one of the songs is based on the historical incident of the rape of the Sabine women. There are many cultures that still have remnants of the old practice of marriage by capture in their wedding ceremonies. In each of them, the match is prearranged, but the husband pretends to take his bride by force, and she feigns resistance.

One example are the Roro of New Guinea. On the wedding day, the groom's party surrounds the bride's home and acts out an assault on it. The bride attempts to run away but is caught. Then a sham battle ensues, with the bride's mother leading the way and crying at the loss of her daughter when she is taken off to the groom (Fielding, 1942).

Marriage by Arrangement

It appears that the most common method of mate selection has been by arrangement. Typically, the parents, often with the aid of certain relatives or professional matchmakers, have chosen the spouse for their child. This form of mate choice is more common when extended kin groups are strong and

important. Essentially, marriage is seen as of group, rather than individual, importance, and economics is often the driving force rather than love between the principals.

Arranged marriages have been considered especially important for the rulers of kingdoms and other nobility. Care had to be taken to preserve bloodlines, enhance wealth, and resolve political issues. It is believed, for instance, that the majority of King Solomon's 700 wives and 300 concubines were acquired for the purpose of political alliances.

Stephens (1963) identifies four major reasons that determine mate choice in societies in which marriages are arranged. The first is *price.* The groom's family may need to pay for the bride, with either money or labor. In some cultures, the situation is reversed, with the bride's family paying a dowry to the husband. In other cases, there is a direct exchange, where both families make payments to each other or simply trade women for each other's sons.

The second consideration is *social status.* That is, the reputation of the family from which the spouse for one's child will come is very important. A third determinant is any *continuous marriage arrangement.* This refers to a set pattern for mate selection, which is carried on from generation to generation. For instance, cousin marriages are preferred in many societies.

The final criteria for mate choice are *sororate and levirate* arrangements, which refer to second marriages and tend to be based on brideprice obligations. These terms are more fully explained later in the [reading]. Stephens also notes nineteen societies (including, for example, some large ones such as China and Renaissance Europe) that have practiced child betrothals or child marriages. This means that the marriage is arranged before puberty and can even be worked out before the child is born.

In addition to marriage by capture, the Yanomamö also practice variety within arranged marriages. The ideal match is between cross-cousins, and the majority of unions fall into this category. Most betrothals are made before the girl is three years of age. Men initiate these arrangements at about the time they become hunters, which is shortly after they turn fifteen. Another acceptable form of mate selection is sister exchange. Two unrelated single males wish to acquire wives and have sisters who are not promised to anyone, so they simply trade sisters (Peters, 1987).

Some societies have provided an "out" for couples who have strong personal preferences that go against the arrangement of their families. This is to permit elopement. Stephens (1963) gives this account of the Iban of Borneo:

> When a young woman is in love with a man who is not acceptable to her parents, there is an old custom called *nunghop bui,* which permits him to carry her off to his own village. She will meet him by arrangement at the waterside, and step into his boat with a paddle in her hand, and both will pull away as fast as they can. If pursued he will stop every now and then to deposit some article of value on the bank, such as a gun, a jar, or a favor for the acceptance of her family, and when he has exhausted his resources he will leave his own sword. When the pursuers observe this they cease to follow, knowing he is cleared out. As soon as he reaches his own village he tidies up the house and spreads the mats, and when his pursuers arrive he gives them food to eat and toddy to drink, and sends them home satisfied. In the meanwhile he is left in possession of his wife. (p. 200)

Following is a detailed look at some of the specific mechanisms of arranged marriages.

Brideprice. Throughout much of human history, marriage has been seen as chiefly an economic transaction. As an old German saying goes, "It is not man that marries maid, but field marries field, vineyard marries vineyard, cattle marry cattle" (Tober, 1984: 12). The purpose of a brideprice is to compensate the family of the bride for the loss of her services. It is extremely common and is indicative of the value of women in those societies. Stephens (1963) reports that Murdock's World Ethnographic Sample yields the following breakdown on marriage payments:

Brideprice—260 societies
Bride service—75 societies
Dowry—24 societies
Gift or woman exchange—31 societies
No marriage payment—152 societies

This means that in 62 percent of the world's societies, a man must pay in order to marry a woman. The price is usually paid in animals, shell money, or other valuable commodities and often exceeds one's annual income. Some cultures prefer payment in service, often many years of labor to the bride's parents, or at least permit it for suitors who cannot afford to pay in goods. One famous example from the Old Testament is that of Jacob, who labored seven years for each of Laban's two daughters, Leah and Rachel.

Dowry. The dowry appears to be an inducement for a man to marry a particular woman and therefore relieve her family of the financial burden of caring for her. Although relatively rare, it is a sign of a culture that places a low value on women. Actually, the key purpose of a dowry is probably to stabilize a marriage, because it is not given to the husband but is something that the bride brings with her into the marriage. For example, in Cyprus before the time of English influence, the expected dowry was often a house. If the husband divorced his wife or mistreated her and she left him, the dowry went with her. Like modern-day wedding gifts, or the bride's trousseau, it was an investment in the marriage and intended to reduce the chances of a breakup (Balswick, 1975).

The dowry has been around for a long time. The Babylonian code of Hammurabi (1955 B.C.E.) clearly stated that the wife's property stayed with her if her husband divorced her and passed on to her children when she died. Ancient Greece and Rome also considered the dowry to be essential in any honorable marriage (Fielding, 1942).

Recent research in the southern Indian state of Kerala (Billig, 1992) differentiates between the traditional dowry and an actual "groomprice." Groomprice is money paid by the bride's family directly to the husband to use as he sees fit. In the 1950s and 1960s, rapid population growth resulted in more younger women looking for husbands a few (average of seven) years older than themselves. This surplus of potential brides increased the value of husbands. Popular revulsion for the groomprice has resulted in a decrease in the age difference (now five years), women lowering their social status expectations for their husband or increasing their own education, and a government outlawing of the practice.

Sororate and Levirate. These terms refer to marriage practices designed to control remarriages after the death of the first spouse. In cultures that practice the sororate, a sister replaces a deceased wife. Assume that a man has paid a good brideprice for his wife but some time later she becomes ill and dies. He has lost his wife and the brideprice. Therefore, to make good on the original bargain, the parents who received the brideprice provide the man with a new wife. This new wife is an unmarried sister or other close relative of the first wife. Here we see how marriage is often more of an economic transaction than it is a personal relationship.

Much more widely practiced has been the levirate. Under this system, it is the husband who dies, and his wife must be married to a brother of the deceased man. There are various reasons for this practice. One is that the wife belonged to her husband as part of his property and as such would be inherited along with the other possessions by a near relative. Another is that it is presumed that women need someone to take care of them, and brothers-in-law (which is the meaning of the Latin word *levir*) should assume that responsibility. It has been reported that the levirate has been practiced by the New Caledonians, the Mongols, the Afghans, the Abyssinians, the Hebrews, and the Hindus, as well as certain Native American and African tribes (Fielding, 1942).

The chief reason that the Hindus and Hebrews practiced the levirate was religious and had to do with the importance of having a son in the family.

Hindu men needed a son to perform certain sacrifices, so if a man died before having one, a boy born to his former wife and brother would carry out those ceremonies in his name (Fielding, 1942).

For the Hebrews, it was also important that every man have a son, so that his name would not die out. There was a ritualized penalty for men who refused to marry their brother's widow and rear a son in his name:

And if the man like not to take his brother's wife, then let his brother's wife go up to the gate unto the elders, and say, My husband's brother refuseth to raise up unto his brother a name in Israel, he will not perform the duty of my husband's brother. Then the elders of his city shall call him, and speak unto him: and if he stand to it, and say, I like not to take her; Then shall his brother's wife come in to him in the presence of the elders, and loose his shoe from his foot, and spit in his face, and shall answer and say, So shall it be done unto that man that will not build up his brother's house. (Deuteronomy 25:7–9).

The punishment for refusing to practice the levirate used to be more severe than the above-quoted ritual. In Genesis, chapter 38, we read of Judah's son Onan and how he was killed by the Lord for refusing to impregnate his dead older brother's wife. The book of Ruth in the Old Testament is also an excellent example of how the levirate worked. It is an account of how Naomi has no more sons for her daughter-in-law Ruth to marry, so she arranges for another male relative, Boaz, to take on the responsibility.

Matchmaking. There are various ways in which two young people can be brought together. Typically, the parents of both boys and girls will work out the details among themselves and then announce it to their children. The initial go-between in Turkey has been the boy's mother, who would inspect possibilities at the public baths and then give reports to her son (Tober, 1984). The popular musical *Fiddler on the Roof* is about father-arranged marriages. Often, hired go-betweens, or matchmakers, assist in making the arrangement. They might act as intermediaries between the families or suggest potential spouses.

Checking for astrological or other religious signs and requirements could also be part of their job.

In the 1800s, bachelor pioneers in the American West would sometimes find a wife by ordering one from a mail-order catalog. Even today, many Asian families publish matrimonial want ads in search of a respectable spouse for their child (Tober, 1984). I recently found the following in the classified section of a Philippine newspaper:

Foreigner: video match a decent friendship marriage consultant office introducing a beautiful single educated Filipina view friendship to marriage.

Ladies: Australian European businessmen newly arrive in town sincerely willing to meet decent Filipina view friendship to marriage. Ambassador Hotel suite 216.

Computer dating services in the United States, Japan, and elsewhere manifest the continued utility of professional matchmaking, even in societies in which the individuals involved make the final decisions themselves. There are also magazines designed for singles that include matrimonial or relationship want ads.

There are immigrants to Western societies who are not comfortable with love-based unions and prefer to have their marriages arranged by their parents or through a mediator. It is estimated, for instance, that up to 90 percent of the marriages in the East Indian community in Edmonton, Alberta, are to some degree arranged (Jimenez, 1992). Some ethnic Indians return to the Indian subcontinent to find a spouse, whereas others allow their parents to find a match locally for them. Some place ads in newspapers such as *India Today* or *India Abroad,* which focus on desired background characteristics such as education, religion, and age. In deference to Western customs, the young people can veto any match that does not appeal to them, and a dowry is rarely accepted.

Free-Choice Mate Selection

…[L]ove gradually became the principal criterion for marriage in the Western world after the Renaissance. The shift from kinship and economic motives to personal ones in mate selection led to the conclusion that the individuals themselves, rather than their parents or others, were best qualified to make the decision. In societies in which the basic family unit is nuclear, both romantic love and free mate choice are more common. This is because extended kin groups are not important enough to see marriage as needing to be group controlled.

Even though free choice is the mate selection method of the modern United States, one should not conclude that it is the most common approach in the world. In a survey of forty societies, Stephens (1963) found only five in which completely free mate choice is permitted. An additional six allowed the young people to choose their spouse, but subject to parental approval. Twelve other cultures had a mix of arranged marriages and free-choice (usually subject to approval) unions, and the final sixteen allowed only arranged marriages.

Moreover, even free choice does not mean that one can marry anyone. All societies have marital regulations. The rule of *exogamy* declares that a person must marry outside his/her group. Typically, this means that certain relatives are unavailable as marriage partners. Exogamous rules are generally the same as the incest taboos of the society, which prohibit sexual intercourse between close blood relatives. Others go beyond that, however. In classical China, two people with the same surname could not marry even if there was no kinship relation (Hutter, 1981).

The rule of *endogamy* declares that a person must marry within his/her group. This rule applies social pressure to marry someone who is similar to oneself in important ways, including religion, race, or ethnic group; social class; and age. These factors have been found to be related to marital compatibility and are precisely the kinds of things considered by parents in arranged marriages. One reason why the divorce rate seems to be higher in free-choice societies may be that many couples ignore endogamy issues and allow romantic love to be practically the sole consideration in mate selection. There is a tendency for marriages to be fairly homogamous, however, even in free-mate-choice societies.

A final factor is *propinquity* (geographical nearness). It is, of course, impossible to marry someone who lives so far away from you that you never meet. At another level, however, this principle refers to a human tendency to be friends with people with whom it is convenient to interact. Let us say that you leave your hometown to attend college elsewhere. You left a boyfriend or girlfriend back at home and you also meet someone new at college. All other things being equal, which one will you marry? Generally, it will be the one at school simply because it is easier.

Some Examples*.* Free mate choice is on the rise in China today. However, it is very different from the courtship pattern in North America. Young people gather information about each other first and check for mutual suitability before going public with their relationship. In fact, dating follows, rather than precedes, the decision to marry. Typically, the couple knows each other for well over two years before marrying. This cautious approach is paying off, as the quality of these marriages seems to be higher than that of arranged unions (Liao & Heaton, 1992).

The Igbo are a people living in present-day Nigeria (Okonjo, 1992). About 55 percent of the Igbo have their marriages arranged, while the remaining 45 percent are in free-choice unions. Most of the latter are younger, indicating a move from arranged to free choice, which we see occurring throughout much of the world today. Regardless of type, premarital chastity is very highly valued among the Igbo.

As the Ibgo move to free mate choice based on love, their various arranged practices are falling into disfavor. Customs that are quickly disappearing include woman-to-woman marriage. In this situation, an older childless woman pays the brideprice to marry a younger female, usually a cousin.

A male mate is chosen for the "wife" to have children with, but they belong to the older female spouse, who has the legal role of "husband."

Another way of securing an heir is *father-to-daughter* marriage. If a man has no sons, he may prohibit a daughter from marrying. She has children from a male mate (not the father) but her sons are considered her father's. Women whose husbands turn out to be impotent are allowed to have a lover from whom to have children, who are considered to be the legal husband's. Other arranged practices seldom practiced anymore are the levirate and child marriages.

CRITICAL THINKING QUESTIONS

1. What four major issues influence mate choice in societies where marriages are arranged? What societal functions do the specific mechanisms of arranged marriages (such as brideprice, dowry, sororate, levirate, and matchmaking) fulfill?
2. Does marriage by free choice mean that a person can really marry *anyone?* What factors (or rules) considerably narrow the field of eligible mates in societies with free-choice mate selection?
3. What are the advantages and disadvantages of marrying for love (in free-choice societies) rather than economic or political considerations (in societies with arranged marriages)? Would marriages in North America be less likely to end in divorce if marriages were arranged?

REFERENCES

Balswick, J. 1975. The function of the dowry system in a rapidly modernizing society: The case of Cyprus. *International Journal of Sociology and the Family,* 5(2): 158–67.

Billig, M. 1992. The marriage squeeze and the rise of groom-price in India's Kerala state. *Journal of Comparative Family Studies,* 23(2): 197–216.

Fielding, W. 1942. *Strange customs of courtship and marriage.* New York: New Home Library.

The Holy Bible. King James Version.

Hutter, M. 1981. *The changing family: Comparative perspectives.* New York: Wiley.

Jimenez, M. 1992. Many Indo-Canadians follow age-old custom. *Edmonton Journal*, (July 26): B3.

Liao, C., and T. Heaton. 1992. Divorce trends and differentials in China. *Journal of Comparative Family Studies*, 23(3): 413–29.

Okonjo, K. 1992. Aspects of continuity and change in mate selection among the Igbo west of the river Niger. *Journal of Comparative Family Studies*, 23(3): 339–60.

Peters, J. 1987. Yanomamö mate selection and marriage. *Journal of Comparative Family Studies*, 18(1): 79–98.

Stephens, W. 1963. *The family in cross-cultural perspective.* New York: Holt, Rinehart & Winston.

Tober, B. 1984. *The bride: A celebration.* New York: Harry N. Abrams.

23

Sex and Temperament in Three Primitive Societies

Margaret Mead

The work of anthropologist Margaret Mead laid the foundation for much of our contemporary sociological research and debate on gender. Are "masculine" and "feminine" traits innate or learned? Do men and women differ because of nature (heredity) or nurture (socialization)? Based on her studies of three "primitive peoples" in New Guinea, Margaret Mead argues that cultural conditioning is more important than biology in shaping behaviour.

We have…considered in detail the approved personalities of each sex among three primitive peoples. We found the Arapesh—both men and women—displaying a personality that, out of our historically limited preoccupations, we would call maternal in its parental aspects, and feminine in its sexual aspects. We found men, as well as women, trained to be cooperative, unaggressive, responsive to the needs and demands of others. We found no idea that sex was a powerful driving force either for men or for women. In marked contrast to these attitudes, we found among the Mundugumor that both men and women developed as ruthless, aggressive, positively sexed individuals, with the maternal cherishing aspects of personality at a minimum. Both men and women approximated to a personality type that we in our culture would find only in an undisciplined and very violent male. Neither the Arapesh nor the Mundugumor profit by a contrast between the sexes; the Arapesh ideal is the mild, responsive man married to the mild, responsive woman; the Mundugumor ideal is the violent aggressive man married to the violent aggressive woman. In the third tribe, the Tchambuli, we found a genuine reversal of the sex attitudes of our own culture, with the woman the dominant, impersonal, managing partner, the man the less responsible and the emotionally dependent person. These three situations suggest, then, a very definite conclusion. If those

Source: From *Sex and Temperament in Three Primitive Societies*, pp. 279–88, by Margaret Mead, copyright © 1935, 1950, 1963, by Margaret Mead. Reprinted by permission of HarperCollins Publishers, Inc./ William Morrow.

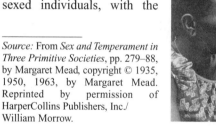

temperamental attitudes which we have traditionally regarded as feminine—such as passivity, responsiveness, and a willingness to cherish children—can so easily be set up as the masculine pattern in one tribe, and in another be outlawed for the majority of women as well as for the majority of men, we no longer have any basis for regarding such aspects of behaviour as sex-linked. And this conclusion becomes even stronger when we consider the actual reversal in Tchambuli of the position of dominance of the two sexes, in spite of the existence of formal patrilineal institutions.

The material suggests that we may say that many, if not all, of the personality traits which we have called masculine or feminine are as lightly linked to sex as are the clothing, the manners, and the form of head-dress that a society at a given period assigns to either sex. When we consider the behaviour of the typical Arapesh man or woman as contrasted with the behaviour of the typical Mundugumor man or woman, the evidence is overwhelmingly in favour of the strength of social conditioning. In no other way can we account for the almost complete uniformity with which Arapesh children develop into contented, passive, secure persons, while Mundugumor children develop as characteristically into violent, aggressive, insecure persons. Only to the impact of the whole of the integrated culture upon the growing child can we lay the formation of the contrasting types. There is no other explanation of race, or diet, or selection that can be adduced to explain them. We are forced to conclude that human nature is almost unbelievably malleable, responding accurately and contrastingly to contrasting cultural conditions. The differences between individuals who are members of different cultures, like the differences between individuals within a culture, are almost entirely to be laid to differences in conditioning, especially during early childhood, and the form of this conditioning is culturally determined. Standardized personality differences between the sexes are of this order, cultural creations to which each generation, male and female, is trained to conform. There remains, however, the problem of the origin of these socially standardized differences.

While the basic importance of social conditioning is still imperfectly recognized—not only in lay thought, but even by the scientist specifically concerned with such matters—to go beyond it and consider the possible influence of variations in hereditary equipment is a hazardous matter. The following pages will read very differently to one who has made a part of his thinking a recognition of the whole amazing mechanism of cultural conditioning—who has really accepted the fact that the same infant could be developed into a full participant in any one of these three cultures—than they will read to one who still believes that the minutiae of cultural behaviour are carried in the individual germ-plasm. If it is said, therefore, that when we have grasped the full significance of the malleability of the human organism and the preponderant importance of cultural conditioning, there are still further problems to solve, it must be remembered that these problems come *after* such a comprehension of the force of conditioning; they cannot precede it. The forces that make children born among the Arapesh grow up into typical Arapesh personalities are entirely social, and any discussion of the variations which do occur must be looked at against this social background.

With this warning firmly in mind, we can ask a further question. Granting the malleability of human nature, whence arise the differences between the standardized personalities that different cultures decree for all of their members, or which one culture decrees for the members of one sex as contrasted with the members of the opposite sex? If such differences are culturally created, as this material would most strongly suggest that they are, if the new-born child can be shaped with equal ease into an unaggressive Arapesh or an aggressive Mundugumor, why do these striking contrasts occur at all? If the clues to the different personalities decreed for men and women in Tchambuli do not lie in the physical constitution of the two sexes—an assumption that we must reject both for the Tchambuli and for our own society—where can we find the clues upon which the Tchambuli, the Arapesh, the Mundugumor, have built? Cultures are manmade, they are built of human materials; they are diverse but comparable structures within which human beings can attain full human stature. Upon what have they built their diversities?

We recognize that a homogeneous culture committed in all of its gravest institutions and slightest usages to a cooperative, unaggressive course can bend every child to that emphasis, some to a perfect accord with it, the majority to an easy acceptance, while only a few deviants fail to receive the cultural imprint. To consider such traits as aggressiveness or passivity to be sex-linked is not possible in the light of the facts. Have such traits, then, as aggressiveness or passivity, pride or humility, objectivity or a preoccupation with personal relationships, an easy response to the needs of the young and the weak or a hostility to the young and the weak, a tendency to initiate sex-relations or merely to respond to the dictates of a situation or another person's advances—have these traits any basis in temperament at all? Are they potentialities of all human temperaments that can be developed by different kinds of social conditioning and which will not appear if the necessary conditioning is absent?

When we ask this question we shift our emphasis. If we ask why an Arapesh man or an Arapesh woman shows the kind of personality that we have considered in the first section of this book, the answer is: Because of the Arapesh culture, because of the intricate, elaborate, and unfailing fashion in which a culture is able to shape each new-born child to the cultural image. And if we ask the same question about a Mundugumor man or woman, or about a Tchambuli man as compared with a Tchambuli woman, the answer is of the same kind. They display the personalities that are peculiar to the cultures in which they were born and educated. Our attention has been on the differences between Arapesh men and women as a group and Mundugumor men and women as a group. It is as if we had represented the Arapesh personality by a soft yellow, the Mundugumor by a deep red, while the Tchambuli female personality was deep orange, and that of the Tchambuli male, pale green. But if we now ask whence came the original direction in each culture, so that one now shows yellow, another red, the third orange and green by sex, then we must peer more closely. And leaning closer to the picture, it is as if behind the bright consistent yellow of the Arapesh, and the deep equally consistent red of the Mundugumor, behind the orange and green that are Tchambuli, we found in each case the delicate, just discernible outlines of the whole spectrum, differently overlaid in each case by the monotone which covers it. This spectrum is the range of individual differences which lie back of the so much more conspicuous cultural emphases, and it is to this that we must turn to find the explanation of cultural inspiration, of the source from which each culture has drawn.

There appears to be about the same range of basic temperamental variation among the Arapesh and among the Mundugumor, although the violent man is a misfit in the first society and a leader in the second. If human nature were completely homogeneous raw material, lacking specific drives and characterized by no important constitutional differences between individuals, then individuals who display personality traits so antithetical to the social pressure should not reappear in societies of such differing emphases. If the variations between individuals were to be set down to accidents in the genetic process, the same accidents should not be repeated with similar frequency in strikingly different cultures, with strongly contrasting methods of education.

But because this same relative distribution of individual differences does appear in culture after culture, in spite of the divergence between the cultures, it seems pertinent to offer a hypothesis to explain upon what basis the personalities of men and women have been differently standardized so often in the history of the human race. This hypothesis is an extension of that advanced by Ruth Benedict in her *Patterns of Culture.* Let us assume that there are definite temperamental differences between human beings which if not entirely hereditary at least are established on a hereditary base very soon after birth. (Further than this we cannot at present narrow the matter.) These differences finally embodied in the character structure of adults, then, are the clues from which culture works, selecting one temperament, or a combination of related and congruent types, as desirable, and embodying this choice in every thread of the social fabric—in the care of the young child, the games the children play, the songs the people sing, the structure of political organization, the religious observance, the art and the philosophy.

Some primitive societies have had the time and the robustness to revamp all of their institutions to fit one extreme type, and to develop educational techniques which will ensure that the majority of each generation will show a personality congruent with this extreme emphasis. Other societies have pursued a less definitive course, selecting their models not from the most extreme, most highly differentiated individuals, but from the less marked types. In such societies the approved personality is less pronounced, and the culture often contains the types of inconsistencies that many human beings display also; one institution may be adjusted to the uses of pride, another to a casual humility that is congruent neither with pride nor with inverted pride. Such societies, which have taken the more usual and less sharply defined types as models, often show also a less definitely patterned social structure. The culture of such societies may be likened to a house the decoration of which has been informed by no definite and precise taste, no exclusive emphasis upon dignity or comfort or pretentiousness or beauty, but in which a little of each effect has been included.

Alternatively, a culture may take its clues not from one temperament, but from several temperaments. But instead of mixing together into an inconsistent hotchpotch the choices and emphases of different temperaments, or blending them together into a smooth but not particularly distinguished whole, it may isolate each type by making it the basis for the approved social personality for an age-group, a sex-group, a caste-group, or an occupational group. In this way society becomes not a monotone with a few discrepant patches of an intrusive colour, but a mosaic, with different groups displaying different personality traits. Such specializations as these may be based upon any facet of human endowment—different intellectual abilities, different artistic abilities, different emotional traits. So the Samoans decree that all young people must show the personality trait of unaggressiveness and punish with opprobrium the aggressive child who displays traits regarded as appropriate only in titled middle-aged men. In societies based upon elaborate ideas of rank, members of the aristocracy will be permitted, even compelled, to display a pride, a sensitivity to insult, that would be deprecated as inappropriate in members of the plebeian class. So also in professional groups or in religious sects some temperamental traits are selected and institutionalized, and taught to each new member who enters the profession or sect. Thus the physician learns the bedside manner, which is the natural behaviour of some temperaments and the standard behaviour of the general practitioner in the medical profession; the Quaker learns at least the outward behaviour and the rudiments of meditation, the capacity for which is not necessarily an innate characteristic of many of the members of the Society of Friends.

So it is with the social personalities of the two sexes. The traits that occur in some members of each sex are specially assigned to one sex, and disallowed in the other. The history of the social definition of sex-differences is filled with such arbitrary arrangements in the intellectual and artistic field, but because of the assumed congruence between physiological sex and emotional endowment we have been less able to recognize that a similar arbitrary selection is being made among emotional traits also. We have assumed that because it is convenient for a mother to wish to care for her child, this is a trait with which women have been more generously endowed by a carefully teleological process of evolution. We have assumed that because men have hunted, an activity requiring enterprise, bravery, and initiative, they have been endowed with these useful attitudes as part of their sex-temperament.

Societies have made these assumptions both overtly and implicitly. If a society insists that warfare is the major occupation for the male sex, it is therefore insisting that all male children display bravery and pugnacity. Even if the insistence upon the differential bravery of men and women is not made articulate, the difference in occupation makes this point implicitly. When, however, a society goes further and defines men as brave and women as timorous, when men are forbidden to show fear and women are indulged in the most flagrant display of fear, a more explicit element enters in. Bravery, hatred of any weakness, of flinching before pain or danger— this attitude which is so strong a component of *some human* temperaments has been selected as the key to masculine behaviour. The easy unashamed display of fear or suffering that is congenial to a different temperament has been made the key to feminine behaviour.

Originally two variations of human temperament, a hatred of fear or willingness to display fear, they have been socially translated into inalienable aspects of the personalities of the two sexes. And to that defined sex-personality every child will be educated, if a boy, to suppress fear, if a girl, to show it. If there has been no social selection in regard to this trait, the proud temperament that is repelled by any betrayal of feeling will display itself, regardless of sex, by keeping a stiff upper lip. Without an express prohibition of such behaviour the expressive unashamed man or woman will weep, or comment upon fear or suffering. Such attitudes, strongly marked in certain temperaments, may by social selection be

standardized for everyone, or outlawed for everyone, or ignored by society, or made the exclusive and approved behaviour of one sex only.

Neither the Arapesh nor the Mundugumor have made any attitude specific for one sex. All of the energies of the culture have gone towards the creation of a single human type, regardless of class, age, or sex. There is no division into age-classes for which different motives or different moral attitudes are regarded as suitable. There is no class of seers or mediums who stand apart drawing inspiration from psychological sources not available to the majority of the people. The Mundugumor have, it is true, made one arbitrary selection, in that they recognize artistic ability only among individuals born with the cord about their necks, and firmly deny the happy exercise of artistic ability to those less unusually born. The Arapesh boy with a tinea infection has been socially selected to be a disgruntled, antisocial individual, and the society forces upon sunny cooperative children cursed with this affliction a final approximation to the behaviour appropriate to a pariah. With these two exceptions no emotional role is forced upon an individual because of birth or accident. As there is no idea of rank which declares that some are of high estate and some of low, so there is no idea of sex-difference which declares that one sex must feel differently from the other. One possible imaginative social construct, the attribution of different personalities to different members of the community classified into sex-, age-, or caste-groups, is lacking.

When we turn however to the Tchambuli, we find a situation that while bizarre in one respect, seems nevertheless more intelligible in another. The Tchambuli have at least made the point of sex-difference; they have used the obvious fact of sex as an organizing point for the formation of social personality, even though they seem to us to have reversed the normal picture. While there is reason to believe that not every Tchambuli woman is born with a dominating, organizing, administrative temperament, actively sexed and willing to initiate sex-relations, possessive, definite, robust, practical and impersonal in outlook, still most Tchambuli girls grow up to display these traits. And while there is definite evidence to show that all Tchambuli men are not, by native endowment, the delicate responsive actors of a play staged for the women's benefit, still most Tchambuli boys manifest this coquettish play-acting personality most of the time. Because the Tchambuli formulation of sex-attitudes contradicts our usual premises, we can see clearly that Tchambuli culture has arbitrarily permitted certain human traits to women, and allotted others, equally arbitrarily, to men.

CRITICAL THINKING QUESTIONS

1. How do female and male personality traits differ among the Arapesh, the Mundugumor, and the Tchambuli?
2. How does Mead explain these differences? What does she mean, for example, when she states that "human nature is unbelievably malleable to cultural conditions"?
3. Most people in North America still describe men as aggressive, strong, confident, and ambitious while characterizing women as emotional, talkative, romantic, and nurturing. Does this mean that biology is more important than environment in shaping our personality and behaviour?

24

Playing by the Rules of the Game: Women's Experiences and Perceptions of Sexual Harassment in Sport

*Vivian Krauchek and Gillian Ranson**

Gender

CLASSIC

CONTEMPORARY

CROSS-CULTURAL

In this reading, Krauchek and Ranson investigate the experiences of female athletes in the male-dominated world of elite sport. Through their interviews of female athletes, they uncover a wide variety of examples of gender harassment of female athletes by their male coaches.

This paper explores the experiences and perceptions of sexual harassment among women athletes coached by men in the male-dominated world of elite sport. Drawing on interviews with 32 female athletes, we focus on the women's own interpretations of the behaviours they encounter, and locate their experiences of sexual harassment within the broader context of gender harassment and discrimination which shapes much of their experience in sport. We consider the possibility of challenging sexual harassment in sport by changing the terms of women's participation.

*The authors would like to thank Barbara Crow, Leslie Miller, Aysan Sev'er and the CRSA reviewers for helpful comments on an earlier draft of this paper. The manuscript of this article was submitted in June 1999 and accepted in August 1999.

Source: Vivian Krauchek and Gillian Ranson. 1999. "Playing by the Rules of the Game: Women's Experiences and Perceptions of Sexual Harassment in Sport." *Canadian Review of Sociology and Anthropology,* 36(4), 585–600. Reprinted by permission of the Canadian Sociology and Anthropology Association.

Sexual harassment has now been established as not merely a personal trouble for individual women but a social problem "rooted in power dynamics" (Sev'er, 1996: 188). However, in spite of the wide variety of sites in which sexual harassment is experienced, much of the scholarly work on the subject has focussed on workplaces and educational institutions.

In this paper, our interest is in the experience of sexual harassment in an environment that has received much less attention. We report here on a study of female athletes coached by men in the male-dominated world of elite sport. Our study is strategic because of the ways coach–athlete relationships, and the sporting context in which they occur, *differ* in important ways from more conventional workplace or educational relationships and settings. First, the authority exerted by the men as coaches is, self-evidently, over women's bodies and the physical performances of those bodies. Second, while the athletes' performances take place in public, much of the "work" to achieve them is not so public. While coaches may share some accountability for their athletes' performances—the "ends" of the relationship—they are generally not accountable for what happens off the field. Brackenridge (1997) describes several features of the coach–athlete relationship that may make female athletes particularly vulnerable to sexual harassment from male coaches: the dependence of the athlete on the coach's expertise—and the heavy pressure *not* to leave the sport or drop out that is placed on highly talented athletes; the construction of coach and team members as "family" and the special intimacy of the coach–athlete relationship; the apolitical, laissez-faire attitude to inequality that makes sport "a particularly active site of social exploitation" (Brackenridge, 1997: 115). On the latter point, Canadian scholars (e.g., Hall et al., 1989; Lenskyj, 1992; Kirby, 1995; Hall, 1995, 1996) point to the general unwillingness of national sports organizations in Canada to view sexual harassment as an institutional, rather than an individual, problem.

Our particular focus on female athletes is not meant to discount the sexual harassment known to have been perpetrated by male coaches against male athletes. It is rather that, as Tomlinson and Yorganci (1997) point out, the relations of power and control that characterize all coach–athlete interactions are particularly acute when the coach is a man and the athlete—competing in male-dominated terrain—is a woman.

SEXUAL HARASSMENT IN SPORT

...Among the earliest scholarly studies of sexual harassment in sport are Lackey's (1990) survey of 264 Nebraska women college and university athletes, and Yorganci's (1993) survey of 149 female athletes in the U.K. Lackey found that at least 20% of the female athletes he surveyed identified harassment as occurring in each of three categories: profanity, intrusive physical contacts (for example, "slapping on the butt"), and demeaning language, in other words language that is "embarrassing,

derogatory, containing sexual innuendoes that male athletes are superior to females" (Lackey, 1990: 23). However, he found his respondents accepted much of the behaviour as "part of the game"; only 17% acknowledged sexual harassment as a problem. In Yorganci's study, 54% of respondents had experienced or knew of someone who had experienced demeaning language, verbal intrusion, physical contact, fondling or pressure to have sexual intercourse from their male coaches. Of these, 43% felt that the behaviour was not sexual harassment. Similar patterns have been reported by Lenskyj (1992), Kirby and Greaves (cited in Smith, 1996), Tomlinson and Yorganci (1997), and Volkwein et al. (1997).

These studies suggest that women in sport, like those studied in other contexts, are not only unwilling to take formal action against their harassers (Fitzgerald et al., 1988; Cairns, 1997; Thomas & Kitzinger, 1997); they are also unwilling to label as sexual harassment many of the behaviours that would certainly be recognized as such both in law and by researchers studying the issue. The various explanations cited for this anomalous situation centre on a recognition of the sporting world as emphatically masculine, and women's participation in it as contingent on their willingness to accept the (masculine) rules of the game.

Male dominance in sport has been demonstrated in the literature on several fronts. Barriers to women's participation in sports, historically on the grounds that it endangered their feminine physiology, have been only slowly and grudgingly removed (Messner, 1992; Hargreaves, 1994). Feminist critics point to the role of the media in sexualizing and trivializing women's athleticism (Lenskyj, 1987; Messner et al., 1993; Hargreaves, 1994; Burton-Nelson, 1994). Other studies note the absence of women in the hierarchies of authority and administration in sport (White & Brackenridge, 1985; Lenskyj, 1992; Hargreaves, 1994; Hall et al., 1989; Hall, 1995, 1996)....

ISSUES IN THE STUDY OF SEXUAL HARASSMENT

...A major problem for researchers is to decide which behaviours should be included in the definition of sexual harassment. Attempts to specify such behaviours (e.g., Fitgerald et al., 1988) have generally proposed a continuum of severity, ranging from the verbal level of sexist and offensive comments, to the more serious level of actual or attempted intercourse. But more recent work by Fitzgerald and her colleagues (Fitzgerald & Hesson-McInnis, 1989; Fitzgerald & Shullman, 1993) suggests that the continuum model over-simplifies what is a multi-dimensional construct. In particular, they draw attention to *gender* harassment as conceptually distinct from the more commonly identified forms of sexual harassment. Gender harassment is exemplified in sexist behaviour or remarks, or gender favouritism (as in the male professor clearly favouring the male students in a co-ed class). There is some dispute about whether the conceptual distinctiveness of gender harassment actually disqualifies it from inclusion in a study of sexual harassment; Gruber (1992), for example, describing his own category of sexual remarks/comments, considers that sexist comments, while contributing to a hostile environment, are not *technically* instances of sexual harassment. However, Fitzgerald and her colleagues clearly locate sexist behaviour, as well as sexually offensive behaviour, within the general category of sexual harassment behaviours known as "conditions of work" or "environment."[1] They argue that until questions about how to study sexual harassment as a *process* are resolved, "[r]esearchers should inquire about the full range of potentially sexually harassing behaviors, from gender harassment to sexual assault" (Fitzgerald & Shullman, 1993: 9).

Exactly how to conduct such inquiry raises the second methodological (and epistemological) question. Critics of much of the survey research on sexual harassment (e.g., Gruber, 1990, 1992; Arvey & Cavanaugh, 1995; Welsh & Nierobisz, 1997) suggest ways to improve surveys. But while useful in helping us to understand the incidence of particular behaviours among large populations, surveys are not always sensitive to the context in which those behaviours occur. More importantly, they are less appropriate tools for exploring individuals' own interpretations of behaviours and contexts.

We draw from the work of Fitzgerald and her colleagues, described above, the need to take account of a wide range of behaviours and contexts. We argue that, in our particular case, local "contexts" of coach–athlete interaction are part of the institutional context of masculine hegemony in sports in which sexual harassment is almost normative. This commits us to a study of sexual harassment which does not bracket off certain specific behaviours for particular attention, but which attempts to explore behaviours and perceptions of behaviours in *both* the local *and* the broader institutional context. In other words, we need to pay close attention to environment, not merely as a category of sexual harassment, but as the place in which it may be cultivated.

We also take seriously the issues related to women's recognition and acknowledgement of sexually harassing behaviours. These issues are critical if social harassment as a problem is to be effectively addressed. A stable finding in the literature, as noted above, is that women generally do *not* see sexual harassment for what it is. To ask, "Why not?" as we wish to do, clearly commits us to a study which also pays close attention to how women *do* see such behaviour, and how they themselves interpret the details and the context of their relationships.

RESEARCH DESIGN AND METHODOLOGY

Our study design is significantly shaped by the two imperatives noted above: the need to pay attention to context, and the need to hear women's own interpretations of it. Our approach was to use a semi-structured interview in which all questions were open-ended. Details of the interview guide are discussed elsewhere (Krauchek, 1999). Briefly, however, we included questions that addressed issues of power and control in the coach–athlete relationship, as well as questions relating to gender and sexuality. While not explicitly asking about sexual harassment, we provided ample opportunity for a discussion of sexually harassing behaviours to emerge. For example, we asked about the coach's coaching style, what he was like outside of sport, whether the athlete's athletic career (or her life) would have looked different had she not worked with the coach, the athlete's image of an ideal coach (and how well the coach in question measured up), whether she had ever thought of quitting (and why), how she would feel about a daughter (or a son) playing with the coach in question.

Interviews were conducted by the first author, herself an athlete who had competed at provincial, national and international levels in her sport, and whose entire sporting career had involved relationships with male coaches. Clearly this experience also informed the interview guide, and shaped "the discourse between interviewer and respondent as they try to make continuing sense of what they are saying to each other" (Mishler, 1986: 53–4). Interviews took place between March and September 1997. All were taped and transcribed verbatim....

EXPERIENCES OF SEXUAL HARASSMENT

In the context of a discussion of sexual harassment by male coaches, it is important to record that of at least some male coaches, only good things were said. Indeed, about a quarter of the women believed that in at least one of their coaches, they had gained a friend and an important figure in their lives. They spoke of some of these coaches as "father figures" whom "everybody really loved," as men to whom they would entrust their children for coaching.

But what also emerged, for about two-thirds of the women, were experiences along the range of sexually harassing behaviours from gender harassment to what Gruber (1992) would call "sexual imposition." A now-retired athlete reported the most serious incident of the study, as follows:

We were coming back on the plane, it was my second year with him, and I was sitting next to him on the plane. I was awakened by him fondling me, I kid you not, and I just kept my eyes closed and was thinking, "This cannot be happening—he cannot be doing this." His hands were all over, he was rubbing my legs and my stomach. I thought, "This can't be happening to me." So I just got up really quickly and went to the bathroom and then sat down in another seat. I guess I just never thought he would take advantage of me while I was sleeping. I trusted him.... I never thought he'd do that. That blew anything that ever happened between us and anything he ever said to me after that. I can't believe he stepped over this boundary.... I was shattered.

At the time, she took no action. More than a year later, she changed coaches. But the incident clearly sensitized her to the prevalence of sexual harassment in sport. As a coach herself now, she actively counsels the teenage girls she encounters in her sport about who to avoid on the coaching circuit, because "many coaches are male predators."

Five of the women talked about what they described as "womanizing" behaviour on the part of a coach, summed up by one of them as follows:

[A]t the banquets when he's got a bit of liquor in him he is incredibly opposite from what he always is. He's flirty and he's always touchy-feely when he's dancing with you. I don't like to dance with him..., he'll take your hand and pull you in anyways.

Though "womanizing" behaviour was described similarly by all five women, their reactions to it varied. One said, albeit with a laugh, "I would charge him." One commented that the behaviour showed a side of the coach that she was "a little sceptical or hesitant about"; it was behaviour that made her "shiver a little bit." One commented that "if someone from the outside was looking in, it might not seem appropriate. She added, however, that as long as the offending coach treated her respectfully as coach to athlete, "I don't have a problem with him." The fourth commented that her coach was "actually pretty fun to be around" even though he could sometimes "cross the line" with behaviour that's "not anything big, just a little peck on the cheek," but "somewhat inappropriate or uncharacteristic for a coach, I think." The fifth remarked that she was really "turned off" by the way a former coach "always went after the athletes on the other teams," and this was one reason why she changed coaches. Yet, asked if she would allow him to coach her daughter, she said, "Oh, yes, I think he's fine."

While all these experiences concerned behaviour that was explicitly sexual, and caused some level of discomfort for all the women concerned, none of them *spoke* of "sexual harassment" even though these were the experiences that ought to have been most likely to warrant the label. And there were some startling differences of interpretation, not only between the individual women, but also in the way individual perceptions could be clearly distinguished from how "someone from the outside" might see things. Knowing that someone else might view certain behaviours as constituting sexual harassment does not necessarily change the insider's view.

The "womanizing behaviour" examples also indicate another dimension of sexual harassment, namely that while individual women may seem to be its overt targets, observation of the behaviour by other women greatly extends its effects. This is one of the ways in which environments become "toxic" (Welsh & Nierobisz, 1997). What is further suggested here is the difficulty of separating "environment" harassment from the more serious forms of sexual intrusion or coercion which target individuals.

Much more common in the interviews, however, were experiences in the category labelled by Fitzgerald and Shullman (1993) as gender harassment, and defined as including sexist remarks and behaviour, and gender favouritism. Some of these comments related to women's bodies, and so could be seen as verging on more sexualized terrain. For example, Ann[2] reported comments about body weight being directed at women rather than men. "When the guys get bulky you don't hear a whole lot about it, but when a girl starts putting on weight…a lot is said and it's embarrassing for women because I think they beat themselves up enough about it." Nadine agreed:

Just the girls would have to go running after workout because in his words, "they were all fat." …He made little comments, "You're being lazy. You're getting fat." It was never like that for the guys, which drove me insane because there were some fat guys compared to the girls—they didn't have to run.

Traci commented:

He's always, always making little comments, like if you see somebody walk by…he'll say, "Oh, look at that," just really negative toward women in general. And then you wonder what he says about you behind your back.

Other comments and reported behaviours included a wide variety of other forms of gender harassment. For example, Ann reported being upset by her coach when, informed of her education plans, he said, "Oh, you don't want to be a doctor. You'll just be a nurse." Clare heard her coach say that "women aren't as tough as men." Sue elaborated the same basic story:

He would say, "I know women, I know athletic women, when you coach them they're going to cry, they're going to sulk, they're wimps, you have to deal with their emotional side."

Gail spoke of an incident with a swim coach before a competition:

He was doing something on the board and a bunch of us were sitting around the board looking at it and we had lots of time for warm-up, but he chose to yell in our direction, but he only said the female names, "Get in the water!" And he said it really nasty. Meanwhile there were three guys standing with us and he never said a word to them. And he was talking to us as if we were kids.

These are only a few of the very many similar stories that emerged during the interviews.

We see them as illuminating the environment in which the more serious and explicitly sexual episodes of harassment occur. Sexual harassment as a *process*, as Fitzgerald and Shullman (1993) point out, is difficult to assess. But attention to environment and context makes it much easier to understand. The woman whose coach makes her feel embarrassed because of her weight has had a different experience from the woman who watches her coach come on to other team members at a banquet. But both experiences grow out of an environment where women are degraded. And it is the behaviour labelled as gender harassment that produces that degradation on a daily basis.

THE BROADER CONTEXT: PLAYING BY MEN'S RULES

This perspective returns us to the broader context of women's participation in sports. Sexual harassment, according to the theoretical analyses outlined earlier, is a means of upholding the masculine hegemony of sport in the face of increasing participation and challenge by women. Yet even the women who do encroach on this male turf do not participate on the same terms. For heuristic purposes, we can specify three possible ideological positions for the women in the male-dominated elite sporting world of our study. They can adopt the male model of sporting participation by becoming "one of the boys"; they can, in the terms of Disch and Kane (1996), adopt the "apologetic" code of conduct that continues to affirm male supremacy by allowing themselves and other women to be "second-class citizens"; or they can challenge the rules of the game.

These positions have serious implications in terms of how women as athletes might respond, both personally and generally, to the sexual harassment of women in sport. We argue that women who resist the masculine rules of the game, and who want to compete in sport on their own terms, are most likely to challenge and confront sexual harassment in all its forms. This

is the transformative potential described earlier by Birrell and Theberge (1994). On the other hand, we see women who are "one of the boys," or who consent to second-class status, as accepting the rules of the game, and by extension unlikely to challenge sexual harassment. It is beyond the scope of our data and this paper to test these propositions, but we see them as theoretically plausible. And as a first attempt at mapping the terrain of women's resistance to, and accommodation of, sexual harassment in sport, we can certainly offer examples from the interviews of the three positions outlined above.

We begin with the "resisters"—those who challenge the rules of the game. Several comments illustrated women's resistance both to men's rules, and to men's perceptions of women as athletes. Ellen's resistance was to her coach's ideas about body weight:

> I know he doesn't think I'm lean enough. But I told him, "I don't care what you think about that"—it's bad for you to be less. He wants us to be 12% body weight.... That's where you start screwing things up. So I always say, "No, I'm never going to be that low."

...Comments representative of the position of "one of the boys," or of women as second-class athletes, were much more common in the interviews. The extent to which women become "one of the boys" is most clearly demonstrated in their talk about pain and injury. The tenet "no pain, no gain" is widely recognized to be a central ideological component of masculinist sport (Connell, 1990; Kidd, 1990; Sabo, 1994; Young et al., 1994). But our interviews suggest the extent to which elite women athletes are also prepared to "suck it up." In most cases of dealing with injury, they "worked through it," "got used to it," "learned to play with it," and "expected it." As Maureen commented, "you have to sacrifice your body" in order to compete. The interviews yielded a long list of descriptions of injuries, including shoulder strains, groin injuries, chronic back injuries, pulled hamstrings, sprained ankles among many others. Pain and injury were thoroughly normalized. According to Traci, "you take eight ibuprofen and anti-inflammatories and you run." Sue recalled staying on the field to play after pulling a hamstring: "I could hardly walk and I didn't leave. I still thought I could make a difference."

...Nowhere, however, was the articulation of women's lower status in the sporting world made more clear than in the strongly stated preferences of several women for men, rather than women, as coaches. While it must be noted that information about gender preferences was volunteered and not deliberately sought, only three of the nine women who raised the issue could see advantages to having a woman as a coach. Much more typical was Traci's comment:

I think it's awful to say it but you sort of respect male coaches more...boys especially look up to male coaches. And it's horrible but I think women do too. And that makes it a lot harder for women to be coaches, to get the same recognition and respect as a male coach does. And that's horrible. But I think a lot of people would agree with me.

Others commented that they had only experienced male coaches, and had no basis of comparison. But this only supported the view of another athlete that "it's almost ingrained in a person that the male is the coach."

Having given examples from our study of the discourse representative of the three ideological positions available to female athletes, we note that our concern is to map the ideological terrain rather than assess the relative strength of each position. In any case, individual women at different times during the interview moved across the ideological space from one position to another. That said, the fact that we heard much more accommodation than resistance has implications for the way the serious problems of sexual harassment in sport might be addressed.

IMPLICATIONS FOR CHANGE

This discussion of the broader institutional context in which our athletes and their coaches interact brings us back to the first theoretical proposition informing the study—the radical feminist claim that sexual harassment constitutes a defence of male turf against intrusion by women, and that women's entry into the male-dominated world of elite sport is conditional and on male terms. Our interviews have suggested that the athletes' experiences, which have included sexual harassment in its most inclusive sense, have occurred in a context in which they generally accept the "rules of the game." Our interviews did not produce any evidence of the specific, sexually coercive behaviour known as quid pro quo harassment. But we suggest that women's tolerance of ongoing gender and "environment" harassment as a condition of their participation in sport and because "it's just something that happens" (Thomas & Kitzinger, 1994) is a quid pro quo of a different kind.

What then of the second theoretical proposition, that women's entry into the sporting world represents resistance that brings with it the potential for transformation of the existing structures of power and control? As we have noted, not all women who do enter the world of elite sport participate on the same terms. Women who construct themselves as "one of the boys," or who acquiesce to second-class status, are unlikely to transform power relations unless the prevailing model of masculine behaviour changes also.

Recognition by men in the sports world that the model needs to change would be helpful, and educational efforts in this direction (such as the mandatory workshops now being offered by Calgary's National Sports Centre for all its athletes) are to be commended. So are initiatives like the Coaching Code of Ethics developed by the Canadian Professional Coaches Association. But while continuing to encourage these efforts, we need to acknowledge that those who are well served by the status quo, as we suggest is the case for men in sports, have little motivation to change. We should not pin all our hopes for ending sexual harassment on work with men.

Drawing on some of the findings of our study, we want to suggest that transformation of the power relations which enable sexual harassment in the sporting world could *also* be effected by changing women—but in a way that we hope might be exciting and emancipatory. We have argued earlier that the female athletes most likely to resist sexual harassment, and the model of behaviour which enables it, are those who are not willing to play by men's rules. We gave examples of women—the resisters—who seemed to want to claim their place in sport on their own terms. These were the women who spoke passionately about their love for their sport; who talked in positive terms about their strong, athletic bodies, their size and speed; who relished the hard work and the competition but who most highly valued the friendships they made on the field.

There is much to work with here—at least partly because elements of this discourse of resistance are available to women who in some situations may self-identify more readily as "one of the boys," or continue to think that female athletes "always kind of suck." Clearly what is needed here is perceptual reframing on a fairly large scale, and on (at least) two levels. The more women are able to celebrate their own sporting achievements, and win them on their own terms, the less likely they are to see themselves as inferior. And the more confidently they claim their place in this way, the less willing they will be to tolerate behaviour like sexual harassment that denigrates or impedes their performance.

CRITICAL THINKING QUESTIONS

1. How do *sexual* harassment and *gender* harassment differ?
2. In your opinion, and with reference to the article, why might female athletes be more prone to harassment than other women?
3. Review the three ways that the authors suggest female athletes can participate in male-dominated elite sports. What other options can you think of? Do you think they are viable?
4. How would you explain the fact that in some of the interviews, most female athletes preferred male coaches even though they were fully aware of their sexist attitudes and behaviours?

NOTES

1. This category is generally contrasted with quid pro quo harassment, defined as sexual cooperation that is coerced by promises of rewards or fear of punishment (Fitzgerald & Hesson-McInnis, 1989: 510).
2. Names have been changed, and other identifying details withheld, to maintain confidentiality.

REFERENCES

Arvey, R., and M. Cavanaugh. 1995. Using surveys to assess the prevalence of sexual harassment: Some methodological problems. *Journal of Social Issues,* 51(1): 39–52.

Birrell, S., and N. Theberge. 1994. Feminist resistance and transformation in sport. In *Women and sport: Interdisciplinary perspectives,* eds. D. Costa, and S. Guthrie, 361–76. Champaign, Ill.: Human Kinetics.

Brackenridge, C. 1997. 'He owned me basically...' Women's experience of sexual abuse in sport. *International Review for the Sociology of Sport,* 32(2): 115–30.

Burton-Nelson, M. 1994. *The stronger women get, the more men love football.* New York: Harcourt Brace & Co.

Cairns, K. 1997. 'Femininity' and women's silence in response to sexual harassment and coercion. In *Sexual harassment: Contemporary feminist perspectives,* eds. A. Thomas, and C. Kitzinger, 91–111. Buckingham: Open University Press.

Connell, R. W. 1990. An iron man: The body and some contradictions of hegemonic masculinity. In *Sport, men and the gender order,* eds. M. Messner and D. Sabo, 83–95. Champaign, Ill.: Human Kinetics Books.

Disch, I., and M. Kane. 1996. When a looker is really a bitch: Lis Olson, sport, and the heterosexual matrix. *Signs,* 21(2): 278–308.

Fitzgerald, L., S. Shullman, N. Bailey, M. Richards, J. Swecker, Y. Gold, M. Ormerod, and L. Weitzman. 1988. The incidence and dimensions of sexual harassment in academia and the workplace. *Journal of Vocational Behavior,* 32: 152–75.

Fitzgerald, L., and M. Hesson-McInnis. 1989. The dimensions of sexual harassment: A structural analysis. *Journal of Vocational Behavior,* 35: 308–26.

Fitzgerald, L., and S. Shullman. 1993. Sexual harassment: A research analysis and agenda for the 1990s. *Journal of Vocational Behavior,* 42: 5–27.

Gruber, J. 1990. Methodological problems and policy implications in sexual harassment/research. *Population Research and Policy Review,* 9: 235–54.

———. 1992. A typology of personal and environmental sexual harassment: Research and policy implications for the 1990s. *Sex Roles,* 26(11–12): 447–63.

Hall, M. A. 1995. Women and sport: From liberal activism to radical cultural struggle. In *Changing methods*, eds. S. Burr, and L. Code, 265–99. Peterborough, Ont.: Broadview.

———. 1996. *Feminism and sporting bodies: Essays on theory and practice.* Champaign, Ill.: Human Kinetics.

Hall, M. A., D. Cullen, and T. Slack. 1989. Organizational elites recreating themselves: The gender structure of national sports organizations. *Quest,* 41: 28–45.

Hargreaves, J. 1994. *Sporting females: Critical issues in the history and sociology of women's sport.* London: Routledge.

Kidd, B. 1990. The men's cultural centre: Sports and the dynamic of women's oppression/men's repression. In *Sport, men and the gender order,* eds. M. Messnet and D. Sabo, 31–43. Champaign, Ill.: Human Kinetics.

Kirby, S. 1995. Not in my backyard: Sexual harassment and abuse in sport. *Canadian Woman Studies,* 15(4): 58–62.

Krauchek, V. 1999. In the hands of the coach? Women's interpretations of athleticism and their relationships with men as coaches. Unpublished Master's thesis, Department of Sociology, University of Calgary.

Lackey, D. 1990. Sexual harassment in sports. *Physical Educator,* 47(2): 22–6.

Lenskyj, H. 1987. Canadian women and physical activity. In *From fair sex to feminism: Sport and the socialization of women in the industrial and post-industrial eras,* eds. J. Mangan and R. Park, 208–31. London: Frank Cass and Co. Ltd.

———. 1990. Power and play: Gender and sexuality issues in sport and physical activity. *International Review for the Sociology of Sport,* 25(3): 235–43.

———. 1992. Sexual harassment: Female athletes' experiences and coaches' responsibilities. *Sports,* 12(6): 1–5.

Messner, M. 1992. *Power at play: Sports and the problem of masculinity.* Boston: Beacon Press.

Messner, M., M. Duncan, and K. Jensen. 1993. Separating the men from the girls: The gendered language of televised sport. *Gender & Society,* 7(1): 121–37.

Mishler, E. 1986. *Research interviewing: Context and narrative.* Cambridge: Harvard University Press.

Sabo, D. 1994. Pigskin, patriarchy and pain. In *Sex, violence and power in sports,* eds. M. Messner, and D. Sabo, 82–8. Freedom, Calif.: The Crossing Press.

Sev'er, A. 1996. Mainstream neglect of sexual harassment as a social problem. *Canadian Journal of Sociology,* 21(2): 185–202.

Smith. B. 1996. Abuse prevalent in elite sport, survey indicates. *The Globe and Mail,* (July 17): A1.

Theberge, N. 1994. Toward a feminist alternative to sport as a male preserve. In *Women, sport and culture,* eds. S. Birrell, and C. Cole, 181–92. Champaign, Ill.: Human Kinetics.

Thomas, A., and C. Kitzinger. 1994. "It's just something that happens": The invisibility of sexual harassment in the workplace. *Gender, Work and Organization,* 1(3): 151–61.

———. 1997. Sexual harassment: Reviewing the field. In *Sexual harassment: Contemporary feminist perspectives,* eds. A. Thomas, and C. Kitzinger, 1–18. Buckingham: Open University Press.

Tomlinson, A., and I. Yorganci. 1997. Male coach/female athlete relations: Gender and power relations in competitive sport. *Journal of Sport and Social Issues,* 21(2): 134–55.

Volkwein, K., F. Schnell, D. Sherwood, and A. Livezey. 1997. Sexual harassment in sport: Perceptions and experiences of American female student-athletes. *International Review for the Sociology of Sport,* 32(3): 283–95.

Welsh, S., and A. Nierobisz. 1997. How prevalent is sexual harassment? A research note on measuring sexual harassment in Canada. *Canadian Journal of Sociology,* 22(4): 505–22.

White, A., and C. Brackenridge. 1985. Who rules sport? Gender divisions in the power structure of British sports organizations from 1960. *International Review for the Sociology of Sport,* 20: 1–11.

Yorganci, I. 1993. Preliminary findings from a survey of gender relationships and sexual harassment in sport. In *Body matters: Leisure images and lifestyles,* ed. C. Brackenridge, 197–203. Brighton: Leisure Studies Association.

Young, K., P. White, and B. McTeer. 1994. Body talk: Male athletes reflect on sport, injury, and pain. *Sociology of Sport Journal,* 11: 175–94.

25

Domestic Violence: A Cross-Cultural View

Elaine Leeder

Domestic violence is a global problem and occurs in both industrialized and developing countries. Elaine Leeder discusses why women and children, especially girls, experience physical abuse in locations as diverse as India, Japan, Vietnam, and Africa. This dark side of family life reflects structural inequality and cultural attitudes about gender.

FAMILY VIOLENCE IN INDIA

The Indian government and feminist organizations are concerned about wife battering, child abuse and neglect, and infanticide, which occur quite regularly there. In Chapter 5 I mentioned bride burnings in India, called "dowry deaths," which occur as a result of rising demands for the dowry given from the bride's side to the groom's family. I also briefly mentioned female infanticide. Those are extreme forms of gender violence. However, in this chapter we focus on the regular and daily patterns of domestic violence that take place in India.

Many forms of domestic violence in India occur as a result of rising industrialization and modernization. Families have rising economic expectations, and the problems are acted out at home. Wife battering is a fairly common occurrence (Rao, 1997). Mild forms of wife beating are

commonplace, and many men and women admit freely in interviews that it is justified if the woman does not "behave herself." Interestingly, though, in one study only 22 percent of the women admitted on surveys to having been beaten; it is unacceptable to admit abuse, yet it seems to be such a common practice that it is not considered worthy of mention. Only women for whom abuse is a serious or chronic problem are willing to admit it. Otherwise it is such an everyday affair that it is not considered a problem.

In rural India, women believe that alcohol and inadequate dowries provoke the abuse. Some drunken husbands beat their wives without provocation, and women who are beaten complain that the problem is exacerbated by the drunken fits of their husbands. Alcohol is widely available, as it is in the United States, and many of the men say that their drinking is due to a feeling of hopelessness caused by poverty. Their lack of options for breaking out of poverty leads them to drink to "forget their troubles."

Also, as dowry demands have escalated in the past 20 years, many parents have been unable to keep up with the inflation. Some girls are kept hostage by their in-laws in an attempt to extract larger amounts of money from the girls' parents. When those demands are not met, the young bride is beaten, often living in terror of what might become of her. Her power is also diminished in the home after she has been beaten. Sometimes "family resources are transferred away from the wife and her children to other members of the household... and the husband and wife are unable to construct a strong marital bond."

It appears that if women have male children they are less likely to be beaten. Having fulfilled societal expectations seems to provide a deterrent to abuse. A rural woman is more likely to be beaten if she has been sterilized. Sterilization is a major form of birth control in rural India; after bearing enough children, a woman often chooses it as contraception. It appears that a man feels freer to beat a woman who has been sterilized, perhaps out of fear of her infidelity.

In rural India, abuse is tolerated under certain circumstances, which include dowry problems, a wife's infidelity, her neglect of household duties, or her disobedience to her husband's dictates. Abuse is also tolerated if a husband beats his wife when he is drunk but is otherwise a good husband. But if a man batters his wife beyond levels considered tolerable for the village, or if he beats her for reasons not considered legitimate by the village, then a village elder or a local monk will intervene to stop the violence.

Finally, we should mention that living outside of marriage is not an option for an Indian woman. There are no alternatives to marriage for Indian women at this time. Although many women work outside of the home, the types of jobs available are limited, pay is quite low, and marriage is considered the norm.

Clearly, wife battering is a prevalent and "normal" family dynamic in India. It is part of the social fabric, so much so that it is not even commented on unless it is extreme. So too is child abuse.

Child abuse has occurred since time immemorial and exists across cultures. Usually it is the poorer classes who get the attention of public health and welfare services. But middle-class practices are more reflective of whether or not abuse is common in a society. In India middle-class families have experienced a greater amount of stress as the country modernizes and industrializes. India is becoming more urban, and this points to a rise in child abuse among Indian families (Segal, 1995, 219). There is intense competition and effort at upward mobility. This also puts stress on the family. In addition, there is a well-established pattern of corporal punishment in raising children. Children are socialized to obey their parents, and there is strict discipline, even though infants are highly indulged (219). The family is highly hierarchical, and now that families are moving away from the joint family, there is less support for raising children and sharing household tasks. All these factors create an environment that's ripe for an increase in child abuse rates.

The use of corporal punishment is so well entrenched in Indian society that even the middle and upper classes admit to using it. In one study of 319 highly educated, college-graduate parents in three cities in India, a full 56.9 percent reported having used "acceptable" forms of violence, while 41.9 percent engaged in "abusive" violence, and 2.9 percent admitted using "extreme" violence on their children (217). Unfortunately we have no specific studies of middle- and upper-class parents in the United States with which to compare this data. Suffice it to say that in the United States we have comparably high rates of child abuse, too (Gelles & Straus, 1986). Remember that in the United States *at least* a million children are abused a year.

Female infanticide and child neglect are also major child abuse issues in India, particularly in rural villages. Barbara Miller (1987) has spent years studying abuse in rural north India and has found significant discrimination against girl children there. There is a strong preference for sons. Boys are needed as economic assets, for farming, and for the money they send home if they move away. They are more likely to stay with their families after marriage and maintain their parents in old age. Girls move away when they marry and cannot contribute to the family upkeep. Sons bring dowries and perform rituals among the Hindus when the father dies; therefore, boys are important to the maintenance of family life, while girls are seen as a drain economically. This strong preference for sons has led to disappointment when a girl is born, withholding of medical care for girls, and preferential feeding of boy children (424).

Infanticide is the killing of a child under one year old, and is the most extreme form of child abuse. *Neonaticide* is the killing of an infant up to 24 hours old, and *feticide* is the abortion of a baby in utero, particularly when it is done as sex selection (425). After a child is 12 months old, the killing is considered a homicide. In north India, the killing of female infants is quite an old phenomenon. The British discovered it as early as 1789 and outlawed it by 1870. In some parts of India during that time, the sex ratio was 118 men to 100 women (426). Nowadays, systematic, indirect female infanticide still exists. Girls are not actively killed; they are just neglected so badly that they die from lack of care. The numbers seem to cross class and caste, with even wealthier families preferring sons. This is also true for well-educated families (427–428).

In India there is also sex-selective abortion. Although there is a lack of definitive data, anecdotal evidence indicates that it is quite widespread. One study found that in one hospital, of the 700 amniocenteses done, 250 were male and 450 were female. A full 430 of the 450 females were aborted, while all the male fetuses were brought to full term (429).

Now that I have presented this data, I urge a suspension of any ethnocentric value judgments. It is true that these figures are disturbing and certainly are contrary to Western-based humanistic values. Let's try to keep a view that is culturally relative, to understand why people would engage in such behavior. Understanding why it is

done, and being aware of one's own bias, might lead us to think of what can be done about it. There are groups working in India and through the United Nations who have declared this problem a public health issue and are trying to prevent or reduce the incidence of these practices.

WIFE BATTERING IN JAPAN

Now let's focus our lens on another part of Asia, this time Japan. In previous chapters we talked about the way the Japanese family is organized, and how unlike it is to families in the United States, even though both countries are highly industrialized. In Japan the incidence of wife battering is quite high. In one study (Yoshihama & Sorenson, 1994), a survey was done of 796 married women, in which more than three-fourths reported at least one type of violence perpetrated by a male intimate partner. This ranged from a slap to an assault with a deadly weapon, from verbal ridicule to restriction of social activities, and from incompliance with contraception to forced, violent sex. About two-thirds of the most serious physically violent incidents resulted in injury (63).

Unlike the United States, Japan has no specific laws against wife battering as a crime, and there is no governmental funding for services that address the problem. Often, if women get help, it is through services intended for other purposes, like homes established under child welfare laws. Fully one-third of the women who use other services, like shelters that protect prostitutes, were actually battered women seeking protection from their abusers (64). A husband's violence is one of the primary reasons women list when they are seeking divorce, and contrary to the myths of the quiet, passive Japanese man, violence is an integral part of family life in Japanese society.

Often, when a woman seeks to end a violent marriage, the violence does not end. This is true in the United States as well as Japan (71). Violence often escalates during the process of separation and divorce. It is as if the man does not want to let go of his property, holding tighter and becoming more abusive as he fears the loss. Male violence in Japan seems to cross all socioeconomic strata and can lead to serious consequences. Women report broken bones, lacerations requiring stitches, ruptured eardrums, and other injuries requiring medical care (72).

Domestic violence in Japan is still an unrecognized problem. There is not even a word for it in Japanese; language has been adapted from the English to refer to it (74). An increasing level of media attention is being focused on the problem at the time of the publication of this book, but the level is far below that with which we are familiar in the West. This is a problem that bears watching closely, to see how well Japan deals with a problem that many countries are starting to grapple with.

DOMESTIC VIOLENCE IN VIETNAM

The Socialist Republic of Vietnam is rich in culture, deep in religion, and ancient yet modern. It is beautiful, with pristine beaches, huge rivers, and rice paddies galore. Eighty percent of the population lives in the rural areas, and it has a 94 percent literacy rate. We in the United States think that Vietnam is a place of war, and it was, in fact, for most of the past century. In 1945 Vietnam became independent of France, fought for its freedom, and then fought against the Americans, who established their presence there after the French pulled out.

The war has had a significant impact on family life in Vietnam. With the revolution in 1945 came the first attempts to change the inferior position of women there. Laws were passed to equalize the rights, positions, and interests of women. Unfortunately, today the vestiges of Confucian ideology still linger. Men act as kings in their homes even while the women in the workforce make more money than their husbands (Quy, 1996). Women are employed in the labor market in great numbers, but still do the "second shift" that's common in the United States. After work at the factory, Vietnamese women spend five to six hours a night on housework at home. This has been called the "invisible violence" of Vietnam, because while there may not be physical violence between men and women, intimidation and fear drive the relationships (266). This inequity occurs for both urban educated and rural poor women. Many women feel that their situation is predestined, in accordance with Confucian ideology.

Then there is the "visible violence" that recently has led to a large number of divorces in Vietnam. One report indicates that as many as 87.5 percent of the divorces in 1992 were a result of violence or violence-related causes (267). There are numerous injuries and deaths related to violence in the home, although exact numbers are not available. What is known is that 17.5 percent of the deaths in Vietnam in 1992 were caused by family violence (271).

One of the reasons given for this problem is low socioeconomic status. Poor men, in particular, feel that it is permissible to take out their frustration and anger on their wives and children (268). Another reason given is the "feudal attitude": the old Confucian ideas of "thinking highly of men and slightly of women" seem to inform beliefs about hitting one's wife (268). Sometimes men take lovers, or even concubines, who come to live in the home with the wife, against the wife's will.

Other reasons for violence are drinking, gambling, adultery, and jealousy (269). Although there are no numbers available on this, the researcher conducted interviews with battered wives who attributed the abusive behavior to a few of these factors. Another reason given was what we would call the "intra-individual theory": that there is "mad blood" in the perpetrator (270). In Vietnam this means that there are people who always feel anxious and angry and tend to shift the blame onto others, especially their next of kin.

In Vietnamese law, men and women are considered equal. Violence toward wives and children is specifically prohibited and is considered a violation of human rights (272), and the government has established a series of local and state programs for intervention. There are also laws against the preference for male children, although as we will see, these have certainly not had much of an impact. Interestingly, however, the incidence of rape in Vietnam seems to be low, specifically as compared with the United States (Goodstein, 1996). The Vietnamese Women's Union plays a role at the local level, watching out for the rights of women (Johnson, 1996).

As in many parts of the world, preference for a son remains strong in Vietnam, especially in light of the family planning policy there, which recommends only two children per family (Haughton & Haughton, 1995). Payments must be made to the government should a family have more than two children, although the sanctions are not as strict as they are in neighboring China. Following the Confucian model, in Vietnam there is still the belief that a son will care for you in old age and that a son is an investment, while a daughter will leave. Even though women in Vietnam are well educated (remember, the literacy rate is 94 percent) and well integrated into the workforce, the Vietnamese still prefer male children.

Another problem related to violence in Vietnam is the trafficking in women (Barry, 1996). Vietnam's traditional values, like fate and filial piety, shape the culture and make it ripe for exploitation by the "sex work" industry. Other countries in the region, like Japan, Thailand, and Australia, have well-established sex industries that have begun moving into Vietnam as the country moves toward economic development (153). Vietnam has a history of sexual exploitation of women, most notably during the Vietnam War, when more than 500,000 women served as prostitutes to the U.S. troops (149). Many were rape victims or war widows needing to earn a living. Now many women are being forced into prostitution as part of the growing sex trade industry. Because prostitution provides immediate cash incentives for the women when other work is not available, it is becoming an increasingly viable option as the country moves toward a more westernized model of economics (153).

Vietnam, although a socialist country with some new elements of capitalism, seems to have similar domestic violence problems as other parts of the world: violence against wives, son sex-preference, and a growing sex trade. It appears that not many places in the world are free of domestic violence.

DOMESTIC VIOLENCE IN AFRICA

In Uganda, violence against one's wife is accepted as legitimate; when it is mentioned, most men just shrug and say, "It's our culture" (Doro, 1999). If a woman attacks her husband, the violence is considered criminal. The U.S. Department of State Uganda Report on Human Rights Practices for 1998 says that violence against women, including rape, is quite common. There are no specific laws against wife battering, although a law passed in 1997 provides protection for families, including wives and children. But it is hard to implement the law since law enforcement officials view the problem the way the public does, as not a problem.

Families in Uganda endure violence in silence, and violence is worse in the countryside than it is in the city (1). According to the Human Rights Report, the pattern is similar in other African countries, too. Women have few rights, neighbors don't want to get involved, and the women lie about their injuries if asked about them at medical facilities.

Several women's organizations in coalition are actively pursuing reform and holding public workshops to lobby for a revision of the Domestic Relations Act. Most of the trouble in getting anything done is related to lack of funding. Many of the countries in Africa do not have adequate funds to handle the many social problems they have, like AIDS, and they have put domestic violence issues on the back burner, because they think, after all, "It is our culture."

Other studies done in Africa are also not comprehensive. One study of domestic violence in Nigeria found that polygamy lends itself more to wife battering than do monogamous marriages (Efoghe, 1990). In this study, more polygamous marriages were violent than were monogamous marriages. Another study, of child sexual abuse in Zimbabwe, found that sexual abuse of children is not as prevalent there as it is internationally, with only about 10 percent of the population being victims of this kind of abuse (Khan, 1995). The authors of the study wonder whether this discrepancy reflects underreporting, or if sexual abuse of children is really not a big problem in Zimbabwe.

Finally, let's remember that Africa and parts of Southwest Asia perform ritual circumcision of girls. In Somalia, Kenya, the Sudan, Tanzania, Ethiopia, Egypt, Uganda, Chad, Mali, Senegal, Cameroon, Zaire, Nigeria, to name just a few, girls are cut and scraped to make their bodies more attractive and marriageable. This practice has been framed as a human rights abuse, as well as a form of child abuse that is being taken up as a problem by the United Nations and the World Health Organization.

CRITICAL THINKING QUESTIONS

1. How is domestic violence similar in India, Japan, Vietnam, and Africa? How does it differ? Also, Leeder notes that rising industrialization and modernization increase the likelihood of family violence. Why, then, is wife battering also common in industrialized countries such as Japan and the United States?

2. Why do most of the women in these countries never complain about domestic violence? What individual, legal, historical, and cultural factors help explain their silence?

3. Leeder urges the reader to suspend "any ethnocentric value judgements" about family violence. What does she mean? And, if we do

so, does this mean that the global community shouldn't interfere with a country?

REFERENCES

Barry, K. 1996. Industrialization and economic development: The costs to women. In *Vietnam women in transition,* ed. K. Barry. New York: St. Martin's Press.

Doro, M. 1999 August 4. Available on the World Wide Web at End Violence@edc-cit.org.

Efoghe, G. B. 1990. Nature and type of marriage as predictors of aggressiveness among married men in Ekpoma, Bendel State of Nigeria. *International Journal of Sociology of the Family*, 20(Spring): 67–78.

Gelles, R., and M. Straus. 1986. Societal change and change in family violence from 1975–1985 as revealed in two national surveys. *Journal of Marriage and the Family*. 48(3):465–80.

Goodstein, L. 1996. Sexual assessment in the U.S. and Vietnam: Some thoughts and questions. In *Vietnam women in transition*, ed. K. Barry. New York: St. Martin's Press.

Haughton, J., and D. Haughton. 1995. Son preference in Vietnam. *Studies in Family Planning.* 26(6): 325–38.

Johnson, M. 1996. Violence against women in the family: The U.S. and Vietnam. In. *Vietnam women in transition,* ed. K. Barry. New York: St. Martin's Press.

Khan, N. 1995. Patterns of child sexual abuse in Zimbabwe: An overview. *Zimbabwe Journal of Educational Research.* 7(2): 181–208.

Miller, B. 1987. Female infanticide and child neglect in rural North India. In *Child survival,* ed. N. Scheper-Hughes, 95–112 Dordrecht: D. Reidel Publishing Co.

Quy, L. 1996. Domestic violence in Vietnam. *Vietnam women in transition,* ed. K. Barry, 263–74. New York: St. Martin's Press.

Rao, V. 1997. Wife beating in rural south India: A qualitative and econometric analysis. *Social Science and Medicine,* 44(8): 1169–1180.

Segal, U. 1995. Child abuse by the middle class: A study of professionals in India. *Child Abuse and Neglect*, 19(2): 217–231.

Yoshihama, M., and S. Sorenson. 1994. Physical, sexual and emotional abuse by male inmates: Experiences of women in Japan. *Violence and Victims,* 9(1): 63–77.

26

Understanding Sexual Orientation

*Alfred C. Kinsey, Wardell B. Pomeroy,
and Clyde E. Martin*

In 1948, Alfred Kinsey and his colleagues published the first modern study of sexuality in the United States—and they raised plenty of eyebrows. For the first time, people began talking openly about sex, questioning many common stereotypes. Here Kinsey reports his finding that sexual orientation is not a matter of clear-cut differences between heterosexuals and homosexuals, but is better described as a continuum by which most people combine elements of both.

THE HETEROSEXUAL–HOMOSEXUAL BALANCE

Concerning patterns of sexual behavior, a great deal of the thinking done by scientists and laymen alike stems from the assumption that there are persons who are "heterosexual" and persons who are "homosexual," that these two types represent antitheses in the sexual world, and that there is only an insignificant class of "bisexuals" who occupy an intermediate position between the other groups. It is implied that every individual is innately—inherently—either heterosexual

or homosexual. It is further implied that from the time of birth one is fated to be one thing or the other, and that there is little chance for one to change his pattern in the course of a lifetime.

It is quite generally believed that one's preference for a sexual partner of one or the other sex is correlated with various physical and mental qualities, and with the total personality which makes a homosexual male or female physically, psychically, and perhaps spiritually distinct from a heterosexual individual. It is generally thought that these qualities make a homosexual person obvious and recognizable to anyone who has a sufficient understanding of such matters. Even psychiatrists discuss "the homosexual personality" and many of them

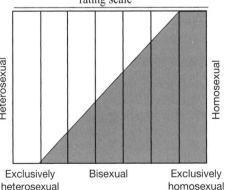

Figure 26.1 Heterosexual–homosexual rating scale

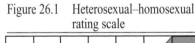

Exclusively
heterosexual

Bisexual

Exclusively
homosexual

Source: From *Sexual Behavior in the Human Male* by Alfred C. Kinsey, Wardell B. Pomeroy, and Clyde E. Martin. Philadelphia: W. B. Saunders Company, 1948, pp. 636–39.

believe that preferences for sexual partners of a particular sex are merely secondary manifestations of something that lies much deeper in the totality of that intangible which they call the personality.

It is commonly believed, for instance, that homosexual males are rarely robust physically, are uncoordinated or delicate in their movements, or perhaps graceful enough but not strong and vigorous in their physical expression. Fine skins, high-pitched voices, obvious hand movements, a feminine carriage of the hips, and peculiarities of walking gaits are supposed accompaniments of a preference for a male as a sexual partner. It is commonly believed that the homosexual male is artistically sensitive, emotionally unbalanced, temperamental to the point of being unpredictable, difficult to get along with, and undependable in meeting specific obligations. In physical characters there have been attempts to show that the homosexual male has a considerable crop of hair and less often becomes bald, has teeth which are more like those of the female, a broader pelvis, larger genitalia, and a tendency toward being fat, and that he lacks a linea alba. The homosexual male is supposed to be less interested in athletics, more often interested in music and the arts, more often engaged in such occupations as bookkeeping, dress design, window display, hairdressing, acting, radio work, nursing, religious service, and social work. The converse to all of these is supposed to represent the typical heterosexual male. Many a clinician attaches considerable weight to these things in diagnosing the basic heterosexuality or homosexuality of his patients. The characterizations are so distinct that they seem to leave little room for doubt that homosexual and heterosexual represent two very distinct types of males.…

It should be pointed out that scientific judgments on this point have been based on little more than the same sorts of impressions which the general public has had concerning homosexual persons. But before any sufficient study can be made of such possible correlations between patterns of sexual behavior and other qualities in

the individual, it is necessary to understand the incidences and frequencies of the homosexual in the population as a whole, and the relation of the homosexual activity to the rest of the sexual pattern in each individual's history.

The histories which have been available in the present study make it apparent that the heterosexuality or homosexuality of many individuals is not an all-or-none proposition. It is true that there are persons in the population whose histories are exclusively heterosexual, both in regard to their overt experience and in regard to their psychic reactions. And there are individuals in the population whose histories are exclusively homosexual, both in experience and in psychic reactions. But the record also shows that there is a considerable portion of the population whose members have combined, within their individual histories, both homosexual and heterosexual experience and/or psychic responses. There are some whose heterosexual experiences predominate, there are some whose homosexual experiences predominate, there are some who have had quite equal amounts of both types of experience [see Figure 26.1].

Some of the males who are involved in one type of relation at one period in their lives may have only the other type of relation at some later period. There may be considerable fluctuation of patterns from time to time. Some males may be involved in both heterosexual and homosexual activities within the same period of time. For instance, there are some who engage in both heterosexual and homosexual activities in the same year, or in the same month or week, or even in the same day. There are not a few individuals who engage in group activities in which they may make simultaneous contact with partners of both sexes.

Males do not represent two discrete populations, heterosexual and homosexual. The world is not to be divided into sheep and goats. Not all things are black nor all things white. It is a fundamental of taxonomy that nature rarely deals with discrete categories. Only the human mind invents categories and tries to force facts into separated pigeon-holes. The living world is a continuum in each and every one of its aspects. The sooner we learn this concerning human sexual behavior the sooner we shall reach a sound understanding of the realities of sex.

CRITICAL THINKING QUESTIONS

1. Why do you think people have long thought of heterosexuality and homosexuality as opposite and mutually exclusive (that is, only in terms of "exclusively heterosexual" or "exclusively homosexual" in the Figure 26.1 on page 170)?
2. Kinsey suggests that anyone's sexual orientation may well change over time. Do you agree? Why or why not?
3. Why do people tend to label someone with any degree of homosexual experience as a "homosexual"? (After all, we don't do the same in the case of any heterosexual experience.)

27

Streets, Strangers, and Solidarity

Tracy Nielsen

Sexuality

CLASSIC

CONTEMPORARY

CROSS-CULTURAL

Nielsen offers many important and engaging insights into the social experiences found in the lesbian subculture. By investigating lesbian interaction in public places, Nielsen reveals how lesbians build nonintimate solidarity through highly sensitive and accurate gaydar.

In New York City, my girlfriend and I were walking, holding hands, down a busy East Village sidewalk. We passed a couple of lesbians. All four of us exchanged quick (knowing) glances and subtle nods. The more femme looking one held my gaze for a prolonged moment and smiled. I remarked, jokingly, to my partner that she must have liked me. A few seconds after we passed each other, we all turned our heads to look back at each other. Being caught in the act of obvious recognition was both exhilarating and a bit embarrassing. My partner called out, "Hey, she's mine." We all laughed and then kept on our way. This passing exchange, so seemingly inconsequential that most people on the street did not notice it, created a surge of validation for four lesbians on a New York City sidewalk. In a world surrounded by heterosexual norms, complete strangers shared a moment of "queer pride."

(Fieldnotes)

Source: Reprinted by permission of the author, 2002.

As unexceptional as this incident may appear, the interactions within it are sociologically significant. The essential role of strangers in building social solidarity in cities has been greatly underestimated. Urban public places have traditionally been viewed as populated by anti-social types who care little about the fellow human beings with whom they share space.

Such an anti-urban attitude is based on a profound misunderstanding of the way urbanites operate. Studious observation of interaction between strangers reveals that, far from being interactional wastelands, public places are sites of rich and dynamic social life (Lofland, 1990). It is difficult to grasp the meaning of fleeting engagements between strangers, such as the one described above, not only because they are short lived, but also because they are so routine that they are often engaged in unconsciously. Marginalized people are necessarily more conscious of their actions than members of dominant groups. I have drawn on this heightened consciousness to illustrate the ways lesbians build nonintimate solidarity, thereby stressing the significance of stranger interaction in the urban public realm.

As an insider in the lesbian subculture, I was able to use a unique empirical method to study the interactional patterns of this group. I actively engaged in participant observation of lesbians in public places in a number of North American cities. After detecting other lesbians on the streets and sharing acknowledgment rituals with them, I stopped them to talk about what had occurred between us and asked them to take part in a survey that I had designed to encourage lesbians to think about their public realm experiences. The empirical materials for this article came from my fieldnotes on these unusual encounters, informal interviews, and completed questionnaires from 38 participants.[1]

SEXUAL IDENTITY AND URBAN SPACES

For gay people, the urban public realm is both challenging and rewarding (Gardner, 1994). In heterosexually dominated urban spaces, gay people often experience the magnified vulnerability and sense of isolation that accompany a stigmatized identity. However, like members of other minorities, when gay people connect, they are more likely to experience moments of heightened civility than people whose identities are in sync with the dominant reality.

Lesbians often possess an enhanced awareness of the presence of other gay people in public places. Interactionally, it is possible to turn this awareness to their advantage. However, lesbians must always be vigilant about the risks that accompany being "out" in a homophobic society.[2] These risks range from breaches in civility, such as staring and harassment, to more serious attacks, such as physical assault. Interesting subcultural rituals have developed over time, as lesbians negotiate the dual processes of building solidarity by recognizing and responding to each other, while dealing

with issues of trust and risk. Strategies used by lesbians revolve around the interrelated concepts of *recognition*, *acknowledgment*, and *encounters*. Signals of recognition (gaydar) and acknowledgment (lesbian interaction rituals) that pass between lesbians often lead to prolonged and more spontaneous engagement (encounters). These interactional episodes, often strategically subtle, have profound effects on the lesbian subculture.

READING STRANGERS' IDENTITIES

The public realm is the world of strangers. City life would not be possible if strangers did not categorize each other so as to define situations and to know how to act toward each other. Habitually drawing on stereotypes or typifications to categorize strangers is a ubiquitous urban phenomenon.[3] Because much of this "ordering of the urban populace" (Lofland, 1973) is automatic and relatively unproblematic, many people are unaware of the influence that these everyday categorization processes have on subsequent social actions and interactions.

Lesbians, however, can take little for granted with respect to their sexual identities. Because a lesbian identity is largely indiscernible, most strangers will assume the "default sexuality" (heterosexuality) unless a lesbian identity is clearly presented to the public world. Although most urbanites tend to have a sophisticated grasp of the diverse identities of the strangers they encounter, based, for example, on age, race, class, and occupation, many are unaware of the signals and cues that represent a lesbian identity.

It would be a mistake to assume that public realm invisibility is an objective for lesbians. The ability to "pass" as straight can be desirable for lesbians who are not out or who feel vulnerable about their sexual orientation. However, it is also common for lesbians to claim that they are troubled by the omnipresent assumption of heterosexuality and therefore to challenge it by designing their presentation of self (Goffman, 1959) towards lesbian visibility. As indicated by this Vancouver lesbian's struggle to explain her presentation of self, impression management is never simple.

I always prefer that people identify me as lesbian—to experience interaction in any other way makes me feel that I am being "accepted" based on an incorrect assumption of heterosexuality. For years I presented myself as a stereotypical dyke, accentuating every possible visual and spatial cue to ensure that I would be recognized by all members of the public. Interestingly, though, I now identify as a more femme lesbian and it rarely occurs to me that I may appear straight. Although I wear make up and have grown my hair to a considerable length, I generally take up a great deal of energy or space in many public settings. I have an open stance, very strong (I hesitate to say masculine) gait and sit most frequently with my legs apart. I also perceive my shoes to be a give-away. I always wear "comfortable" (read: masculine or male-identified) shoes.

The desire to be visible to other lesbians has resulted in an elaborate impression management system in the lesbian subculture. The signalling and receiving behaviour that takes place between gay people in the public realm has been playfully named "gaydar" by the gay/lesbian subculture. Many heterosexuals express disbelief when gay people say they can, in the words of one survey participant, "*spot the queers a mile away*."[4] Those who do think they can detect lesbians often rely on superficial stereotypes. However, lesbians are aware that reading a lesbian identity requires a more finely tuned grasp of coding signals than the presence of masculine traits on a female body. Lesbians are a diverse subculture. If lesbians relied on simplistic readings to detect other lesbians, they would overlook the majority of lesbians in public places. A survey participant discusses the complexity of the New York City subculture.

In New York, there are so many types of lesbians that gaydar is quite complicated. There are the women who wear baggy pants and oversized shirts. Then you have the ones who dress alternatively and have many piercings and tattoos. Then I also see the business/professional types. Then you have the athletic types.... Come to think of it, lesbians are just as diverse as heterosexuals.

Although gaydar is unique to the gay subculture, this concept illustrates the tentative and contingent nature of stranger interaction in general. In attempting to make sense of situations, urbanites continually test their conceptions of strangers.[5] Through expressions given and given off (Goffman, 1959), lesbians signify their identities to an audience (i.e., lesbian strangers). The presence of "surface signs" may make a lesbian take a second look at a stranger for more "subtle signs" to confirm a gaydar reading. Surface signs are those more obvious cues signifying a lesbian identity that even some outsiders can discern (e.g., very short hair, a butch appearance or public displays of affection between women). Subtle signs include those cues whose meanings are clear mainly to insiders (e.g., strong stance, lesbian insignia, or prolonged eye contact).

Strangers assess each other's roles and identities using cues based on appearance (e.g., clothing, hairstyles, and jewellery), behaviour (e.g., actions, facial expressions, and body language) and space (e.g., where they are located in the city).[6] A lesbian from New York City made the following humorous observation about appearential cues.

Sometimes I need a set of cues for my gaydar to go off. Short hair, of course, makes me think twice, especially if it is spiky, slicked back, anything butch. In NYC it can get tricky because straight women have co-opted many dyke looks. If a woman has long hair but has piercings in places other than her ears or tattoos I might think she's a dyke. The other things that make me think "hmmm" are clunky black shoes or boots, those damn rainbows, shirts that say "dyke" are pretty easy, baggy jeans hanging off someone's hips, thick black leather belts, torn clothing that looks like it was found under a rock and anything that is considered, by the outside world, as belonging to men.

Although strangers often gain first impressions from appearance cues, appearances can be deceiving. Thus, deeper cues must often be used. A Winnipeg lesbian stressed the importance of assessing behavioural cues.

I think there is more than just clothes and hair—it is a combination that includes body language. A straight woman can wear masculine attire but I have my doubts that she is gay because the *cues are broader*. For example, I have a co-worker who I am sure is a lesbian (it turns out she has a female "roommate" and they seem more involved than sharing house bills). This woman will wear stereotypical feminine clothing but her "sporty" gait makes me think she'd be more comfortable in a ball field. She seems a bit more masculine in voice, manner and body movement. To me this is a common giveaway. Straight women rarely express their body language in that way (and when they do I usually think they are bisexual or closeted).

Like all urbanites, lesbians also assess spatial cues in making lesbian identity placements. As gay/lesbian spaces become more popular as hangouts, these cues can be misleading. As a New Yorker points out:

I am more likely to assume that someone is queer if she is in a lesbian space (i.e., bar, bookstore, pride march) but in the East Village of Manhattan, I do recognize that there are many queer-friendly exceptions even within those spaces.

With the exception of very clear cues such public displays of affection (PDAs) between women, most signals of a lesbian identity are ambiguous. Perhaps for this reason, many lesbians find themselves looking beyond appearential, behavioural, and spatial cues for an attitudinal variable. A lesbian from Toronto put it this way:

I believe there are a thousand hidden cues that we give to one another that we then interpret as a feeling. But there is a feeling I get when I discover another lesbian. I am having a hard time narrowing it down.... It's a look, a feeling, a vibe that they send you that says, I see you, I recognize you. Now I don't believe in ESP so I think it must be a form of nonverbal communication, but it's hard to put my finger on exactly what it is.

All urbanites interpret signals from strangers that are so subtle that describing them is very difficult. These cues are often picked up subconsciously. Because lesbians are motivated to recognize other lesbians, they find it easier to verbalize the nature of these intangible cues. Lesbians often say that their radar picks up a "dyke energy" or "lesbian vibe." A Winnipeg lesbian expressed it

this way: "I identify women as lesbian (I admit it) based on hair, clothes, and mannerisms but also their 'essence.' Lesbians have an indescribable trait that just screams 'I'm a lesbian!'"

A critical reader might ask why lesbians are so concerned about recognizing other lesbians in public places. Although it might be tempting to dismiss gaydar as a frivolous notion, the emotional responses elicited by sighting other lesbians captures the significance of gaydar for the lesbian community. Consider these comments from survey respondents from Minneapolis, Toronto, and New York, respectively.

I feel affirmed, energized and empowered and proud of myself and the lesbians I encounter. It makes me feel that I'm not alone in the world and that I am okay.

I look for lesbians everywhere. Especially at straight functions. It's kind of a game and it makes the experience less lonely. I get thrilled to see lesbians and will work to connect with them in some manner. There is definitely a feeling I get when I discover another lesbian. It's so damn exciting!

Seeing a queer person in a crowd of strangers is like seeing a friend, even if we don't connect, I feel comforted and less alone.

If lesbians engage their "dyke spotting" abilities and invest these sightings with a heightened importance, can we conclude that the process of gaydar ends with recognition and the fleeting "warm and fuzzy" feelings that accompany spotting a "friend" in a crowd of hostile strangers?

ACKNOWLEDGING STRANGERS

The assessment of strangers' identities is, in fact, simply one step in a dynamic interactional process. Symbolic interactionists suggest that all social action stems from these initial categorizations. However, a strong urban norm dictates that strangers appear to pay little heed to each other. Goffman's (1963) concept of "civil inattention" describes the urban interaction ritual in which trust and mutual respect are routinely secured in instances of co-presence between strangers. In a quick scanning of a stranger's eyes, we assess the other's identity and in an equally quick "dimming of the lights" (looking away) we convey respect for the sacredness of the other's self.

Using gaydar can lead to situations of heightened civility where gay strangers momentarily eschew the norms of civil inattention that structure the urban world as they become more attentive to each other based on shared marginalized sexual identity. This "reciprocal responsiveness" (Couch, 1989) takes varied forms. The smallest exchanges between lesbian strangers involve ritualistic mutual acknowledgement. I refer to these actions as "acknowledgement rituals" to capture their habitual nature.

Returning to the scenario described at the beginning of the article, we find that once the four lesbians had read each other's identities, a number of actions followed. These rituals would not likely have been shared among heterosexual strangers. Six lesbian interaction rituals took place on the New York City sidewalk: prolonged eye contact, nodding, smiling, subtle checking out, brief words, and low-level flirting. These rituals have developed historically in lesbian subcultures as ways to show that recognition has occurred and to take that recognition further by displaying solidarity. A Winnipeg lesbian described a number of these rituals.

It is all in the eyes! Initially eye contact and then a subtle smile. If possible, then a longer look to figure out why I think she is or isn't. If I am with another queer person, then we play the "Is She or Isn't She?" game. If it is at all appropriate in the setting, I will engage in low-level flirting. Some lesbians of course carefully avoid any acknowledgment but those who have at least some comfort with who they are make eye contact, smile knowingly, nod hello.

Rituals of acknowledgement in public places are not unique to lesbians. Strangers often find occasion to nod or smile at each other and even to exchange brief greetings. It is the motivation behind the increased interactional civility between lesbians that is unique. In a world where lesbian identity can be problematic, strangers send signals of identity validation to each other

through mutual acknowledgment in the form of small gestures filled with amplified meaning. Certain characteristics of these rituals make them specific to the subculture as in the "Is She or Isn't She?" game described above. The persistent use of folk terms such as "the knowing smile," "the butch nod," or "the subtle check out" to describe the ways lesbians respond to each other suggests their ubiquity in the lesbian subculture.

The interactions described in the opening scenario could not have taken place without the most basic of rituals: eye contact. Mutual eye contact is "perhaps the most direct and purest reciprocity which exists anywhere" (Simmel, 1970: 301). In the simplest gestures the most profound messages are sent. It is for this reason that the eye is said to be the window to the soul.

Civil inattention is often altered when lesbians are co-present. Lesbians repeatedly state that they can detect another lesbian by the intensity of the eye contact she makes. Despite the apparent simplicity and brevity of this ritual, its message is profound and its effects in guiding social action enormous. Folk terms for this slightly longer eye contact include "the knowing look," "the prolonged glance," or "the lingering gaze." In a very short time, lasting only a second or two, lesbians convey in "the look" that a secret knowledge is shared. As a Toronto resident put it, "If you catch a woman looking at you (twice or in a cautious but lingering way—apart from the 'through you' stares of public transit) then it is a signal that you are being checked out and read as queer or whatever."

Due to its secretive nature, lesbians often describe intense or prolonged eye contact as exciting. A Winnipeg lesbian observes, "Making eye contact with dykes conjures up feeling of pleasure, delight, a sense of power that we know something about each other that maybe other people on the street don't recognize—or if they recognize it they are not part of it."

Eye contact is both a behavioural cue of recognition and an action of acknowledgment. One way that lesbians determine the accuracy of a gaydar reading is by assessing the quality and length of eye contact they receive from a stranger. In the scenario below, described by a Toronto lesbian, eye contact is the only cue available. It is such a powerful cue, however, that it is enough to solidify a gaydar reading.

My first experience recognizing a lesbian came about when I was 16 years old. A new teacher had come to our school. She dressed femmy, had a good figure and long blond hair. I was in the empty hall going through my locker when she came out of her classroom. It was just she and me in the hallway. I looked up at her and our eyes locked. And I knew, and I knew that she knew. I was almost knocked over with the surprise of it all. I started to laugh and she started to laugh and we just stood there in the hallway smiling and laughing and seeing each other. The bell rang and the hallway filled with students. So what was it? It wasn't her look or anything she wore. It wasn't situational, the high-school hallway. It was the way she looked at me. Like she knew who I was. Like we shared something. It was also wild to know this thing that I was sure no one else in the school knew. That she was willing to let herself be recognized by recognizing me. That was my first real experience with recognizing a lesbian stranger: it was strange and joyful. Later when I told my gay friends about the experience, I couldn't really explain how I knew, but I was and still am 100% certain. I knew because she told me [in the way she looked at me].

Few lesbians, I suspect, would read this story without emotion. This moment, described so lucidly, captures the essence of what gaydar means to many lesbians. Neither of the lesbians in the scenario was "out," in the full meaning of the term, and yet they shared a brief moment of solidarity that placed them outside the heterosexual norm.

Prolonged or intense eye contact seals an identity placement made through assessment of cues. Further rituals (e.g., smiling, nodding, or exchanging greetings) follow eye contact. If the situation is conducive, more spontaneous actions, such as low-level flirting, may take place.[7] These rituals of recognition and acknowledgement temporarily imbue public places with lesbian meaning. Hence, they can ease the difficulties that lesbians experience in negotiating a hetero-sexist society. Are engagements between lesbian strangers always so subtle and ritualistic?

ENCOUNTERS

Anti-urbanites view the idea of stranger interaction as an oxymoron (Lofland, 1990). The following quote sums up an attitude toward the public realm that continues to influence both the sociological imagination (Mills, 1959) and common-sense beliefs about urbanite interaction:

On the street, in the subway, on the bus [the city dweller] comes in contact with hundreds of people. But these brief incidental associations are based neither on sharing of common values nor on a co-operation for a common purpose. They are formal in the most complete sense of the term in that they are empty of content. (Spykman, 1926: 58)

Is this pessimistic conjecture a reality? Not so, according to urban ethnographers.[8] On the contrary, a moral order underlies the apparent chaos and impersonality of city streets. This "interaction order" (Goffman, 1983) is sustained differently from the morality found in primary groups. Strangers on city streets do not display the kinds of close interaction found in smaller settings; that would be impossible. Yet civil intentions can be detected between strangers, affirming the existence of a collective urban civility.

Being openly gay in public places carries a degree of risk. Despite this fact, or perhaps because of it, gay people may find more opportunities than heterosexuals to engage in encounters. Heightened civility between lesbian strangers, then, moves beyond politeness and a collective effort to sustain an orderly society. Such actions also send messages of solidarity. Once the transitory actions of mutual acknowledgement take place, openings in the norms of silence between strangers may be created where lesbians make contacts that are spontaneous and enduring in nature. These encounters range from small gestures of helping behaviour to more sustained interactions, such as making friends or romantic connections.

Lesbians often state that they are more willing to help a stranger if they perceive her to be gay. They may look for reasons to assist a woman they have tagged as lesbian in order to connect. Two lesbians, from Minneapolis and Vancouver, respectively, illustrate this point.

I always try to be extra nice to the dykes who checkout at my register (give them free stuff, talk more, flirt, etc.). There is a lot of negativity and homophobia out there, so I smile and make eye contact a lot. Sometimes I try to start conversation if it is reasonable.

I decided in my mind which of the staff at a bookstore I shopped at in Vancouver were lesbians based on which ones were more overtly friendly to me when I was buying or browsing through lesbian-themed books. When I worked in retail and lesbians (or women I assumed or suspected were lesbians) came into the store, I was much more friendly to them than to general customers.

Always aware of safety issues, lesbians are often subtle in their interactions with lesbian strangers. Although the events described below by a New Yorker do not typify normal subway riding behaviour, the incident is unexceptional. Though no words are exchanged, the meaning of the nonverbal communication is clear.

My girlfriend and I were riding the subway home, and it was fairly late. A very interesting couple sat across from us holding hands. The younger of the two was an androgynous, butchy dyke, and her girlfriend was much older and clearly femme. My girlfriend was holding my hand and we all very subtly, casually glanced at each other. They were getting off the subway at the same stop as us, and when the subway doors opened, the butchy dyke stood at the opening *holding the door* until her girlfriend, *my* girlfriend and *myself* had safely exited. The funny thing is, we would have made it through the door just fine on our own, I mean we'd definitely done it many times before…*but*, it was simply the *beauty*, and *respect* and *recognition* and *pride* of the gesture that really struck me. The subway is definitely one of the scariest places to be out, because you are surrounded by some of the scariest people in New York ya know? It was just so beautiful how this woman *without* words made such as huge statement to me and my girl, by showing concern and recognizing us.

The exchange among the four subway riders can be interpreted as a silent honouring of the boldness of being "out" in one of the cities "scariest places." In a marginalized subculture, signals of solidarity are political in nature, even when not intended as political statements. Through displays of solidarity, the subculture is strengthened and heterosexual hegemony is challenged.

Political and safety issues aside, strangers connect for the pure pleasure of engaging with fellow human beings (Lofland, 1990). Nonintimate social interaction, although qualitatively different from intimate social interaction, can be deeply satisfying. In fact, these encounters have certain advantages, not the least of which are that differences are not immediately threatening and group dynamics do not come into play. Jane Jacobs has referred to "sidewalk terms" to capture the nature of these types of social engagements. In public places, it is possible to connect with people "without unwelcome entanglements, without boredom, necessity for excuses, explanations, fears of giving offence, embarrassments respecting impositions or commitments and all such paraphernalia of obligations which accompany less limited relationships. It is possible to be on excellent sidewalk terms with people who are very different from oneself" (Jacobs, 1961: 62).

Sidewalk connections are made easily among lesbians because they share a symbolic culture that facilitates the breaking down of boundaries. A New Yorker recalls an encounter with a stranger that transformed her bus riding experience. Take notice of the way the interaction unfolded. The mutual reading of identity cues (assisted by subtle actions) was followed by acknowledgement, which led to an encounter.

I was on a city bus. It was extremely crowded with people pushing and shoving their way home. A woman sat down next to me and, although we did not initially acknowledge one another, I read her as a dyke right away. She was middle-aged, with a short haircut and style that I read as 70s feminist lesbian. I realize that I did something I often do when I see others I perceive as queer. I picked up my backpack so that the rainbow beads on the zipper were visible. Whether or not any conversation takes place, I feel a sense of connection with others when I know they've recognized a common sign. I got out my book and began reading. I noticed the woman next to me peering over at the page. Normally I'd be irritated by this, but I was interested to connect with this woman I perceived to be "family" in this straight crowd. I acknowledged her glance by looking back in a friendly way. She mentioned her surprise to see the book and said she [had known] the author long ago. We spoke about the book and about where one might buy the book and she mentioned that she hosts a poetry night at Bluestockings [a lesbian bookstore collective] once a month. We got off the bus at the same stop and went our separate ways...but, speaking with her even just briefly created a sense of connection to the community in me that stayed with me the whole day.

The fact that this episode took place in an ordinary public place is important. The creation of "free territories" in the city is a resistance tactic of marginalized people (Lyman & Scott, 1970). Lesbian territories are spaces where lesbians can interact, free from heterosexual constraints. In more restrictive times, lesbians and gays forged urban spaces in underground places such as bars (Nestle, 1997). With the advent of the gay rights movement, many lesbian spaces, such as coffee shops, bookstores, and urban neighbourhoods with large numbers of lesbians living in them, have become available (Valentine, 1995). Recently, however, the gay community, refusing to be ghettoized, has emphasized the right to be "out" in heterosexually dominated public places.

Considering the historical restriction of lesbian interaction to specified spaces, it is no surprise that interacting as lesbians in nongay public places is exciting. This strategy of being visible in public has become progressively, politically significant.

Such visibility reacts against the confined space of the "closet," which has been perhaps the most compelling metaphor for visibility and identity within gay and lesbian narratives. The closet symbolizes the space of denial, darkness, confinement. To come out depends on emerging from the spatial structures of the closet and into the public, onto the street. Therefore, the process of attaining an authentic gay identity relies on the movement from one space to another—from the closet to the street (Polchin, 1997: 386).

As lesbians struggle to express themselves freely in public places, the connection between lesbian visibility and street level solidarity continues to grow in importance. Each time lesbians engage with each other in public places, they strengthen the subculture and challenge the right of heterosexuals to dominate those spaces. These interactions infuse a lesbian reality into a society that would otherwise render lesbians invisible. The significance of gaydar and the interactions that follow, then, cannot be underestimated nor dismissed as the trivial imaginings of an elitist subculture. They are parts of the dynamic identity and community building processes that occur on city streets. As Giddens (1984) has argued, it is through the collective actions of individual social actors that structures of society are created and recreated. Indeed Goffman (1967: 91) expressed it best when he observed: "The gestures which we sometimes call empty are perhaps in fact the fullest things of all."

CRITICAL THINKING QUESTIONS

1. What is gaydar and how would a person know when they have it?
2. Nielsen suggests that lesbians often find interactions with other lesbians in a nongay public place exciting. As a budding sociologist, how would you explain such a reaction?
3. What rituals do heterosexual couples use to signal their interest in or attraction to each other? Do you believe these cues have changed over time? If so, how? If not, why not?
4. With reference to the article, discuss the quotation "The gestures which we sometimes call empty are perhaps in fact the fullest things of all."

NOTES

1. This article is drawn from my Ph.D. dissertation. For details of the methodology, theoretical outcomes, and in-depth quotations from participants see Nielsen (2002), "Streets Strangers and Solidarity: A Study of Lesbian Interaction in the Public Realm." Unpublished dissertation. University of Manitoba.
2. The word "out" is used by gays and lesbians to refer to being open (i.e., "out of the closet") about their sexual identity.

3. Outright condemnation of stereotyped thinking is unrealistic. Although it is tempting to relegate stereotyping to the rigid attitudes of prejudiced people, in reality all people must employ stereotypes to organize the kaleidoscopic flow of events around them. A more realistic approach is to confront the dual reality of these "enabling conventions" (Goffman, 1971) as both distorters of reality and doorways to social engagement.

4. Note that as part of the "gay pride" movement, gays and lesbians have re-appropriated pejorative labels such as queer, dyke, fag, and homo. By adopting these labels for their own use, the subculture has reduced their power to stigmatize.

5. Turner's (1990) concept of "role making" describes the way that social actors impose meanings on situations through the process of testing the inferences they make about others in social situations.

6. For a detailed analysis of the ways that strangers use these different types of cues (appearential, behavioural, and spatial) in making sense of the chaotic "world of strangers" see Lofland (1973).

7. For an explanation of why low-level flirting takes on ritualistic qualities in the lesbian subculture as both a gaydar cue and a recognition strategy, see Nielsen (2002). The dissertation outlines the details of these rituals and the situational variables that affect whether they take place (i.e., safety, spatial concerns, racial variables, and outness levels).

8. Urban ethnographers have steadily chipped away at the pervasive belief in the emptiness of urban interaction. See Lofland (1998) for an overview of these ethnographic studies.

REFERENCES

Couch, C. 1989. *Social processes and relationships.* New York: General Hall.

Giddens, A. 1984. *The constitution of society: Outline of the theory of structuration.* Cambridge: Polity Press.

Gardner, C. B. 1994. A family among strangers: Kinship claims among gay men in public places. In *The community of the streets,* eds. L. Lofland, and S. Cahill, 95–120. London: JAI Press Inc.

Goffman, E. 1959. *The presentation of self in everyday life.* New York: Anchor.

———. 1963. *Behavior in public places.* New York: Free Press of Glencoe.

———. 1967. *Interaction ritual.* New York: Pantheon Books.

———. 1971. *Relations in public.* New York: Basic Books.

———. 1983. The interaction order. *American Sociological Review,* 48: 1–17.

Jacobs, J. 1961. *The death and life of great American cities.* New York: Vintage Books.

Lofland, L. 1973. *A world of strangers: Order and action in urban public space.* New York: Basic Books.

———. 1990. Social interaction: Continuities and complexities in the study of nonintimate sociality. In *Sociological perspectives on social psychology,* eds. K. Cook, G. Fine, and J. House, 176–201. Boston: Allyn and Bacon.

———. 1998. *The public realm: Exploring the city's quintessential social territory.* New York: Basic Books.

Lyman, S., and M. Scott. 1970. Territoriality: A neglected sociological dimension. In *Social psychology through symbolic interactionism,* eds. G. Stone, and H. Faberman, 214–26. Massachusetts: Xerox College Publishing.

Mills, C. W. 1959. *The sociological imagination.* London: Oxford University Press.

Nestle, J. 1997. Restriction and reclamation: Lesbian bars and beaches in the 1950s. In *Queers in space: Communities, public places, resistance,* eds. G. Ingram, A. Bouthilette, and Y. Retter, 61–8. Seattle: Bay Press.

Nielsen, T. 2002. Streets, strangers and solidarity: A study of lesbian interaction in the public realm. Unpublished dissertation. Winnipeg: University of Manitoba.

Polchin, J. 1997. Having something to wear: The landscape of identity on Christopher Street. In *Queers in space: Communities, public places, resistance,* eds. G. Ingram, A. Bouthilette, and Y. Retter, 381–90. Seattle: Bay Press.

Simmel, G. 1970. On visual interaction. In *Social psychology through symbolic interactionism,* eds. G. Stone, and H. Farberman, 300–02. Massachusetts: Xerox College Publishing.

Spykman, N. 1926. A social philosophy of the city. In *The urban community: Selected papers from the proceedings of the American Sociological Society,* ed. E. Burgess. Chicago: University of Chicago Press.

Turner, R. 1990. Role-taking: Process versus conformity. In *Life as theatre: A dramaturgical sourcebook,* eds. D. Brissett, and C. Edgley, 85–100. New York: Aldine de Gruyter.

Valentine, G. 1995. Out and about: Geographies of lesbian landscapes. *International Journal of Urban and Regional Research,* 19: 96–112.

28

Revisiting the Heterosexual Presumption: How Parents Reconstruct Their Sons' Earlier Lives after Learning that They Are Gay

David Aveline

In this article, Aveline investigates how parents reconstruct their son's early experiences growing up upon learning that he is gay. To reach his conclusions, Aveline interviewed 80 parents of gay men. His research revealed a great deal about parents' retroactive perceptions of their sons' lives and how parents' erroneous interpretations reinforce society's presumption of heterosexuality.

How many gays and lesbians are there in Canada? Using Kinsey's research from the 1940s (Kinsey, Pomeroy, and Martin, 1948), many have claimed the proportion to be 10 percent of the population. More recent evidence, based on such sources as the 2003 Canadian Community Health Survey, gives a much lower estimate of 1.7%.[1] Because of the continued stigmatization of gays and lesbians, however, which leads many to remain in the closet, it is likely that the proportion is higher than this. Sociologists who study the family remain interested in sexual orientation since this stigma has an impact not only upon gays and lesbians but upon their siblings, aunts, uncles, children, and parents. With this in mind, I interviewed 80 parents of gays in the late 1990s

(Aveline, 1998) and asked them what impact having a gay son had had upon their lives.

One particular aspect I was interested in was how parents come to terms with having wrongly interpreted their son's sexual orientation in the past. Generally, a son will tell his parents he is gay, or the parents may discover this for themselves. I imagined that, because parents typically do not anticipate such news, two things might result from such an event. First, parents might feel that the future they had always imagined (weddings, daughters-in-law, grandchildren) would be forever changed. Second, they might look back at the past and realize that the reality they had always taken for granted was false. Having assumed that their sons were heterosexual, these parents would long have defined all of their sons' interests, traits, and behaviours as such. Friendships with girls in early adolescence may have been seen as budding romantic interests, moodiness may have been dismissed as "girl

Source: D. Aveline. 2005. "Revisiting the Heterosexual Presumption: How Parents Reconstruct Their Sons' Earlier Lives After Learning that They Are Gay." Unpublished Ph.D. dissertation. Published by permission.

troubles," and close male friends may have been seen as mere "buddies." Now, the new information that their sons were gay would have revealed all these assumptions to have been false.

Parents typically expect their children to be no different from others'; they expect them to reach adolescence, date, go steady, become engaged, marry, and father children like most. This automatic defining of sons' activities and interests as heterosexual is what Davies (1997) called the "heterosexual presumption." We typically attribute heterosexual interests to everyone we meet, by default; such attributions are maintained until signs meaningful to the attributors indicate otherwise. Without a perceived appearance of either homosexuality or heterosexuality, people are typically assumed to be "naturally" heterosexual and thus to conform to an assumed social order. Even if people do not consciously think of others as "heterosexuals," they are at least likely to take opposite-sex sexual or romantic interests for granted. This assumption of heteronormativity fits within what Schutz (1970) called "the natural attitude," or people's taken-for-granted assumptions about the way the world operates.

Believing that the coming-out crisis would compel parents to make sense of their false assumptions of their sons' sexual orientation in their growing years, I interviewed 80 parents of gay men and focused on two questions.[2] First, if First, if parents do reconstruct the past upon learning that their sons are gay, what, if anything, is taken as evidence of earlier homosexuality? as evidence of earlier homosexuality? Assuming that many parents might recall events and behaviours that they see as indicative of homosexuality, their recollections would likely reflect their present underlying beliefs about homosexuality and gay people in general. For example, if parents believe that gay men are typically effeminate, will they selectively focus on indicators of feminine behaviour? Assuming that parents' core beliefs about homosexuality are drawn from the wider culture, and assuming that media images and long-held beliefs about gay men are part of

that culture, what parents see as evidence may reflect those wider beliefs.

Second, how might parents come to terms with having wrongly interpreted a significant part of their sons' earlier lives? Few relationships are as close as that between parent and child, and parents often pride themselves on truly knowing the needs and struggles of their children. When sons come out as gay, parents may feel that they have not known them as well as they thought; that their sons' "true" needs had somehow not been apparent to them, their struggles had somehow been missed, and substantial parts of their lives had been carried out in secrecy. As a result, many parents might feel the need to justify their past interpretations to themselves and others for not having seen what "really was" or what "must have been." To this extent, parents may reinterpret not only the past but also the basis of their original interpretations. How they interpret the circumstances of and reasons for their wrong interpretations may in turn reflect the ways in which they operate under the heterosexual presumption.

WHAT THE PARENTS RECALLED

In recalling their gay sons' growing-up years, parents did not pinpoint any particular trait as an indicator of homosexuality; nevertheless, they felt that there was something that set their sons apart from other boys. The single most commonly reported indicator was "difference"; 15 parents (18.8%) used the word "different" when initially describing their sons in their growing years. They were different from their brothers, different from other boys in the neighbourhood, different from average boys, or simply different. None of the parents said that they had associated this difference with homosexuality at the time, and two even mentioned specifically that this had never occurred to them. Several parents, however, did say that they now realized what this difference "really meant," considering their sons' newly disclosed sexual orientation.

Thirty parents (37.5%) named traits and behaviours they thought were atypical of boys. Sons were "gentle," "sensitive," and "tender." Others were "musically inclined," "fashion conscious," and "into theatre." Still others were "neat," "organized," and accomplished cooks. Despite any wider societal associations of such things with femininity, these parents readily defended their sons' behaviours as being within the bounds of gender normativity. They said that they originally saw their sons' atypical gender behaviour as compatible with perceived recent trends toward less rigid gender roles, implying that in modern times boys need not necessarily be restricted to traditional roles. Sensitivity, one mother suggested, was a desirable masculine trait.

When parents mentioned their sons' early relationships with girls, they described them either as too close or as not close enough. Eleven parents (13.8%) said that their sons gravitated too intensely toward girls as children, or that their best friends were always girls. These parents and others saw their sons as having been, in contrast, too distant from girls later on in life. Nineteen parents (23.8%) referred to their sons' teenage and young-adult dating habits, seeing their sons as having been unwilling to commit themselves, awkward, or entirely disinterested.

Relationships with boys or men were also seen as having been too close or not close enough. Three parents whose sons disclosed their sexual identities as adults mentioned that their sons had always shared houses or apartments with other men, and that the arrangements had appeared too domestic or too intimate. One father, for example, mentioned that his son had bought a house with another man and that their house was tastefully decorated with antiques. He added that he had not "realized" until much later what this arrangement "really meant." In contrast, parents who said that their sons had not been close enough to boys—implying that they had failed to bond with them properly as peers—not only implied this in saying that they were too close to girls, but discussed the matter almost entirely in terms of their sons' participation or interest in sports.

Major sports such as hockey, basketball, and baseball have long been thought of as arenas of male bonding. As a result, parents have long encouraged their sons to participate. Perhaps also as a result, participation or interest in sports has often been considered part and parcel of a male heterosexual persona and thus essential to heterosexual development (Young, 1995). It is therefore not surprising that sports came up often in the parents' stories. Twenty parents (25%) mentioned sports of one kind or another, reporting that their sons were not interested in or simply disliked them altogether. Still, they defended their sons' dislike of sports on the grounds that the boys had other interests, were too busy with other things, or were overly shy.

HOW THE PARENTS RECALLED THE PAST

How people come to terms with what they originally thought versus what they "now know" suggests another level of interpretation of what led them to the original interpretation in question. Not only might people reinterpret past events for what they "really meant"; they might also reinterpret the reasons that had led them to think of those events in particular ways at the time they took place. This suggests two levels of reinterpretation: (a) one of what past events "really meant," and (b) one of why events were interpreted as they were when they occurred.

Virtually all parents recounted events, traits, or behaviours from their sons' growing years. Although some gave only simple descriptions, the majority either offered second-level interpretations of what they thought at the time or implied such interpretations in their words. An examination of their stories yielded three broad types of second-level interpretations: (a) *revelations,* or "I never noticed until now"; (b) *confirmations,* or "So! I was right"; and (c) *justifications,* or "How could I have known?"

Revelations were interpretations that focused on particular past events, suggesting that their "true meanings" had either been missed or misinterpreted at the time. This was apparent when parents related incidents that they thought in retrospect were obvious indicators of their sons' sexual orientation and said that they had missed interpreting them as such or that they had interpreted them in some other way. One mother, for example, had believed that her son had stopped dating because of bad experiences with girls. Once she knew that her son was gay, however, she revisited that time and reinterpreted it accordingly. Parents relating such stories not only said that they had had "blinders on" or had been "in denial," but called themselves "dumb," "innocent," or simply uninformed. These explanations appeared to be given as reasons why they had been unable, at the time, to see what "must have been." Second were confirmations: Parents related incidents that, to them, were either obvious indicators of earlier homosexuality or raised questions about it. Once these parents learned that their sons were gay, those incidents became confirmed in their minds as true indicators of earlier homosexuality. One father, for example, said he had always wondered why his son was reluctant to shower after swimming practice. Once he knew that his son was gay, he "realized" that this was an indicator of developing homosexuality. Confirmations differ from revelations in that, in the former case, parents claimed that their original interpretations had been correct and that they had either noted them at the time or suspended them pending further evidence.

Justifications differ from both revelations and confirmations in that parents gave reasons as to why they had not seen past events as indicators of their sons' early homosexuality. The justifications that parents offered for their "oversights" were either internal, i.e., failings within themselves, or external, i.e., failures within organizations or society itself. In the case of internal justifications, parents most commonly said that such things as their sons' frequent dating, interest in sports, or, simply, appearance of masculinity threw them off the track. Other parents cited what they defined as their own ignorance or lack of

perceptiveness. Parents citing external justifications referred either to their church's failure to talk about homosexuality or to the fact that homosexuality was simply not discussed in their own growing years, or they blamed society in general for its failure to prepare parents for having gay sons. Several parents said that because they had been very religious they had taken for granted the church's teachings that life is laid out like a plan for those who believe in God. Their religiosity, they suggested, had prevented them from thinking about life in any way other than in terms of the accepted heterosexual family cycle.

Whether revelations, confirmations, or justifications, the parents' second-level interpretations typically appeared to accompany or were implicit in their recollections of past occurrences. It was apparent that the parents felt a need to interpret their own interpretations of the past so as to come to terms with it.

CULTURAL PARADIGMS FOR INTERPRETING HOMOSEXUALITY

It is ironic that little reported evidence of early homosexuality in sons came from actual homosexual behaviour. One mother who overheard her son talking on the telephone about dating another boy, and another who recalled her son talking about a boy he met at camp "as a girl would talk about a boyfriend," are notable exceptions. Although actual homosexual behaviour—i.e., sexual activity or same-sex dating—might be strong evidence of a homosexual orientation, it is unlikely that parents in general would observe it directly or define it as such if they did, especially in their sons' earlier growing years. Not only might same-sex sexual activity before puberty be dismissed as mere experimentation, but gay identities are rarely crystallized at such a young age; thus, such activity would likely not be linked to sexual orientation. Later on, according to the Central Toronto Youth Services (Schneider, 1989), gay adolescents often do what they can to conceal their sexual and romantic activities from their parents. With little "true" evidence of homosexuality, the question remains of what, if anything, can be taken as evidence of earlier homosexuality by parents attempting to make sense of the past.

If the past may be looked upon as a mine of information that may be used for sense-making in the present, then atypical gender behaviour is the ore that the parents mined. Boys typically like sports; their sons did not. Boys typically choose other boys as playmates; their sons preferred the company of girls. Boys are typically aggressive and assertive; their sons were sensitive and artistic. Their sons "must have been" homosexual in their growing years not because they engaged in homosexual behaviour nor because they felt as though they were gay, but because they did not act like typical boys. Atypical gender behaviour, to these parents, foreshadowed later homosexuality.

One might ask why retrospective indicators of homosexuality came overwhelmingly from atypical gender behaviour. One answer surely lies in western cultural history, in which an ingrained cultural script links feminine behaviour and male homosexuality. Because heterosexuality involves two sexes, it is characterized by morphological and gender-rooted differences thought to complement each other. As homosexuality involves only one sex, differences considered an inextricable part of sexual relations elude those trying to make sense of it in those terms. As a result, the differences rooted in heterosexuality are often projected onto homosexual relationships; femininity and passivity in one partner are thus thought of as a necessity. In this respect, assumptions of heteronormativity are generalized even to homosexuality: Heterosexuality involves two sexes; homosexuality must, therefore, somehow involve compensatory differences.

Perhaps as a result, cultural constructions of the feminine male homosexual are pervasive. Effeminate gay men have been portrayed in media and folklore—often to the exclusion of more masculine representations (Russo, 1981), and the notion of their prevalence was even given early scientific legitimacy (West, 1955), rooting such images still deeper in culture. It is therefore not surprising that atypical gender behaviour in the form of femininity would be noticed by parents and conflated with homosexuality. To the extent that parents were motivated to make sense of their sons' growing years, they seemed to focus upon evidence available to them, and that evidence was drawn from culture. If a culture reinforces the link between feminine male behaviour and male homosexuality, then the two will indicate each other reflexively. It is this reflexivity the parents invoked in their efforts to make sense of their sons' growing years.

Even though these parents adduced much atypical gender behaviour as evidence of their sons' developing homosexuality, one must be cautious about concluding that such an association exists. Boys who turn out to be heterosexual may also exhibit traits such as sensitivity or a gentle nature, and they may also be equally uninterested in hockey or basketball. Because heterosexuality is not stigmatized, however, parents would have no need to make sense of such traits in terms of their relationship to sexual orientation; thus, these traits would more likely be taken at face value. On the other hand, because effeminacy has been built up as a cultural indicator of homosexuality, it is far more likely to be noticed among gay men.

Canada has come a long way in its outlook on sexual orientation. It now extends marriage benefits to gays and lesbians in seven provinces and one territory, and will likely do so in all in the near future. With such benefits come an eventual lessening of stigma and an opportunity for other Canadians to see how gays, lesbians, and their families live. What will this do to society's heterosexual presumption? Canadians are now aware enough of religious diversity to not assume that everyone is Christian. Will they eventually become aware enough of sexual orientation to not assume that everyone is—or that their sons and daughters will automatically grow up to be—heterosexual?

CRITICAL THINKING QUESTIONS

1. As a sociologist, how would you explain the predominance of the *heterosexual presumption?*
2. Were you surprised to find out that parents often reinterpreted their son's early behaviours and experiences with sexuality once they found out he was gay? Why?
3. Do you agree with Aveline's suggestion that as Canada's laws continue to expand the rights of gays, the presumption of heterosexuality will decrease? Discuss.

NOTES

1. The 2003 Canadian Community Health Survey of 135 000 Canadians, which included a question on sexual orientation, found that 1.0% considered themselves homosexual and 0.7% considered themselves bisexual. The proportion of homosexual and bisexual respondents was highest in Quebec and lowest in Alberta and Saskatchewan. (For a summary of this survey, see **www.statcan.ca/Daily/English/040615/d040615b.htm**).

2. This research was part of a larger project, funded by the Social Science Research Council, that investigated the lives and concerns of parents of gay men. Subject interviews were audiotaped, transcribed, and analyzed for their recurring themes. For a larger discussion of the method, see Aveline (1998).

REFERENCES

Aveline, D. 1998. "My son, my son!" How parents adapt to having a gay son. Ph.D. dissertation, Indiana University.

Davies, P. 1997. The role of disclosure in coming out among gay men. In *Modern Homosexualities,* eds. K. Plummer. New York, NY: Routledge, 75–83.

Kinsey, A., E.B. Pomeroy, and C.F. Martin. 1948. *Sexual behavior in the human male.* Philadelphia: W. B. Saunders.

Russo, V. 1981. *The celluloid closet.* New York: Harper & Row.

Schneider, M. 1988. *Often invisible: Counselling gay and lesbian youth.* Toronto: Central Toronto Youth Services.

Schutz, A. 1970. *On phenomenology and social relations.* Chicago: University of Chicago Press.

West, D. 1955. *Homosexuality.* London: Penguin Books.

Young, P. D. 1994. *Lesbians and gays and sports.* New York: Chelsea House Publishers.

HELPFUL WEBSITES

PFLAG: Canadian Chapter of Parents and Friends of Lesbians and Gays **www.pflagcanada.ca**

PRIDENET: A resource guide of gay, lesbian, bisexual, and transgendered persons in Canada **www.pridenet.com/canada. html**

EGALE: A Canadian national organization for gay, lesbian, bisexual, and transgendered people **www.cglcc.ca/news_JIBPride1911 04.asp**

29

Homosexual Behavior in Cross-Cultural Perspective

*J. M. Carrier**

Although sexuality is a biological process, the meaning of sexuality is culturally variable. Carrier shows that attitudes toward homosexuality are far from uniform around the world. Some societies are quite accommodating about sexual practices that other societies punish harshly.

The available cross-cultural data clearly show that the ways in which individuals organize their sexual behavior vary considerably between societies (Westermarck, 1908; Ford & Beach, 1951; Broude & Greene, 1976). Although biological and psychological factors help explain variations of sexual behavior between individuals within a given society, intercultural variations in patterns of human sexual behavior are mainly related to social and cultural differences occurring between societies around the world. The purpose of this chapter is to consider what kinds of variations in homosexual behavior occur between societies, and to determine which sociocultural factors appear to account for the variance of the behavior cross-culturally.[1]

*The author is particularly indebted to Evelyn Hooker for her invaluable comments and criticism; and to the Gender Identity Research Group at UCLA for an early critique of the ideas presented in this paper.

THE CROSS-CULTURAL DATA

Data available on homosexual behavior in most of the world's societies, past or present, are meager. Much is known about the dominant middle-class white populations of the United States, England, and northern European countries where most scientific research on human sexual behavior has been done, but very little is known about homosexual behavior in the rest of the world. The lack of knowledge stems from the irrational fear and prejudice surrounding the study of human sexual behavior, and from the difficulties associated with the collection of information on a topic that is so personal and highly regulated in most societies.

Most of the cross-cultural information on sexual behavior has been gathered by Western anthropologists. The quality of the information collected and published, however, varies considerably. Based on a survey of the literature, Marshall and Suggs (1971) report that: "Sexual behavior is occasionally touched upon in anthropological publications but is seldom the topic of either articles or monographs by anthropologists." Broude and Greene (1976), after coding the sexual attitudes and practices in 186 societies using the Human Relations Area Files, note:[2]

> ...information of any sort on sexual habits and beliefs is hard to come by.... [W]hen data do exist concerning sexual attitudes and practices, they are often sketchy and vague; what is more, such information is usually suspect in terms of its reliability, either because of distortions on the part of the subjects or because of biases introduced by the ethnographer....

Cross-cultural data on homosexual behavior is further complicated by the prejudice of many observers who consider the behavior unnatural, dysfunctional, or associated with mental illness, and by the fact that in many of the societies studied the behavior is stigmatized and thus not usually carried out openly. Under these circumstances, the behavior is not easily talked about. At the turn of the twentieth century such adjectives as disgusting, vile, and detestable were still being used to describe homosexual behavior; and even in the mid-1930s some anthropologists continued to view the behavior as unnatural. In discussing sodomy with some of his New Guinea informants, Williams (1936), for example, asked them if they "had ever been subjected to an unnatural practice." With the acceptance of the view in the mid-1930s that homosexual behavior should be classified as a mental illness (or at best dysfunctional), many anthropologists replaced "unnatural" with the medical model. This model still finds adherents among researchers at present, especially those in the branch of anthropology referred to as psychological anthropology.

Because of the prejudice with which many researchers and observers approached the subject, statements about the reported absence of homosexual behavior, or the limited extent of the behavior where reported, should be viewed with some skepticism. Mead (1961) suggests that statements of this kind "can only be accepted with the greatest caution and with very careful analysis of the personality and training of the investigator." She further notes that: "Denials of a practice cannot be regarded as meaningful if that practice is verbally recognized among a given people, even though a strong taboo exists against it."

This chapter will mainly utilize the published research findings of empirical studies which have considered homosexual behavior in some detail. It will examine homosexual behavior in preliterate, peasant, and complex modern societies in all the major geographical regions of the world.[3] Where necessary, these findings will be supplemented with information found in accounts given by travelers, missionaries, and novelists.

SOCIOCULTURAL FACTORS

A number of sociocultural factors help explain variations of homosexual behavior between societies. Two of the most important are cultural attitudes and proscriptions related to cross-gender behavior, and availability of sexual partners.[4] The latter is in turn related to such variables as segregation of sexes prior to marriage, expectations with respect to virginity, age at marriage, and available economic resources and/or distribution of income.

Cross-Gender and Homosexual Behavior

Different expectations for male persons as opposed to female persons are culturally elaborated from birth onward in every known society. Although behavioral boundaries between the sexes may vary culturally, male persons are clearly differentiated from female persons; and progeny is assured by normative societal rules which correlate male and female gender roles with sexual behavior, marriage, and the family. There is a general expectation in every society that a majority of adult men and women will cohabit and produce the next generation. Social pressure is thus applied in the direction of marriage. The general rule is that one should not remain single.

The cross-cultural data on human sexual behavior suggest that a significant relationship exists between much of the homosexual behavior reported cross culturally and the continuing need of societies to deal with cross-gender behavior. Feminine male behavior, and the set of anxieties associated with its occurrence in the male part of the population, appears to have brought about more elaborate cultural responses temporally and spatially than has masculine female behavior. There are no doubt many reasons why this is so, but it appears to be related in general to the higher status accorded men than women in most societies; and, in particular, to the defense role that men have historically played in protecting women and children from outsiders.

Societies in which homosexual behavior can be linked to cultural responses to cross-gender behavior may be categorized according to the type of response made. Three major cultural types have been identified: those societies which make a basic accommodation to cross-gender behavior, those societies which outlaw the behavior as scandalous and/or criminal, and those societies which neither make an accommodation to such behavior nor outlaw it but instead have a cultural formulation which tries to ensure that cross-gender behavior does not occur.

Accommodating Societies

Societies making an accommodation to cross-gender behavior in one form or another have been reported in many different parts of the world. Munroe et al. (1969), for example, put together a list of societies having what they call "institutionalized male transvestism...the permanent adoption by males of aspects of female dress and/or behavior in accordance with customary expectations within a given society." Their list includes Indian societies in North and South America, island societies in Polynesia and Southeast Asia, and preliterate and peasant societies in mainland Asia and Africa. Although reported for both sexes, male cross-gender behavior appears in the literature more often than female.

A folk belief exists in some of these societies that in every generation a certain number of individuals will play the gender role of the opposite sex, usually beginning at or prior to puberty and often identified at a very early age. The Mohave Indians of the American Southwest, for example, used to hold the following belief—typical of many Indian societies in North America—about cross-gender behavior of both sexes:

> Ever since the world began at the magic mountain...it was said that there would be transvestites. In the beginning, if they were to become transvestites, the process started during their intrauterine life. When they grew up they were given toys according to their sex. They did not like these toys however. (Devereux, 1937)

In southern Mexico one group of Zapotec Indians believes that "effeminate males" are born not made: "Typical comments include: But what can we do; he was born that way; he is like God made him. A related belief also exists that...it is a thing of the blood" (Royce, 1973). In Tahiti, the belief exists that there is at least one cross-gender behaving male, called a *mahu* in all villages: "When one dies then another substitutes.... God arranges it like this. It isn't allowed (that there should be) two *mahu* in one place" (Levy, 1973).

Cross-gender behavior is accepted in other societies because it is believed that some supernatural event makes people that way prior to birth, or that the behavior is acquired through some mystical force or dream after birth. In India, for example, the following belief exists about the *Hijadas,* cross-gender behaving males thought to be impotent at birth who later have their genitals removed:

> When we ask a *Hijada* or an ordinary man in Gujarat "Why does a man become a *Hijada*?" the usual reply is "One does not become a *Hijada* by one's own will; it is only by the command of the *mata* that one becomes a *Hijada*." The same idea is found in a myth about the origin of the *Hijadas.* It is said that one receives the *mata's* command either in dreams or when one sits in meditation before her image. (Shah, 1961)

Among the Chukchee of northeastern Asia, a role reversal was accepted because of an unusual dream or vision:

Transformation takes place by the command of the *ka'let* (spirits) usually at the critical age of early youth when shamanistic inspiration first manifests itself. (Bogores, 1904)

Among the Lango in Africa:

A number of Lango men dress as women, simulate menstruation, and become one of the wives of other males. They are believed to be impotent and to have been afflicted by some supernatural agency. (Ford & Beach, 1951)

Although not necessarily accepted gladly, the various folk beliefs make the behavior acceptable, and a certain number of cross-gender behaving individuals are to be expected in every generation. Expectations about the extent to which the opposite gender role is to be played, however, appear to have changed over time with acculturation. Affected individuals in the past often were required to make a public ritualized change of gender and cross-dress and behave in accordance with their new identity. Among the Mohave, for example, there was an initiation ceremony and it was important for the initiate "to duplicate the behavior pattern of his adopted sex and make 'normal' individuals of his anatomic sex feel toward him as though he truly belonged to his adopted sex" (Devereux, 1937). The *mahu* in Tahiti were described in the latter part of the eighteenth century as follows:

These men are in some respects like the Eunichs [*sic*] in India but are not castrated. They never cohabit with women but live as they do. They pick their beard out and dress as women, dance and sing with them and are as effeminate in their voice. (Morrison, 1935)

Affected individuals in most societies at present are allowed a choice as to the extent they want to play the role; e.g., how far they want to identify with the opposite sex, whether they want to cross-dress or not, etc. Levy (1973) notes, for example, that in Tahiti: "Being a *mahu* does not now usually entail actually dressing as a woman." The North American Indian societies who used to have initiation ceremonies discontinued them long ago;

and, although expectations about cross-gender behaving individuals persist, only remnants of the original belief system are remembered currently. They continue, however, to be tolerant and "there apparently is no body of role behavior aimed at humiliating boys who are feminine or men who prefer men sexually" (Stoller, 1976).

The link between cross-gender behavior and homosexual behavior is the belief that there should be concordance between gender role and sexual object choice. When a male behaves like a female, he should be expected therefore to want a male sexual partner and to play the female sex role—that is, to play the insertee role in anal intercourse or fellatio. The same concordance should be expected when a female behaves like a male. As a result of beliefs about concordance, it is important to note that a society may not conceptualize the sexual behavior or its participants as "homosexual."

There is some evidence in support of this linking of gender role and homosexual behavior in societies making an accommodation and providing a social role for cross-gender behaving individuals. Kroeber (1940), for example, concluded from his investigations that: "In most of primitive northern Asia and North America, men of homosexual trends adopted women's dress, work, and status, and were accepted as nonphysiological but institutionalized women." Devereux's Mohave informants said that the males who changed their gender role to female had male husbands and that both anal intercourse and fellatio were practiced, with the participants playing the appropriate gender sex role. The informants noted the same concordance for females who behaved like males.

Unfortunately, the anthropological data do not always make clear whether cultural expectations in a given society were for concordance between gender role and erotic object; or, in terms of actual behavior, how many cross-gender behaving individuals chose same sex, opposite sex, or both sexes as erotic objects. In the paper I just quoted, Kroeber also concluded: "How far invert erotic practices accompanied the status is not always clear from the data, and it probably varied. At any rate, the North American attitude toward the berdache stresses not his erotic life but his social status; born a male, he became accepted as a woman socially."

Many anthropologists and other observers confounded their findings by assuming an equivalence between "transvestite" and "homosexual."[5] Thus, when an informant described cross-gender behavior, they may have concluded without foundation that a same-sex erotic object choice was part of the behavior being described, and that they were eliciting information on "homosexuals." Angelino and Shedd (1955) provide supporting evidence. They reviewed the literature on an often used anthropological concept, berdache, and concluded that the "term has been used in an exceedingly ambiguous way, being used as a synonym for homosexualism, hermaphroditism, transvestism, and effeminism." They also note that the meaning of berdache changed over time; going from kept boy/male prostitute, to individuals who played a passive role in sodomy, to males who played a passive sex role and cross-dressed.

In spite of the confusion between "transvestite" and "homosexual," the available data suggest that in many of the societies providing a social role for cross-gender behavior, the selection of sexual partners was based on the adopted gender role; and, though they might be subjected to ridicule, neither partner in the sexual relationship was penalized for the role played.

The *mahu* role in Tahiti provides a contemporary look at how one Polynesian society continues to provide a social role for cross-gender behavior. According to Levy (1973), villagers in his area of study do not agree on the sexual behavior of the *mahu*—some "believe that *mahu* do not generally engage in homosexual intercourse." Information from both *mahu* and *non-mahu* informants, however, leads to the conclusion that probably a majority of the *mahus* prefer adolescent males with whom they perform "ote moa" (literally,

"penis sucking"). The following are some aspects of the role and the community response to it:

It is said to be exclusive. Its essential defining characteristic is "doing woman's work," that is, a role reversal which is *publicly demonstrated*—either through clothes or through other public aspects of women's role playing. Most villagers approve of, and are pleased by, the role reversal. But homosexual behavior is a covert part of the role, and it is disapproved by many villagers. Men who have sexual relations with the *mahu*…do not consider themselves abnormal. Villagers who know of such activities may disapprove, but they do not label the partners as unmanly. The *mahu* is considered as a substitute woman for the partner. A new word, *raerae*, which reportedly originated in Papeete, is used by some to designate nontraditional types of homosexual behavior. (Levy, 1973)

It should also be noted that in Levy's village of study *mahus* were the only adult men reported to be engaging in homosexual intercourse.

Another contemporary example of a social role for cross-gender behavior is the *Hijada* role provided cross-gender behaving males in northwestern India. Given slightly different names by different observers (*Hijaras, Hinjras,* and *Hijiras*), these males appear to be playing the same role. There is general agreement on the fact that they cross-dress, beg alms, and collect dues at special ceremonies where they dance and sing as women. There is a considerable difference of opinion, however, as to whether they engage in homosexual intercourse or in any sexual activity for that matter. From the available data, it appears that they live mostly in towns in communes, with each commune having a definite jurisdiction of villages and towns "where its members can beg alms and collect dues" (Shah, 1961). They are also reported to live separately by themselves. From the findings of Carstairs (1956) and Shah (1961), one can at least conclude that the *Hijadas* living alone are sexually active:

Carstairs is wrong in considering all the Hijadas as homosexual, but there seems to be some truth in his information about the homosexuality of the Deoli Hijada (Note: Deoli is the village of Carstairs' study.)

Faridi and Mehta also note that some Hijadas practice "sodomy." This, however, is not institutionalized homosexuality. (Shah, 1961)

The finding by Opler (1960) that "they cannot carry on sexual activities and do not marry" may apply to the majority of *Hijadas* living in communes. The question of what kind of sexual behavior the *Hijadas* practice, if any, cannot be answered definitively with the data available. That they are still a viable group in India is confirmed by a recent Associated Press release:

About 2000 eunuchs dressed in brightly colored saris and other female garb were converging on this northern town from all over India this weekend for a private convention of song, dance and prayer.
Local reaction to the gathering was mixed. "They're perverts," commented a local peanut vendor. "We should have nothing to do with them. They should be run out of town."
A New Delhi social worker...said they sometimes supplement their income as paid lovers of homosexuals. (Excerpts from AP, February 6, 1979)

Disapproving Societies

Societies in which cross-gender behavior produces strong emotional negative reactions in large segments of the population tend to have the following commonalities: (1) negative reactions produced by the behavior are essentially limited to the male part of the population and relate mainly to effeminate males; (2) cross-gender behavior is controlled by laws which prohibit cross-dressing, and by laws and public opinion which consider other attributes associated with the behavior as scandalous; (3) gender roles are sharply dichotomized; and (4) a general belief exists that anyone demonstrating cross-gender behavior is homosexual.

A number of complex modern and peasant societies in the Middle East, North Africa, southern Europe, and Central and South America have the commonalities listed. The author's research in Mexico (Carrier, 1976 and 1977) illustrates how homosexual behavior in these societies appears

to be linked to social responses to cross-gender behavior. The comments that follow are limited to male homosexual behavior. Female homosexuality is known to exist in these societies, but too little is known about the behavior to be included in the discussion.

Mexican Homosexual Behavior. The Mexican mestizo culture places a high value on manliness. One of the salient features of the society is thus a sharp delimitation between the roles played by males and females. Role expectations in general are for the male to be dominant and independent and for the female to be submissive and dependent. The continued sharp boundary between male and female roles in Mexico appears to be due in part to a culturally defined hypermasculine ideal model of manliness, referred to under the label *machismo*. The ideal female role is generally believed to be the reciprocal of the macho (male) role.[6]

As a consequence of the high status given manliness, Mexican males from birth onward are expected to behave in as manly a way as possible. Peñalosa (1968) sums it up as follows: "Any signs of feminization are severely repressed in the boy." McGinn (1966) concludes: "The young Mexican boy may be severely scolded for engaging in feminine activities, such as playing with dolls or jacks. Parents verbally and physically punish feminine traits in their male children." The importance of manly behavior continues throughout the life span of Mexican males.

One result of the sharp dichotomization of male and female gender roles is the widely held belief that effeminate males basically prefer to play the female role rather than the male. The link between male effeminacy and homosexuality is the additional belief that as a result of this role preference effeminate males are sexually interested only in masculine males with whom they play the passive sex role. Although the motivations of males participating in homosexual encounters are without question diverse and complex, the fact remains that in Mexico cultural pressure is brought to bear on effeminate males to play the passive insertee role in sexual intercourse, and a kind of de facto cultural approval is given (that is, no particular stigma is attached to) masculine males who want to play the active insertor role in homosexual intercourse.

The beliefs linking effeminate males with homosexuality are culturally transmitted by a vocabulary which provides the appropriate labels, by homosexually oriented jokes and word games (*albures*), and by the mass media. The links are established at a very early age. From early childhood on, Mexican males are made aware of the labels used to denote male homosexuals and the connection is always clearly made that these homosexual males are guilty of unmanly effeminate behavior.

The author's data also support the notion that prior to puberty effeminate males in Mexico are targeted as sexual objects for adolescent and adult males, and are expected to play the passive insertee sex role in anal intercourse. Following the onset of puberty, they continue to be sexual targets for other males because of their effeminacy. The consensus of my effeminate respondents in Mexico is that regardless of whether they are at school, in a movie theater, on the downtown streets, in a park, or in their own neighborhood, they are sought out and expected to play the anal passive sex role by more masculine males. As one fourteen-year-old respondent put it, in response to the question of where he had looked for sexual contacts during the year prior to the interview: "I didn't have to search for them...they looked for me."

The other side of the coin is represented by masculine male participants in homosexual encounters. Given the fact that effeminate males in Mexico are assumed homosexual and thus considered available as sexual outlets, how do the cultural factors contribute to the willingness of masculine males to play the active insertor sex role? The available data suggest that, insofar as the social variables are concerned, their willingness to participate in homosexual encounters is due to the relatively high level of sexual awareness

that exists among males in the society, to the lack of stigmatization of the insertor sex role, and to the restraints that may be placed on alternative sexual outlets by available income and/or by marital status. The only cultural proscriptions are that "masculine" males should not play the passive sex role and should not be exclusively involved with homosexual intercourse.

The passive sex role is by inference—through the cultural equivalence of effeminacy with homosexuality—prescribed for "effeminate" males. It becomes a self-fulfilling prophecy of the society that effeminate males (a majority?) are eventually, if not from the beginning, pushed toward exclusively homosexual behavior. Some do engage in heterosexual intercourse, and some marry and set up households; but these probably are a minority of the identifiably effeminate males among the mestizos of the Mexican population.

Brazilian Homosexual Behavior. Both Young (1973) and Fry (1974) note the relationship between cross-gender behavior and homosexuality in Brazil.

> Brazilians are still pretty hung-up about sexual roles. Many Brazilians believe in the *bicha/bofe* (femme/butch) dichotomy and try to live by it. In Brazil, the average person doesn't even recognize the existence of the masculine homosexual. For example, among working-class men, it is considered all right to fuck a *bicha,* an accomplishment of sorts, just like fucking a woman. (Young, 1973)
>
> In the simplest of terms, a male is a man until he is assumed or proved to have "given" in which case he becomes a *bicha*. With very few exceptions, males who "eat" *bichas* are not classified as anything other than "real men." Under this classificatory scheme they differ in no way from males who restrict themselves to "eating" females. (Note: the male who gives is an insertee, the one who eats is an insertor.) (Fry, 1974)

Southern European Homosexual Behavior. Contemporary patterns of male homosexual behavior in Greece appear similar to those observed by the author in Mexico. An American anthropologist who collected data on homosexual behavior in Greece while working there on an archaeological project (Bialor, 1975) found, for example, that preferences for playing one sex role or the other (anal insertor or anal insertee) appear to be highly developed among Greek males. Little or no stigma is attached to the masculine male who plays the active insertor role. The social setting in modern Greece also appears to be strikingly similar to that in modern Mexico. Karlen (1971) describes it as follows:

> The father spends his spare time with other men in cafes; society is a male club, and there all true companionship lies. Women live separate, sequestered lives. Girls' virginity is carefully protected, and the majority of homicides are committed over the "honor" of daughters and sisters. In some Greek villages a woman does not leave her home unaccompanied by a relative between puberty and old age. Women walk the street, even in Athens, with their eyes down; a woman who looks up when a man speaks to her is, quite simply, a whore. The young male goes to prostitutes and may carry on homosexual connections; it is not unusual for him to marry at thirty having had no sexual experience save with prostitutes and male friends. (p. 16)

In an evaluation of the strategy of Turkish boys' verbal dueling rhymes, Dundes, Leach, and Ozkok (1972) make the following observations about homosexual behavior in Turkey:

> It is extremely important to note that the insult refers to *passive* homosexuality, not to homosexuality in general. In this context there is nothing insulting about being the active homosexual. In a homosexual relationship, the active phallic aggressor gains status; the passive victim of such aggression loses status. It is important to play the active role in a homosexual relationship; it is shameful and demeaning to be forced to take the passive role.

Moroccan Homosexual Behavior. The author does not know of any formal studies of homosexual behavior in Morocco. The available information suggests, however, that contemporary patterns of homosexual behavior in Morocco are similar to those in Mexico; that is, as long as Moroccan males play the active, insertor sex role in the relationship, there is never any question of their being considered homosexual. Based on his field work in Morocco shortly after the turn of

the century, Westermarck (1908) believed that "a very large proportion of the men" in some parts of the country were involved in homosexual activity. He also noted that: "In Morocco active pederasty is regarded with almost complete indifference, whilst the passive sodomite, if a grown-up individual, is spoken of with scorn. Dr. Polak says the same of the Persians." Contemporary patterns of homosexual behavior in the Islamic Arab countries of North Africa are probably similar to those in Morocco....

DISCUSSION

Heterosexual intercourse, marriage, and the creation of a family are culturally established as primary objectives for adults living in all of the societies discussed above. Ford & Beach (1951) concluded from their cross-cultural survey that "all known cultures are strongly biased in favor of copulation between males and females as contrasted with alternative avenues of sexual expression." They further note that this viewpoint is biologically adaptive in that it favors perpetuation of the species and social group, and that societies favoring other nonreproductive forms of sexual expression for adults would not be likely to survive for many generations.

Homosexual intercourse appears to be the most important alternative form of sexual expression utilized by people living around the world. All cultures have established rules and regulations that govern the selection of a sexual partner or partners. With respect to homosexual behavior, however, there appear to be greater variations of the rules and regulations. And male homosexual behavior generally appears to be more regulated by cultures than female homosexual behavior. This difference may be the result of females being less likely than males to engage in homosexual activity; but it may also just be the result of a lack of data on female as compared with male homosexual behavior cross-culturally.

Exclusive homosexuality, however, because of the cultural dictums concerning marriage and the family, appears to be generally excluded as a sexual option even in those societies where homosexual behavior is generally approved. For example, the two societies where all male individuals are free to participate in homosexual activity if they choose, Siwan and East Bay, do not sanction exclusive homosexuality.[7] Although nearly all male members of these two societies are reported to engage in extensive homosexual activities, they are not permitted to do so exclusively over their adult life span. Davenport (1965) reports "that East Bay is a society which permits men to be either heterosexual or bisexual in their behavior, but denies the possibility of the exclusively homosexual man." He notes that "they have no concept and therefore no word for the exclusive homosexual." There are not much data available on the Siwans, but it has been reported that whether single or married Siwan males "are expected to have both homosexual and heterosexual affairs" (Ford & Beach, 1951).

In East Bay there are two categories of homosexual relationships. One category appears similar to that found in a number of Melanesian societies; an older man plays the active (insertor) sex role in anal intercourse with younger boys "from seven to perhaps eleven years of age." Davenport notes:

> The man always plays the active role, and it is considered obligatory for him to give the boy presents in return for accommodating him. A man would not engage his own son in such a relationship, but fathers do not object when friends use their young sons in this way, provided the adult is kind and generous. (p. 200)

The other category is between young single men of the same age group who play both sex roles in anal intercourse. The young men, however, "are not regarded as homosexual lovers. They are simply friends or relatives, who, understanding each other's needs and desires, accommodate one another thus fulfilling some of the obligations of kinship and friendship." This category may be related to several social factors which limit heterosexual contacts of young single men. First, the population is highly masculine with a male/female ratio of 120:100 in

the fifteen- to twenty-five-year-old age group. Second, females have historically been brought in as wives for those who could afford the bride price. Third, sexual relations between unmarried individuals and adultery are forbidden. Both relationships are classed as larcenies and "only murder carries a more severe punishment." At first marriage a bride is expected to be a virgin. Chastity is highly valued in that it indicates adultery is less likely to occur after marriage. And fourth, there is "an extensive system for separating the sexes by what amounts to a general social avoidance between men and women in all but a few situations." From early adolescence on, unmarried men and boys sleep and eat in the men's house; and married men spend much of their time there during the day. Davenport notes that both masturbation and anal copulation are socially approved and regarded as substitutes for heterosexual intercourse by members of the society. Female homosexual activity is not reported in East Bay.

Among Siwan males the accepted homosexual relationship is "between a man and a boy but not between adult men or between two young boys" (Bullough, 1976). They are reported to practice anal intercourse with the adult man always playing the active (insertor) sex role. In this society, boys are more valued than girls. Allah (1917) reports that

> ...[the] bringing up of a boy costs very little whereas the girl needs ornaments, clothing, and stains. Moreover the boy is a very fruitful source of profit for the father, not for the work he does, but because he is hired by his father to another man to be used as a catamite. Sometimes two men exchange their sons. If they are asked about this, they are not ashamed to mention it.

Homosexual activity is not reported for Siwan females.

The way in which cross-gender behavior is linked to homosexual behavior, and the meaning ascribed to the "homosexual" behavior by participants and significant others, differ between the three categories of societies identified in this study. What is considered homosexuality in one culture may be considered appropriate behavior within prescribed gender roles in another, a homosexual act only on the part of one participant in another, or a ritual act involving growth and masculinity in still another. Care must therefore be taken when judging sexual behavior cross-culturally with such culture-bound labels as "homosexual" and "homosexuality."

From a cultural point of view, deviations from sexual mores in a given society appear most likely to occur as a result of the lack of appropriate sexual partners and/or a result of conditioning in approved sexual behavior which is limited by age or ritual (for example, where homosexual intercourse is only appropriate for a certain age group and/or ritual time period and inappropriate thereafter). Homosexual activity initiated by sociocultural variables may over time through interaction with personality variables, produce an outcome not in accordance with the sexual mores of the society.

The findings presented in this chapter illustrate the profound influence of culture on the structuring of individual patterns of sexual behavior. Whether from biological or psychological causation, cross-gender behaving individuals in many societies must cope with a cultural formulation which equates their behavior with homosexual activity and thus makes it a self-fulfilling prophecy that they become homosexually involved. There are also individuals in many societies who might *prefer* to be exclusively homosexual but are prevented from doing so by cultural edicts. From whatever causes that homosexual impulses originate, whether they be biological or psychological, culture provides an additional dimension that cannot be ignored.

CRITICAL THINKING QUESTIONS

1. What type of society tends to be accepting of homosexuality? What kind of society is disapproving of this sexual orientation? Why?
2. What insights can be drawn from this article that help to explain violence and discrimination directed toward gay people in Canadian society?
3. Are data about sexuality easily available to researchers? Why not?

NOTES

1. Homosexual behavior or activity will be used here to describe sexual behavior between individuals of the same sex; it may have nothing to do with sexual object choice or sexual orientation of the individual involved. Additionally, the terms "sex role" and "gender role" will be used to describe different behavioral phenomena. As Hooker (1965) points out, they "are often used interchangeably, and with resulting confusion." Following her suggestion the term "sex role," when homosexual practices are described, will refer to typical sexual performance only. "The gender connotations (M-F) of these performances need not then be implicitly assumed." The term "gender role" will refer to the expected attitudes and behavior that distinguish males from females.

2. The Human Relations Area Files (HRAF) contain information on the habits, practices, customs, and behavior of populations in hundreds of societies around the world. These files utilize accounts given not only by anthropologists but also by travelers, writers, missionaries, and explorers. Most cross-cultural surveys of sexual behavior, like those of Ford and Beach and Broude and Greene, have been based on HRAF information. A major criticism of the HRAF information on sexual behavior relates to the difficulty of assessing the reliability of the data collected in different time periods by different people with varying amounts of scientific training as observers.

3. "Preliterate" refers to essentially tribal societies that do not have a written language; "peasant" refers to essentially agrarian literate societies; and "complex modern" refers to highly industrialized societies.

4. In one of the first scholarly surveys of homosexual behavior done by an anthropologist, Westermarck (1908) concluded that: "A very important cause of homosexual practices is absence of the other sex."

5. The confounding of transvestism with homosexuality still occurs. For example, Minturn, Grosse, and Haider (1969) coded male homosexuality with transvestism in a recent study of the patterning of sexual beliefs and behavior, "because it is often difficult to distinguish between the two practices, and because they are assumed to be manifestations of the same psychological processes and to have similar causes."

6. The roles described represent the normative cultural ideals of the mestizoized national culture. Mestizos are Mexican nationals of mixed Indian and Spanish ancestry. They make up a large majority of the population, and their culture is the dominant one.

7. Both societies are small, each totaling less than 1,000 inhabitants. The Siwans live in an oasis in the Libyan desert. The people of East Bay (a pseudonym) live in a number of small coastal villages in an island in Melanesia.

REFERENCES

Allah, M. 1917. Siwan customs. *Harvard African Studies,* 1: 7.

Angelino, A., and C. Shedd. 1955. A note on berdache. *American Anthropologist,* 57: 121–25.

Associated Press. 1979. Eunuchs gather for convention in India. *Panipat,* February 6, 1979.

Bialor, P. 1975. Personal communication.

Bogores, W. 1904. The Chukchee. *Memoirs of American Museum of Natural History,* 2: 449–51.

Broude, G., and S. Greene. 1976. Cross-cultural codes on twenty sexual attitudes and practices. *Ethnology,* 15(4): 410–11.

Bullough, V. 1976. *Sexual variance in society and history,* 22–49. New York: John Wiley.

Carrier, J. 1976. Cultural factors affecting urban Mexican male homosexual behavior. *Archives of Sexual Behavior,* 5(2): 103–24.

———. 1977. Sex-role preference as an explanatory variable in homosexual behavior. *Archives of Sexual Behavior,* 6(1): 53–65.

Carstairs, G. 1956. Hinjra and Jiryan: Two derivatives of Hindu attitudes to sexuality. *British Journal of Medical Psychology,* 2: 129–32.

Davenport, W. 1965. Sexual patterns and their regulation in a society of the southwest Pacific. In *Sex and behavior,* 164–207. New York: John Wiley.

Devereux, G. 1937. Institutionalized homosexuality of the Mohave Indians. In *The problem of homosexuality in modern society,* 183–226. New York: E. P. Dutton.

Dundes, A., J. Leach, and B. Ozkok. 1972. The strategy of Turkish boys' verbal dueling. In *Directions in sociolinguistics: The ethnography of communication.* New York: Holt.

Ford, C. S., and F. A. Beach. 1951. *Patterns of sexual behavior.* New York: Harper & Row.

Fry, P. 1974. Male homosexuality and Afro-Brazilian possession cults. Unpublished paper presented to Symposium on Homosexuality in Crosscultural Perspective, 73rd Annual Meeting of the American Anthropological Association, Mexico City.

Hooker, E. 1965. An empirical study of some relations between sexual patterns and gender identity in male homosexuals. In *Sex research: New developments,* 24–5. New York: Holt.

Karlen, A. 1971. *Sexuality and homosexuality: A new view.* New York: W. W. Norton.

Kroeber, A. 1940. Psychosis or social sanction. *Character and Personality,* 8: 204–15. Reprinted in *The nature of culture,* 313. Chicago: University of Chicago Press, 1952.

Levy, R. 1973. *Tahitians.* Chicago: University of Chicago Press.

Marshall, D., and R. Suggs. 1971. *Human sexual behavior,* 220–21. New York: Basic Books.

McGinn, N. 1966. Marriage and family in middle-class Mexico. *Journal of Marriage and Family Counseling,* 28: 305–13.

Mead, M. 1961. Cultural determinants of sexual behavior. In *Sex and internal secretions,* 1433–79. Baltimore: Williams & Wilkins.

Minturn, L., M. Grosse, and S. Haider. 1969. Cultural patterning of sexual beliefs and behavior. *Ethnology,* 8(3): 3.

Morrison, J. 1935. *The journal of James Morrison.* London: Golden Cockerel Press.

Munroe, R., J. Whiting, and D. Hally. 1969. Institutionalized male transvestism and sex distinctions. *American Anthropologist,* 71: 87–91.

Opler, M. 1960. The Hijadas (hermaphrodites) of India and Indian national character: A rejoinder. *American Anthropologist,* 62(3): 505–11.

Peñalosa, F. 1968. Mexican family roles. *Journal of Marriage and Family Counseling,* 30: 680–89.

Royce, A. 1973. Personal communication.

Shah, A. 1961. A note on the Hijadas of Gujarat. *American Anthropologist,* 63(6): 1325–30.

Stoller, R. 1976. Two feminized male American Indians. *Archives of Sexual Behavior,* 5(6): 536.

Westermarck, E. 1908. On homosexual love. In *The origin and development of the moral ideas.* London: Macmillan.

Williams, F. 1936. *Papuans of the trans-fly.* London: Oxford University Press.

Young, A. 1973. Gay gringo in Brazil. In *The gay liberation book,* eds. L. Richmond and G. Noguera, 60–7. San Francisco: Ramparts Press.

30

Education and Inequality

Samuel Bowles and Herbert Gintis

Education has long been held to be a means to realizing U.S. ideals of equal opportunity. As Lester Ward notes at the beginning of this selection, the promise of education is to allow "natural" abilities to win out over the "artificial" inequalities of class, race, and sex. Samuel Bowles and Herbert Gintis claim that this has happened very little in the United States. Rather, they argue, schooling has more to do with maintaining existing social hierarchy.

Universal education is the power, which is destined to overthrow every species of hierarchy. It is destined to remove all artificial inequality and leave the natural inequalities to find their true level. With the artificial inequalities of caste, rank, title, blood, birth, race, color, sex, etc., will fall nearly all the oppression, abuse, prejudice, enmity, and injustice, that humanity is now subject to.
—Lester Frank Ward, Education, *1872*

A review of educational history hardly supports the optimistic pronouncements of liberal educational theory. The politics of education are better understood in terms of the need for social control in an unequal and rapidly

Source: From *Schooling in Capitalist America: Educational Reform and the Contradictions of Economic Life* by Samuel Bowles and Herbert Gintis. Copyright © 1976 by Basic Books, Inc. Reprinted with permission of Basic Books, Inc., a division of HarperCollins Publishers, Inc.

changing economic order. The founders of the modern U.S. school system understood that the capitalist economy produces great extremes of wealth and poverty, of social elevation and degradation. Horace Mann and other school reformers of the antebellum period knew well the seamy side of the burgeoning industrial and urban centers. "Here," wrote Henry Barnard, the first state superintendent of education in both Connecticut and Rhode Island, and later to become the first U.S. Commissioner of Education, "the wealth, enterprise and professional talent of the state are concentrated...but here also are poverty, ignorance, profligacy and irreligion, and a classification of society as broad and deep as ever divided the plebeian and patrician of ancient Rome."[1] They lived in a world in which, to use de Tocqueville's words, "...small aristocratic societies...are formed by some manufacturers in the midst of the immense democracy of our age [in which]...some men are opulent and a multitude…are wretchedly poor."[2] The rapid rise of the factory system, particularly in New England, was celebrated by the early school reformers; yet, the alarming transition from a relatively simple rural society to a highly stratified industrial economy could not be ignored. They shared the fears that de Tocqueville had expressed following his visit to the United States in 1831:

> When a workman is unceasingly and exclusively engaged in the fabrication of one thing, he ultimately does his work with singular dexterity; but at the same time he loses the general faculty of applying his mind to the direction of the work.… [While] the science of manufacture lowers the class of workmen, it raises the class of masters.… [If] ever a permanent inequality of conditions…again penetrates into the world, it may be predicted that this is the gate by which they will enter.[3]

While deeply committed to the emerging industrial order, the farsighted school reformers of the mid-nineteenth century understood the explosive potential of the glaring inequalities of factory life. Deploring the widening of social divisions and fearing increasing unrest, Mann, Barnard, and others proposed educational expansion and reform. In his Fifth Report as Secretary of the Massachusetts Board of Education, Horace Mann wrote:

> Education, then beyond all other devices of human origin, is the great equalizer of the conditions of men—the balance wheel of the social machinery.… It does better than to disarm the poor of their hostility toward the rich; it prevents being poor.[4]

Mann and his followers appeared to be at least as interested in disarming the poor as in preventing poverty. They saw in the spread of universal and free education a means of alleviating social distress without redistributing wealth and power or altering the broad outlines of the economic system. Education, it seems, had almost magical powers:

> The main idea set forth in the creeds of some political reformers, or revolutionizers, is, that some people are poor because others are rich. This idea supposed a fixed amount of property in the community…and the

problem presented for solution is, how to transfer a portion of this property from those who are supposed to have too much to those who feel and know that they have too little. At this point, both their theory and their expectation of reform stop. But the beneficent power of education would not be exhausted, even though it should peaceably abolish all the miseries that spring from the coexistence, side by side, of enormous wealth and squalid want. It has a higher function. Beyond the power of diffusing old wealth, it has the prerogative of creating new.[5]

The early educators viewed the poor as the foreign element that they were. Mill hands were recruited throughout New England, often disrupting the small towns in which textile and other rapidly growing industries had located. Following the Irish potato famine of the 1840s, thousands of Irish workers settled in the cities and towns of the northeastern United States. Schooling was seen as a means of integrating this "uncouth and dangerous" element into the social fabric of American life. The inferiority of the foreigner was taken for granted. The editors of the influential *Massachusetts Teacher,* a leader in the educational reform movement, writing in 1851, saw "…the increasing influx of foreigners…" as a moral and social problem:

> Will it, like the muddy Missouri, as it pours its waters into the clear Mississippi and contaminates the whole united mass, spread ignorance and vice, crime and disease, through our native population?
>
> If…we can by any means purify this foreign people, enlighten their ignorance and bring them up to our level, we shall perform a work of true and perfect charity, blessing the giver and receiver in equal measure.…
>
> With the old not much can be done; but with their children, the great remedy is *education.* The rising generation must be taught as our own children are taught. We say *must be* because in many cases this can only be accomplished by coercion.[6]

Since the mid-nineteenth century the dual objectives of educational reformers—equality of opportunity and social control—have been intermingled, the merger of these two threads sometimes so nearly complete that it becomes impossible to distinguish between the two. Schooling has been at once something done for the poor and to the poor.

The basic assumptions which underlay this commingling help explain the educational reform movement's social legacy. First, educational reformers did not question the fundamental economic institutions of capitalism: Capitalist ownership and control of the means of production and dependent wage labor were taken for granted. In fact, education was to help preserve and extend the capitalist order. The function of the school system was to accommodate workers to its most rapid possible development. Second, it was assumed that people (often classes of people or "races") are differentially equipped by nature or social origins to occupy the varied economic and social levels in the class structure. By providing equal opportunity, the school system was to elevate the masses, guiding them sensibly and fairly to the manifold political, social, and economic roles of adult life.

Jefferson's educational thought strikingly illustrates this perspective. In 1779, he proposed a two-track educational system which would prepare individuals for adulthood in one of the two classes of society: the "laboring and the learned."[7] Even children of the laboring class would qualify for leadership. Scholarships would allow "...those persons whom nature hath endowed with genius and virtue..." to "...be rendered by liberal education worthy to receive and able to guard the sacred deposit of the rights and liberties of their fellow citizens."[8] Such a system, Jefferson asserted, would succeed in "...raking a few geniuses from the rubbish."[9] Jefferson's two-tiered educational plan presents in stark relief the outlines and motivation for the stratified structure of U.S. education which has endured up to the present. At the top, there is the highly selective aristocratic tradition, the elite university training future leaders. At the base is mass education for all, dedicated to uplift and control. The two traditions have always coexisted although their meeting point has drifted upward over the years, as mass education has spread upward from elementary school through high school, and now up to the post-high-school level.

Though schooling was consciously molded to reflect the class structure, education was seen as a means of enhancing wealth and morality, which would work to the advantage of all. Horace Mann, in his 1842 report to the State Board of Education, reproduced this comment by a Massachusetts industrialist:

> The great majority always have been and probably always will be comparatively poor, while a few will possess the greatest share of this world's goods. And it is a wise provision of Providence which connects so intimately, and as I think so indissolubly, the greatest good of the many with the highest interests in the few.[10]

Much of the content of education over the past century and a half can only be construed as an unvarnished attempt to persuade the "many" to make the best of the inevitable.

The unequal contest between social control and social justice is evident in the total functioning of U.S. education. The system as it stands today provides eloquent testimony to the ability of the well-to-do to perpetuate in the name of equality of opportunity an arrangement which consistently yields to themselves disproportional advantages, while thwarting the aspirations and needs of the working people of the United States. However grating this judgment may sound to the ears of the undaunted optimist, it is by no means excessive in light of the massive statistical data on inequality in the United States. Let us look at the contemporary evidence.

We may begin with the basic issue of inequalities in the years of schooling. As can be seen in [Figure 30.1], the number of years of schooling attained by an individual is strongly associated with parental socioeconomic status. This figure presents the estimated distribution of years of schooling attained by individuals of varying socioeconomic backgrounds. If we define socioeconomic background by a weighted sum of income, occupation, and educational level of the parents, a child from the ninetieth percentile may expect, on the average, five more

FIGURE 30.1 Educational Attainments Are Strongly Dependent on Social Background
Even for People of Similar Childhood IQs

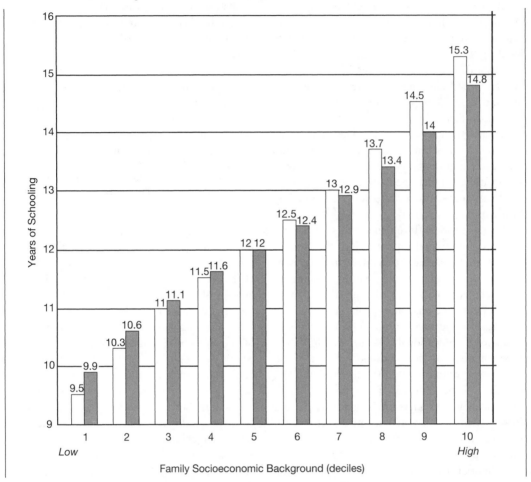

Notes: For each socioeconomic group, the left-hand bar indicates the estimated average number of years of schooling attained by all men from that group. The right-hand bar indicates the estimated average number of years of schooling attained by men with IQ scores equal to the average for the entire sample. The sample refers to "non-Negro" men of "nonfarm" backgrounds, aged 35–44 years in 1962.

Source: Samuel Bowles and Valerie Nelson, "The 'Inheritance of IQ' and the Intergenerational Transmission of Economic Inequality," *The Review of Economics and Statistics,* vol. LVI, no. 1 (Feb. 1974).

years of schooling than a child in the tenth percentile.[11]

...We have chosen a sample of white males because the most complete statistics are available for this group. Moreover, if inequality for white males can be documented, the proposition is

merely strengthened when sexual and racial differences are taken into account.

Additional census data dramatize one aspect of educational inequalities: the relationship between family income and college attendance. Even among those who had graduated from high school in the early 1960s, children of families earning less than $3,000 per year were over six times as likely *not* to attend college as were the children of families earning over $15,000.[12] Moreover, children from less well-off families are *both* less likely to have graduated from high school and more likely to attend inexpensive, two-year community colleges rather than a four-year B.A. program if they do make it to college.[13]

Not surprisingly, the results of schooling differ greatly for children of different social backgrounds. Most easily measured, but of limited importance, are differences in scholastic achievement. If we measure the output of schooling by scores on nationally standardized achievement tests, children whose parents were themselves highly educated outperform the children of parents with less education by a wide margin. Data collected for the U.S. Office of Education Survey of Educational Opportunity reveal, for example, that among white high-school seniors, those whose parents were in the top education decile were, on the average, well over three grade levels in measured scholastic achievement ahead of those whose parents were in the bottom decile.[14]

Given these differences in scholastic achievement, inequalities in years of schooling among individuals of different social backgrounds are to be expected. Thus one might be tempted to argue that the close dependence of years of schooling attained on background displayed in the left-hand bars of [Figure 30.1] is simply a reflection of unequal intellectual abilities, or that inequalities in college attendance are the consequences of differing levels of scholastic achievement in high school and do not reflect any additional social class inequalities peculiar to the process of college admission.

This view, so comforting to the admissions personnel in our elite universities, is unsupported by the data, some of which is presented in [the figure]. The right-hand bars of [the figure] indicate that even among children with identical IQ test scores at ages six and eight, those with rich, well-educated, high-status parents could expect a

much higher level of schooling than those with less-favored origins. Indeed, the closeness of the left-hand and right-hand bars in [the figure] shows that only a small portion of the observed social class differences in educational attainment is related to IQ differences across social classes.[15] The dependence of education attained on background is almost as strong for individuals with the same IQ as for all individuals. Thus, while [the figure] indicates that an individual in the ninetieth percentile in social class background is likely to receive five more years of education than an individual in the tenth percentile, it also indicates that he is likely to receive 4.25 more years schooling than an individual from the tenth percentile with the same IQ. Similar results are obtained when we look specifically at access to college education for students with the same measured IQ. Project Talent data indicates that for "high ability" students (top 25 percent as measured by a composite of tests of "general aptitude"), those of high socioeconomic background (top 25 percent as measured by a composite of family income, parents' education, and occupation) are nearly twice as likely to attend college than students of low socioeconomic background (bottom 25 percent). For "low ability" students (bottom 25 percent), those of high-social background are more than four times as likely to attend college as are their low-social background counterparts.[16]

Inequality in years of schooling is, of course, only symptomatic of broader inequalities in the educational system. Not only do less well-off children go to school for fewer years, they are treated with less attention (or more precisely, less benevolent attention) when they are there. These broader inequalities are not easily measured. Some show up in statistics on the different levels of expenditure for the education of children of different socioeconomic backgrounds. Taking account of the inequality in financial resources for each year in school and the inequality in years of schooling obtained, Jencks estimated that a child whose parents were in the top fifth of the income distribution receives roughly twice the educational resources in dollar terms as does a child whose parents are in the bottom fifth.[17]

The social class inequalities in our school system, then, are too evident to be denied. Defenders of the educational system are forced back on the assertion that things are getting better; the inequalities of the past were far worse. And, indeed, there can be no doubt that some of the inequalities of the past have been mitigated. Yet new inequalities have apparently developed to take their place, for the available historical evidence lends little support to the idea that our schools are on the road to equality of educational opportunity. For example, data from a recent U.S. Census survey reported in Spady indicate that graduation from college has become no less dependent on one's social background. This is true despite the fact that high-school graduation is becoming increasingly equal across social classes.[18] Additional data confirm this impression. The statistical association (coefficient of correlation) between parents' social status and years of education attained by individuals who completed their schooling three or four decades ago is virtually identical to the same correlation for individuals who terminated their schooling in recent years.[19] On balance, the available data suggest that the number of years of school attained by a child depends upon family background as much in the recent period as it did fifty years ago.

Thus, we have empirical reasons for doubting the egalitarian impact of schooling.... We conclude that U.S. education is highly unequal, the chances of attaining much or little schooling being substantially dependent on one's race and parents' economic level. Moreover, where there is a discernible trend toward a more equal educational system—as in the narrowing of the black education deficit, for example—the impact on the structure of economic opportunity is minimal at best.

CRITICAL THINKING QUESTIONS

1. Does Bowles and Gintis's description of the American education system apply to the Canadian system? How are the two systems similar? How are they different?
2. In what respects, according to Bowles and Gintis, has schooling supported the capitalist economic system? How has such support shaped the content of the educational system?
3. What are Bowles and Gintis's conclusions about the relationship between schooling and natural ability? between schooling and social background?

NOTES

1. H. Barnard, *Papers for the Teacher: 2nd Series* (New York: F. C. Brownell, 1866), pp. 293–310.
2. A. de Tocqueville, as quoted in Jeremy Brecher, *Strike!* (San Francisco: Straight Arrow Books, 1972), pp. xi, xii.
3. Ibid., p. 172.
4. Horace Mann as quoted in Michael Katz, ed., *School Reform Past and Present* (Boston: Little, Brown, 1971), p. 141.
5. Ibid., p. 145.
6. *The Massachusetts Teacher* (Oct., 1851), quoted in Katz, pp. 169–70.
7. D. Tyack, *Turning Points in American Educational History* (Waltham, Mass.: Blaisdell, 1967), p. 89.
8. Ibid., p. 10.
9. Ibid., p. 89.
10. Mann, quoted in Katz, p. 147.
11. This calculation is based on data reported in full in Samuel Bowles and Valerie Nelson, "The 'Inheritance of IQ' and the Intergenerational Transmission of Economic Inequality," *The Review of Economics and Statistics,* 56, 1 (Feb., 1974). It refers to non-Negro males from nonfarm backgrounds, aged 35–44 years. The zero-order correlation coefficient between socioeconomic background and years of schooling was estimated at 0.646. The estimated standard deviation of years of schooling was 3.02. The results for other age groups are similar.
12. These figures refer to individuals who were high-school seniors in October 1965, and who subsequently graduated from high school. College attendance refers to both two- and four-year institutions. Family income is for the twelve months preceding October 1965. Data is drawn from U.S. Bureau of the Census, *Current Population Reports,* Series P-60, No. 183 (May, 1969).
13. For further evidence, see ibid.; and Jerome Karabel, "Community Colleges and Social Stratification," *Harvard Educational Review,* 424, 42 (Nov., 1972).
14. Calculation based on data in James S. Coleman et al., *Equality of Educational Opportunity* (Washington, D.C.: U.S. Government Printing Office, 1966), and the authors.

15. The data relating to IQ are from a 1966 survey of veterans by the National Opinion Research Center; and from N. Bayley and E. S. Schaefer, "Correlations of Maternal and Child Behaviors with the Development of Mental Ability: Data from the Berkeley Growth Study," *Monographs of Social Research in Child Development,* 29, 6 (1964).

16. Based on a large sample of U.S. high-school students as reported in John C. Flannagan and William W. Cooley, *Project Talent, One Year Follow-up Study,* Cooperative Research Project, No. 2333 (Pittsburgh: University of Pittsburgh, School of Education, 1966).

17. C. Jencks et al., *Inequality: A Reassessment of the Effects of Family and Schooling in America* (New York: Basic Books, 1972), p. 48.

18. W. L. Spady, "Educational Mobility and Access: Growth and Paradoxes," in *American Journal of Sociology,* 73, 3 (Nov. 1967); and Peter Blau and Otis D. Duncan, *The American Occupational Structure* (New York: John Wiley, 1967). More recent data support the evidence of no trend toward equality. See U.S. Bureau of Census, op. cit.

19. Ibid., Blau and Duncan.

31

Any Changes Since Residential School?

CLASSIC

CONTEMPORARY

CROSS-CULTURAL

Jacqueline Hookimaw-Witt

Hookimaw-Witt reviews the residential school experience of Native children and explores how the education system is partly responsible for the destruction of their culture and loss of self-esteem.

The social situation Native people find themselves in on reserves is often blamed on a lack of education. The thought behind this suggestion is that "education" itself is neutral and automatically leads to a rise of the standard of living. I discuss that the situation we Native people are in is partly due to that very "education," which, as a continuation of residential schools, is still breaking down our cultures and societies. Education for Native people can be successful only when it has grown within the culture of the people.

In this article I wish to discuss the legacy of the residential school in a different light. As well as physical and emotional abuse suffered by the Native children who were placed in these schools, there was also an onslaught on our culture and identity through the content taught in school and the way it was taught. I would even say

Source: Jacqueline Hookimaw-Witt. 1998. Any changes since residential school? *Canadian Journal of Native Education*, 22(2): 159–70. Abridged with the permission of the Canadian Journal of Native Education, University of Alberta and University of British Columbia.

that "education" is partly responsible for the destruction of our cultures and the loss of self-esteem and thus has contributed directly to the problems in our community today. The content and methods of teaching have not changed in modern schools that now "help" us to "catch up." I therefore try to examine how education itself not only has not helped to prevent the social problems we have today, but has actually created them, and that when we do not change the basis of education for Native people, the process started by residential schools will still continue.

The basis for the following analysis of the problem can easily be summarized in the quote that refers to a researcher in the Arctic who was approached by an Elder:

An Elder approached me and asked what I was doing in the community. I explained that I was conducting research on dominant influences on Aboriginal student decision making, which might lead to reducing the Native student drop-out rate. He had an enigmatic response to my answer as he asked what the community would lose this time. I asked him to elaborate on his response and he said, every time the white man comes and offers us something, the Aboriginal people lose something. He said that at first the white man offered us Christianity, but he took our Native spirituality. Then he offered us his stores, his food, his goods, but we lost our traditional way of life and traditional diets. Then he offered us education, but we lost our language and culture. Now when I see a white man doing something for our good, I worry about what we will lose. (Common & Frost, 1994: 306)

Two major factors can be extracted from this statement. First, the help offered to so-called under-developed people never comes without a price. There is no real development in a scenario like this. It is, rather, that our own development is stopped and we have to adjust to something alien that is offered to us. The price is always that instead of developing our ways and adjusting them to the new environment, we have to given them up. Second, education per se is not neutral. Educational institutes have to follow curricula, and these curricula are used for "legitimation. Social groups are given legitimacy…through which social and cultural ideologies are built, recreated and maintained" (Apple & Weis, 1983: 516).

It is self-evident that the social groups and cultural ideologies Apple and Weis (1983) are referring to are not based in the culture of the Native people, but in the culture of those who suggest this kind of education. What the people who "help" us usually ignore is that we did not grow up completely uneducated, that we do not need a new education system. The only need is an adjustment of the existing system to new realities, if there are any. The content to be taught in school would not necessarily qualify to fall under the categories of new "realities," because the determination of content to be taught is usually based on a political decision.

Referring to the content, Apple (1990) rephrases the question of "*what* knowledge is most worth into *whose* knowledge is most worth" (p. viii), expressing that curricula are not neutral and that the knowledge taught in schools is not neutral when he reminds that it should hardly have to be said, but perhaps is worth remembering, that

education is not a neutral activity. It is profoundly political" (Apple, 1995: ix).

The political nature of education is explained above where it is stated that curricula are used for legitimation of social groups (Apple & Weis, 1983). Non-Native people must remember that the social groups and cultural ideologies are theirs, not ours, and when they suggest *their* education as means of healing our past wounds, they are suggesting that we give up our identity, which reopens the wounds rather than healing them.

Why the education offered to Native people is ultimately destroying Native cultures is also explained by Apple (1995):

Our formal institutions of education—because they cannot escape their history and their social conditions in which they are situated—are intimately linked with the social conditions in which they are situated—are intimately linked with the social divisions of paid and unpaid labour in this society. (p. ix)

It should be understood that these conditions are not the original conditions in Native societies, and that it is western society that is duplicated by the education that is offered to us. This underlines my statement that our societies are destroyed by the education system that is offered to us. The destruction of culture is also mentioned by Apple (1995) when he says that

the curriculum itself is always a choice from a wider universe of knowledge and values. Thus schooling is deeply implicated in cultural politics, with some groups having the power to declare their knowledge, values, and histories (i.e., "official knowledge"), while others are marginalized. (p. ix)

This power is taken away from us, because it is not the Native people themselves who decide on the content of teaching. The content is already decided on in the curricula the schools must follow when they are to be recognized.

The effect of these school politics can immediately be seen in the high dropout rates of Native students. The immediate analysis for school dropout is again based on the economic conditions in western society, as most of the dropouts are found among the economically poor people of this society (for me mainstream society). Apple (1989) therefore concludes that

it would not be an overstatement to say that our kind of economy, with its growing inequalities, its structuring of what are more and more alienating, deskilled, and meaningless jobs, its emphasis on profit no matter what the social cost—"naturally" *produces* the conditions that lead to dropping out. The phenomenon of the dropout is not an odd aberration that randomly arises in our school system. It is structurally generated, created out of the real and unequal relations of economic, political, and cultural resources and power that organize this society. Solutions to it will require that we no longer hide ourselves from this reality. The first step is looking at our economy honestly and recognizing how the class, race, and gender relations that structure it operate. (p. 220)

Looking into our communities, this analysis based on economic conditions seems to fit the case of Native youths dropping out of school. After all, the few jobs available in our communities are hardly a motivation for the youths to put an effort into their education. However, Apple (1989) also mentions cultural resources, and I will use this as a bridge to what I think is the real problem in Native education: lack of exposure to our own culture.

One explanation for the failure of Native youths in the school system has been that Native youths simply could not compete with the other youths in school because of their "cultural deprivation," meaning that our culture is so inferior to mainstream culture that we simply cannot succeed in a necessary education as long as we hold onto our culture. This led to the evaluation of a consultant for our community who was writing a proposal for the establishment of a solvent abuse treatment center. Although he emphasized the importance of including Native content in the curriculum, he stated that "Native culture and spirituality alone are not enough" (Kells, 1995) to survive in the modern world.

This observation was based on his misinterpretation of the educational goal the National Indian

Brotherhood set for Native people in 1973, namely, to reinforce Indian identity *and* to provide the training necessary for making a good living in modern society (National Indian Brotherhood, 1972). Kells (1995) interpreted this as "parallel teaching," concluding that education based on Native culture is not sufficient for survival in the so-called modern world. This is not what the National Indian Brotherhood (1972) intended to suggest. In their paper, they established the basis for Native education, stating that

unless the child learns the forces that shape him: the history of his people, their values and customs, their language, he will never really know himself or his potential as a human being.... The lessons he learns at school, his whole school experience should reinforce and contribute to the image he has of himself as an Indian. (p. 9)

I interpret the reference to the whole school experience as an indication of the importance of basing the school curriculum entirely in Native culture, no matter what content is taught. This means that "western" skills to be learned are still learned on the basis of the Native perspective, which would also include Native learning and teaching styles. The basis for education is here defined as being the culture of the Native people, from where they draw their identity. Only when this is understood by Native children can they develop their potential as human beings. The learning of skills for survival in the *other*, western reality are learned from a Native basis. The Native child, like any other child, needs a reference point to her or his own cultural environment when he or she wants to understand the meanings of the skills taught to him or her. Western skills and values are learned by comparing the *other* cultural reality with one's own. A parallel teaching that does not provide this point of reference, that in fact suggests that certain skills do not exist in our culture (rather than pointing out that they are different), will therefore fail....

The Royal Commission on Aboriginal People (Government of Canada, 1996) confirms my understanding of the NIB's educational goal that although we do have to include knowledge of the *other* culture in our curriculum, it still has to be based in our own culture: "Education must develop children and youth as Aboriginal citizens, linguistically and culturally competent to assume responsibilities in their nations.... Youth that emerge from school must be grounded in a strong positive Aboriginal identity" (p. 5). Their recommendation is, therefore, to establish "a curriculum that instills a proud Aboriginal identity and competence as an Aboriginal person" (p. 5). This Aboriginal identity and competence as an Aboriginal person can be reached only when the curriculum is based on the culture from which the youths draw their identity. A parallel teaching as suggested by Kells (1995) lacks this basis.

I would interpret the cultural deprivation that was so often quoted as the major factor of school dropout by people from different cultures (Ogbu, 1989) as Native people being deprived of the security of their own culture (by being forced into an alien education system), and not as the lack of survival skills their own culture would offer.

Ogbu (1989) analyzes the reasons for school dropout on the basis of cultural differences. He counts Native people with those *involuntary minorities* who were "brought into" the country's society by "slavery, conquest or colonization" (p. 187). Native people can definitely be identified in this group, as they were colonized in their own country. The lack of motivation of children from involuntary minorities to succeed in the education system is explained as the children from this group having come "to realize or believe that it requires more than education, and more than individual effort and hard work, to overcome the barriers. Consequently, they develop a folk theory of getting ahead which differs from white Americans" (p. 188).

Although this statement might explain school dropout based on different behaviour by the youths of involuntary minorities, Ogbu's (1989) conclusion of the development of a folk theory cannot be applied to Native youth. The means of coping with difficulties in school and the different

behaviour of Native youths cannot be identified as folk theory but as the culture in which the Native youths were raised. Although it may be true that the Native youths realized that getting on in society required more than education, they did not develop their attitude toward western education on this basis. Ogbu does not consider our culture here. We had our culture long before the Europeans came to this country. Referring to our own interpretations of life, there also needs to be a definition of getting ahead, because a good life in Native culture always includes spirituality and is not merely based on economic aspirations. Dropping out of school by Native youths may certainly not be based only on the realization that the capitalist vision of life is only a dream, but also on the lack of Native culture and spirituality within the educational system.

However, Ogbu's (1989) conclusion that the problem of dropping out of school has to be analyzed on the cultural basis of the minorities can be used as explanation why the alien school system cannot be used to solve the problems of Native people:

> At the moment, the definition and explanation of the school adjustment and academic performance problems of the minorities are based on a white middle-class cultural model, not the cultural model of the minorities which influence the latter's school orientations and behaviors. However, such definitions and explanations are incomplete until they incorporate the minorities' own notion of schooling which influences their school behavior. And until such an incorporation is made, social policies or remedial problems based on the definitions such as those embedded in the dropout literature are not likely to be particularly effective. (p. 201)

This would explain why the school system offered to us Native people cannot be successful. It is not based on our own cultural values and traditions....

All the Elders I interviewed agreed that the education presently offered to our children is part of the problem in our communities. They all emphasized that education would have to be based on our own culture and that the other content, that of western culture, can be included, rather than the reverse of just including some Native cultural teaching in an altogether non-Native educational system. The importance is the foundation on which the education system is based.

This realization led to the suggestion of Indian control of Indian education. I frequently found during my time in universities that even this concept would have to be defined. Many Native people do not realize any more that mere control of the education system that was forced on us will not change the success rate of education in Native communities. Haig-Brown (1995) warns that "though it is generally asserted that Native control of Native education would be a positive move, educators, researchers, and writers only cursorily articulate the assumptions behind this belief and rarely debate their validity" (p. 21).

The way I read this statement is that Native control of Native education is only valuable for Native people when the whole education system changes and is based on Native culture. The control of an altogether alien—and for Native cultures destructive—education system cannot keep at bay the damage that this system is causing our cultures....

Having established the importance of a cultural basis for our education system, I now try to explain why a Native cultural basis for our education system was not popular in the past, why nowadays many non-Native people might still view our cultures as inferior, and coupled with this thought, that we therefore need the help of an alien education system.

I heard much about racism and anti-racism while I attended universities. The anti-racism groups, although probably well-meaning, usually thought that they were opening a path for minorities to be accepted into *society*, basing this belief on the wrong assumption that there is actually only one society, and that the other groups are marginal or minority groups. They would certainly be shocked by the thoughts that go through my mind whenever they present their ideology. In my opinion, this assumption is as racist as the one that

we as Native people are inferior to other people due to the color of our skin. The wrong assumption is that all minority groups strive toward being accepted into *society*. For me that would mean assimilation. Why would Native people want to be assimilated? The only reason for wanting to be assimilated into an alien society would be an acknowledgement that the other society is superior to ours. This would mean that our culture is inferior as well, and this view feeds directly into the attitude expressed in the help we supposedly receive from the education system that is forced on us.

The concept on which I base the following explanations is that of *cultural difference*, which is explained by Bhabha (1988):

> The revision of history of critical theory rests on the notion of cultural difference, not cultural diversity. Cultural diversity is an epistemological object—culture as an object of empirical knowledge—whereas cultural difference is the process of the enunciation of culture as knowledgeable, authoritative, adequate to the construction of systems of cultural identification. (p. 206)

The suffix *able* in knowledge*able* is interpreted by Witt (1998) as the ability of each culture to enable the people to survive; the ability to create one's own programs without having to borrow from other cultures. This would certainly include that Native people can develop their own education system.

However, this *ability* is unfortunately not attributed to our culture. The way our culture is interpreted can, in my opinion, be traced to the unfortunate hierarchy of cultures exemplified in the work of Habermas (1979), who identifies four distinct stages of cultural evolution: *Neolithic societies*, *archaic civilizations*, *developed civilizations*, and the *modern age*. These stages are characterized by different principles of organization determining the kinds of institutions possible, the extent to which productive capacities will be utilized, and the capacity of societies to adapt to complex circumstances. The identification of stages of evolution necessarily also contains that notion that there is ultimately only one stage into which all cultures would develop. In fact this would defuse cultural difference altogether, because the differences would only be between stages of development, not between whole different cultures. Thus our Native cultures would ultimately develop the same way as any other culture, and the ultimate highest stage would be identified as the western culture of today. I consider an analysis like this racist and ethnocentric, as it is based on the opinion that one particular culture is superior to all others....

As in the quote by Bhabha (1988) above, the emphasis today should be on cultural difference rather than on analysis of which culture is inferior and which is superior. Western people should not fool themselves into believing they are acting as good Samaritans. The fact that other cultures are destroyed has not changed, only the methods have changed or, as Minh-Ha (1989) puts it, "tactics have changed since the colonial times, and indigenous cultures are no longer (overtly) destroyed" (p. 265). The emphasis is on the term *overtly*, because cultures are still destroyed by actions like "removal-relocation-reeducation-redefinition, the humiliation of having to falsify your own reality, your own voice" (p. 265).

The humiliation of having to falsify one's own reality lies in the suggestion that our problems can be solved by leaving our own culture behind, which would be the ultimate goal of education based on western cultural values. That the different cultures are not expressions of different developments but expressions of different realities can be concluded from the following: "Culture is the only facet of the human condition and of life in which knowledge of the human reality and the human interest in self-perfection and fulfillment merge into one. Culture is...the natural enemy of alienation. It constantly questions the self-appointed wisdom, serenity and authority of the Real" (Bauman, 1973: 176).

This tells me two things. One, *the Real* is different in any given culture, meaning that my reality is different from that of non-Native people; second,

I will not accept any self-appointed wisdom from westerners just because they claim that this is the truth because it has been researched on a "scientific" basis. This so-called science is culture as well....

As mentioned above, reality can be challenged, and it can be explained by culture. The challenge does not, however, work only one way. As much as non-Natives can challenge my reality, I can challenge their reality. As a Native woman I consider myself as much *human* as anyone from a different culture, and thus claim the right to define my own reality. This reality is, of course, also formed by the environment that surrounds the people who developed that particular culture. Culture can also be seen as means of survival in a particular environment, and "if culture is looked at as a system, it must be accepted that each is a workable means of adaptation to a given environment" (Arsenberg & Niehoff, 1971: 67)....

I conclude with the following. The negative social and economical situation Native people find themselves in today cannot be referred to as *cultural deprivation*, nor can it be improved by education that is based on a different, supposedly *superior* or *more developed* culture. The idea that this kind of education is the solution to problems in Native communities is based on an attitude toward Native culture that is, unfortunately, still widely prevalent among non-Native people. The attitude is detectable in the...statement that "these people need education" and in a statement made during a presentation in one of my university courses that "these people do not know anything about science," which referred to a classroom situation with immigrant children. Statements like this show either ignorance about educational concepts from other cultures, or feelings of superiority of the speaker, or both. This attitude is probably based on the evaluation of different cultures as exemplified in Habermas' (1979) model of cultural development. However, this model cannot be applied to all the cultures of the world, because it would distort differences in cultures and would state that all human development will ultimately be the same. This would make Native people underdeveloped white people. The attitude of the residential schools, which destroyed much of Native cultures in Canada, does not differ at all from the attitude exhibited in Habermas' model. If, as it is agreed, the residential school system was detrimental to our people, then logically any educational system that is based on the same assumptions—those of the inferiority of Native cultures—would have the same detrimental effects. Although it is true that people need education, the basis of that education will have to be defined. Education cannot be seen as neutral. It is geared to replicate society. The question is, which society? Eager educators must get used to the idea that there is no single society, but many societies, and that people who are called minorities or marginal still have the right to determine their own fate.

CRITICAL THINKING QUESTIONS

1. Discuss the assertion that education is never socially or politically neutral. How can the original decision to implement the residential school system be seen as the result of social and political motivations?
2. Review Hookimaw-Witt's discussion of *cultural deprivation*. What does this concept mean? In your opinion, can it be used to explain the social and economic position of Native peoples today? If so, how? If not, why not?
3. Residential schools have been closed for some time. What, if any, improvements can you see in how Native children are educated today?

REFERENCES

Apple, M. W. 1989. American realities: Poverty, economy and education. In *Dropouts from school: Issues, dilemmas, and solutions*, eds. L. Weis, E. Farrar, and H. G. Petrie, 205–20. Albany, N.Y.: SUNY Press.

Apple, M. W. 1990. *Ideology and curriculum,* 2nd ed. New York: Routledge.

Apple, M. W. 1995. Preface. In *Taking control: Power and contradiction in First Nations adult education*, ed. C. Haig-Brown, ix. Vancouver, B.C.: University of British Columbia Press.

Apple, M. W., and L. Weis. 1983. *Ideology and practice in schooling*. Philadelphia: Temple University Press.

Arsenberg, C. M, and A. H. Niehoff. 1971. *Introducing social change: A manual for community development*. Chicago, Ill.: Aldine.

Bauman, Z. 1973. *Culture as praxis*. Boston: Routledge & Kegan Paul.

Bhabha, H. 1988. Cultural diversity and cultural difference. In *The post-colonial studies reader,* eds. B. Ashcroft, G. Griffiths, and H. Tiffin, 206–09. New York: Routledge.

Common, R., and L. Frost. 1994. *Teaching wigwams: A modern version of Native education*. Muncey, Ont.: Anishinabe Kendaasiwin.

Government of Canada. 1996. *Report of the Royal Commission on Aboriginal People*. Ottawa: Canadian Communication Group.

Habermas, J. 1979. *Communication and the evolution of society*. Boston: Beacon.

Haig-Brown, C. 1995. *Taking control: Power and contradiction in First Nations adult education*. Vancouver, B.C.: University of British Columbia Press.

Hookimaw-Witt, J. 1998. *Keenabonanoh Keemoshominook Kaeshe Peemishishik Odaskiwakh [We stand on the graves of our ancestors]: Native interpretations of Treaty #9 with Attawapiskat Elders*. Unpublished master's thesis, Trent University.

Kells & Associates. 1995. *The Jules Mattinas healing lodge and treatment center in Attawapiskat*. Proposal to Nishnawbe Aski Health Planning Group. Ottawa: Author.

National Indian Brotherhood. 1973. *Indian control of Indian education*. Ottawa: Assembly of First Nations.

Ogbu, J. U. 1989. The individual in collective adaptation: A framework for focusing on academic underperformance and dropping out among involuntary minorities. In *Dropouts from school: Issues, dilemmas, and solutions*, eds. L. Weis, E. Farrar, and H.G. Petrie, 181–204. Albany, N.Y.: SUNY Press.

Witt, N. W. 1998. *Opening the healing path: The cultural basis for a solvent abusers' treatment program for the Attawapiskat First Nation*. Unpublished doctoral dissertation, OISE/UT.

32

Japanese Mothers as the Best Teachers

Keiko Hirao

The Japanese government has tried to encourage fathers to share in their children's upbringing, including placing advertisements in major newspapers that read "We don't call a man a father if he doesn't participate in childcare." Nonetheless, employed mothers rather than employed fathers are the ones who leave the labour force to devote a major part of their lives to their young children's education.

...The intensity and the depth of involvement of many Japanese mothers in their children's education has received considerable attention (Boocock 1991; Ellington 1992; Uno 1993; White 1987). The phenomenon of the *kyōiku mama* (education mother), in which a woman devotes a major part of her life to her child's academic career, is both praised as the source of Japanese students' impressive academic success and criticized for depriving children of their free time. The description of the *kyōiku mama* phenomenon, however, has been limited by a lack of attention to how Japanese education has been privatized in the past 20 years and how the role of *kyōiku mama* has been shaped and influenced by the reality of the educational system in Japan.

According to a survey by the Ministry of Education, over 35 percent of schoolchildren

Source: Keiko Hirao, "Mothers as the Best Teachers: Japanese Motherhood and Early Childhood Education." In *Women's Working Lives in East Asia*, ed. Mary C. Brinton, 180–203. Copyright © 2001: Stanford University Press. Published by permission.

attend *juku* (private educational institutions) that provide supplemental academic training (Ministry of Education 1994). The rate of attendance is highest among older children: in 1993, an amazing 67 percent of Japanese ninth graders were enrolled. Between 1985 and 1993, juku attendance increased from 17 to 24 percent for elementary school children and from 47 to 60 percent for middle school children. These *juku* statistics, however, tell only a small part of the story, which includes correspondence courses, tutoring services, and various private lessons available to children. When these services are included, 82 percent of all Japanese schoolchildren are enrolled in one or a combination of private educational programs (Ministry of Education 1994).

... A recent notable development in educational competition and the *kyōiku mama* phenomenon in Japan is that ever-younger children are becoming involved in educational activities outside of school. Approximately 42 percent of Japanese preschool children are enrolled in some kind of educational program outside of kindergarten and day nurseries (Ministry of Health and Welfare 1991). As Norma Field notes, childhood in contemporary Japan has become streamlined as a series of preparatory steps to productive adulthood (Field 1995), and parents—especially mothers—play a vital role as the agents of human capital investment.

DATA

This chapter is based on interviews conducted on the parenting behaviors of mothers in the Tokyo area during 1991–1992 and in Nagoya (Aichi Prefecture) in 1994–1995. The samples for the Tokyo interviews were recruited through three parenting classes sponsored by local governments and play-group networks. The parenting classes involved approximately 80 participants in total. As I served as the coordinator/instructor, I was able to request the names of participants who were willing to cooperate in the interviews. I then added to the samples through snowball sampling methods. Twenty women from the classes were contacted for the in-depth interviews. I also utilized the discussions in the classes as a means of participant observation. Because the parenting classes were offered in the daytime, the participants were limited to full-time housewives and part-time workers. The format of the interview was mostly open-ended, with some structured questions about personal background....

DEVELOPMENT OF EARLY EDUCATION PROGRAMS: AN OBSESSION WITH PRODIGIES

The educational role played by Japanese mothers starts when children are very young. Kindergartens and nursery schools expect mothers to incorporate an educational agenda into the routine of daily life (Allison 1996). The intensity of this responsibility is illustrated by the recent development of *soki-kyōiku,* early educational programs that are given either at home or at private, extra-school institutions. These are geared explicitly toward the development of cognitive skills in preschool children.

These programs are "extra-school" in the sense that they are independent from formal kindergartens and accredited day nurseries. Kindergartens and day nurseries operate under the auspices of the Ministry of Education and the Ministry of Health and Welfare, respectively. Because more than 93 percent of preschool children are enrolled in one or the other of these institutions, kindergartens and day nursery programs have now become comparable to formal schools. Private enterprises that provide educational services for preschoolers can be compared to the preschool version of *juku* for school-aged children. *Juku* is distinguished from extracurricular activities as it is administered outside the school system. In the same manner, early education programs function externally to the formal system of kindergarten and nursery schools.

... The course content offered in the extra-preschool curriculums varies widely, ranging from music lessons to reading and writing, simple mathematics to foreign languages. Some courses are purely academically oriented, some specialize in preparatory training for entrance examinations for prestigious elementary schools, and others emphasize artistic skills and music lessons. Many boast a combination of some or all of these benefits.

Kumon, a prominent *juku,* for example, invites preschoolers to work on mathematics, English, and Japanese. Founded by Toru Kumon in 1958 in Osaka as a small neighborhood *juku* for schoolchildren, Kumon is now one of the largest *juku* establishments in Japan, with more than 18,000 branch classroom locations all over the country and a total enrollment of 1.5 million (Kumon Kyōiku Kenkyukai 1998).

During the late 1980s, Kumon expanded its programs to include the enrollment of preschoolers.

In 1990, they started a correspondence course through which they delivered monthly educational kits such as videos, flash cards, and workbooks to children between the ages of two and five. In the mid-1980s, Kumon began to commend their high achievers. Among them were preschool children who could work out differential and integral calculus. These youngsters had already finished the high school level mathematics curriculum, and some of their mothers were reported to have started the program while they were pregnant.

The Association of Early Childhood Development, founded by Masaru Ibuka, the founder of Sony, states its mission as assisting in the sound development of the mother–child relationship. Its operation includes developing teaching materials, such as electronically prerecorded flash cards called "talking cards." Courses are offered to children aged 12 to 24 months old. Courses are also available to pregnant women on how to enhance the potential abilities of their unborn children....

The Child Academy, founded by Makoto Shichida, offers comprehensive programs such as storytelling, flash-card learning, haiku, arts and crafts, and music. The Ishii School of Kanji Education focuses on the teaching of reading and writing Chinese characters for preschoolers, offering correspondence courses as well as instruction in classrooms....

The spur for early education began in 1976 when Ibuka published a sensational book titled *Yochien de wa Ososugiru* ("Kindergarten Is Too Late"). This book became a best-seller and was followed by a flood of publications that advocated early intervention in order to develop the cognitive and verbal skills of infants. Such publications include Shichida's *Miraculous Education for the Zero-Year-Old* (1983) and *Tips on Raising an Intelligent Baby* (1985), *Mitsuishi's Creating Prodigies* (1988), and *Ōshima's Prenatal Education* (1988). The acceleration of early education can be seen through the titles of Ibuka's successive books: *Kindergarten Is Too Late* (1976), followed by *Zero-Year-Old* (1991) and *From Embryo* (1992). We can see the shift in the messages. Kindergarten was too late in the 1970s. But in the 1990s mothers were instructed to be concerned about their children's academic achievements *from conception.*

The accelerated education in Japan parallels, to some extent, the proliferation of educational programs for preschool children in the United States. Programs with heavy educational components for prekindergarten children are also on the increase in the United States. The well-publicized "superkid" practice by Glenn Doman, *How to Teach Your Baby to Read* (1964) and *How to Multiply Your Baby's Intelligence* (1984), for example, resonates with many of the publications by Ibuka, Shichida, and Ishii. They share the common premises that children's IQ is not fixed at birth but is determined by environment and intellectual stimulation, that children's potential for learning has long been underestimated, and that intellectual growth is very rapid during early childhood. In other words, the cognitive potential of children, according to both Doman and Ishii, can be significantly boosted by early intervention programs....

PRESCHOOLERS AS A NEW MARKET

...Once education for preschoolers proved to be a profitable business for *juku* industries, other sectors began to enter the market. For example, a company that sells underwear and other home-related products through direct-mail catalogs decided to go into the extra-preschool education business in 1992. They converted their customer list into a mailing list through which they delivered educational materials each month for children under the age of six. It is not unusual, especially in urban areas, for mothers of newborn babies to receive a direct-mail advertisement of courses offered to "enhance the academic ability" of their offspring. The early education "boom" was thus driven by the supply of these services.

Ironically, this development took place outside the public school system just as the Ministry of Education was trying to relax school schedules to remedy the excessive competition for entrance examinations. The public schools have taken to heart the criticism that excessive academic competition causes poor health among children, school violence, and bullying. Contrary to the common belief that Japanese schools are driving their students with relentless pressure for academic success, they are now shifting their emphasis to "creativity," "sociability," and "whole development" and away from rote learning. Approximately one-fourth of the time spent at Japanese schools is now devoted to nonacademic activities, such as recess and club activities (Stevenson 1992). Moreover, the Ministry of Education decided to reduce the time spent in school by 70 hours per year for elementary school students and 35 hours for junior high school students. The ministry also stipulates in the new curriculum guidelines that the content be cut by 30 percent, beginning in 2002.

In spite of the ministry's attempt to give children more free time and develop their creativity, the reforms have not extended to broad changes in the entrance examination system for colleges. As a result, many parents feel that school classrooms have become a place to confirm what children already know instead of a center for learning and mastering new subjects. This concern has prompted them to plan ahead out of the fear of having their children fall behind.

For example, Natsuko, who is age 36 and has three school-aged children, comments that

> I was too naive when I was raising my first child. You can't believe how smart today's children are. Most first graders already know several *kanji* [Chinese characters], not to mention being able to read and write *hiragana* [the Japanese phonetic syllabary]. My daughter was the only one in the class who could not write her name. Although we are told that teachers don't expect children to have mastered these things by the time they enter school, the fact that all the other children already know them makes the slow starters fall behind.

Another problem with the educational reforms is that all schools must meet minimum standards, but private schools are not bound by the curriculum guidelines stipulated by the Ministry of Education. That is, private schools can use more advanced materials than those used in public schools. They can also allocate more hours to important subjects, such as English, which carries more weight in the college entrance exams. Given that a sizable portion of students admitted to the University of Tokyo, the most prestigious university in the Japanese educational hierarchy, come from private high schools with admission tracks tied to their own attached junior high schools, parents are reminded that educational competition starts at a very young age. Many of these schools push their curricula forward so that students can devote their entire senior year in high school to preparing for college entrance examinations. Private elementary schools are also attractive to parents who worry that their children will not fare well in the intense competition for junior high schools: many of these private institutions provide an admission track all the way up to high school. Consequently, the age for competition has been lowered, and the competition for a better school career has involved young preschool children.

Chisato is married to a computer engineer and has a three-year-old son. She is planning to send him to a private elementary school. He is attending a weekly preparatory program for the screening test. He also has to do workbook exercises at home with his mother. Chisato comments on their decision as follows:

> I know it is a pity that a small boy like him has to work so hard, but it is for his own good. It is much easier to push him now than it will be later. If he can avoid the pressure of the entrance examination for junior high and high school, he can devote more time to developing his talents during the 12 years [he is in school full-time].

Kumiko, who is married to a physician, had a son just three weeks before I interviewed her. When I asked her how she felt about having a baby, she said,

> I am glad Satoshi was born in April. Of course it's the best time for having a baby! The weather is nice,

and I can take him outside and let him breathe fresh air. You know, oxygen is very important for brain development. Also, he will be one of the oldest in his class [the school year starts in April in Japan], and that will make him ahead of most children. Kids born in spring have better school records. I think that's why children born in April and May are overrepresented among students in the University of Tokyo.

I wish I had asked her where she got this idea about the birth month and the chance of being accepted to the University of Tokyo. When I met her a year later, she had put Satoshi in an enrichment class for infants run by one of the large *juku* establishments. She escorted Satoshi every week and joined an hour-long class with him. She commented bashfully,

Well, I don't mean to raise him as a "super kid." It's just a play group sort of program where children play with toys and listen to songs and so on. I just think it is important to let him play with other babies, because he has to know how to cooperate and socialize with his peers by the time he goes to kindergarten.

Although Kumiko's example may be an extreme case, there are three points that represent the ideas shared by many *kyōiku mama* today. First, a child has to go through keen academic competition in order to obtain a decent educational background. Second, a child's educational success depends on how much the parent puts into it. Third, the younger the child, the better the time for preparation. It is almost always the mother who is responsible for seeing to the provision of these opportunities and who is expected to be closely involved in the process....

JAPANESE WOMEN IN THE COMMUNITY

While the publication trends in popular books set the tenor of public discourse on "good parenting," they also mirror what the public wants to read. The increased demands for parenting advice reflect the social context in which adult socialization takes place for young Japanese mothers.

Adult Socialization and the Role of the Mass Media

Assuming the parental role is a totally fresh endeavor for most Japanese women, who generally become mothers without any firsthand experience of taking care of small children (given that Japanese families typically now have few children). Unlike in the United States, babysitting is not a socially accepted way for teenagers to earn money. So it is not unusual for a mother to start parenting with no experience in changing diapers or bathing babies. Parenting, or mothering specifically, is a performance without rehearsal.

Japanese women learn parenting from several socializing agents: parents and in-laws, friends, neighbors, older siblings, books, magazines, television programs, parenting courses sponsored by local governments, and kindergartens and daycare centers. Among these sources, the mass media is of increasing importance as a socializing agent. When asked where they obtained information on infant care, 35 percent of mothers surveyed in Tokyo named the mass media (books, magazines, and television) as the primary source of information, 34 percent named friends, and 17 percent answered kindergartens and daycare centers (Shirasa 1990). Parents and kin networks still play a major role in providing emotional support, but apparently they are somewhat secondary in the transmission of parenting knowledge.

Given the rapid pace at which childrearing practices have changed over the past decades, it is understandable that what grandmothers did 30 years ago is not often applicable to today's childrearing. For example, women in their 60s raised children when bottle-feeding was predominant; it was regarded as superior and as the "modern" way of feeding. Now the trend has reversed. Today more mothers opt for breast-feeding if it is possible (Katsuura-Cook 1991).

The arrival of parenting magazines is a rational consequence of this "information gap." They began to be published in the early 1980s and now provide detailed, up-to-date information on chil-drearing practices based on children's ages. Opposite to the decline in the birth rate, the circulation of parenting magazines has steadily increased. The total circulation of the major 12 parenting magazines is estimated to be as high as 2,710,000 (Shiomi 1996). Almost all of these parenting magazines contain advertisements and paid publications by companies that provide extra-preschool curricula and educational materials. No single issue appears without their advertisements and their sponsored articles on early intervention programs.

The effect of the mass media on the early education boom can be seen in a survey that showed a positive relationship between mothers' reliance on published materials for parenting know-how and their attitudes toward extra-preschool curricula. The more they are exposed to parenting information through the mass media, the more they are likely to be influenced to provide enrichment "stimulus" through extra-preschool curricula (Shirasa 1990). These mothers are also more likely to feel uneasy about their child's development if other children of the same age are more advanced in writing Chinese characters and in computations. Thus reliance on the mass media for parenting information seems to go hand in hand with the popularization of early education.

Isolation and Anxiety: Childrearing behind Closed Doors

Another prominent aspect in the lives of Japanese mothers who stay at home full-time is their isolation with their children. Because the social spheres of Japanese men and women tend to be so distinctly separated, there are very few opportunities for full-time housewives of salaried workers to socialize. The husband is busy with long working hours and rarely has spare time to help around the home with chores and childcare. Baby-sitters are not readily available in the neighborhood, and commercialized

services are often too expensive. A mother is not qualified to have her baby enrolled in an accredited daycare center if she is not working or does not have another "legitimate" reason, such as illness. Commenting on her days with her baby, Toshiko, a full-time housewife married to a "salaryman," says: "A day, a week, and a month could easily pass without talking to any adult except for people in the market or with a salesperson who comes to our door to sell educational toys and *futon*."

In spite of the great emphasis placed on close mother–child relationships in Japanese families, literature in psychology and sociology has long ignored the situation of young mothers. The focus of attention has always been on *children* and on how the mother–child relationship affects the development of a child's personality, well-being, and so on. Little has been written or known about how the mother–child relationship affects mothers.

The isolation of mothers from other adult interaction is another precondition for the development of the early education boom. Ironically, extra-preschool courses provide lonely mothers with a place to meet people. Toshiko said that she decided to put her son in an enrichment program because she wanted to meet people and make friends. The "friends" she was talking about were not for her son, but for herself. Kumiko, mentioned earlier in this chapter, also said that chatting with other mothers in the waiting room while their children took classes provided a nice change of pace.

Many mothers are aware of the suffocation of lonely childrearing and many of them do try to get out of the isolation. Ochiai (1989) argues that a new type of network among mothers is emerging in urban areas in response to the lack of support from husbands and kin. They are of a spontaneous nature, usually composed of mothers who meet each other in neighborhood parks or parenting classes sponsored by the local government. These neighborhood networks provide mutual support in parenting and supplement kin networks. However, my observation is that much of what Ochiai calls "networks" tend to be exclusive, rarely involve fathers, and limit concerns to matters revolving around children.

Yoshiko used to work as a secretary at a trading company until she became pregnant. She decided to leave her job and take care of her son at home. The change in her lifestyle and the routines of a full-time housewife were "a kind of culture shock" to her. She described her days as follows:

I usually take my son to a neighborhood park in the morning so that he can play with other children. Mothers chat while children play in the sandbox. If the kids move to the swings, we move with them and chat around the swing, or slides, or whatever. Then we usually go to one of the mothers' houses, order pizza or noodles for lunch, and then chat in the afternoon while the children play in the house. When daddies are on business trips, we sometimes eat supper together. The members are the same and the topic of our conversation is the same. At first I enjoyed being with these people, but I am getting tired of it. It's so suffocating!

After several months, she decided to have her son enroll in Suzuki violin and Kumon so that she could avoid this situation.

I was getting tired of this, but did not want to be ostracized and to be left alone with my kid. Having a private lesson for him gave me a good excuse for keeping some distance from other mothers. They won't feel bad about me if I just say, "I can't join you today because I have to take my kid to a violin lesson."

Again, extra-preschool courses are meeting the demands of their patrons. They provide a place to meet other mothers—and to avoid them.

"A GOOD MOTHER" AS A STATUS: THE CULTURAL CONTRADICTIONS IN WOMEN'S ROLES

Mothers receive mixed and conflicting message[s] [about] labor force participation: you have to be a good mother, but childrearing will not occupy you for your entire life. On the one hand, mothers are pressed to stay home at least until their children reach the age of three. On the other hand, mothers are aware that they have to be prepared to pursue their "own lives," for their children will grow up and leave the nest. Men and women, especially those who have pursued higher education, have been exposed to contemporary cultural values that emphasize the significance of achievement....

Over 80 percent of Japanese women join the labor force upon graduating from school, but more than 80 percent of these women have withdrawn from the labor force for one year or longer by the time they reach the age of 34. The probability of leaving one's job is not necessarily lower for women with higher education (Brinton 1993; Hirao 1997). That is, highly educated women are as likely to be out of the labor force as their less-educated counterparts during the prime parenting years. Moreover, the probability of coming back to the labor force after initial "retirement" is not necessarily higher for four-year university graduates (Hirao 1998). In other words, Japanese women's human capital is very much underutilized in the labor force.

The most striking thing that I noticed throughout my interviews was the frustration shared by many young mothers. "What depresses me is the social trend that gives praise to career women," said Yuko, a graduate from a prestigious four-year university. She used to work at a large department store as a sales assistant and resigned from her job when she had her second daughter.

They say it's good to be "at the top," pursue your career, and earn money. Super moms who can handle both work and family appear as attractive figures in TV dramas. I used to have self-confidence, I was always at the top both in school and work. My grades were higher than those of my male classmates. I thought I was in a career track until I left it to take care of my kids. Now, I ask myself, "What am I doing here?" I feel trapped and left behind by the rest of the world.

Emiko, who also has two children, expresses her frustration more clearly.

I used to have everything except kids; study, work, travel, and love. I was imbued with the pleasure of achieving what I deserved. But now, I am doing nothing but raising children, feeding them, bathing them, chasing them around, and yelling at them. My speculation is that, in spite of the primacy given to mothering by childcare experts, the perceived value of childrearing is declining.

These women, particularly those with higher education, have experienced an egalitarian school environment and have internalized, to some extent, the idea that it is crucial even for women to have status in society. Upon becoming mothers, however, the role of mother becomes their primary social identity.

Ohinata (1982) reports changes in mothers' attitudes toward the value of childcare. She compared the attitude of two cohorts of highly educated mothers, one in their 60s and the other in their 30s. Both cohorts shared the idea that childrearing is physically and emotionally demanding. A significant difference was observed, however, in how they viewed the value of childrearing. A majority (74 percent) of the older cohort agreed that childrearing is a worthwhile and wonderful job, while only 40 percent of the younger cohort shared this view. The majority (61 percent) of the younger cohort asserted that their reasons to live exist outside childrearing, while only 20 percent of the older cohort expressed this view.

The ambivalence toward parenting among young mothers is a natural consequence of changing lifestyles. Being a mother no longer necessarily provides a sense of achievement. Becoming a "good mother," however, is a different story. The ideology of the good mother has exerted a strong normative force on Japanese women during the last two decades. This is because mother and child have been seen as an inseparable pair, the mother and child relationship has been conceptualized as an extension of a mother's "self," a substantial proportion of a child's achievement is believed to result from his or her "effort" rather than from innate individual capabilities, and a child's outcomes have become more easily measurable at an early stage of childhood (e.g., school records and results in entrance examinations to prestigious elementary schools).

Mothers can learn where their child stands relative to other children at quite an early stage through various assessments. The results are thought to reflect how hard the child—and the mother—worked. When we take into account the presumably close psychological proximity between mother and child in Japan and the beliefs related to the causal link between maternal care and child outcomes, it is logical to see being a good mother as a status, one that is achievable depending on how much effort one makes.

Natsumi works part-time as a shop clerk in a confectionery store. She feels that her parenting is constantly being assessed. In her view, "'a good child' is necessary for becoming 'a good mother.'"

When I talk with other mothers, I often feel that they are evaluating each other's "worth" by the "quality" of the child. A good child is what makes you proud. It isn't your career, your achievement, or what you do as an individual. These things don't count in the world of mothers!

Tomoe, a physician's wife and the full-time mother of one daughter, described early intervention programs as "addictive."

I wasn't serious when I started sending my daughter to a *yoji kyoshitsu*. I was just curious about the program when I saw their flyer in the newspaper. After I enrolled her, however, I soon learned that such a program has an addictive power. She liked going there, and it was exciting to see how quickly and how much a child can learn. This excitement makes you feel as if it was you who took the test and scored so well. Once you feel this excitement, it is very hard to stop; you don't want to feel that you have failed in something.

The *kyoiku mama* syndrome is not an irreversible process: Tomoe began to notice that she was seeking a vicarious sense of achievement.

One day, I was telling my daughter to do her homework. She must have thought I was nagging her too much. She stared at me and said, "Mom, it's my homework, not yours. Don't talk to me like that." I realized that I was pushing her too hard and that being an extreme *kyoiku mama* can be its own form of child abuse.

CRITICAL THINKING QUESTIONS

1. The Japanese government has tried to reduce the extreme competitiveness to enter university. Why have these efforts been largely unsuccessful?
2. How are Japanese mothers, but not fathers, socialized to be active participants in their children's early education? Also, how is the isolation of mothers one of the reasons for their involvement in the early-education boom?
3. What is the cultural contradiction about gender roles that educated mothers encounter in Japanese society? Do you think that Canadian mothers experience the sacme contradictions? Why or why not?

REFERENCES

Allison, Anne. 1996. *Permitted and prohibited desires: Mothers, comics, and censorship in Japan.* Boulder, Colo.: Westview Press.

Boocock, Sarane Spence. 1991. The Japanese preschool system. In *Windows on Japanese Education,* ed. Edward R. Beauchamp, 97–126. New York: Greenwood Press.

Brinton, Mary C. 1993. *Women and the economic miracle: Gender and work in postwar Japan.* Berkeley: University of California Press.

Doman, Glenn. 1964. *How to teach your baby to read.* New York: Random House.

———. 1984. *How to multiply your baby's intelligence.* New York: Doubleday.

Ellington, Lucien. 1992. *Education in the Japanese life-cycle.* Lewiston, N.Y.: E. Mellen Press.

Field, Norma. 1995. The child as laborer and consumer: The disappearance of childhood in contemporary Japan. In *Children and the politics of culture,* ed. Sharon Stephens, 51–78. Princeton, N.J.: Princeton University Press.

Hirao, Keiko. 1997. Work histories and home investment of married Japanese women. Ph.D. diss., University of Notre Dame, Department of Sociology.

———. 1998. Saishushoku no taiming: Kekkon/shussan taishokugo no rodoshijo saisanyu katei no hasado bunseki (Hazard analyses on the timing of re-entry to the labor force). Paper presented at the annual meetings of the Japanese Sociological Society, Kwansei Gakuin University, Nishinomiya, Japan.

Ibuka, Masaru. 1976. *Yochien dewa ososugiru* (Kindergarten is too late). Tokyo: Goma Shobo.

———. 1992. *Zerosai* (Zero-year-old). Tokyo: Gomashobo.

———. 1992. *Taijikara* (From embryo). Tokyo Tokumashobo.

Katsuura-Cook, Noriko. 1991. *Nihon no kosodate, Amerika no kosodate* (Childrearing in Japan and the United States). Tokyo: Saiensu.

Kumon Kyoiku Kenkyukai. 1998. *Company profiles.* Tokyo: Kumon Kyoiku Kenkyukai.

Ministry of Education, Japan. 1994. *Survey report on Juku and other extra-school programs.* Tokyo: Author.

Ministry of Health and Welfare, Japan. 1991. *Survey on children's environment.* Tokyo: Government Printing Office.

Mitsuishi, Yukiko, 1988. *Tensaiji o tsukuru!* (Creating prodigies). Tokyo: Foyu.

Ochiai, Emiko. 1989. *Kindai kazoku to feminizumu* (Modern families and feminism). Tokyo: Keisoshobo.

Ohinata, Masami. 1982. Hahaoya no shinriteki antei to jusoku o motomete (For the mental stability and fulfillment of mothers). In *Ikuji noiroze* (Childrearing depression). Tokyo: Yuhikaku.

Oshima, Kiyoshi. *Taikyo* (Prenatal education) Tokyo: Gomashobo.

Shichida, Makoto. 1983. *Kiseki ga okiru shichidashiki zerosai kyoiku* (Miraculous education for zero-year-olds). Tokyo: Homeido.

———. 1985. *Akachan wo kashikoku sodateru himitsu* (Tips on raising an intelligent baby). Tokyo: Nihon Keizai Shimbunsha.

Shiomi, Toshiyuki. 1996. *Yoji kyoiku sangyo to kosodate* (Education industry and childrearing). Tokyo: Iwanami Shoten.

Shirasa, Izumi. 1990. Soki kyoiku ni kansuru kahoaoya no taido (Attitude of mothers on early education). Master's paper, University of Tokyo.

Stevenson, Harold W. 1992. Learning from Asian schools. *Scientific American* 267 (December): 70–76.

Uno, Kathleen S. 1993. The death of "Good wife, wise mother"? In *Postwar Japan as history,* ed. Andrew Gordon. Berkeley: University of California Press.

White, Merry. 1987. *The Japanese educational challenge: A commitment to children.* New York: Free Press.

33

The Souls of Black Folk

W. E. B. Du Bois

Minority Populations

CLASSIC

CONTEMPORARY

CROSS-CULTURAL

W. E. B. Du Bois, a pioneering U.S. sociologist and the first African American to receive a doctorate from Harvard University, describes how a colour-conscious society casts black people as "strangers in their own homes." One result, Du Bois explains, is that African Americans develop a "double consciousness," seeing themselves as Americans but always gazing back at themselves through the eyes of the white majority, as people set below and apart by colour.

Between me and the other world there is ever an unasked question: unasked by some through feelings of delicacy; by others through the difficulty of rightly framing it. All, nevertheless, flutter round it. They approach me in a half-hesitant sort of way, eye me curiously or compassionately, and then, instead of saying directly, How does it feel to be a problem? they say, I know an excellent colored man in my town; or, I fought at Mechanicsville; or, Do not these Southern outrages make your blood boil? At these I smile, or am interested, or reduce the boiling to a simmer, as the occasion may require. To the real question, How does it feel to be a problem? I answer seldom a word.

Source: From *The Souls of Black Folk* by W. E. B. Du Bois (New York: Penguin, 1982; orig. 1903), pp. 43–53.

And yet, being a problem is a strange experience—peculiar even for one who has never been anything else, save perhaps in babyhood and in Europe. It is in the early days of rollicking boyhood that the revelation first bursts upon one, all in a day, as it were. I remember well when the shadow swept across me. I was a little thing, away up in the hills of New England, where the dark Housatonic winds between Hoosac and Taghkanic to the sea. In a wee wooden schoolhouse, something put it into the boys' and girls' heads to buy gorgeous visiting-cards—ten cents a package—and exchange. The exchange was merry, till one girl, a tall newcomer, refused my card—refused it peremptorily, with a glance. Then it dawned upon me with a certain suddenness that I was different from the others; or like, mayhap, in heart and life and longing, but shut out from their world by a vast veil. I had thereafter no desire to tear down that veil, to creep through; I held all beyond it in common contempt, and lived above it in a region of blue sky and great wandering shadows. That sky was bluest when I could beat my mates at examination-time, or beat them at a foot-race, or even beat their stringy heads. Alas, with the years all this fine contempt began to fade; for the words I longed for, and all their dazzling opportunities, were theirs, not mine. But they should not keep these prizes, I said; some, all, I would wrest from them. Just how I would do it I could never decide: by reading law, by healing the sick, by telling the wonderful tales that swam in my head—some way. With other black boys the strife was not so fiercely sunny: Their youth shrunk into tasteless sycophancy, or into silent hatred of the pale world about them and mocking distrust of everything white; or wasted itself in a bitter cry, Why did God make me an outcast and a stranger in mine own house? The shades of the prison-house closed round about us all: walls strait and stubborn to the whitest, but relentlessly narrow, tall, and unscalable to sons of night who must plod darkly on in resignation, or beat unavailing palms against the stone, or steadily, half hopelessly, watch the streak of blue above.

After the Egyptian and Indian, the Greek and Roman, the Teuton and Mongolian, the Negro is a sort of seventh son, born with a veil, and gifted with second-sight in this American world—a world which yields him no true self-consciousness, but only lets him see himself through the revelation of the other world. It is a peculiar sensation, this double-consciousness, this sense of always looking at one's self through the eyes of others, of measuring one's soul by the tape of a world that looks on in amused contempt and pity. One ever feels his twoness—an American, a Negro; two souls, two thoughts, two unreconciled strivings; two warring ideals in one dark body, whose dogged strength alone keeps it from being torn asunder.

The history of the American Negro is the history of this strife, this longing to attain self-conscious manhood, to merge his double self into a better and truer self. In this merging he wishes neither of the older selves to be lost. He would not Africanize America, for America has too much to teach the world and Africa. He would not bleach his Negro soul in a flood of white Americanism, for he knows that Negro blood has a message for the world. He simply wishes to make it possible for a man to be both a Negro and an American, without being cursed and spit upon by his fellows, without having the doors of Opportunity closed roughly in his face.

This, then, is the end of his striving: to be a coworker in the kingdom of culture, to escape both death and isolation, to husband and use his best powers and his latent genius. These powers of body and mind have in the past been strangely wasted, dispersed, or forgotten. The shadow of a mighty Negro past flits through the tale of Ethiopia the Shadowy and of Egypt the Sphinx. Through history, the powers of single black men flash here and there like falling stars, and die sometimes before the world has rightly gauged their brightness. Here in America, in the few days since Emancipation, the black man's turning hither and thither in hesitant and doubtful striving has often made his very strength to lose effectiveness, to seem like absence of power, like weakness. And yet it is not weakness—it is the contradiction of double aims. The double-aimed struggle of the black artisan on the one hand to escape white contempt for a nation of mere hewers of wood and drawers of water, and on the other hand to plough and nail and dig for a poverty-stricken horde—could only result in making him a poor craftsman, for he had but half a heart in either cause. By the poverty and ignorance of his people, the Negro minister or doctor was tempted toward quackery and demagogy; and by the criticism of the other world, toward ideals that made him ashamed of his lowly tasks. The would-be black *savant* was confronted by the paradox that the knowledge his people needed was a twice-told tale to his white neighbors, while the knowledge which would teach the white world was Greek to his own flesh and blood. The innate love of harmony and beauty that set the ruder souls of his people a-dancing and a-singing raised but confusion and doubt in the soul of the black artist; for the beauty revealed to him was the soul-beauty of a race which his larger audience despised, and he could not articulate the message of another people. This waste of double aims, this seeking to satisfy two unreconciled ideals, has wrought sad havoc with the courage and faith and deeds of ten thousand thousand people, has sent them often wooing false gods and invoking false means of salvation, and at times has even seemed about to make them ashamed of themselves.

Away back in the days of bondage they thought to see in one divine event the end of all doubt and disappointment; few men ever worshipped Freedom with half such unquestioning faith as did the American Negro for two centuries. To him, so far as he thought and dreamed, slavery was indeed the sum of all villainies, the cause of all sorrow, the root of all prejudice; Emancipation was the key to a promised land of sweeter beauty than ever stretched before the eyes of wearied Israelites. In song and exhortation swelled one refrain—Liberty; in his tears and curses the God he implored had Freedom in his right hand. At last it came, suddenly, fearfully, like a dream. With one wild carnival of blood and passion came the message in his own plaintive cadences:

> Shout, O children!
> Shout, you're free!
> For God has bought your liberty!

Years have passed away since then,—ten, twenty, forty; forty years of national life, forty years of renewal and development, and yet the swarthy spectre sits in its accustomed seat at the Nation's feast. In vain do we cry to this our vastest social problem:

> Take any shape but that, and my firm nerves
> Shall never tremble!

The Nation has not yet found peace from its sins; the freedman has not yet found in freedom his promised land. Whatever of good may have come in these years of change, the shadow of a deep disappointment rests upon the Negro people—a disappointment all the more bitter because the unattained ideal was unbounded save by the simple ignorance of a lowly people.

The first decade was merely a prolongation of the vain search for freedom, the boon that seemed ever barely to elude their grasp, like a tantalizing will-o'-the-wisp, maddening and misleading the headless host. The holocaust of war, the terrors of the Ku-Klux Klan, the lies of carpet-baggers, the disorganization of industry, and the contradictory advice of friends and foes, left the bewildered serf with no new watchword beyond the old cry for freedom. As the time flew, however, he began to grasp a new idea. The ideal of liberty demanded for its attainment powerful means, and these the Fifteenth Amendment gave him. The ballot, which before he had looked upon as a visible sign of freedom, he now regarded as the chief means of gaining and perfecting the liberty with which war had partially endowed him. And why not? Had not votes made war and emancipated millions? Had not votes enfranchised the freedmen? Was anything impossible to a power that had done all this? A million black men started with renewed zeal to vote themselves into the kingdom. So the decade flew away, the revolution of 1876 came, and left the half-free serf weary, wondering, but still inspired. Slowly but steadily, in the following years, a new vision began gradually to replace the dream of political power—a powerful movement, the rise of another ideal to guide the unguided, another pillar of fire by night after a clouded day. It was the ideal of "book-learning"; the curiosity, born of compulsory ignorance, to know and test the power of the cabalistic letters of the white man, the longing to know. Here at last seemed to have been discovered the mountain path to Canaan; longer than the highway of Emancipation and law, steep and rugged, but straight, leading to heights high enough to overlook life.

Up the new path the advance guard toiled, slowly, heavily, doggedly; only those who have watched and guided the faltering feet, the misty minds, the dull understandings, of the dark pupils of these schools know how faithfully, how piteously, this people strove to learn. It was weary work. The cold statistician wrote down the inches of progress here and there, noted also where here and there a foot had slipped or some one had fallen. To the tired climbers, the horizon was ever dark, the mists were often cold, the Canaan was always dim and far away. If, however, the vistas disclosed as yet no goal, no resting-place, little but flattery and criticism, the journey at least gave leisure for reflection and self-examination; it changed the child of Emancipation to the youth with dawning self-consciousness, self-realization, self-respect. In those sombre forests of his striving his own soul rose before him, and he saw himself, darkly as through a veil; and yet he saw in himself some faint revelation of his power, of his mission. He began to have a dim feeling that, to attain his place in the world, he must be himself, and not another. For the first time he sought to analyze the burden he bore upon his back, that dead-weight of social degradation partially masked behind a half-named Negro problem. He felt his poverty; without a cent, without a home, without land, tools, or savings, he had entered into competition with rich, landed, skilled neighbors. To be a man is hard, but to be a poor race in a land of dollars is the very bottom of hardships. He felt the weight of his ignorance, not simply of letters, but of life, of business, of the humanities; the accumulated sloth and shirking and awkwardness of decades and centuries shackled his hands and feet. Nor was his burden all poverty and ignorance. The red stain of bastardy, which two centuries of systematic legal defilement of Negro women had stamped upon his race, meant not only the loss of ancient African chastity, but also the hereditary weight of a mass of corruption from white adulterers, threatening almost the obliteration of the Negro home.

A people thus handicapped ought not to be asked to race with the world, but rather allowed to give all its time and thought to its own social problems. But alas! while sociologists gleefully count his bastards and his prostitutes, the very soul of the toiling, sweating black man is darkened by the shadow of a vast despair. Men call the shadow prejudice, and learnedly explain it as the natural defence of culture against barbarism, learning against ignorance, purity against crime, the "higher" against the "lower" races. To which the Negro cries Amen! and swears that to so much of this strange prejudice as is founded on just homage to civilization, culture, righteousness, and progress, he humbly bows and meekly does obeisance. But before that nameless prejudice that leaps beyond all this he stands helpless, dismayed, and well-nigh speechless; before that personal disrespect and mockery, the ridicule and systematic humiliation, the distortion of fact and wanton license of fancy, the cynical ignoring of the better and the boisterous welcoming of the worse, the all-pervading desire to inculcate disdain for everything black, from Toussaint to the devil—before this there rises a sickening despair that would disarm and discourage any nation save that black host to whom "discouragement" is an unwritten word.

But the facing of so vast a prejudice could not but bring the inevitable self-questioning, self-disparagement, and lowering of ideals which ever accompany repression and breed in an atmosphere of contempt and hate. Whisperings and portents came borne upon the four winds: Lo! we are diseased and dying, cried the dark hosts; we cannot write, our voting is vain; what need of education, since we must always cook and serve? And the Nation echoed and enforced this self-criticism saying: Be content to be servants, and nothing more; what need of higher culture for half-men? Away with the black man's ballot, by force or fraud—and behold the suicide of a race!

Nevertheless, out of the evil came something of good—the more careful adjustment of education to real life, the clearer perception of the Negroes' social responsibilities, and the sobering realization of the meaning of progress.

So dawned the time of *Sturm und Drang:* Storm and stress today rocks our little boat on the mad waters of the world-sea; there is within and without the sound of conflict, the burning of body and rending of soul; inspiration strives with doubt, and faith with vain questionings. The bright ideals of the past—physical freedom, political power, the training of brains and the training of hands— all these in turn have waxed and waned, until even the last grows dim and overcast. Are they all wrong, all false? No, not that, but each alone was over-simple and incomplete—the dreams of a credulous race-childhood, or the fond imaginings of the other world which does not know and does not want to know our power. To be really true, all these ideals must be melted and welded into one. The training of the schools we need today more than ever—the training of deft hands, quick eyes and ears, and above all the broader, deeper, higher culture of gifted minds and pure hearts. The power of the ballot we need in sheer self-defence—else what shall save us from a second slavery? Freedom, too, the long-sought, we still seek, the freedom of life and limb, the freedom to work and think, the freedom to love and aspire. Work, culture, liberty—all these we need, not singly but together, not successively but together, each growing and aiding each, and all striving toward that vaster ideal that swims before the Negro people, the ideal of human brotherhood, gained through the unifying ideal of Race; the ideal of fostering and developing the traits and talents of the Negro, not in opposition to or contempt for other races, but rather in large conformity to the greater ideals of the American Republic, in order that some day on American soil two world-races may give each to each those characteristics both so sadly lack. We the darker ones come even now not altogether empty-handed: There are today no truer exponents of the pure human spirit of the Declaration of Independence than the American Negroes; there is no true American music but the wild sweet melodies of the Negro slave, the American fairy tales and folklore are Indian and African; and, all in all, we black men seem the sole oasis of simple faith and reverence in a dusty desert of dollars and smartness. Will America be poorer if she replace[s] her brutal dyspeptic blundering with light-hearted but determined Negro humility? or her coarse and cruel wit with loving jovial good-humor? or her vulgar music with the soul of the Sorrow Songs?

Merely a concrete test of the underlying principles of the great republic is the Negro Problem, and the spiritual striving of the freedmen's sons is in the travail of souls whose burden is almost beyond the measure of their strength, but who bear it in the name of an historic race, in the name of this the land of their fathers' fathers, and in the name of human opportunity.

CRITICAL THINKING QUESTIONS

1. What does Du Bois mean by the "double consciousness" of African Americans?
2. Du Bois writes that people of colour aspire to realizing a "better and truer self." What do you think he imagines such a self to be?
3. What are some of the reasons, according to Du Bois, that Emancipation (from slavery in 1863) brought disappointment to former slaves, at least in the short run?
4. Does this essay seem optimistic or pessimistic about the future of race relations? Why?

34

Aboriginal Identity:
The Need for Historical and
Contextual Perspectives

Jean-Paul Restoule

Restoule explores Canadian Aboriginal identities from legal and historical perspectives as well as the personal and subjective experiences of Aboriginal peoples.

Employing a perspective that distinguishes between "identity" and "identifying" demonstrates the limitations inherent in typical conceptions of cultural identity. Identifying is situational and historical, shaped by the time and place in which it occurs, whereas identity is thought to transcend history and social situations. Identity is represented in the Indian Act and its definition of "Indian." Métis efforts for recognition as an Aboriginal people in their own right is seen as identifying. The potential harm of identity is demonstrated by the Crown's arguments in the case for Gitksan-Wet'suwet'en Aboriginal title.

I recently attended a conference where a number of us were discussing issues concerning Aboriginal identity. We talked about how our parents had tried

Source: Jean-Paul Restoule. 2000. "Aboriginal Identity: The Need for Historical and Contextual Perspectives." *Canadian Journal of Native Education*, 24(2), 102–12. Abridged with the permission of the Canadian Journal of Native Education, University of Alberta and University of British Columbia.

to hide any semblance of their Aboriginal identity and how in our experience today it was not only acceptable, but indeed desirable to be Aboriginal. In our experience dreamcatchers were everywhere and Aboriginal plays and events in the city were sold out. "What happened?" we asked each other. Then someone pointed out that where she came from there was not the luxury to talk about identifying as Aboriginal as if it were a choice. Shame about being Aboriginal continued to exist in her community. Most of the people from her community would hide their Aboriginality if possible. For many of them it was not even an option. They were "known" as Aboriginal people. Also, in her experience the issues of drug abuse, AIDS, diabetes, unemployment, spousal abuse, and others were seen as more pressing concerns than identity.

Her words had quite an impact on me. How can some of us talk about the struggle for identity when on a daily basis so many of us struggle just to survive? Is writing about these matters really helping to change anything? I keep coming back to this idea that some of the people in her community would hide their Aboriginality if they could. Understanding what influences our pride or shame in identifying as Aboriginal people is important. How we feel about ourselves contributes to and arises from the issues my colleague felt were more urgent to discuss than identity. I have seen examples where pride in Aboriginal identity is the basis for fighting addiction and where shame in identity is a factor in developing a habit of substance abuse (Restoule, 1999). It is important to explore what identifying as Aboriginal means and what is gained and lost in attempting to erase that identity, as well as what it means to change the referents of what is meant by Aboriginal identity.

IDENTITY AND IDENTIFYING

The term *identity* expressed popularly, as well as in academic circles, implies a fixed nature over a given time period. In psychology, identity is often qualified as, for example, sex-role identity or racial identity (Sutherland, 1989). These qualities are assumed to have some continuity over time for the individual. In Piaget's work, identity refers to a state of awareness that something holds its value despite surface appearances to the contrary (Sutherland, 1989). In logic, identity refers to two words, properties, or statements that are so similar that they can substitute one for the other in an equation without altering the meaning (Sutherland 1989). In sum, identity has been conceived to mean sameness. For social scientists discussing cultural identity, the sameness inherent in the definition of identity refers to the shared norms, traits, and habits of members of a cultural group at one historical moment. Unfortunately, there are educators, lawyers, and policymakers who make the error of assuming Aboriginal identity must hold over several generations.

To talk about Aboriginal identity assumes a sameness and continuity that belies the fluidity and change that Aboriginal people experience and demonstrate. When this assumed permanence of character is run through institutions like the education and court systems "Aboriginal identity" can be constrictive and colonizing. I return to this idea below with a discussion of the case for Gitksan-Wet'suwet'en Aboriginal title. If we change the focus from *identity* to *identifying*, we move from noun to verb and set off a potentially liberating way of conceiving and talking about self-definition. *Identity* implies fixedness; that the "things" that make one Indian remain the same and should be the same as those things associated with Indianness by the Europeans at the time of historical "first" contact. Identity places power in the observer who observes Aboriginal people from the outside and defines them, giving them an identity. *Identifying* shifts control to the self, and motivations come to the fore. This perspective favors a set of referents that are put into action at the historical time one identifies as an Aboriginal person and in the contextual place where one identifies. Identifying is a process of being and becoming what one is in the moment. The power is placed in the self, for the Aboriginal person who emphasizes his or her Indigenous roots at a particular place and time. This allows for the salient components of an Aboriginal identity to be expressed as the actor feels is expedient, allowing for cultural change and adaptation. Identifying is situational and historical, whereas identity is thought to transcend history and social situations.

In this article I use a number of examples to make clearer the distinction between identity and identifying. Dunn's (2001) research on the Métis of the Red River region shows that the tension between identity and identifying existed even in the 1800s. I provide a brief overview of Canadian legislation defining "Indians" as an example of identity as I characterize it above. As a point of contrast, Métis participation in the Constitutional Conferences of the 1980s and the Royal Commission on Aboriginal Peoples (RCAP, 1996) demonstrate identifying.

Employing a perspective that distinguishes between identity and identifying might help us problematize typical conceptions of cultural identity limited in their ability to reflect the situational and contextual identifying that exists in contemporary Aboriginal life. To demonstrate the limitations of an identity perspective, I look at Fitzgerald's (1977) notion of cultural identity as an interplay between color, culture, and class. This conception of cultural identity, I feel, is fairly typical. I refer to work by Valentine (1995) and Pinneault and Patterson (1997) to demonstrate that identity/identifying is indeed contextual and is shaped by the time and place in which it occurs....

LIMITATIONS OF IDENTITY IN ABORIGINAL NORTH AMERICA

Identity is a complicated concept. Cultural identity is often conceived as an interplay between biology, socioeconomic status, and cultural knowledge. Fitzgerald (1977), in his study of Maori students, refers to these three components as color, culture, and class. To Fitzgerald color represents a biological connection to the original peoples. In other words, it is the blood connection, the lineage that can be traced to Aboriginal communities and families. By culture Fitzgerald means knowledge of the traditions, language, and ceremonies or the "markers" of the race. Class stands for socioeconomic position in the greater society. Society is perceived as the greater economic and political entity where many cultures coexist. Each culture participates in the larger society where it is located, although the cultural norms of the group may be distinct from the rest of the society.

Race is often conflated with class, so that a racial group or cultural group is likely to be thought of as occupying a particular class position in relation to the greater society. Power is maintained by barriers that keep racial groups from advancing socioeconomically. Although certain

individuals may succeed in being upwardly mobile, much of the group continues to experience difficulty. As Fitzgerald (1993) observed, "The central tensions between groups do not seem to be essentially cultural but originate in inequalities over power and participation in society. More and more, groups are trying to invent cultures through identity assertions" (p. 221). Identity tends to be more persistent and stable over time, whereas cultures are in a constant state of reinvention. This is because identity often has to do with how the out-group culture views the in-group. Fitzgerald (1977) found that some Maoris he studied validated their right of acceptance in the Maori group by overemphasizing their biological connections and/or class position, especially if they knew little about the culture. I suspect this to be the case among Aboriginal people in Canada. Those who know little about the Aboriginal culture to which they claim a connection probably will emphasize their blood ties to an Aboriginal culture. Claiming to be born "Ojibwe" or "Blackfoot" does not necessarily entail a familiarity with the music, ceremonies, or language. This is a reality of living in a dispersed culture where there have been generations of increased pressure not to exhibit these cultural knowledges.

The interplay of biology, culture, and class cannot maintain its integrity when applied to Aboriginal cultures in North America. Perhaps in the mid-nineteenth century most Aboriginal people could be slotted by class, culture, and biology such that the categories remained relatively stable. Aboriginal persons for the most part were not only able to demonstrate who they were related to (biology), but also could make their way in their culture and were probably lower-class citizens in relation to the class structure of British North America. Today these factors are not necessarily applicable to each Aboriginal person, and it is impossible to predict with any certainty one's placement in each of these categories. For example, today many Aboriginal people may be slotted into lower socioeconomic categories in relation to Canadian class structure, but individual Aboriginal people are not necessarily reducible to a particular class. Also, many people with Aboriginal cultural knowledge have no ties to their home communities or to an officially recognized community. Conversely, many Aboriginal people with blood ties to Aboriginal communities have little or no Aboriginal cultural knowledge. The instability of these categories is evident when one looks at contemporary Aboriginal people on Turtle Island today.

IDENTIFYING AS SITUATIONAL AND CONTEXTUAL

Fitzgerald's (1977) observation that "cultural identity has relevance only in a situation of cultural homogeneity" (p. 59) appears to be supported by the research of both Valentine (1995) and Pinneault and Patterson (1997). Valentine lived and worked among the Anishinabe of Lynx Lake, Ontario where the community is composed almost entirely of Aboriginal families. As Valentine explains,

> In southern Ojibwe communities, where forced contact with the White matrix society has been long standing, Native people tend to define themselves vis-à-vis the "other." Thus, if something is "White" then it is necessarily "not-Indian" and vice versa.... In the north, where there has been relatively little and generally recent contact with Whites, the Native people define themselves internally. In a situation such as that in Lynx Lake, it is moot to ask if one element or another is "White" or even "borrowed." If the people are using it, the item is being used "Natively." The question asked by the people of Lynx Lake is "Will X be useful to us?" not "Will the use of X compromise our Nativeness?" (p. 164)

Here the question of what is Aboriginal is raised only in comparison with cultures outside the community.

Contrast the Lynx Lake community with Pinneault and Patterson's (1997) work in urban schools in the Niagara region of Ontario. Here Pinneault and Patterson counsel youth who struggle with debunking myths and labels or with trying to find where they fit in. Pinneault and Patterson describe the situation thus.

> Attempt to put yourself in the following story. You are living in a land which is the first and only foundation of your philosophy, spiritual beliefs, historical patterns, cultural distinction, and ancestral connections. At the same time, you never see a reflection of yourself within the philosophy of others, the educational system, popular culture, or day-to-day events within the community. Stereotyping remains entrenched in most societal situations and you are constantly in a position of needing to defend your rights and position. When you are able to visualize yourself, it is through the interpretation of others who have little understanding of who you are. You are constantly being defined and redefined from an outside system. (p. 27)

Many students in the south are struggling with the creation of safe places to increase self-esteem and build understanding and acceptance of some of the Aboriginal cultural traditions. Obviously identity issues come to the fore when there is sustained contact between culturally different groups, and especially when they are valued differently on the social scale.

Another way to understand the differences between the disparate groups in Niagara and Lynx Lake is to discuss identifying rather than identity. Identifying in Niagara has different meanings and consequences than it does in Lynx Lake. Aboriginal people in Lynx Lake do not identify as "Native" in Lynx Lake because the homogeneous nature of the population makes it redundant to do so. The identity of the people in the distant communities is not different necessarily. Rather the factors that influence an Aboriginal person's choice to identify change from one region to another are different....

LEGISLATIVE DEFINITIONS AS IDENTITY

The Indian Act has been the source of many problems in the history of Aboriginal survival. It has been the legal support for violence enacted against Aboriginal peoples in the form of regulations imposed on personal mobility, language use, and participation in cultural activities. Relevant to this discussion is its peculiar claim of distinction as a rare piece of legislation that sets out in law a definition of a people. This definition has had a profound impact not only in how we are understood by non-Aboriginal people, but also in how we have come to understand ourselves.…

In early legislation designed to contain potential violence between Aboriginal people and newcomers, a broad definition of *Indian* was set into law. For example, the 1850 Indian Protection Act defined Indians broadly:

> The following classes of persons are and shall be considered as Indians belonging to the Tribe or body of Indians interested in such lands: First—All persons of Indian blood, reputed to belong to the particular Body or Tribe of Indians interested in such lands, and their descendants. Secondly—All persons intermarried with any such Indians and residing amongst them, and the descendants of all such persons. Thirdly—All persons residing among such Indians, whose parents on either side were or are Indians of such Body or Tribe, or entitled to be considered as such: And Fourthly—All persons adopted in infancy by any such Indians, and residing in the Village or upon the lands of such Tribe or Body of Indians, and their descendants.

The only important distinction was between European and Indian. Interestingly enough, early definitions of Indian like this one allowed for men and women of European descent who lived with an Aboriginal community to be considered Indian before the law. What mattered more than blood (although this too was important) was the evidence that one lived as an Indian. One would have to assume this distinction was relatively simple to make in the nineteenth century. Otherwise the definition would have been drafted differently.

As laws governing Indian lands were consolidated, the definition of an Indian in law was redrafted to exclude more Aboriginal people and to encourage the assimilation of registered Indians into the Canadian body politic (RCAP, 1996). Assimilation is genocide according to the United Nations Genocide Convention, signed by Canada in 1949 and unanimously adopted in Parliament in 1952. Chrisjohn and Young with Maraun (1997) have argued that Canada could be tried in violation of the genocide convention for the operation of residential schools. The Canadian Civil Liberties Union, in debates held before Canada enabled legislation in 1952, recognized the potential for Canada's transfer of Indian children to residential schools to be seen as genocide (Churchill, 1997). Enfranchisement was also a key tool of assimilation or genocide.

Enfranchisement, along with definitions privileging patrilineal descent, reduced the number of Indians eligible for the Register. The children of interracial marriages were counted as Indians only when the father was Indian. Native women who married non-Native men were removed from the Register and often distanced from their communities. Over the years there were many ways Indians could lose their status. Some examples include earning a university degree, requesting the right to vote in a federal election, or requesting removal from the Indian Register for a share of the monies that would have gone to the band on their behalf. Most significantly, Indian women who married non-Indian men were enfranchised involuntarily, and the children of these marriages were ineligible for status. Clearly the goal of the Gradual Enfranchisement Act, and its subsequent absorption into the Indian Act, was assimilation (RCAP, 1996).

The Métis, as an Aboriginal people, found themselves caught in the middle of the changing legal definitions. The numbers of Métis who would have been entitled to receive the benefits of Indian status in 1850 were gradually reduced by arbitrary legislation. Great pains were taken to extinguish Métis claims to Aboriginal title, and they were not accorded any benefits in exchange for the land. This does not mean that only "full-blooded" Indians were entitled to be registered. What mattered was whether it was one's father or mother who was officially recognized as Indian. Often these non-status Indians would align themselves politically with the cultural Métis, who had for the most part been denied any rights as Aboriginal people. This denial occurred despite Métis treaties with Canada in the Manitoba Act and the Dominion Lands Act(s).

BEING AND BECOMING MÉTIS AS AN EXAMPLE OF IDENTIFYING

The Métis provide an interesting example of how colonial definitions are played out and affect self-definitions. Most people believe that Métis means simply "mixed" denoting the mixing of the blood of European and Indian parents in their child. The word has been used to designate various groups with a tie to Aboriginal peoples present on the continent before European settlement. How were the new populations that were a result of the new interrelationships between Indian and non-Indian characterized or written about in the earliest times? How did Métis, which originally meant simply mixed, come to mean specific kinds of mixes and in specific times and locations?

Dunn (2001), a descendant of the Red River Métis and consultant to the RCAP, has an excellent Web site (www.otherMétis.net) that catalogues the many terms and names that have been used to describe the intermixing of European and Aboriginal peoples. It is important to note that there is little evidence of what these groups of people under discussion preferred to be called in the nineteenth century, and few records of what they called themselves exist. Most of these terms were used by colonial bureaucrats and traders who thought it important enough and necessary to write about this growing and influential population in their particular region.... The diversity of names used indicates at least two important points. First, the groups now known as Métis were seen as a distinct social fact by most of the social groups sharing the same region. Second, the names accorded these groups of "mixed-race"

people are ways for people external to the group to make an identity for them. Obviously some terms are meant to be disparaging. Dunn's ancestors were called Half-breed by the government officials of the day. At the same time, Dunn's great-great-grandfather used the term *Natives of the country* when referring to his group. In any case, as Dunn points out, "the external application of terminology does not guarantee that the term accurately communicates the expression of an internal identity" (para. 22). Identity is a process of being and becoming, and nouns cannot adequately be used to describe identity; rather they merely serve to label and fix a group of persons (Peterson & Brown, 1985). The attributes of the group that make it identifiable as distinct from others are constantly changing, and the words that are used to fix the group also change their referents. The use of the word Métis was taken up by these groups of "mixed blood" or "ancestry" and applied in different ways and for different ends.

At the constitutional conferences in the mid-1980s the leader of the Métis National Council (1986) stated:

> Surely it is more than racial characteristics that makes a people. What about a common history, culture, political consciousness? Our origins, like that of any people when traced back far enough, are mixed, but once we evolved into a distinct aboriginal people, the amount of this much or that much ancestry mattered less than being Métis.

Note that he stressed the acceptance of the community and identification with the community.

This distinction was promoted by the 1996 *Report of the Royal Commission on Aboriginal Peoples*, although it made some concessions for the Congress of Aboriginal Peoples definition of Métis, which is based solely on Aboriginal ancestry (blood). The RCAP (1996) recommendation is as follows:

> ... 4.5.2 Every person who (a) identifies himself or herself as Métis and (b) is accepted as such by the nation of Métis people with which that person wishes

to be associated, on the basis of criteria and procedures determined by that nation be recognized as a member of that nation for purposes of nation-to-nation negotiations and as Métis for that purpose. (vol. 4: 203)

This definition, although leaving the choice of political affiliation to the individual claimant, is broad enough to include both Métis National Council and Native Council of Canada/Congress of Aboriginal Peoples members.

It should be noted that the Commission's recommendation above is made in respect to the sphere of political rights. The Commission (1996) recognizes that the identification of Aboriginal communities for legal purposes has taken a different approach. Essentially, after some analysis, the Commission laid out three elements that seemed to be acceptable to courts in determining membership in an Aboriginal community:

- some ancestral family connection (not necessarily genetic) with the particular Aboriginal people;
- self-identification of the individual with the particular Aboriginal people; and
- community acceptance of the individual by the particular Aboriginal people. (vol. 4: 297–98)

A fourth element was mentioned as also being of relevance in some cases: "a rational connection, consisting of sufficient objectively determinable points of contact between the individual and the particular Aboriginal people" (vol. 4: 298). Acceptable criteria include residence, family connections, cultural ties, language, and religion (vol. 4: 298).

In many ways it seems as if we have come full circle. Early attempts to legislate who is an Indian were broad and inclusive and allowed for anyone living in an Aboriginal community to qualify as Indian under the law. Definitions became increasingly exclusive, causing inequities and suffering and dissension among Aboriginal peoples. The RCAP (1996) recommended that all Aboriginal peoples be entitled to rights as members of an Aboriginal community. But

history has seen individuals with Aboriginal "blood" migrate to urban areas where they may not live in Aboriginal communities that are located in a tight geographical configuration. As sound and fair as it may appear for legal reasoning to recognize only Aboriginal communities and members of those communities, in practice it may again turn out to be a politically expedient way of reducing the numbers of Aboriginal people whom the government must recognize. In the end it really may be up to the individuals in communities of interest to decide what factors of their personality and culture make them distinctly Aboriginal and continue a process of being and becoming that cannot be legislated.

THE IMPACT OF IDENTITY

Once when I was talking to a friend and tenant at a native housing co-op where I worked, I told her that my lack of knowledge on a particular issue was because I was not a politically active person. She replied, "For an Indian, being born is political." I realize now that she meant that from the time we are born, as Indians we are in a particular relationship with the Canadian state by virtue of the treaties, the Indian Register, and the Indian Act. She also meant that because the state had been seeking our disappearance for centuries, each time one more of us is born we are directly in opposition to the goals of the state. Each of us through our birth proved we would not disappear. When we are born, we are defined by the state as a particular kind of Indian. Either we are eligible for the Indian Register and designated a Status Indian, or we are denied the rights that this heritage should lend itself to. There were times when not being registered was an advantage because the strict enforcement of the Indian Act imposed many measures on recognized Indians. The drawback, of course, was that many identifiable Indians were disallowed connections with their extended families and some of the treaty rights their ancestors had negotiated.

Using strictly the legal view of Indianness, in my family's experience, my father was born an Indian, later "earned the right not to be an Indian" through enfranchisement, and many years later was seen as a Status Indian once again. I was not born an Indian and was given Indian Status only after passage of the amended Indian Act of 1985. Receiving that card in the mail made me question a lot of things, and it caused me to look at my family in a new way. I was confused about how we had an identity decided for us. Why was it not a given that we could define for ourselves who we were?

The issue of Aboriginal identity is most often played out in Canadian law. Aboriginal "difference" from others is used to maintain inequities in power when it is convenient for those with power (Macklem, 1993). However, when our difference results in what is seen as privilege, arguments are made that treating Aboriginal people differently is "un-Canadian" because it is in opposition to the stated goal of equality among individuals before the law. There is a constructed image of what Indians are supposed to be that has to be played into or against in order to make advances in Canadian institutions, especially courts of law (Crosby, 1992; Razack, 1998). If we do not appear Indian enough or do not exhibit enough of the traits that are somewhat expected of Indians, then we will be judged to be no longer different enough from the Euro-Canadian assumption of the mainstream, and thus no longer Aboriginal. We will, in fact, be assumed to have assimilated into the assumed mainstream Canadian norm.

This line of logic has been argued by lawyers for the Crown in the case for Gitksan-Wet'suwet'en Aboriginal title (Crosby, 1992). The Crown argued that because the contemporary Gitksan eat pizza from microwaves and drive cars, they have essentially given up their Aboriginality. Indian rights flow only to those who meet the criteria for authenticity established by the Eurocentric courts (Crosby, 1992). Sustained colonization has caused many Aboriginal people to move away from a subsistence economy to a market economy, often without their choice. Many of the traditional ways of life seen from the Eurocentric position as "authentic Indian ways" have been altered by the imposition of colonial policies and laws, and then these very charges are used against us as arguments that we are no longer Aboriginal people.

The criteria accepted in the legal system, however, are often limited to material "stuff." What makes one Aboriginal is not the clothes one wears or the food one eats, but the values one holds. There is more to Aboriginal cultures than "fluff and feathers" (Doxtator, 1992). Johnston (1995), an Ojibwe ethnologist, recalls the time a young student in an elementary school, having spent five weeks learning about tipis, buskskin, canoes, and so much other stuff, asked him, "Is that all there is?" Johnston wanted people to know that there was more to Anishinabe culture than mere stuff, and this led him to write books like *Ojibway Heritage* (1976), *Ojibway Ceremonies* (1982), and *The Manitous* (1995). Unfortunately, in museums, movies, and courts of law it is the stuff that is exhibited. We are not Indian unless we prove that we still cling to the stuff that defined us in the eyes of others over 100 years ago. This conception will continue as long as we talk about identity and not identifying.

An interesting exercise is to turn these arguments around and apply them to the Eurocentric arguments for our assimilation. Does the lawyer who said the Gitksan-Wet'suwet'en drive cars realize that Europeans did not drive cars at the point of contact either? Was this lawyer wearing the same clothes his forefathers wore in 1763? Does this lawyer use the number zero? I think the use of zero may be been a case of cultural adoption, not unlike the Aboriginal people who adopt the use of snowmobiles. The culture that made the law is privileged to adapt and change over time, whereas the Aboriginal cultures are denied this same privilege. Although it may not be the stated objective of the law, the result is often the maintenance of in-equitable relations of power. Keeping Indians in the place they had at confederation is a goal of the consolidated Indian Act of 1876.

CONCLUSION

The Indian Act had as its goal nothing less than the assimilation of Aboriginal people in Canada (RCAP, 1996). A key strategy in achieving this goal was increasingly to limit who is an Indian by law and to change the status of those who were already on the list through enfranchisement. In this law "Indians" are identical to one another, but "different" from the Canadian power major-ity. The writers of legislation did not consider our cultures and histories important. Our identity as Indians was invented. Although at times we have used this identity to our own interests, forming coalitions across cultures to seek political gains (such as inclusion in the Constitution Act, 1982), we have also used these invented identities against one another, allowing these government categories to intrude on our social and cultural affairs (Coates, 1999). In our lives, in our work, in our efforts to educate others, let us identify as Aboriginal people from our inside place, from ourselves, our communities, our traditions. Let us not allow others to decide our identity for us.

ACKNOWLEDGMENTS

I would like to thank the anonymous reviewers of an earlier draft for their comments.

CRITICAL THINKING QUESTIONS

1. From a sociological perspective, why would possessing a positive self-identity influence how you lived your life?

2. With reference to the article, what role has the government played in the development of Aboriginal identity in Canada?
3. Review the similarities and differences between the concepts of *identity* and *identifying*. Why is the distinction important?
4. Review some of the recommendations for the *Report of the Royal Commission on Aborig-inal Peoples* (1996) as described in the article. Can you find any examples from your own community where these recommendations have been implemented?

REFERENCES

Chrisjohn, R., S Young, with M. Maraun. 1997. *The circle game: Shadows and substance in the Indian residential school experience in Canada*. Penticton, B.C.: Theytus.

Churchill, W. 1997. *A little matter of genocide: Holocaust and denial in the Americas 1492 to the present*. San Francisco, CA: City Lights Books.

Coates, K. 1999. Being Aboriginal. In *Futures and identities: Aboriginal peoples in Canada*, ed. M. Behiels, 23–41. Montreal: Association for Canadian Studies.

Crosby, M. 1992. Construction of the imaginary Indian. In *Vancouver anthology: The institutional politics of art*, ed. S. Douglas, 267–91. Burnaby, B.C.: Talonbooks.

Doxtator, D. 1992. *Fluff and feathers: An exhibit of the symbols of Indianness*. Brantford, Ont.: Woodland Cultural Centre.

Dunn, M. 2001, January. Métis identity—A source of rights? Paper presented at Trent University. [Online]. Available: **http://www.otherMétis.net/index.html/Papers/trent/ trent1.html#Terminology**. Retrieved January 4, 2001,

Fitzgerald, T. K. 1977. *Education and identity: A study of the New Zealand Maori graduate*. Wellington: New Zealand Council for Educational Research.

Johnston, B. 1976. *Ojibway heritage*. Toronto: McClelland and Stewart.

———. 1982. *Ojibway ceremonies*. Toronto: McClelland and Stewart.

———. 1995. *The Manitous: The spiritual world of the Ojibway*. Toronto: Key Porter Books.

Macklem, P. 1993. Ethnonationalism, Aboriginal identities, and the law. In *Ethnicity and Aboriginality: Case studies in ethnonationalism*, ed. M. D. Levin, 9–28. Toronto: University of Toronto Press.

The Métis Nation. 1986. 2(1): Winter.

Peterson, J., and J. S. H. Brown (eds.). 1985. *The new peoples: Being and becoming Métis in North America*. Winnipeg: University of Manitoba Press.

Pinneault, A., and C. Patterson. 1997. Native support circles in urban schools. *Orbit*, 28(1): 27–9.

Razack, S. 1998. *Looking white people in the eye: Gender, race and culture in courtrooms and classrooms*. Toronto: University of Toronto Press.

Restoule, J. P. 1999. Making movies, changing lives. Aboriginal film and identity. In *Futures and identities: Aboriginal peoples in Canada,* ed. M. Behiels, 180–89. Montreal: Association for Canadian Studies.

Royal Commission on Aboriginal Peoples. 1996. *Report of the Royal Commission on Aboriginal Peoples*. Ottawa: Ministry of Supply and Services.

Sutherland, N. S. 1989. *The international dictionary of psychology*. New York: Continuum.

Valentine, L. P. 1995. *Making it their own: Severn Ojibwe communicative practices*. Toronto: University of Toronto Press.

Minority Populations

CLASSIC

CONTEMPORARY

CROSS-CULTURAL

35

Ethnically Heterogamous Marriages: The Case of Asian Canadians

Jessie M. Tzeng

Tzeng's research investigates Canadian trends in interracial marriages. Findings suggest that while many believe their decision regarding whom to marry to be completely autonomous, it is in fact influenced by many social factors—whether they realize it or not.

INTRODUCTION

In an ethnically diverse society, such as Canada, the increases in intersection of group affiliations may promote intermarriage. A person often belongs to several social groups; for example, people live in a neighborhood, have an occupation, belong to an ethnic group, are members of a religious group, and have a socioeconomic status. Thus, the increasing social interactions among individuals of different backgrounds in modem society promote intergroup relations which in turn foster intermarriage (BIau, Beeker, and Fitzpatrick, 1984). In addition, the apparent growth of cultural pluralism, which stresses the acceptance of various ethnicities within a society, also shortens the social distances among persons of different ethnic backgrounds and may encourage intermarriage.

Many recent empirical studies suggest that various kinds of intermarriage have become more common over the course of this century (Kitano, Yeung, Chai, and Hatanaka, 1984; Lieberson and Waters, 1988; Kalmijn, 1993). However, the question of who marries whom remains a complicated mate-selection process for inter-married couples. The traditional theory of homogamy (like attracts like) is insufficient to explain interracial assortative mating because individuals in interracial relationships face unconventional and unique challenges when compared to couples in interracial relationships. To better understand the mechanism behind interracial marriage selection, one needs to further explore the forces of pull and push in the decision to intermarry and the role which achieved socioeconomic status plays in the process of interracial assortative mating.

Dynamics in Intermarriage: Forces of Pull and Push

In principle, there are two major forces, pull and push, operating simultaneously in the interracial assortative mating. Young people today may

Source: J. M. Tzeng. 2000. Ethnically Heterogamous Marriages: The Case of Asian Canadians. *Journal of Comparative Family Studies*, 31(3), 321–37. Published by permission.

assume that their choice of mate is completely autonomous; however, many factors, in fact, do place limits on autonomy, whether we consciously recognize their impact or not. One of the major influences on marital autonomy is the principle of endogamy, which requires a person to choose a partner from his or her own group (Larson, Goltz, and Hobart, 1994). This is one of the major pull sources constraining individuals from marrying someone outside their own group. Historically both family and society strongly opposed intermarriage. Almost all racial and ethnic groups have resisted intermarriage to protect and maintain their ethnic identities. Though there was no law prohibiting marriages between individuals from different racial and ethnic groups in Canada, intermarriage taboo exists not only in the importance of maintaining purity of one's own race or consistency of socialization for the younger generations, but also in the prevention of creating incompatible norms between members of diverse ethnic groups (Tinker, 1973; Merton, 1941). In this vein, it is said to be extremely difficult for a child of an intermarriage when it comes to selecting a role model for his or her identity; thus, those who oppose intermarriage believe marriage across racial and ethnic boundaries inevitably leads to a loss of identity among minority groups and signifies that a group is disintegrating, both socially and culturally (Goldstein and Segall, 1991).

Looking back in history, despite the persistence of negative attitudes and reactions toward intermarriage, people continue to intermarry, which may be a result of the following favorable push factors. First, recent social, economic and political environment changes provide some evidence that the society has become more open and tolerant to racial and cultural heterogeneity (Spickard, 1989; Goldstein and Segall, 1991). Namely, a higher rate of interracial marriage is possible because social proximity is common across many areas of social life, thereby providing evidence of shortening social distances between different racial and ethnic groups. Second, significant changes in the racial and ethnic distributions of the population will inevitably increase the probability of intermarriage. As the opportunities for individuals to come into contact with someone outside their own group increase, so does the likelihood of intermarriage. Third, research suggests that individuals from various racial and ethnic groups with higher socioeconomic status are more likely to enter intermarriage (Glick, 1970; Tinker, 1973; Fitzpatrick and Gurak, 1979; Sung, 1990). For example, the recent success in socioeconomic achievement obtained by Japanese, Chinese, and Jews in the United States is consistent with their higher out-marriage rates (Kitano, et. al., 1984; Mayer, 1985). On the one hand, individuals with higher socioeconomic status are more appealing to potential partners in the marriage market, both within and outside their own ethnic group. Since everyone is searching for a "better half" as a marriage partner, individuals from racial and ethnic groups with favorable socioeconomic positions increase their chance of out-marrying. On the other hand, this may also suggest that individuals from various racial and ethnic groups with higher socioeconomic status have a more liberal attitude toward marriage and are less likely to be bounded by traditional family or cultural norms, and thus are more likely to select mates outside their own group. Overall, it is argued that the number of interracial marriages will continue to rise as physical and social barriers between peoples diminish and the traditional approaches to mate selection will be replaced by the individual's choice (Sung, 1990).

Given the expansion of education and of women's participation in the labor force in the past few decades, young adults of all races are increasingly more likely to meet their potential spouses in school or at work. As a result of the current social forces, we are tempted to argue that the push force will play a more significant role than the pull force in an individual's marital choice.

The Significance of Achieved Status and Mate Selection

Some empirical evidence supports the theory of homogamy (that persons marry others either with similar ascribed family background or, increasingly, with similar achieved socioeconomic status). Couples who share similar cultural resources, either from ascribed or from achieved status, are more likely to enjoy similar views or agree with each other on certain issues and behaviors. On the one hand, the ascribed cultural characteristics from one's family of origin, including social class, religion, and race/ethnicity, are believed to have a major impact on an individual's choice of a future partner (Hollingshead, 1950). Among the many ascribed cultural characteristics used to describe the process of assortative mating, race and ethnicity is one of the most significant characteristics to represent one's cultural heritage. In particular, persons who were born and raised in Asian families have very distinctive cultural traits, such as unique physical appearance, languages, subcultures, values, norms, lifestyles, attitude, customs, and beliefs, all of which contribute to the uniqueness of their personalities, attitudes, social activities, and social circles and eventually affect their preference or choice of future mates.

On the other hand, the achieved cultural characteristics associated with individuals' socioeconomic status, such as language capability of the host society, educational attainment, and labor-market experience, are obtained by individuals through external institutions outside the home over time. The role of one's socioeconomic resources is becoming more important than race and ethnicity in the process of mate selection, due to the great expansion of education in the second half of the twentieth century, the greater flexibility in social mobility, and the changing role of women in the labor force.

For Asian immigrants, language ability is an important achieved characteristic clearly related to the assimilation process (White, Biddlecom, and Guo, 1993), because most Asian countries from which immigrants come do not use English or French as their official languages. Not only is the ability to speak English and/or French in Canada necessary for survival and assimilation in the host society, it helps to shorten the distance and to increase contact between individuals from different racial and ethnic groups. If immigrants lack knowledge of the official language, then there are cumulative as well as social and cultural barriers between immigrant groups and the host society (Stevens and Schoen, 1988). According to Murstein's (1970) stimulus-value-role theory of marital choice, marital choice involves a series of sequential stages: stimulus, value, and role; and, at any given point of the relationship, its viability can be determined as a function of the equality of exchange subjectively experienced by its participants. Without language capability, one cannot effectively go through the three stages of marital choice: interacting with each other, sharing values, and defining roles. In addition, the most obvious channel for communication between spouses is language, and when there is no common language between the potential marital partners, the channels of communication are blocked; thus, the odds of intermarriage will be small (Sung, 1990). Accordingly, Asian immigrants' knowledge of English and/or French will facilitate their propensity to intermarry in Canada (Castonguay, 1982).

In addition, numerous studies show that an individual's educational attainment and labor-market experience have become influential predictors in the process of marriage selection (Mare, 1991; Kalmijn, 1991, 1993; Qian and Preston, 1993; Schmitt, 1971; Hout, 1982). Educational attainment probably is one of the most significant social influences on the marriage process in many ways (Qian and Preston, 1993). Since education is often looked upon as being a key determinant of long-term socioeconomic status, research shows that the level of schooling varies positively with the propensity to marry (South, 1991). Following the exchange theory of mate selection (Merton, 1941), the higher the educational attainment of individuals, the more desirable they are in the marriage market, thus increasing their chances to marry. In addition, there has been a high level of marriage homogamy by education in the U.S. as well as in Canada (Sweet and Bumpass, 1987; Schoen and Wooldredge, 1989; Mare, 1991; lshwaran, 1992). Most people tend to many those with a similar level of education, due to their comparable values, goals, interests, and outlooks on life.

Among the most significant social changes in the recent decades has been the increasing participation of women in the labor force (Cherlin, 1992; Bianchi and Spain, 1986). The labor-market experience of women may have two opposite effects on the overall propensity to marry. On the one hand, the new economic independence gained by employed women reduces the comparative gains from marriage, thereby reducing the propensity to marry (Becker, 1981). On the other hand, women's full-time labor-force participation may be viewed as potential marital capital which will contribute to the total family income, thus increasing their desirability in the marriage market.

In view of people's general interest to marry up and/or marry homogamously, the high educational attainment and labor-force participation of Asians may affect their odds of marrying someone outside their own group. However, for many individuals of Asian origin, the newly learned cultural traits may be in great conflict or competition with traditional cultural characteristics. Individuals with Asian background have one of the strongest family traditions and kinship ties, and it is extremely important for the members in each group to preserve and pass their cultural heritage from one generation to the next. Marriage, for most Asian families, is important for its effect on family continuity and for maintaining the family line, not just for two individuals (Tinker, 1973). If, among Asian groups, the family tradition still plays an important role (even implicitly) in the individual's choice of spouse,

then the increasing trend of interracial marriage expected for Asian groups due to their high socioeconomic achievement would have been offset or lessened to a certain degree.

How one balances or weighs the two cultural forces when it comes to the individual's choice of a marital partner may vary with different groups and change over time. Thus, in this paper, I investigate the association between socioeconomic achievement and intermarriage for Asians in Canada and examine the changes in the importance of an individual's achieved socioeconomic status on his or her propensity to intermarry.

INTERMARRIAGE IN CANADA

This paper is aimed toward a better understanding of recent unique patterns in interracial marriage for Asians in Canada. Canada is widely regarded as an ethnoracially complex but remarkably ordered society of immigrants and refugees, aboriginal peoples, and colonizing groups (Fleras and Elliott, 1992). The immigrant population represented 16% (4.3 million persons) of Canada's population in 1991, almost unchanged since 1951, when the immigration population was 15% (Badets and Chui, 1994). Although the proportion of immigrants living in Canada has remained stable for the past 50 years, the distribution of immigrant population has become much more diverse now than it was a few decades ago. For example, in 1961, 90% of immigrants in Canada were from Europe, partly because immigration policy had systematically excluded non-white people; however, the proportion of European immigrants dropped significantly to less than a quarter in 1991. Among the new immigrant population, people reporting Asian origins were the fastest-growing group between 1981 and 1991. In 1991, more than 40% of immigrants came from Asia and the Pacific, while only 21% were from Europe (Statistics Canada, 1993). The shift in the source of immigrants from European to non-European countries has altered Canada's ethnic and linguistic composition and has created a greater diversity in the new "Canadian mosaic."[1]

Given Canada's new multicultural mosaic, one might expect to observe an ever-increasing trend in marriages among various racial and ethnic groups if current migration flow remains unchanged. Migration, indeed, is a major factor leading to interracial unions (Sung, 1990). If Asians or other racial and ethnic groups had not migrated to Canada, intermarriage would be less likely to occur. In the late 1980s, about 14% of the total married couples in Canada involved one foreign-born spouse, and 9% of the marriages were made up of two foreign-born persons (Dumas, 1990). The rate of interracial marriage would, no doubt, be even higher if I included second and later immigrant generations, as many studies have shown that generational differences account for a great deal of out-marriages (Tinker, 1973; Pagnini and Morgan, 1990). Compared to its southern neighbor, Canada has a higher rate of intermarriage than the U.S.,[2] mainly due to the following reasons. First, in the United States, racial intermarriage was legally restricted until 1967, while in Canada, no legal sanction was imposed on interracial marriage. Despite the fact that the U.S. Supreme Court's decision declaring its law on racial intermarriage unconstitutional, the social mores and the disfavor placed on interracial marriage by all major racial, religious, and ethnic groups have had major impact on an individual's choice of marital partner (Eshleman and Wilson, 1995). Second, most studies in Canada employ place of birth or countries of origin as the main source of identification of interracial marriages. This source allows a broader definition for interracial marriage than the self-identified race and ethnicity variable used in the U.S. studies. Third, the higher rate of intermarriage in Canada may also be directly attributed to its increasingly diverse immigrant population in recent years. For example, one out of six Canadians is a first-generation immigrant who is usually single and thus eligible for marriage (Statistics Canada, 1988), which also increases the opportunity for interracial marriage.

As a result of increasing Asian immigration to Canada in the past two decades, those reporting single Asian origins represented about 5% of the total population in 1991, and this trend is likely to persist with current immigration policies. Nevertheless, not only has systematic empirical research on intermarriage for individuals with Asian origins rarely been conducted in Canada, but also little attention has been paid to married couples' socioeconomic status in the study of interracial marriages. Among the limited empirical research on interracial marriage for Asians in North America (mostly in the U.S.), studies are predominately descriptive in nature (Burma, 1963; Tinker, 1973; Kitano et al., 1984; Romano, 1988; Sung, 1990) and lack multivariate analyses linking Asians' socioeconomic achievement and interracial marriage. Recent studies in marriages have described the tendency for persons to choose partners of similar educational attainment (Mare, 1991), occupation (Hout, 1982), and other social standings. In addition, in his recent research, Kalmijn (1991, 1993) suggests that educational homogamy has increased its importance over social origin homogamy, such as class and race, in marriage selection in the U.S. during recent decades. Thus, the focus of this paper is to examine the patterns and changes in intermarriage for Asians in Canada from 1981 to 1991, focusing on the effects of married couples' individual characteristics and socioeconomic status on intermarriage.

DATA AND METHOD

Sample

To examine intermarriage for various Asian Groups in Canada, it would have been more fruitful to use the individual file from recent Canadian censuses, which would provide detailed information on the respondent's ethnic origin[3], place of birth, and other individual characteristics. However, the individual identification codes in each census file were removed from public access and the data was randomly rearranged to ensure its total confidentiality. Thus, it is impossible to identify married couples from this data structure. As a result of this constraint in using individual census records, I have resorted to the family census file for this analysis.

FINDINGS

Changes and Temporal Patterns of In- and Out-marriages

Table 35.1 presents descriptive statistics on selective spouses' characteristics for Asian in- and out-marriages in Canada for 1981 and 1991. Contrary to the popular belief, in-marriage rates for Asians

TABLE 35.1:   Descriptive Statistics for Selective Variables

	1981			*1991*		
Variables	*In-mar.*	*Out-mar. Husband*	*Out-mar. Wife*	*In-mar.*	*Out-mar. Husband*	*Out-mar. Wife*
Marriage Rate	75.5	12.8	11.7	80.1	9.7	10.2
Husband's Age	42.0	42.2	42.8	45.3	42.2	43.6
Wife's Age	38.2	37.8	38.8	41.4	38.8	39.8
Years of Immigration (Husband)						
≤10	64.1	42.7	18.9	45.7	24.9	10.6
>10	35.9	56.4	30.1	49.9	70.8	32.7
n/a	.9	51.0	4.4	4.4	56.7	
Years of Immigration (Wife)						
≤10	71.6	30.8	45.1	48.7	12.1	30.4
>10	28.4	24.7	53.4	46.5	29.8	64.8
n/a	44.5	1.5	4.8	58.1	4.8	
Official Language (Husband)						
English and/or French	89.2	98.7	98.5	88.2	98.6	99.1
Neither	10.8	1.3	1.5	11.8	1.4	.9
Official Language (Wife)						
English and/or French	81.1	97.8	98.1	82.8	98.9	98.1
Neither	18.9	2.2	1.9	17.2	1.1	1.9
Education (Husband)						
<12	25.7	14.5	12.6	28.1	15.1	16.4
12–13	29.9	36.1	46.1	22.3	19.9	24.3
14+	44.4	49.3	41.3	49.6	65.0	59.3
Education (Wife)						
<12	36.1	23.3	12.1	35.8	16.0	15.1
12–13	33.4	48.0	52.4	27.1	30.8	26.3
14+	30.5	28.6	35.4	37.1	53.2	58.6
Employment Status (Husband)						
Not employed	13.4	9.7	3.9	18.7	10.8	10.9
Part-time	3.3	2.2	3.9	4.3	5.8	5.6
Full-time	83.3	88.1	92.2	77.0	83.3	83.4
Employment Status (Wife)						
Not employed	37.0	34.4	35.9	33.6	24.9	25.8
Part-time	13.2	15.4	21.4	11.1	20.0	17.5
Full-time	49.8	50.2	42.7	55.4	55.2	56.7

increased from 75.5% in 1981 to 80.1% in 1991. Accordingly, both male and female out-marriage rates were somewhat lower in 1991 than in 1981, with male out-marriage rates dropping twice as much as female out-marriage rates (3.1% vs 1.5%) during the 10-year period. As a result, Asian women have a slightly higher out-marriage rate than Asian men in 1991; however, the gaps in out-marriage rates between Asian men and women are small in both time periods. Thus, a significant gender difference in intermarriage found in other studies (Tinker, 1973; Kitano et. al., 1984) is not evident for Asian men and women in our data.

The average ages for husbands and wives in our sample are 42.3 and 38.27 in 1981; 43.7 and 40 in 1991. The respondents in our sample are in their middle age because the age composition of the immigrant population differs markedly from that of non-immigrants in Canada (Fleras and Elliott, 1992). The immigrant population in Canada is older than the native-born population because most people who immigrate to Canada do so when they are adults. More specifically, the in-married couples in 1981 were about 3 years younger than those couples in 1991. However, the changes in the age distributions are within 1 year for both male and female out-marriers from 1981 to 1991. The average differences between husbands and wives in all marriage types range from 3.3 to 4.4 years.

In both time periods, there are more out-married couples than in-married couples who have no children in their family, and the proportions are higher in 1991 than in 1981. In particular, female out-marriers have the highest proportion of being childless—32% and 38.2% in 1981 and 1991, respectively. In addition, male out-marriers in 1981 and female out-marriers in 1991 have the lowest proportions of having more than 3 children in their families. Nevertheless, the majority of couples have 1 or 2 children in their families regardless of marriage types. For all marriages, about one-third of the couples

have children under the age of 6. This is consistent with the literature in that intermarried couples tend to have fewer children due to their concern about adjustment problems for their children or their lack of time to have children if both of them are highly devoted to the labor force (Eberhard and Waldron, 1977; Sung, 1990).

The majority of Asians who married within group had been in Canada less than 10 years by the time of survey in 1981. In 1981, more than 50% of male (56.4%) and female (53.4%) out-marriers had been in the country for more than 10 years. However, for those who many within group in 1991, about half of them had been in Canada for more than 10 years and the other half had been in the country for less than 10 years. In addition, among out-marriers, 70.8% of men and 64.8% of women had been living in Canada for more than 10 years by the time of survey in 1991.

As to language capability, those who were unable to speak either English or French were more likely to marry within the Asian group. About 10% of men and 20% of women who had no knowledge of English or French were in in-marriages. On the other hand, more than 98% of the out-marriers were able to speak English, French, or both English and French in 1981 and 1991.

The lower half of Table 35.1 describes couples' labor-force characteristics for both in- and out-marriages. The overall educational attainment increased for all Asians during the period of 1981–1991. For in-marriages, the proportion of husbands and wives with more than 14 years[4] of schooling increased more than 5% from 1981 to 1991. The upward shift in educational achievement was even more significant for Asian out-marriers. The proportions of male and female out-marriers who were in the highest educational category increased from 49.3% to 65% and from 35.4% to 58.6% in the 10-year period, respectively.

The changes in the labor-force participation for husbands and wives show somewhat different patterns during this period. There was about a 5–6% decrease in full-time employment for both in- and out-married Asian males. On the contrary, the proportions of full-time employment increased from 49.8% to 55.4% for wives in in-marriages and from 42.7% to 56.7% for female out-marriers. In addition, the proportions of housewives for Asian females in both types of marriages declined, especially for female out-marriers.

The Effects of Individual Characteristics and Socioeconomic Factors on Intermarriage

In other analysis not shown here I estimated models that only include the effects of married couples' ages, the difference in age, and the respondents' duration of immigration on the probability of interracial marriage (Model I). Then, I added the variables indicating spouses' socioeconomic characteristics, such as individual's knowledge of the official language (i.e., English and/or French) in Canada, educational attainment, employment status, and the symmetrical positions of both spouses on educational attainment and employment status (model II, i.e., models in Table 35.2). In both years, scale deviances[5] drop significantly from model I to model II (Scale deviance {(model I model II)} = -129.5 and -616.3 in 1981 and 1991, respectively), with 15 degrees of freedom, which indicates the significant effects of spouses' socioeconomic characteristics in predicting the propensity of interracial marriage for Asians in Canada.

Thus, the following discussion will be focused on model II (shown on Table 35.2) for both years. The multivariate analyses presented in Table 35.2 examine the effects of both Asian husbands' and wives' social demographic and socioeconomic characteristics on the log odds of interracial marriage in 1981 and 1991, respectively. For models in Table 35.2, I report the logit coefficients, beta, and their standard deviations, se (beta).

Age

The results show that the effect of husband's age on the odds of interracial marriage is much stronger in 1991 than in 1981 except for the oldest age group. Husbands who were 35–44 or 45–54 years old are about 66% ($100[\exp(-1.079)-1]$) or 65% ($(10)[\exp(-1.050)-1]$) less likely to be intermarried than those who were 15–24 years of age in 1991. Wife's age consistently shows a negative effect on the probability of intermarriage in both years. Namely, older wives are less likely than those who were 15–24 years old to marry out, especially for those who were older than 65 years of age in 1981 and those who were 55–64 years of age in 1991. I also examine the effect of age homogamy on intermarriage. The results indicate that age-heterogamous Asian couples are more likely than age-homogamous couples (i.e., wife's age is equal to or less than 3 years younger than her husband's) to intermarry in both years. Especially in 1991, older wife–younger husband couples are about 62% ($100[\exp(0.481)-1]$) more likely to intermarry than age-homogamous couples.

Years of Immigration

The results also indicate the durations of immigration for both husband and wife significantly predict whether they enter intermarriage or not. Couples in which either one of the spouses or both spouses had been in Canada for more than 10 years are much more likely to be intermarried than those couples who had been in the country for less than 10 years. For example, if both spouses had been in Canada for more than 10 years, they are at least 5 times (1981: $100[\exp(1.859)-1]$; 1991: $100[\exp(1.954)-1]$) more likely to marry out than those had been in the country less than 10 years. The effects of durations of immigration on the log odds of entering intermarriage have remained quite stable during the 10-year period.

TABLE 35.2:   Logistic Models of Asian Interracial Marriages in Canada

	1981		*1991*	
	beta	se(beta)	beta	se(beta)
Husband's Age				
(15–24)				
25–34	0.057	0.452	−0.761	0.208
35–44	−0.446	0.503	−1.079	0.227
45–54	0.006	0.558	−1.050	0.252
55–64	−0.019	0.640	−0.592	0.281
65+	1.386	0.760	0.027	0331
Wife's Age				
(15–24)				
25–34	−0.363	0.272	−0.042	0.138
35–44	−0.556	0.349	−0.375	0.167
45–54	−0.428	0.440	−0.495	0.202
55–64	−0.308	0.555	−0.737	0.248
65+	−1.625	0.768	−0.390	0.301
Age Homogamy				
(Husband–Wife = 0–3)				
Husband–Wife >3	0.167	0.158	0.138	0.068
Husband–Wife <0	0.212	0.199	0.481	0.081
Years of Immigration (>10 Yrs)				
(Neither)				
Husband only	1.982	0.256	1.866	0.123
Wife only	1.234	0.196	1.854	0.110
Both	1.859	0.166	1.954	0.086
Official Language				
(Both)				
Husband only	−2.069	0.531	−1.795	0.260
Wife only	−1.311	1.134	−0.984	0.388
Neither	−1.715	0.492	−2.074	0.257
Husband's Education				
(≤11)				
12–13	0.704	0.233	0.231	0.097
14+	0.467	0.280	0.336	0.117
Wife's Education				
(≤11)				
12–13	0.448	0.193	0.475	0.090
14+	0.114	0.255	0.744	0.109
Educational Homogamy				
(H = W)				
H > W	0.098	0.180	0.135	0.071
H < W	0.755	0.194	0.550	0.085
H's Employment Status				
(Not employed)				
Part-time	−0.162	0.601	0.398	0.175
Full-time	−0.454	0.793	0.275	0.258
W's Employment Status				
(Not employed)				
Part-time	0.093	0.194	0.325	0.092
Full-time	0.513	0.774	−0.045	0.243

TABLE 35.2: *(Continued)*

	1981		1991	
	beta	*se(beta)*	*beta*	*se(beta)*
Employment Homogamy (H – W)				
H > W	0.751	0.756	0.155	0.228
II <- W	−0.858	0.655	0.429	0.222
Scaled Deviance	1586.2	8812	–	–
Degrees of Freedom	1	738	10	567

Official Language

Furthermore, the ability to speak either English and/or French increases one's probability to marry someone outside the Asian group. As shown from both years, when either one of the spouses or neither of the spouses speak the official languages, the chance of out-marrying is reduced. Although the negative effects on the probability of intermarriage have lessened from 1981 to 1991 for couples with only one of the spouses speaking the official languages, they are still highly significant. In addition, when neither spouse speaks one of the official languages, couples are about 87% less likely to intermarry than those couples who both have the ability to speak English or French in 1991. The ability to negotiate life in the host society using the official languages helps the immigrants to achieve social and economic assimilation, which in turn can facilitate intermarriage (White et al., 1993).

Education

The results from the lower panel of Table 35.2 show that the odds of interracial marriage vary positively with the educational attainment of husbands and wives for both years. In particular, the magnitude of the effects of wife's educational attainment is about twice that of husband's in 1991. The models also indicate that educational heterogamous couples are, in general, more likely than homogamous couples to experience interracial marriage, especially when the wife has more years of schooling. Apparently, the high levels of marriage homogamy by education found in recent years for married couples in North America are not witnessed in the intermarried Asian couples in Canada.

Employment Status

The odds of interracial marriage are not affected by husband's and wife's employment status in 1981. However, the odds of out-marriage vary positively with husband's and wife's employment status in 1991, except for wife's full-time employment. And employment-heterogamous couples are also more likely to be intermarried than employment-homogamous couples in 1991, especially when wives work more than their husbands. The effects of employment heterogamy are consistent with that of educational heterogamy on intermarriage. That is, couples in which wives work more than their husbands are about 54% more likely to be intermarried than employment-homogamous couples in 1991.

CONCLUSIONS

Our results indicate the increasingly significant roles which the achieved socioeconomic characteristics play in interracial assortative mating. Our study first builds on previous work by examining the effect of social demographic variables such as husband's and wife's age, age heterogamy, and years of immigration on Asian intermarriage in Canada from 1981 to 1991. The results are, in large part, in agreement with prior research. I find older individuals and those without any knowledge of English or French are less likely to marry out. Whereas, the propensity to intermarry is higher for age-heterogamous couples and when either one or both spouses have been in Canada for more than 10 years.

I then examined the effects of couples' socioeconomic characteristics on the odds of intermarriage. Our results indicate that educational attainment positively affects one's probability of interracial marriage. In addition, couples in which wives have higher educational achievement are also more likely to intermarry than educational homogamous couples. As for the effect of labor-force experience, I did not observe the same main effects of husband's and wife's employment status on intermarriage for both 1981 and 1991. In particular, the employment effect is not significant in 1981. On the contrary, in 1991 employment-heterogamous couples are more likely to be inter-married than employment-homogamous couples, especially when wives work more than their husband.

Thus, the results suggest age-, educational-, and employment-heterogamous Asian couples vary positively with the odds of intermarriage. In particular, the most unconventional couples, in which the wife is older, more educated, and with a higher level of labor-force participation than the husband, are more likely to be intermarried. These results may suggest that Asian women do have more to gain by intermarriage (Tinker, 1973). In general, older ages of the wives in intermarriage are highly correlated with their higher educational attainment and labor-market experience. Also, highly educated or full-time employed Asian women are more likely to inter-marry due to their quest for a more egalitarian marriage and their desire to avoid traditional

constraints set upon an Asian wife if she were to marry within her cultural group.

However, to my surprise, the rates of Asian intermarriage did not increase from 1981 to 1991, as I originally thought. The reasons for these decreasing rates may be due to the following: First, there is a larger selection as well as a more balanced sex ratio within one's own ethnic group as more Asian-origin groups immigrate to Canada. Most prior research suggests that population size and a balanced sex ratio positively correlate with in-marriage (Besanceney, 1965; Alba and Golden, 1986: Sung, 1990). Second, with a growing consciousness of multi-culturalism in the Canadian society, many racial and ethnic minorities, including Asians, are increasingly aware of their cultural and linguistic heritage as a positive component of personal identity and are anxious to remain culturally distinct, which may pose cultural constraints on intermarriage (Fleras and Elliott, 1992). Though I observe a declining trend in intermarriage over this 10-year period, it is premature to predict a downward trend in Asian intermarriage in Canada, because I only include the first generation, foreign-born Asians in this sample, which usually has much lower out-marriage rates than later generations of immigrants. In addition, there may exist a large variation in the patterns of intermarriage for various Asian ethnic groups, which was not captured in this study.

CRITICAL THINKING QUESTIONS

1. Judging from the married people that you know, do you believe that the principle of *endogamy* still prevails? Provide examples to support your answer.
2. One of the findings revealed in the article is that people of higher socioeconomic status are more likely to intermarry. As a sociologist, why do you think this is the case?

3. According to Tzeng, how has the increasing participation of women in the labour force influenced rates of intermarriage?

NOTES

1. Although people of British (Anglophones) and French (Francophones) backgrounds are still the largest ethnic groups in Canada, neither of them account for a majority of the population (Statistics Canada, 1993).
2. About 2.2% of all marriages were interracial in the 1990s (U.S. Bureau of the Census, 1993).
3. Respondent's race-ethnicity was not included in Canadian censuses.
4. The reason I did not use 12 years of schooling as the dividing criterion for different educational categories is that secondary school may include grade 13 in some provinces in Canada.
5. Scale deviance describes the lack of fit of a given unsaturated model versus saturated model, i.e., Scale Deviance = $-2\log(L2/L1)$. where $L2$ is the maximum likelihood of the model understudy, and $L1$ is the maximum likelihood of the saturated model. Under regularity conditions, the difference in scale deviances has approximately a chi-squared distribution, with degrees of freedom equal to the difference between the numbers of parameters in the two models (Agresti, 1990).

REFERENCES

Agresti, A. 1990. *Categorical data analysis*. New York: Wiley-Interscience.

Alba, R. & R. M. Golden. 1956. Patterns of ethnic marriage in the United States. *Social Forces* 65: 202–23.

Badets, J., and T. W. Chui. 1994. Canada's changing immigrant population. Statistics Canada-Catalogue No. 96–311E. Scarborough, Ontario: Prentice Hall.

Becker, G. S. 1981. *A treatise on the family*. Cambridge: Harvard University Press.

Besanceney, P. H. 1965. On reporting rates of intermarriage. *American Journal of Sociology,* 70 (6): 717–21.

Bianchi, S. M. and D. Spain. 1986. *American women in transition*. New York: Russell Sage Foundation.

Blau, P. M., C. Beeker, and K. M. Fitzpatrick. 1984. Intersecting social affiliations and intermarriage. *Social Forces,* 62 (3): 585–605.

Burma J. H. 1963. Interethnic marriage in Los Angeles, 1948–1959. *Social Forces,* 42 (1): 156–65.

Castonguay, C. 1982. Intermarriage and language shift in Canada. 1971 and 1976. *Canadian Journal of Sociology,* 7 (3): 263–77.

Cherlin, A. J. 1992. *Marriage, divorce, remarriage*. Cambridge: Harvard University Press.

Dumas, J. 1990. Report on the demographic situation in Canada. 1988. Statistics Canada-Catalogue No. 91-209E. Ottawa: Statistics Canada.

Eberhard, M., and J. Waldron. 1977. Intercultural marriage and child rearing. In *Adjustment in Intercultural Marriage*, eds. W. S. Tseng et al. Honolulu: University of Hawaii Press.

Eshleman, R. J., and S. J. Wilson. 1995. *The Family*. Canadian Edition. Scarborough, Ontario: Allyn & Bacon Canada.

Fitzpatrick, J. T., and D. T. Gurak. 1979. *Hispanic intermarriage in New York City*. 1975. New York: Fordham University Hispanic Research Center.

Fleras, A., and J. L. Elliott. 1992. *Multiculturalism in Canada: The challenge of diversity*. Scarborough. Ontario: Nelson Canada.

Glick, P. 1970. Intermarriage among ethnic groups in the United States. *Social Biology,* 17(4): 293–298.

Goldstein, J., and A. Segall. 1991. Ethnic intermarriage and ethnic identity. In *Continuity & change in marriage and family*, ed. Jean E. Veerers. Toronto: Holt, Rinehart and Winston.

Hollingshead, A. B. 1950. Cultural factors in the selection of marriage mates. *American Sociological Review,* 15: 619–27.

Hout, M. 1982. The association between husbands' and wives' occupations in two-earner families. *American Journal of Sociology,* 88: 397–409.

Ishwaran, K. 1992. *Family and marriage: Cross-cultural perspectives*. Toronto: Thompson Educational Publishing.

Kalmijn. M. 1991. Status homogamy in the United States. *American Journal of Sociology,* 97(2): 496–523.

—— 1993. Trends in Black/White intermarriage. *Social Forces,* 72(1): 119–46.

Kitano, H. H., Y. Wai-Tsang, L Chai, and H. Hatanaka. 1984. Asian-American interracial marriage. *Journal of Marriage and the Family,* 46(1): 179–90.

Larson, I. E., W. Goltz, and C. W. Hobart. 1994. *Families in Canada*. Scarborough, Ontario: Prentice Hall.

Lieberson, S. and M. C. Waters. 1985. *From many strands: Ethnic and racial groups in contemporary America*. New York: Russell Sage.

Mare. R. D. 1991. Five decades of educational assortative mating. *American Sociological Review,* 56, 15–32.

Mayer. E. 1985. *Love and tradition: Marriage between Jews and Christians*. New York: Plenum Press.

Merton, R. K. 1941. Intermarriage and social structure: Fact and theory. *Psychiatry,* 4: 361–374.

Murstein, B. 1970. Stimulus—Value—Role: A theory of marital choice. *Journal of Marriage and the Family,* 32: 465–81.

Pagnini, D. I., and S. P. Morgan. 1991. Intermarriage and social distance among U.S. immigrants at the turn of the century. *American Journal of Sociology,* 96 (2): 405–32.

Qian, Z., and S. H. Preston. 1993. Changes in American marriage, 1972 to 1987: Availability and forces of attraction by age and education. *American Sociological Review,* 58: 482–495.

Romano, D. 1988. *Intercultural marriage: Promises & pitfalls.* Yarmouth, Maine: Intercultural Press.

Schoen, R., and J. Wooldredge. 1989. Marriage choices in North Carolina and Virginia, 1969–71 and 1979–81. *Journal of Marriage and the Family,* 51: 465–81.

Schmitt. R. C. 1971. Recent trends in Hawaiian interracial marriage rates by occupation. *Journal of Marriage and the Family,* 33: 373–74.

South, S. J. 1991. Sociodemographic differentials in mate selection preferences. *Journal of Marriage and the Family,* 53: 928–40.

Spickard, P. R. 1989. *Mixed blood: Intermarriage and ethnic identity in twentieth-century America.* Madison, WI: University of Wisconsin Press.

Statistics Canada. 1988. Marriage and conjugal life in Canada. Statistics Canada - Demography Division. Ottawa: Statistics Canada.

—— 1993. Ethnic origin and occupied private dwellings. *The Daily,* Statistics Canada - Catalogue No. 96-304E. Ottawa: Statistics Canada.

Stevens, G. and R. Schoen. 1988. Linguistic intermarriage in the United States. *Journal of Marriage and the Family,* 50: 267–79.

Sung, B. L. 1990. *Chinese American intermarriage.* New York: Center for Migration Studies.

Sweet, J. A., and L. L., Bumpass. 1987. *American families and households.* New York: Russell Sage Foundation.

Tinker, J. N. 1973. Intermarriage and ethnic boundaries: The Japanese American case. *Journal of Social Issues,* 29(2): 49–66.

Tucker, M. B., and C. Mitchell-Kernan. 1990. New trends in Black American interracial marriage: The social structural context. *Journal of Marriage and the Family,* 52(1): 209–218.

U.S. Bureau of the Census. 1993. Current population reports. Series P-25, no. 455. Population projections of the United States, by age, sex, race, and hispanic origin: 1993 to 2050. Washington, D.C.: U.S. Department of Commerce.

White, M, J., A. E. Biddlecom, and G. Shenyang. 1993. Immigration, naturalization, and residential assimilation among Asian Americans in 1980. *Social Forces,* 72 (1): 93–117.

36

The Functions of Crime

Emile Durkheim

Deviance

CLASSIC

CONTEMPORARY

CROSS-CULTURAL

Common sense leads us to view crime, and all kinds of deviance, as pathological—that is, as harmful to social life. Despite the obvious social costs of crime, however, Durkheim argues that crime is normal because it is part of all societies. Furthermore, he claims that crime makes important contributions to the operation of a social system.

...Crime is present not only in the majority of societies of one particular species but in all societies of all types. There is no society that is not confronted with the problem of criminality. Its form changes; the acts thus characterized are not the same everywhere; but, everywhere and always, there have been men who have behaved in such a way as to draw upon themselves penal repression.... There is, then, no phenomenon that presents more indisputably all the symptoms of normality, since it

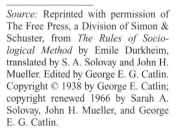

Source: Reprinted with permission of The Free Press, a Division of Simon & Schuster, from *The Rules of Sociological Method* by Emile Durkheim, translated by S. A. Solovay and John H. Mueller. Edited by George E. G. Catlin. Copyright © 1938 by George E. Catlin; copyright renewed 1966 by Sarah A. Solovay, John H. Mueller, and George E. G. Catlin.

appears closely connected with the conditions of all collective life. To make of crime a form of social morbidity would be to admit that morbidity is not something accidental, but, on the contrary, that in certain cases it grows out of the fundamental constitution of the living organism; it would result in wiping out all distinction between the physiological and the pathological. No doubt it is possible that crime itself will have abnormal forms, as, for example, when its rate is unusually high. This excess is, indeed, undoubtedly morbid in nature. What is normal, simply, is the existence of criminality....

Here we are, then, in the presence of a conclusion in appearance quite paradoxical. Let us make no mistake. To classify crime among the phenomena of normal sociology is not to say merely that it is an inevitable, although regrettable, phenomenon, due to the incorrigible wickedness of men; it is to affirm that it is a factor in public health, an integral part of all healthy societies. This result is, at first glance, surprising enough to have puzzled even ourselves for a long time. Once this first surprise has been overcome, however, it is not difficult to find reasons explaining this normality and at the same time confirming it.

In the first place crime is normal because a society exempt from it is utterly impossible. Crime, we have shown elsewhere, consists of an act that offends certain very strong collective sentiments. In a society in which criminal acts are no longer committed, the sentiments they offend would have to be found without exception in all individual consciousnesses, and they must be found to exist with the same degree as sentiments contrary to them. Assuming that this condition could actually be realized, crime would not thereby disappear; it would only change its form, for the very cause which would thus dry up the sources of criminality would immediately open up new ones.

Indeed, for the collective sentiments which are protected by the penal law of a people at a specified moment of its history to take possession of the public conscience or for them to acquire a stronger hold where they have an insufficient grip, they must acquire an intensity greater than that which they had hitherto had. The community as a whole must experience them more vividly, for it can acquire from no other source the greater force necessary to control these individuals who formerly were the most refractory. For murderers to disappear, the horror of bloodshed must become greater in those social strata from which murderers are recruited; but, first it must become greater throughout the entire society. Moreover, the very absence of crime would directly contribute to produce this horror; because any sentiment seems much more respectable when it is always and uniformly respected.

One easily overlooks the consideration that these strong states of the common consciousness cannot be thus reinforced without reinforcing at the same time the more feeble states, whose violation previously gave birth to mere infraction of convention—since the weaker ones are only the prolongation, the attenuated form, of the stronger. Thus robbery and simple bad taste injure the same single altruistic sentiment, the respect for that which is another's. However, this same sentiment is less grievously offended by bad taste than by robbery; and since, in addition, the average consciousness has not sufficient intensity to react keenly to the bad taste, it is treated with greater tolerance. That is why the person guilty of bad taste is merely blamed, whereas the thief is punished. But, if this sentiment grows stronger, to the point of silencing in all consciousnesses the inclination which disposes man to steal, he will become more sensitive to the offenses which, until then, touched him but lightly. He will react against them, then, with more energy; they will be the object of greater opprobrium, which will transform certain of them from the simple moral faults that they were and give them the quality of crimes. For example, improper contracts, or contracts improperly executed, which only incur public blame or civil damages, will become offenses in law.

Imagine a society of saints, a perfect cloister of exemplary individuals. Crimes, properly so called, will there be unknown; but faults which appear venial to the layman will create there the same scandal that the ordinary offense does in ordinary consciousnesses. If, then, this society has the power to judge and punish, it will define these acts as criminal and will treat them as such. For the same reason, the perfect and upright man judges his smallest failings with a severity that the majority reserve for acts more truly in the nature of an offense. Formerly, acts of violence against persons were more frequent than they are today, because respect for individual dignity was less strong. As this has increased, these crimes have become more rare; and also, many acts violating this sentiment have been introduced into the penal law which were not included there in primitive times.[1]

…Crime is, then, necessary; it is bound up with the fundamental conditions of all social life, and by that very fact it is useful, because these conditions of which it is a part are themselves indispensable to the normal evolution of morality and law.

Indeed, it is no longer possible today to dispute the fact that law and morality vary from one social type to the next, nor that they change within the same type if the conditions of life are modified. But, in order that these transformations may be possible, the collective sentiments at the basis of morality must not be hostile to change, and consequently must have but moderate energy. If they were too strong, they would no longer be plastic. Every pattern is an obstacle to new patterns, to the extent that the first pattern is inflexible. The better a structure is articulated, the more it offers a healthy resistance to all modification; and this is equally true of functional, as of anatomical, organization. If there were no crimes, this condition could not have been fulfilled; for such a hypothesis presupposes that collective sentiments have arrived at a degree of intensity unexampled in history. Nothing is good indefinitely and to an unlimited extent. The authority which the moral conscience enjoys must not be excessive; otherwise no one would dare criticize it, and it would too easily congeal into an immutable form. To make progress, individual originality must be able to express itself. In order that the originality of the idealist whose dreams transcend his century may find expression, it is necessary that the originality of the criminal, who is below the level of his time, shall also be possible. One does not occur without the other.

Nor is this all. Aside from this indirect utility, it happens that crime itself plays a useful role in this evolution. Crime implies not only that the way remains open to necessary changes but that in certain cases it directly prepares these changes. Where crime exists, collective sentiments are sufficiently flexible to take on a new form, and crime sometimes helps to determine the form they will take. How many times, indeed, it is only an anticipation of future morality—a step toward what will be! According to Athenian law, Socrates was a criminal, and his condemnation was no more than just. However, his crime, namely, the independence of his thought, rendered a service not only to humanity but to his country.…

From this point of view the fundamental facts of criminality present themselves to us in an entirely new light. Contrary to current ideas, the criminal no longer seems a totally unsociable being, a sort of parasitic element, a strange and unassimilable body, introduced into the midst of society. On the contrary, he plays a definite role in social life.

CRITICAL THINKING QUESTIONS

1. On what grounds does Durkheim argue that crime should be considered a "normal" element of society?
2. Why is a society devoid of crime an impossibility?
3. What are the functional consequences of crime and deviance?

NOTE

1. Calumny, insults, slander, fraud, etc.

Deviance	**37**
CLASSIC	
CONTEMPORARY	The Rebels: A Brotherhood of Outlaw Bikers
CROSS-CULTURAL	*Daniel R. Wolf*

Using a classic social research strategy, fieldwork, Wolf reviews his experiences as a member of the outlaw biker gang, the Rebels.

ENTERING THE WORLD OF THE OUTLAW

"All the world likes an outlaw. For some damn reason they remember 'em."

—Jesse James

A midnight run shatters the night air. Thirty Harley-Davidson motorcycles stretch out for a quarter-mile, thundering down the highway. The pack moves in tight formation, advancing as a column of staggered twos. Veteran riders make sure there are fifteen yards between themselves and the bikes they are riding behind, three yards and a 45-degree angle between themselves and the bikes they are riding beside. Thirty men ride in boots and jeans, leathers and cut-off denim jackets, beards and long hair, tattoos and earrings, buck knives and chain belts. Each rider follows the grimacing skull on the back patch of the rider in front of him. Some ride with their ol' ladies,

"jamming in the wind" with a laid-back coolness bordering on arrogance, a combination of speed, grace, and power. The lead biker snaps his wrist to full throttle and the supercharged V-twin engines heat up and pound out the challenge. Each biker is locked into the tunnel vision of his own world. He feels the heavy metal vibrations in every joint of his body, but he can no longer hear the rumble of his own machine, just a collective roar. Headlamps slice open just enough darkness to let the sculptured metal of extended front ends slide through. Cool blackness clips over high-rise handlebars, whips their faces, then quickly swallows the red glare of tail-lights. A grey blur of pavement that represents instant oblivion passes six inches beneath the soles of their boots. At a hundred miles an hour the inflections of the road surface disappear, eye sockets are pushed back, and tears flow. Riders hurtle down the highway, in total control of their own destinies, wrapped in the freedom of high sensation. They are the Rebels: Caveman, Blues, Tiny, Wee Albert, Gerry, Slim, Tramp, Danny, Onion, Jim Raunch, Ken, Voodoo,

Source: From *The Rebels: A Brotherhood of Outlaw Bikers* by Daniel R. Wolf. Toronto: University of Toronto Press, 1991, pp. 3–21. Reprinted by permission of the publisher.

Larry, Killer, Whimpy, Clayton, Steve, Indian, Armand, Crash, Big Mike, Smooth Ed, Yesnoski, Snake, Dale the Butcher, Saint, and Terrible Tom.

Outlaw motorcycle clubs originated on the American west coast following the Second World War. With names such as the Booze Fighters and their parent club the 13 Rebels, the Galloping Gooses, Satan's Sinners, and the Winos, they rapidly spread across the United States and into Canada in the early 1950s; Canada's first outlaw club was the Canadian Lancers in Toronto, Ontario. Today, outlaw motorcycle clubs are an international social phenomenon. As of 1990 the outlaw club subculture had spread into eleven other countries, including the European nations of Great Britain, West Germany, France, Switzerland, Austria, Belgium, Denmark, and the Netherlands in the mid-sixties and early seventies, and then into Australia, New Zealand, and Brazil in the mid-seventies and early eighties.

What is or is not considered deviant by society, and how society reacts to that deviance, always involves the process of social definition. Technically, the label "outlaw motorcycle club" designates a club that is not registered with the American Motorcycle Association (AMA) or the Canadian Motorcycle Association (CMA), which are the respective governing bodies for the sport of motorcycling in the United States and Canada. The AMA and CMA are themselves affiliated with the Fédération Internationale Motorcycliste (FIM), the international coordinating body for motorcycling whose headquarters are located in Paris, France. A motorcycle club that is registered with the AMA or CMA obtains a club charter from those parent bodies that allows the club and its members to participate in or sponsor sanctioned motorcycle events—mainly racing competitions. AMA or CMA registration further aligns the club with the legal and judicial elements of the host society; some clubs will go one step further and incorporate themselves as "registered societies" with the local state or provincial authorities. Non-registered clubs are labelled "outlaw" and considered as the 1 per cent deviant

fringe that continues to tarnish the public image of both motorcycles and motorcyclists. For its part, the outlaw-biker community graciously accepted the AMA's "one percenter" label as a means of identifying a "righteous outlaw." Today, many outlaw club members wear 1% badges as a supplement to their club colours; or, as Sonny Barger, president of the Hell's Angels, first did in the sixties, they make a very personal and uncompromising statement on where they stand on the issue of being an outlaw by having the 1% logo tattooed on their shoulders.

Historically, the initial and most dramatic definition of outlaw clubs occurred in response to the world's first motorcycle riot in the rural town of Hollister, California, on 4 July 1947. Approximately five hundred non-affiliated bikers disrupted an AMA-sponsored Gypsy Tour and competition events involving 2500 affiliated bikers by drinking and racing in the streets of the host town of Hollister. The ineffective efforts of a numerically insufficient seven-man police force, in conjunction with the sometimes provocative vigilante tactics of indignant local residents, caused the motorcyclists to coalesce as a mob. At the height of the riot, bikers rode their motorcycles into bars and restaurants and through traffic lights, tossed bottles out of upper-floor windows, and got rid of the beer they had been drinking in the streets (indecent exposure). The unruly behaviour lasted for approximately thirty-six hours, from July 4th to 5th; the world's first motorcycle riot ended with the departure of many of the partyers on the evening of the first day and the arrival on the second of an auxiliary police force of thirty-two officers.

The national exposure that was given the Hollister incident by *Life* magazine and others resulted in the stigmatization of an image: the motorcyclist as deviant. *Life's* account started a mass-media chain reaction that saw the Hollister incident grow considerably in its sensationalistic portrayal, and, as a result, the image of the motorcyclist as deviant become more defined and immutable. In 1949, Frank Rooney wrote a short narrative entitled "Cyclist Raid," based on *Life's* one-hundred-and-fifteen-word documentary; in 1951, "Cyclist Raid" was published in *Harper's* magazine. The *Harper's* serial was read by Stanley Kramer, a Hollywood producer, who immortalized the "motorcycle riot" in the movie *The Wild One,* released in 1953. The anti-hero image of the motorcyclist was cast in the person of Marion Brando, while Lee Marvin personified the motorcyclist as villain. Interestingly enough, the striped shirt that Lee Marvin wore in the movie was later bought by a member of the Hell's Angels Motorcycle Club (MC)—a symbolic indication of events to come. The movie was to titillate the North American media with its "factual" account of a "menacing element of modern youth": A little bit of the surface of contemporary American life is scratched in Stanley Kramer's "The Wild One"…and underneath is opened an ugly, debauched and frightening view of a small, but particularly significant and menacing element of modern youth.…

The subject of its examination is a swarm of youthful motorcyclists who ride through the country in wolf-pack fashion and terrorize the people of one small town.… These "wild ones" resent discipline and show an aggressive contempt for common decency and the police. Reckless and vandalistic, they live for sensations, nothing more—save perhaps the supreme sensation of defying the normal world. (Crowther, *New York Times,* 31 December 1953)

Audiences who like their facts dished up with realism, no matter how painful, might pay attention to "The Wild One"—a picture that is factual.… It displays a group of hoodlums, motorcyclists who ride around the country with a contempt for the law and a fondness for annoying people, who take over a small town…a slice of contemporary Americana at its worst. (Hartung, *Commonweal,* 3 February 1954)

The above "factual" accounts were based on viewing a Stanley Kramer movie production whose script was written by John Paxton; Paxton's script was based on Kramer's reading of Frank Rooney's serialized story in *Harper's* magazine; Rooney's short story was in turn based on his

reading of *Life's* one-hundred-and-fifteen-word report—complete with photo—which itself was originally construed by adding four major distortions to a brief press-wire release.

By contemporary standards the amount of property damage and civic duress incurred in Hollister was minimal. In actuality there were only thirty-eight arrests (out of approximately three or four thousand bikers), fighting was mostly confined to the bikers, and no one was killed, maimed, or even gang-kissed. "Wino Willie" Forkner is a biker who has ridden Harleys since he was a teenager in the 1930s. He had returned from the Second World War after fighting the Japanese as a waist gunner and engineer for the American Seventh Air Force. He attended the Hollister incident as a charter member of the Booze Fighters MC:

The worst thing that happened was that a bunch of guys wanted to break Red Daldren out of jail. I was in a bar and somebody came in and said there were about 500 bikers ready to break him out, and I thought, "Shit, that's all we need, something like that." So I ran down to where the crowd was assembling and told 'em, "Hell, old Red's drunk and he needs a good night's sleep. Leave him stay—he'll be out in the morning." Then I turned around and went back to the bar, and damned if the cops didn't come and nail me for inciting a riot [the charges were dropped]…but no big bad things happened. There were a few broken windows that we paid for. ("Wino Willie" Faukner, interview in *Easyriders,* September 1986: 107)

However, as *Life* was to point out twenty-five years after the Hollister riot, the significance of the media chain reaction was its very real consequences: "The *Wild One* became a milestone in movie history, launching the cult of gang violence in films. It also helped create an image of motorcycling that non-violent bike riders have been trying to live down for a quarter of a century now" *(Life,* September 1972: 32). After the Hollister incident and, more to the point, after the movie, the AMA issued its now famous statement about 1 per cent of the motorcycling public, specifically clubs like the Booze Fighters, being a deviant criminal fringe element.

There is a tendency to view the Hollister motorcycle riot and its subsequent national media coverage as the genesis of the "outlaw biker"—it was the birth of an image. In effect, the outlaw biker image that was created served as a frame of reference for many young and restless rebels who copied the celluloid vision in search of both a thrill and a cause. Historically, outlaw motorcycle clubs have operated in the shadows of several different media stereotypes, all of which have been variations on the theme of "social menace." In the 1950s bikers were depicted as social rebels and deviants; in the sixties and seventies the clubs were seen as subcultures of violence and drugs. The contemporary image adds a spectre of organized crime. In 1984 the Criminal Intelligence Service of Canada (CISC) declared that outlaw motorcycle gangs had become as much of an organized-crime threat to Canada as the traditional Mafia. According to the CISC report, outlaw clubs "are involved in practically all major crime activities from murder to white-collar crime." At the annual meeting of Canadian police chiefs in 1985, outlaw motorcycle clubs were again acknowledged as the number-one concern in the area of organized crime; media headlines carried the claim: "Bikers more powerful than Mafia" (Canadian Press release, *Edmonton Journal,* 15 August 1985: Al2). How law-enforcement agencies have come to view outlaw motorcycle clubs is summarized in the following profile contained in an application for a search warrant made out by a member of the City of Calgary police department's Special Strike Force:

Outlaw Motorcycle Gangs have over the years evolved into highly sophisticated "organized crime" bodies, involved in drug manufactured/distribution/trafficking, prostitution, "gun running," fencing of stolen property and strong arm debt collection.

Law enforcement agencies across Canada have recognized that outlaw motorcycle gangs as "organized crime" bodies pose the single most serious threat to the country.

An outlaw motorcycle gang is "Any group of motorcycle enthusiasts who have voluntarily made a commitment to band together and abide by their organization's rigorous rules enforced by violence, who engage in activities that bring them and their club into serious conflict with society and the law."

It is their involvement as a group in criminal activities and antisocial behaviour which sets them apart from other organized groups. (Detective Brendan Alexander Kapuscinski, City of Calgary police force, "Application for Warrant to Search and Seize," 1988: 2)

"If the Cops are the Good Guys," writes the representative of an American federal law-enforcement training centre, "then it's hard to imagine a more archetypal Bad Guy than the outlaw motorcyclist!" (Ayoob, 1982: 26). North Americans typically react with an interesting mixture of apprehension and fascination to the fearsome images of aggression, revolt, anarchy, and criminal abandon that are used to portray outlaw-biker gangs.

Ironically, the appeal of outlaw clubs to their members is very different from what the public understands. Outlaw bikers view themselves as nothing less than frontier heroes, living out the "freedom ethic" that they feel the rest of society has largely abandoned. They acknowledge that they are antisocial, but only to the extent that they seek to gain their own unique experiences and express their individuality through their motorcycles. Their "hogs" become personal charms against the regimented world of the "citizen." They view their club as collective leverage that they can use against an establishment that threatens to crush those who find conventional society inhibiting and destructive of individual character. In an interesting twist of stereotypes the citizen becomes the bad guy, or at least weak, and the outlaw becomes the hero. Bikers make much of the point that the differential treatment—harassment—accorded outlaw clubs by law-enforcement agencies runs counter to the basic principles of self-determination. They protest that a truly democratic society should be able to tolerate diversity and accommodate an awareness that drifting away from society's conventions is very different from opting out of society's laws. Somewhere between the convenient stereotype of "criminal deviants" used by the police and the stylized self-conscious image outlaws have of themselves as "frontier heroes" lies the story of real people.

The Rebels Motorcycle Club is an outlaw club. It began in 1969 as a small club of motorcycle enthusiasts who rode their Harley-Davidsons on the streets of Edmonton, Alberta, a mid-sized Canadian city with a population of approximately 700,000 people. Today (1990), the Rebels MC is a federation of four clubs—located in the provinces of Alberta and Saskatchewan—that maintains informal social and political ties with the Hells Angels MC. Becoming a Rebel means being part of a tightly knit voluntary association that operates as a secret society within an organizational framework that includes a political structure, a financial base, a geographical territory, a chain of command, a constitution, an elaborate set of rules, and internal mechanisms for enforcing justice and compliance from within.

At its best a veteran club will operate with the internal discipline and precision of a paramilitary organization, which is completely necessary if it hopes to beat the odds and survive. These men close their world to the outside, turning to each other for help and guidance. They protect themselves with a rigid code of silence that cloaks their world in secrecy. Thus, despite the fact that outlaw motorcycle clubs are found in every major urban centre in Canada and the United States—there are approximately 900 clubs—*the subculture had remained ethnographically unexplored.*

As a doctoral graduate student in anthropology at the University of Alberta, Edmonton, I wanted to study the "Harley tribe." It was my intent to obtain an insider's perspective on the emotions and the mechanics that underlie the outlaw bikers' creation of a subcultural alternative. My interest in outlaw motorcycle clubs was not entirely theoretical; it was also a personal challenge. Brought up on the streets of a lower-class neighbourhood, I saw my best friend—with whom I broke into abandoned buildings as a kid—sent to prison for grand theft auto, and then shot down in an attempted armed robbery. Rather than be crushed

like that, I worked in meat-packing plants and factories for thirteen hours a day and put myself through university. I also bought myself a British-made Norton motorcycle. My Norton Commando became a "magic carpet ride" of thrills and excitement that I rode with lean women who were equally hungry to get their share. But it was more than that. I rode my motorcycle in anger; for me it became a show of contempt and a way of defying the privileged middle class that had put me down and had kept my parents "in their place." I felt that the Establishment had done me no favours and that I owed it even less. At that time I saw outlaw bikers as a reflection of my own dark side. I made them the embodiment of my own youthful rebellion and resentment. In retrospect, I believe that it was this aspect of my non-academic background—the fact that I had learned to ride and beat the streets—that made it possible for me to contemplate such a study, and eventually to ride with the Rebels.

At the time of beginning my fieldwork I had been riding British-made motorcycles for three years and had talked briefly to members of the King's Crew MC in Calgary. But this was not enough to comprehend the outlaw-biker community or to study it. My impression of outlaw bikers was narrow and incomplete and, in that sense, almost as misleading as the stereotype held by most "citizens." I was physically close to the scene, but far removed from a balanced understanding; that understanding would only come from "being there."

I customized my Norton, donned some biker clothing, and set off to do some fieldwork. My first attempts at contacting an outlaw club were near disasters. In Calgary, I met several members of the King's Crew MC in a motorcycle shop and expressed an interest in "hanging around." But I lacked patience and pushed the situation by asking too many questions. A deviant society, especially one that walks on the wild side of illegal activities, will have its own information network for checking out strangers. I found out quickly that outsiders, even bikers, do not rush into a club, and that anyone who doesn't show the proper restraint will be shut out. That was mistake number one. Days later, I carelessly got into an argument with a club "striker," a probationary member, that led to blows in a bar-room skirmish. He flattened my nose and began choking me. Unable to get air down my throat and breathing only blood through my nostrils, I managed a body punch that luckily found his solar plexus and loosened his grip. I then grabbed one of his hands and pulled back on the thumb till l heard the joint break. Mistake number two. It was time to move on. I packed my sleeping-bag on my Norton and headed west for Vancouver with some vague and ridiculous notion of meeting up with the Satan's Angels, now a chapter of the Hell's Angels.

Riding into Burnaby (Greater Vancouver) I discovered that an outlaw biker has to learn a whole new set of rules for dealing with the law. I had decided to modify my public identity in order to facilitate participant observation of a deviant group; I could not expect any favours from legal authorities and I would have to learn how to cope with what might be termed differential treatment—bikers use the term "harassment"—on the part of police officers. I saw the flashing red light in my rear-view mirror moments before I heard the siren. I had been looking for the Admiral Hotel, a bar where the Satan's Angels hung out. I started to gear down when I noticed that the RCMP (Royal Canadian Mounted Police) cruiser was only three feet from my rear tire. I continued to slow down and hoped that he knew what he was doing. I pulled into the parking lot behind the Admiral bar, got of my bike, and turned around to approach the officer. As I reached for my wallet he immediately ordered me to turn around and put my hands behind my head. I froze in what was probably 90 per cent uncertainty and 10 per cent defiance. When I didn't move he unlatched the holster that held his pistol; he gripped the weapon and then reached inside his car and grabbed the radio mike to call for a backup. Within moments a second cruiser was on the scene. He lined me up with the car's headlights, turned on the high

beams, and then began the standard shakedown. Upon request I produced my operator's licence, vehicle registration, and insurance, and was then asked where I was from, what club I rode with, if I had a criminal record, and if I had ever been in trouble with the law before. As I answered the questions, wondering what kind of trouble I was in now, a third cruiser pulled up, turned on its bright lights, and two more officers joined in. At that time some of my identification read "Daniel" and some read "Danny," which prompted a series of questions about aliases and a radio check about outstanding arrest warrants and vehicle registration. When this failed to produce any evidence against me, I was asked if I was carrying any weapons or drugs. The answer to both questions was "no" and the whole situation began to seem absurd. I was being put on stage under the spotlights of three police cruisers in a back alley drama directed by five RCMP officers. Meanwhile, the Satan's Angels that I'd come to meet were relaxing and having some cool beers in the bar across the alley. I began to laugh at the irony, which was mistake number three. "Put your hands up against that wall!" yelled a constable who was angered by my apparent disdain for he law. One officer searched through the pockets of my leathers and jeans while another rummaged through the leather saddle-bags on my bike. After the bike and body search, I asked the officers if motorcycle clubs were a major problem in their area. I was told they weren't, "but some guys figure they're king shit when you pull them over, and you've got to remember that no matter how tough you are, there's always someone tougher!" I was then asked how long I was staying, and I replied that it depended on my financial situation. I answered straightforwardly and stated that I was carrying credit cards and a little more than three hundred dollars, as the police already knew—having counted it. Only then did one of the officers explain: "When he asked you how long you're staying, what he's saying is that this road leads to Harvey Avenue, which leads to the highway out of town!"

I had sewn a secret pocket into the sleeve of my leather jacket. It contained a letter from the [Social Sciences and Humanities Research Council]…(SSHRC) addressed to the RCMP that identified myself and my research. The officers failed to find it, and I wasn't about to reveal it. My research goal was to find out and experience what happens within the outlaw-biker scene, not be told what happens from the outside. Three days earlier I had talked to a Vancouver city police officer who knew me as a researcher: "I'll save you a whole lot of trouble, maybe even your neck, and explain this whole biker thing to you," he said. "They're all just psychologically unstable. That's all you have to know; otherwise none of it makes any sense."

"Those cops [at the Admiral Hotel] were setting you up," Steve, the Rebels MC sergeant at arms, would explain some months later. "They were just waiting for you to make a stupid move and they've got you by the balls. They could have beaten the shit outta you, and you'd have five cops as witnesses. Well, it would've been tough shit for you!" I learned that one does not play the role of Jesse James when being pulled over by "the man," especially on a "club run," or motor-cycle tour, where police can make a shakedown last up to two hours. One learns to avoid all eye contact and restrict all verbal responses to a monosyllabic "no" or "yes." Over the next few years I got lots of practice; that first summer I was pulled over and interrogated fifteen times— on only one of these occasions was I actually charged with an offence, a speeding violation.

While touring through the British Columbia interior I joined up with three members of the Tribesmen MC from Squamish, BC, whom I met at a Penticton hamburger stand. From the Tribesmen I learned that gaining entry into a club would take time. The time factor meant that my best chance of success lay in studying the Rebels in the familiar confines of my own back yard in Edmonton. "You don't make friends with members of a club," cautioned Lance of the Tribesmen. "You let them make friends with you."

Lance pointed out that in order to ride with a club I would have to be accepted by all the members, get to know some of the members personally, and at least one member well enough that he would be willing to sponsor me and take responsibility for my actions. A critical suggestion emphatically made by all three Tribesmen was "Get yourself a hog [Harley-Davidson]!"

These first experiences "in the field" made it clear that I couldn't study any club I wanted, at any time that suited me. There was a good reason for this, as I discovered later. Restricting contacts with non-club members was a key to club survival. With time I realized that maintaining strict boundaries is a central theme that underlies all aspects of club life. This fact presented a major ethical dilemma. I could not do a study if I explained my research goal at the outset. However, an "undercover" strategy contravened a fundamental ethical tenet in which I believed, that no research should be carried out without the informants' full awareness. I devised an alternative strategy that satisfied myself, my thesis committee, and the guidelines that the University of Alberta had set down for ethical research. The plan was that initially I would attempt to establish contact with the Rebels as a biker who also happened to be a university— anthropology—student. If I were successful in achieving sufficient rapport and mutual trust with club members, I would officially ask the Rebels MC for permission to conduct a study. The bottom line was that it would be the Rebel club members I rode with who would make the final decision as to whether or not the study would go beyond my personal files.

This strategy was not without risks. Outlaw clubs are aware that they are under constant police surveillance, often by special police units, such as the RCMP's E-squad in Vancouver or the City of Calgary's Strike Force. I learned that the Edmonton Rebels suspected that a biker who had recently attempted to gain entry into their club as a "striker" was an agent of the RCMP. After repeated attempts, the police have long since discovered that infiltrating an outlaw club is a long, arduous, and risky process when it is being done for "professional" reasons. "Infiltration of the gangs is difficult. 'They have an internal discipline that makes it dangerous,' said a police officer. 'It's an area we have trouble infiltrating. The conditions of initiation make it almost impossible....' 'They are scary,' said one police intelligence officer, who asked not to be identified. 'We've had two or three informants killed, found tied to trees up north with bullet holes in them'" (Canadian Press release, *Edmonton Journal,* 29 September 1979).

In the United States the FBI had gone so far as to have several agents start up their own club in order to bypass the striker (probation) period that screens out bogus bikers. The Edmonton police play a wide variety of angles in order to update their information on the Rebels. On one occasion, two plain-clothes officers wore media badges at a biker rally protesting mandatory helmet legislation in order to move freely among the club members and take pictures. If the Rebels discovered my research motive before I was ready to tell them, it would have been difficult to communicate any good intentions, scientific or otherwise. There existed the distinct possibility that more than just the study would have been terminated prematurely. I lived with that possibility for three years.

I fine-tuned my image before I approached the Rebels. This was going to be my final make-it-or-forget-it attempt. I purchased an old 1955 Harley-Davidson FL, a "panhead," which I customized but later sold in favour of a mechanically more reliable 1972 Electraglide, a "shovelhead." I had grown shoulder-length hair and a heavy beard. I bought a Harley-Davidson leather jacket and vest, wore studded leather wristbands and a shark's-tooth pendant, and sported a cut-off denim jacket with assorted Harley-Davidson pins and patches, all symbolic of the outlaw-biker world-view. While I was still very nervous about approaching the Rebels, I had become more comfortable with myself. My public image expressed what I now felt was my personal character. There was no pretension. As far as I was concerned, I was a genuine biker who was intrigued with the notion of riding with an outlaw club.

I discovered that I was a lot more apprehensive than I thought as I sat at the opposite end of the Kingsway Motor Inn and watched the Rebels down their drinks. The loud thunder of heavy-metal rock music would make initiating a delicate introduction difficult if not impossible; and there were no individual faces or features to be made out in the smoky haze, only a series of Rebel skull patches draped over leather jackets in a corner of the bar that outsiders seemed to warily avoid. It was like a scene out of a western movie: hard-faced outlaws in the bar, downing doubles while waiting for the stagecoach to arrive. I decided to go outside and devise an approach strategy, including how I would react if one of the Rebels turned to me and simply said, "Who invited you?" I had thought through five different approaches when Wee Albert of the Rebels MC came out of the bar to do a security check on the "Rebel iron" in the parking lot. He saw me leaning on my bike and came over to check me out. For some time Wee Albert and I stood in the parking lot and talked about motorcycles, riding in the wind, and the Harley tradition. He showed me some of the more impressive Rebel choppers and detailed the jobs of customizing that members of the club had done to their machines. He then checked out my "hog," gave a grunt of approval, and invited me to come in and join the Rebels at their tables. Drinking at the club bar on a regular basis gave me the opportunity to get to know the Rebels and gave them an opportunity to size me up and check me out on neutral ground. I had made the first of a long sequence of border crossings that all bikers go through if they hope to get close to a club.

Wee Albert became a good buddy of mine, and he sponsored my participation in club runs and at club parties. In addition to my having a Sponsor, my presence had to be voted on by the membership as a whole at their weekly Wednesday meeting, if two of the twenty-five members voted "no," then I wasn't around. The number of close friends that I had in the club increased and I was gradually drawn into the Rebel brotherhood. Measured in terms of social networking, brotherhood meant being part of a high frequency of interpersonal contacts that were activated over a wide range of social situations. Among the activities that I took part in were drinking and carousing in the club bar, assisting members in the chopping (customizing) and repair of motorcycles, loaning and borrowing money, shooting pool and "bullshitting" at the clubhouse, exchanging motorcycle parts along with technical information and gossip at a motorcycle shop owned by two club members, going on a duck hunt and on fishing trips, making casual visits and receiving dinner invitations to members' homes, general partying and riding together, providing emotional support, and, when necessary, standing shoulder-to-shoulder in the face of physical threat. Brotherhood, I came to learn, is the foundation of the outlaw-club community. It establishes among members a sense of moral, emotional, and material interdependence; feelings of commitment arise out of a sense of sharing a common fate. The enduring emotion of brotherhood is comradeship. To a "patch holder" (club member) brotherhood means being there when needed; its most dramatic expression occurs when brothers defend each other from outside threats. I vividly remember sitting with the Rebels in the Kingsway Motor Inn bar, trying to sober up quickly while I mentally acted out what I thought would be my best martial-arts moves. I looked down at my hand: I had sprained my thumb the night before while sparring in karate. My right hand was black, blue, swollen, and useless. I watched nervously as sixty-five members of the Canadian Airborne Regiment strutted into the bar. Their walk said that they were looking for us and a brawl. I came to view brotherhood as both a privilege and a tremendous personal responsibility.

I watched my own identity change as the result of experiences I had on my own as a biker and those I shared with club members. These often involved the process of public identification, or labelling, and other reactions by outsiders. I learned that a lone biker on the highway is vulnerable. I was run off the road three times over a four-year period. On one of those occasions I was forced off a mountain road into the side of a cliff and nearly catapulted into oblivion. Another lesson was that an outlaw biker has to be ready for "the heat to come down" at the most unexpected times. For instance, while I was washing my bike at a car wash, the owner phoned the police about a suspicious-looking biker. The police came, searched my bike, and I was arrested and charged with carrying a concealed and illegal weapon—a switch-blade. I felt sure that I would have a criminal record long before, and maybe instead of, a PhD. Fortunately, I discovered that a good lawyer, who is "owed a favour" by the crown prosecutor, can get the charges dropped—in this case, three minutes prior to the start of the trial. I learned that a police officer will follow an outlaw biker for five miles to give him a ticket for doing 35 mph in a 30-mph zone. A biker could be given a ticket for a balding tire or because his custom handlebars were one-half of an inch too high above the motorcycle's seat. I recall being turned down by insurance companies for vehicle coverage, refused admittance to private camp-grounds, and kicked off a public beach by Penticton police who thought we intended to incite a riot. I found that associating with outlaw patch holders could be an invitation to danger. While riding with the club, I and some patch holders were pulled over by a cruiser and warned that members of the Highway Kings MC were out gunning for Rebels with shotguns. None of these situations could have been acted out in a detached manner. My involvement demanded the intensity of a highly emotional reaction. Each encounter was an escalation towards an outlaw-biker identity. My record of personal encounters with citizens and the police, especially those that were threatening, enabled me to understand and articulate the biker's perspective on drifting away from the Establishment and being drawn into the club. Sometimes, as I watched the faces of the Rebels, I could see the hardening of an attitude—"us-against-the-world."

Gradually my status changed from being a "biker" with a familiar face to being a "friend of the club." There were no formal announcements. Tiny just yelled across at me one afternoon while we were starting up our bikes, "Hey! 'Coyote!' No way I'm riding beside you. Some farmer is going to shoot our asses off and then say he was shooting at varmints." This was a reference to the coyote skin I had taken to wearing over my helmet. Wee Albert looked at me, grinned, and said "That's it, 'Coyote.' From now on that'll be your club name." Most of the patch holders had club names, such as Spider or Greaser. These names are reminders of club association. More important, they separate the individual from his past, giving him the opportunity to build a new persona in terms of group-valued traits. Pseudonyms give members an aura; they draw upon a collective power. They are no longer just Rick, Allan, or Bill; they are Blues, Terrible Tom, and Caveman; they are outlaw bikers!

As a "friend of the club" I took part informally in political rhetoric concerning the club's future, such as debates concerning the hot issue of club expansion. This position of trust with the Rebels brought me into contact with other outlaw clubs such as the King's Crew of Calgary, the Spokesmen of Saskatoon, the Bounty Hunters of Victoria, the Gypsy Wheelers of White Rock, and the Warlords of Edmonton. Through these inter-club contacts I became familiar with the political relationships of conflict and alliance that exist among outlaw clubs. Meeting members of different clubs also provided me with the comparative data I needed to isolate those aspects of behaviour and organization that were shared by all clubs, and helped to explain how some clubs were different and why. My long-term association with the Rebels gave me a valuable historical perspective that included insights into the developmental sequence of clubs. I was able to describe how new clubs form, why few emergent clubs beat the odds and survive, and how a chosen few clubs achieved long-term success and expansion while all that remains of other clubs is their colours hanging upside down as trophies on the wall of a rival's clubhouse.

If the Rebels had at any time refused permission for the study, I would have destroyed all the data I had collected and closed the investigation. The fact that I had established myself as a friend of the club was no reason for the members to agree to become scientific units of analysis. Rejection of the study appeared more and more imminent as I grew to sense and share members' distrust of outsiders. I had come to appreciate some of the multifaceted advantages of having a negative public stereotype—however unrealistic. When outsiders look at an outlaw biker, they do not see an individual, all they see is the club patch that he wears on the back of his leathers. The negative image that comes with the Rebel skull patch discourages unnecessary intrusions by outsiders. "That way I'm not bothered," explained Steve of the Rebels, "and I don't have to tell the guy 'Fuck off, cunt!'" The patch becomes part of the biker's threat display: it effectively keeps violence to a minimum by warding off those outsiders who might otherwise choose to test the mettle of the bikers. For the majority of outsiders, the prospect of having to initiate even the briefest of encounters with an outlaw biker brings forth emotions ranging from uneasiness to sheer dread. Ironically, the more I got to know the members and the greater the bonds of trust and brotherhood, the less I expected that they would approve of the study. "The best public relations for us," according to Indian of the Rebels, "is no public relations!" I found it increasingly difficult to live with the fact that the closer I came to my destination of knowing the Rebels, the further distant became my goal of doing an ethnographic study.

One night, during a three-week Rebel run to the west coast, I was sharing a beer with Tiny while sitting on the porch of the Bounty Hunters' clubhouse. We were watching officers of the Victoria police force who were watching us from their cruisers in the street and from a nearby hotel—binoculars between closed curtains. "You know, Coyote," grumbled a 6-foot, 275-pound Tiny in a very personable tone, "I've talked with some of the guys and we think that you should strike [enter probationary membership] for the club. The way I see it, it shouldn't take you more than a year to earn your colours [club patch]." The pressure was now on and building for me to make a move that would bring me even closer to the club. I had made a commitment to myself that under no circumstances would I attempt to become a full-fledged member without first revealing my desire to do a study on the club. It was time to disengage. It was time for me to sell my study to the Rebels, but I was at a loss as to what to say. I had been a brother through good times and bad, thick and thin; but to distance myself from the Rebels by announcing a study done for outsiders of a way of life I had shared with them against the world seemed nothing short of a betrayal. Entering the field as a biker and maintaining relations of trust and friendship during the course of fieldwork prevented my leaving the field with my notes. I had accomplished what I had hoped to during my fieldwork, but at this point there was no way out. There was no formula for disengagement of the field project. As far as I was concerned, I had lost a three-year gamble.

Weeks of personal frustration and near-depression later, I had an incredible stroke of luck. Wee Albert, who took great pleasure in talking about "what it means to be a Rebel and a brother," approached me and said, "Being an anthropologist you study people, right? Well, have you ever thought of maybe doing a study on the club? Chances are it probably wouldn't carry [club approval], but maybe. I'd like to see it happen." I told Wee Albert that I'd consider it and approach the executive members with the proposal. The door of disengagement was open; Wee Albert had provided me with an honourable way out. Whether or not it would be a successful

disengagement—the approval of an ethnography—remained to be seen.

I first talked to Ken and Steve about the prospect of "doing an anthropological study." Ken, president, and Steve, sergeant at arms, were both friends of mine and well-respected club officers, but their most positive response was a shrug of the shoulders and "We'll see." Ken decided to bring up the proposed study at a meeting of the club executive. The officers of the club discussed the proposal among themselves and determined that no harm would be done if they presented it one week later to the general membership at a club meeting. For me it was the longest night of the year as I waited for the decision. The issue was hotly debated, a vote was held, and the study approved. Why? Granting me permission for the study was done as a "personal favour": "You have come into favour with a lot of the members and been nothing but good to the club. All in all you've been a pretty righteous friend of the club. But there was a lot of opposition to your study, especially from guys like T.T. [Terrible Tom] and Blues. The way I see it the vote went the way it did because you were asking us a favour. You didn't come in promising us the moon, you know, money from books and that sort of thing. You promised us nothing so we did it as a personal favour" (Wee Albert). Any offers of economic remuneration on my part would have been interpreted as an insult; the Rebels were doing me a favour. I strongly suspect that any researcher who buys his or her way into a closed society—with promises of money or royalties—will garner information that is at best forced, at worst fabricated. However, I did give the "victims" of the four-and-one-half-hour questionnaire a twenty-six-ounce bottle of Alberta Springs (Old Time Sipping Whisky) and a Harley-Davidson beer mug. "Fair return" for the club as a whole was a bound copy of my thesis, which found a home in the Rebels' clubhouse.

I continued to ride with the Rebels for another year and a half, during which time I carried out formal data-gathering procedures. These included extensive open-ended interviews with a number of Rebel patch holders and ended with the administration of a four-hour-long structured questionnaire to six members. Interestingly enough, Blues, a Rebel who was both a friend and a staunch opponent of the study, was one of the six. "The club is all I have. It means everything to me. It's with me all the time. I feel leery about talking to anybody about it. If I wasn't 100 per cent for you I wouldn't be here. If you'd been asking these questions three years ago [when I initially made contact with the Rebels MC], well no fucking way. We've been burned before, but never again!" Blues's trust and vote of confidence brought me a tremendous degree of personal satisfaction.

The theoretical framework and methodological approach that I use in [my] book are based on a cognitive definition of culture. Culture is here defined as the rules and categories of meaning and action that are used by individuals to both interpret and generate appropriate behaviour. I therefore view the outlaw-biker subculture as a human experience. It is a system of meaning in which I, as an anthropologist, had to involve myself in order to develop an adequate explanation of what was being observed. That is, in order to understand the biker subculture, or any culture for that matter, one must first try to understand it as it is experienced by the bikers themselves. Only then can one comprehend both the meaning of being an outlaw and how that meaning is constructed and comes to be shared by bikers. Only by first seeing the world through the eyes of the outlaws can we then go on to render intelligible the decisions that they make and the behaviours they engage in. Those meanings, decisions, and behaviours may lead you to applaud outlaw bikers as heroes. Alternatively, they may lead you to condemn them as villains. Labelling them as heroes or villains is a subsequent value judgment that the reader has the option of making. That value judgment is quite separate from first knowing outlaw bikers – my job as an ethnographer.

In order to operationalize this theoretical position of capturing an insider's perspective, I adopted a research methodology that closely resembles that of a symbolic interactionist. That is, within the overall framework of participant observation I emphasize analysis that is proximate—events are described in terms of variables that are close to the immediate situation in which the actors find themselves; processual—events are viewed as an emerging step-by-step reality whose completion requires actors to meet a series of contingencies; and phenomenological—events are explained in a manner that pays serious attention to how the actors experience them (Lofland, 1969: 296–97). By blending the methodological strategy of participant observation with the perspective of symbolic interactionism (Visano, 1989: 3, 29), I hope to replicate for the reader the experienced natural world as it unfolds for the outlaw biker.

CRITICAL THINKING QUESTIONS

1. Discuss the significance of the "one percenter" label for bikers.
2. Do you think that the image of the "biker" has changed since the Hollister incident in 1947? If so, in what ways? If not, why do you feel that the image has remained stable over time?
3. Has Wolf's presentation of the Rebels changed how you look at bike gangs? If so, how? If not, why not?

REFERENCES

Agar, M. 1986. *Speaking of ethnography.* Beverly Hills, Calif.: Sage.

Ayoob, M. 1982. Outlaw bikers. *Police Product News*, 6(5).

Forkner, W. 1986. "Wino" Willie Forkner: All the old romance retold. *Easyriders* 16(159).

Kapuscinski, B. A. 1988. Application for warrant to search and seize. Attorney-General of the Province of Alberta: 2.

Keiser, L. R. 1979. *The Vice Lords: Warriors of the streets.* Toronto: Holt, Rinehart and Winston. Lofland, J. 1969. *Deviance and identity.* Englewood Cliffs. N.J.: Prentice-Hall.

Maanen, J. van. 1988. *Tales of the field: On writing ethnography.* Chicago: University of Chicago Press.

Visano, L. 1989. Researching deviance: An interactionist account. Paper presented at the Canadian Sociology and Anthropology Association annual conference, Quebec City.

CLASSIC

CONTEMPORARY

CROSS-CULTURAL

38

Prostitution: A Worldwide Business of Sexual Exploitation

Melissa Farley

Some prostitutes and academic feminists contend that prostitution should be legalized: "Sex workers" would have greater autonomy over their earnings and could report violence from pimps (men who economically benefit from a prostitute's earnings) and johns (customers); as well, international sex trafficking would decrease. Others, like Melissa Farley, argue that legalizing prostitution would legitimize and increase women's sexual exploitation around the world.

Prostitution is many kinds of violence against women, but it is often not clearly understood as such. Because prostitution/trafficking is so profitable, the factors that propel women into sex businesses are sometimes concealed. This article reviews evidence for the extreme violence that occurs in prostitution and the physical and psychological harm that results from that violence.

DENIAL

Institutions such as prostitution and slavery, which have existed for thousands of years, are so deeply embedded in cultures that they become

Source: Melissa Farley. 2001. "Prostitution: The Business of Sexual Exploitation." In *Encyclopedia of Women and Gender,* Vol. 2, ed. J. Worell, pp. 879–91. New York: Academic Press.

invisible. In Mauritania, for example, there are 90,000 Africans enslaved by Arabs. Human rights activists travel to Mauritania to report on slavery, but because they do not observe precisely the stereotype of what they think slavery should look like (for example, if they do not see bidding for shackled people on auction blocks), then they conclude that the Africans working in the fields in front of them are voluntary laborers who are receiving food and shelter as salary.

In a similar way, if observers do not see exactly what the stereotype of "harmful" prostitution is—for example, if they do not see a girl being trafficked at gunpoint from one state to another or if all they see is a streetwise teenager who says, "I like this job, and besides, I'm making a lot of money," then they do not see the harm. Prostitution tourists go to the prostitution zones of Amsterdam, Atlanta, Phnom Pehn, Moscow, or Havana and see smiling girls waving at them from glass cages or strip clubs. The customers decide that prostitution is a free choice.

If we describe women as "sex workers" then we are accepting conditions that in other employment would be correctly described as sexual harassment, sexual exploitation, or rape. if prostitution is transformed into "commercial sex work," then the brutal exploitation of those prostituted by pimps becomes an employer–employee relationship. And the predatory, pedophiliac purchase of a human being by the john becomes just an everyday business transaction.

The myth that prostitution is a free choice is a major obstacle to understanding the harm of prostitution. Most people in prostitution have few or no other options for obtaining the necessities of life. One woman interviewed by Ine Vanwesenbeeck in the Netherlands described prostitution as "volunteer slavery," clearly articulating both the appearance of choice and the overwhelming coercion behind that choice. Sexual exploitation seems to happen with the "consent" of those involved. But real consent involves the option to make other choices. In prostitution, the conditions necessary for choice— physical safety; information, equal power with customers, and real alternatives—are absent. Women in prostitution tend to be the ones who have the fewest options.

The social and legal refusal to acknowledge the harm of prostitution is stunning. Normalization of prostitution by researchers, public health agencies, and the media is a significant barrier to addressing the harm of prostitution. In 1988, for example, the World Health Organization described prostitution as "dynamic and adaptive sex work, involving a transaction between seller and buyer of a sexual service." Continuing this trend a decade later, the International Labor Organization normalized prostitution as the "sex sector" of Asian economies despite citing surveys that indicated that, for example, in Indonesia, 96% of those interviewed wanted to leave prostitution if they could. Lin Lim commented, "many groups, sometimes including government officials,

have an interest in maintaining the sex sector." Libertarian ideology obfuscates the harm of prostitution, defining it as a form of sex.

In the social sciences as well, the harm of prostitution becomes invisible. The psychological literature of the 1980s blamed battered women for their victimization, describing them as "masochistic," a theoretical perspective that was later rejected for lack of evidence. However, the notion that prostituted women (who are also battered women) have personality characteristics that lead to their victimization is still promoted. Karl Abraham saw prostitution as a woman's act of hostility against her father, based on an oedipal fixation. And the sexologists, from Alfred Kinsey to Havelock Ellis to Masters and Johnson, formulated their theories of human sexuality by observing johns with prostitutes, thus normalizing prostitution-like sexuality.

Since the 1980s, there has been huge growth in socially legitimized pimping in the United States: strip clubs, nude dancing, escort services, tanning salons, massage parlors, phone sex, and computer sex. Many people do not realize that these permutations of the commercial sex industry are, in fact, prostitution. The lines between prostitution and nonprostitution have become blurred. New employees may assume they are going to dance, waitress, or tend bar, but find that the real money comes from prostituting after work. Lisa Sanchez has pointed out that the amount of physical contact between dancers and customers has escalated since the 1980s, although earnings have decreased. In addition to watching a stage show, in most strip clubs customers can buy either a table dance performance by the dancer directly in front of them or a lap dance where the dancer sits on the customer's lap while she wears few or no clothes and grinds her genitals against his. Although he is clothed, he usually expects ejaculation. Sometimes the table dance or lap dance is in front of the customer on the main floor of the club. It may also take place behind a curtain or in a private room. The more private the sexual performance, the more it costs, and the more likely that violent sexual harassment or rape will occur. Although the typical lap-dancing scenario does not involve skin-to-skin sexual contact, for a larger tip some dancers allow customers to touch their genitals, or they masturbate or fellate johns. Used condoms are often found in lap dance clubs.

Different kinds of exploitation and abuse overlap and combine to harm women. Catharine MacKinnon has pointed out that "a great many instances of sexual harassment in essence amount to solicitation for prostitution." The words used to humiliate prostituted women are the same verbal abuse used by men when they are beating up or raping nonprostituting women. Racially constructed ideas about women in sex tourism have a greater and greater effect on the ways women of color are treated at home. For example, Asian American women reported rapes after men viewed pornography of Asian women. A vast range of abuse makes up a continuum of violence in which women are first hurt in early childhood.

CHILD ABUSE AND PROSTITUTION

The prostitution of children is aggressively made invisible. For example, commenting that the connection between childhood sexual abuse and prostitution has been "exaggerated," Peter Davies and Rayah Feldman described the prostituted boys they interviewed in the United Kingdom as having an average age of under 18, with 97% of them younger than the legal age of consent. In other words, their interviewees were legally minors.

Another example of this invisibility is the common belief in Taiwan that the island's 100,000 child prostitutes want to prostitute because it pays for their "expensive tastes" in clothes and jewelry. Pimps are considered the children's bodyguards. Prejudice against indigenous people in Taiwan bolsters this denial of

harm to their children, who comprise most of the children in prostitution.

In many parts of the world, a younger rather than older person is a preferred commodity, for several reasons. First, the culturally advocated pedophiliac sexuality in some countries (the Netherlands, India, the United States) channels men's sexual desire to younger and younger girls. Second, children are more easily controlled than adults by pimps and are more easily coerced by johns into behaviors that adults might resist. Third, there is the widespread but mistaken belief in some locales that younger children are safer for the customer since they are believed to be less likely to have HIV (Thailand, Zambia).

Most women over the age of 18 in prostitution began prostituting when they were adolescents. Adele du Plessis, a social worker who worked with homeless and prostituted children in Johannesburg, South Africa, reported that she could not refuse her agency's services to 21-year-olds because she understood them to be grownup child prostitutes. Estimates regarding the age of recruitment into prostitution vary, but early adolescence is the most frequently reported age of entry into any type of prostitution. Researcher Debra Boyer interviewed 60 women prostituting in escort, street, strip club, phone sex, and massage parlors (brothels) in Seattle, Washington. All of them began prostituting between the ages of 12 and 14. In another study, 89% had begun prostitution before the age of 16. Of 200 adult women in prostitution interviewed by Mimi Silbert, 78% began prostituting as juveniles and 68% began when they were younger than 16.

The artificial distinction between child and adult prostitution obscures the continuity between the two. On a continuum of violence and relative powerlessness, the prostitution of a 12-year-old is more horrific than the prostitution of a 20-year-old, not because the crimes committed against her are different, but because the younger person has less power. In other respects, the experiences of sexual exploitation, rape, verbal abuse, and social contempt are the same, whether the person being prostituted is the legal age of a child or the legal age of an adult. The antecedent poverty and attempts to escape from unbearable living conditions (violence at home or the economic violence of globalization) are similar in child and adult prostitution.

One woman interviewed by Boyer said, "We've all been molested. Over and over, and raped. We were all molested and sexually abused as children, don't you know that? We ran to get away. They didn't want us in the house anymore. We were thrown out, thrown away. We've been on the street since we were 12, 13, 14."

The chronic, systematic nature of violence against girls and women may be seen more clearly when incest is understood as child prostitution. Use of a child for sex by adults, with or without payment, is prostitution of the child. When a child is incestuously assaulted, the perpetrator's objectification of the child victim and his rationalization and denial are the same as those of the john in prostitution. Incest and prostitution cause similar physical and psychological symptoms in the victim.

Child sexual abuse is a primary risk factor for prostitution. Familial sexual abuse functions as a training ground for prostitution. One young woman told Mimi Silbert and Ayala Pines, "I started turning tricks to show my father what he made me." Andrea Dworkin described sexual abuse of children as "boot camp" for prostitution. Research and clinical reports have documented the widespread occurrence of childhood sexual abuse and chronic traumatization among prostituted women. From 60% to 90% of those in prostitution were sexually assaulted in childhood.

Multiple perpetrators of sexual abuse were common, as was physical abuse in childhood. Sixty-two percent of women in prostitution reported a history of physical abuse as children. Evelina Giobbe found that 90% of prostituted women had been physically battered in childhood; 74% were sexually abused in their families, with 50% also having been sexually abused by someone outside the family. Of 123 survivors of prostitution at the Council for Prostitution Alternatives in Portland, 85% reported a history of incest, 90% a history of physical abuse, and 98% a history of emotional abuse.

In the 1980s, Silbert and Pines published a number of groundbreaking studies that documented the role of child sexual abuse as an antecedent to prostitution. These authors and others have noted the role of pornography in the recruitment of children into prostitution and in teaching them how to act as prostitutes. Eighty percent of a group of prostituted women and girls in Vancouver, Canada, reported that while working as prostitutes, they had been upset by someone trying to coerce them into imitating pornography.

Prostituting adolescents grow up in neglectful, often violent families. Although not all sexually abused girls are recruited into prostitution, most of those in prostitution have a history of sexual abuse as children, usually by several people. For example, in a pilot study of prostituted women in Vancouver, Melissa Farley and Jackie Lynne reported that 88% of 40 women had been sexually assaulted as children, by an average of five perpetrators. This latter statistic (those assaulted by an average of five perpetrators) did not include those who responded to the question "If there was unwanted sexual touching or sexual contact between you and an adult, how many people in all?" with "tons" or "I can't count that high" or "I was too young to remember." Sixty-three percent of those whose experiences were recorded in this study were First Nations women.

Survivors directly link physical, sexual, and emotional abuse as children to later prostitution. Seventy percent of the adult women in prostitution in one study stated that their childhood sexual abuse affected their decision to become prostitutes. They described family abuse and neglect as not only causing direct physical and emotional harm, but also creating a cycle of victimization that affected their futures. For example, one woman interviewed by Joanna Phoenix stated that by the time she was 17, "all I knew was how to be raped, and how to be attacked, and how to be beaten up, and that's all I knew. So when he put me on the game [pimped her] I was too down in the dumps to do anything. All I knew was abuse."

When she is sexually abused, the child is reinforced via attention, food, and money for behaving sexually in the way the perpetrator wishes. The perpetrator's seductive manipulation of the child causes immense psychological harm. In addition, many children are threatened with violence if they do not perform sexually.

Angela Browne and David Finkelhor described traumatic sexualization as the inappropriate conditioning of the child's sexual responsiveness and the socialization of the child into faulty beliefs and assumptions about sexuality. Traumatic sexualization leaves the girl vulnerable to additional sexual exploitation and is a critical component of the grooming process for subsequent prostitution. Some of the consequences of childhood sexual abuse are behaviors that are prostitution-like; a common symptom of sexually abused children is sexualized behavior.

Sexual abuse may result in different behaviors at different stages of the child's development. Sexualized behaviors are likely to be prominent among sexually abused preschool-age children, submerge during the latency years, and then re-emerge during adolescence as behavior described as promiscuity, prostitution, or sexual aggression.

Sexual abuse causes extreme damage to children's self-esteem. Frank Putnam noted that the child may incorporate the perpetrator's perspective, eventually viewing herself as good for nothing but sex, which is to say, she may adopt the perpetrator's view that she is a prostitute. According to John Briere, this constricted sense of self of the sexually abused child and the coercive refusal of the perpetrator to respect the child's physical boundaries may result in her subsequent difficulties in asserting boundaries, in impaired self-protection, and a greater likelihood of being further sexually victimized, including becoming involved in prostitution.

The powerlessness of having been sexually assaulted as a child may be related to the frequent discussions of control and power by women who are prostituting. The emotional and physical helplessness of the sexually abused child may be re-enacted in the prostitution transaction, with vigilant attention to the tiniest shard of control. Payment of money for an unwanted sex act in prostitution may make the girl or woman feel more in control when compared to the same experience with no payment of money. For example, one woman said that at age 17, she felt safer and more in control turning tricks on the street than she did in her home with her stepfather who raped her.

Children commonly run away from homes in which they are being sexually abused. If there is no safe place to escape to, the child or adolescent is left extremely vulnerable to further sexual exploitation and assault. Mimi Silbert reported that 96% of the adults she interviewed had been runaway children before they began prostituting. Louie and colleagues found that more than half of 50 prostituting Asian girls aged 11 to 16 ran away because of family problems.

Children in prostitution are recruited from runaway and homeless populations. For example, John Lowman described the average Canadian prostitute as having entered prostitution between the ages of 13 and 19, usually after running away from home. Pimps exploit the vulnerability of runaway or thrown-out children in recruiting them to prostitution. In Vancouver, 46% of homeless girls had received offers of "assistance to help them work in prostitution." One 13-year old who had run away from home was given housing by a pimp, but only in exchange for prostituting.

A survey of 500 homeless youths by Barbara Lucas and Lena Hackett in Indianapolis found that at first only 14% acknowledged that they were "working as prostitutes." This survey reveals the importance of the wording of questions about prostitution. When the Indiana adolescents were later asked nonjudgmental questions about specific behaviors, they responded as follows: 32% said that they had sex to get money; 21% said they had sex for a place to stay overnight; 12% exchanged sex for food; 10% exchanged sex for drugs; and 6% exchanged sex for clothes. In other words, a total of 81%, not 14%, of these 500 homeless adolescents were prostituting. The following wordings for inquiry about prostitution are suggested: "Have you ever exchanged sex for money or clothes, food, housing, or drugs?" or "Have you ever worked in the commercial sex industry: dancing, escort, massage, prostitution, pornography, video, internet, or phone sex?"

Like heterosexual adolescent girls, gay male adolescents' prostitution behavior is likely to be a re-enactment of earlier sexual abuse. Homophobia also plays a role in the prostituting of gay young men. Gay youth may have been thrown out of their homes because of their sexual orientation. Furthermore, in many cities, prostitution was the only available entry into the gay community; it was an activity where boys could "practice" being gay. Thus gay adolescent boys may develop an identity that links their sexual orientation to prostitution.

SOCIOECONOMIC CONTRIBUTION TO ENTRY INTO PROSTITUTION

According to Julia Davidson, "Prostitution is an institution in which one person has the social and economic power to transform another human being into the living embodiment of a masturbation fantasy." In addition to gender, poverty is a precondition for prostitution. The economic vulnerability and limited career options of poor women are significant factors in their recruitment into prostitution. Of 854 people in prostitution from nine countries (Canada, Colombia, Germany, Mexico, South Africa, Thailand, Turkey, United States, and Zambia), Melissa Farley and colleagues found that 75% were currently or previously homeless. PROMISE, a California agency serving women in prostitution, reported that 67% of those requesting services were currently or formerly homeless.

Lack of education was frequently a precursor to entering prostitution. Seventy percent of West Bengal Indian women wanted to escape prostitution, but the cultural and economic factors that channeled them into prostitution prevented that: a

6% literacy rate, beatings, starvation, rape by family members, and sexual exploitation at their jobs. As reported by Molly Chattopadhyay and her colleagues, women in most jobs in West Bengal, India, were required to permit sexual exploitation in order to stay employed. The most frequent reason given by these women for leaving their last job was that prostitution would provide "better pay for what they had to do anyway."

RACISM AND COLONIALISM IN PROSTITUTION

Women in prostitution are purchased for their appearance, including skin color and characteristics based on ethnic stereotyping. Throughout history, women have been enslaved and prostituted based on race and ethnicity, as well as gender and class.

Entire communities are affected by the racism that is entrenched in prostitution. For example, legal prostitution, such as strip clubs and stores that sell pornography (that is, pictures of women in prostitution) tends to be zoned into poor neighborhoods, which in many urban areas in the United States also tend to be neighborhoods of people of color. The insidious trauma of racism continually wears away at people of color and makes them vulnerable to stress disorders. Families who have been subjected to race and class discrimination may interface with street networks that normalize hustling for economic survival. Sex businesses create a hostile environment in which girls and women are continually harassed by pimps and johns. Women and girls are actively recruited by pimps and are harassed by johns driving through their neighborhoods. As Vednita Nelson pointed out, there is a sameness between the abduction into prostitution of African women by slavers and today's cruising of African American neighborhoods by johns searching for women to buy.

Compared to their numbers in the United States as a whole, women of color are overrepresented in prostitution. For example, in Minneapolis, a city that is 96% White European American, more than half of the women in strip club prostitution are women of color. Furthermore, African American women are arrested for prostitution solicitation at a higher rate than others charged with this crime.

Colonialism exploits not only natural resources, but also the people whose land contains those resources. Especially vulnerable to violence from wars or economic devastation, indigenous women are brutally exploited in prostitution (for example, Mayan women in Mexico City, Hmong women in Minneapolis, Karen women in Bangkok, and First Nations women in Vancouver).

Once in prostitution, women of color face barriers that prevent escape. Among these is an absence of culturally sensitive advocacy services. Other barriers faced by all women escaping prostitution are the lack of services that address emergency needs (for example, shelters, drug/alcohol detoxification, and treatment of acute posttraumatic stress disorder, or PTSD). There is a similar lack of services that address long-term needs, such as treatment of depression and chronic posttraumatic stress disorder (PTSD), vocational training, and long-term housing.

TRAFFICKING IS INTERNATIONAL PROSTITUTION

Prostitution always involves marketing, and trafficking is the marketing of prostitution. Women in prostitution are transported to the most lucrative market. The United Nations estimated that two million women, girls, and boys were trafficked into prostitution in 1999. Trafficking (moving girls and women across international borders) can not exist without an acceptance of prostitution in the receiving country. Many governments protect commercial sex businesses because of the massive profits (estimated at $56 billion per year). For example, the International Labor Organization called on poor countries to take economic advantage of "the

sex sector," that is, prostitution and trafficking. Governments frequently have chosen to protect the demand for prostitution, rather than adopting complex solutions, which would involve prevention through community education programs and penalization of traffickers, pimps, and customers. Governments have failed to address the root cause of prostitution, which is the unequal status of women.

In 1999, Thailand, Vietnam, China, Mexico, Russia, Ukraine, and the Czech Republic were primary source countries for trafficking of women into the United States. Source countries vary according to the economic desperation of women, promotion of prostitution/trafficking by corrupt government officials who issue passports and visas, and criminal connections in both the sending and the receiving country, such as gang-controlled massage parlors and the lack of laws to protect women who immigrate. The economic interdependence of countries and multinational corporations (globalization) promotes prostitution and trafficking by creating conditions for women to sell their own sexual exploitation at far better rates of pay than other forms of labor, according to Tanya Hernandez. Pimps and traffickers take advantage of the unequal status of women and girls in the source country by exploiting sexist and racist stereotypes of women as property, commodities, servants, and sexual objects.

Researcher Donna M. Hughes analyzed the ways in which economic devastation in Russia exacerbated pre-existing gender inequality, promoting sex businesses, including trafficking. Russian women have been scapegoated for keeping jobs that some believe they should have given up to men (the Russian Minister of Labor Melikyan stated that all women should be unemployed before a single man lost his job); domestic violence is at epidemic proportions; and sexual harassment on the job is commonplace. Under these conditions, almost any opportunity to leave Russia, even one that involves trafficking/prostitution, seems tolerable.

International prostitution includes prostitution tourism ("sex tourism"), arranged marriages with foreign women who are sexually objectified and kept in domestic servitude ("mail-order brides"), and recently, promotion of sexual exploitation by internet pimping and online prostitution, as described by Hughes.

The interconnectedness of racism and sexism in prostitution is vividly apparent in sex tourism. Colonialism in Asia and the Caribbean, according to Hernandez, promoted a view of women of color as natural-born sex workers, sexually promiscuous and immoral by nature. Over time, women of color came to be viewed as "exotic others," defined as inherently hyper-sexual on the basis of race and gender. The prostitution tourist, reading between the lines of travel brochures, denies the racist exploitation of women in "native cultures," as in Ryan Bishop and Lillian Robinson's analysis of the Thai sex business: "Indigenous Thai people are seen as Peter-Pan-like, children who are sensual and never grow up. Thus travel brochures assure sex tourists that they are simply partaking of the Thai culture, which just happens to be 'overtly sexual.'"

PERVASIVE VIOLENCE IN PROSTITUTION

Prostitution is like rape. It's like when I was 15 years old and I was raped. I used to experience leaving my body. I mean that's what I did when that man raped me. I looked up at the ceiling and I went to the ceiling and I numbed myself... because I didn't want to feel what I was feeling. I was very frightened. And while I was a prostitute I used to do that all the time. I would numb my feelings. I wouldn't even feel like I was in my body. I would actually leave my body and go somewhere else with my thoughts and with my feelings until he got off and it was over with. I don't know how else to explain it except that it felt like rape. It was rape to me. (*Giobbe,* 1991, p. 144)

Sexual violence and physical assault are normative experiences for women in prostitution. Silbert and Pines reported that 70% of women in prostitution were raped. The Council for Prostitution Alternatives in Portland reported that prostituted women were raped an average of once a week.

According to Ine Vanwesenbeeck, in the Netherlands, 60% of prostituted women suffered physical assaults, 70% experienced verbal threats of physical assault, 40% experienced sexual violence, and 40% had been forced into prostitution and/or sexual abuse by acquaintances. Most young women in prostitution were abused or beaten by pimps as well as johns. Eighty-five percent of women interviewed by Ruth Parriott had been raped in prostitution. Of 854 people in prostitution in nine countries, 71% had experienced physical assaults in prostitution, and 62% had been raped in prostitution, according to Farley and colleagues.

According to Jody Miller, 94% of those in street prostitution had experienced sexual assault and 75% had been raped by one or more johns. In spite of these reports of extreme violence, there is a widespread belief that the concept of rape does not apply to prostitutes. Some people assume that when a prostituted woman was raped, it was part of her job and that she deserved or even asked for the rape. Nothing could be farther from the truth.

Like battering, prostitution is domestic violence. Giobbe compared pimps and batterers and found similarities in the ways they used extreme physical violence to control women, the ways they forced women into social isolation, used minimization and denial, threats, intimidation, verbal and sexual abuse, and had an attitude of ownership. The techniques of physical violence used by pimps are often the same as those used by batterers and torturers.

The level of harassment and physical abuse of women in strip club prostitution has drastically increased in the past 20 years. Touching, grabbing, pinching, and fingering of dancers removes any boundary that previously existed between dancing, stripping, and prostitution. in 1998, Kelly Holsopple summarized the verbal, physical, and sexual abuse experienced by women in strip club prostitution, which included being grabbed on the breasts, buttocks, and genitals, as well as being kicked, bitten, slapped, spit on, and penetrated vaginally and anally during lap dancing.

TRAUMA SYMPTOMS AMONG WOMEN IN PROSTITUTION

Recruitment into prostitution begins with what Kathleen Barry has called seasoning; brutal violence designed to break the victim's will. After control is established, pimping tactics shift to brainwashing and other forms of psychological control. Pimps establish emotional dependency as quickly as possible, beginning with changing a girl's name. This obliterates her identity, separates her from her past, and isolates her from her community. The purpose of pimps' violence is to convince women of their worthlessness and social invisibility, as well as physically controlling them.

Escape from prostitution becomes more and more difficult as the woman is repeatedly overwhelmed with terror. She is forced to commit acts that are sexually humiliating and that cause her to betray her own principles. The contempt and violence aimed at her are eventually internalized, resulting in a virulent self-hate that then makes it even more difficult to defend herself. Survivors report a sense of contamination, of being different from others, and self-loathing, which lasts many years after getting out of prostitution. Judith Herman and Lenore Terr have each described the complexity of repetitive behaviors found in survivors of chronic trauma. Traumatic re-enactments of abuse are common, along with psychobiological dysfunction, including self-destructive thoughts and behaviors, self-contempt, feelings of shame and worthlessness, substance abuse, eating disorders, and sexual aversions or compulsions.

Dissociation is the psychological process of banishing traumatic events from consciousness. It is an emotional shutting down, which occurs during extreme stress among prisoners of war who are being tortured, among children who are being sexually assaulted, and among women who are

being battered, raped, or prostituted. The emotional distancing necessary to survive rape and prostitution is the same technique used to endure familial sexual assault. Most women report that they cannot engage in prostitution unless they dissociate. Being drunk or high has been described as chemical dissociation.

One woman described the link between johns' behavior and her dissociation while she was prostituting in a strip club:

> You start changing yourself to fit a fantasy role of what they think a woman should be. In the real world, these women don't exist. They're not really looking at you. You become this empty shell. You're not you. You're not even there. (*Farley, unpublished interview,* 1998)

People in prostitution also suffer from posttraumatic stress disorder (PTSD). Symptoms of PTSD include anxiety, depression, insomnia, irritability, flashbacks, emotional numbing, and hyperalertness. Farley and colleagues found that 68% of 854 people in prostitution from nine countries met diagnostic criteria for PTSD, suggesting that the traumatic consequences of prostitution were similar across different cultures. The following are two examples of PTSD.

Saundra Sturdevant and Brenda Stolzfus interviewed an Okinawan woman who had been purchased by U.S. military personnel during the Vietnam War. Many years later, she still became extremely agitated and had visions of sexual assault and persecution on the 15th and 30th of each month, the days that had been Army paydays. Another woman who spoke to Farley described symptoms of PTSD that were a consequence of violence in prostitution: "I wonder why I keep going to therapists and telling them I can't sleep, and I have nightmares. They pass right over the fact that I was a prostitute and I was beaten with two-by-four boards, I had my fingers and toes broken by a pimp, and I was raped more than 30 times. Why do they ignore that?"

Over time, the violence of prostitution, the constant humiliation, the social indignity, and the misogyny result in personality changes that

Judith Herman has described as complex post-traumatic stress disorder (CPTSD). Symptoms of CPTSD include changes in consciousness and self-concept, changes in the ability to regulate emotions, shifts in systems of meaning, such as loss of faith, and an unremitting sense of despair. Sexual feelings are severely damaged in prostitution. Once out of prostitution, 76% of a group of women interviewed by Ruth Parriott reported that they had great difficulty with intimate relationships.

PHYSICAL HEALTH CONSEQUENCES OF PROSTITUTION

Chronic health problems result from physical abuse and neglect in childhood, sexual assault, battering, untreated health problems, and overwhelming stress. Prostituted women suffer from all of these. Many of the chronic physical symptoms of women in prostitution are similar to the physical consequences of torture. In a 1985 study by the Canadian government, the death rate of those in prostitution was found to be 40 times higher than that of the general population.

A lack of attention to pervasive physical and sexual violence has resulted in failures of the health care system for all women. Those in prostitution lacked access to social and medical services that were available to other women. Fear of arrest and social contempt made it difficult for prostituted women to seek emergency shelter or medical treatment.

Although the majority of research on prostituted women's health from 1980 to 2000 focused exclusively on HIV or other sexually transmitted diseases (STDs), some research has addressed non-HIV-related health problems. Prostituted women had an increased risk of cervical cancer and chronic hepatitis. Incidence of abnormal Pap screens was several times higher than the state average in a Minnesota study of prostituted women's health. Childhood rape was associated with increased incidence of cervical dysplasia

in Ann Coker and colleagues' study of women prisoners, many of whom had been in prostitution.

Half of the women interviewed in San Francisco in 1998 by Farley and Barkan reported physical health problems, including joint pain, cardiovascular symptoms, respiratory symptoms, neurological problems, and HIV (8%). Seventeen percent stated that, if it were accessible, they would request immediate hospital admission for drug addiction or emotional problems. Many acute and chronic problems were directly related to violence. In addition to poor nutrition, gastrointestinal problems, and pneumonia, Eleanor Miller reported that women in prostitution had bruises, broken bones, cuts, and abrasions that resulted from beatings and sexual assaults. One woman said about her health:

> I've had three broken arms, nose broken twice, (and) I'm partially deaf in one ear.... I have a small fragment of a bone floating in my head that gives me migraines. I've had a fractured skull. My legs ain't worth shit no more; my toes have been broken. My feet, bottom of my feet, have been burned; they've been whopped with a hot iron and clothes hanger... the hair on my pussy had been burned off at one time.... I have scars. I've been cut with a knife, beat with guns, two by fours. There hasn't been a place on my body that hasn't been bruised somehow, some way, some big, some small. (*Giobbe,* 1992, p. 126)

Frida Spiwak reported that 70% of 100 prostituted girls and women in Bogota had physical health problems. In addition to STDs, their diseases were those of poverty and despair: allergies, respiratory problems, and blindness caused by glue sniffing, migraines, symptoms of premature aging, dental problems, and complications from abortion. Adolescent girls and boys in prostitution surveyed by D. Kelly Weisberg reported STDs, hepatitis, pregnancies, sore throats, flu, and repeated suicide attempts. Women who serviced more customers in prostitution reported more severe physical symptoms. The longer women were in prostitution, the more they suffered symptoms of STDs.

Globally, the incidence of HIV seropositivity among prostituted women and children is devastating. Homeless children are at highest risk for

HIV, for example, in Romania and Colombia. Peter Piot noted that half of new AIDS cases are in the under-25 age group, and that girls are likely to become infected at a much younger age than boys, in part because of the acceptance of violence against women and girls in most cultures....

CRIMINAL JUSTICE RESPONSES TO PROSTITUTION

It is commonly assumed that the greater the legal tolerance of prostitution, the easier it is to control public health. Public health in this context refers primarily to STDs in johns rather than to the psychological and physical health of prostituted women.

Legalized prostitution involves state, county, or city ordinances that regulate prostitution, for example, issuing zoning permits, requiring STD tests, and collecting taxes. In effect, the state operates as the pimp. In Nevada, state regulations determine geographic location and size of brothels, as well as activities of women outside the brothel. Prostituted women are only allowed into nearby towns from 3 to 4 p.m., are restricted to certain locations, and are even prohibited from talking to certain persons. Respondents in South Africa and Zambia were asked whether they thought they would be safer from sexual and physical assault if prostitution were legal. A significant majority (68%) said "no." The implication was that regardless of the legal status of prostitution, those in it knew that they would continue to experience violence.

The HIV epidemic has brought with it the advocacy of another legal approach to prostitution: decriminalization, or the cessation of enforcement of all laws against prostitution. Decriminalization of prostitution has been promoted by sex businesses as a way to remove the social stigma associated with prostitution. Decriminalization would normalize commercial sex, but it would not reduce the trauma and the humiliation of being prostituted. Compared to illegal prostitution, decriminalization would facilitate men's access to women and children.

Stating that "prostitution is not a desirable social phenomenon," the Swedish government in 1999 criminalized the behavior of pimps and johns but not those who were prostituting. Noting that "it is not reasonable to punish the person who sells a sexual service [because] in the majority of cases this person is a weaker partner who is exploited," the Swedish government allocated social welfare monies to "motivate prostitutes to seek help to leave their way of life." This progressive interventionist approach reflects the Swedish interest in countering growth of commercial sex businesses.

In the United States, although there is legislative concern about forced trafficking, there are few legal remedies for women who enter prostitution because of educational neglect, emotional abuse, or lack of economic alternatives. Some women in prostitution do not appear to have been forced or coerced. Public policies that offer legal, financial, and social assistance only to those who can prove violent force, or who are under age eighteen, or who crossed international borders, do not address the core of violence that is present in all types of prostitution. Legal responses to prostitution are inadequate if they fail to include johns, as well as pimps and traffickers, as perpetrators.

The state of Florida passed a remarkably progressive law that addresses some of the forces propelling girls and women into prostitution. The Florida law specifically prohibits inducement into prostitution by sexual abuse, by pornography, or by exploiting the need for food, shelter, safety, or affection.

CONCLUSION

Commercial sex businesses are a multibillion dollar global market that includes strip clubs, massage parlors, phone sex, online prostitution, internet pimping of women and children, adult and child pornography, street, brothel, and escort prostitution. One's political perspective will determine whether prostitution is viewed primarily as a public health issue, as an issue of zoning and property values (which parts of town should house strip clubs and pornography stores?), as vocational choice, as sexual liberation, as freedom of speech (does the webmaster have the right to sell internet photographs of prostituted women being raped?), as petty crime, as domestic violence, or as human rights violation.

For the vast majority of the world's prostituted women, prostitution is the experience of being hunted, dominated, harassed, assaulted, and battered. Intrinsic to prostitution are numerous violations of human rights: sexual harassment, economic servitude, educational deprivation, job discrimination, domestic violence, racism, classism, vulnerability to frequent physical and sexual assault, and being subjected to body invasions that are equivalent to torture.

Demand creates supply in prostitution. Because men want to buy sex, prostitution is assumed to be inevitable, therefore "normal." Men's ambivalence about the purchase of women, however, is reflected in the scarcity of research interviews with johns and in their desire to remain hidden. In a series of interviews with johns conducted by women prostituting in massage parlors, Elizabeth Plumridge noted that, on the one hand, the men believed that commercial sex was a mutually pleasurable exchange, and on the other hand, they asserted that payment of money removed all social and ethical obligations. A john interviewed by Neil McKeganey and Marina Barnard said: "It's like going to have your car done, you tell them what you want done, they don't ask, you tell them you want so and so done."

Programs that assist women in prostitution can not succeed in the long run unless social systems that keep women subordinate also change. Jacquelyn White and Mary Ross observed that violent behaviors against women have been associated with attitudes that promote men's beliefs that they are entitled to sexual access to women, that they are superior to women, and that they have license for sexual aggression. Prostitution myths are a component of attitudes that normalize sexual violence. Martin Monto found that johns' acceptance of commodified sexuality was strongly associated with their acceptance of rape myths, violent sex, and less frequent use of condoms with women in prostitution. A widespread acceptance among men of what has been described as nonrelational sexuality may be a contributing factor to the normalization of prostitution. According to sociologist Kathleen Barry, in today's culture we do not distinguish that is exploitative or coercive from sex that is positive human experience. This blurring results in what Barry has called the prostitution of human sexuality.

Prostitution must be exposed for what it really is: a particularly lethal form of male violence against women. The focus of research, prevention, and law enforcement in the next decades must be on the demand side of prostitution.

CRITICAL THINKING QUESTIONS

1. Many people believe that prostitution is a free choice. Farley argues that this belief is false. Why? What is your view of this issue?
2. How does prostitution reflect an intersection of race, sex, and class oppression?
3. In terms of the legal status of prostitution, how do decriminalization and legalization differ? Why is Farley opposed to both? Do you agree or disagree with her position?

REFERENCES

Abraham, K. 1953. *Selected papers on psychoanalysis.* New York: Basic Books.

Baldwin, M. A. 1999. A million dollars and an apology: Prostitution and public benefits claims. *Hastings Women's Law Journal,* Winter 1999, 189–224.

Barry, K. 1995. *The prostitution of sexuality.* New York: New York University Press.

Bishop, R., and Robinson, L. S. 1998. *Night market: Sexual cultures and the Thai economic miracle.* New York and London: Routledge.

Boyer, D., Chapman, L., and Marshall, B. K. 1993. Survival Sex in King County: Helping Women Out. *Report Submitted to King County Women's Advisory Board, March 31, 1993.* Seattle: Northwest Resource Associates.

Briere, J. 1992. *Child abuse trauma: Theory and treatment of the lasting effects.* Sage: Newbury Park.

Browne, A, and Finkelhor, D. 1986. Impact of child sexual abuse: A review of the research. *Psychological Bulletin 99*(1), 66–77.

Burkett, E. 1997. God created me to be a slave. *New York Times Magazine 12*, 56–60.

Chattopadhyay, M., Bandyopadhyay, S., and Duttagupra, C. 1994. Biosocial factors influencing women to become prostitutes in India. *Social Biology 41*(3–4), 252–259.

Coker, A., Patel, N., Krishnaswami, S., Schmidt, W., and Richter, D. 1998. Childhood forced sex and cervical dysplasia among women prison inmates. *Violence Against Women 4*(5), 595–608.

Crowell, N. A., and Burgess, A. W. (eds.) 1996. *Understanding violence against women.* Washington, D.C.: National Academy Press.

Davidson, J. O. 1998. *Prostitution, power, and freedom.* Ann Arbor: University of Michigan Press.

Davis, N. 1993. *Prostitution: An international handbook on trends, problems, and policies.* London: Greenwood Press.

Dworkin, A. 1997. *Prostitution and male supremacy in life and death.* New York: Free Press.

Farley, M., and Barkan, H. 1998. Prostitution, violence and post-traumatic stress disorder. *Women & Health 27*(3), 37–49.

Farley, M., Baral, I., Kiremire, M., and Sezgin, U. 1998. Prostitution in five countries: Violence and posttraumatic stress disorder. *Feminism & Psychology 8*(4), 415–426.

Finstad, L, and Hoigard, C. 1993. Norway. In *Prostitution: An international handbook on trends, problems, and policies* (N. Davis, ed.). London: Greenwood Press.

Giobbe, E. 1993. An analysis of individual, institutional and cultural pimping. *Michigan Journal of Gender & Law 1*, 33–57.

Giobbe, E., Harrigan, M., Ryan, J., and Gamache, D. 1990. *Prostitution: A matter of violence against women.* Minneapolis, MN: WHISPER.

Herman, J. L. 1992. *Trauma and recovery.* New York: Basic Books.

Hernandez, T. K. 2001. Sexual harassment and racial disparity: The mutual construction of gender and race. *Journal of Gender, Race & Justice 4*, 183.

Hoigard, C., and Finstad, L. 1986. *Backstreets: Prostitution, money and love.* University Park, PA: Pennsylvania State University Press.

Holsopple, K. 1998. Stripclubs according to strippers: Exposing workplace violence. Unpublished paper.

Hughes, D. M. 2000. The "Natasha" trade: The transnational shadow market of trafficking in women. *Journal of International Affairs 53*(2), 625–651.

Hughes, Donna M. 1999. *Pimps and predators on the Internet—Globalizing the sexual exploitation of women and children.* Kingston, Rhode Island: The Coalition Against Trafficking in Women.

Hunter, S. K. 1994. Prostitution is cruelty and abuse to women and children. *Michigan Journal of Gender and Law 1*, 1–44.

Lim, L. L., ed. 1998. *The sex sector: The economic and social bases of prostitution in southeast Asia.* Geneva: International Labor Organization.

Louie, L., Joe, K., Luu. M., and Tong, B. 1991. Chinese American adolescent runaways. Paper presented at Annual Convention of the Asian American Psychological Association, San Francisco.

Lowman, J. 1992. Canada. In *Prostitution: An international handbook on trends, problems, and policies* (N. Davis, Ed.). Westport, CT: Greenwood Press.

Lucas, B., and Hackett, L. 1995. *Street youth: On their own in Indianapolis.* Health Foundation of Greater Indianapolis, IN.

MacKinnon, C. A. 1993. Prostitution and civil rights. *Michigan Journal of Gender and Law 1*, 13–31.

MacKinnon, C. A., and Dworkin, A. 1997. *In harm's way: The pornography civil rights hearings.* Cambridge: Harvard University Press.

McKeganey, N., and Barnard, M. 1996. *Sex work on the streets: Prostitutes and their clients.* Buckingham, Scotland: Milton Keynes Open University Press.

Miller, E. M. 1986. *Street woman.* Philadelphia: Temple University Press.

Ministry of Labour in cooperation with the Ministry of Justice and the Ministry of Health and Social Affairs, Government of Sweden. 1998. Fact Sheet. Secretariat for Information and Communication, Ministry of Labour. Tel +46-8-405 11 55, fax +46-8-405 12 98. Artiklnr, A98.004.

Munro, M. 1999. *Prostitution and human commodification: A study of arrested clients of female street prostitutes.* Chicago: American Sociological Association.

Murphy, P. 1993. *Making the connections: Women, work and abuse: Dramatic insight into the lives of abuse victims and practical recommendations for their successful return to work.* Orlando, FL: Paul M. Deutsch Press.

Nelson, V. 1993. Prostitution: Where racism and sexism intersect. *Michigan Journal of Gender & Law 1*, 81–89.

Parriott, R. 1994. *Health experiences of twin cities women used in prostitution.* Minneapolis, MN.: Unpublished survey initiated by WHISPER.

Piot, P. 1999. Remarks at United Nations Commission on the Status of Women, United Nations Press Release, March 3, New York.

Plumridge, E. W., Chetwynd. J. W., Reed, A., and Gifford, S. J. 1997. Discourses of emotionality in commercial sex: The missing client voice. *Feminism & Psychology 7*(2), 165–181.

Putnam, F. 1990. Disturbances of 'self' in victims of childhood sexual abuse. In *Incest-related syndromes of adult psychopathology* (R. Kluft, Ed.), pp. 113–131. Washington, D.C.: American Psychiatric Press.

Root, M. 1996. Women of color and traumatic stress in 'domestic captivity': Gender and race as disempowering statuses. In *Ethnocultural aspects of posttraumatic stress disorder: Issues, research, and clinical applications* (Mirsella, A. J., Friedman, M. J., Gerrity, E. T., and Scurfield, R. M., Eds.) Washington, D.C.: American Psychological Assn.

Sanchez, L. 1998. Boundaries of legitimacy: Sex, violence, citizenship, and community in a local sexual economy. *Law and Social Inquiry 22*, 543–580.

Silbert, M. H., and Pines, A. M. 1983. Early sexual exploitation as an influence in prostitution. *Social Work 28*, 285–289.

Silbert, M. H., and Pines, A. M. 1984. Pornography and sexual abuse of women. *Sex Roles 10*(11–12), 857–868.

Special Committee on Pornography and Prostitution. 1985. *Pornography and Prostitution in Canada 350.*

Sturdevant, S., and Stolzfus, B. 1992. *Let the good times roll: Prostitution and the US military in Asia.* New York: The New Press.

Terr L C. 1991. Childhood traumas: An outline and overview. *American Journal of Psychiatry 148*, 10–20.

Vanwesenbeeck, I. 1994. *Prostitutes' well-being and risk.* Amsterdam: VU Boekhandel/Uitgeverij Press.

Weisberg, D. 1985. *Children of the night: A study of adolescent prostitution.* Lexington, MA.: Lexington Books.

White, J. W., and Koss, M. P. 1993. Adolescent sexual aggression within heterosexual relationships: Prevalence, characteristics, and causes. In *The juvenile sex offender* (H. E. Barbaree, W. L. Marshall and D. R. Laws, Eds.). New York: Guilford Press.

39

The Protestant Ethic and the Spirit of Capitalism

Max Weber

In perhaps his most well-known treatise, Max Weber argues that a major factor in the development of the capitalist economic system was the distinctive world view of early, ascetic Protestantism, especially Calvinism and Puritanism. In this excerpt from his classic analysis, Weber explains that religious ideas about work and materials initially fostered capitalism's growth, but ultimately capitalism was able to stand on its own without religious supports.

A product of modern European civilization, studying any problem of universal history, is bound to ask himself to what combination of circumstances the fact should be attributed that in Western civilization, and in Western civilization only, cultural phenomena have appeared which (as we like to think) lie in a line of development having *universal* significance and value.... All over the world there have been merchants, wholesale and retail, local and engaged in foreign trade....

But in modern times the Occident has developed, in addition to this, a very different form of capitalism which has appeared nowhere else: the rational capitalistic organization of (formally) free labour. Only suggestions of

it are found elsewhere. Even the organization of unfree labour reached a considerable degree of rationality only on plantations and to a very limited extent in the *Ergasteria* of antiquity. In the manors, manorial workshops, and domestic industries on estates with serf labour it was probably somewhat less developed. Even real domestic industries with free labour have definitely been proved to have existed in only a few isolated cases outside the Occident....

Rational industrial organization, attuned to a regular market, and neither to political nor irrationally speculative opportunities for profit, is not, however, the only peculiarity of Western capitalism. The modern rational organization of the capitalistic enterprise would not have been possible without two other important factors in its development: the separation of business

Source: From *The Protestant Ethic and the Spirit of Capitalism* by Max Weber, copyright © 1988, Prentice-Hall, Inc. Reprinted by permission.

from the household, which completely dominates modern economic life, and closely connected with it, rational book-keeping....

Hence in a universal history of culture the central problem for us is not, in the last analysis, even from a purely economic view-point, the development of capitalistic activity as such, differing in different cultures only in form: the adventurer type, or capitalism in trade, war, politics, or administration as sources of gain. It is rather the origin of this sober bourgeois capitalism with its rational organization of free labour. Or in terms of cultural history, the problem is that of the origin of the Western bourgeois class and of its peculiarities, a problem which is certainly closely connected with that of the origin of the capitalistic organization of labour, but is not quite the same thing. For the bourgeois as a class existed prior to the development of the peculiar modern form of capitalism, though, it is true, only in the Western hemisphere.

Now the peculiar modern Western form of capitalism has been, at first sight, strongly influenced by the development of technical possibilities. Its rationality is today essentially dependent on the calculability of the most important technical factors. But this means fundamentally that it is dependent on the peculiarities of modern science, especially the natural sciences based on mathematics and exact and rational experiment. On the other hand, the development of these sciences and of the technique resting upon them now receives important stimulation from these capitalistic interests in its practical economic application. It is true that the origin of Western science cannot be attributed to such interests. Calculation, even with decimals, and algebra have been carried on in India, where the decimal system was invented. But it was only made use of by developing capitalism in the West, while in India it led to no modern arithmetic or book-keeping. Neither was the origin of mathematics and mechanics determined by capitalistic interests. But the *technical* utilization of scientific knowledge, so important for the living conditions of the mass of people,

was certainly encouraged by economic considerations, which were extremely favourable to it in the Occident. But this encouragement was derived from the peculiarities of the social structure of the Occident. We must hence ask, from *what* parts of that structure was it derived, since not all of them have been of equal importance?

Among those of undoubted importance are the rational structures of law and of administration. For modern rational capitalism has need, not only of the technical means of production, but of a calculable legal system and of administration in terms of formal rules. Without it adventurous and speculative trading capitalism and all sorts of politically determined capitalisms are possible, but no rational enterprise under individual initiative, with fixed capital and certainty of calculations. Such a legal system and such administration have been available for economic activity in a comparative state of legal and formalistic perfection only in the Occident. We must hence inquire where that law came from. Among other circumstances, capitalistic interests have in turn undoubtedly also helped, but by no means alone nor even principally, to prepare the way for the predominance in law and administration of a class of jurists specially trained in rational law. But these interests did not themselves create that law. Quite different forces were at work in this development. And why did not the capitalistic interests do the same in China or India? Why did not the scientific, the artistic, the political, or the economic development there enter upon that path of rationalization which is peculiar to the Occident?

For in all the above cases it is a question of the specific and peculiar rationalism of Western culture.... It is hence our first concern to work out and to explain genetically the special peculiarity of Occidental rationalism, and within this field that of the modern Occidental form. Every such attempt at explanation must, recognizing the fundamental importance of the economic factor, above all take account of the economic conditions. But at the same time the opposite correlation must not be left out of consideration. For though the development of economic rationalism is partly dependent on rational technique and law, it is at the same time determined by the ability and disposition of men to adopt certain types of practical rational conduct. When these types have been obstructed by spiritual obstacles, the development of rational economic conduct has also met serious inner resistance. The magical and religious forces, and the ethical ideas of duty based upon them, have in the past always been among the most important formative influences on conduct. In the studies collected here we shall be concerned with these forces.

Two older essays have been placed at the beginning which attempt, at one important point, to approach the side of the problem which is generally most difficult to grasp: the influence of certain religious ideas on the development of an economic spirit, or the *ethos* of an economic system. In this case we are dealing with the connection of the spirit of modern economic life with the rational ethics of ascetic Protestantism. Thus we treat here only one side of the causal chain....

...[T]hat side of English Puritanism which was derived from Calvinism gives the most consistent religious basis for the idea of the calling.... For the saints' everlasting rest is in the next world; on earth man must, to be certain of his state of grace, "do the works of him who sent him, as long as it is yet day." Not leisure and enjoyment, but only activity serves to increase the glory of God according to the definite manifestations of His will.

Waste of time is thus the first and in principle the deadliest of sins. The span of human life is infinitely short and precious to make sure of one's own election. Loss of time through sociability, idle talk, luxury, even more sleep than is necessary for health, six to at most eight hours, is worthy of absolute moral condemnation. It does not yet hold, with Franklin, that time is money, but the proposition is true in a certain spiritual sense. It is infinitely valuable because every hour lost is lost to labour for the glory of God. Thus inactive contemplation is also valueless, or even directly reprehensible if it is at the expense of one's daily work....

[T]he same prescription is given for all sexual temptation as is used against religious doubts and a sense of moral unworthiness: "Work hard in your calling." But the most important thing was that even beyond that labour came to be considered in itself the end of life, ordained as such by God. St. Paul's "He who will not work shall not eat" holds unconditionally for everyone. Unwillingness to work is symptomatic of the lack of grace.

Here the difference from the mediæval viewpoint becomes quite evident. Thomas Aquinas also gave an interpretation of that statement of St. Paul. But for him labour is only necessary *naturali ratione* for the maintenance of individual and community. Where this end is achieved, the precept ceases to have any meaning. Moreover, it holds only for the race, not for every individual. It does not apply to anyone who can live without labour on his possessions, and of course contemplation, as a spiritual form of action in the Kingdom of God, takes precedence over the commandment in its literal sense. Moreover, for the popular theology of the time, the highest form of monastic productivity lay in the increase of the *Thesaurus eccleslœ* through prayer and chant.

...For everyone without exception God's Providence has prepared a calling, which he should profess and in which he should labour. And this calling is not, as it was for the Lutheran, a fate to which he must submit and which he must make the best of, but God's commandment to the individual to work for the divine glory. This seemingly subtle difference had far-reaching psychological consequences, and became connected with a further development of the providential interpretation of the economic order which had begun in scholasticism.

It is true that the usefulness of a calling, and thus its favour in the sight of God, is measured primarily in moral terms, and thus in terms of the importance of the goods produced in it for the community. But a further, and, above all, in practice the most important, criterion is found in private profitableness. For if that God, whose hand the Puritan sees in all the occurrences of life, shows one of His elect a chance of profit, he must do it with a purpose. Hence the faithful Christian must follow the call by taking advantage of the opportunity. "If God show you a way in which you may lawfully get more than in another way (without wrong to your soul or to any other), if you refuse this, and choose the less gainful way, you cross one of the ends of your calling, and you refuse to be God's steward, and to accept His gifts and use them for Him when He requireth it: you may labour to be rich for God, though not for the flesh and sin."…

The superior indulgence of the *seigneur* and the parvenu ostentation of the *nouveau riche* are equally detestable to asceticism. But, on the other hand, it has the highest ethical appreciation of the sober, middle-class, self-made man. "God blesseth His trade" is a stock remark about those good men who had successfully followed the divine hints. The whole power of the God of the Old Testament, who rewards His people for their obedience in this life, necessarily exercised a similar influence on the Puritan who…compared his own state of grace with that of the heroes of the Bible.…

Although we cannot here enter upon a discussion of the influence of Puritanism in all…directions, we should call attention to the fact that the toleration of pleasure in cultural goods, which contributed to purely aesthetic or athletic enjoyment, certainly always ran up against one characteristic limitation: They must not cost anything. Man is only a trustee of the goods which have come to him through God's grace. He must, like the servant in the parable, give an account of every penny entrusted to him, and it is at least hazardous to spend any of it for a purpose which does not serve the glory of God but only one's own enjoyment. What person, who keeps his eyes open, has not met representatives of this viewpoint even in the present? The idea of a man's duty to his possessions, to which he subordinates himself as an obedient steward, or even as an acquisitive machine, bears with chilling weight on his life. The greater the possessions the heavier, if the ascetic attitude toward life stands the

test, the feeling of responsibility for them, for holding them undiminished for the glory of God and increasing them by restless effort. The origin of this type of life also extends in certain roots, like so many aspects of the spirit of capitalism, back into the Middle Ages. But it was in the ethic of ascetic Protestantism that it first found a consistent ethical foundation. Its significance for the development of capitalism is obvious.

This worldly Protestant asceticism, as we may recapitulate up to this point, acted powerfully against the spontaneous enjoyment of possessions; it restricted consumption, especially of luxuries. On the other hand, it had the psychological effect of freeing the acquisition of goods from the inhibitions of traditionalistic ethics. It broke the bonds of the impulse of acquisition in that it not only legalized it, but (in the sense discussed) looked upon it as directly willed by God.…

As far as the influence of the Puritan outlook extended, under all circumstances—and this is, of course, much more important than the mere encouragement of capital accumulation—it favoured the development of a rational bourgeois economic life; it was the most important, and above all the only consistent influence in the development of that life. It stood at the cradle of the modern economic man.

To be sure, these Puritanical ideals tended to give way under excessive pressure from the temptations of wealth, as the Puritans themselves knew very well. With great regularity we find the most genuine adherents of Puritanism among the classes which were rising from a lowly status, the small bourgeois and farmers while the *beati possidentes,* even among Quakers, are often found tending to repudiate the old ideals. It was the same fate which again and again befell the predecessor of this worldly asceticism, the monastic asceticism of the Middle Ages. In the latter case, when rational economic activity had worked out its full effects by strict regulation of conduct and limitation of consumption, the wealth accumulated either succumbed directly to the nobility, as in the time before the Reformation, or monastic discipline threatened to break down, and one of the numerous reformations became necessary.

In fact the whole history of monasticism is in a certain sense the history of a continual struggle with the problem of the secularizing influence of wealth. The same is true on a grand scale of the worldly asceticism of Puritanism. The great revival of Methodism, which preceded the expansion of English industry toward the end of the eighteenth century, may well be compared with such a monastic reform. We may hence quote here a passage from John Wesley himself which might well serve as a motto for everything which has been said above. For it shows that the leaders of these ascetic movements understood the seemingly paradoxical relationships which we have here analysed perfectly well, and in the same sense that we have given them. He wrote:

I fear, wherever riches have increased, the essence of religion has decreased in the same proportion. Therefore I do not see how it is possible, in the nature of things, for any revival of true religion to continue long. For religion must necessarily produce both industry and frugality, and these cannot but produce riches. But as riches increase, so will pride, anger, and love of the world in all its branches. How then is it possible that Methodism, that is, a religion of the heart, though it flourishes now as a green bay tree, should continue in this state? For the Methodists in every place grow diligent and frugal; consequently they increase in goods. Hence they proportionately increase in pride, in anger, in the desire of the flesh, the desire of the eyes, and the pride of life. So, although the form of religion remains, the spirit is swiftly vanishing away. Is there no way to prevent this—this continual decay of pure religion? We ought not to prevent people from being diligent and frugal; *we must exhort all Christians to gain all they can, and to save all they can; that is, in effect, to grow rich.*

As Wesley here says, the full economic effect of those great religious movements, whose significance for economic development lay above all in their ascetic educative influence, generally came only after the peak of the purely religious enthusiasm was past. Then the intensity of the search for the Kingdom of God commenced gradually to pass over into sober economic virtue; the religious roots died out slowly, giving way to utilitarian worldliness. Then, as Dowden puts it, as in *Robinson Crusoe,* the isolated economic man who carries on missionary activities on the side takes the place of the lonely spiritual search for the Kingdom of Heaven of Bunyan's pilgrim, hurrying through the market-place of Vanity....

A specifically bourgeois economic ethic had grown up. With the consciousness of standing in the fullness of God's grace and being visibly blessed by Him, the bourgeois business man, as long as he remained within the bounds of formal correctness, as long as his moral conduct was spotless and the use to which he put his wealth was not objectionable, could follow his pecuniary interests as he would and feel that he was fulfilling a duty in doing so. The power of religious asceticism provided him in addition with sober, conscientious, and unusually industrious workmen, who clung to their work as to a life purpose willed by God.

Finally, it gave him the comforting assurance that the unequal distribution of the goods of this world was a special dispensation of Divine Providence, which in these differences, as in particular grace, pursued secret ends unknown to men....

One of the fundamental elements of the spirit of modern capitalism, and not only of that but of all modern culture: Rational conduct on the basis of the idea of the calling, was born—that is what this discussion has sought to demonstrate—from the spirit of Christian asceticism. One has only to re-read the passage from Franklin, quoted at the beginning of this essay, in order to see that the essential elements of the attitude which was there called the spirit of capitalism are the same as what we have just shown to be the content of the Puritan worldly asceticism, only without the religious basis, which by Franklin's time had died away....

Since asceticism undertook to remodel the world and to work out its ideals in the world, material goods have gained an increasing and finally an inexorable power over the lives of men as at no previous period in history. Today the spirit of religious asceticism—whether finally, who knows?—has escaped from the cage. But victorious capitalism, since it rests on mechanical foundations, needs its support no longer. The rosy blush of its laughing heir, the Enlightenment, seems also to be irretrievably fading, and the idea of duty in one's calling prowls about in our lives like the ghost of dead religious beliefs. Where the fulfilment of the calling cannot directly be related to the highest spiritual and cultural values, or when, on the other hand, it need not be felt simply as economic compulsion, the individual generally abandons the attempt to justify it at all. In the field of its highest development, in the United States, the pursuit of wealth, stripped of its religious and ethical meaning, tends to become associated with purely mundane passions, which often actually give it the character of sport.

No one knows who will live in this cage in the future, or whether at the end of this tremendous development entirely new prophets will arise, or there will be a great rebirth of old ideas and ideals, or, if neither, mechanized petrification, embellished with a sort of convulsive self-importance. For of the last stage of this cultural development, it might well be truly said: "Specialists without spirit, sensualists without heart; this nullity imagines that it has attained a level of civilization never before achieved."

But this brings us to the world of judgments of value and of faith, with which this purely historical discussion need not be burdened....

Here we have only attempted to trace the fact and the direction of its influence to their motives in one, though a very important point. But it would also further be necessary to investigate how Protestant Asceticism was in turn influenced in its development and its character by the totality of social conditions, especially economic. The modern man is in general, even with the best will, unable to give religious ideas a significance for culture and national character which they deserve. But it is, of course, not my aim to substitute for a one-sided materialistic an equally one-sided spiritualistic causal interpretation of culture and of history. Each is equally possible, but each, if it does not serve as the preparation, but as the conclusion of an investigation, accomplishes equally little in the interest of historical truth.

CRITICAL THINKING QUESTIONS

1. What are the distinctive characteristics of the religious orientation that Weber called the "Protestant ethic"? In what ways did those characteristics promote the development of the capitalist economic system?
2. In what respects do early Calvinists with a "calling" differ from today's "workaholics"?
3. In what sense does Weber's analysis differ from the materialist orientation of Karl Marx (Reading 52), who suggested that productive forces shape the world of ideas?

Religion

40

Canada's Mythical Religious
Mosaic: Some Census Findings

CLASSIC

CONTEMPORARY

CROSS-CULTURAL

Reginald W. Bibby

*Bibby finds that many Canadians believe that since Canada is a multicultural society it
must also feature considerable religious diversity. However, national census data suggest
that Canada's "religious mosaic" is largely a myth. Bibby's research reveals that
Christianity continues to enjoy a significant numerical majority in Canada and that new
religions are finding it difficult to attract new members. In fact, the author suggests that
Canada is characterized by an extremely narrow spectrum of religious diversity and that
it is dominated by Catholic and Protestant "companies."*

Canada historically has been a country of immigrants. Similar to the United States, much of its early population growth from the seventeenth century onward was due to the arrival of people from France and England, and increasingly from around the world. Since the 1960s, there has been a shift in the dominant origins of immigrants, with a majority now coming from Asia and other Third World countries, rather than Europe.

In the face of such cultural group diversity, Canada has taken pride in defining itself as a mosaic, a "community of communities." Such a self-definition is more than mere rhetoric. In 1971, the federal government unveiled its official policy of multiculturalism, complete with an array of programs aimed at enabling citizens of all backgrounds to participate fully in Canadian life, and to perpetuate their national cultures to the extent they so desired. In 1988, these twin ideals were enshrined in the *Multiculturalism Act* that

states the Canadian government is committed to a policy "designed to preserve and enhance the multicultural heritage of Canadians while working to achieve the equality of all Canadians."

A widely held assumption is that the cultural diversity of Canadians is translating into increasing religious diversity, as people arriving from other countries bring with them an array of different religions. Data from Canada's latest national census calls such an assumption into question.

The statistical gathering body of the Canadian government, known as *Statistics Canada,* carries out a major national census in the second year of each new decade that includes the item "What is your religion?" The question has been asked dating back to the first national census in 1871. Select runs of the 1991 census data that shed some important light on religious identification patterns among culturally diverse Canadians were made available to the author in 1996. What follows is a brief summary of key findings relating to religious identification and some of its key family- and cultural-group correlates.

Source: R. W. Bibby. 2000. "Canada's Mythical Religious Mosaic: Some Census Findings." *Journal for the Scientific Study of Religion,* 39(2), 235–39.

RELIGIOUS IDENTIFICATION

The 1991 census found that 88% of Canadians continue to "think" that they are Catholic (46%), Protestant (36%), or adherents of Other Faiths (6%). An examination of religious identification over time shows that the proportion of the population who regard themselves as Catholics has remained fairly constant over time, while the proportion who identify themselves as Protestants has declined. The overall "Christian" total, including Eastern Orthodox, was 98% in 1871, 96% in 1931, and 84% in 1991. The remaining 16% of the populace consists primarily of those who report they have no religion (12%); this category only became a methodological possibility in 1971 through the introduction of self-enumeration. Overtime, the Jewish total has remained a constant 1%, while those identifying with Other Faiths (including, in Statistics Canada's classification scheme, atheists and agnostics) has increased only marginally, from 2% to 3%.

THE ROLE OF THE FAMILY IN TRANSMITTING RELIGIOUS IDENTIFICATION

The key source of religious identification continues to be parents. People who marry partners of the same faith are inclined to pass that faith on to their children—reporting in the census that their children have the same religious identification as they do. This intergenerational pattern also holds in the case of cohabitation, as well as for the offspring of both female and male lone parents. It also is equally true in situations where parents do not identify with any religion.

Where there are exceptions to the rule, parents usually indicate that their children see themselves as having no religion. However, in the Other Faith and No Religion parental instances, some "switching" of offspring to Catholicism or Protestantism is acknowledged—2% to 4% by Other Faith and No Religion couples and, among lone parent "nones," 6% by females and 12% by males.

To the extent that identification changes, a key variable appears to be intermarriage and "intercohabitation." Catholics in particular, along with Protestants, tend to be the big winners numerically when relationships cross religious lines, while the "No Religion" category and other religious groups tend to experience significant net losses. The reasons are fairly straightforward. When people of different religions marry or cohabit, the religion of women predominates, even in the case of women who have no religious preference. Women in such relationships tend to raise their children in their own tradition, and are matched only by men when Catholic men marry Protestant women. A very important singular exception to this pattern is when women with Other Faith preferences intermarry: in such cases, they—along with Other Faith men—are inclined to raise their children in *their partner's* tradition.

The most numerous intermarriage and "intercohabitation" arrangements involve Catholic and Protestant women, who in effect "recruit" large

TABLE 40.1: Religious Identification of Canadians, *1871–1991*

	1871	1901	1931	1961	1991
Identification					
Catholic	42%	42	41	47	46
Protestant	56	56	54	49	36
Eastern Orthodox	<1	<1	1	1	2
Jewish	<1	<1	1	1	1
Other Faiths	2	2	2	1	3
No Religion	<1	<1	<1	<1	12

numbers of offspring at the expense of the "No Religion" and Other Faith categories. These gains offset the frequent losses that occur when Catholic and Protestant men become involved with women who have no religious preference. Yet Catholic and Protestant men typically "add" offspring when they marry or cohabit with women who identify with other world faiths.

CULTURAL GROUP AFFINITIES

As a result of such intermarriage patterns, Christianity continues to be overwhelmingly dominant in Canada. Despite the stimulus of immigration, other major world religions are having considerable difficulty making significant numerical inroads in Canada.

The 1991 census reveals that some 65 to 75% of the affiliates of Islam, Buddhism, Hinduism, and Sikhism are immigrants, compared to about 13% in the case of both Catholics and Protestants. The census further shows that less than 2% of Canadians of British, French, German, and Italian origins *combined* are identifying with religions other than Christianity. Individuals who are identifying with Islam, Buddhism, Hinduism, and Sikhism are primarily people with Middle East and Asian cultural roots. Affiliates with European backgrounds do not exceed 3% in any of these faith instances.

In order to sustain their numbers and grow, faith groups such as these have to be able to replace their aging immigrants with offspring (birth) and resident Canadians (proselytism). To date there is little indication that such demographic developments are occurring in the numbers required.

Asian includes Middle East, South Asian, East Asian; European includes British, French, and other Western European.

For a complete listing of affiliation figures for all religious groups, broken down by province, gender, age, education, ethnicity, and language, see Statistics Canada, *Religions in Canada,* Ottawa: Science and Technology Canada, 1993. 1991 Census of Canada, Catalogue Number 93-319.

Smaller religions in the "Other Faith" category are faring even worse. For all the media hype about disenchanted and disaffiliated Canadians turning to a wide range of religious options in the last half of this century—what sociologists dub "new religions" or "para-religious groups"—the census reveals that relatively few people are actually identifying with the available alternatives. In a nation of close to 30 million people, less than 5,000 individuals are identifying with religions including New Age, Scientology, and Theosophy. Such data suggest that Canada has an extremely tight "religious market" dominated by Catholic and Protestant "companies." New entries find the going extremely tough.

TABLE 40.2: Religious Identification of Children* by Parental Identification and Marital Status

Parental Identification	Married Partner Same	Common-Law Partner Same	Female Lone Parent	Male Lone Parent
Catholic	99%	95	93	94
Protestant	95	87	87	85
Eastern Orthodox	98	98	82	85
Jewish	99	97	95	88
Other Faiths	94	89	86	57
No Religion	98	97	94	88

*As reported by parents for children living at home.

TABLE 40.3: Religious Identification of Children by Religious Identification of Mothers and Fathers

Religion of:Religion of Children

Mother/Father	No. of Couples	Catholic	Protestant	Eastern Orthodox	Jewish	Other Faiths	No Religion	Totals**
Catholic/Protestant	259,130	70%	11	*	*	*	9	100
Protestant/Catholic	254,105	42	44	*	*	*	14	100
Catholic/East Orthodox	12,735	54	1	39	*	*	6	100
East Orthodox/Catholic	8,625	62	4	28	*	*	7	101
Catholic/Jewish	3,070	38	2	*	25	*	35	100
Jewish/Catholic	2,055	28	1	1	45	*	25	100
Catholic/Other Faiths	7,600	57	1	*	*	21	20	99
Other Faiths/Catholic	3,195	58	4	*	*	12	26	100
Catholic/No Religion	82,745	67	3	*	*	*	30	100
No Religion/Catholic	35,050	40	3	*	*	*	57	100
Protestant/East Orthodox	10,300	2	55	29	*	*	14	100
East Orthodox/Protestant	6,595	4	47	36	*	*	13	101
Protestant/Jewish	3.555	2	38	*	26	*	34	100
Jewish/Protestant	2,520	1	23	*	52	*	24	100
Protestant/Other Faiths	5,735	1	45	*	*	26	28	100
Other Faiths/Protestant	3,220	2	42	*	*	26	29	99
Protestant/No Religion	126,935	1	58	*	*	*	41	100
No Religion/Protestant	35,115	2	27	*	*	*	71	100
Other Faiths/No Religion	4,415	3	5	*	*	22	70	100
No Religion/Jewish	1,225	2	6	*	29	*	62	99
No Religion/Other faiths	2,365	5	4	*	*	22	70	101

*Less than 1%.
**Because of rounding on the part of Statistics Canada, some totals do not equal 100.

DISCUSSION

The net result of these patterns of socialization and switching is that the vast majority of Canadians are continuing to identify with the numerically dominant Christian groups. Demographically at 82% strong, Catholics and Protestants have a large numerical advantage over other religious groups when it comes to issues of cultural maintenance arid intermarriage. Even with a national policy of multiculturalism, smaller cultural and religious groups find themselves absorbing many parts of the dominant ways of life in this country. In the case of socialization and marriage, groups whose members typically comprise less than 1% of the national population usually find that their children befriend, date, and frequently marry people from other cultural and religious groups. Apparent gains through increased immigration are neutralized by assimilation.

Numerically dominant Catholics arid Protestants who marry and live with people of other religious persuasions tend to experience net gains when it comes to the religious identification of offspring. It needs to be emphasized that the key issue is not whether or not the partner "converts" to the other's faith; what is more important, numerically speaking, is how the children are raised. And here the patterns are fairly clear: the religion of the woman dominates. Given the large Catholic and Protestant numbers, the end result is that the population tends to gravitate toward Catholic and Protestant identifications.

This pattern is particularly evident when Catholics and Protestants marry people of Other

TABLE 40.4: Cultural Group Origins of Affiliates of Select World Religions

Cultural Group Origin*	World Religions				
	Islam	Buddhist	Hindu	Sikh	Totals
Total - Single Origin	90%	93	90	94	91
Asian Regions	75	89	77	91	81
European	3	3	2	2	3
Other Countries	12	1	11	1	7
Total - Multiple Origins	10	7	10	6	9
Grand Total	100	100	100	100	100

*The census differentiates between "single origin" where only one national group heritage is cited, versus more than one.

Faiths, excluding Judaism. Regardless of whether the Other Faith partner is female or male, the inclination is for the ensuing offspring to be raised as Catholics or Protestants—or No Religion. Put bluntly, most smaller groups are losing many of their children and grandchildren to the Catholic and Protestant traditions. Alternately, they do not affiliate with any group.

It's true that there has been an increase in recent decades in the number of people arriving from countries where other world faiths are dominant. It also is true that widespread secularization has led to a decline in individual participation and organizational influence. Nonetheless, the vast majority of Canadians in the 90s continue to "think" they are Catholic or Protestant, and "think" that they are raising "Catholic" and "Protestant" children. Other world religions are having difficulty growing, due to both the tendency of their children to "defect" to Christian groups and their inability to recruit "outsiders." Even the Religion Nones are showing a net loss to the "somethings" when intermarriage and intercohabitation occur—if not immediately, then intergenerationally.

Secularization may have drastically reduced the influence that Catholic and Protestant groups have in Canada. But tradition and assimilation appear to function to keep identification with Christianity at a very high level. From the standpoint of numbers, the heralded emerging religious mosaic, so far at least, is largely a myth.

CRITICAL THINKING QUESTIONS

1. Given that Canadian law, as embodied in the *Multiculturalism Act* (1988), confirms the national support for cultural diversity, were you surprised to find out that Christian faiths continue to enjoy such a monopoly? As a sociologist, how would you explain such stability in religious faith over time?

2. With reference to the article, what influences do *intermarriage* and *intercohabitation* have on parents' decisions regarding the religious tradition in which to raise their children?

3. Bibby suggests that although secularization is diminishing the influence of religion in people's lives, religion is still identified as an important element by many of today's families. Do you see the influence of religion increasing or decreasing over the next hundred years? Why?

41

Women and Islam

Jane I. Smith

Religion

CLASSIC

CONTEMPORARY

CROSS-CULTURAL

Many Westerners have a vague notion that women in Iran, Saudi Arabia, and other Islamic societies are relentlessly controlled by men. Although this stereotype has some truth, a more realistic account of the relationship between Islam and the sexes must begin with a basic understanding of this unfamiliar religion. In this article, Jane Smith provides an overview of Islamic tenets, explores some of the variations that divide the vast Islamic world, and assesses the relative social standing of the sexes—as Muslims themselves understand it.

To attempt to talk about women in Islam is of course to venture into an area fraught with the perils of overgeneralization, oversimplification, and the almost unavoidable limitations of a Western bias. The first problem is simply one of raw numbers. There are perhaps close to half a billion Muslim women inhabiting all major areas of the world today. Is it possible to say anything that holds true for all of them, let alone for their sisters over the past fourteen centuries of Islam?

Then one must consider all the various elements that comprise the picture of Islamic womanhood. Many of these elements are directly related to the religion of Islam itself, such as past and present legal realities, roles permitted and enforced as a result of Muslim images of women, and the variety of Islamic and hetero-Islamic rites and practices in which Islamic women have traditionally participated. Other elements contributing to the full picture of women in Islam—such as education, political rights, professional employment opportunities, and the like—have less to do with the religion per se but are still influenced by it.

The Holy Qur'ān (sometimes transliterated as "Koran") still forms the basis of prevailing family law in most areas of the Muslim world. It has always been and still is considered to be the last in a series of divine revelations from God given in the seventh century C.E. to humanity through the vehicle of his final prophet Muhammad. The Qur'ān is therefore the literal and unmitigated word of God, collected and ordered by the young Muslim community but untainted with the thoughts and interpretations of any persons, including Muhammad himself. It is obvious, then, why the regulations formulated by the Qur'ān in regard to women have been adhered to with strictness and why changes in Muslim family law are coming about only very slowly in the Islamic world.

Source: Reprinted by permission of the State University of New York Press, from *Women in World Religions* by Arvind Sharma and Katherine K. Young (eds.), © State University of New York. All rights reserved.

The circumstances of women in pre-Islamic Arabia are subject to a variety of interpretations. On the one hand, certain women—soothsayers, priestesses, queens, and even singular individuals—did play powerful roles in society. On the other hand, whatever the earlier realities for women in terms of marriage, divorce, and inheritance of property, it is clear that the Qur'ān did introduce very significant changes that were advantageous for women. Contemporary Muslims are fond of pointing out, quite correctly, that Islam brought legal advantages for women quite unknown in corresponding areas of the Western Christian world. What, then, does the Qur'ān say about women?

The earliest messages of the Qur'ān, and the twin themes that run through all the chapters, are of the realities of the oneness of God and the inevitability of the day of judgment. All persons, men and women, are called upon to testify to those realities.... Religiously speaking, then, men and women are fully equal in the eyes of God according to the Qur'ān.

Before looking at the specifics of the legal injunctions for women, it is necessary to consider two verses that have caused a great deal of consternation to Westerners. One is 2:228, which says literally that men are a step above women, and the other is 4:34, clarifying that men are the protectors of women (or are in charge of women) because God has given preference to one over the other and because men provide support for women. Perhaps because these verses have been so troublesome for non-Muslims (especially feminists), they have been subject to an enormous amount of explanation and interpretation by contemporary Muslim apologists eager to present a defense of their religion. These writers, men and women, affirm that it is precisely because men are invested with the responsibility of taking care of women, financially and otherwise, that they are given authority over the females of their families. And that, affirm many Muslim women today, is exactly the way it should be. We will return to this perspective

later, particularly in light of what a desire for liberation means—and does not mean—for many Muslim women....

According to the Qur'ān, a man may marry up to four wives, so long as he is able to provide for each equally. He may marry a Muslim woman or a member of the Jewish or Christian faith, or a slave woman. A Muslim woman, however, may marry only one husband, and he must be a Muslim. Contemporary Muslim apologists are quick to point out that these restrictions are for the benefit of women, ensuring that they will not be left unprotected. In Islam, marriage is not a sacrament but a legal contract, and according to the Qur'ān a woman has clearly defined legal rights in negotiating this contract. She can dictate the terms and can receive the dowry herself. This dowry (*mahr*) she is permitted to keep and maintain as a source of personal pride and comfort.

Polygamy (or more strictly polygyny, plurality of wives) is practiced by only a small percentage of the contemporary Muslim population, and a man with more than two wives is extremely rare. Many countries are now taking steps to modify the circumstances in which a husband may take more than one wife, although only in two countries, Turkey and Tunisia, are multiple marriages actually illegal. Other countries have made such moves as requiring the husband to have the permission of the court (as in Iraq and Syria) or to get the permission of the first wife (as in Egypt), or permitting the wife to write into her marriage contract that she will not allow a cowife (as in Morocco and Lebanon). It seems reasonable to expect that other countries will make changes and modifications. It is interesting to note that while for some finances have dictated monogamy — most husbands have simply not been able to afford more than one wife—changing economic realities may again dictate that a man contemplate the possibility of having several wives to work and supply income for the family.

Muslim women traditionally have been married at an extremely young age, sometimes even before puberty. This practice is related, of course, to the historical fact that fathers and other male relatives generally have chosen the grooms themselves, despite the guarantee of the Qur'ān that marriage is a contract into which male and female enter equally. While it is true that technically a girl cannot be forced into a marriage she does not want, pressures from family and the youth of the bride often have made this prerogative difficult to exercise. Today, the right of a male member of the family to contract an engagement for a girl against her wishes has been legally revoked in most places, although it is still a common practice, especially in rural areas....

In the contemporary Islamic world, divorce rates vary considerably from one country to the next. Muslim apologists insist that divorce is not nearly as common in Islamic countries as it is, for example, in the United States. This statement is generally true, although in some countries, such as Morocco, the rate is high and continues to grow. Often what is really only the breaking of the engagement contract is included in divorce statistics, skewing the measure. Many countries are now considering serious changes in divorce procedures. The simultaneous triple repudiation generally has been declared illegal, and in many countries divorce initiated by either party, the man or the woman, must take place in the court of law. Other countries add special stipulations generally favorable to the woman. It remains true, however, that men can divorce for less cause than women, and often divorces hung up in courts with male judges can prove enormously difficult for women to gain.

In accordance with Islamic law, custody of the children traditionally has gone to the father at some time between the age of seven and nine for boys and between seven and puberty for girls, depending on the legal school. This practice too is slowly changing, and in most areas women who have been divorced by their husbands are allowed to keep their sons until puberty and their daughters until they are of an age to be married.

It is considered one of the great innovations of the Qur'ān over earlier practices that women are permitted to inherit and own property. Non-Muslims have generally found great difficulty with the Qur'ānic stipulation that a woman is allowed to inherit property but that the inheritance should be only half that of a male. According to the Islamic understanding, however, the rationale is precisely that which applies to the verse saying that men are in charge of women. Because women are permitted to keep and maintain their own property without responsibility for taking care of their families financially, it is only reasonable that the male, who must spend his own earning and inheritance for the maintenance of women, should receive twice as much....

According to the Qur'ān, women should not expose themselves to public view with lack of modesty. It does not say that they should be covered specifically from head to toe, nor that they should wear face veils or masks or other of the paraphernalia that has adorned many Islamic women through the ages. The Qur'ān also suggests that the wives of the Prophet Muhammad, when speaking to other men, should do so from behind a partition, again for purposes of propriety. It has been open to question whether this statement is meant to apply to all women. In the early Islamic community, these verses were exaggerated and their underlying ideas elaborated and defined in ways that led fairly quickly to a seclusion of women which seems quite at odds with what the Qur'ān intended or the Prophet wanted. When the community in Medina was established, women participated fully with men in all activities of worship and prayer. Soon they became segregated, however, to the point where an often-quoted *hadith* (no doubt spurious) attributed to Muhammad has him saying that women pray better at home than in the mosque, and best of all in their own closets. Today a number of contemporary Muslim writers are urging a return to the practices of the young Muslim community, with women no longer segregated from the mosque or relegated to certain rear or side portions as they generally have been, but participating fully in worship with men....

What is popularly known as "veiling" is part of the general phenomenon of the segregation of women and yet is also distinctly apart from it. The two are increasingly seen as separate by contemporary Islamic women seeking to affirm a new identity in relation to their religion. Veils traditionally have taken a number of forms: a veil covering the face from just below the eyes down; a *chador* or *burka* covering the entire body, including the face, often with a woven screen in front through which women can see but not be seen; and a full face mask with small slits through the eyes, still worn in some areas of the Arabian Gulf. These costumes, so seemingly oppressive to Western eyes, at least have allowed women to observe without being observed, thus affording their wearers a degree of anonymity that on some occasions has proven useful.

The general movement toward unveiling had its ostensible beginning in the mid-1920s, when the Egyptian feminist Huda Sha'rawi cast off her veil after arriving in Egypt from an international meeting of women. She was followed literally and symbolically by masses of women in the succeeding years, and Egyptian women as well as those in other Middle Eastern countries made great strides in adopting Western dress. At the present time in the history of Islam, however, one finds a quite different phenomenon. Partly in reaction against Western liberation and Western ideals in general, women in many parts of the Islamic world are self-consciously adopting forms of dress by which they can identify with Islam rather than with what they now see as the imperialist West. Islamic dress, generally chosen by Muslim women themselves rather than forced upon them by males, signals for many an identification with a way of life that they are increasingly convinced represents a more viable alternative than that offered by the West....

We see, then, that while legal circumstances for women have undergone some significant changes in the past half-century, the dictates of the Qur'ān continue to be enormously influential in the molding of new laws as well as in the personal choices of Muslim men and women....

I have stressed here the insistence of the Qur'ān on the religious and spiritual equality of men and women. And aside from some unfortunate *hadith* with very weak chains of authority suggesting that the majority of women will be in the Fire on the Day of Judgment because of their mental and physical inferiority, religious literature in general, when talking about human responsibility and concomitant judgment, makes women full partners with men under the divine command to live lives of integrity and righteousness....

Of course, women do participate in many of the activities and duties considered incumbent on all good Muslims, but generally these practices have a somewhat different function for them than for men. Prayer for women, as we have said, is usually in the home rather than in the mosque, and does not necessarily follow the pattern of the regularized five times a day. Participation in the fast itself is normally the same as for the men (except when women are pregnant, nursing, or menstruating), but the particular joys of preparing the fast-breaking meals are for the women alone. While the husband determines the amount of money or goods to be distributed for almsgiving, another responsibility of all Muslims, it is often the wife who takes charge of the actual distribution.

The last duty incumbent on Muslims after the testimony to the oneness of God and prophethood of his apostle Muhammad, the prayer, the fast, and paying the almstax is the pilgrimage once in a lifetime to the holy city of Mecca. Women do participate in this journey, and as transportation becomes easier and the care provided for pilgrims in Saudi Arabia becomes more regularized with modernization, increasing numbers of females join the throngs which gather to circumambulate the Xaaba at Mecca each year....

Saints in Islam are both male and female. One is normally recognized as a saint not by any process of canonization but because of some miraculous deed(s) performed or through a dream communication after death with a living person requesting that a shrine be erected over his or her tomb. Often a woman is favored with these dreams and after the construction of the shrine she becomes the carekeeper of the tomb, a position of some honor and responsibility....

While women in the Islamic world have been segregated and secluded, and historically have been considered second-class citizens by the vast majority of males in the community, they have not been totally without power. They have been able to maintain a degree of control over their own lives and over the men with whom they live through many of the religious practices described above. The fact that they alone have the ability to bear children, the influence they continue to play in the lives of their sons, and the power they have over their sons' wives are subtle indications that there are certain checks and balances on the obvious authority invested by the Qur'ān in men. From sexuality to control of the network of communications in the family to manipulation of such external agencies as spirits and supernatural beings, women have had at their control a variety of means to exert their will over the men in their families and over their own circumstances. The subtle means of control available to women throughout the world have of course been exploited: withholding sexual favors (a questionable but often-quoted *hadith* says that if a woman refuses to sleep with her husband, the angels will curse her until the morning), doing small things to undermine a husband's honor such as embarrassing him in front of guests, indulging in various forms of gossip and social control, and the like....

Until fairly recently, education for women in the Muslim world has been minimal. Girls were given the rudiments of an Islamic education, mainly a little instruction in the Qur'ān and the traditions so as to be able to recite their prayers properly. Beyond that their training was not academic but domestic. In the late nineteenth and early twentieth century, Islamic leaders awoke with a start to the reality that Muslims were significantly behind the West in a variety of ways, including technology and the education necessary to understand and develop it. Many of these leaders recognized that if Islamic nations were to compete successfully in the contemporary world, it had to be with the aid of a well-educated and responsible female sector. Thus, this century has seen a number of educational advances for women, and in some countries, such as Egypt, Iraq, and Kuwait, women constitute very significant numbers of the university population. Nonetheless, illiteracy in many Muslim nations continues to be high, and the gap between male and female literacy rates is even increasing in some areas. In Saudi Arabia, where at present the economic resources are certainly available, large numbers of Saudi girls are receiving a full education, though separated from boys, and are taught either by men through television transmission or by women.

In education as in most areas of life, the male understanding of women as encouraged by certain parts of the Islamic tradition continues to play an important role. The Qur'ān does state, along with the stipulation that women can inherit only half of what men inherit, that the witness (in the court of law) of one man is equal to that of two women. This unfortunately has been interpreted by some in the history of Islam to mean that women are intellectually inferior to men, unstable in their judgment, and too easily swayed by emotion. Such perspectives are certainly not shared by all but nonetheless have been influential (and in some places are increasingly so today) in making it difficult for a woman to have access to the same kinds of educational opportunities that are available to men. Certain subjects are deemed "appropriate" for a woman to study, particularly those geared to make her the best and most productive wife, mother, and female participant in the family structure.

The prevalent view, confirmed by the Qur'ān, is that women should be modest and should neither expose themselves to men nor be too much in public places, where they will be subject to men's observation or forced to interact with males not in their immediate families. This view obviously has contributed to the difficulties of receiving a full education and of securing employment outside the home. More employment opportunities are open to women today than in the past, however, and in many countries women hold high-level positions in business, government, civil service, education, and other sectors. Statistics differ greatly across the Islamic world and are difficult to assess because they often fail to take into account the rural woman who may work full-time in the fields or other occupation outside the house but does not earn an independent salary....

Saudi Arabia presents an interesting case study of the confrontation of Islamic ideas with contemporary reality. Women are greatly inhibited in the labor arena; because of conservative religious attitudes they must be veiled and covered, are not permitted to drive or even ride in a taxi with a strange man, and in general are unable to participate on the social and professional level with males. However, in a country in which production is both necessary and economically possible and which suffers from a lack of manpower, the use of women in the work force or increased importation of foreign labor seem the only two (both undesirable) alternatives. Thus more Saudi women are working, and because of their right to inherit, are accumulating very substantial amounts of money. It is interesting to note the rapid rate of construction of new banks exclusively for women in places like Jiddah and Riyadh.

The aforementioned Qur'ān verse about the witness of two women being equal to that of one man and the supporting literature attesting to female intellectual, physical (and in fact sometimes moral) inferiority have made it difficult for Muslim women to achieve equal political rights. In most Arab countries (except Saudi Arabia and certain of the Gulf States), as well as in most other parts of the Islamic world, women have now been given the vote. Centuries of passivity in the political realm, however, have made it difficult for women to take advantage of the opportunities now available to them. In some countries, such as Egypt, women are playing major political roles,

but generally women politicians find little support from men or even from other women for their aspirations. This is not to underestimate the strong current in Islamic thinking which encourages the full participation of women in politics, as well as in the educational and professional fields.

Like an intricate and complex geometric pattern on a Persian rug or a frieze decorating a mosque, the practices, roles, opportunities, prescriptions, hopes, and frustrations of Islamic women are woven together in a whole. The colors are sometimes bold and striking, at other times muted and subtle. Some contemporary Muslim women are progressive and aggressive, no longer content to fit the traditionally prescribed patterns. Others are passive and accepting, not yet able to discern what new possibilities may be open to them, let alone whether or not they might want to take advantage of such opportunities. Some are Westernized as their mothers and grandmothers were and have every intention of staying that way, while others are increasingly clear in their feelings that the West does not have the answers and that Islam, particularly the Islam of the Qur'ān and the community of the Prophet Muhammad, is God's chosen way for humankind. For the latter, their dress, their relationships with their husbands and families, and their verbal assent to Islamic priorities reflect this conviction that the time has come to cease a fruitless preoccupation with things Western and to reaffirm their identity as Muslim women.

It is difficult for Western feminists to grasp exactly what the Muslim woman may mean by "liberation." For many Islamic women, the fruits of liberation in the West are too many broken marriages, women left without the security of men who will provide for them, deteriorating relations between men and women, and sexual license that appears as rank immorality. They see the Islamic system as affirmed by the Qur'ān as one in which male authority over them ensures their care and protection and provides a structure in which the family is solid, children are inculcated with lasting values, and the balance of responsibility between man and woman is one in which absolute equality is less highly prized than cooperation and complementarity.

The new Islamic woman, then, is morally and religiously conservative and affirms the absolute value of the true Islamic system for human relationships. She is intolerant of the kind of Islam in which women are subjugated and relegated to roles insignificant to the full functioning of society, and she wants to take full advantage of educational and professional opportunities. She may agree, however, that certain fields of education are more appropriate for women than others, and that certain professions are more natural to males than to females. She participates as a contributor to and decisionmaker for the family, yet recognizes that in any complex relationship final authority must rest with one person. And she is content to delegate that authority to her husband, father, or other male relative in return for the solidarity of the family structure and the support and protection that it gives her and her children.

That not all, or even most, Muslim women subscribe to this point of view is clear. And yet, at the time of this writing, it seems equally clear that, if Western observers are to understand women in the contemporary Islamic world, they must appreciate a point of view that is more and more prevalent. The West is increasingly identified with imperialism, and solutions viable for women in the Islamic community are necessarily different from the kinds of solutions that many Western women seem to have chosen for themselves. For the Muslim the words of the Qur'ān are divine, and the prescriptions for the roles and rights of females, like the other messages of the holy book, are seen as part of God's divinely ordered plan for all humanity. Change will come slowly, and whatever kinds of liberation ultimately prevail will be cloaked in a garb that is—in one or another of its various aspects—essentially Islamic.

CRITICAL THINKING QUESTIONS

1. In what formal ways does Islam confer on men authority over women?
2. In what formal and informal ways does Islam give power to women to affect their own lives and the lives of men?
3. From a Muslim perspective, what are some of the problems with Western living and, particularly, Western feminism?

Aging
and the
Elderly

CLASSIC

CONTEMPORARY

CROSS-CULTURAL

42

Growing Old in Inuit Society

Lee Guemple

Guemple's intention in "Growing Old in Inuit Society" is to investigate how, in precontact Inuit society, the elderly were loved and revered but were also killed or allowed to die by their family and friends. This apparent contradiction, at least to Westerners, allows a glimpse into the rich diversity of human adaptation.

The treatment the Inuit (Eskimo) traditionally accorded their old people during the precontact period has been a source of some consternation to members of the Euro–North American cultural tradition because of a seeming paradox. We know that Inuit lavished care and concern on their old people and invested considerable interest in them. But we also know that they sometimes abandoned them on the trail (Freuchen, 1961: 194–203) and that they stood ready at times even to help them to dispose of themselves by drowning or strangulation (Rasmussen, 1908: 127). Our own notion of what people are like makes it difficult for us to see how they could be so affectionate in one context and cold-hearted in another, when the chips were down.

The aim of this essay is to try to resolve the paradox; to show how the attitude of love and affection is not incompatible with the idea of killing one's own parents or helping them to kill themselves. To do so we must make a brief foray into the cognitive universe of the Inuit—into their own notion of how the world (of people and things) works. Only then can we fathom how they manage to mix sentiment with seeming cruelty without a sense of contradiction.

First, however, it will be useful to offer some background material on aging in Inuit society. Inuit have no generic term for "senior citizens." Instead, they use one term for an old man, *ituq*, and another for an old woman, *ningiuq*. These terms are used mainly while speaking about the old people, seldom when speaking to them.

It is difficult to establish the age in years at which people are consigned to old age. Like us, Inuit associate adulthood with work status, and old age constitutes a kind of "retirement" from full participation in community affairs. But Inuit do not keep vital statistics like we do. We cannot reckon

Source: Reprinted with permission from Lee Guemple 1980. "Growing Old in Inuit Society". In Victor Marshall (ed.), *Aging in Canada: Social Perspectives* (pp. 95–101). Fitzhenry and Whiteside Ltd., Markham, Ontario.

an age of retirement for them. Besides, everyone is encouraged to continue working for as long as possible so that retirement comes not by convention, but by the gradual process of biological aging. While doing research in the Belcher Islands Inuit community, I was able to calculate the mean age at which men acquire the label of *ituq* at about fifty years of age (Guemple, 1969). Women seem to maintain the status of adult somewhat longer, but will ordinarily pass over into being classed as *ningiuq* at age sixty or so.

Men become old when they can no longer hunt on a year-round basis but pass on the task of routine hunting to younger members of the household—generally a mature son or son-in-law. Hunting in winter is very demanding and because of its importance to the maintenance of life it is the crucial determinate of male status. At somewhere around fifty years of age a man can no longer sustain the strength and stamina to perform this task on a regular basis and will "retire." His withdrawal can be gradual but is often dramatic.

Women's allocated tasks are both more varied and less strenuous with the result that advancing age does not limit their effectiveness nearly as much as it does men's. Women routinely share work among themselves and the heavy work is often passed along to mature girls even in early adulthood while the older women tend to younger children and infants. Loss of strength and agility will not quickly be noticed in a woman. She will simply spend more time at home, performing other routine tasks such as cooking or sewing. The transition to old age is thus more gradual and comes later in the lifecycle than it does for men.

The onset of old age is hastened by debilitating diseases and may be slowed by what I have elsewhere called "renewal" (Guemple, 1969). The major forms of physical impairment that affect premature entry into old age are arthritis and blindness. The cold, damp character of the traditional igloo and tent tend to promote arthritis; and the incidence of blindness due to trachoma and glaucoma is relatively high. Men also suffer a relatively high incidence of corneal abrasion and snow blindness which can often lead to partial impairments of sight. In the recent past tuberculosis has also taken a considerable toll, particularly in those people who have been sent out to hospital to have portions of lungs or bones removed to rid them of infection.

Old age can also be delayed in some instances. Men often accomplish this by extraordinary effort in hunting during the spring and summer seasons when the demands of production are not so great; and they sometimes undergo symbolic renewal by taking younger women as wives in their maturity. Women cannot aspire to marry younger men in their later years; but they can and frequently do assert they are still able to perform their primary functions by seeking to adopt children. It is said that adopting a child makes an old woman feel young again; and while the primary aim of adoption is not stated to be renewal, it is the only reason given that makes very much sense.[1]

Old people are well cared for in Inuit society because they can draw upon two interlocking social institutions as sources of support: the household and the community at large. Members of a household share equitably; so long as there are younger workers in the household to work on behalf of their elders their interests are seen to with great care and devotion (Gubser, 1965: 122; Hawkes, 1916: 117). The rules of residence stipulate that young hunters stay home until they marry, and so an aging elder can expect to have his son do much of his hunting for him. When the daughters marry their husbands will come to live in the household, and they are answerable to their fathers-in-law, at least until after the first child is born. They may also remain in the household of an in-law if there is need and relations between the son-in-law and other household members are cordial.

Old people can expect some support from the community at large so long as they are able to contribute to the fund of resources from which others draw. Inuit rules of sharing enjoin that successful hunters share a portion of their catch with those who were less successful; and mature hunters are generally only too happy to be able to offer support to other community members, since it is the single source of prestige in the local hunting community. In return, the old people offer the produce of the hunting of their sons or sons-in-law or, as circumstances permit, they offer the help in sewing and gathering wood by their daughters, and they themselves will pitch in to help in any way they can to the general good. Men often offer work in repair jobs, executing technically difficult parts of various pieces of technology where knowledge and patience are particularly needed. They go for short hunting trips around camp, and often school young hunters on how to set snares, stalk land animals, etc. Women contribute their domestic labour for sewing, cooking, cleaning, baby tending, and so on. In the evenings, the old people, as keepers of the sacred and secular lore of this non-literate society, maintain a sense of tradition by telling stories and offering advice which experience shows to be particularly applicable to some predicament.

This system seems to work well so long as old people have someone to rely on to make their contribution to the community pool; and the institutional structure appears to break down only when the old people are left stranded by the departure of their children from the household and the community for one reason or another for an extended period of time. In that context, members of the community at large gradually come to view the old couple as parasitic and begin to complain about their dependency. So far as I am aware, community members would not flatly refuse to feed old people in such a situation; but they often receive a lesser share or the least desirable portion. And they may from time to time suffer the indignity of being gossiped about or verbally abused for their failure to contribute adequately.

As the couple grows into old age, one or the other will die leaving the survivor to move in with a son or daughter or with some more distant relative. The children generally accept the added

burden gracefully; though more distant relatives may find it a bit inconvenient to be saddled with a sibling or cousin in old age. The Inuit of the Canadian North never collected material possessions as a form of wealth. The need to be continually on the move prevented the accumulation of luxuries. But men with ambition often collected people as a kind of "wealth"; and old men or women who were not too feeble were generally welcome in the household of an influential hunter if they had no children to care for them. Seldom were old people to be found in utterly desperate straits unless the entire community was impoverished.

If old people were well treated and cared for by their fellows in the traditional culture, they appear also to have been the objects of startling cruelties. Inuit are known to have abandoned their old people on the trail from time to time with very little ceremony; and there are even cases where the children stood ready to help them end their lives if asked to do so. Such behaviour strikes us as terribly inconsistent and begs for an explanation.

The well-documented facts are that Inuit sometimes abandon their old people. This was generally done either by leaving them behind while on the trail or by allowing them to go off on their own to make an end to themselves. When old people were abandoned, it was most often done out of necessity, seldom out of indifference to the old (Burch, 1975: 148–50; Gubser, 1965: 122; Jenness, 1922: 236; Low, 1906: 165; Spencer, 1959: 252), though cases of apparently cruel treatment are known (Stefánsson, 1914: 130).

Freuchen (1961: 200–03) describes a typical case with his usual dramatic flair: a couple is travelling from one community to another accompanied by their immature children and an old woman, the wife's mother. Sometime during the night, the old lady, having faced an arduous day on the trail, decides the burden of living is too heavy for her to carry any longer, that she should now end the struggle to survive, that she has become a millstone to her children and grandchildren. She tells the two adults that she can go on no longer. They try to dissuade her, but she persists. Finally they agree, and in the morning they pack their gear and depart with only a word or two of farewell, leaving the old lady behind in the igloo, alone with her thoughts and her few meagre possessions.

Other examples appear to be even more unfathomable. An old man, perhaps nettled over some incident which has led to a quarrel or an insult to his sense of dignity, calls his two sons to him and tells them that he is old and useless, the butt of community jokes. Because of this, he has decided that, with their help, he will do away with himself. The sons encourage him to think positively, to remember the joys of playing with his grandchildren, and so on, but he insists that he has seen enough of life and wishes to be rid of it. Eventually, they leave off pleading, and under his direction, fetch a seal skin line and, wrapping the middle around his neck a couple of turns, take the ends and strangle him.

The conventional explanation of these situations is that the old are stoic about death and embrace the notion of their dying fearlessly and with resignation, when they feel they are no longer useful. So the sons or daughters accept the old person's decision with very little coaxing.

There are a number of problems with this formulation of their reaction to the possibility of death. For one thing, it assumes that life in the Arctic is a continuous struggle for survival which people perceive and respond to by a sort of stoic resignation. While this notion is one of *our* favourite themes, it is certainly not part of the Inuit repertoire. They do not see their lives as endangered by their marginal situation. They know its hazards well and have what are to them adequate means for coping with them. It is strangeness that creates a sense of threat, not familiarity; so their situation strikes us as threatening. The Inuit do not perceive it to be so.

How then are we to explain their casual acceptance of the death of loved ones, particularly the old? The answer is that old people do not, in Inuit cosmology, really die. In order to understand this statement, it will be necessary to set aside momentarily our consideration of old age as such and examine briefly the Inuit conception of the underlying character of people, whether old or young. That inquiry will provide us with the basis for solving the riddle of their indifference to death.

Inuit believe that the essential ingredient of a human being is its name. The name embodies a mystical substance which includes the personality, special skills, and basic character which the individual will exhibit in life. Without that substance he will die; and should he exchange his name substance for another through a ritualized renaming process, he will become a different person.

The name substance is derived from other humans, but is not thought of as biological in character; and it bears little resemblance to units of heredity such as genes or of some more metaphorical analogue of biological inheritance such as "blood." The name substance is induced into the body within three or four days after birth; and the process of naming a child is viewed by Inuit as one in which a ritual specialist divines what particular name substance has entered its body. Often the name is that of some recently deceased community member, frequently a relative of the child. But it is never the substance of a parent or sibling of the child and the most frequent "choices" of names are those belonging to members of the grandparent generation. The names of children who are sickly are sometimes changed shortly after birth, and shamans and a few others change their names in adulthood and thus become different persons; but most people keep their given names throughout their lifetimes. At death, the name separates from the body but remains within the vicinity of the body or of the place of death for three or four days during which time it is thought to be dangerous to living humans. After that time, it is thought to return to the underworld to wait till it can enter the body of a newborn child. Names thus cycle as do the social identities which are attached to them.

Names are never exclusively held by individuals in Inuit society. Three or sometimes four individuals may bear the same name and thus be the same person in principle. We might express this idea in a different way and say that from the standpoint of the Inuit community at large, the society consists of a limited number of names each having its own social identity—personal history, personality, work skills, attributes, and attitudes, etc.—attached to it. The identities are shared out in the community among its members on roughly a one-for-four basis, and cycle. At birth, individuals step into one of these well-established identities and bear them in latent form until they come to full expression in adulthood. During their lifetimes, they may contribute to their shape; and at death, they pass their part of the identities on to the next generation fully formed. These identities are indestructible; they neither die nor dissipate, but instead go on endlessly cycling through one generation after another.

Since the name substance is not inherited from the parents and not passed on to one's own biological posterity, parents contribute little to the children's identities except body substance which, to Inuit, is of little significance. And, since the social identity comes to the individual fully formed, it is not something the individual or the community were believed to be able to change in any major way, though in special cases it was possible to actually change identities.

We are now in a position to see why Inuit are relatively casual about the death of old people even if they are bound tightly to them in life. Children permit their parents to do away with themselves because they are not attached to them as we are to our parents. Every individual shares a community of spirit with others, but in Inuit society, that community is with those who bear the same name, not those who share the same blood or some metaphorical analogue. Sentiments link parents and children together, but these can never be binding because parents and children share nothing more vital than those sentiments.

A more compelling reason for the seeming indifference to the death of the parents is related to their understandings about the fate of the person concerned. In our cosmology, the death of an individual means at best his departure to another place, at worst the end of all being, the end of all subjective experience of self. In either case, it is a mystery that makes life precious, that makes us rather bear those ills we have than fly to others. In Inuit cosmology, the persona is the one enduring, immutable substance. Whatever else may happen, Inuit know that their persona live on, not in consciousness, but certainly as fully formed social entities. It is this fact of their existence, and not a resigned stoicism, that make them indifferent to death when the body becomes infirm and the will to live weakens.

The treatment of the old we have described here and the cosmological order we have explored to explain what give[s] them confidence and courage in facing old age and death is part of a tradition that is now on the verge of extinction across the Arctic as conversion to Christianity and the transition to modern living conditions gradually replace the aboriginal customs and beliefs. Modern-day old people of the North live in pre-fab homes, draw old age and disability pensions, take their sustenance from the shelf at the store, and receive their medical care from the local nursing station or hospital. These benefits have done much to make old age comfortable materially; and old men and women alike are quick to express their gratitude for these amenities. That the cosmological explanations we offer serve them as well in death as the material comforts we lavish on them in life is a little more difficult to assert with confidence.

CRITICAL THINKING QUESTIONS

1. How do the definitions of old age differ for men and women in traditional Inuit society? Are there similar factors influencing our definitions of old age in contemporary Canadian society?

2. Discuss the significance of a name in Inuit society and how it helps explain their somewhat indifferent approach to death.

3. Guemple concludes by questioning how the transition of Inuit society into a more modern and materialist one may affect their cosmological understanding of death. What do you feel are some of the other costs associated with this transition? Elderly Inuit today benefit from greater material wealth, but do you feel that the benefits outweigh the costs?

NOTE

1. The principal reason given for adoption [of children] by older women is that the adoption will provide someone to take care of the adopter "when they are old." But this same reason is given when the prospective adopter is in her sixties and the child is but one or two years of age. Further, the same reason is given by older women who have numerous children of their own, in some cases children already grown to maturity, and ready to care for the parent.

REFERENCES

Burch, E. 1975. *Eskimo kinsmen: Changing family relationships in Northwest Alaska.* New York: West Publishing Company (American Ethnological Society Monograph No. 59).

Freuchen, P. 1961. *Peter Freuchen's book of the Eskimos.* Cleveland: World.

Gubser, N. J. 1965. *The Nunamiut Eskimo: Hunters of caribou.* New Haven: Yale University Press.

Guemple, L. 1969. Human resource management: The dilemma of the aging Eskimo. *Sociological Symposium,* 2: 59–74.

Hawkes, E. W. 1916. *The Labrador Eskimo: Canada Department of Mines, Geological Survey Memoir 91.* Anthropological Series No. 14. Ottawa: Government Printing Bureau.

Jenness, D. 1922. *The life of the Copper Eskimos. Report of the Canadian Arctic islands.* Ottawa: Government Printing Bureau.

Low, A. P. 1906. *Report on the Dominion Government expedition to Hudson Bay and the Arctic islands.* Ottawa: Government Printing Bureau.

Rasmussen, K. 1908. *People of the polar north.* London: Kegan Paul, Trench, Trubner.

Spencer, R. F. 1959. *The North Alaskan Eskimo.* Washington: Smithsonian Institute. Bureau of American Ethnology, Bulletin 171.

Stefánsson, B. W. A. 1914. *The Stefánsson-Anderson Arctic expedition of the American Museum.* Anthropological Papers of the American Museum of Natural History. Volume 14, Part I.

Aging
and the
Elderly

CLASSIC

CONTEMPORARY

CROSS-CULTURAL

43

Aging Families:
Have Current Changes and
Challenges Been "Oversold"?

Carolyn J. Rosenthal

In this discussion of the changing structure of Canadian families, Rosenthal reviews some apocalyptic predictions about the future in light of recent research findings.

INTRODUCTION

Apocalyptic demography is typically invoked in relation to state-supported pension and health-care programs. Is there also an apocalyptic demography of the family, or what one might call apocalyptic thinking about the family? How is population aging reflected at the level of the family? What aspects of these demographic and associated changes have been "oversold"? Once we have identified how families are changing, we may then ask whether these changes are indeed apocalyptic and, further, what the real challenges are.

Source: Excerpted from "Aging Families: Have Current Changes and Challenges Been 'Oversold'?" by Carolyn J. Rosenthal in *The Overselling of Population Aging: Apocalyptic Demography, Intergenerational Challenges, and Social Policy* edited by Ellen M. Gee and Gloria M. Gutman. Copyright © Oxford University Press Canada 2000. Reprinted by permission of Oxford University Press Canada.

Most, though not all, of the major changes in contemporary families, as compared to families in the past, are related to demographic changes. Over the course of this century, there have been significant changes in family structure, patterns of marriage and divorce, the occurrence and timing of various family life-course events, and women's paid labour force participation. Increases in life expectancy have resulted in families typically including elderly members. The dynamic aspect of this is a much increased overlap of lives between familial generations. During the past century, widowhood became a typical experience for women—a normative life event. Divorce began to increase when Canadian laws were liberalized in the late 1960s. Female employment began to rise sharply in the early 1970s, with a resultant trend to dual-earner families replacing the traditional male breadwinner/female homemaker family as the normative pattern in husband-wife families.

Apocalyptic thinking about these changes in families has focused mainly on caregiving—either the increased likelihood that middle-aged adults will be faced with an older parent who requires care or the increased likelihood that older people who need care will not have family to whom to turn. In various places in this chapter I will argue that empirical research fails to support such apocalyptic thinking and its related claims. At the same time, I will frequently offer the reminder—and plea—that there is more to family life than caregiving and that we very much need research that goes beyond caregiving in studying what these changes mean to families and family life.

THE CHANGING STRUCTURE OF FAMILIES

How has the structure of families changed? What are the challenges associated with these changes? Have these challenges been overstated? Identifying changes in family structure is not simply a matter of academic interest. Policy-makers and the general public are very interested in the implications of these changes. Anne Martin-Matthews and I (1993) have used the term "structural potential" to denote how family structure creates the potential for experiencing various types of family role demands. This is distinguished from actually facing demands and providing help or care, an issue to which I will turn later in this chapter.

The Increasing Likelihood of Having an Older Parent Alive

Almost all young adult Canadians have living parents (Table 43.1). A majority have a living parent until ages 55–9, when about 4 in 10 are still in the adult child role. At ages 60–4, only 2 in 10 still occupy this role. It is also important to note that from age 45 onward, a majority of men and women who do have a parent alive have only one

parent, a situation that potentially increases responsibility on adult children. If one is ultimately interested in the potential burden placed on adult children by having older parents, it is important to consider the structural feature of having a living parent in the context of that parent's age. Table 43.1 shows that among those in their late thirties and early forties, the average age of parents is relatively young. If we take age 75 and older as the time when health downturns typically occur (Marshall et al., 1983), then we may expect Canadian men and women in their thirties and early forties to have healthy parents who do not require help. Even in their late forties, children are unlikely to have mothers whose age suggests the need for help. Fathers are in a vulnerable age group by this time in their children's lives, but, typically, these fathers will still have their wives to provide such help as is needed. Adult children in their early fifties have parents nearing age 80 and very substantial minorities have only one parent. By age 55 and over, a majority have only one parent alive and that parent is typically over age 80. In other words, by age 50 and more clearly by age 55, we might speculate that the structural potential for needing to help parents may well translate into actual help provision.

The Increasing "Generational Overlap" of Lives

To this point I have presented cross-sectional data on the likelihood of having a parent alive at different ages, a likelihood that has increased over the course of this century. This is clearly seen when we examine the increase in the likelihood of a middle-aged adult having a surviving parent. Gee (1990) compares the proportion of three Canadian birth cohorts having a surviving parent at age 50 and age 60. Among Canadians born in 1910, only 33 per cent of individuals at age 50 had a surviving parent. This rose to 49 per cent of those born in 1930 and is expected to rise to 60 per cent of those born in 1960. The likelihood

TABLE 43.1: Percentage of Canadians with Parent/s Alive, by Age and Gender

Age	35–9		40–4		45–9		50–4		55–9		60–4	
Number of Parents	Women	Men	Women	Men	Women	Men	Women	Men	Women	Men	Women	Men
0	8.9	7.5	14.7	14.6	20.7	26.4	46.6	41.0	60.6	62.3	79.4	82.0
1	35.8	36.1	46.2	41.4	52.2	46.7	39.3	46.2	34.6	33.4	17.6	16.8
2	55.3	56.4	39.1	44.0	27.1	26.8	14.1	12.8	4.8	4.3	2.7	1.2
Age of mother (x)	64.2	65.1	69.8	69.3	74.4	73.3	77.5	78.2	82.0	82.8	85.8	86.4
Age of father (x)	66.8	67.7	72.4	72.0	75.6	76.8	79.0	79.3	82.5	84.1	85.9	86.0

Source: General Social Survey of Canada, 1990.

of having a surviving parent at age 60 has increased from 8 per cent of those born in 1910 to 16 per cent for those born in 1930 and is predicted to rise to 23 per cent for those born in 1960. It has thus become the majority pattern to have a surviving parent at age 50 and it is becoming more common to have one even at age 60. A related phenomenon is the growing likelihood that young adults still have a grandparent alive. These are, in my view, very positive changes.... The longer duration of grandparents' presence in a family ought to create benefits in terms of family cohesion and continuity. It certainly creates the opportunity to be an adult grandchild and for grandparents to have relationships with their grandchildren that extend into the latter's adulthood. Yet research on adult grandchildren is extremely limited. What are the challenges of having older family members? The one challenge that has received extensive research attention is caregiving—the burden on middle generations imposed by older family members with chronic illness or disability who require care. This is an important issue, but surely caregiving is only one aspect of a broad spectrum of family relations.

Changing Patterns of Marriage, Widowhood, and Divorce

Table 43.2 presents data on marital status at different ages for three cohorts of women in order to provide

an indication of changing patterns. Among today's elderly women, widowhood is an expectable life event (Martin-Matthews, 1987), while the normative marital status among older men is married (Table 43.2). Divorce was almost unknown among older women who were aged 65–74 in 1991. Similar patterns are seen in the following cohort (women aged 55–64 in 1991), although members of this cohort are somewhat less likely to be widowed as they enter old age, largely due to the declines in mortality rates of males in mid-life. Among those outside of marriage, however, women in this cohort are somewhat less likely to be widowed and more likely to be divorced compared to the previous cohort (Rosenthal et al., forthcoming).

Since the liberalization of Canadian divorce laws in the late 1960s, divorce rates have increased markedly. Divorce has an impact on older families in two ways—directly (i.e., the individual has experienced divorce) and indirectly (i.e., one's children have experienced divorce). Divorce in the adult child generation may increase needs for support from older parents, particularly for the parents of the custodial child (Gladstone, 1988). Conversely, for others, maintaining contact with grandchildren may become problematic. Some grandparents face serious barriers to maintaining relationships with grandchildren following middle-generation divorce, and indeed we read quite a bit about this situation in articles about the

TABLE 43.2: Marital Status Trends, Women,
1961–1991: Percentage Distributions by
Cohort and Marital Status

Marital Status	1971	1981	1991	Cohort
Married: Age in 1991				
65–74	48.9	51.1	53.9	Born 1917–26
55–64	69.9	72.8	71.8	Born 1927–36
45–54	83.8	83.1	77.2	Born 1937–46
Widowed: Age in 1991				
65–74	39.6	37.8	34.8	Born 1917–26
55–64	18.6	17.1	14.6	Born 1927–36
45–54	6.9	5.9	4.7	Born 1937–46
Divorced: Age in 1991				
65–74	0.9	2.1	4.0	Born 1917–26
55–64	1.6	3.5	7.1	Born 1927–36
45–54	1.9	5.1	9.2	Born 1937–46

Source: Statistics Canada, *The Nation* (1993), Catalogue No. 93-310, p. 33.

grandparent rights movement. We also read (especially in the U.S. press and literature) about grandparents who become surrogate parents, for example, when the adult child is a drug addict. Between these two extremes, however, is what I speculate is the majority of grandparents, who join in the struggle that is part of the aftermath of divorce—trying to help adult children through the difficult divorce transition, trying to provide continuity and stability for grandchildren, trying to maintain relationships in non-custodial situations, in short, trying to muddle through.

Divorce may also be experienced directly, not simply as a parent or grandparent. Having the marital status of "divorced" is rare among today's elderly but will be somewhat more common in the cohort about to enter old age. It is difficult to predict precisely the proportion of women in the future who will enter old age as divorced persons because some of today's divorced women will remarry.

What impact will these changes have on older people? Divorce legally severs some kin relationships; for example, daughters-in-law

become ex-daughters-in-law. Remarriage, on the other hand, creates new relatives; for example, the remarriage of a daughter brings not only a new son-in-law but perhaps stepgrandchildren. One's own remarriage may bring not only a new spouse but stepchildren. We do not know very much, though, about the extent to which such relationships become attenuated following the dissolution of marriage through death or divorce. Nor do we know much about the extent to which kin acquired later in the life course, that is in mid-life or later life, are supportive and/or remain so following the death of the "linking" person. (For example, if a woman remarries in her fifties and is married for 15 years before her "new" spouse dies, what relationship would be maintained between her and her stepchildren after she is widowed?) Riley and Riley (1993) refer to a "latent matrix of kin relationships," created by increasing longevity and increasing prevalence of divorce and remarriage. Matilda Riley (1983: 451) argues that the "kinship structure has become more extensive and complex, the temporal and spatial boundaries of the family have been altered, and the opportunities for close family relationships have proliferated." Riley's concept of a latent matrix is similar to the concept of "structural potential" that I referred to earlier (Martin-Matthews & Rosenthal, 1993). Uhlenberg (1993), however, argues that although divorce may lead to a larger web of relationships, research suggests that divorce weakens many types of family relationships. Therefore, although there may be notable exceptions, in the general case the expansion of relationships in reconstituted families does not translate into increased support for older people. Having said this, however, I think we need a lot more research on what happens to kin relationships following divorce or death of the "linking" individual. For example, we need research beyond that which simply tells us that this type of relative provides less support than another type of relative (e.g., blood kin).

The "Shrinking" Supply of Children

We hear regularly that the birth rate has fallen and that the average family size (i.e., number of children) has decreased. But what does this mean with respect to actual families, who are not "averages," and to potential support for older people? Uhlenberg (1993: 225) points out that while it is true that over the long term the demographic transition means a reduced average number of children for the elderly, "assertions about the future supply of children for the elderly can be misleading unless two important questions are addressed: What changes in family size make a significant difference? What is the timing of changes in the family size of the elderly?" Uhlenberg argues that:

Although total support received from children is positively related to number of children, the marginal benefits from each additional child beyond the second or third is small. The most critical distinction regarding family size is between having none versus having some, and the second-most important distinction is between having one compared with having two or more. Thus, interest in changing family size should pay less attention to changes in mean number and more attention to proportion with zero or only one child. (Ibid)

...Gee (1995) argues that, in old age, it is the number of surviving children, not the number of children ever born, that is critical. The 1990 Canadian General Social Survey showed that 21 per cent of all men and 24 per cent of all women aged 75 and over have no surviving children (remarkably similar to the U.S. figure for childlessness among women aged 85 and over...). The trends described here indicate that upcoming cohorts of old and middle-aged adults, particularly the parents of the baby boom, will be more likely than their predecessors to be able to draw upon support from children. The challenges engendered by changes in fertility rates need to be viewed in historical perspective (many are not new) and linked to cohort analysis. It is fair to say that alarm calls about the shrinking supply of children are an overstatement—if not a distortion of reality.

The Changing Structure of Multigenerational Families

All of the changes discussed so far combine to produce changes in the generational structure of families. For at least 20 years, social scientists have described the generational structure of families as becoming "long and thin." Bengston et al. (1990) use the term "beanpole" family to describe a family form that contains several generations—four or even five—but relatively few people in each generation. This structure implies a heavy burden on middle generations to care for younger and older generation members, with the prospect of someone in old age caring for someone in very old age. This structure is said to have become increasingly common and, indeed, to be the prototypical family form....

What about the beanpole family type? Uhlenberg asks "how accurate is the often repeated assertion that four- and five-generation families are becoming increasingly common as a result of increased longevity?" He points out that no estimates for the population based on representative samples exist to back up this claim. Rossi and Rossi (1990), based on their study of 1400 adults in Boston, contend that popular beliefs about the prevalence of multi-generational families are exaggerated. Data from the National Survey of Families and Households in the United States (Winsborough et al., 1991) suggest that about one-third of adults aged 45–64 are members of four-generation families. All indications are that very few individuals are or ever will be part of a five-generation family. Moreover, Uhlenberg concludes that the four-generation family will not be the dominant lineage type. Therefore, while the beanpole family, in the sense of generational depth, is probably more common than in the past, we need to be cautious about making sweeping statements about its prevalence....

The Scattering of the Family

Another component of apocalyptic thinking at the level of family change is that, should older people require care, their children will be too far away to provide it. This view encompasses assumptions about both living arrangements and wider geographic dispersion.

Considering living arrangements first. [S]ince about 1960 there has been a trend for older Canadians to live either as a married couple or alone. This trend in living alone is especially pronounced among women (Connidis, 1989; Wister, 1985). Between 1961 and 1991, the proportion of women aged 65 and over living alone more than doubled, from 16 per cent to 34 per cent. Among widowed women, the proportion living alone is close to 80 per cent (Martin-Matthews, 1991: 79). In my view, this is a positive rather than a negative change, one that reflects not only changing norms but, more fundamentally, the opening up of options to women in that Old Age Security and subsidized housing make independent living possible. "One woman, one kitchen" seems to be a strong cultural preference in North America. We have enough evidence that older people like to see their children regularly but do not want to share the same household that we can put to rest arguments promoting shared living between older parents and adult children as an optimal arrangement for most older people....

The fact that most older people do not live in the same household as their children, however, does not necessarily mean that they do not live near their children. Assumptions and statements about the decreasing proximity of older parents and adult children because of increased rates of geographic mobility have perhaps been more common in the U.S. than in Canada, but these statements are not rare in Canada. Proximity is an important issue because it is strongly related to contact and the exchange of help (although much less related to emotional closeness and support). Uhlenberg (1993) shows that mobility rates in the United States were considerably lower in the 1970s and 1980s than they were in the 1950s and 1960s. The data, therefore, do not show a trend that would produce greater dispersion of kin over time. Moreover, the 1987–8 National Survey of

Families and Households found that about three-quarters of older people who have an adult child have a child living within 25 miles. This is almost identical to the percentage of older parents with a child living nearby that was reported by Ethel Shanas in 1968 and—to add some Canadian data—very similar to the percentages Victor Marshall, Jane Synge, and I found in our Hamilton study in 1980 (Rosenthal, 1987). We found that, among people aged 70 and over who had children, about two-thirds lived either in the same household or the same city as a child, and just about 90 per cent lived within an hour and one-half travel time of a child.

This is not to say that older people do not have a child who lives at some distance from them. Most studies only examine the proximity of the nearest child; this obscures the reality that, when people have more than one child, they may have some children close by and others more distant.... In other words, total family dispersion is very unusual, no dispersion beyond one and one-half hours' travel time is characteristics of a large minority of older families, and—importantly— partial dispersion is the most common pattern. We also need to be aware that proximity is something we typically measure at one point in time. In real life, however, proximity is fluid. Adult children may move to another city, only to move back to their city of origin later on. Older parents may make a retirement move to another city. Or, they may move at retirement or later on to be closer to a child. In sum, the geographic dispersion issue seems to have been oversold. My intention here is not to underrate the experience of geographically distant children and parents, particularly when the parents need care; it is simply to emphasize that this is far from the typical experience and it is not on a sharp rise.

Increased Participation of Women in the Paid Labour Force

A well-known trend that must be considered when discussing changing families is the trend towards increased female labour force participation. Consider, for example, women's labour force participation at ages 45–54. Among women who were aged 45–54 in 1991, 72 per cent were in the paid labour force, up from 56 per cent among women of those ages in 1981 and 44 per cent in 1971. Especially noteworthy are the increases in paid employment among married women and women with children at home. These trends mean that combining work and family roles has become much more common than in the past. By 1994, dual-earner families made up 60 per cent of all husband-wife families, compared with 33 per cent in 1967 (Statistics Canada, 1996)....

One major change that has not been overstated with regard to its occurrence is the increased likelihood that adult Canadians will have a parent alive and the related increased generational overlap of lives. These changes create the structural potential for experiencing care-related needs from older parents, but to what degree does this structural potential translate into actually experiencing such demands? Has the extent to which this potential translates into actual demands been oversold? I address this question in the next section.

THE OVERSELLING OF THE DEPENDENCY BURDEN ON FAMILIES

We saw earlier that the structural potential to have aging parents who require help exists for a large percentage of Canadian women. Much media attention is currently given to the potential burden of old family members on those in middle generations. A particularly difficult version of this is the burden and conflict experienced by middle-generation adults who have care responsibilities for family members in both older and younger generations.

While the care-related needs of older parents may present a daunting challenge for families, empirical research suggests that issues of prevalence and burden have been overstated. While the chances are we will all experience the death of our parents, there is great variability in the need for and extent of involvement of adult children, and in the duration of care. We will not all become primary caregivers, many of us will provide only a little or no care to our parents, some of us will have intense involvement for a very short period of time and still others will have intermittent periods of involvement as parents move in and out of health crises.

The Extent of Provision of Help to Parents

There has been an enormous amount of research on caregiving over the past two decades, but it is important to note that much of this research uses non-representative samples and focuses only on primary caregivers, and only on elders who need substantial amounts of care. This does not give us much of a perspective on how much help adult children typically provide to older parents. Data from the 1990 Canadian General Social Survey (Rosenthal et al., 1996) show that only small proportions of adult Canadian sons and daughters actually help parents once a month or more. Respondents were asked about five kinds of help: housework, transportation, personal care, financial support, and outside work/household maintenance. Across five-year age categories from age 35 to age 64, from 11 to 22 per cent of daughters and 7 to 12 per cent of sons provided at least one of these types of help monthly or more often. Based on these data, we may say that only small minorities of adult children can be considered to be "active" helpers.

Personal care is arguably the most important type of help to examine, both because it may signify that the parent is highly dependent and because it is the most demanding and intensive type of care. Very small percentages of daughters provided personal care monthly or more often, although the percentages increased with age; at ages 35–49, between 1.2 and 2.0 percent of daughters provided personal care. This rose to 5.6 per cent at ages 50–4 and 7 per cent at ages

55–9, then dropped to 0 per cent at ages 60–4. Among sons, a high of 1 percent provided personal care at least monthly.

When we talk about dependency and need for help in the family context, we are usually referring to informal care. An additional type of dependency, however, is the need for financial assistance.... Data from the General Social Survey indicate that very small percentages of Canadian daughters or sons provide financial assistance to parents: the highest proportion in any age group to provide financial support monthly or more was 2 per cent of daughters and 3 per cent of sons. The percentages who had provided financial support in the past year were not much higher—4 per cent of daughters and 5 per cent of sons. Whatever increases we might see in the future, this type of help is very uncommon at present, and speculation about the future must be placed in this context. For example, even if the percentages giving this type of help doubled, small proportions of adult children would be involved.

The "Sandwich Generation"

The particular manifestation of the need to help older parents that has caught the public imagination is the woman facing care demands from parents and children—popularly termed the "sandwich generation." David Foot (1996), in his best-selling book, *Boom, Bust, and Echo*, devotes a chapter to how demographics can affect family life, but the only issue specifically related to older family members is the sandwich generation—the increased likelihood that one will have an aged parent in declining health and in need of assistance, occurring in the context of being "sandwiched" or pulled between the needs of one's parents and children. When people read Foot's book—and many Canadians have read it— the message about aging families they receive is that more and more women are being sandwiched. However, Foot makes the leap from the demographic fact that women have the family

structure that makes multiple and conflicting demands potentially possible to the assumption that they actually experience such demands.

It is ironic that Foot highlights the sandwich generation issue as emblematic of the impact of demographic change on older families, since it is becoming well established that this is one aspect of demographic change that has been overstated (Rosenthal et al., 1996; Spitze & Logan, 1990; Uhlenberg, 1993).... In our analysis of 1990 General Social Survey data, Anne Martin-Matthews, Sarah Matthews, and I (Rosenthal et al., 1996) found that the proportion of women with the structural potential to be sandwiched between the roles of adult child and parent of a dependent child (defined as a child in the household) dropped from 71 percent among women aged 35–9 to 51 percent among women aged 45–9 and to 24 per cent among women aged 50–4. The most difficult combination of roles is paid worker, adult child, and parent of a dependent child. This role config-uration holds the greatest structural potential for competing demands, should an older parent need care. This combination dropped from 42 per cent in the 40–4 age group to 35 per cent for women in their later forties and to very small proportions after that.

Among women with the structural potential to be sandwiched, what proportion actually provides tangible help to parents? Among daughters who had a parent alive and a child at home, the high-est percentage in any age group who helped a parent at least monthly was 13 per cent. In the potentially most problematic group, those who had a living parent, a child at home, and a paid job, the highest percentage in any age group who helped a parent at least monthly was 7 per cent....

The fact that few adult children seem to be providing assistance at any one point in time does not mean the family is a great untapped resource that can provide much more free labour so that society can save money on the formal health-care system. Creating this impression is one of the dangers of presenting this kind of data (although, clearly, I have had other purposes in mind)....

Women's Labour Force Participation and the "Caregiving Crunch"

The trend to female employment has led to the concern that women will no longer be available to fulfil their traditional roles of family care- givers to older parents, based on the seemingly logical speculation that employment reduces availability of women to provide family care. Myles (1991) uses the term "caregiving crunch" to refer to the crisis stemming from the decreased supply of informal caregivers as a result of women's increased employment outside the home. Myles refers to a crisis in caregiving, the result of the "dramatic decline in the amount of unpaid working time available to the women who have traditionally performed these tasks." Myles sees this caregiving crunch as the next crisis of the welfare state, one that we are already experiencing. A caregiving crunch is very famil- iar to women who combine employment with family responsibilities, whether those are for older or younger family members. Research has documented the strains on such women, includ- ing the impact of care responsibilities on employment careers (Martin-Matthews & Rosenthal, 1993). It is important to recognize, however, that most employed women whose parents require care continue in paid employ- ment. Further, they appear to provide as much help to parents as their non-employed peers. In other words, the "crunch" does not seem to result in a decreased amount of care to older people. In an analysis of 1996 General Social Survey data (Rosenthal et al., 1999), there were minimal differences between employed and non- employed women in the type of help provided to parents and in the amount of time spent helping parents. This issue needs more examination, and I am not implying that everything is fine because employed women seem to provide care despite their job responsibilities. The point is that the so-called "caregiving crunch," to the extent that it exists, is not yet a crisis for the state; it may well be a crisis, however, for those women faced with these multiple demands. The question becomes one of appropriate policy directions. While policies that provide work- place flexibility and support for employed care- givers are important, it is equally or more important to provide policies that create options to family-provided care.

CONCLUSION

While family structure is changing, some aspects of these changes have been oversold—namely, the shrinking supply of children, the beanpole family, and geographic dispersion. On the other hand, families are more likely to have senior- generation members alive. We have tended to accept speculations about the implications of these changes—implications about the growing dependency burden on families—without testing them against empirical data. In examining three of these assumptions—that most adult children are swamped by the need to help parents, that the sandwich generation is a common predicament, and that women's employment is having a profound impact on care provision—we can see they have been oversold. Demographic change in families is not leading us into the apocalypse. It is important to maintain this perspective, in part because it means government programs to assist people who are in these situations are not likely to face massive hordes of caregivers but rather a comparatively small but highly needy segment of the population at any one point in time.

How do we counteract the tendency towards thinking apocalyptically about changes in older families? First of all, we need to identify care- fully what is really happening and to pay atten- tion to cohorts and trends over time. Second, we need to investigate the implications of these trends, rather than simply speculate about what they might be. Third, we need to look beyond averages, a point that is well demonstrated by examining the data on number of children ever born to different cohorts of women. To the extent that we have been able to address these issues, the apocalyptic position appears greatly overstated and indeed unsupportable. This is not to say that families are not changing, for they are changing significantly. The point is rather that they are not changing in ways that set kin relations adrift....

It is important to uncover the realities of social organization and social life, and for this reason we need to understand how the family is changing and what the implications of those changes are. However, there is a real danger that findings may be wrongly interpreted and/or used in support of policies that would not be good for families. I recognize that in much of my own work, for example, work that asks what the changes in family structure mean for support to older people, the implicit or explicit dependent variable is family support. This is a perfectly legitimate and important question. However, it is vital that our questions do not stop there. Whether families are or will be capable of providing needed support to older relatives must take second place to the question of who should be responsible for the care of older people. My position, one that is growing stronger over the years as I continue to learn more about older families, is that the care of the elderly is a public, not a private, issue and that responsibility lies with the state. Within that framework, we may then examine the role families might play if they are able and willing.

CRITICAL THINKING QUESTIONS

1. What are some of the key challenges facing the Canadian family as our population ages?
2. What role, if any, do you feel the Canadian government should take in assisting the elderly?
3. What role, if any, do you feel extended families should take in assisting their aging relatives?
4. In your opinion, who benefits from media attention focusing on the potential burden of older family members on middle-generation adults?

REFERENCES

Bengston, V. L., C. J. Rosenthal, and L. Burton. 1990. Families and aging: Diversity and heterogeneity. In *Handbook of aging and the social sciences,* eds. R. H. Binstock, and L. K. George, 263–87. New York: Academic Press.

Connidis, I. 1989. *Family ties and aging.* Toronto: Butterworths.

Foot, D. K., with Daniel Stoffman. 1996. *Boom, bust, and echo: How to profit from the coming demographic shift.* Toronto: Macfarlane Walter and Ross.

Gee, E. M. 1990. Demographic change and intergenerational relations in Canadian families: Findings and social policy implications. *Canadian Public Policy,* 16(2): 191–99.

———. 1995. Families in later life. In *Family over the life course: Current demographic analysis,* eds. Roderic Beaujot, Gee, Fernando, Rajulton, and Zenaida Ravanera, 7–113. Ottawa: Statistics Canada Demography Division.

Gladstone, J. 1988. Perceived changes in grandmother-grandchild relations following a child's separation or divorce, *Gerontologist,* 28(1): 66–72.

Marshall, V. W., C. J. Rosenthal, and J. Synge. 1983. Concerns about parental health. In *Older women,* ed. Elizabeth W. Markson, 253–73. Lexington, Mass.: Lexington Books.

Martin-Matthews, A. 1987. Widowhood as an expectable life event. In *Aging in Canada: Social Perspectives,* 2nd ed., ed. V. W. Marshall, 343–66. Markham, Ont.: Fitzhenry and Whiteside.

———. 1991. *Widowhood in later life.* Toronto: Butterworths.

Martin-Matthews, A., and C. J. Rosenthal. 1993. Balancing work and family in an aging society: The Canadian experience. In *Annual review of gerontology and geriatrics,* vol. 13, eds. G. Maddox, and M. P. Lawton, 96–119. New York: Springer.

Myles, J. 1991. Women, the welfare state and caregiving. *Canadian Journal on Aging,* 10(2): 82–5.

Riley, M. W. 1983. The family in an aging society: A matrix of latent relationships. *Journal of Family Issues,* 4: 439–54.

Riley, M. W., and J. W. Riley. 1993. Connections: Kin and cohorts. In *The changing contract across generations,* eds. V. L. Bengston, and W. A. Achenbaum. New York: Aldine de Gruyter.

Rosenthal, C. J. 1987. Aging and intergenerational relations in Canada. In *Aging in Canada: Social perspectives,* 2nd ed., ed. V. W. Marshall, 311–42. Markham, Ont.: Fitzhenry and Whiteside.

Rosenthal, C. J., A. Martin-Matthews, and S. Matthews. 1996. Caught in the middle? Occupancy in multiple roles and help to parents in a national probability sample of Canadian adults. *Journal of Gerontology: Social Sciences,* 51B(6): S274–83.

Rosenthal, C. J., A. Martin-Matthews, L. Hayward, and M. Denton. 1999. Women's multiple roles: How constraining is employment on the provision of parent care? Paper presented at the 52nd Annual Scientific Meeting of the Gerontological Society of America, San Francisco.

Rosenthal, C. J., M. Denton, A. Martin-Matthews, and S. French. Forthcoming. Changes in work and family over the life course: Implications for economic security of today's and tomorrow's older women. In *Independence and economic security in old age,* eds. F. Denton, D. Fretz, and B. Spencer. Vancouver: University of British Columbia Press.

Rossi, A. S., and P. H. Rossi. 1990. *Of human bonding: Parent-child relations across the life course.* New York: Aldine de Gruyter.

Spitze, G., and J. R. Logan. 1990. More evidence on women (and men) in the middle. *Research on Aging,* 12: 182–98.

Statistics Canada. 1996. *Characteristics of dual-earner families 1994.* Ottawa: Minister of Industry, Catalogue No. 13-215-XPB.

Uhlenberg, P. 1993. Demographic change and kin relationships in later life. In *Annual Review of Gerontology and Geriatrics*, vol. 13, eds. G. Maddox, and M. P. Lawton, 219–38. New York: Springer.

Winsborough, H., L. Bumpass, and W. Aguilino. 1991. *The death of parents and the transitions to old age.* National Survey of Families and Households Working Paper No. 39. Madison: University of Wisconsin.

Wister, A. 1985. Living arrangement choices among the elderly. *Canadian Journal on Aging,* 4(3): 127–44.

44

Our Aging World

Frank B. Hobbs and Bonnie L. Damon

The average age in societies around the world is rising. Even now, demographers report, the eighty-and-over age group is the fastest-growing portion of the elderly population. Frank B. Hobbs and Bonnie L. Damon describe the growing number of elderly persons worldwide, compare the growth of the elderly population in developed and developing countries, and raise important questions about the future implications of our aging world.

POPULATION AGING IS WORLDWIDE

To set the aging of the United States in context it is useful to look at aging in the rest of the world. Fertility rates and infant and maternal mortality from infectious and parasitic diseases has declined. The world's nations generally have improved other aspects of health and education. All of these factors have interacted so that every major region in the world shows an increased proportion of the population that will be sixty-five or older by 2020.

There were 357 million persons aged sixty-five and over in the world in 1994 (see Table 44.1). They represent 6 percent of the world's population. By the year 2000, there would be about 418 million elderly. The annual growth rate for the elderly was 2.8 percent in 1993–94 (compared with an average annual for the total world population of 1.6 percent). Such growth

Source: From *65+ in the United States*. U.S. Bureau of the Census. Current Population Reports, Special Studies P23–90 (Washington, D.C.: Government Printing Office 1996), pp. 24–27.

is expected to continue far into the twentieth-first century.

Numerical growth of the elderly population is worldwide. It is occurring in both developed and developing countries. The average annual growth rate in 1993–94 of persons sixty-five years and over was 3.2 percent in developing countries, compared with 2.3 percent in the developed world. In absolute numbers, from 1993 to 1994, the net balance of the world's elderly population (sixty-five years and over) increased by over 1,000 persons every hour. Of this increase, 63 percent occurred in developing countries.

Over half (55 percent) of the world's elderly lived in developing nations in 1994. These developing regions could be home to nearly two-thirds (65 percent) of the world's elderly by the years 2020. Thirty nations had elderly populations of at least 2 million in 1994....Current population projections indicate there will be fifty-five such nations by 2020.

Among countries with more than 1 million population, Sweden has the highest proportion of

315

people aged sixty-five and over, with 18 percent in 1994—about the same as the state of Florida. Sweden also has the highest proportion aged eighty and over with 5 percent. The Caribbean is the oldest of the major developing countries, with 7 percent of its population sixty-five or older in 1994.

By 2020, the elderly will constitute from one-fifth to nearly one-fourth of the population of many European countries. For example, Census Bureau projections indicate that 23 percent of Germany's population would be elderly, compared with 22 percent for Italy, Finland, Belgium, Croatia, Denmark, and Greece. The elderly population of twelve additional European countries with more than 1 million population will constitute at least one-fifth of the total country population. The United States would be 16 percent.

Japan's population age sixty-five and over is expected to grow dramatically in the coming decades. According to projections, the percentage of Japan's population that is elderly could grow from 14 percent (17.1 million) in 1994 to 17 percent (21.0 million) in 2000 and to 26 percent (32.2 million) by 2020....This is a rapid rise in a short time. Japan's population eighty years and over also is projected to grow very rapidly, from 3 percent of their total population in 1994 to 7 percent by 2020. Already the Japanese are reducing retirement benefits and making other adjustments to prepare for the economic and social results of a rapidly aging society.

In 1994, the world had an estimated 61 million persons aged eighty or older. That number is expected to increase to 146 million by the year 2020. Persons eighty years and over constituted only 1 percent of the world's total population in 1994 and more than 20 percent of the world's elderly (28 percent in developing countries, 16 percent in developing nations).

DEVELOPED COUNTRIES NOW HAVE MOST OF THE WORLD'S OLDEST POPULATION

Although the developed countries of the world represented only 22 percent of the total world population in 1994, the majority of the world's population aged eighty and over live in developed countries. However, it is projected that by 2020, the majority will live in developing countries. For many nations, the eighty-and-over age group will be the fastest growing portion of the elderly population. In 2000, 26 percent of the elderly in

TABLE 44.1: World Population by Age and Sex, 1994 and 2000

	Population (millions)			Percentage of Total			
Year and Age	Both Sexes	Male	Female	Both Sexes	Male	Female	Males per 100 Females
1994							
All ages	5,640	2,841	2,798	100.0%	100.0%	100.0%	101.5
Under 15 years	1,790	917	873	31.7	32.3	31.2	105.1
15 to 64 years	3,492	1,771	1,722	61.9	62.3	61.5	102.9
65 years and over	357	153	204	6.3	5.4	7.3	75.2
2000							
All ages	6,161	3,103	3,057	100.0	100.0	100.0	101.5
Under 15 years	1,877	962	915	30.5	31.0	29.9	105.2
15 to 64 years	3,866	1,959	1,907	62.7	63.1	62.4	102.8
65 years and over	418	182	236	6.8	5.9	7.7	77.1

Source: U.S. Bureau of the Census, International Data Base.

the United States would be eighty or older, which, among countries with a population size of at least 5 million, would rank sixth, behind Sweden, Denmark, Switzerland, Cuba, and the United Kingdom.

In 1994, China had the largest number of persons aged eighty or older, followed by the United States (see Table 44.2). Nine additional countries had over 1 million persons eighty years and over in 1994. By 2020, this list is expected to include thirteen additional countries, ten of which are developing countries. In many developing countries, the population eighty and over in 2020 is likely to at least quadruple from 1994. This

highlights the problems governments may have in planning support services for this burgeoning population group.

The rapid growth of the oldest old has various health and economic implications for individuals, families, and governments throughout the world. The oldest old often have severe chronic health problems which demand special attention. The nature and duration of their illnesses are likely to produce a substantial need for prolonged care. Developing nations already have diluted resources. They are the most limited in being able to provide preventive measures and, in future years, supportive services. The United

TABLE 44.2: Projected Population for Countries with More than One
Million Persons Aged 80 Years and Over, 1994 and 2020

Country/Area	Rank		Population Aged 80 Years and Over (in thousands, based on rank in 1994)	
	1994	2020	1994	2020
China, Mainland	1	1	9,010	28,737
United States	**2**	**2**	**7,760**	**13,007**
India	3	3	4,021	12,639
Japan	4	4	3,597	9,362
Russia	5	5	3,317	7,191
Germany	6	6	3,313	5,889
France	7	8	2,563	3,754
United Kingdom	8	9	2,342	3,400
Italy	9	7	2,221	4,142
Ukraine	10	12	1,421	2,923
Spain	11	13	1,287	2,488
Brazil	*	10	*	3,132
Indonesia	*	11	*	3,034
Mexico	*	14	*	2,296
Poland	*	15	*	1,877
Turkey	*	16	*	1,751
Canada	*	17	*	1,595
Thailand	*	18	*	1,477
Pakistan	*	19	*	1,385
Romania	*	20	*	1,264
South Korea	*	21	*	1,221
Vietnam	*	22	*	1,199
Argentina	*	23	*	1,072
Iran	*	24	*	1,039

*Indicates population 80 years and over in 1994 was less than 1 million.
Source: U.S. Bureau of the Census, International Data Base.

States and other countries face enormous invest-ments and payments to maintain current levels of services for the oldest old.

CRITICAL THINKING QUESTIONS

1. What are some of the reasons for the growth of aging populations worldwide?
2. In the 1990s, the majority of the world's population aged eighty and over lived in developed countries. How is this expected to change by 2020? As the average length of life continues to increase in both developed and developing countries, who, if anyone, is responsible for improving the quality of extended life?
3. Hobbs and Damon observe that "the United States and other countries face enormous investments and payments to maintain current levels of services for the old." What, specifically, are examples of such investments and payments? Who will pay for the necessary services for elderly populations—individuals? families? government? corporations? people in the labor force? others?

45

The Social Structure of Medicine

Talcott Parsons

Talcott Parsons, one of the most influential U.S. sociologists during the twentieth century, contributed greatly to the development of structural-functional analysis. In this selection, he examines the significance of health and illness within a social system, with particular attention to the social roles of physicians and patients.

A little reflection will show immediately that the problem of health is intimately involved in the functional prerequisites of the social system.... Certainly by almost any definition health is included in the functional needs of the individual member of the society so that from the point of view of functioning of the social system, too low a general level of health, too high an incidence of illness, is dysfunctional. This is in the first instance because illness incapacitates for the effective performance of social roles. It could of course be that this incidence was completely uncontrollable by social action, an independently given condition of social life. But insofar as it is controllable, through rational action or otherwise, it is clear that there is a functional interest of the society in its control, broadly in the minimization of illness. As one special aspect of this, attention may be called to premature death. From a variety of points of view, the birth and rearing of a child constitute a "cost" to the society, through pregnancy, child care, socialization, formal training, and many other channels. Premature death, before the individual has had the opportunity to play out his full quota of social roles, means that only a partial "return" for this cost has been received.

All this would be true were illness purely a "natural phenomenon" in the sense that, like the vagaries of the weather, it was not, to our knowledge, reciprocally involved in the motivated interactions of human beings. In this case illness

Source: From *The Social System* by Talcott Parsons. Copyright © 1951, copyright renewed 1979 by Talcott Parsons. Reprinted with the permission of The Free Press, a Division of Simon & Schuster.

would be something which merely "happened to" people, which involved consequences which had to be dealt with and conditions which might or might not be controllable but was in no way an expression of motivated behavior.

This is in fact the case for a very important part of illness, but it has become increasingly clear, by no means for all. In a variety of ways motivational factors accessible to analysis in action terms are involved in the etiology of many illnesses, and conversely, though without exact correspondence, many conditions are open to therapeutic influence through motivational channels. To take the simplest kind of case, differential exposure, to injuries or to infection, is certainly motivated, and the role of unconscious wishes to be injured or to fall ill in such cases has been clearly demonstrated. Then there is the whole range of "psychosomatic" illness about which knowledge has been rapidly accumulating in recent years. Finally, there is the field of "mental disease," the symptoms of which occur mainly on the behavioral level....

Summing up, we may say that illness is a state of disturbance in the "normal" functioning of the total human individual, including both the state of the organism as a biological system and of his personal and social adjustments. It is thus partly biologically and partly socially defined....

Medical practice...is a "mechanism" in the social system for coping with the illnesses of its members. It involves a set of institutionalized roles.... The immediately relevant social structures consist in the patterning of the role of the medical practitioner himself and, though to common sense it may seem superfluous to analyze it, that of the "sick person" himself....

The role of the medical practitioner belongs to the general class of "professional" roles, a subclass of the larger group of occupational roles. Caring for the sick is thus not an incidental activity of other roles though, for example, mothers do a good deal of it—but has become functionally specialized as a full-time "job." This, of course, is by no means true of all societies. As an occupational role it is

institutionalized about the technical content of the function which is given a high degree of primacy relative to other status-determinants. It is thus inevitable both that incumbency of the role should be achieved and that performance criteria by standards of technical competence should be prominent. Selection for it and the context of its performance are to a high degree segregated from other bases of social status and solidarities.... Unlike the role of the businessman, however, it is collectivity-oriented not self-oriented.

The importance of this patterning is, in one context, strongly emphasized by its relation to the cultural tradition. One basis for the division of labor is the specialization of technical competence. The role of physician is far along the continuum of increasingly high levels of technical competence required for performance. Because of the complexity and subtlety of the knowledge and skill required and the consequent length and intensity of training, it is difficult to see how the functions could, under modern conditions, be ascribed to people occupying a prior status as one of their activities in that status, following the pattern by which, to a degree, responsibility for the health of her children is ascribed to the mother-status. There is an intrinsic connection between achieved statuses and the requirements of high technical competence....

High technical competence also implies specificity of function. Such intensive devotion to expertness in matters of health and disease precludes comparable expertness in other fields. The physician is not, by virtue of his modern role, a generalized "wise man" or sage—though there is considerable folklore to that effect—but a specialist whose superiority to his fellows is confined to the specific sphere of his technical training and experience. For example one does not expect the physician as such to have better judgment about foreign policy or tax legislation than any other comparably intelligent and well-educated citizen. There are of course elaborate subdivisions of specialization within the profession.... The physician is [also] expected to treat an objective problem in objective, scientifically justifiable terms. For example, whether he likes or dislikes the particular patient as a person is supposed to be irrelevant, as indeed it is to most purely objective problems of how to handle a particular disease.

...The "ideology" of the profession lays great emphasis on the obligation of the physician to put the "welfare of the patient" above his personal interests, and regards "commercialism" as the most serious and insidious evil with which it has to contend. The line, therefore, is drawn primarily vis-à-vis "business." The "profit motive" is supposed to be drastically excluded from the medical world. This attitude is, of course, shared with the other professions, but it is perhaps more pronounced in the medical case than in any single one except perhaps the clergy....

An increasing proportion of medical practice is now taking place in the context of organization. To a large extent this is necessitated by the technological development of medicine itself, above all the need for technical facilities beyond the reach of the individual practitioner, and the fact that treating the same case often involves the complex co-operation of several different kinds of physicians as well as of auxiliary personnel. This greatly alters the relation of the physician to the rest of the instrumental complex. He tends to be relieved of much responsibility and hence necessarily of freedom, in relation to his patients other than in his technical role. Even if a hospital executive is a physician himself he is not in the usual sense engaged in the "practice of medicine" in performing his functions any more than the president of the Miners' Union is engaged in mining coal.

As was noted, for common sense there may be some question of whether "being sick" constitutes a social role at all—isn't it simply a state of fact, a "condition"? Things are not quite so simple as this. The test is the existence of a set of institutionalized expectations and the corresponding sentiments and sanctions.

There seem to be four aspects of the institutionalized expectation system relative to the sick role. First is the exemption from normal social role responsibilities, which of course is relative to the nature and severity of the illness. This exemption requires legitimation by and to the various actors involved and the physician often serves as a court of appeal as well as a direct legitimatizing agent. It is noteworthy that like all institutionalized patterns the legitimation of being sick enough to avoid obligations can not only be a right of the sick person but an obligation upon him. People are often resistant to admitting they are sick and it is not uncommon for others to tell them that they *ought* to stay in bed. The word generally has a moral connotation. It goes almost without saying that this legitimation has the social function of protection against "malingering."

The second closely related aspect is the institutionalized definition that the sick person cannot be expected by "pulling himself together" to get well by an act of decision or will. In this sense also he is exempted from responsibility—he is in a condition that must "be taken care of." His "condition" must be changed, not merely his "attitude." Of course the process of recovery may be spontaneous but while the illness lasts he can't "help it." This element in the definition of the state of illness is obviously crucial as a bridge to the acceptance of "help."

The third element is the definition of the state of being ill as itself undesirable with its obligation to want to "get well." The first two elements of legitimation of the sick role thus are conditional in a highly important sense. It is a relative legitimation so long as he is in this unfortunate state which both he and alter hope he can get out of as expeditiously as possible.

Finally, the fourth closely related element is the obligation—in proportion to the severity of the condition, of course—to seek *technically competent* help, namely, in the most usual case, that of a physician and to *cooperate* with him in the process of trying to get well. It is here, of course, that the role of the sick person as patient becomes articulated with that of the physician in a complementary role structure.

It is evident from the above that the role of motivational factors in illness immensely broadens the scope and increases the importance of the institutionalized role aspect of being sick. For then the problem of social control becomes much more than one of ascertaining facts and drawing lines. The privileges and exemptions of the sick role may become objects of a "secondary gain" which the patient is positively motivated, usually unconsciously, to secure or to retain. The problem, therefore, of the balance of motivations to recover becomes of first importance. In general motivational balances of great functional significance to the social system are institutionally controlled, and it should, therefore, not be surprising that this is no exception.

A few further points may be made about the specific patterning of the sick role and its relation to social structure. It is, in the first place, a "contingent" role into which anyone, regardless of his status in other respects, may come. It is, furthermore, in the type case temporary. One may say that it is in a certain sense a "negatively achieved" role, through failure to "keep well," though, of course, positive motivations also operate, which by that very token must be motivations to deviance....

The orientation of the sick role vis-à-vis the physician is also defined as collectively-oriented. It is true that the patient has a very obvious self-interest in getting well in most cases, though this point may not always be so simple. But once he has called in a physician the attitude is clearly marked, that he has assumed the obligation to cooperate with that physician in what is regarded as a common task. The obverse of the physician's obligation to be guided by the welfare of the patient is the latter's obligation to "do his part" to the best of his ability. This point is clearly brought out, for example, in the attitudes of the profession toward what is called "shopping around." By that is meant the practice of a patient "checking" the advice of one physician against that of another without telling physician A that he intends to consult physician B, or if he comes back to A that he has done so or who B is. The medical view is that if the patient is not satisfied with the advice his physician gives him he may properly do one of two things, first he may request a consultation, even naming the physician he wishes called in, but in that case it is physician A not the patient who must call B in, the patient may not see B independently, and above all not without A's knowledge. The other proper recourse is to terminate the relation with A and become "B's patient." The notable fact here is that a pattern of behavior on the part not only of the physician but also of the patient, is expected which is in sharp contrast to perfectly legitimate behavior in a commercial relationship. If he is buying a car there is no objection to the customer going to a number of dealers before making up his mind, and there is no obligation for him to inform any one dealer what others he is consulting, to say nothing of approaching the Chevrolet dealer only through the Ford dealer.

The doctor-patient relationship is thus focused on these pattern elements. The patient has a need for technical services because he doesn't—nor do his lay associates, family members, etc.— "know" what is the matter or what to do about it, nor does he control the necessary facilities. The physician is a technical expert who by special training and experience, and by an institutionally validated status, is qualified to "help" the patient in a situation institutionally defined as legitimate in a relative sense but as needing help....

CRITICAL THINKING QUESTIONS

1. Does Parsons understand illness as a biological condition, that is, "something that happens to people"? What are the social elements in health and illness?

2. According to Parsons, what are the distinctive characteristics of the social role of the physician?

3. What are the major elements of "the sick role"? In what respects does Parsons view the social roles of physicians and patients as complementary? Can you see ways in which they may be in conflict?

46

"Even If I Don't Know What I'm Doing I Can Make It Look Like I Know What I'm Doing": Becoming a Doctor in the 1990s

Brenda L. Beagan

Health and Medicine

CLASSIC

CONTEMPORARY

CROSS-CULTURAL

Beagan's article investigates how medical students are trained at Canadian universities. Her analysis provides revealing insight into how medical students incorporate new professional identities as they move through their studies.

For most medical students, a remarkable and important transformation occurs from the time they enter medical school to the time they leave.... They become immersed in the culture, environment and lifestyle of the school. They slowly lose their initial identity and become redefined by the new situation. Medical students have to look for something to hang on to. And that something is provided: their new identity as 'doctor.'
— Shapiro (1987: 27)

When students enter medical school they are lay people with some science background. When they leave four years later they have become physicians; they have acquired specialized knowledge and taken on a new identity of medical

Source: Brenda L. Beagan. 2001. "Even If I Don't Know What I'm Doing I Can Make It Look Like I Know What I'm Doing": Becoming a Doctor in the 1990s. *Canadian Review of Sociology and Anthropology,* 38(3), 275–92. Reprinted by permission of the Canadian Sociology and Anthropology Association.

professional. What happens in those four years? What processes of socialization go into the making of a doctor?

Most of what we know about how students come to identify as future-physicians derives from research conducted when students were almost exclusively male, white, middle- or upper-class, young and single—for example, the classics *Boys in White* (Becker, Geer, Strauss, & Hughes, 1961) and *Student Physician* (Morton, Reader, & Kendall, 1957). When women and students of colour were present in this research it was in token numbers. Even when women and non-traditional students were present, as in Sinclair's (1997) recent ethnography, their impact on processes of professional identity formation and the potentially distinct impact of professional socialization on these students have been largely unanalysed. What does becoming a doctor look like in a medical school of the late 1990s, where many students are female, are of diverse racial and cultural backgrounds, are working-class, gay and/or parents?

This study draws on survey and interview data from students and faculty at one Canadian medical school to examine the processes of professional identity formation and how they are experienced by diverse undergraduate medical students in the late 1990s. As the results will show, the processes are remarkably unchanged from the processes documented 40 years ago.

RESEARCH METHODS AND PARTICIPANTS

The research employed three complementary research strategies: A survey of a third-year class (123 students) at one medical school, interviews with 25 students from that class, and interviews with 23 faculty members from the same school.[1] Third-year students were chosen because in a traditional medical curriculum the third year is a key point for students, an important transition as they move out of the classroom to spend the majority of their time working with patients— patients who may or may not call them "doctor," treat them as doctors, and reflect them back to themselves as doctors (cf. Coombs, 1978; Haas & Shaffir, 1987)....

Survey respondents also identified faculty members who they believed were "especially interested in medical education." Twenty-three faculty interviews were conducted. All interviews took 60–90 minutes following a semi-structured interview guide, and were tape-recorded and transcribed. The interview transcripts were coded inductively using broad categories such as "pressures toward conformity," and "conflicts experienced," and using codes such as "language of medicine" derived from the literature. Initial broad codes were later subdivided into narrower codes.

...[T]he students who completed the survey were evenly divided by gender and were heterogeneous in "race"/ethnicity, as well as in self-identified social class background.[2] Twenty students (28%) self-identified as members of "minority groups," all identifying racial or cultural groups.

The students interviewed were slightly less heterogeneous in "race"/ethnicity and first language, and were somewhat more likely to be in committed relationships. The purposive sample of faculty members and administrators was predominately male, English-speaking and of European origin— reflective of the school's faculty more generally.

FIRST EXPERIENCES BECOME COMMONPLACE

When identifying how they came to think of themselves as medical students, participants described a process whereby what feels artificial and unnatural initially comes to feel natural simply through repetition. For many students, a series of "first times" were transformative moments.

Denise:[3] I think there are sort of seminal experiences. The first cut in anatomy, the first time you see a patient die, first time you see a treatment that was really aggressive and didn't work.... First few procedures that I conducted myself, first time I realized that I really did have somebody's life in my hands.... It seems like a whole lot of first times. The first time you take a history, the first time you actually hear the murmur. There are a lot of "Ah-ha!" sort of experiences.

Part of the novelty is the experience of being entitled—even required—to violate conventional social norms, touching patients' bodies, inquiring about bodily functions, probing emotional states: "You have to master a sense that you're invading somebody, and to feel like it's all right to do that, to invade their personal space...."

CONSTRUCTING A PROFESSIONAL APPEARANCE

Students are quite explicitly socialized to adopt a professional appearance: "When people started to relax the dress code a letter was sent to everybody's mailbox, commenting that we were not to show up in jeans, and a tie is appropriate for men." Most students, however, do not require such reminders; they have internalized the requisite standards.

Dressing neatly and appropriately is important to convey respect to patients, other medical staff, and the profession. It probably also helps in patients taking students seriously (survey comment).

Asked whether or not they ever worry about their appearance or dress at the hospital, 41% of the survey respondents said they do not, while 59% said they do.

There were no statistically significant differences by gender, class background or "minority" status, yet gendered patterns emerged when students detailed their concerns in an open-ended question. Most of the men satisfied their concerns about professional appearance with a shave and a collared shirt, perhaps adding a tie: "I do make sure that I am dressed appropriately when I see patients i.e. well-groomed, collared shirt (but no tie)." Women, on the other hand, struggled with the complex messages conveyed by their clothing, trying to look well-dressed yet not convey sexual messages. For women, "dressed up" normally means feminine while a professional image is intended to convey competence. Striking a balance at the intersection can be difficult: "Is it professional enough? Competent looking?… I do not want to appear 'sexy' on the job." As one student noted, while both men and women sometimes violate standards of professional dress, men's violations tend to involve being too informal; women's may involve dressing too provocatively, thereby sexualizing a doctor-patient encounter.

CHANGES IN LANGUAGE, THINKING AND COMMUNICATION SKILLS

Acquiring a huge vocabulary of new words and old words with new meanings—what one student called "medical-ese"—is one of the central tasks facing medical students, and one of the major bases for examining them (Sinclair, 1997). Students were well aware of adopting the formal language of medicine.

Dawna: All of a sudden all I can think of is this lingo that people won't understand. My brother told me the other day, "Sometimes I just don't understand what you are talking about anymore." I don't realize it! I'll use technical terms that I didn't think that other people wouldn't know.

The language of medicine is the basis for constructing a new social reality. Even as it allows communication, language constructs "zones of meaning that are linguistically circumscribed" (Berger & Luckmann, 1966: 39). Medical language encapsulates and constructs a worldview wherein reducing a person to body parts, tissues, organs and systems becomes normal, natural, "the only reasonable way to think" (Good & Good, 1993: 98–9). Students described this as learning to pare away "extraneous" information about a patient's life to focus on what is clinically relevant.

Becky: I see how it happens.… The first day of medicine we're just people. We relate by asking everything about a person, just like you'd have a conversation with anybody. And then that sort of changes and you become focussed on the disease…because right now there's just too much. It's overwhelming I'm hoping that as I learn more and become more comfortable with what I know and I can apply it without having to consciously go through every step in my mind, that I'll be able to focus on the *person* again.

In part through the language of medicine students learn a scientific gaze that reduces patients to bodies, allowing them to concentrate on what is medically important—disease, procedures, and techniques (Haas & Shaffir, 1987).

Not surprisingly, students may simultaneously lose the communication abilities they had upon entering medical school.

Dr. W.: Their ability to talk to people becomes corrupted by the educational process. They learn the language of medicine but they give up some of the knowledge that they brought in.… The knowledge of how to listen to somebody, how to be humble, how to hear somebody else's words.… It gets overtaken by the agenda of medical interviewing.

Another faculty member noted that students' communication skills improved significantly during their first term of first year, but "by the end of fourth year they were worse than they had been before medical school."

LEARNING THE HIERARCHY

Key to becoming a medical student is learning to negotiate the complex hierarchy within medicine, with students positioned at the bottom. A few faculty saw this hierarchy as a fine and important tradition facilitating students' learning.

> Dr. U.: You're always taught by the person above you. Third-year medical students taught by the fourth-year student.... Fourth-year student depends on the resident to go over his stuff. Resident depends on maybe the senior or the chief resident or the staff person. So they all get this hierarchy which is wonderful for learning because the attendings can't deal with everybody.

Students, and most faculty, were far less accepting of this traditional hierarchy—particularly of students' place in it.

Both faculty and students pointed out the compliance the hierarchical structure inculcates in students, discouraging them from questioning those above them.

> Dr. G.: If they don't appear compliant and so on they will get evaluated poorly. And if you get evaluated poorly then you might not get a good residency position. There's that sort of thing over their shoulders all of the time...the fear.

For students being a "good medical student" means not challenging clinicians.

> Valerie: If I ever saw something blatantly sexist or racist or wrong I hope that I would say something. But you get so caught up in basically clamming up, shutting up, and just taking it.... Is it going to ruin my career, am I going to end up known as the fink, am I going to not get the [residency] spot that I want because I told?

Though virtually every student described seeing things on the wards that they disagreed with, as long as there was no direct harm to a patient they stayed silent and simply filed away the incident in their collection of "things not to do when I am a doctor."

Other researchers have noted that medical students develop an approach geared to getting along with faculty, pleasing them whatever their demands (Becker et al., 1961: 281; Bloom, 1973: 20; Sinclair, 1997: 29). Some students, however, had *internalized* the norm of not criticizing clinicians, adopting an unspoken "code of silence" not just to appease faculty, but as part of being a good physician. In particular, one should never critique a colleague in front of patients.

> Mark: As students we all critique the professors and our attendings.... But I don't think we'd ever do that in front of a patient. It's never been told to us not to. But most of us wouldn't do that. Even if a patient describes something their doctor has prescribed to them or a treatment they've recommended which you know is totally wrong, maybe even harmful, I think most of us, unless it was really harmful, would tend to ignore it and just accept, "This is the doctor and his patient. What happens between them is okay."

These students had developed a sense of alliance with other members of the profession rather than with lay people and patients—a key to professional socialization. Several faculty referred to good medical students as "good team players' (cf. Sinclair, 1997), invoking a notion of belonging.

> Dr. M.: That sense of belonging, I think, is a sense of belonging to the profession.... You're part of the process of health care.... I mean, you haven't a lot of the responsibility, but at least you're connected with the team.

For some students, too, the desire to present a united front for patients was expressed as being a good team player: "You have to go along with some things...in front of the patient. For teams it wouldn't be good to have the ranks arguing amongst themselves about the best approach for patient care." To remain good team players, many students, residents and physicians learn to say nothing even when they see colleagues and superiors violating the ethics and standards of the profession; such violations are disregarded as matters of personal style (Light, 1988).

RELATIONSHIP TO PATIENTS

As students are learning their place in the hierarchy within medicine, they are simultaneously learning an appropriate relationship to patients. Within the medical hierarchy students feel powerless at the bottom. Yet in relation to patients even students hold a certain amount of power. In the interviews there were widely diverging views on the degree of professional authority physicians and student-physicians should display.

Some faculty drew a very clear connection between professionalism and the "emotional distancing" Fox documented in medicine in 1957, describing students developing a "hard shell" as a "way of dealing with feelings" to prevent over-identifying with patients. Emotional involvement and over-identification are seen as dangerous; students must strike a balance between empathy and objectivity, learning to overcome or master their emotions (Conrad, 1988; Haas & Shaffir, 1987): "I only become of use if I can create some distance so that I can function."

> Dr. E.: Within the professional job that you have to do, one can be very nice to patients but there's a distancing that says you're not their friend, you're their doctor.

In contrast, several faculty members rejected the "emotional distancing" approach to medicine in favour of one based in egalitarian connection.

> Dr. V.: I reject that way of dealing with it.... When I'm seeing a patient I have to try to get into understanding what's bothering them. And in fact it's a harder job, I mean I need to understand well enough so I can help them to understand. 'Cause the process of healing is self-understanding.

These faculty members talked about recognizing and levelling power or sharing power. They saw professional distancing as the loss of humanitarianism, the adoption of a position of superiority, aloofness, emphasizing that clinicians need to know their patients as something more than a diagnosis. Women were slightly over-represented among those expressing the egalitarian perspective, but several male clinicians also advocated this position.

PLAYING A ROLE GRADUALLY BECOMES REAL

Along with emotional distancing, Fox (1957) identified "training for uncertainty" as key to medical socialization, including the uncertainty arising from not knowing everything, and not knowing enough. Alongside gathering the knowledge and experience that gradually reduces feelings of uncertainty, students also grow to simply tolerate high levels of uncertainty. At the same time they face routine expectations of certainty—from patients who expect them "to know it all" and faculty who often expect them to know far more than they do and who evaluate the students' competence (Haas & Shaffir, 1987). Students quickly learn it is risky to display lack of certainty; impression management becomes a central feature of clinical learning (Conrad, 1988). Haas and Shaffir (1987: 110) conclude that the process of professionalization involves *above all* the successful adoption of a cloak of competence such that audiences are convinced of the legitimacy of claims to competence.

Robert Coombs argues that medical professional socialization is partly a matter of *playing* the role of doctor, complete with the props of white coat, stethoscope, name tag, and clipboard (1978: 222). The symbols mark medical students off as distinct from lay people and other hospital staff, differentiating between We and They. Students spoke of "taking on a role" that initially made them feel like "total frauds," "impostors."

> Erin: It was really role-playing. You were doing all these examinations on these patients which were not going to go into their charts, were not going to ever be read by anybody who was treating the people so it really was just practice. Just play-acting.

They affirmed the importance of the props to successful accomplishment of their role play— even as it enhanced the feeling of artifice: "During third year when we got to put the little white coat on and carry some instruments around the hospital, have a name tag…it definitely felt like role-playing."

Despite feeling fraudulent, the role play allows students to meet a crucial objective: demonstrating to faculty, clinical instructors, nurses and patients that they know something. They quickly learn to at least look competent.

Nancy: Even if I don't know what I'm doing I can make it *look* like I know what I'm doing.... It was my acting in high school.... I get the trust of the patient....

RESPONSES FROM OTHERS

The more students are treated by others as if they really were doctors the more they feel like doctors (cf. Coombs, 1978). In particular, the response from other hospital personnel and patients can help confirm the student's emerging medical professional identity.

Rina: The more the staff treats you as someone who actually belongs there, that definitely adds to your feeling like you do belong there.... It's like, "Wow! This nurse is paging me and wants to know *my* opinion on why this patient has no urine output?!"

For many students patients were the single most important source of confirmation for their emerging identity as physicians. With doctors and nurses, students feel they can easily be caught out for what they don't know; with patients they feel fairly certain they can pull off a convincing performance, and they often realize they *do* know more than the average person.

One response from others that has tremendous impact is simply being called doctor by others (Konner, 1987; Shapiro, 1987). Survey results show 68% ($n = 48$) of students had been called doctor at least occasionally by people other than family or friends. All but two fully recalled the first time they were called doctor and how they felt about it. *Not* being called doctor—especially when your peers *are*—can be equally significant. In previous accounts, being white and being male have greatly improved a medical student's chances of being taken for a doctor (Dickstein, 1993; Gamble, 1990; Kirk, 1994; Lenhart, 1993).

In this study, although social class background, minority status and first language made no difference, significantly more men than women were *regularly* called doctor and significantly more women had *never* been called doctor.[4]

These data suggest a lingering societal assumption that the doctor is a man. According to the interviews, women medical students and physicians are still often mistaken for nurses. Two of the male students suggested the dominant assumption that a doctor is a man facilitates their establishing rapport with patients and may ease their relationships with those above them in the medical hierarchy: "I've often felt because I fit like a stereotypical white male, that patients might see me as a bit more trustworthy. A bit more what they'd like to see. Who they want to see." Goffman notes that the part of a social performance intended to impress others, which he calls the "front," and which includes clothing, gender, appearance and manner, is predetermined: "When an actor takes on an established social role, usually he finds that a particular front has already been established for it" (1959: 27). In this case it appears that the role doctor, or medical student, still carries an attached assumption of maleness.

SECONDARY SOCIALIZATION: SUBSUMING THE FORMER SELF?

The fact that roles carry with them established expectations heightens the potential for clashes with the identity characteristics of new incumbents. Education processes, inevitably processes of secondary socialization, must always contend with individuals' already formed and persistent selves, selves established through primary socialization. As Berger and Luckmann (1966: 129) note, "Whatever new contents are now to be internalized must somehow be superimposed upon this already present reality."

In his study of how medical students put together identities as spouses, parents, and so on with their developing identities as physicians, Broadhead

(1983) stresses the need for individuals to "articulate" their various identities to one another, sorting out convergences and divergences of attitudes, assumptions, activities and perspectives that accompany different subject positions.

In this research, most students indicated that medicine had largely taken over the rest of their lives, diminishing their performance of other responsibilities. While 55% of survey respondents thought they were doing a good job of being a medical student, many thought they were doing a poor to very poor job of being a spouse (26%) or family member (37%); 46% gave themselves failing grades as friends. Fewer than a quarter of respondents thought they were doing a good job of being an informed citizen (18%) or member of their religion, if they had one (17%).

What emerged from most interviews and from the survey was a picture of medical school dominating all other aspects of daily life. Overwhelmingly, students talked about sacrifice.

Lew: You just sacrifice so much. I don't know about people who don't have children, but I value my family more than anything, and, and I cannot—I didn't know you had to sacrifice that much.

Many students had given things up, at least temporarily: musical instruments, art, writing, sports activities, volunteer activities. Some students spoke of putting themselves on hold, taking on new medical-student identities by subsuming former identities.

This sacrifice of self-identity can be quite serious. Several faculty and students suggested students from non-Western, non-Caucasian cultural backgrounds need to assimilate: "Students from other cultures leave behind a lot of their culture in order to succeed. There's a trade-off." Similarly, faculty and students suggested gay and lesbian students frequently become more "closeted" as they proceed through undergraduate training. One clinician said of a lesbian fourth-year student, "Now all of a sudden her hair's cut very business-like and the clothes are different.... She's fitting into medicine. Medicine isn't becoming a component

of her, she's becoming a component of the machine." Some faculty suggested women in medicine may need to relinquish their identity as women in order to fit in as physicians.

Dr. Q.: The women who are in those positions are white men. You just have to look at the way they dress. They're wearing power suits often with ties, you know, they're really trying to fit the image. [One of the women here] recently retired and in the elevator in the hospital they talked about her as one of the boys. So that's the perception of the men is that this is not a woman, this is one of the boys.

Women, they argued, become more-or-less men during medical training, "almost hyper-masculine in their interactions," "much more like men in terms of thought processes and interactions with people."

In addition to letting go of gender identity, sexual identity and cultural identity, some students described losing connections to their families and old friends after entering medical school. Often this was due to time constraints and diverging interests, but for some there was also a growing social distance as they moved into a new social status and education level. Lance was disconnecting from his working-class family:

Lance: My family actually were very unsupportive [when I got into medicine]. They didn't even know what I was doing. And there's still this huge gap between them and myself because they don't want to understand what's going on in my world, and their world seems quite simple, simplistic to me.... I see that gap getting larger over time.

Relationships with family, friends from outside of medicine, and anyone else who cannot relate to what students are doing every day are put "on the back burner." Intimate relationships are frequent casualties of medical school.

Thus some students do not or cannot integrate their medical student identities with their former sense of self; rather they let go of parts of themselves, bury them, abandon them, or put them aside, at least for a while. Another option for students who experience incongruities between their medical-student identities and other aspects of themselves is to segregate their lives. Because human beings have the ability to reflect on our own actions, it becomes possible to experience a segment of the self as distinct, to "detach a part of the self and its concomitant reality as relevant only to the role-specific situation in question" (Berger & Luckmann, 1966: 131). In this research 31% of survey respondents felt they are one person at school and another with friends and family. Perhaps as a consequence, many students maintain quite separate groups of friends, within medicine and outside medicine. Indeed, some faculty stressed the importance of maintaining strong outside connections to make it through medical school without losing part of yourself.[5]

DIFFERENCE AS A BASIS FOR RESISTANCE

Elsewhere I have argued that intentional and unintentional homogenizing influences in medical education neutralize the impact of social differences students bring into medicine (Beagan, 2000). Students come to believe that the social class, "race," ethnicity, gender and sexual orientation of a physician is not—and should not be relevant during physician-patient interactions. Nonetheless, at the same time those social differences can provide a basis for critique of and resistance to aspects of medical professional socialization. A study of medical residents found that those most able to resist socialization pressures minimized contact and interaction with others in medicine; maintained outside relationships that supported an alternative orientation to the program; and entered their programs with a "relatively strong and well-defined orientation" (Shapiro & Jones, 1979: 243). Complete resocialization requires "an intense concentration of all significant interaction within the [new social] group" (Berger & Luckmann, 1966: 145); it is also facilitated by minimal contradictions between the previous social world and the new world.

In this research, age played a clear role in students' ability to resist some aspects of professional socialization. Older students usually had careers before medicine, which helped put medical school in a different perspective. Often medicine was one of a range of possible things they could be doing with their lives—important, but not worth sacrificing for: "There are other things that are more important to me than this, so if at any point this conflicted too much with those things, I would give it up." One student suggested that being older entering medicine meant she had her goals and self-identity more clearly established. Most older students were in committed relationships with non-medical partners and had clear priorities about maintaining non-medical activities and connections, rather than abandoning them under the onslaught of medical school demands.

> Robin: I resolved that I wouldn't let my close friends go by the wayside.... My partner is important to me, and I wouldn't always make him take a back seat to what I was doing.... It was like an ultimatum. If this program won't allow me to do those things, which I thought were reasonable things, then I just wasn't willing to do it.

These outside commitments helped them minimize interactions with their new social group.

The strongest basis for resisting professional socialization, however, came from having a working-class or impoverished family background. Most of the working-class students said they are not seen as particularly praiseworthy within their families—if anything they are somewhat suspect. They expressed a sustained anti-elitism that keeps them from fully identifying with other medical professionals. Janis, for example, insisted that she is not "one of Them," that she came from the other side of the tracks and still belongs there, that she could never fit in at medical school, could never be "a proper med student." She feels very uncomfortable with social functions at school and sees herself as utterly different from her classmates and preceptors: "Let's just say I don't share Dr. Smith's interest in yachting in the Caribbean, you know what I mean? (laughing)."

Lance, who spent his summers working on fishing boats to pay for medical school, described most of his classmates as "the pampered elite." He resists the required dress code because it epitomizes elitism.

Lance: A lot of people, the first thing they did when we started seeing patients was throw on a nice pair of shoes and grab the tie and button up. I've never worn a tie. And I never will.... To me, it symbolizes everything that sets the doctor and the patient apart. It's like...'I'm somewhat better than everyone else'.... It gets in the way of good communication. I think you want a level of respect there, but you don't want that B.S. that goes with it.

Although the number of working class students was small, the data showed quite clearly that they tended to be among the least compliant with the processes of secondary socialization encountered in medical school.

Lance: I think I'm very much different from my classmates...more outspoken, definitely.... Other people tend to say the right thing because they're a little afraid of the consequences. I don't care.... It comes from my background, you know, fishing. I've seen these tough, hard guys, think they're pretty something, but they're puking their guts out being seasick. It kind of reduces to the common denominator.

CONCLUSION

What is perhaps most remarkable about these findings is how little has changed since the publication *of Boys in White* (Becker et al., 1961) and *Student Physician* (Merton et al., 1957), despite the passage of 40 years and the influx of a very different student population. The basic processes of socializing new members into the profession of medicine remain remarkably similar, as students encounter new social norms, a new language, new thought processes, and a new world view that will eventually enable them to become full-fledged members of "the team" taking the expected role in the medical hierarchy.

Yet, with the differences in the 1990s student population, there are also some important differences in experiences. The role of medical student continues to carry with it certain expectations of its occupant. At a time when medical students were almost exclusively white, heterosexually identified, upper- or middle-class men, the identity may have "fit" more easily than it does for students who are women, who are from minority racial groups, who identify as gay or lesbian or working-class. If role-playing competence and being reflected back to yourself as "doctor" are as central to medical socialization as Haas and Shaffir (1987) suggest, what does it mean that women students are less likely than their male peers to be called doctor? This research has indicated the presence of a lingering societal assumption that Doctor = Man. Women students struggle to construct a professional appearance that male students find a straightforward accomplishment. Women search for ways to be in relationship with their patients that are unmarked by gender. Despite the fact that they make up half of all medical students in Canada, women's experiences of medical school remain different. In this research, almost half (6 of 14) of the women students interviewed indicated that they do not identify themselves as medical students in casual social settings outside school lest they be seen as putting on airs; none of the male students indicated this. It remains for future research to determine whether gender differences in the "fit" of the physician role make a difference to medical practice.

Interestingly, it is commonly assumed that the source of change in medical education will be the next generation of physicians—in other words, the current crop of medical students and residents (cf. Sinclair, 1997: 323–24). Over and over again I heard the refrain, "Surely the new generation of doctors will do things differently." This was the response to the hierarchy that stifles questioning or dissent through fear; to the inhumane hours expected of student interns and residents; to the need to show deference to superiors; to the need to pretend competence and confidence; to the need to sacrifice family, friends and outside interests to succeed in medicine. Yet, there have been many new generations of doctors in the past 40 years…with remarkably little change. Why should we expect change now? Students, residents and junior physicians have very little power in the hierarchy to bring about change. Moreover, if they have been well socialized, why would we expect them to facilitate change? As one physician suggested, those who fit in well in medical school, who thrive on the competition and succeed, those are the students who return as physicians to join the faculty of the medical school. The ones who did not fit in, the ones who hated medical school, the ones who barely made it through—they are unlikely to be involved enough in medical education to bring about change.

Medical training has not always been good for patients (see Beagan, 2000). Nor has it been particularly good for medical students in many ways. Yet efforts at change on a structural level seem to have made little overall difference. In fact medical schools have a history of revision and reform without change (Bloom, 1988). Sinclair suggests moves toward entire new educational processes, such as the move to problem-based learning in medical schools throughout North America, simply "realign existing elements in the traditional training" (1997: 325). Furthermore, additions of new and very different components of the curriculum—such as classes on social and cultural aspects of health and illness, communication courses, and courses critiquing the social relations of the medical profession—are often seriously undermined in clinical teaching (Sinclair, 1997). Again, further empirical research should investigate the impact of such curriculum changes on professional socialization.

Finally, this research shows that the same sources of differentiation that mark some students as not quite fitting in also serve as sources of resistance against medical socialization. Older students, gay students who refuse to be closeted, and students who come from poverty or from working-class backgrounds, may be more likely than others to "do medical student" differently. Whether that translates into "doing doctor" differently is a matter for further empirical research. Future research needs to examine how these "different" students, these resisting students, experience residency and professional practice, whether and how they remain in medical practice.

CRITICAL THINKING QUESTIONS

1. One new experience for medical students is learning *medical-ese*. Have you faced a similar process during your postsecondary education? Explain.
2. Why do you think that the traditional hierarchy in medical schools (i.e., faculty at the top, students at the bottom) is seen by many as a good thing?
3. Discuss the process of playing the role of doctor. Does this process help us understand the training of young medical students? If so how? If not, why?
4. Which groups of students were most likely to resist professional socialization? Why would this be the case?

NOTES

1. In order to gain access to the research site, it was agreed that the medical school would remain unnamed. The school in question was in a large Canadian city with a racially and ethnically diverse population. It followed a traditional undergraduate curriculum.
2. At this medical school classes have been 40%–50% female for about 15 years (Association of Canadian Medical Colleges, 1996: 16); the class studied here was 48% female. Using subjective assessment of club photos, over the past 15 years about 30% of each class would be considered "visible minority" students, mainly of Asian and South Asian heritage.
3. All names are pseudonyms.
4. Never been called doctor, 14% of women, 0% of men; occasionally or regularly, 57% of women, 78% of men (Cramer's V = 0.32).
5. All of the gay/lesbian faculty and students described themselves as leading highly segregated lives during medical school.

REFERENCES

Association of Canadian Medical Colleges. 1996. *Canadian medical education statistics,* Vol. 18.

————. 2000. Neutralizing differences: Producing neutral doctors for (almost) neutral patients. *Social Science & Medicine,* 51(8): 1253–65.

Beagan, B. L. Forthcoming. Micro inequities and everyday inequalities: "Race," gender, sexuality and class in medical school. *Canadian Journal of Sociology.*

Becker, H. S., B. Geer, A. L. Strauss, and E. C. Hughes. 1961. *Boys in white: Student culture in medical school.* Chicago: University of Chicago Press.

Berger, P. L., and T. Luckmann. 1966. *The social construction of reality: A treatise in the sociology of knowledge.* New York: Doubleday and Co.

Bloom, S. W. 1973. *Power and dissent in the medical school.* New York: The Free Press.

————. 1988. Structure and ideology in medical education: An analysis of resistance to change. *Journal of Health and Social Behavior,* 29: 294–306.

Broadhead, R. 1983. *The private lives and professional identities of medical students.* New Brunswick, N.J.: Transaction.

Conrad, E. 1988. Learning to doctor: Reflections on recent accounts of the medical school years. *Journal of Health and Social Behavior,* 29: 323–32.

Cooley, C. H. 1964. *Human nature and the social order.* New York: Schocken.

Coombs, R. H. 1978. *Mastering medicine.* New York: Free Press.

Dickstein, L. J. 1993. Gender bias in medical education: Twenty vignettes and recommended responses. *Journal of the American Medical Women's Association,* 48(5): 152–62.

Fox, R. C. 1957. Training for uncertainty. In *The student-physician: Introduction studies in the sociology of medical education,* eds. R. K. Merton, G. G. Reader, and E. L. Kendall, 207–44. Cambridge, Mass.: Harvard University Press.

Gamble, V. N. 1990. On becoming a physician: A dream not deferred. In *The black women's health book: Speaking for ourselves,* ed. E. C. White, 52–64. Seattle: Seal Press.

Goffman, E. 1959. *The presentation of self in everyday life.* New York: Doubleday.

Good, B. J., and M. J. DelVecchio Good. 1993. "Learning medicine." The constructing of medical knowledge at Harvard medical school. In *Knowledge, power, and practice: The anthropology of medicine and everyday life,* eds. S. Lindbaum, and M. Lock, 81–107. Berkeley: University of California Press.

Haas, J., and W. Shaffir. 1987. *Becoming doctors: The adoption of a cloak of competence.* Greenwich, Conn.: JAI Press.

Hojat, M., J. S. Gonnella, and G. Xu. 1995. Gender comparisons of young physicians' perceptions of medical education, professional life, and practice: A follow-up study of Jefferson college graduates. *Academic Medicine,* 70: 305–12.

Hostler, S. L., and R. P. Gressard. 1993. Perceptions of the gender fairness of the medical education environment. *Journal of the American Medical Women's Association,* 48: 51–4.

Kirk, J. 1994. A feminist analysis of women in medical schools. In *Health, illness, and health care in Canada,* 2nd ed., eds. B. S. Bolaria, and H. D. Dickenson, 158–82. Toronto: Harcourt Brace.

Konner, M. 1987. *Becoming a doctor: A journey of initiation in medical school.* New York: Viking.

Lenhart, S. 1993. Gender discrimination: A health and career development problem for women physicians. *Journal of the American Medical Women's* Association, 48(5): 155–59.

Light, D. W. 1988. Toward a new sociology of medical education. *Journal of Health and Social Behavior,* 29: 307–22.

Mead, G. H. 1934. *Mind, self, and society: From the standpoint of a social behaviorist.* Chicago: University of Chicago Press.

Merton, R. K., G. G. Reader, and P. L. Kendall 1957. *The student physician: Introductory studies in the sociology of medical education.* Cambridge, Mass.: Harvard University Press.

Shapiro, E. C., and A. B. Jones. 1979. Women physicians and the exercise of power and authority in health care. In *Becoming a physician: Development of values and attitudes in medicine,* eds. E. Shapiro, and L. Lowenstein, 237–45. Cambridge: Bellinger.

Shapiro, M. 1987. *Getting doctored: Critical reflections on becoming a physician.* Toronto: Between the Lines. Sinclair, S. 1997. *Making doctors: An institutional apprenticeship.* New York: Berg.

Health
and
Medicine

CLASSIC

CONTEMPORARY

CROSS-CULTURAL

47

Crack and Prostitution: Gender, Myths, and Experiences

Patricia G. Erickson, Jennifer Butters, Patti McGillicuddy, and Ase Hallgren

In this article, Erickson et al. report on their research into crack-using women who work in the sex trade to support their drug use. Their findings reveal the harsh realities of the streets and how socially marginalized these women are. The authors conclude that the increasing availability and use of crack have particularly serious consequences for poor women who are, or become, sex-trade workers.

This paper presents the results from in-depth interviews with 30 crack-using women also working in the sex trade to support their drug use. The gender roles perspective highlights traditional beliefs from past decades about the appeal of cocaine to women, its effects on their sexuality, and the reasons they become prostitutes.

Who wants to be a crack head when you think about it? Who wants to fucking stand on the corner in the fucking −18C and sell their body for a piece of rock that's going to be gone in fucking 10 minutes? ("Jenny," age 25)

The woman who sells her body for drugs is the most dependent person in the world.

(Germaine Greer, *The Whole Woman*, p.6)

Source: P.G. Erickson, J. Butters, P. McGillicuddy, and A. Hallgren, 2000. "Crack and Prostitution: Gender, Myths, and Experiences". *Journal of Drug Issues, 30*(4), 767–88.

INTRODUCTION

The image of the crack-using prostitute has come to epitomize the ultimate shame and sexual degradation of women, but this portrayal is merely the latest in a long series of linkages between "fallen women" and substance use (Carstairs, 1998). The drug use experience of women has long been interpreted through the lens of ingrained cultural assumptions about their "remarkable vulnerability" to addiction and their inevitable downfall once they succumb to intoxicating temptations (Fillmore, 1984). In the early decades of the past century, indulgence in alcohol, tobacco, marijuana, and heroin for pleasure or "highs" was subject to severe social disapproval, while consuming the same substances in medicinal form was acceptable (Gomberg, 1982).

In the early 1980s, the gender roles perspective articulated a broader view on substance use within the framework of women's normative role as nurturer and caregiver (Colten & Marsh, 1984).

Concern about women who use alcohol or other drugs is seen as rooted in the perception that such behavior impairs the performance of their primary role; thus, they are viewed as more sick and deviant than male substance users (Marsh, 1982). Women who engage in illicit drug use are doubly deviant because they are not only breaking the law but also engaging in a predominantly male activity (Erickson & Watson, 1990). The negative sanctions applied to women who depart from mainstream standards serve as a form of social control and warning to all women to stay in their place (Rosenbaum, 1981). Like women who reject the housewife role for less traditional pursuits, women who use cocaine pose a particular threat to the gender role expectations of society.

The primary focus of this paper is the impact of crack addiction on poor women who were in, or became involved in, the sex trade. Building on the tradition of studies linking drug-using women with prostitution (Erickson & Watson, 1990), recent research has examined this latest manifestation in the crack era (lnciardi, Lockwood, & Pottieger, 1993; Maher, 1997). Maher and Daly (1996, pp. 483–484) describe how women in the street-level sex trade were affected by increased crack consumption in a New York neighborhood: "The market became flooded with novice sex workers, the going rate for sexual transactions decreased, and 'deviant' sexual expectations by dates increased, as did the levels of violence and victimization." Studies in several U.S. locales made similar observations; common practices include women repeatedly turning tricks for $5 or $10, just enough for another "rock" of crack, accepting dangerous dates, engaging in a variety of sexual practices beyond oral sex and intercourse, and servicing multiple partners in crack houses for a hit of crack (Bourgois & Dunlap, 1993; Inciardi, 1993; Pottieger & Tressell, 1999a). Like Fagan (1994), Sterk, Dolan, and Hatch (1999) contend that many of these acts go beyond conventional understandings of prostitution and constitute abusive sexual encounters.

This paper will present the results of an intensive interview study with 30 women who are heavily involved in crack use and obtain it primarily by selling or trading sex. We examine experiences in the effects of crack and the meanings of addiction for these women.

Sample and Method

Locating respondents who are engaged in activities that are both illegal and highly deviant is challenging. While studies of treatment samples have been the primary source of generalizations about illicit drug users in the past, their failure to reflect the much larger pool of unidentified users has led to more emphasis on community-based recruitment (Erickson & Alexander, 1989). Drug researchers have developed methods of locating low-profile subjects through an adaptation of qualitative and ethnographic techniques pioneered in the broader study of deviant populations (Douglas, 1972). Along with the time required to gain trust, a large element of self-selection is involved in such recruitment; cocaine use and prostitution have been studied this way (e.g. Goldstein, 1979; Erickson, Adlaf, Smart, & Murray, 1987). Since crack use is even more rare than cocaine use and lodged in groups that are quite inaccessible to random-sample household surveys, more targeted fieldwork is required.

While hidden populations of crack users have most often been studied in treatment or street samples, both approaches have strengths and limitations (Pottieger, Tressell, Surrall, Inciardi, & Chitwood, 1995). Treatment programs provide more ready access in safer settings, and their participants may be more ready to allow researchers access to their histories and experiences. They will not, however, be representative of those crack users at large on the street where ongoing use and income-generating activities are still paramount. A number of street studies of female crack users have been conducted, some utilizing large samples of several hundred women (Fagan, 1994; Pottieger & Tressler, forthcoming), others focusing on in-depth and sometimes repeated interviews with smaller samples (Maher & Daley, 1996; Sterk et al., 1999). It is clear that with empathy and persistence, researchers are able to locate women who use crack and gain the trust necessary for them to tell their stories honestly.

The site of this study was an inner-city neighborhood of Toronto known as "East Downtown," which had become notable for its street market in crack cocaine in the early 1990s. One author [Erickson] had gained some field presence and credibility in the area by undertaking some earlier collaborative research with local service-agency staff on violence in the crack trade (Erickson et al., 1996; Erickson, Butters, & German, 2000). These ongoing connections with health care providers in the area, combined with a growing concern for the impact of crack on residents and, in particular, the use of crack by some women living and working on these streets, led to this collaborative study.

Between November 1996 and February 1997, 30 women were recruited on the basis of being known heavy crack users for some years. The approach was made by a trusted local street worker who knew the women well [co-author Hallgren]. A trained person, also known and respected in the community, conducted the interviews in a local drop-in centre. The women were paid $20 and provided with food, soft drinks, and cigarettes. No names were recorded, and the identity of the women remained unknown to the research team. Most of the interviews, which took about one hour to complete, were tape recorded and transcribed, but in a few cases, at the participant's request, verbatim responses were recorded by hand. The women divulged information about many aspects of their lives related to drug use, experience with violence, and the sex trade, and appeared to be honest and open in their responses. While this particular group of women cannot be said to represent female crack users in general, it does reflect the range of characteristics and backgrounds of such women in this area of Toronto.

While a contrast to more conventional, middle-class users (Erickson, Adlaf. Smart, & Murray. 1994; Murphy & Rosenbaum, 1997), such a sample may be considered quite appropriate for providing insights into thc world of the poor, female crack user.

The demographic and drug-use profile of the 30 women in our study is the following. The average age of the Toronto East Downtown sample was 31, ranging from 22 to 52 years. The majority (17) of participants were White; seven were Native Canadian, five were Black, and one was East Indian. While 27 had been pregnant and 25 had given birth, all of their children were living with relatives, had been taken into care, or were grown up. All the women interviewed lived in the area, some most of their lives, with an average time spent of seven years. While 17 women had some form of relatively stable housing such as an apartment or room, the rest were homeless, living either on the street or transiently in neighborhood shelters. Although we did not probe their educational or occupational histories in depth, very few mentioned any previous conventional jobs other than housewife, and all but one had a criminal arrest record that would have further limited employment options. All of the participants acknowledged past as well as recent or current involvement in prostitution, identifying it as their major source of income. For less than half of the women, other forms of petty crime, drug selling, and panhandling, as well as some form of welfare benefit, were additional sources of income. While we did not ask the question directly, most of the women volunteered a history of childhood or adolescent physical and/or sexual abuse.

While all the women were current crack users at the time of the interview, using it for an average of eight and one-half years (the range of time these women had been using crack was between two and 13 years), they also had a poly-drug use history. All had used cannabis, 28 had also used powder cocaine, and 27 had used numerous prescription drugs; 25 had used LSD, 14 had used speed, and 11 had used heroin. Age of first drug use was 14 years on average and ranged from eight to 26 years. Most also continued to use alcohol, marijuana, and prescription drugs in the past year and past month, with very few exclusively using crack. This profile is similar to the street samples described by Fagan (1994), Maher and Daley (1996), Sterk et al. (1999), and Pottieger and Tressler (forthcoming), with the primary demographic distinction being the higher proportion of White participants in our Canadian sample. The social disadvantage of the women in all these studies is evident, regardless of location.

In the next sections, we shall present the women's introduction to crack, their perceptions of its effects, and what they like and dislike about it.

Experience of Crack Use

The women were asked what was going on in their lives when they first were exposed to crack and what had led them to try it. Responses fell mainly in two categories. About half—16 women—identified some particularly traumatic or difficult chronic personal situations. These included the death of family members, serious illness, divorce, miscarriage, losing their children, experiencing a rape or other form of abuse, and suffering from stress, depression, or other serious mental instability. Sometimes it was a combination of things:

Three things in a row- I got raped; I came home and found my partner of 11 years in bed with my best friend; then I lost my child.

Crack's "bad press" could be an incentive to someone who was looking for escape:

I was just out of a bad, an abusive relationship. I tried to kill myself...I was lonely and depressed. I was watching TV one day, COPS or something, and saw it (crack) being done. I actually drove my car to__ and asked for a rock. And so I started on my own.

A second set of responses referred to crack coming along when the women were already quite drug-involved; for example:

Me and my husband were both (methamphetamine) addicts. We had got arrested for dealing speed and then when I came out of jail all of a sudden this new drug was around, crack cocaine. And I went off the speed immediately and started smoking the crack.

Other women who switched their drug of choice to crack had previously been doing powder cocaine or injecting heroin. Its ready availability in their circles made crack easy to try. Finally, a third and smaller group of other responses were offered by women who simply tried it because it was around, others were doing it, or they described themselves as young and naïve.

They liked the rush, the relaxation, and the numbing effects on their emotions while still keeping them mentally alert. They could articulate many positive aspects of crack, but they also recognized its down side. Their more negative comments included that "crack wears you out," and that it made them sick, led to weight loss, and destroyed their lungs. Feelings of paranoia, depression, and memory loss were also mentioned. The worst aspect identified was coming down from a crack high, or "jonesing" as they termed it, when their supply ran out.

Are these women addicted to crack? From their own perspective, 27 of the 30 women answered that they were. Their expressions of craving and what they will do to get crack appear to substantiate their personal assessment. The question, "do you *get* all the crack you want?" produced these typical replies:

There's never enough.
The thing about crack cocaine is you never get enough.
One [hit] is too many and a thousand is never enough.
You never get all the drugs you need or want.

When asked what they do if they can't get crack, responses varied, with many women pointing out that "there's always some way to get it" if you are desperate enough:

You'll do anything to get it, that one hit on the pipe.
You want the crack so bad you'd do anything.

EXPERIENCE OF PROSTITUTION

For some women, life on the street started quite late, often after leaving an abusive relationship and having no money. "Cynthia," a 45-year-old woman with three grown children who has spent four years on the streets in Toronto East Downtown, provided this account:

> Since I started crack it's been a whole different life for me. I didn't live on the street before, until I was 40 years old. I didn't start hooking until I was 40 years old. After being a wife and a mother for so many years, then all of a sudden you're into hooking and you are doing that to pay for your crack.

For others, getting involved in drug use and prostitution started at an early age. "Marlene," a 25-year-old woman who had been working in the area for the past two years, described this sequence:

> I've been doing it (prostitution) since I was 16 years old, that's like what I know best. I started prostitution to support my habit for alcohol and marijuana...when you have so many people touching your body, I did the drugs first. I got addicted (to crack) when I was 18 and I've never stopped since that.

While some had started prostitution to support themselves, as a way to survive on the streets, or to pay for other drugs, at this stage all of these women acknowledged spending most of what they earned now on crack. These are some responses to a question asking, why do you work in the sex trade?

> To support my habit...that's not initially why I started. Because I don't have any other way of getting money. I'm addicted to crack cocaine and I have no other source of income.

Central to an understanding of the sex–crack dynamic is that stopping crack use was not considered a serious option by these women. Only a minority (nine) even identified their drug use as a problem. To most, it is the solution—they continue to use because it's what makes their lives bearable or interesting. Selling sex is the means to this end.

The sexual marketability of these women may have been reinforced by the effect of cocaine on body image and body weight. By keeping thin and subject to sexual objectification, crack-using women reflect the historical assertion that "women's social value has been inseparable from their bodies" (Brown & Jasper, 1993, p. 18). However, their subordination extended beyond simply selling sex. Some of the women recounted sexual deviations beyond what they considered normal heterosexual services for the trade (i.e., genital and oral sex), with which, nevertheless, they had complied, or been forced to perform:

> I've done a lot of things for crack. Sure I've sucked a dick for crack. Sure I've been with four men one time. I had to.

In the context of street prostitution in an area with a high volume of crack consumption going on, many of the customers will also be using crack. Some of the women did sex-for-crack exchanges, what they called "freaking," in crack houses. Others serviced well-off male professionals who paid for crack and expected to get high and have sex as part of the overall transaction. This gave the women ample opportunity to observe the differential effect of crack on women and men. The Swiss psychiatrist, Hans Maier, in his 1926 treatise on cocaine addiction, believed that cocaine reduced the sexual potency of men but had this effect on women: "In women there is, without exception, an increase in both the physical and psychological components of sexual drive. There is an exaggerated sensitivity to sexual stimuli... [she] often makes direct sexual advance to any man who happens to be present" (Maier, 1926: tr. Kalant, 1987, p. 82). While the women in our study universally and emphatically denied that crack stimulated their own sexual arousal, they saw it affecting men quite differently:

> Men get extremely horny where a lot of women don't. Men want sex when they're on it and I can't stand it.

The women also thought that men tended to get violent on crack and that this added additional risk when sex was being traded for crack or money to male crack users, a major segment of their clientele.

Crack markets are characterized by a high degree of systemic violence (Goldstein, 1985), and prostitution is an occupation that also entails a high degree of personal risk of violence (Erickson & Watson, 1990); the combination of the two is dangerous and can be lethal. Maher and Daly (1996) noted that three of the 45 women in their study were murdered. "Sally," a 34-year-old respondent who had worked in the Toronto East Downtown for 10 years, said, "I risk my life every day," and provided some examples:

There have been fights with knives over crack, over 20 pieces in a crack house, I was almost raped because I did not want to give this guy a blowjob after he gave me a toke...I had my jaw broken (by my boyfriend) when I was partying with this girl. [Why?] Because I smoked without him.

Three quarters of the women in our study reported being hurt as a result of their involvement with crack, most of them experiencing multiple incidents of violence. Nevertheless, these women acknowledge their feelings of vulnerability in their responses to the question "What is the most pressing issue to women on the street?":

There is always the fear of being beaten, robbed or killed.

Rape. It's happened to me twice this year, when I've been intoxicated.

The effects of a form of post-traumatic stress related to a history of assault and abuse may indeed contribute to the need to continue to use crack (Ledray, 1994), and the effects of abuse may become compounded for women of color (McGillicuddy, 1993). That these women survive on the street and cope as well they do after many years of crack and other drug use reflects their ability to be streetwise and handle numerous threatening situations. Some take a certain pride or satisfaction in the various ways their lives have evolved. "Cynthia," who came to crack later in life than most, described herself this way:

I've always been someone who liked to live dangerously, sort of on the edge...I know it sounds strange for you to hear me say this, but I wouldn't change the experience that I've had, on the whole. I've learned so much.

"Rosa" described crack as a kind of catalyst:

My daughter's father was very abusive, and for some strange reason, cocaine gave me the courage to tell him to get the fuck out of my life.

Despite these assets of interpersonal skills and the excitement of the street life that clearly appeals to many of the women, their awareness of the dangers is realistic. [Two women working in the area were murdered soon after we did this study, and another was shot in a back alley in May, 2000.]

EXPERIENCE OF MOTHERHOOD

Virtually all of the women (25 of the 30) in this study are mothers. The number of children these women have had ranges from one to eight, with the majority giving birth to between one and three children; about five of them have more. In each case, none of the children are currently living with their mother but are instead being cared for by other relatives (including grandparents, aunts, fathers, sisters), have been adopted, or have been placed in foster care. In addition, some are already adults, and one woman said her daughter was on the streets.

Why are these children not with their mothers? A variety of reasons were given in response to this question. Some revolved quite clearly around issues of substance abuse:

I gave her up for adoption. She's not with me because I couldn't stop using crack. Best thing for her. I didn't want to do to her what my mother did to me, so I just figured I would just, you know, give her to Children's Aid. Then the youngest one, I went back to using and my mom took the babies and I'm still using.

My 12-year-old was taken away because I was only 14 [when she was born], my 10-year-old I sent down to my mother when she was 5, my son was born with crack in his system so the Children's Aid were involved but his grandmother took him.

[My] other daughter and son are with my little sister because of my addiction.

Many of these women recognized on their own that active mothering and cocaine use were incompatible. They were not in the position of being able to provide adequate care for their children because of their substance use—crack use in particular—and the lifestyle that went with it. They were often fortunate in having other family members available to take on the care of their children.

While these women have not given up cocaine use for the sake of their children, they have been able to make, or at least accept, the choice not to be the primary caregiver.

IMAGES OF SELF

Cooley's (1902) discussion of the "looking-glass self" suggests that self-concepts are the reflection of others' perceptions of us; in essence we are, or become, what we think others think we are. More contemporary formulations have extended this notion to a consideration of stigma (Goffman, 1963) and shame (Fossum & Mason, 1986). Since crack users and prostitutes are typically regarded with much disdain, the combination of the two identities places individuals at the extreme of stigmatization. Sometimes, external perceptions translate into self-concepts and may aid in the understanding of deviant subgroups such as the women in this study. While we did not explore this relationship in depth, we are concerned with the extent to which perceptions of others become internalized and contribute to a self-fulfilling prophecy or act as barriers to seeking help.

When the respondents in this study were asked how they felt others in their neighborhood perceived them, their vulnerability to derogatory and demeaning self-images was quite evident. Some perceptions were tied closely to crack use:

They see me as a crack-head and like a nobody. And that is true, they do, they look at me like a nobody and it really pees me off. You see me sometimes, how angry I get in that church when they start talkin' about me and putting me down 'cause they're no better than me.

Other responses identify images that revolve as much or more so around prostitution:

... as a drug addict, prostitute drug addict, basically that's what they think.

As a tramp. But I don't care, though, because I'm addicted to crack. I'm addicted to it, eh? I can't help myself, what they think of me 'cause whatever they think about me, I don't have time to think because my mind is just busy on the next toke.

The ability to resist such ingrained and widespread perceptions held by others poses a significant challenge to these women, and accepting the labels is perhaps the path of least resistance. However, it may also be a contributing factor to the downward spiral in which these women find themselves. If these images are internalized, then the doors to treatment and life-changing options may also be perceived as pointless. And this may in fact be one of the greatest dangers these women face.

OPTIONS FOR CHANGE?

What might make a difference in these women's lives? We asked them about their prior experience with treatment, their views on different forms of drug access, and what sorts of services they thought would be helpful to women like them. While seeking treatment had been part of the drug-use history of 22 of the women, their reasons were predominantly either to "get some rest and rehab," or to respond to some external threat, such as the loss of their children or their housing, or to reduce jail time. The short-term nature of most of these interventions and the return to life on the streets did not present a successful picture of treatment outcome.

When asked what a free supply of drugs would do to their current way of life, 23 said they would stop other illegal activities and leave the street:

Absolutely. I'm not a law breaker by choice. I much prefer not to be putting my ass on the line, so to speak.

Definitely. I wouldn't have time to do it. I'd be too busy getting high.

Not surprisingly, given that any form of cocaine maintenance has almost never been discussed even in drug-treatment or drug-policy circles, most women had not thought about such an alternative (Erickson & Cheung, 1999). For poor women, there would still be the issue of where they would get money to live. Therefore, prostitution and other illegal acts may not necessarily subside. We also asked them if they would take a "crack substitute" if one were available: 18 said they would, seven said they wouldn't, and three were undecided. The negative responses were geared mainly to not wanting to stop crack or not wishing to substitute one addictive drug for another.

The women were more expansive when offered the chance to suggest the kinds of services they would like to see offered in the community. They enumerated a number of simple needs like places to shower, do laundry, and sleep safely when they were exhausted. Most of the women, 24 of 30, also would like to see more health services geared to their needs, and many also mentioned counseling—often defined as just someone to talk to—on a 24-hour basis. These are some of the examples they elaborated:

> A hotline for women, someone to offer support
> Counseling to get back on track
> A roof over my head 3 to 4 nights a week.
> A year's treatment out of the city
> Somewhere to call your own
> An understanding, good ear
> Somewhere to go and be safe

In other words, being treated like human beings with the same needs as everyone else.

SUMMARY AND CONCLUSION

Our study of 30 crack-using prostitutes refutes the view that cocaine makes these women "sexually licentious," as was believed in earlier eras (Carstairs, 1998: Maier, 1926, in tr. Kalant, 1987). It is clear that they work in the sex trade to get money and/or crack to support their own usage when few other sources of income are available to them. Far from enjoying sex while intoxicated, they describe it as aversive. Nor was their use of crack the main impetus to a career on the streets—most were involved in both the drug and sex trades previously, but crack intensified that life and led to more dangerous and perverse sexual activities. This is similar to the conclusions of Maher and Daly (1996) and others. Nor has research on women who use crack and lead otherwise conventional lives indicated any particularly positive effect of cocaine on their sexual activities (Erickson et al., 1994). Nevertheless, it is possible that women in the lower echelon of the sex trade, many of whom have histories of early childhood and adolescent sexual and physical abuse, may be less inclined to take pleasure in sex, irrespective of cocaine use.

The other prevailing stereotype, that crack-using women are unfit mothers, was in a sense upheld by the women themselves. Most had given up their children or had them taken away, but none disputed the appropriateness of this decision. This did not mean that they had no feelings for their children—quite the opposite. We would argue that they were acting, insofar as they were able, in the best interests of their children.

The policy of legal and social suppression of crack has helped it to find ready markets in vulnerable portions of the population. Nevertheless, there is no simple answer to these women's problems, such as legalizing the supply of the drug. As they say, "you can never have enough." Unlike methadone maintenance for heroin users, there is no "cocadone" that alleviates withdrawal symptoms or provides a longer-acting substitute (Erickson & Cheung, 1999). Effective intervention strategies for problem cocaine use depend, in part, on motivation for change—noticeably absent in most of this population, who lack the stakes in conformity that provide self- and informal controls over the most excessive use-patterns (Waldorf, Reinarman, & Murphy, 1991). Moreover, these women are characterized by the poverty and lack of social support that predicts poor compliance and relapse in the management of chronic conditions generally (McLellan, Lewis, O'Brien, & Kleber, 2000). Strategies that would provide a safer environment for use of drugs, along with community outreach of health and social services, might have more individual and social benefit for such women than drug-focused policy options.

The pervasive violence and fear of violence that these women experience speaks to the importance of improving the working conditions on the street and providing safe shelters and support for these women. While they are unlikely to choose a life without crack in their present situation, some of the riskier aspects of their existence might be ameliorated by nonjudgmental approaches to meeting their basic needs. As the above discussion indicated, abstinence-oriented treatment is not a particularly appealing or an effective approach for these women. Whether a longer-term investment, geared to their lifestyle, and treating crack addiction as a chronic medical condition might produce a more favorable result remains to be tried (McLellan et al., 2000). Our participants are positively inclined to more services and support in their immediate community. These types of broad harm-reduction measures, such as housing, medical attention, and safer work conditions, might realistically focus on keeping the women alive and HIV negative rather than ending their crack addiction.

ACKNOWLEDGMENTS

This project was funded by the Drug Abuse Prevention Program of the Department of Public Health, Toronto, and facilitated by Teresa Damaso.

CRITICAL THINKING QUESTIONS

1. Review the authors' discussion of how traditional gender-role behaviours influence the public's perception of female crack-using prostitutes.

2. In the article the authors describe some of the challenges researchers face when investigating illegal-drug users. Speculate on some of the challenges researchers might confront when investigating prescription-drug use among the middle class.

3. Of the 30 women interviewed as part of this research, only 9 felt that their drug use was a *problem*; to most of the women, it was in fact a *solution*. Explain this apparent contradiction from the sociological perspective.

REFERENCES

Bourgois, P., and E. Dunlap. 1993. Exorcising sex-for-crack: An ethnographic perspective from Harlem. In *Crack pipe as pimp: An ethnographic investigation of sex-for-crack exchanges,* ed. M. Rather. New York: Lexington Books.

Brown, Catrina, and Karin Jasper. 1993. *Consuming passions: Feminist approach to weight preoccupation and eating disorders.* Toronto: Second Story Press.

Butters, J., A. Hallgren, and P. McGillicuddy. 1997. *Poor women and crack use in downtown Toronto.* Research Report.

Carstairs, C. 1998. Innocent addicts, dope fiends and nefarious traffickers: Illegal drug use in 1920s English Canada. *Journal of Canadian Studies, 33,* 145–62.

Colten, M., and J. Marsh. 1984. A sex-roles perspective on drug and alcohol use by women. In *Sex roles and psychopathology.* ed. C. Widom. New York: Plenum.

Cooley, Charles. 1902. *Human nature and the social order.* New York: Scribner.

Douglas, J. 1972 *Research on deviance.* New York: Random House.

Erickson. P., F. Adlaf, R. Smart, and G. Murray. 1994. *The steel drug: Cocaine and crack in perspective* (2nd ed.). New York: Lexington Books.

Erickson, P., and B. Alexander. 1989. Cocaine and addictive liability. *Social Pharmacology, 3,* 249–70.

Erickson, P., J. Butters, B. Fischer, E. Fehrman, D. Haans, and B. Poland. 1996. Exploring drug market violence in a more peaceable society. Appendix G in the Draft Report of the Drugs–Violence Task Force, U.S. Sentencing Commission, Washington, DC.

Erickson, P., J. Butters, and B. German. 2000. Flexing crack in Toronto: A deviant pathway for poor, homeless drug users. Paper presented at the International Conference on Deviant Pathways, Porto, Portugal, January.

Erickson. P., and Y. Cheung. 1999. Harm reduction among cocaine users: Reflections on individual intervention and community social capital. *International Journal of Drug Policy, 10,* 235–46.

Erickson, P., and V. Watson. 1990. Women, illicit drugs and crime. *Research Advances in Alcohol and Drug Problems, 10,* 859–77.

Fagan, J. 1994. Women and drugs revisited: Female participation in the cocaine economy. *Journal of Drug Issues, 24,* 179–225.

Fillmore, K. 1984. When angels fall: Women's drinking as cultural preoccupation and as reality. In *Alcohol problems in women,* eds. S. Wilsnack and L. Beckman. New York: Guilford Press.

Fossum, Merle, and Marilyn Mason. 1986. *Facing shame.* New York: Norton.

Goffman, Erving. 1963. *Stigma: Notes on the management of spoiled identity.* Englewood Cliffs, NJ: Prentice-Hall.

Goldstein, P. 1979. *Prostitution and drugs.* Lexington, Massachusetts: Lexington Books.

——1985. The drugs/violence nexus: A tripartite conceptual framework. *Journal of Drug Issues, 21,* 345–67.

Gomberg, E. 1982. Historical and political perspectives: Women and drug use. *Journal of Social Issues, 38,* 9–23.

Humphries, D. 1999. *Crack mothers: Pregnancy, drugs and the media.* Columbus, OH: The Ohio State University.

Inciardi, J. 1993. King rats, chicken heads, slow necks, freaks and blood suckers: A glimpse of Miami sex-for-crack market. In *Crack pipe as pimp: An ethnographic investigation of sex-for-crack exchanges,* ed. M. Ratner. New York: Lexington Books.

Kalant, O. [tr.] 1987. *Maier's cocaine addiction [Der Kokainismus 1926].* Toronto: Addiction Research Foundation.

Ledray, Linda. 1994. *Recovery from rape.* Holt and Company, New York.

McGillicuddy, Patricia. 1993. Embodied and emboldened: Dealing with sexual violence. In *Consuming passions: Feminist approach to weight preoccupation and eating disorders,* ed. C. Brown and K. Jasper. Toronto: Second Story Press.

McLennan. A., D. Lewis, C. O'Brien, and H. Kleber. 2000. Drug dependence, a chronic mental illness: Implications for treatment, insurance and outcome evaluation. *Journal of the American Medical Association, 284,* 1689–95.

Maher, L. 1997. *Sexed work: Gender, race and resistance in a Brooklyn drug market.* Oxford: Clarendon Press.

Maher. L., and K. Daly. 1996. Women in the street-level drug economy: Continuity or change? *Criminology, 34,* 465–91.

Marsh, J. 1982. Public issues and private problems: Women and drug use. *Journal of Social Issues, 38,* 153–65.

Murphy. S., and M. Rosenbaum. 1997. Two women who used cocaine too much: Class, race, gender, crack and coke. In *Crack in America: Demon drugs and social justice,* eds. C. Reinarman and H. Levine. California: University of California Press.

Pottieger. A., and P. Tressell. Social relationships of crime-involved women cocaine users. *Journal of Psychoactive Drugs.*

——1999a. Dimensions of sex trading among women cocaine users. Paper presented at the Annual Meeting of the American Society of Criminology, Washington, D.C., November 1998.

——1999b. Barriers to treatment for crime-involved cocaine-dependent women. Paper presented at the Annual Meeting of the American Sociological Association, New York, August 1996.

Pottieger. A., P. Tressell, H. Surrall, J. Inciardi, and D. Chitwood. 1995. Drug use patterns of adult crack users in street and residential treatment samples. *Journal of Psychoactive Drugs, 27,* 27–38.

Rosenbaum, M. 1981. Sex roles among deviants: The woman addict. *International Journal of the Addictions, 16,* 859–77.

Sterk, C., K. Dolan, and S. Hatch. 1999. Epidemiological indicators and ethnographic realities of female cocaine use. *Substance Use and Misuse, 34,* 2057–72.

Waldorf, D., C. Reinarman, and S. Murphy. 1991. *Cocaine changes: The experience of using and quitting.* Philadelphia: Temple University Press.

Health
and
Medicine

CLASSIC

CONTEMPORARY

CROSS-CULTURAL

48

Female Genital Mutilation

Efua Dorkenoo and Scilla Elworthy

Women's organizations around the world focus on a variety of women's health-related issues and problems, including domestic violence, rape, sexual harassment, and poverty. In this selection, Efua Dorkenoo and Scilla Elworthy examine the complex cultural issues surrounding female genital mutilation, a practice that has received international attention since the early 1990s.

THE FACTS

…[F]emale genital mutilation covers four types of operation:

1. *Circumcision,* or cutting of the prepuce or hood of the clitoris, known in Muslim countries as Sunna (tradition). This, the mildest type, affects only a small proportion of the millions of women concerned. It is the only type of mutilation that can correctly be called circumcision, though there has been a tendency to group all kinds of mutilations under the misleading term "female circumcision."

2. *Excision,* meaning the cutting of the clitoris and of all or part of the labia minora.

3. *Infibulation,* the cutting of the clitoris, labia minora and at least part of the labia majora. The two sides of the vulva are then pinned together by silk or catgut sutures, or with thorns, thus obliterating the vaginal introitus except for a very small opening, preserved by the insertion of a tiny piece of wood or a reed for the passage of urine or menstrual

blood. These operations are done with special knives, with razor blades or pieces of glass. The girl's legs are then bound together from hip to ankle and she is kept immobile for up to forty days to permit the formation of scar tissue.

4. *Intermediate,* meaning the removal of the clitoris and some parts of the labia minora or the whole of it. Various degrees are done according to the demands of the girl's relatives.…

Most frequently these operations are performed by an old woman of the village or by a traditional birth attendant and only rarely by qualified nurses or doctors. The age at which the mutilations are carried out varies from area to area, and according to whether legislation against the practice is foreseen or not. It varies from a few days old (for example, the Jewish Falashas in Ethiopia, and the nomads of the Sudan) to about seven years (as in Egypt and many countries of Central Africa) or—more rarely—adolescence, as among the Ibo of Nigeria. Most experts are agreed that the age of mutilation is becoming younger, and has less and less to do with initiation into adulthood.[1]

Source: From "Female Genital Mutilation," by Efua Dorkenoo and Scilla Elworthy, in *Female Genital Mutilation: Proposals for Change,* an MRG Report, 92/3. Reprinted with permission.

FIGURE 48.1   Female genital mutilation in Africa

Physical Consequences

Health risks and complications depend on the gravity of the mutilation, hygienic conditions, the skill and eyesight of the operator, and the struggles of the child. Whether immediate or long term, they are grave.[2] Death from bleeding is not uncommon, while long-term complications include chronic infections of the uterus and vagina, painful menstruation, severe pain during intercourse, sterility and complications during childbirth. Though evidence has yet to be collected, it is also likely that bleeding or open wounds increase the likelihood of HIV transmission and AIDS.

There is great difficulty in obtaining accurate research on the sexual experiences of mutilated women, because the majority are reluctant to speak on the subject and are generally ambivalent on questions of sexual enjoyment.[3] However, in all types of mutilation, even the "mildest" clitoridectomy, a part of a woman's body containing nerves of vital importance to sexual pleasure is amputated.

Psychological Consequences

Even less research has been done to date on the psychological consequences of these traditions. However, many personal accounts and research findings contain repeated references to anxiety prior to the operation, terror at the moment of being seized by an aunt or village matron, unbearable pain, and the subsequent sense of humiliation and of being betrayed by parents, especially the mother. On the other hand, there are references to special clothes and good food associated with the event, to the pride felt in being like everyone else, in being "made clean," in having suffered without screaming.

To be different clearly produces anxiety and mental conflict. An unexcised, non-infibulated girl is despised and made the target of ridicule, and no one in her community will marry her. Thus what is clearly understood to be her life's work, namely marriage and child-bearing, is denied her. So, in tight-knit village societies where mutilation is the rule, it will be the exceptional girl who will suffer psychologically, unless she has another very strong identity which she has lost.[4]

There is no doubt that genital mutilation would have overwhelming psychological effects on an unmotivated girl, unsupported by her family, village, peers and community. To those from other cultures unfamiliar with the force of this particular community identity, the very concept of amputation of the genitals carries a shock value which does not exist for most women in the areas concerned. For them, not to amputate would be shocking.

These observations concern social-psychological factors rather than the central question, namely, what effects do these traumatic operations have on little girls at the moment of operation and as they grow up? The fact is that we simply don't know. We do not know what it means to a girl or woman when her central organ of sensory pleasure is cut off, when her life-giving canal is stitched up amid blood and fear and secrecy, while she is forcibly held down and told that if she screams she will cause the death of her mother or bring shame on the family.

THE PRACTICE

The Area Covered

The countries where one or more forms of female genital mutilation are practised number more than twenty in Africa, from the Atlantic to the Red Sea, the Indian Ocean and the eastern Mediterranean. Outside Africa, excision is also practised in Oman, South Yemen and in the United Arab Emirates (UAE). Circumcision is practised by the Muslim populations of Indonesia and Malaysia and by Bohra Muslims in India, Pakistan and East Africa.[5]

On the map of Africa, an uninterrupted belt is formed across the centre of the continent, which then expands up the length of the Nile. This belt, with the exception of the Egyptian buckle, corresponds strikingly with the pattern of countries that have the highest child mortality rates (more than 30 percent for children from one to four years of age).[6] These levels reflect deficiencies of medical care, of clean drinking water, of sanitary infrastructure and of adequate nutrition in most of the countries.

The gravity of the mutilations varies from country to country. Infibulation is reported to affect nearly all the female population of Somalia, Djibouti and the Sudan (except the non-Muslim population of southern Sudan), southern Egypt, the Red Sea coast of Ethiopia, northern Kenya, northern Nigeria and some parts of Mali. The most recent estimate of women mutilated is 74 million.[7]

Ethnic groups closely situated geographically are by no means affected in the same way: For example, in Kenya, the Kikuyu practise excision and the Luo do not; in Nigeria, the Yoruba, the Ibo and the Hausa do, but not the Nupes or the Fulanis; in Senegal, the Woloff have no practice of mutilation. There are many other examples.

As the subject of female genital mutilation began to be eligible at least for discussion, reports of genital operations on non-consenting females have appeared from many unexpected parts of the world. During the 1980s, women in Sweden were shocked by accounts of mutilations performed in Swedish hospitals on daughters of immigrants. In France, women from Mali and Senegal have been reported to bring an *exciseuse* to France once a year to operate on their daughters in their apartments.[8] In July 1982 a Malian infant died of an excision performed by a professional circumciser, who then fled to Mali. In the same year, reports appeared in the British press that excision for non-medical reasons had been performed in a London private clinic.

Legislation

In Africa. Formal legislation forbidding genital mutilation, or more precisely infibulation, exists in the Sudan. A law first enacted in 1946 allows for a term of imprisonment up to five years and/or a fine. However, it is not an offence (under Article 284 of the Sudan Penal Code for 1974) "merely to remove the free and projecting part of the clitoris."

Many references have been made to legislation in Egypt, but after researching the available materials, all that has been traced is a resolution signed by the Minister of Health in 1959, recommending only partial clitoridectomy for those who want an operation, to be performed only by doctors.[9]

In late 1978, largely due to the efforts of the Somali Women's Democratic Organization (SWDO), Somalia set up a commission to abolish infibulation. In 1988 at a seminar held in Mogadishu, it was recommended that SWDO should propose a bill to the competent authorities to eradicate all forms of female genital mutilation.

In September 1982, President Arap Moi took steps to ban the practices in Kenya, following reports of the deaths of fourteen children after excision. A traditional practitioner found to be carrying out this operation can be arrested under the Chiefs Act and brought before the law.

Official declarations against female genital mutilation were made by the late Captain Thomas Sankara and Abdou Diouf, the heads of state in Burkina Faso and Senegal respectively.

In Western Countries. A law prohibiting female excision, whether consent has been given or not, came into force in Sweden in July 1982, carrying a two-year sentence. In Norway, in 1985, all hospitals were alerted to the practice. Belgium has incorporated a ban on the practice. Several states in the U.S.A. have incorporated female genital mutilation into their criminal code.

In the U.K., specific legislation prohibiting female circumcision came into force at the end of 1985. A person found guilty of an offence is liable to up to five years' imprisonment or to a fine. Female genital mutilation has been incorporated into child protection procedures at local authority levels. As yet no person has been committed in the English courts for female circumcision but since 1989 there have been at least seven local authority legal interventions which prevented parents from sexually mutilating their daughters or wards.

France does not have specific legislation on female sexual mutilation but under Article 312–3 of the French Penal Code, female genital mutilation can be considered as a criminal offence. Under this code, anybody who exercises violence or seriously assaults a child less than fifteen years old can be punished with imprisonment from ten to twenty years, if the act of violence results in a mutilation, amputation of a limb, the loss of an eye or other parts of the body or has unintentionally caused the death of the child.

In 1989, a mother who had paid a traditional woman exciser to excise her week-old daughter, in 1984, was convicted and given a three-year suspended jail sentence. In 1991 a traditional exciser was jailed for five years in France.

Contemporary Practices

Opinions are very divided as to whether the practice is disappearing because of legislation or social and economic changes. Esther Ogunmodede, for instance, believes that in Nigeria, Africa's most populous country, the tradition is disappearing but extremely slowly, with millions of excisions still taking place. She reports that in areas where the operations are done on girls of marriageable age, they are "running away from home to avoid the razor." This confirms Fran Hosken's assertion that operations are being done at earlier and earlier ages, in order that the children should be "too young to resist." Fran Hosken does not think that the custom is dying out, and she indisputably has the best published range of information concerning all the countries where the practice is known.

An interesting development took place in Ethiopia during the years of civil warfare which only ended in 1991. When the Eritrean People's Liberation Front (EPLF) occupied large areas from January 1977 to December 1978, among many other reforms they categorically and successfully forbade genital mutilation and forced marriage. In fact, the reason given for the large numbers of young women in the EPLF army was that they were running away from home in other parts of Ethiopia to avoid forced marriage and the knife.[10] Although it appears the practice continues in remote areas, because the consciousness of Eritrean women has changed dramatically during the war years, it is easier to persuade men and women to let go of this practice.

Since 1983, the number of educational programmes initiated to raise public awareness of the health risk associated with female genital mutilation at local, national and international levels have increased. The media have played a major role in bringing this issue from the domestic to the public domain. As a result of these efforts it can be said that the taboo surrounding even public mention of the practice has at last been broken. There is an increase in public awareness of the harmful effects of female genital mutilation.

It has been noted that female genital mutilation is becoming unpopular amongst the urban elite in some African countries. In Sierra Leone, for example, Koso-Thomas claims that urban men are willing to marry uncircumcised women, in particular when the marriage is not pre-arranged.[11]

In general, among urban educated women, reasons often cited against female genital mutilation include the pointlessness of mutilation, health risks and reduction of sexual sensitivity. The last reason points to a changing attitude towards women's fundamental human rights amongst urban Africans.

In the main, the practice continues to be widespread among large sectors and groups within Africa. Those in favour of the practice are noted in the 1986 UN study to be a passive majority who refer back to traditional society, without necessarily sharing that society's values.[12] In some cases, the practice appears to be spreading to population groups who traditionally never practised female genital mutilation, as observed with city women in Wau, Sudan, who regard it as fashionable, and among converted Muslim women in southern Sudan who marry northern Sudanese men.[13] Furthermore, even in areas where some groups are turning against the practice, the absolute numbers affected may be increasing. Rapid population growth in Africa means greater numbers of female children are born, who in turn are exposed to the risk of mutilation.

THE ISSUES

Female genital mutilation is a complex issue, for it involves deep-seated cultural practices which affect millions of people. However, it can be divided into (at least) four distinct issues.

Rights of Women

Female genital mutilation is an extreme example of the general subjugation of women, sufficiently extreme and horrifying to make women and men question the basis of what is done to women, what women have accepted and why, in the name of society and tradition.

The burning of Indian widows and the binding of the feet of Chinese girl children are other striking examples, sharp enough and strange enough to throw a spotlight on other less obvious ways in which women the world over submit to oppression. It is important to remember that all these practices are, or were, preserved under centuries of tradition, and that foot-binding was only definitively stopped by a massive social and political revolution (replacing the many traditions which it swept away by offering an entirely new social system, revolutionary in many aspects: land ownership, class system, education, sex equality, etc.) which had been preceded by years of patient work by reformers.

Thus, to be successful, campaigns on female genital mutilation should consider carefully not only eliminating but also replacing the custom. (The example of Eritrea, previously quoted, is illuminating here.) Furthermore, such success may be predicated on long-term changes in attitudes and ideologies by both men and women.

A major international expression of the goal of equal rights for women was taken in December 1979, when the U.N. General Assembly adopted the Convention on the Elimination of All Forms of Discrimination Against Women. This came into force in September 1981. The comprehensive convention calls for equal rights for women, regardless of their marital status, in all fields: political, economic, social, cultural and civil. Article 5(a) obliges states' parties to take:

All appropriate measures to modify the social and cultural patterns of conduct of men and women, with a view to achieving the elimination of prejudices and customary and all other practices which are based on the idea of the inferiority or superiority of either of the sexes or on stereotyped roles for men and women.

To succeed in abolishing such practices will demand fundamental attitudinal shifts in the way that society perceives the human rights of women. The starting point for change should be educational programmes that assist women to recognize their fundamental human rights. This is where UNESCO, the U.N. Centre for Human Rights and international agencies could help by supporting awareness-building programmes.

Rights of Children

An adult is free to submit her or himself to a ritual or tradition, but a child, having no formed judgement, does not consent but simply undergoes the operation (which in this case is irrevocable) while she is totally vulnerable. The descriptions available of the reactions of children—panic and shock from extreme pain, biting through the tongue, convulsions, necessity for six adults to hold down an eight-year-old, and death—indicate a practice comparable to torture.

Many countries signatory to Article 5 of the Universal Declaration of Human Rights (which provides that no one shall be subjected to torture, or to cruel, inhuman or degrading treatment) violate that clause. Those violations are discussed and sometimes condemned by various U.N. commissions. Female genital mutilation, however, is a question of torture inflicted not on adults but on girl children, and the reasons given are not concerned with either political conviction or military necessity but are solely in the name of tradition.

The Declaration of the Rights of Children, adopted in 1959 by the General Assembly, asserts that children should have the possibility to develop physically in a healthy and normal way in conditions of liberty and dignity. They should have adequate medical attention, and be protected from all forms of cruelty.

It is the opinion of Renée Bridel, of the Fédération Internationale des Femmes de Carrières Juridiques, that "One cannot but consider Member States which tolerate these practices as infringing their obligations as assumed under the terms of the Charter [of the U.N.].[14]

In September 1990, the United Nations Convention on the Rights of the Child went into force. It became part of international human rights law. Under Article 24(3) it states that: "States Parties shall take all effective and appropriate measures with a view to abolishing traditional practices prejudicial to the health of children." This crucial article should not merely remain a paper provision, to be given lip service by those entrusted to implement it. Members of the U.N. should work at translating its provisions into specific implementation programmes at grass-roots level. Much could be learned (by African states in particular) from countries with established child protection systems.

The Right to Good Health

No reputable medical practitioner insists that mutilation is good for the physical or mental health of girls and women, and a growing number offer research indicating its grave permanent damage to health and underlining the risks of death. Medical facts, carefully explained, may be the way to discourage the practice, since these facts are almost always the contrary of what is believed, and can be shown and demonstrated.

Those U.N. agencies and government departments specifically entrusted with the health needs of women and children must realize that it is their responsibility to support positive and specific preventative programmes against female genital mutilation, for while the practice continues the quality of life and health will inevitably suffer. However, this approach, if presented out of context, ignores the force of societal pressures which drive women to perform these operations, regardless of risk, in order to guarantee marriage for their daughters, and to conform to severe codes of female behaviour laid down by male-dominated societies.

The Right to Development

The practice of female genital mutilation must be seen in the context of underdevelopment,[15] and the realities of life for the most vulnerable and exploited sectors—women and children. International political and economic forces have frequently prevented development programmes from meeting the basic needs of rural populations. With no access to education or resources, and with no effective power base, the rural and urban poor cling to traditions as a survival mechanism in time of socio-economic change.

In societies where marriage for a woman is her only means of survival, and where some form of excision is a prerequisite for marriage, persuading her to relinquish the practice for herself or for her children is an extraordinarily difficult task. Female (and some male) African analysts of development strategies are today constantly urging that the overall deteriorating conditions in which poor women live be made a major focus for change, for unless development affects their lives for the better, traditional practices are unlikely to change.

DIRECTIONS FOR THE FUTURE

The mutilation of female genitals has been practised in many areas for centuries. The greatest determination, combined with sensitivity and understanding of local conditions, will be needed if it is to be abolished. In every country and region where operations are carried out, the situation is different, as is the political will, whether at local or national levels. In Western countries the way forward is relatively clear. In Africa the problem is more profound and the economic and political conditions vastly more difficult, while international agencies have hardly begun to explore their potential role.

What all three have in common is that, to date, nearly all programmes have been individual or *ad hoc* efforts, with little integration into other structures, with minimal evaluation or monitoring, and lacking in long-term goals and strategies. To achieve real change will require more resources, more detailed planning, and more real, sustained commitment from governments and international organizations.

CRITICAL THINKING QUESTIONS

1. What are the four types of female genital mutilation? How widespread are these practices?
2. What do Dorkenoo and Elworthy mean when they describe female genital mutilation as a "complex" issue? Do they feel that this practice can be abolished or not?
3. Many Western countries have denounced female genital mutilation as barbaric. But what about comparable practices in Canada and other Western nations? Even though they are voluntary, are silicone breast transplants, facelifts, or liposuction more "civilized" in making women's bodies more acceptable to men?

NOTES

1. Fran Hosken, *The Hosken Report—Genital and Sexual Mutilation of Females* (third enlarged/revised edition, Autumn, 1982, published by Women's International Network News, 187 Grant St, Lexington, Mass. 02173, USA). This is the most detailed and comprehensive collection of information available.
2. The consequences of sexual mutilations on the health of women have been studied by Dr. Ahmed Abu-el-Futuh Shandall, Lecturer in the Department of Obstetrics and Gynaecology at the University of Khartoum, in a paper entitled, "Circumcision and Infibulation of Females" (*Sudanese Medical Journal,* Vol. 5, No. 4, 1967); and by Dr. J.A. Verzin, in an article entitled "The Sequelae of Female Circumcision," (*Tropical Doctor,* October, 1975). A bibliography on the subject has been prepared by Dr. R. Cook for the World Health Organization.
3. Readers interested to read more about research on the sexual experience of circumcised women may want to read Hanny Lightfoot-Klein, *Prisoners of Ritual: An Odyssey into Female Genital Mutilation in Africa* (New York, The Haworth Press, 1989).
4. These feelings of rejection are clearly articulated by Kenyan girls in "The Silence over Female Circumcision in Kenya," in *Viva,* August, 1978.
5. Q.R. Ghadially, "Ali for 'Izzat': The Practice of Female Circumcision among Bohra Muslims," *Manushi,* No. 66, New Delhi, India, 1991.
6. See map of Childhood Mortality in the World, 1977 (Health Sector Policy Paper, World Bank, Washington, D.C., 1980).
7. See Hosken for details and estimates of ethnic groups involved.
8. *F Magazine,* No. 4, March, 1979 and No. 31, October, 1980.
9. Marie Assaad, *Female Circumcision in Egypt—Current Research and Social Implications* (American University in Cairo, 1979), p. 12.
10. "Social Transformation of Eritrean Society," paper presented to the People's Tribunal, Milan, 24–26 May 1980, by Mary Dines of Rights and Justice.
11. Koso-Thomas, *The Circumcision of Women: A Strategy for Elimination* (London, Zed Books, 1987).
12. UN Commission on Human Rights, Report of the Working Group on Traditional Practices Affecting Women and Children, 1986.
13. Ellen Ismail et al., *Women of the Sudan* (Bendestorf, Germany, EIS, 1990).
14. *L'enfant mutilé* by Renée Bridel, delegate of the FIFCJ to the UN, Geneva, 1978. See also Raqiya Haji Dualeh Abdalla, *Sisters in Affliction* (London, Zed Press, 1982) and Asma El Dareer, *Woman Why Do You Weep?* (London, Zed Press, 1982).
15. Belkis Woldes Giorgis, *Female Circumcision in Africa,* ST/ECA/ATRCW 81/02.

49

The Vertical Mosaic: An Analysis of Social Class and Power in Canada

John Porter

In this chapter from the highly regarded book The Vertical Mosaic, *Porter highlights the importance of studying Canadian social class structures. Porter traces the Canadian belief that there are no clearly defined classes in Canada back to the frontier environment and the settlement of Canada.*

THE CANADIAN MIDDLE CLASS IMAGE

One of the most persistent images that Canadians have of their society is that it has no classes. This image becomes translated into the assertion that Canadians are all relatively equal in their possessions, in the amount of money they earn, and in the opportunities which they and their children have to get on in the world. An important element in this image of classlessness is that, with the absence of formal aristocracy and aristocratic institutions, Canada is a society in which equalitarian values have asserted themselves over authoritarian values. Canada, it is thought, shares not only a continent with the United States, but also a democratic ideology which rejects the historical class and power structures of Europe.

Source: From *The Vertical Mosaic* by John Porter. Toronto: University of Toronto Press, 1965, pp. 3–6. Reprinted with the permission of the publisher.

Social images are one thing and social realities another. Yet the two are not completely separate. Social images are not entirely fictional characters with only a coincidental likeness to a real society, living or dead. Often the images can be traced to an earlier historical period of the society, its golden age perhaps, which, thanks to the historians, is held up, long after it has been transformed into something else, as a model way of life. As well as their historical sources, images can be traced to their contemporary creators, particularly in the world of the mass media and popular culture. When a society's writers, journalists, editors, and other image-creators are a relatively small and closely linked group, and have more or less the same social background, the images they produce can, because they are consistent, appear to be much more true to life than if their group were larger, less cohesive, and more heterogeneous in composition.

The historical source of the image of a classless Canada is the equality among pioneers in the frontier environment of the last century. In the early part of the [twentieth] century there was a similar equality of status among those who were settlers in the west, although, as we shall see, these settlers were by no means treated equally. A rural, agricultural, primary producing society is a much less differentiated society than one which has highly concentrated industries in large cities. Equality in the rural society may be much more apparent than real, but the rural environment has been for Canada an important source of the image of equality. Later we shall examine more closely how the historical image has become out of date with the transformation of Canadian society from the rural to the urban type.

Although the historical image of rural equality lingers, it has gradually given way in the urban industrial setting to an image of a middle level classlessness in which there is a general uniformity of possessions. For families these possessions include a separate dwelling with an array of electrical equipment, a car, and perhaps a summer cottage. Family members, together or as individuals, engage in a certain amount of ritualistic behaviour in churches and service clubs. Modern advertising has done much to standardize the image of middle class consumption levels and middle class behaviour. Consumers' magazines are devoted to the task of constructing the ideal way of life through articles on child-rearing, home-making, sexual behaviour, health, sports, and hobbies. Often, too, corporations which do not produce family commodities directly will have large advertisements to demonstrate how general social well-being at this middle level is an outcome of their own operations.

That there is neither very rich nor very poor in Canada is an important part of the image. There are no barriers to opportunity. Education is free. Therefore, making use of it is largely a question of personal ambition. Even university education is available to all, except that it may require for some a little more summer work and thrift. There

is a view widely held by many university graduates that they, and most other graduates, have worked their way through college. Consequently it is felt anyone else can do the same.

In some superficial respects the image of middle class uniformity may appear plausible. The main values of the society are concerned with the consumption of commodities, and in the so-called affluence that has followed World War II there seem to have been commodities for everybody, except, perhaps, a small group of the permanently poor at the bottom. Credit facilities are available for large numbers of low-income families, enabling them, too, to be consumers of commodities over and above the basic necessities of life. The vast array of credit facilities, some of them extraordinarily ingenious, have inequalities built into them, in that the cost of borrowing money varies with the amount already possessed. There are vast differences in the quality of goods bought by the middle income levels and the lower income levels. One commodity, for instance, which low-income families can rarely purchase is privacy, particularly the privacy of a house to themselves. It is perhaps the value of privacy and the capacity to afford it which has become the dividing line between the real and the apparent middle class.

If low-income families achieve high consumption levels it is usually through having more than one income earner in the household. Often this is the wife and mother, but it may be an older child who has left school, and who is expected to contribute to the family budget. Alternatively, high consumption levels may be achieved at a cost in leisure. Many low-income family heads have two jobs, a possibility which has arisen with the shorter working day and the five-day week. This "moonlighting," as it is called in labour circles, tends to offset the progress which has been made in raising the level of wages and reducing the hours of work. There is no way of knowing how extensive "moonlighting" is, except that we know that trade unions denounce it as a practice which tends to take away the gains which have been obtained for workers. For large segments of the population, therefore, a high level of consumption is obtained by means which are alien to a true middle class standard. [When]…we…examine closely the distribution of income, we …see what a small proportion of Canadian families were able to live a middle class style of life in the middle 1950s, the high tide of post-war affluence.

At the high end of the social class spectrum, also in contrast to the middle level image, are the families of great wealth and influence. They are not perhaps as ostentatious as the very wealthy of other societies, and Canada has no "celebrity world" with which these families must compete for prestige in the way Mills has suggested is important for the very rich in American society.[1]

Almost every large Canadian city has its wealthy and prominent families of several generations. They have their own social life, their children go to private schools, they have their clubs and associations, and they take on the charitable and philanthropic roles which have so long been the "duty" of those of high status. Although this upper class is always being joined by the new rich, it still contributes, as we shall see later, far more than its proportionate share to the elite of big business.

The concentration of wealth in the upper classes is indicated by the fact that in Canada in 1955 the top one per cent of income recipients received about 40 per cent of all income from dividends.

Images which conflict with the one of middle class equality rarely find expression, partly because the literate middle class is both the producer and the consumer of the image. Even at times in what purports to be serious social analysis, middle class intellectuals project the image of their own class onto the social classes above and below them. There is scarcely any critical analysis of Canadian social life upon which a conflicting image could be based. The idea of class differences has scarcely entered into the stream of Canadian academic writing despite the fact that class differences stand in the way of implementing one of the most important values of western society, that is equality.[2] The fact, which we shall see later, that Canada draws its intellectuals either from abroad or from its own middle class, means that there is almost no one producing a view of the world which reflects the experience of the poor or the underprivileged. It was as though they did not exist. It is the nature of these class differences and their consequences for Canadian society that [we]…seek to explore.

Closely related to differences in class levels are differences in the exercising of power and decision-making in the society: Often it is thought that once a society becomes an electoral democracy based on universal suffrage, power becomes diffused throughout the general population so that everyone participates somehow in the selection of social goals. There is, however, a whole range of institutional resistances to the transfer of power to a democratic political system.…[3]

CRITICAL THINKING QUESTIONS

1. Is Porter's assertion that Canadians believe they exist within a classless society still valid today? Why or why not?

2. Porter's work was published in 1965. Do any of his observations continue to be revealing in a contemporary analysis of Canadian society?

3. According to Porter, does democracy ensure the equal allocation of power and influence within society? Why or why not?

NOTES

1. C. W. Mills, *The Power Elite* (New York, 1956), chap. 4.

2. Nor does class appear as a theme in Canadian literature. See R. L. McDougall, "The Dodo and the Cruising Auk," *Canadian Literature*, no. 18 (Autumn 1963).

3. For a comparative study of social mobility see S. M. Lipset and R. Bendix, *Social Mobility in Industrial Society* (Berkeley, 1959).

50

Does the Vertical Mosaic Still Exist? Ethnicity and Income in Canada, 1991

Jason Z. Lian and
David Ralph Matthews

Social Stratification

CLASSIC

CONTEMPORARY

CROSS-CULTURAL

Lian and Matthews review Porter's work and explore it using contemporary data. The authors find that race (particularly visible minorities) has become the fundamental basis for income inequality in Canada.

This paper updates our knowledge about the relationship between ethnicity and social class in Canada using *The Public Use Microdata File for Individuals* drawn from the 1991 Census of Canada. We provide three levels of analysis. First, we examine the relationship between ethnicity and education by ethnic group. Second, we examine the "return to education" in terms of income for those of various ethnic groups. Third, we use log-linear regression to examine the relationship between ethnicity, education, and income while controlling for the effects of a variety of other social variables. We find that, at most

*This is a revised version of a paper presented at the Canadian Ethnic Studies Association, Biennial Meeting, Gimli, Manitoba, October 1995. We thank Margaret Denton, John Fox, and Wulong Gu for helpful suggestions and comments. The manuscript of this article was submitted in February 1997 and accepted in July 1997.

Source: Jason Z. Lian and David Matthews. 1998. Does the Vertical Mosaic Still Exist? Ethnicity and Income in Canada, 1991. *Canadian Review of Sociology and Anthropology*, 35(4), 461–81. Reprinted by permission of the Canadian Sociology and Anthropology Association.

educational levels, Canadians of French ethnicity now earn significantly more than those of British ethnicity when other variables are controlled. With this exception, for those of European ethnic backgrounds there are now virtually no significant differences in income within educational levels when other social variables are controlled. However, those who belong to visible minorities have significantly lower incomes than other Canadians at all educational levels. Race is now the fundamental basis of income inequality in Canada.

In 1965, John Porter described Canadian society as a "vertical mosaic" stratified along ethnic lines (1965: 60–103). Porter argued that the British and French, as the first ethnic groups to come into Canada, became the "charter groups" and to a considerable extent dictated the circumstances under which other ethnic groups were subsequently permitted to enter. He argued that "entrance status" was generally granted to those of other ethnic groups who were willing to accept lower level occupational roles (63–73) and that, as a result, "immigration and ethnic affiliation... have been important factors in the formation of social classes in Canada" (73). Porter used census data from the 1931 to 1961 period to demonstrate that the British dominated the French in all of the most prestigious occupational categories, and that other ethnic groups were generally distributed in a hierarchy below them.

Since then, considerable effort has been expended by researchers to support or refute Porter's thesis and to examine the extent to which ethnic social class mobility has occurred as previous immigrants overcame their "entrance status" and moved up the social class hierarchy. Proponents of the vertical mosaic thesis have argued that differences in occupational status among Canadian ethnic groups remain substantial. Over the past thirty years, they have demonstrated that, for the two charter groups, the occupational status of the British has remained significantly higher than that of the French (Royal Commission, 1969: 34–45; Breton & Roseborough, 1971; Boyd et al., 1981). They have argued that among other groups, Jews and those from the north and west of Europe are generally in favourable positions, South Europeans and visible minorities are generally in disadvantaged positions, and Aboriginal Peoples are at the bottom of the Canadian occupational hierarchy (Reitz, 1980; Porter, 1985; Jabbra & Cosper, 1988; Li, 1988; Lautard & Guppy, 1990). Thus, in 1984, Lautard and Loree could still claim that "occupational inequality is still substantial enough to justify the use of the concept 'vertical mosaic' to characterize this aspect of ethnic relations in Canada" (343).

In contrast, a number of other researchers have argued that the influence of ethnicity in the process of social mobility was and/or is minimal in Canada, and that ethnic affiliation did not operate as a significant block to social mobility as Porter had suggested. Most such works have examined the relationship between ethnicity and occupation, while controlling for a range of other variables. Using such methods, they have argued that the association between ethnicity and

occupational status was minimal and declining (Pineo, 1976; Darroch, 1979; Ornstein, 1981) and that the contention of the vertical mosaic thesis that the status of immigrants groups has been rigidly preserved is "patently false" (Tepperman, 1975: 156). Other researchers have suggested that a convergence process in occupational status among ethnic groups in Canada has become more apparent since Porter's original analysis (Reitz, 1980: 150–53), the relationship between ethnic origin and class position has been in flux (Nakhaie, 1951), and that gains by non-charter groups have been significantly greater than those of the charter groups (Boyd et al., 1981; Pineo & Porter, 1985: 382–83). Porter, himself, has argued that the situation he described in 1965 may have been in existence only for a relatively short period in Canadian history (Pineo & Porter, 1985: 390). It is also argued that, to the extent that any ethnic status hierarchy remains, Porter's status hierarchy of ethnic groups has changed dramatically with the British dropping from the top to the middle and the Asians moving to the top with the Jews (Herberg, 1990). As a result, it has been stated recently that ethnicity is no longer a drawback for social mobility in Canada (Isajiw, Sev'er & Driedger, 1993).

In many such works, the relation of education and ethnicity has come under considerable scrutiny. Thus, proponents of the ethnic inequality thesis have argued that the Canadian education system has been a mechanism to reproduce social inequality (Shamai, 1992: 44–5) and that educational opportunity was not equally accessible to all groups (Li, 1988: 77–96). Alternatively, those who have been critical of the ethnic inequality thesis have argued that there is little evidence of ethnic inequality in education in Canada and that a *"contest-achieved"* system of status attainment is operating (Herberg, 1990). Indeed, Porter was himself involved in work which argued that non-charter groups have gained significantly in educational achievement compared to the British

(Pineo & Porter, 1985: 384) and that the educational system has worked to help minority Canadians overcome the disadvantages of their background (391).

The general conclusion of this body of work would seem to be that there is a collapsing of the vertical mosaic. However, there is growing evidence (see Li, 1988; Reitz, 1980; Agocs & Boyd, 1993) that Canada has retained what Geschwender and Guppy have called a "colour-coded vertical mosaic" (1995: 2). Such works suggest that, whereas ethnic stratification has lessened among white European groups, differences between racial groups have persisted and that, in effect, Canada's mosaic has been reduced to a division based principally on skin colour (1995: 2).

This paper will examine the evidence for and against ethnic inequality in Canada with respect to income distribution, using *The Public Use Microdata Files for Individuals* (PUMFI) provided by Statistics Canada, which constitutes a 3% sample of the 1991 Census. Such files have been made available since 1971, but the 1991 PUMFI provides both a more extensive list of ethnic groups and a more detailed categorization of other variables that may be employed as controls than were available in previous issues. Thus, the present paper is able to provide more current information on the relationship between ethnicity and income than most previous studies, and also is able to identify ethnicity more precisely and use more stringent control variables in the analysis.

To carry out the analysis we have used those respondents in the PUMFI who were in the "working population," and from this group have eliminated those respondents for whom data were not available or who had zero or negative earnings.[1] These latter reductions reduce the number of respondents in the working population sample by 4.78%, nearly half of whom had zero or negative earnings in 1990. As a result of these adjustments, the average earnings of the sample increased by approximately 4%, but the ethnic composition

changed very little.... Thus, for purposes of the present study which focuses on ethnicity, our sample was not affected significantly.

ETHNICITY AND EDUCATION

In any study of ethnic stratification and mobility, education is seen as a critically important intervening variable between ethnicity and income. A fundamental question in such studies is whether educational achievement is distributed equally among ethnic groups. Earlier we noted the diverging positions on this subject in Canada—some argued that the educational system has functioned to reproduce the existing socio-economic hierarchy in favour of the dominant groups (Li, 1988: 73–7; Shamai, 1992: 53–5), and others argued that the educational system has functioned as a source of upward mobility for Canadian minority groups since the early decades of this century (Herberg, 1990).

It is not possible to test this issue fully using data from a single time period. However, data from the 1991 PUMFI show a considerable variation in education among ethnic groups when compared with the Canadian average and this variation remains even when one separates out the Canadian born from the foreign born. This indicates that, among native-born Canadians, educational achievement is unevenly distributed by ethnicity....

In 1991, approximately 30% of the employed labour force in Canada had less than secondary education, just over 54% had secondary or non-university post-secondary education, and almost 17% had post-secondary education. About two-thirds of the European groups and half of the visible minority groups were close to this Canadian average. However, several Southern European groups (Italians, Greeks, Portuguese), Vietnamese, and Aboriginal Peoples had proportionally more persons with this lower educational level while Arabs, West Asians, Jews and Filipinos were under-represented in the lower educational groups.

At the other extreme, in terms of post-secondary (university) education most European groups were around the national average, Poles were moderately above and Jews were nearly three times likely to have a university degree than were those of European origin *per se*. With the exception of the Black/Caribbean and Aboriginal groups who ranked substantially below the national level, the remaining visible minority groups had high rates of university education. This was particularly the case for those of Arab, West Asian, South Asian, Chinese, Filipino and Other East and Southeast Asian ethnic backgrounds.

To some considerable degree this latter finding is a reflection of Canadian immigration policy since the 1970s, which has favoured those with high levels of education and training. Thus, Arab, West Asian, South Asian, Filipino, and Vietnamese foreign born were generally better educated than their Canadian-born counterparts. This relationship held for most other groups with the notable exception of the Greek, Italian, and Balkan ethnic groups among whom the native born were generally better educated than recent immigrants.

EDUCATION AND INCOME DIFFERENCES AMONG ETHNIC GROUPS

While differences in education by ethnic group, particularly among the Canadian-born, are an indication of possible ethnic discrimination, the more significant indication is whether the "returns for education" are also unequal among ethnic groups. That is, does similar education (at whatever level) generate significantly different incomes among the ethnic groups?...

At the national level, those with secondary education earned about 50% more than those without secondary education and those with university education earned about 150% more than those without secondary education.... However, there are extreme ethnic differences at all three educational levels.

The following analyses are all based on comparisons with the national average for each of the educational categories. Looking first at the two "charter groups," workers of British origin with non-secondary education earned 3% more than the national average for this educational level, those with secondary education earned 7% more, while those with university education earned 8% more. In comparison, workers of French ethnicity with non-secondary education earned 12% more than the national average, those with secondary education earned 1% less and those with university education earned 4% more. Thus, in contrast to Porter's finding that the French were rewarded significantly less than the British for their educational achievement, at the lower educational level they now have a significant edge over the British, and are above the national average in income at the higher educational levels.

Those of Western European ethnic background earned considerably higher incomes than the Canadian average in each of the education categories, the exception being university educated persons of Dutch and German ethnic backgrounds who earned only marginally more. Eastern Europeans also tended to earn more than the Canadian average, with Hungarians and Ukrainians earning substantially more at all levels. Persons of Polish ethnicity with lower as well as middle levels of education earned more than average, but better educated persons of Polish ethnicity earned less.

For those whose Jewish ethnic background was recorded, those with the lowest level of education earned 9% more than the Canadian average income for that level, while those with university education earned 19% more than the Canadian university educated average income. However, those with secondary education earned 4% less than the average Canadians at their educational level.

The pattern for Southern Europeans is mixed. At the lowest educational level, most of these ethnic groups earned above the Canadian average income with those of Italian, Portuguese, Greek, and Balkan origin earning considerably higher than that average. However, at higher educational levels Southern Europeans were generally disadvantaged.

However, it is when we consider visible minorities that the largest discrepancies between education and income are apparent. At the lower education levels all 10 visible minority groups earned less than an average Canadian with similar education, ranging from 5% less for those of Arab ethnicity to 33% less for those of Filipino ethnic background and 42% less for Aboriginal Peoples. Likewise, among those with secondary education, all 10 visible minority groups earned substantially less than the comparable Canadian average. Similarly, amongst those with post-secondary education, while those of Black and Chinese ethnicity earned only somewhat less than the Canadian average, those in the other eight visible minority groups received earning[s] substantially below that level.

The overall conclusion to be drawn from these two tables is that persons of European background generally receive above average income for their educational level with the exception of persons with higher education from some Eastern and Southern European ethnic groups. Indeed, persons from many such ethnic backgrounds now receive incomes relative to education that are higher than for either of the two "charter groups." *However, for visible minorities a very different picture emerges. For all visible ethnic groups and at all educational levels, the rewards for education are substantially below the Canadian average.*

ETHNICITY AND INCOME DIFFERENCES WITHIN EDUCATIONAL CATEGORIES, TAKING INTO ACCOUNT OTHER VARIABLES

Although the preceding analysis has provided strong indications that the rewards for education vary by ethnic group and particularly that workers of visible minorities receive comparatively less than other workers with similar education, it is possible that these results are not due to ethnicity *per se* but to a range of other factors such as the age composition, marital status, or

period of immigration of workers from various ethnic groups. Thus, if one wants to measure directly the effect of ethnicity on earnings within educational categories, it is necessary to take into account the effect of these other earnings-related variables.

To do this, we developed a semi-logarithmic regression model of earnings determination with interaction terms constructed of ethnicity and education, controlling for gender; age and age squared; marital status; province of residence; metropolitan versus non-metropolitan area of residence; geographic mobility in the past five years; period of immigration; knowledge of official languages; occupational level; industrial sector; weeks worked and weeks worked squared; and full versus part-time weeks worked. Controlling for these factors in a semi-logarithmic regression yields an adjusted R square of 0.58007, indicating that 58% of the variations in log earnings have been accounted for by the variables included in the model.

Because of the dominant position of the British in Canadian society both numerically and socio-economically, we have used them as the base line category in the regression for an estimation of the net log earnings of the other ethnic groups at each educational level. While persons of British ethnicity with "no degree, certificate, or diploma" were used as the reference category for all other interactive categories of ethnicity and education in the regression, for easy interpretation, we have converted the partial coefficients for the other ethnic groups as deviations from those of their category of "no degree, certificate, or diploma" for the British. The coefficients derived in this manner have been converted into percentages and displayed in Table 50.1

As an example of how to interpret the table, we would note that the 3.1% in the cell for French with "no degree, certificate, or diploma" indicates that workers of French ethnic origin earned 3.1% more than their British counterparts with comparable education when all the dimensions in our model have been taken into account. Similarly,

TABLE 50.1: Adjusted Earnings[1] of Persons of Different Ethnic Origins[2] as Percentage Differences from Those of Persons of British Origin by Educational Level, Canada, 1990

				Highest Degree Obtained						
Ethnic Origin	No Degree, Certificate, or Diploma	High School Graduation Certificate	Trades Certificate	Other Non-University Certificate	University Certificate below Bachelor Level	Bachelor's Degree(s)	University Certificate above Bachelor Level	Master's Degree(s)	Earned Doctorate	Degree in Medicine[3]
British[4]		13.2***	16.8***	21.3***	27.3***	39.6***	47.4***	58.3***	76.6***	141.7***
French	3 1**	1.7**	3 0**	5.3**	8 1**	2.3*	2.8	1.2	5.4	4.2
Dutch	0.5	2.8	1.6	-2.0	-18.4***	-3.9	-3.9	-12.4*	1.9	-40.6**
German	3.7**	-0.5	-2.1	0.7	3.7	-2.6	-3.4	-7.0	-3.4	-14.7
Other W European	14.0**	5.2	1.0	14.3**	16.2	0.9	-7.4	2.4	6.1	-24.4
Hungarian	-2.4	-2.1	-1.3	-11.3**	-18.7	-2.0	4.4	11.4	-17.0	8.3
Polish	-3.6	-1.1	1.8	1.1	-19.2*	0.6	-3.0	-14.4**	-6.1	-12.5
Ukrainian	2.7	3.1	2.7	4.0**	-14.4**	5.6*	-2.2	-3.4	-13.8	6.3
Balkan	2.4	-3.6	-2.0	5.3	4.6	-2.1	-5.6	-5.8	-8.6	-3.4
Greek	-6.3**	-6.6**	0.4	-1.7	-32.5**	-9.3	-15.7	-2.4	-25.9	-50.1**
Italian	-0.6	2.7**	-0.0	7.1**	8.3	-1.1	-2.1	3.6	-1.8	-26.4*
Portuguese	11.0**	3.1	4.8	2.8	-22.5**	-4.9	5.3	0.6	–	41.7
Spanish	4.1	-14.4**	0.7	-6.0	-13.1	-14.7	0.5	-20.2	48.5	14.6
Jewish	21.9**	8.0**	3.3	3.1	3.2	4.4	6.7	0.7	6.7	-2.2
Arab	1.4	-6.2*	-12.6**	1.6	-22.7**	-17.8**	-22.3**	-18.1**	1.6	-27.7**
West Asian	-5.4	-10.4**	-5.3	-0.6	-10.2	-7.5	-15.6	-18.2**	-25.7	-30.5*
South Asian	2.9	-3.9*	-8.6**	-4.1	-0.7	-17.7**	-12.8*	-18.9**	-6.8	-15.9*
Chinese	-4.4**	5 3**	-3.3	-5.6**	-6.6	-7.3**	-14.1**	-10.3**	-26.3**	-15.2*
Filipino	-6.4	-2.1	-12.5**	-8.2*	-7.5	-12.4**	-12.5	-20.9*	–	13.0
Vietnamese	0.8	-11.9**	-19.7**	3.2	-19.3**	-12.7*	-39.2**	-6.9	-7.0	-42.7**
Other E & SE Asian	-4.2	-10.2**	-3.7	-6.8	20.2*	-14.6**	-10.1	-12.1	-27.5	-35.1**
Latin American	3.7	-11.7**	-2.3	-29.8**	-7.8	-24.4**	-31.1**	-18.7	-30.4	-40.6
Black	-8.1**	-3.1	-3.3	-10.4**	-3.7	-10.0**	10.6	-12.4	-10.3	-10.2
Aboriginal	-18.8**	-16.0**	-20.0**	-24.7**	-1.9	-8.0	-24.2	-20.2	-49.4	-76.7**
Others	-2.7**	-0.3	-1.7*	-0.9	0.3	-3.7**	-2.5	-6.7**	-2.6	-7.2

Source: Public Use Microdata File for Individuals, 1991 Census of Canada.

1. Controlling for gender, age, marital status, province of residence, metropolitan/non-metropolitan area, geographic mobility, period of immigration, knowledge of official languages, occupation, industrial sector, weeks worked, and part-time/full-time weeks worked.
2. The earnings of workers of various ethnic origins are expressed as percentage differences from the earnings of workers of British origin in the same educational category....
3. Including degrees in medicine, dentistry, veterinary medicine, and optometry.
4. The category of "no degree, certificate, or diploma" for the British is the base category for other categories for the British....

*Significant at 0.10
**Significant at 0.05

persons of British origin with "no degree, certificate, or diploma" are used as the base category for their British counterparts at other levels of education. Thus, for example, workers of British origin with "high school graduate certificates" earned 13.2% more than their counterparts of British origin, who had "no degree, certificate, or diploma," when all the other factors in our [regression] were taken into account. As also noted, this difference is significant at the 0.05 level.

Looking first at the two "charter groups," it is obvious that the net economic returns to education for workers of British origin is significant, with each advancing educational category providing progressively higher returns. It is clear that the economic value of education for persons of British origin in the Canadian labour market is beyond doubt.

However, of more significance is the somewhat surprising finding that, after the other factors are controlled, persons of French origin at *all* educational levels had earnings above that for persons of British origin. Moreover, at the Bachelor's degree level and below, these differences of income between the French and the British are statistically significant. Hence, whatever may have been the situation in the past, it is clear that any suggestion that today the French are discriminated against in terms of the returns they receive for their education, is clearly not the case. Indeed, especially at lower levels, the French are significantly favoured over the British in terms of this relationship.

Among Europeans, whether from the north, east, or south of Europe, most ethnic groups had approximately the same income levels as their British counterparts with similar education. Notable exceptions were the Dutch and Poles who, in several of the upper educational levels earned significantly less, and those of Jewish ethnicity in the lowest educational categories who earned significantly more. The most significant discrepancies occurred, not in relation to any ethnicity, but in terms of certain educational categories. Thus, where respondents held either a "university certificate below the bachelor's level" or a "degree in medicine," persons from continental Europe were quite likely to have incomes significantly below that of the British when other factors were taken into account. The frequency of such discrepancies in these two categories suggests that this may have to do with the evaluation of educational qualification at these levels rather than just ethnicity.

In sharp contrast to the situation for Europeans, adjusted earnings of visible minorities were much lower than for the British at most educational levels. Compared to their British counterparts, out of the 10 educational categories, most visible minority groups earned less than their British counterparts in the majority of categories. Moreover, in many of the educational categories, visible minorities earned *significantly* less than their British counterparts.

Given this obvious evidence of discrimination against all visible minority groups, it is difficult to single out any one or two groups as being more hard done by than others. Perhaps persons of Chinese background might fit this category as they earned less than those of British ethnicity in all 10 educational categories and significantly less than the British in 8 of the 10 educational categories. However, Aboriginal Peoples and West Asians also earned less in 10 categories, and most other visible minority groups earned less in nine of them. While the Arabs might seem better off amongst visible minorities in that they earned lower in only 7 categories, they were significantly less in all 7, a level of earnings discrimination surpassed only by those of Chinese ethnicity.

Whereas one might have thought that increased level of education would lead to lower levels of discrimination, there is little in Table 32.1 to support such a position. From high school to doctorate there is clear evidence of lower earnings amongst visible minorities compared to their British counterparts at the same educational level. Thus, all visible minorities earned less than the British at the high school graduate level, at the level of bachelor's degree holder, master's degree holder and, with the exception of Arabs, at the level of doctorate degree holder. Likewise, all visible minorities who held degrees in medicine earned less than their British counterparts, as did all but the Blacks among those who held a university certificate above bachelor's but below master's level. Moreover, in the majority of cases *these differences were either significant or highly significant. In sum, it is clear from these findings that educational achievement at any level fails to protect persons of visible minority background from being disadvantaged in terms of the income they receive.*

SUMMARY AND DISCUSSION

We began this paper with the question, "Does the 'vertical mosaic' still exist?" It has been our assumption that the most appropriate place to look for evidence to either support or refute the vision of Canadian society as a "vertical mosaic" is through an examination of the relationship between ethnicity and income, first controlling for educational level, and then controlling for other key social variables so that this relationship can be measured more directly and precisely.

Our conclusion is that, by 1991, for the majority of ethnic groups in Canada there is no evidence that the traditionally accepted image of a vertical mosaic still remains. Among the two charter groups, the French now earn more for comparable education than their British counterparts when other factors are controlled. Likewise, many ethnic groups from all parts of Europe who had entered Canada with generally little education and hence occupied lower income positions, have now moved up the educational and income hierarchies and there is very little evidence of discrimination against any such ethnic groups.

On the other hand, there is also clear evidence that visible minorities have not fared well. When education and a range of other social variables are controlled, Aboriginal Peoples still remain mired at the bottom of Canadian society. Almost all Asian groups and most of those of Latin American and Middle Eastern ethnicity were also similarly disadvantaged.

In sum, the evidence indicates that similar educational qualifications carried different economic values in the Canadian labour market for individuals of different "racial" origins. All visible minority groups had below-average earnings in each of the categories, while most of those of European ethnicity had above-average earnings.

It is possible that there are some other variables than "race" which systematically operate to discriminate against people of colour in Canadian society. However, the 1991 *Public Use Microdata File for Individuals* permits more "controls" for other possible variables than has ever previously been possible in such a large data set based on Canadian society. Thus, we have controlled for most of the other competing factors and their interaction effects which might conceivably affect the fundamental relationship between education and income that lies at the centre of our analysis. If there are other factors which might affect this relationship, we cannot easily discern what these might be. More importantly, the large literature on the relationship between education, income, and ethnicity in Canada which we have reviewed provides no clue of any other factor or factors which might have such a significant influence.

Consequently, whereas we began this paper with the question, "Does the vertical mosaic still exist?," we must end it with an even more serious question, namely, "Is Canada a racist society?" Canadians have long prided themselves on their policy of ethnic pluralism in contrast to the "melting pot" of the United States. We have also generally seen ourselves as a more racially tolerant society than the American one. However, our data suggest that there are limits to our tolerance of cultural and racial divisions. While we are apparently willing to accept cultural differences (particularly from a wide range of European cultures) in terms of the income received relative to level of education, we show no such tolerance for those who are racially "visible" from the white majority in Canadian society. All our evidence suggests that, while our traditional "vertical mosaic" of ethnic differences may be disappearing, it has been replaced by a strong "coloured mosaic" of racial differences in terms of income rewards and income benefits. While this does not necessarily mean that we have racial discrimination when it comes to other social benefits such as location of residence, access to public facilities, and the extreme forms of discrimination that have characterized some other societies, our evidence leads us to conclude that there *is* some considerable level of racial discrimination in Canada in terms of financial rewards for educational achievement. In this respect at least, yes, we are a racist society.

CRITICAL THINKING QUESTIONS

1. Does contemporary data support Porter's original work in *The Vertical Mosaic*? If so, how? If not, why not?
2. Given the evidence presented in the article, do you feel that Canada is a racist society? What evidence from your own community supports your position?
3. What role, if any, does a person's level of education have on income in Canada?

NOTES

1. The analysis is based on 425,107 cases. The 1991 PUMFI contains 809,654 cases. Respondents who did not work in 1990 (nearly half of whom were under age 15) have been excluded, thereby dropping the sample to 446,478 cases representing the working population of Canada in 1990. A small number of persons were on employment authorizations or Minister's permits or were refugee claimants. As the income of such persons could have been significantly affected by factors atypical of the Canadian labour market, they have been excluded, thereby reducing the sample to 443,161 cases. Also eliminated were a small number of cases with missing information on education, age, marital status, geographic mobility, and period of immigration (i.e., the factors of earning determination used in this study), thereby reducing the sample to 439,959 cases. Finally, to estimate the net effect of ethnicity on

earnings with educational categories, we employed linear least-squares regression with logarithms of earnings as the dependent variable..., and this meant persons with zero or negative earnings had to be eliminated. This further reduced the sample to 425,107 persons.

REFERENCES

Agocs, C., and M. Boyd. 1993. The Canadian ethnic mosaic recast for the 1990s. In *Social inequality in Canada: Patterns, problems, policies,* eds. J. Curtis, E. Grabb, and N. Guppy, 330–60. Scarborough, Ont.: Prentice-Hall Canada Inc..

Barringer, H., and G. Kassebaum. 1989. Asian Indians as a minority in the United States: The effects of education, occupations and gender on income. *Sociological Perspectives,* 32(4): 501–20.

Beggs, J. J. 1995. The institutional environment: Implications for race and gender inequality in the U.S. labour market. *American Sociological Review,* 60 (August): 612–33.

Boyd, M., J. Goyder, F. E. Jones, H. A. McRoberts, P. C. Pineo, and J. Porter. 1981. Status attainment in Canada: Findings of the Canadian mobility study. *Canadian Review of Sociology and Anthropology,* 18(5): 657–73.

Breton, R., and H. Roseborough. 1971. Ethnic differences in status. In *Canadian society: Sociological perspectives,* eds. B. R. Blishen, F. E. Jones, K. D. Naegele, and J. Porter, 450–68. Toronto: Macmillan of Canada Ltd.

Darroch, A. G. 1979. Another look at ethnicity, stratification and social mobility in Canada. *Canadian Journal of Sociology,* 4(1): 1–24.

Featherman, D. L., and R. M. Hauser. 1978. *Opportunity and change.* New York: Academic Press.

Fox, B. J. and J. Fox. 1986. Women in the labour market, 1931–81: Exclusion and competition. *The Canadian Review of Sociology and Anthropology,* 23(1): 1–21.

Geschwender, J. A., and N. Guppy. 1995. Ethnicity, educational attainment and earned income among Canadian-born men and women. *Canadian Ethnic Studies,* 27(1): 67–84.

Halvorsen, R., and R. Palmquist. 1980. The interpretation of dummy variables in semilogarithmic equations. *American Economic Review,* 70(3): 474–75.

Herberg, E. N. 1990. The ethno-racial socioeconomic hierarchy in Canada: Theory and analysis of the new vertical mosaic. *International Journal of Comparative Sociology,* 31(3–4): 206–20.

Isajiw, W. W., A. Sev'er, and L. Dreidger. 1993. Ethnic identity and social mobility: A test of the "drawback model." *Canadian Journal of Sociology,* 18(2): 177–96.

Jabbra, N. W., and R. L. Cosper. 1988. Ethnicity in Atlantic Canada: A survey. *Canadian Ethnic Studies,* 20(3): 6–27.

Lautard, E. H., and N. Guppy. 1990. The vertical mosaic revisited: Occupational differentials among Canadian ethnic groups. In *Race and ethnic relations in Canada,* ed. P. S. Li, 189–208. Toronto: Oxford University Press.

Lautard, E. H., and D. J. Loree. 1984. Ethnic stratification in Canada, 1931–1971. *Canadian Journal of Sociology,* 9: 333–43.

Li, P. S. 1988. *Ethnic inequality in a class society.* Toronto: Thompson Educational Publishing Inc.

Nakhaie, M. R. 1995. Ownership and management position of Canadian ethnic groups in 1973 and 1989. *Canadian Journal of Sociology,* 20(2): 167–92.

Ornstein, M. D. 1981. The occupational mobility of men in Ontario. *The Canadian Review of Sociology and Anthropology,* 18(2): 181–215.

Pineo, P. C. 1976. Social mobility in Canada: The current picture. *Sociological Focus,* 9(2): 109–23.

Pineo, P. C., and J. Porter. 1985. Ethnic origin and occupational attainment. In *Ascription and achievement: Studies in mobility and status attainment in Canada,* eds. M. Boyd, J. Goyder, F. E. Jones, H. A. McRoberts, P. C. Pineo, and J. Porter, 357–92. Ottawa: Carleton University Press.

Porter, J. 1965. *The vertical mosaic.* Toronto: University of Toronto Press.

Reitz, J. G. 1980. *The survival of ethnic groups.* Toronto: McGraw-Hill Ryerson, Ltd.

Royal Commission on Bilingualism and Biculturalism, Canada. 1969. *Report of the Royal Commission on Bilingualism and Biculturalism,* Vol. 3A. Ottawa: Queen's Printer.

Sandefur, G. D., and W. J. Scott. 1983. Minority group status and the wages of Indian and Black males. *Social Science Research,* 12(1): 44–68.

Shamai, S. 1992. Ethnicity and educational achievement in Canada: 1941–1981. *Canadian Ethnic Studies,* 24(1): 41–57.

Statistics Canada. 1993. *Standard occupational classification, 1991.* Ottawa: Ministry of Industry, Science and Technology.

———. 1994. *User documentation for public use microdata file for individuals, 1991 Census.* Catalogue No.: 48-030E. Ottawa: Statistics Canada.

Tepperman, L. 1975. *Social mobility in Canada.* Toronto: McGraw-Hill Ryerson.

Winn, C. 1988. The socio-economic attainment of visible minorities: Facts and policy implications. In *Social inequality in Canada: Patterns, problems, policies,* eds. J. Curtis, E. Grabb, N. Guppy, and S. Gilbert, 195–213. Scarborough, Ont.: Prentice-Hall Canada.

51

Social Stratification

The Uses of Global Poverty: How Economic Inequality Benefits the West

CLASSIC

CONTEMPORARY

CROSS-CULTURAL

Daina Stukuls Eglitis

Why don't rich nations do more to reduce the severe poverty that paralyzes much of the world? This selection argues that people in rich countries, including the United States, actually benefit from global poverty in several ways.

In the global village, there stand a wide variety of homes, from the stately mansion on the hill, to the modest abode blessed with electricity and running water, to the adequate but unheated (or uncooled) hut, to the flood-prone, tattered shanty cobbled together from gathered scrap. Those who live on the hill are aware of their neighbors, as their neighbors are aware of them. Most inhabitants of the global village recognize that wealth and the accompanying opportunities for education, health care, and consumption are not evenly divided and that a substantial gap exists between the more and less materially blessed populations. Not everyone agrees on why that is the case.

Consider the following comparisons of life in the global village: In 1999, the gross national income in purchasing power parity (GNI PPP)[1] in the United States was $31,910. In Germany the figure was $23,510, and in Australia, $23,850. By contrast, the GNI PPP of China was $3,550, in Indonesia it was $2,660, and in Pakistan, $1,860. On the bottom tier of states, we find countries like

Nigeria with a GNI of $770 and Sierra Leone with just $440. If we use the GNI PPP as a yardstick of economic power and the well-being of populations, we may begin to construct a picture of a global system characterized by the massive maldistribution of wealth, economic security, and purchasing power. Our village is one characterized by deep and fundamental stratification.

What have been the responses of well-off states to this global class system with its extremes of wealth and poverty? Not surprisingly, perhaps, political rhetoric has consistently elevated the goal of spreading the prosperity enjoyed by the advanced industrial states of the West around the globe. In remarks made at the United States Coast Guard Academy commencement ceremony in 1989, President George Bush phrased it this way: "What is it that we want to see? It is a growing community of democracies anchoring international peace and stability, and a dynamic free-market system generating prosperity and progress on a global scale.... If we succeed, the next decade and the century beyond will be an era of unparalleled growth, an era which sees the

Source: Prepared by the author for this book.

flourishing of freedom, peace, and prosperity around the world."

If shared global prosperity was the goal, it seems safe to say that while there was some modest progress made in areas like Latin America, Eastern Europe, and parts of Asia, "we" did not really succeed, because the global wealth gap is still massive and growing. The rich countries remain rich, and the poor countries, for the most part, remain trapped in desperate, dire poverty.

This has not changed.

Another thing that has not changed is the rhetorical commitment to spreading the wealth.

In a speech in Coventry, England, in December 2000, President Bill Clinton laid out a "prescription for how the United States might help close the gap between rich and poor nations." And in his farewell address to the nation in January 2001, the President declared that "the global gap requires more than compassion. It requires action." As of 2002, President George W. Bush has not addressed the question of non-Western development specifically, though it seems relatively safe to say that he too will join the political chorus of support for global prosperity, although his administration seems destined to be defined by a focus on war rather than development.

Western rhetoric, assistance programs, and advice seem to support the goal of global prosperity and its extension to the 1.3 billion who live on less than $1 per day and those millions or even billions more who eke out a sparse existence just above the threshold of absolute poverty. But the reality of prosperity has touched only a relative few countries, while the struggle to meet basic needs touches many more. Social indicators like the GNI PPP highlight the differences we find in our village. But what explains them? Why does global poverty exist and persist? Why does a global class system with a thin layer of rich states and a broad strata of poor countries exist and persist? What explains why some villagers inhabit houses on the mount while others squat in mud huts below? Possible answers are many. This article explores one way of understanding the yawning gap between the planet's wealthiest and poorest states.

In 1971, sociologist Herbert Gans published an article entitled "The Uses of Poverty: The Poor Pay All."[2] In the article, Gans utilized a conservative theoretical perspective in sociology, functionalism, to inquire about the persistence of poverty in America. The functionalist perspective takes as its starting point the position that essentially all institutions and social phenomena that exist in society contribute in some manner to that society—that is, they are functional for society. If they did not contribute to the social order, the functionalists maintain, they would disappear. Using this perspective, functionalists may inquire about, for instance, the functions, both obvious and hidden (or manifest and latent, to use sociologist Robert Merton's terms), of institutions like the education system or the family or social phenomena like punishment for deviance. These social theorists assume that institutions or phenomena exist because they are functional, and hence their guiding question is, What function do they serve?

Gans posed a similar question about poverty, asking, What are the uses of poverty? Clearly, the notion that poverty is functional for society as a whole is ludicrous: Who would suggest that it is functional for those who endure economic deprivation? So Gans offered a modified functionalist analysis: "...instead of identifying functions for an entire social system, I shall identify them for the interest groups, socioeconomic classes, and other population aggregates with shared values that 'inhabit' a social system. I suspect that in a modern heterogeneous society, few phenomena are functional or dysfunctional for the society as a whole, and that most result in benefits to some groups and costs to others."

Gans sought to explain the existence and persistence of poverty in modern, wealthy America by highlighting the way that the existence of poverty has benefits for the nonpoor—not just "evil" individuals like the loan shark or the slum lord, but for "normal" members of nonpoor classes. He identified thirteen "uses" of poverty, including the notions that the existence of a poor class "ensures that society's 'dirty work' will be done," that "the poor buy goods others do not want and thus prolong the economic usefulness of such goods," and "the poor can be identified and punished as alleged or real deviants in order to uphold the legitimacy of conventional norms." He was not arguing that poverty is good. He was suggesting that understanding poverty's existence and persistence mean recognizing that the poor have positive social and economic functions for the nonpoor. Thus, one would conclude that the elimination of poverty, while elevated as a societal goal, would be, in practice, costly to the nonpoor.

While Gans's theoretically based inquiry into poverty was focused on America's poor, the same question might be asked about the existence of global poverty: What are the "uses" of global poverty for the better-off countries of the world economic system? The purpose of such an inquiry would be, as it was in Gans's inquiry, not to use a functionalist analysis to legitimate poverty or the highly skewed distribution of wealth in the global system, but to contribute to a deeper understanding of why it continues to exist by explaining how its persistence confers benefits on well-off states and their inhabitants.

The argument is not that advanced states are consciously conspiring to keep the poor states destitute: Well-off countries have historically sought to offer help to less developed countries. In reality, however, there are limited incentives for the better-off states to support the full industrial and technological (and even democratic) development of all the states in the global system. To the degree that the existence of a class of poor states is positively functional for wealthy states, we can begin to imagine why development and assistance programs that help ensure survival, but not prosperity, for poor populations are quite characteristic of Western policy.

This article notes eleven "uses" of global poverty. Global poverty is not, from this perspective, functional for the global community as a whole. The notion that the poverty of billions who live in economically marginal states is globally "useful" would be absurd. But it is not absurd to ask how the existence of a class of poor states serves wealthy states. In fact, asking such a question might contribute to a better understanding of the dual phenomena of global poverty and the global "class" system.

Point 1: The existence of global poverty helps ensure the wealth of affordable goods for Western consumers

The cornucopia of decently priced goods of reasonable quality enjoyed by Western consumers is underpinned by the low-wage work done in low-income countries. The labels on the clothing you are wearing right now likely contain the familiar words "Made in China" or perhaps "Made in Pakistan." Your clothing is probably of reasonable quality, and you likely paid a reasonable (but not necessarily cheap) price for it.

The Western consumer of textiles such as off-the-rack clothing is a beneficiary of a globalized manufacturing process that has seen the movement of manufacturing to low-wage areas located in poor states that provide ready pools of workers needy enough to labor for pittance. In China, the average hourly wage of apparel workers is about 23 cents. This benefits the consumer of that apparel. The worker herself (workers in this industry are usually female) derives less benefit: The average hourly wage needed to meet basic needs in China, according to Women's Edge, an advocacy group, is 87 cents.[3]

Another way that the impoverished workers of the third world help reduce the cost of goods coming to Western consumers is through their agricultural labor. For instance, the comparably (and sometimes illegally) low wages paid to many poor migrant farm workers from Mexico and Central America in states like California contribute to America's ample and reasonably priced food supply.

Stories about low-wage workers in developing countries have, in recent years, emerged in the Western press and provoked some expressions of outrage and the formation of groups like United Students Against Sweatshops. These expressions have been small and limited. Imagine, however, the outrage if popular sports shoes, already pricey, climbed another $50 in cost as a result of manufacturers opting for well-paid, unionized labor. Or imagine if the price of a head of iceberg lettuce, America's favorite vegetable, suddenly doubled in price to $3.00. Which outrage would be more potent?

Point 2: The existence of global poverty benefits Western companies and shareholders in the form of increased profit margins

Labor costs typically constitute a high percentage of a company's expenditures. By reducing labor costs, companies can both keep prices reasonable (which benefits, as noted, the consumer) and raise profit margins. Not surprisingly, then, companies are not likely to locate in—and are more likely to leave—locations where wages are relatively high. The use of poor female workers in the third world is, in this respect, especially "beneficial" to companies. Women comprise about 80 percent of workers in Export Processing Zones and are often paid 20 percent to 50 percent less than male counterparts. The less costly the workforce, the greater the opportunity for profit. Not coincidentally, countries with an ample supply of poor workers willing to work for miserable wages are also countries with lax safety and environmental regulations, which also keeps down the costs to the Western employer and pushes up the profits. Hence, companies benefit directly from the existence of economically deprived would-be workers willing (or not in a position to be unwilling) to work for paltry wages in potentially hazardous, or at least very unpleasant, conditions.

Point 3: The existence of global poverty fosters access to resources in poor states that are needed in or desired by the West

Poor states may sell raw goods at low prices to Western states, which can transform the resource into a more valuable finished product. The position of the poor states in the world economy makes it less likely that they can derive the full benefit of the resources they possess for the government and people. The case of oil in resource-rich but desperately poor Nigeria is an example. Seven major foreign oil companies operate in Nigeria, all representing interests in wealthy states. The vast majority of benefits from Nigeria's oil has accrued not to the country's people, but to the companies (and consumers) of the wealthy states. There is no attempt to hide this: John Connor, head of Texaco's worldwide exploration and production, talking about a massive oil strike in January 2000, stated that the successful conclusion of the well test "sets the stage for development of a world-class project that will add substantially to the company's resource base."[4] Clearly, the failure of Nigeria's people to benefit from the country's resources is also linked to a succession of corrupt governments, but the poverty of the masses and the powerful position of oil companies help to ensure that resistance to exploitation of resources for the benefit for non-Nigerian interests will be marginal.

Point 4: The existence of global poverty helps support Western medical advances

The poor provide a pool of guinea pigs for the testing of medicines developed for use primarily in the West. The beneficiaries are not the poor themselves but Western consumers of advanced medicine (60 percent of profits are made in the United States, which leads the world in drug consumption) and the pharmaceutical companies, which stand astride a $350 billion (and growing) industry. A series of reports in the *Washington Post* in December 2000 documents the disturbing practice of conducting drug trials on ill inhabitants of poor states. For instance, an unapproved antibiotic was tested by a major pharmaceutical company on sick children during a meningitis epidemic in Nigeria. The country's lax regulatory oversight, the sense among some doctors that they could not object to experiment conditions for political or economic reasons, the dearth of alternative health care options, combined with the desire of the company to rapidly prepare for the market a potential "blockbuster" drug underpinned a situation in which disease victims were treated as test subjects rather than patients. This case highlights the way that nonpoor states actually benefit from the existence of poor states with struggling, sick populations. A reporter for the series noted that "companies use the tests to produce new product and revenue streams, but they are also responding to pressure from regulators, Congress, and lobbyists for disease victims to develop new medicines quickly. By providing huge pools of human subjects, foreign trials help speed new drugs to the marketplace—where they will be sold mainly to patients in wealthy countries."[5]

Point 5: The existence of global poverty contributes to the advancement of Western economies and societies with the human capital of poor states.

Poorer states like India have become intellectual feeders of well-educated and bright individuals whose skills cannot be fully rewarded in less developed states. The magnetic draw of a better life in economies that amply reward their human capital pulls the brightest minds from their countries of origin, a process referred to as "brain drain." Advanced economies such as the United States and England are beneficiaries of brain drain. The United States has moved to take advantage of the pool of highly educated workers from the developing world: Congress has passed legislation increasing the number of H-1B visas, or "high-tech visas," to bring up to 600,000 workers

to the United States over the next several years. The United States and England offer attractive opportunities to highly educated workers from poorer states. Notably, high-tech companies often pay the foreign workers less than their domestic equivalents would demand.

Point 6: The existence of global poverty may contribute to the pacification of the Western proletariat, or "Workers of the World, a Blue Light Special!"

To some degree, the broad availability of good, inexpensive merchandise may help obscure class divisions in the West, at least in the arena of consumption. It is clear that those with greater wealth can consume more high-quality goods, but low-end "designer" merchandise is accessible to the less well-off in cathedrals of consumption such as Wal-Mart. At K-Mart, for instance, Martha Stewart peddles her wares, intended to transform "homemaking chores…into what we like to call 'domestic art.'" Thanks in part to the low-wage workers in places like China, these goods are available to the unwashed masses (now washed by Martha's smart and cozy towels) as well as to better-situated homemakers. Consumption appears to be one of the great equalizers of modern society. (It is worth noting, though, that many members of the Western working class are also "victims" of global poverty, since many jobs have gone abroad to low-wage areas, leaving behind, for less educated workers, positions in the less remunerative and less secure service industry or leaving former industrial workers jobless.)

Point 7: Global poverty benefits the West because poor countries make optimal dumping grounds for goods that are dangerous, expired, or illegal

Wealthy countries and their inhabitants may utilize poorer states as repositories for dangerous or unwanted material such as nuclear waste. The desperation of cash-strapped states benefits better-off countries, which might otherwise have difficulty ridding themselves of the dangerous by-products of their industrial and consumer economies. For instance, in December 2000, the Russian Parliament, in an initial vote on the issue, overwhelmingly supported the amendment of an environmental law to permit the importation of foreign nuclear waste. The alteration of the law was supported by the Atomic Ministry of the Russian Federation, which suggested that over the next decade, Russia might earn up to $21 billion from the importation of spent nuclear fuel from states like Japan, Germany, and South Korea. Likely repositories of the radioactive refuse are Mayak and Krasnoyarsk, already among the most contaminated sites on the planet.

India has also emerged as a dumping ground for hazardous junk from the world's industrial giants. The western Indian city of Alang, for instance, is host to the world's largest shipbreaking yard, where Western-owned ships are sent for dismantling and, ostensibly, recycling. The process of "breaking" the old vessels, however, endangers workers and the environment because it releases asbestos, PCBs, and other toxic wastes.[6]

Point 8: The existence of global poverty provides jobs for specialists employed to assist, advise, and study the world's poor and to protect the "better-off" from them

Within this group of specialists we find people in a variety of professions. There are those who are professional development workers, operating through organizations like the United States Agency for International Development (USAID) to further "America's foreign policy interests in expanding democracy and free markets while improving the lives of the citizens of the developing world."[7] The Peace Corps is also built around the goal of bringing Western "know-how" to the poor with volunteer programs that promote entrepreneurship and agricultural development.

Academics in fields as diverse as economics, sociology, international affairs, political science, and anthropology study, write about, and "decipher" the lives of the poor and the condition of poor states. Texts on development, articles debating why poverty persists, and books from university presses are only some of the products of this research. Journalists and novelists can build careers around bringing colorful, compelling representations of the poor to the warm living rooms of literate, well-off consumers. Still others are charged with the task of protecting wealthy states from "invasions" of the poor: U.S. border patrols, for instance, employ thousands to keep those seeking better fortunes out of U.S. territory.

Point 9: Global poverty benefits inhabitants of wealthy countries, who can feel good about helping the global poor through charitable work and charitable giving.

From the celebrity-studded musical production "We are the World" to trick-or-treating for UNICEF, those who inhabit the wealthy corners of the world feel good about themselves for sharing their good fortune. The Web site of World Vision, a faith-based charity that offers the opportunity to sponsor poor children, features a speak-out area for contributors. On that site, a young Canadian sponsor wrote, "A few days ago I woke up early and turned the TV on…looking at those children made me realize I could help them. I thought if I have enough money to pay for the Internet, cell phone, and a couple of other things I didn't need, I said to myself, [then] why not give that money to people who need it instead of spending it all in [*sic*] luxury and things that are not really important…. I immediately picked up the phone and called to sponsor a child! I am happy. I can help someone who needs it!"[8]

Apparently, we need not feel guilt about consuming many times what the unfortunate inhabitants of the world's poor states do if only we are willing to give up a few of our luxuries to help them. Indeed, not only do the poor not inspire guilt, they may inspire positive feelings: As the World Vision writer notes, she feels "happy" because she can "help someone who needs it." No less a figure than the world's richest man, Bill Gates, is also "dedicated to improving people's lives by sharing advances in health and learning with the global community" through the Gates Foundation.[9]

A related point is that the poor we see on television or hear about in news or music give those of us in wealthy countries the opportunity to feel good about ourselves, regardless of our position in the socioeconomic structure of our own states. Consider the memorable lines from the 1985 Band-Aid song, "Do They Know It's Christmas?" which was produced by British pop artist Bob Geldof as a charitable act to raise money for Ethiopia's famine victims: "And the Christmas bells that ring there are the clanging chimes of doom. Well, tonight, thank God, it's them instead of you." Indeed, even the underpaid blue- or pink-collar worker in the West can relate to that sentiment.

Point 10: The poverty of less-developed states makes possible the massive flow of resources westward.

Imagine if large and largely poor countries like China, Nigeria, and India consumed at U.S. rates. At present, Americans consume a tremendously disproportionate share of the world's resources. With their profligate use of all manner of resources, most notably fossil fuels, Americans are the greediest consumers of natural resources on the planet. On both an absolute and per capita basis, most world resources flow westward. Notably, an October 4, 2000, article in the *Seattle Times* reported that bicycles, long a characteristic and popular means of transport for Chinese commuters, are losing popularity: "Increasingly, young Chinese are not even bothering to learn to ride bikes, because growing wealth has unleashed a plethora of transportation choices, public and private."[10] The new transportation of choice is still

largely public buses or private taxis; the Chinese have not yet graduated to mass private cars. But it is interesting to ponder whether there would be enough (affordable) oil for everyone if the Chinese, with their growing population and prosperity, became a country of two-vehicle families or developed a taste and market for gas-guzzling sports utility vehicles. In this case, the West likely benefits from the fact that few can afford (at least at present) to consume at the rate its people do.

Point 11: The poorer countries, which reproduce at rates higher than Western states, are useful scapegoats for real and potential global environmental threats.

What is the bigger environmental threat to our planet? Is it the rapid growth of the populations of developing states or the rapid consumption of resources by the much smaller populations of developed states? The overdevelopment of the West may well be the bigger threat, though the growth of populations in third-world countries, which is often linked to conditions of underdevelopment, such as a lack of birth control and the need to have "extra" children as a hedge against high child mortality rates, makes an attractive alternative explanation for those who would not wish to fault the SUV-driving, disposable-diaper using, BBQ-loving American consumer for threats to the global environment. While some Western policymakers express concern about the environmental threats emerging from rapid population growth or the use of "dirty" technology in developing states, there is comparably little serious attention given to the global threat presented by the profligate consumption by Western states. The poor divert attention from the environmental problems caused by Western overconsumption.

I have talked about eleven ways that the continued existence of global poverty benefits those who reside in wealthy states. The argument I have offered to explain the persistence of a strata of poor states and the yawning global gap highlights the idea that while global poverty (and the status quo) is beneficial to the wealthy West, serious steps to alleviate it will not be taken. It is surely the case that poverty does not have to exist. But while we in the West derive the benefits and bonuses of these economic inequalities, it seems likely that our efforts to support, advise, and assist the less developed states will remain at levels that are financially and politically convenient and feasible, and will target survival rather than true prosperity for those outside our gated, privileged, greedy Western neighborhood. In Gans's words, "Phenomena like poverty can be eliminated only when they become dysfunctional for the affluent or powerful, or when the powerless can obtain enough power to change society."

CRITICAL THINKING QUESTIONS

1. The author describes several ways in which people in rich nations benefit from global poverty. Which do you find most convincing? Why?
2. What weaknesses do you find in the arguments? Explain.
3. Do you think that rich countries provide assistance to poor countries? If so, in what ways? If not, why?

NOTES

1. The figures in this paragraph come from the Population Research Bureau Web site at **http://www.prb.org**, which provides excellent demographic data. According to the PRB, the "GNI PPP per capita is gross national income in purchasing power parity divided by mid-year population.... GNI PPP refers to gross national income converted to 'international' dollars using a purchasing power parity conversion factor. International dollars indicate the amount of goods or services one could buy in the United States with a given amount of money. GNI PPP provides an indicator of the welfare of people that is comparable across countries free of price and exchange rate distortions that occur when GNI is converted using market exchange rates."

2. *Social Policy,* July/August 1971.

3. Information on issues of trade and Chinese women is available at **http://www.womensedge.org**. The information cited is from the April 2000 Web issue of *Notes from the Edge.*

4. "Texaco in massive oil strike in Nigeria" in *The Namibian*, available online at **http://www.namibian.com.na/Netstories/2000/ January/Marketplace/texaco.html**.

5. Stephens, Joe, "As Drug Testing Spreads, Profits and Lives Hang in Balance," *Washington Post*, (December 2000): A1.

6. Information on both issues is available at the Web site of the environmental group Greenpeace at **http://www.greenpeace.org**.

7. The Web site address is **http://www.usaid.gov**.

8. The charity's Web site address is **http://www.worldvision.org**.

9. The foundation is at **http://www.gatesfoundation.org**.

10. The article is cited at the Web site of the Competitive Enterprise Institute: **http://www.cei.org/CHNReader.asp?ID=1227**.

52

Alienated Labor

Karl Marx

The human species, argues Karl Marx, is social by nature and expresses that social nature in the act of production. But within the capitalist economic system, Marx claims, the process of production denies human nature, rather than affirming it. The result is what he terms "alienated labor."

...[We] have shown that the worker sinks to the level of a commodity, and to a most miserable commodity; that the misery of the worker increases with the power and volume of his production; that the necessary result of competition is the accumulation of capital in a few hands, and thus a restoration of monopoly in a more terrible form; and finally that the distinction between capitalist and landlord, and between agricultural laborer and industrial worker, must disappear, and the whole of society divide into the two classes of property *owners* and *propertyless* workers....

Source: "Alienated Labor," by Karl Marx from *Karl Marx: Early Writings,* trans. and ed. by T. B. Bottomore. Copyright © 1963, McGraw-Hill Companies. Reprinted by permission of The McGraw-Hill Companies.

Thus we have now to grasp the real connexion between this whole system of alienation—private property, acquisitiveness, the separation of labor, capital and land, exchange and competition, value and the devaluation of man, monopoly and competition—and the system of *money....*

We shall begin from a *contemporary* economic fact. The worker becomes poorer the more wealth he produces and the more his production increases in power and extent. The worker becomes an ever cheaper commodity the more goods he creates. The *devaluation* of the human world increases in direct relation with the *increase in value* of the world of things. Labor does not only create goods; it also produces itself and the worker as a *commodity,* and indeed in the same proportion as it produces goods.

373

This fact simply implies that the object produced by labor, its product, now stands opposed to it as an *alien being,* as a *power independent* of the producer. The product of labor is labor which has been embodied in an object and turned into a physical thing; this product is an *objectification* of labor. The performance of work is at the same time its objectification. The performance of work appears in the sphere of political economy as a *vitiation*[1] of the worker, objectification as a *loss* and as *servitude to the object,* and appropriation as *alienation.*

So much does the performance of work appear as vitiation that the worker is vitiated to the point of starvation. So much does objectification appear as loss of the object that the worker is deprived of the most essential things not only of life but also of work. Labor itself becomes an object which he can acquire only by the greatest effort and with unpredictable interruptions. So much does the appropriation of the object appear as alienation that the more objects the worker produces the fewer he can possess and the more he falls under the domination of his product, of capital.

All these consequences follow from the fact that the worker is related to the *product of his labor* as to an *alien* object. For it is clear on this presupposition that the more the worker expends himself in work the more powerful becomes the world of objects which he creates in face of himself, the poorer he becomes in his inner life, and the less he belongs to himself. It is just the same as in religion. The more of himself man attributes to God the less he has left in himself. The worker puts his life into the object, and his life then belongs no longer to himself but to the object. The greater his activity, therefore, the less he possesses. What is embodied in the product of his labor is no longer his own. The greater this product is, therefore, the more he is diminished. The *alienation* of the worker in his product means not only that his labor becomes an object, assumes an *external* existence, but that it exists independently, *outside himself,* and alien to him, and that it stands opposed to him as an

autonomous power. The life which he has given to the object sets itself against him as an alien and hostile force.

Let us now examine more closely the phenomenon of *objectification;* the worker's production and the *alienation* and *loss* of the object it produces, which is involved in it. The worker can create nothing without *nature,* without the *sensuous external world.* The latter is the material in which his labor is realized, in which it is active, out of which and through which it produces things.

But just as nature affords the *means of existence* of labor, in the sense that labor cannot *live* without objects upon which it can be exercised, so also it provides the *means of existence* in a narrower sense; namely the means of physical existence for the *worker* himself. Thus, the more the worker *appropriates* the external world of sensuous nature by his labor the more he deprives himself of *means of existence,* in two respects: First, that the sensuous external world becomes progressively less an object belonging to his labor or a means of existence of his labor, and secondly, that it becomes progressively less a means of existence in the direct sense, a means for the physical subsistence of the worker.

In both respects, therefore, the worker becomes a slave of the object; first, in that he receives an *object of work,* i.e., receives *work,* and secondly, in that he receives *means of subsistence.* Thus the object enables him to exist, first as a *worker* and secondly, as a *physical subject.* The culmination of this enslavement is that he can only maintain himself as a *physical subject* so far as he is a *worker,* and that it is only as a *physical subject* that he is a worker.

(The alienation of the worker in his object is expressed as follows in the laws of political economy: The more the worker produces the less he has to consume; the more value he creates the more worthless he becomes; the more refined his product the more crude and misshapen the worker; the more civilized the product the more barbarous the worker; the more powerful the work the more feeble the worker; the more the work manifests intelligence the more the worker declines in intelligence and becomes a slave of nature.)

Political economy conceals the alienation in the nature of labor insofar as it does not examine the direct relationship between the worker (work) and production. Labor certainly produces marvels for the rich but it produces privation for the worker. It produces palaces, but hovels for the worker. It produces beauty, but deformity for the worker. It replaces labor by machinery, but it casts some of the workers back into a barbarous kind of work and turns the others into machines. It produces intelligence, but also stupidity and cretinism for the workers.

The direct relationship of labor to its products is the relationship of the worker to the objects of his production. The relationship of property owners to the objects of production and to production itself is merely a *consequence* of this first relationship and confirms it. We shall consider this second aspect later.

Thus, when we ask what is the important relationship of labor, we are concerned with the relationship of the *worker* to production.

So far we have considered the alienation of the worker only from one aspect; namely, *his relationship with the products of his labor.* However, alienation appears not merely in the result but also in the *process of production,* within *productive activity* itself. How could the worker stand in an alien relationship to the product of his activity if he did not alienate himself in the act of production itself? The product is indeed only the *résumé* of activity, of production. Consequently, if the product of labor is alienation, production itself must be active alienation—the alienation of activity and the activity of alienation. The alienation of the object of labor merely summarizes the alienation in the work activity itself.

What constitutes the alienation of labor? First, that the work is *external* to the worker, that it is not part of his nature; and that, consequently, he does not fulfill himself in his work but denies himself, has a feeling of misery rather than well-being, does not develop freely his mental and physical energies but is physically exhausted and mentally debased. The worker, therefore, feels himself at home only during his leisure time, whereas at work he feels homeless. His work is not voluntary but imposed, *forced labor.* It is not the satisfaction of a need, but only a *means* for satisfying other needs. Its alien character is clearly shown by the fact that as soon as there is no physical or other compulsion it is avoided like the plague. External labor, labor in which man alienates himself, is a labor of self-sacrifice, of mortification. Finally, the external character of work for the worker is shown by the fact that it is not his own work but work for someone else, that in work he does not belong to himself but to another person.…

We arrive at the result that man (the worker) feels himself to be freely active only in his animal functions—eating, drinking and procreating, or at most also in his dwelling and in personal adornment—while in his human functions he is reduced to an animal. The animal becomes human and the human becomes animal.

Eating, drinking, and procreating are of course also genuine human functions. But abstractly considered, apart from the environment of human activities, and turned into final and sole ends, they are animal functions.

We have now considered the act of alienation of practical human activity, labor, from two aspects: (1) the relationship of the worker to the *product of labor* as an alien object which dominates him. This relationship is at the same time the relationship to the sensuous external world, to natural objects, as an alien and hostile world; (2) the relationship of labor to the *act of production* within *labor.* This is the relationship of the worker to his own activity as something alien and not belonging to him, activity as suffering (passivity), strength as powerlessness, creation as emasculation, the *personal* physical and mental energy of the worker, his personal life (for what is life but activity?), as an activity which is directed against himself, independent of him and not belonging to him. This is *self-alienation* as against the [afore]mentioned alienation of the *thing.*

We have now to infer a third characteristic of *alienated labor* from the two we have considered. Man is a species-being not only in the sense that he makes the community (his own as well as those of other things) his object both practically and theoretically, but also (and this is simply another expression for the same thing) in the sense that he treats himself as the present, living species, as a *universal* and consequently free being.

Species-life, for man as for animals, has its physical basis in the fact that man (like animals) lives from inorganic nature, and since man is more universal than an animal so the range of inorganic nature from which he lives is more universal. Plants, animals, minerals, air, light, etc. constitute, from the theoretical aspect, a part of human consciousness as objects of natural science and art; they are man's spiritual inorganic nature, his intellectual means of life, which he must first prepare for enjoyment and perpetuation. So also, from the practical aspect, they form a part of human life and activity. In practice man lives only from these natural products, whether in the form of food, heating, clothing, housing, etc. The universality of man appears in practice in the universality which makes the whole of nature into his inorganic body: (1) as a direct means of life; and equally (2) as the material object and instrument of his life activity. Nature is the inorganic body of man; that is to say nature, excluding the human body itself. To say that man *lives* from nature means that nature is his *body* with which he must remain in a continuous interchange in order not to die. The statement that the physical and mental life of man, and nature, are interdependent means simply that nature is interdependent with itself, for man is a part of nature.

Since alienated labor (1) alienates nature from man; and (2) alienates man from himself, from his own active function, his life activity; so it alienates him from the species. It makes *species-life* into a means of individual life. In the first place it alienates species-life and individual life, and secondly, it turns the latter, as an abstraction, into the purpose of the former, also in its abstract and alienated form.

For labor, *life activity, productive life,* now appear to man only as *means* for the satisfaction of a need, the need to maintain his physical existence. Productive life is, however, species-life. It is life creating life. In the type of life activity resides the whole character of a species, its species-character; and free, conscious activity is the species-character of human beings. Life itself appears only as a *means of life.*

The animal is one with its life activity. It does not distinguish the activity from itself. It is *its activity.* But man makes his life activity itself an object of his will and consciousness. He has a conscious life activity. It is not a determination with which he is completely identified. Conscious life activity distinguishes man from the life activity of animals. Only for this reason is he a species-being. Or rather, he is only a self-conscious being, i.e., his own life is an object for him, because he is a species-being. Only for this reason is his activity free activity. Alienated labor reverses the relationship, in that man because he is a self-conscious being makes his life activity, his *being,* only a means for his *existence.*

CRITICAL THINKING QUESTIONS

1. Does Marx argue that work is inevitably alienating? Why does work within a capitalist economy produce alienation?
2. In what different respects does labour within capitalism alienate the worker?
3. Based on this analysis, under what conditions do you think Marx would argue that labour is not alienating?

NOTE

1. Debasement.

53

McJobs: McDonaldization and the Workplace

George Ritzer

A decade ago, George Ritzer coined the term "McDonaldization" to refer to a set of organizational principles—including efficiency, uniformity, predictability, and control— that play an important part in today's society. Here, he describes the way McDonald's and similar organizations control not just their workers, but also their customers.

In recent years the spread of McDonaldized systems has led to the creation of an enormous number of jobs. Unfortunately, the majority of them can be thought of as McDonaldized jobs, or "McJobs." While we usually associate these types of positions with fast-food restaurants, and in fact there are many such jobs in that setting (over 2.5 million people worked in that industry in the United States in 1992 [Van Giezen, 1994]), McJobs have spread throughout much of the economy with the growing impact of McDonaldization on work settings which had previously experienced relatively little rationalization.

It is worth outlining some of the basic realities of employment in the fast-food industry in the United States since those jobs serve as a model for employment in other McDonaldized settings (Van Giezen, 1994). The large number of people

Source: Reprinted by permission of Sage Publications Ltd. from George Ritzer, *The McDonaldization Thesis: Explorations and Extensions*, Copyright © 1998 Sage Publications.

employed in fast-food restaurants accounts for over 40 percent of the approximately 6 million people employed in restaurants of all types. Fast-food restaurants rely heavily on teenage employees— almost 70 percent of their employees are twenty years of age or younger. For many, the fast-food restaurant is likely to be their first employer. It is estimated that the first job for one of every fifteen workers was at McDonald's; one of every eight Americans has worked at McDonald's at some time in his or her life. The vast majority of employees are part-time workers: The average work week in the fast-food industry is 29.5 hours. There is a high turnover rate: Only slightly more than half the employees remain on the job for a year or more. Minorities are over-represented in these jobs—almost two-thirds of employees are women and nearly a quarter are non-white. These are low-paid occupations, with many earning the minimum wage, or slightly more. As a result, these jobs are greatly affected by changes in the minimum wage: An upward revision has an important effect on the income of these workers. However, there is a real danger that many workers would lose their positions as a result of such increases, especially in economically marginal fast-food restaurants.[1]

Although the McDonaldization of society is manifest at all levels and in all realms of the social world, the work world has played a particularly pivotal role in this. On the one hand, it is the main source of many of the precursors of McDonaldization, including bureaucracies, scientific management, assembly lines, and so on. More contemporaneously, the kinds of jobs, work procedures, and organizing principles that have made McDonald's so successful have affected the way in which many businesses now organize much of their work. In fact, it could well be argued that the primary root of the McDonaldization of the larger society is the work world. On the other hand, the McDonaldization of the larger society has, in turn, served to further rationalize the work world. We thus have a self-reinforcing and enriching process that is speeding the growth and spread of McDonaldization.

The process of McDonaldization is leading to the creation of more and more McJobs.[2] The service sector, especially at its lower end, is producing an enormous number of jobs, most of them requiring little or no skill. There is no better example of this than the mountain of jobs being produced by the fast-food industry. However, new occupational creation is not the only source of McJobs: Many extant low-level jobs are being McDonaldized. More strikingly, large numbers of middle-level jobs are also being deskilled and transformed into McJobs.

McJobs are characterized by the five dimensions of McDonaldization. The jobs tend to involve a series of simple tasks in which the emphasis is on performing each as efficiently as possible. Second, the time associated with many of the tasks is carefully calculated and the emphasis on the quantity of time a task should take tends to diminish the quality of the work from the point of view of the worker. That is, tasks are so simplified

and streamlined that they provide little or no meaning to the worker. Third, the work is predictable: employees do and say essentially the same things hour after hour, day after day. Fourth, many nonhuman technologies are employed to control workers and reduce them to robotlike actions. Some technologies are in place, and others are in development, that will lead to the eventual replacement of many of these "human robots" with computerized robots. Finally, the rationalized McJobs lead to a variety of irrationalities, especially the dehumanization of work. The result is the extraordinarily high turnover rate described above and difficulty in maintaining an adequate supply of replacements.[3]

The claim is usually made by spokespeople for McDonaldized systems that they are offering a large number of entry-level positions that help give employees basic skills they will need in order to move up the occupational ladder within such systems (and many of them do). This is likely to be true in the instances in which the middle-level jobs to which they move—for example shift leader, assistant manager, or manager of a fast-food restaurant—are also routinized and scripted. In fact, it turns out that this even holds for the positions held by the routinized and scripted instructors at [McDonald's training program at] Hamburger University who teach the managers, who teach the employees, and so on. However, the skills acquired in McJobs are not likely to prepare one for, help one to acquire, or help one to function well in, the far more desirable postindustrial occupations which are highly complex and require high levels of skill and education. Experience in routinized actions and scripted interactions do not help much when occupations require thought and creativity....

At the cultural level, large numbers of people in the United States, and increasingly throughout much of the rest of the world, have come to value McDonaldization in general, as well as its fundamental characteristics. McDonaldization, as well as its various principles, has become part of our value system. That value system has, in turn, been translated into a series of principles that have been exported to, adopted by, and adapted to, a wide range of social settings....

...For example, the behavior of customers at fast-food restaurants is being affected in much the same way as the behavior of those who work in those restaurants....

The constraints on the behavior of employees and customers in McDonaldized systems are of both a structural and a cultural nature. Employees and customers find themselves in a variety of McDonaldized structures that demand that they behave in accord with the dictates of those structures. For example, the drive-through window associated with the fast-food restaurant (as well as other settings such as banks) structures both what customers in their cars and employees in their booths can and cannot do. They can efficiently exchange money for food, but their positions (in a car and a booth) and the press of other cars in the queue make any kind of personal interaction virtually impossible. Of course, many other kinds of behavior are either made possible, or prohibited, by such structures. In Giddens's (1984) terms, such structures are both enabling and constraining.

At a cultural level, both employees and customers are socialized into, and have internalized, the norms and values of working and living in a McDonaldized society. Employees are trained by managers or owners who are likely, themselves, to have been trained at an institution like McDonald's Hamburger University (Schaaf, 1991). Such institutions are as much concerned with inculcating norms and values as they are with the teaching of basic skills. For their part, customers are not required to attend Hamburger University, but they are "trained" by the employees themselves, by television advertisements, and by their own children who are often diligent students, teachers, and enforcers of the McDonald's way. This "training," like that of those employees who attend Hamburger University, is oriented not only to teaching the "skills" required to be a customer at a fast-food restaurant (e.g. how to queue up in order to order food), but also the norms and values

of such settings as they apply to customers (e.g. customers are expected to dispose of their own debris; they are not expected to linger after eating). As a result of such formal and informal training, both employees and customers can be relied on to do what they are supposed to, and what is expected of them, with little or no personal supervision....

...McJobs are not simply the deskilled jobs of our industrial past in new settings; they are jobs that have a variety of new and distinctive characteristics.... Industrial and McDonaldized jobs both tend to be highly routinized in terms of what people do on the job. However, one of the things that is distinctive about McDonaldized jobs, especially since so many of them involve work that requires interaction and communication, especially with consumers, is that what people *say* on the job is also highly routinized. To put this another way, McDonaldized jobs are tightly scripted: They are characterized by *both* routinized actions (for example, the way McDonald's hamburgers are to be put down on the grill and flipped [Love, 1986: 141–2]) and scripted interactions (examples include, "May I help you?"; "Would you like a dessert to go with your meal?"; "Have a nice day!"). Scripts are crucial because, as Leidner (1993) points out, many of the workers in McDonaldized systems are interactive service workers. This means that they not only produce goods and provide services, but they often do so in interaction with customers.

The scripting of interaction leads to new depths in the deskilling of workers. Not only have employee actions been deskilled; employees' ability to speak and interact with customers is now being limited and controlled. There are not only scripts to handle general situations, but also a range of subscripts to deal with a variety of contingencies. Verbal and interactive skills are being taken away from employees and built into the scripts in much the same way that manual skills were taken and built into various technologies. At one time distrusted in their ability to *do* the right thing, workers now find themselves no longer trusted to *say* the right thing. Once able to create distinctive interactive styles, and to adjust them to different circumstances, employees are now asked to follow scripts as mindlessly as possible....

One very important, but rarely noted, aspect of the labor process in the fast-food restaurant and other McDonaldized systems is the extent to which customers are being led, perhaps even almost required, to perform a number of tasks without pay that were formerly performed by paid employees. For example, in the modern gasoline station the driver now does various things for free (pumps gas, cleans windows, checks oil, even pays through a computerized credit card system built into the pump) that were formerly done by paid attendants. In these and many other settings, McDonaldization has brought the customer *into* the labor process: The customer *is* the laborer! This has several advantages for employers such as lower (even nonexistent) labor costs, the need for fewer employees, and less trouble with personnel problems: Customers are far less likely to complain about a few seconds or minutes of tedious work than employees who devote a full work day to such tasks. Because of its advantages, as well as because customers are growing accustomed to and accepting of it, I think customers are likely to become even more involved in the labor process.

This is the most revolutionary development, at least as far as the labor process is concerned, associated with McDonaldization. As a result of this dramatic change, the analysis of the labor process must be extended to what customers do in McDonaldized systems. The distinction between customer and employee is eroding, or in postmodern terms "imploding," and one can envision more and more work settings in which customers are asked to do an increasing amount of "work." More dramatically, it is also likely that we will see more work settings in which there are no employees at all! In such settings customers, in interaction with nonhuman technologies, will do *all* of the human labor. A widespread example is the ATM in which customers (and the technology)

do all of the work formerly done by bank tellers. More strikingly, we are beginning to see automated loan machines which dispense loans as high as $10,000 (Singletary, 1996). Again, customers and technologies do the work and, in the process, many loan-officer positions are eliminated. Similarly, the new automated gasoline pumps allow (or force) customers to do all of the required tasks; in some cases and at certain times (late at night) no employees at all are present.

In a sense, a key to the success of McDonaldized systems is that they have been able to supplement the exploitation of employees with the exploitation of customers. Lest we forget, Marx "put at the heart of his sociology—as no other sociology does—the theme of exploitation" (Worsley, 1982: 115). In Marxian theory, the capitalists are seen as simply paying workers less than the value produced by the workers, and as keeping the rest for themselves. This dynamic continues in contemporary society, but capitalists have learned that they can ratchet up the level of exploitation not only by exploiting workers more, but also by exploiting a whole new group of people—consumers. In Marxian terms, customers create value in the tasks they perform for McDonaldized systems. And they are not simply paid less than the value they produce, they are paid *nothing at all*. In this way, customers are exploited to an even greater degree than workers....

While no class within society is immune to McDonaldization, the lower classes are the most affected. They are the ones who are most likely to go to McDonaldized schools, live in inexpensive, mass-produced tract houses, and work in McDonaldized jobs. Those in the upper classes have much more of a chance of sending their children to non-McDonaldized schools, living in custom-built homes, and working in occupations in which they impose McDonaldization on others while avoiding it to a large degree themselves.

Also related to the social class issue...is the fact that the McDonaldization of a significant portion of the labor force does not mean that all, or even most, of the labor force is undergoing this process. In fact, the McDonaldization of some of the labor force is occurring at the same time that another large segment is moving in a postindustrial, that is, more highly skilled, direction (Hage & Powers, 1992). Being created in this sector of society are relatively high-status, well-paid occupations requiring high levels of education and training. In the main, these are far from McJobs and lack most, or all, of the dimensions discussed at the beginning of this [reading]. The growth of such postindustrial occupations parallels the concern in the labor process literature with flexible specialization occurring side by side with the deskilling of many other jobs. This points to a bifurcation in the class system. In spite of appearances, there is no contradiction here; McDonaldization and postindustrialization tend to occur in different sectors of the labor market. However, the spread of McJobs leads us to be dubious of the idea that we have moved into a new postindustrial era and have left behind the kind of deskilled jobs we associate with industrial society.

CRITICAL THINKING QUESTIONS

1. Describe ways in which McDonaldization is evident in many familiar settings (not just the workplace, but perhaps shopping malls and even university campuses). What elements of McDonaldization can you find?
2. In what ways does a McDonaldized setting control not just workers but also customers? Why do organizations want to control customers?
3. Why does McDonaldization seem to appeal to many people? Do you think this process is good or harmful for society as a whole? Why?

NOTES

This chapter combines a paper, "McJobs," published in Rich Feller and Garry Walz (eds.), *Career Transitions in Turbulent Times* (Greensboro, N.C.: ERIC/CASS Publications, 1996) and the Invited Plenary Address, International Labour Process Conference, Blackpool, England, April, 1995.

1. Although a study by Katz and Krueger (1992) indicates an employment *increase* accompanying a rise in the minimum wage.
2. As we will see below, other kinds of high-status, high-paying postindustrial occupations are also growing.
3. There are, of course, many other factors involved in turnover.

REFERENCES

Giddens, A. 1984. *The constitution of society: Outline of the theory of structuration.* Berkeley: University of California Press.

Hage, J., and C. H. Powers. 1992. *Post-industrial lives: Roles and relationships in the 21st century.* Newbury Park, Calif.: Sage.

Leidner, R. 1993. *Fast food, fast talk: Service work and the routinization of everyday life.* Berkeley: University of California Press.

Love, J. 1986. *McDonald's: Behind the arches.* Toronto: Bantam Books.

Schaaf, D. 1994. Inside Hamburger University. *Training*, December: 18–24.

Singletary, M. 1996. Borrowing by the touch. *Washington Post*, (30 March): C1, C2.

Van Giezen, R. W. 1994. Occupational wages in the fast-food restaurant industry. *Monthly Labor Review*, August: 24–30.

Worsley, P. 1982. *Marx and Marxism.* Chichester: Ellis Horwood.

54

The Changing Colour of Poverty
in Canada

*Abdolmohammad Kazemipur
and Shiva S. Halli*

*Kazemipur and Halli investigate the issue of poor or low-income immigrants. They reveal
that immigrants are consistently overrepresented among Canada's poor; moreover, immigrants belonging to visible-minority groups are the most likely to suffer poverty.*

Using the 1991 and 1996 Canadian census data, the
present study addresses the issue of poor or low-
income immigrants, a topic largely overlooked in
previous immigration research. The authors found
that, compared to native-born Canadians, immigrants were consistently overrepresented among
the poor, and that this overrepresentation had a
clear ethnic and racial colour, with visible-minority
immigrants experiencing the most severe conditions. For them, the logistic regression models
show, the odds of poverty are noticeably higher,
even after controlling for all other relevant variables. The poverty rates of different generations of
immigrants also show an unexpected pattern, in
which those who have migrated during their
adolescent years experience unusually severe
poverty conditions. A comparison of the situation

in 1991 and 1996 shows that human capital endowments are becoming less rewarding for immigrants.

In the last two decades of the 20th century,
like many other industrial nations, Canada went
through some radical transformations, influenced
by two major forces—one economic, the other
political. The Canadian economy has been shifting away from a structure based on manufacturing to one dependent on information processing,
and from one dependent on domestic resources
to one increasingly operating in a global scene.
This development has influenced many aspects
of Canadian society, but particularly its occupational structure, income distribution, and regional
inequality (Marchak, 1991; Rifkin, 1995). In the
political arena, a new wave of conservatism,
which some have called Neoliberalism (Abu-
Laban, 1998) and others New Right (Marchak,
1991), has swept across the country, forcing major
Canadian social institutions—such as education,
health care, occupations, the social safety net and
the taxation system—to depart from their postwar
paths of development. Despite having dynamics

Source: A. Kazemipur and S.S. Halli. 2001. "The Changing
Colour of Poverty in Canada." *Canadian Review of Sociology
and Anthropology,* 38(2), 217–38.

of their own, these two trends—economic and political—have converged in at least one area, eroding the middle class and generating a bipolar structure in the economy, job market, and income distribution (Teeple, 1995). The essence of this development is well captured in a commonly expressed metaphor that the industrial societies are leaving a pyramid shape in favour of an hourglass one (Portes and Rumbaut, 1996).

One area in which the effects of the new economic and political circumstances have been more visible is in immigration policy and the social and economic experiences of immigrants. This has partly to do with the nature of the Neoliberal prescriptions that, according to Abu-Laban (1998: 194), "have a tendency to create discourses of enemies and scapegoats, transforming what were once seen as victims into victimizers (e.g., single mothers, the poor, immigrants and so on are blamed for stealing 'our' welfare, 'our' social and educational services, or 'our' jobs)." In many Western countries, she argues, "such discourses relating to immigrants have resulted in both a tightening of criteria for formal citizenship, and a tightening of immigration controls vis-à-vis certain groups and nationals—typically those from countries of the Third World" (194). The clear implication of this proposition is that, in an era of Neoliberal politics, with its associated fiscal conservatism and priority of deficit reduction, the vulnerable groups such as immigrants are more likely to suffer disproportionately.

The present study tries to shed some light on the validity of the above proposition by empirically examining the experience of poverty by immigrants to Canada and the factors behind it. The choice of poverty as the topic is justified based on two facts. First, in an era marked by transition from a "pyramid"- to an "hourglass"-shaped social structure, a larger number of people may find themselves at the lower level of social structure and income scale, as reflected in the constant rise of poverty levels in Canada since the late 1980s. A study of poverty, therefore, will address a social problem that more and more people will be struggling with. Second, in the particular case of immigrants, most of the previous research has treated them as one homogeneous sub-population, masking the enormous diversity that exists among them. The plight of low-income immigrants has gone largely unnoticed in serious academic research, though it has received some attention in the popular media.

The central questions with which we are concerned are: 1) What is the magnitude of poverty among immigrants, compared to non-immigrants? 2) What is the composition of poor immigrants, in terms of ethnic origin, location of residence, period of migration, and age at arrival? 3) What are the causes of poverty among immigrants, and are they different from those of non-immigrants? and finally, 4) How has immigrants' experience of poverty and its causative factors changed during the period of the Neoliberal swing in Canadian politics? In what follows, we first introduce an overarching conceptual framework for understanding the causes of poverty among immigrants. This framework has an eclectic nature; it includes conceptual elements taken from various theoretical approaches. This allows for an examination of the relative significance of the different factors emphasized by different perspectives. Then we address the methodological issues and describe the nature of the data used. The article concludes with a presentation of the findings, and the implications for future research.

THE CONCEPTUAL FRAMEWORK

The paucity of research on poverty among immigrants has hindered the development of theories specifically formulated to address this issue. This theoretical shortage is certainly, at least partly, a result of the paucity of research on poverty in Canada. But it has also been reinforced by the long-held view that the problem of poverty among immigrants is not any more serious than among the native-born. Against this background, it is understandable why the poverty of immigrants has never come to the foreground, nor ever been high in the immigration-research agenda. To these factors of theoretical significance, one may add a possible third factor of a more practical nature: an unconscious reluctance among researchers to raise an issue that could be easily used against immigrants and in favour of more restrictive immigration policies. The result, whatever the causes, is the current lack of a well-developed theory of immigrant poverty.

The paucity of specific theories of poverty, however, does not mean that we are left in a theoretical vacuum. Indeed, there exists a rich literature on the general economic performance of immigrants that has useful implications for the study of poverty. Examining the validity of John Porter's thesis of the "vertical mosaic," Lautard and Loree (1984), for instance, found that the occupational inequality among ethnic groups in Canada was substantial enough to justify the use of the notion of a "vertical mosaic," and that the differences observed "do not seem to be explainable by the effects of differences in regions and differences in education" (342). In a search for factors that can explain these persisting patterns of inequality, Grant and Oertel (1998: 70) suggest three possibilities: "A slower rate of acquisition of unobservable skills (such as language proficiency and awareness of cultural norms specific to Canada); a higher degree of discrimination with the rising percentage of visible minorities among immigrants; or a change in the structure of employment in Canada in favour of lower-paid service occupations." This proposition, indeed, encompasses three major theoretical approaches employed in the previous research on the economic performance of immigrants: one that emphasizes the individual factors such as assimilation and human capital; another that stresses the economic environment of the host society at the time of immigrants' arrival; and a third that highlights the social environment in the receiving country, along with factors such as discrimination, as predictors of immigrants' performance. Over time, each of these theoretical approaches has branched out into various versions, with slight differences. Below, we introduce the variations of these perspectives in more detail, along with their implications for the issue of concern in this study, that is, poverty.

Assimilation Thesis

The *assimilation thesis* considers poverty of immigrants as a passing phenomenon due to immediate post-migration difficulties, a problem that eases up with longer stay in the new home. The assimilation theory would hypothesize that over time immigrants produce better economic records, as they become increasingly familiar with their new environments, develop better communication skills, and become more realistic in their expectations. In other words, in their early years after arrival immigrants face the harshest situation. This harshness, however, subsides as time allows for more assimilation to take place. It follows that the situation is even more favourable for the second generation of immigrants, as for them such a process starts from childhood and even from birth. As far as poverty is concerned, the most vulnerable immigrants—that is, those with a high risk of poverty—are to be found among those in their early years of arrival, those with little or no knowledge of the official languages, and those who migrated at an older age.

Entrance Status Thesis

While the early "assimilationists" paid more attention to cultural and ideational processes (see Park and Burgess, 1924; Gordon, 1964), the later ones put more emphasis on economic factors. Porter (1965) suggested "the entrance status thesis," in which immigrants start from the lowest jobs in the market and move their way up the occupational hierarchy, leaving the entrance status jobs for the newly arrived immigrants. In this perspective, immigrants' economic perform-ance is a function of their occupational ranking, itself a function of their duration of stay in the host society and the existence of consecutive waves of immigrants. Those immigrants who are in the early years of their arrival, according to this view, are more likely to have higher poverty rates, but this likelihood diminishes with longer stays and movement to more rewarding jobs.

Human Capital Thesis

This perspective puts more emphasis on human capital endowments of immigrants as determi-nants of their economic performance. A low-income status, according to this thesis, can result from factors such as low education, low job skills, old age, poor health, and low geographical mobility. A low education, for example, can suppress one's chance of admission into well-paid jobs that demand a highly skilled labour force; old age can be detrimental when success-ful performance in a job requires mastery of modern technology; low geographical mobility, both nationally and internationally, tends to deprive one of the job opportunities available elsewhere. Borjas (1994), for instance, has attrib-uted the lower level of economic achievement among recent immigrants in the United States to the fact that they have come mostly from devel-oping countries, and with low levels of educa-tional qualifications and occupational skills (Massey et al., 1994).

Discrimination Thesis

Despite the significance of human capital factors, many studies have shown that an explanation merely based on such factors runs the risk of being too static and fairly simplistic. Some have raised the possibility that the lower economic achievement of recent immigrants may be attrib-uted not to their lower level of human capital endowment but to the diminishing returns for it. Gordon (1995: 530), for example, attributes the

lower educational attainments of second genera-tion immigrants to the diminishing returns for their education: "[against] a background of envi-ronmental disadvantages, institutional racism, and doubts about the likely rewards for qualifi-cations, educational attainments have been uneven." Basran and Zong (1999), on the other hand, argue that even when the educational attainments are high for immigrants, they are not recognized accordingly. They show that large numbers of immigrants in Canada have occupa-tions inferior, in terms of both prestige and finan-cial gains, to those for which they are trained, due to the fact that their credentials are not recog-nized appropriately.

The studies cited above clearly imply that the positive impact of human capital factors can be intercepted by other factors such as discrimina-tion, both at interpersonal and institutional levels. Among all possible types of discrimination, one based on race and ethnic characteristics is found to be most common and persistent, as well as more conducive to poverty. This relationship is well captured in an observation by Dunk (1999) that "it is no historical accident...that skin colour and poverty are related."

Empirical studies of the impact of discrimina-tion on the economic performance of immigrants in Canada have yielded mixed results. A report by the Economic Council of Canada (1991), for instance, claimed that there was no substantial discrimination against immigrants, and in partic-ular against visible minorities. This report was later criticized for its flawed statistical and meas-urement methods, two of which being the use of country of birth instead of ethnic and racial origins, and the smallness of the. samples—as low as a dozen for some ethnic groups (Reitz and Breton, 1994). More rigorous treatment of the problem in later research resulted in an opposite finding. In a study to measure the "market value of race," for example, Li (1999: 126) found that "non-white origin creates a penalty for all visible minorities in the labour market." He attributed such a penalty to a range of mechanisms, from refusing to recognize the non-white immigrants' credentials, to their lower likelihood of being hired, higher chances of being screened out in the job-application process owing to their language characteristics, accent, and deviation from the language standard of the dominant group. Along this line, Reitz and Breton (1994:122) found "consistent and substantial net earnings disadvantages" for both adult immigrants and immigrants raised in Canada. The expression of the opposing views in regard to whether immigrants face discrimination in Canada justifies their inclusion in our analysis. However, due to the fact that discrimination does not easily lend itself to direct observation, and that its impact is often confounded by other variables, the findings of this study on discrimination need to be approached cautiously. The variables included in census data are only indirect proxies for discrimination.

Period Effect Thesis

In addition to assimilation, human capital, and discrimination, the period in which one migrated can also affect one's economic performance. Commenting on the experiences of recent immigrants to the United States, Gans (1992) remarked:

> . . . the long-term periods of economic growth, the first that began after the Civil War and the second that started after World War II, are not likely to return soon. The first helped to spur the arrival of the new European immigrants and enabled them to find more or less steady jobs so that many of them or their children could escape poverty by the end of the 1920s. The second enabled the descendents of that immigration to move at least into the upper-working and lower-middle classes, and in many cases, firmly into the middle class. Even if periods of long-term economic growth return, they will probably not be equally labour-intensive. No-one expects a revival in physical labour, and even many low-level service jobs may be computerized, sent abroad, or left undone. Such trends have special meaning for the new immigration and its second generation since, among other things, they could lead to what I have earlier called second-generation decline (181).

In Canada, likewise, the post–World War II decades were especially prosperous, providing newly arrived immigrants with plenty of opportunities. Shorter periods of waiting to get into a first job, the rarity of employment terminations, and the prevalence of full-time occupations enabled immigrants to have an early financial take-off and establish themselves more easily. Such an economic environment, however, is totally nonexistent for those immigrants who have landed in Canada since the mid-1970s. There is, therefore, a higher likelihood for these groups of immigrants to be poorer than their preceding peers.

The theoretical propositions discussed above guide the present study. While some of these propositions are derived from competing theoretical perspectives, as mentioned earlier, we have attempted to include all of them in our conceptual model to verify them empirically. Figure 54.1 encapsulates the conceptual synthesis that we use in the present study.

FIGURE 54.1 The Conceptual Model of the Causes of Poverty among Immigrants

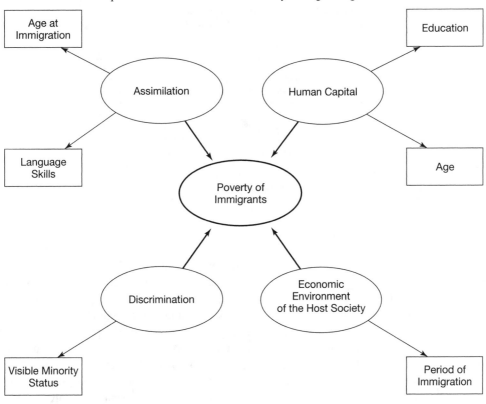

DATA AND METHODOLOGY

The data used in this study consist of the individual Public Use Micro Files (PUMFs) of Canada's 1991 and 1996 censuses.

A word is needed on the notion of poverty and the way it is defined. Like most discussions of poverty in Canada during the last 25 years, this study has employed Statistics Canada's "Low Income Cut-Offs" (LICOs), which are calculated for communities and for families of various sizes within those communities. Table 54.1 contains the poverty lines for the census year 1996. It is important to note that not all researchers agree upon the legitimacy of using LICOs as poverty status indicators. Whether LICOs should be used as indicators of poverty, or should simply be considered as indicators of low income, is still debated (see, for instance, Sarlo, 1992, 1994; Fellegi, 1997). Such a debate is not new, and is certainly not confined to Canada. It is a part of a larger and yet unsettled debate among academics and policy makers on the measure of poverty (see Ruggles, 1990; Kazemipur and Halli, 2000). An examination of the debate surrounding this issue, however, is beyond the scope of this study. Even if the reader does not consider low-income and poverty as equivalent, the trends and patterns found in this study will still remain pertinent to low-income, if not poor, immigrants.

TABLE 54.1: Low-Income Cut-offs for Families and Unattached
Individuals (1986-based), in Dollars, 1996

	Size of Area of Residence				
Family Size	500,000 or More	100,000 to 499,999	30,000 to 99.999	Small Urban Areas	Rural Areas (Farm and Non-farm)
1	15,819	13,895	13,574	12,374	10,769
2	21,442	18,835	18,399	16,771	14,600
3	27,256	23,941	23,387	21,318	18,556
4	31,383	27,561	26,927	24,547	21,364
5	34,287	30,114	29,419	26,818	23,343
6	37,219	32,686	31,932	29,109	25,337
7 or More	40,029	35,159	34,347	31,311	27,252

Source: Statistics Canada (1998).

FINDINGS

Table 54.2 shows the magnitude of poverty for immigrants in Canada in 1996. To provide a better view of the possible impacts of location and ethnicity, poverty rates are reported by city and ethnic origin. Poverty rates of non-immigrants are also included, to compare and to isolate the particular effect of immigrant status. The values that are highlighted specify those groups of immigrants who have poverty rates higher than their non-immigrant counterparts of the same ethnic origin and living in the same city. The table is also divided into three sections based on the geographical origins of the ethnic groups. The top section shows the rates for western and northwestern Europe, the middle section for southern and eastern Europe, and the bottom section for the developing countries.

The first thing to note is the overall magnitude of poverty rates in the three sections of Table 54.2, which reveal a number of consistent patterns. First, a cursory look at the distribution of the cases in the table shown in boldface—that is, the ethnic groups in which immigrants have higher poverty rates than non-immigrants of the same ethnic origin—shows that they occur with much higher frequencies in the middle and bottom sections. To be more specific, considering the

three centres of concentration of immigrants, i.e., Montreal, Toronto and Vancouver, out of a total of fifteen groups in this category, seven groups (47%) show higher rates of poverty for immigrants as compared to non-immigrants of the European ethnic origin. The proportion is 26 out of 30 (or 87%) for the middle section, and 18 out of 33 (or 57%) for the bottom section. At face value, this may indicate that immigrants of eastern and southern European origin are the most disadvantaged groups. This implication, however, is qualified when the magnitude of poverty is taken into consideration. The poverty rates for the eastern and southern European groups vary mostly in the range of 20s and 30s, while those of visible minorities in the bottom section vary in the range of 40s and 50s, with one higher than 60. Also, it should be noted that the poverty rates of the non-immigrants in the bottom section are so noticeably high that being an immigrant hardly aggravates the poverty level. Except for variations in the range of poverty rates, this pattern exists for all three cities.

Second, in addition to the differential rates of poverty for immigrants and non-immigrants, the severity of poverty for certain groups is particularly noticeable. A search for the groups with poverty rates of more than 50% in all

TABLE 54.2: Poverty Rates by Ethnic Origin, CMA and Immigration Status, 1996

	Montreal		Toronto		Vancouver		All other CMAs	
	Non-immigrants	Immigrants	Non-immigrants	Immigrants	Non-immigrants	Immigrants	Non-immigrants	Immigrants
British	26.6	22.7	15.1	14.5	18.4	17	17.1	13.3
French	20.5	27.3	16.4	18.6	21.8	28.6	19.7	17.7
Dutch (Netherlands)	13.5	13.2	9.9	12.9	14.9	21.3	12.4	12.5
German	20.7	15.9	12.3	15.9	19.2	17.4	14.5	16.2
Other Western European	19.3	21.3	15.4	14.2	21.9	18.6	12.0	14.2
Hungarian (Magyar)	18	27.2	18.8	27.8	28.6	36.6	13.8	19.9
Polish	32.7	37.1	17.7	30.2	23.9	31.1	15.3	22.0
Ukrainian	25.6	29.8	14.5	32	20.9	36.6	15.7	20.1
Balkan	26.2	37.1	13.4	25.8	15	41.7	16.2	33.2
Greek	28.8	31.7	19.7	21.5	19.5	24	19.0	16.3
Italian	19.9	23.2	11.7	17.2	15.3	18.8	11.0	15.3
Portuguese	25.3	24	19.5	19.7	15.6	18.3	16.9	14.2
Spanish	53.5	52.8	49.3	43.8	45.2	36	67.1	48.6
Jewish	19.7	29.5	8.3	20.5	10.7	13.5	10.4	22.3
Other European	20.3	42.7	14.6	23.4	22.7	27.8	17.5	20.5
African	70.7	62.6	57.8	55.2	36.4	45.5	57.6	65.6
Lebanese	54.9	53	38.4	45.6	27.3	30.8	42.4	46.6
Other Arab	47.9	54.6	35.5	46.1	38.5	46.4	44.9	50.1
West Asian	38.8	48.1	45.8	47.3	61.8	50.4	50.8	59.7
South Asian	51.4	54.9	27.6	32.6	20.2	23.9	23.4	25.9
Chinese	37.7	45.9	22.1	33.4	19.5	39.5	19.2	31.5
Filipino	28.8	27.5	18.8	23.3	16.1	22.2	18.4	22.4
Vietnamese	41.1	40.5	47.5	38.7	72.2	52	43.3	41.2
Other East/Southeast Asian	56.9	49.8	15.5	36.7	22.4	35.7	28.7	42.2
Latin/Central/South American	69.2	58.7	40.7	35.7	52	44.8	49.2	45.3
Caribbean	58.4	53.4	44.7	32.5	25.9	17.6	41.2	32.6
Total	24	39.6	16	27.7	18.3	29.9	18.2	23.9

CMAs yields an alarming result: one western/ north western European group, 21 southern/eastern European (particularly Spanish), and 103 visible minorities, four of which show a 100% poverty rate (i.e., West Asian non-immigrants in Quebec City, West Asian immigrants in Sherbrooke–Trois-Rivières, Spanish non-immigrants in Hamilton, and Lebanese immigrants in Regina–Saskatoon).

It should be noted, however, that more than 60% of the Spanish reported a Latin American country as their place of birth. This is to say that the most disadvantaged group in the middle section of Table 54.2 is more closely associated with the developing world than with Europe.

The immigrant groups with the highest rates of poverty have another thing in common: the majority of them arrived in Canada since the late 1960s. This commonality can be related to their higher rates of poverty in two ways. First, they arrived after the postwar economic boom in Canada, hence their lower economic performance and higher poverty rates. Second, they are still new immigrants, with a low level of familiarity with Canada, and are still building up their careers. The former possibility alludes to what may be called the "period effect"; the latter, to the "assimilation effect." By showing the poverty rates of different cohorts of immigrants, Table 54.3 allows an empirical examination of these possibilities.

Table 53.3 reports the poverty rate of immigrants by their period of immigration. The last row of the table contains the overall poverty rates for those who migrated in seven different periods. The poverty rate starts at 21.3% for those who arrived before 1946, and consistently declines in three subsequent categories, reaching its lowest level in the 1960s (14.2%). It then rises noticeably. This trend clearly supports the period effect, as it is perfectly synchronized with the postwar periods of economic boom and bust in Canada. This general confirmation should be qualified, however, with a reminder that the best way to isolate the period effect is through the use of longitudinal data. In the absence of such data, the period effect can be confounded by other variables, thus obscuring the findings.

When it comes to testing the assimilation effect, however, Table 54.3 is more reliable. One implication of assimilation theory was that immigrants who migrated at an earlier age would show better economic performance, owing to their familiarity with the social environment and market demands in their new homes, access to job-searching social networks, better language skills, less severe cultural conflict, and recognized education. It follows that the poverty rates of immigrants should increase as their age at migration increases. The average poverty rates of immigrants by their age at migration shown in the last two columns of Table 54.3 support this argument, though with some qualification. The poverty rates for all immigrants reported in the first column yields the surprising result that those who migrated at a younger age are as, or more, disadvantaged than their parents, as far as their poverty is concerned. The exclusion of those under 16, with the justification that they are not at the employment age and therefore do not yet earn income, improves the results to some extent. It clearly shows that those who migrated at age 0–4, who can be considered analogous to second-generation immigrants, have the lowest rate of poverty. The poverty rate then rises as the age at migration increases. The only anomaly in this trend is the poverty rate of those who migrated at age 13–19, for whom the poverty rate exceeds those of the age groups immediately before and after them. This anomaly persists regardless of the period of immigration, and it clearly runs in contrast to the expectation derived from the assimilation theory. It therefore demands an explanation. In the absence of any previous study on this issue, one can only speculate about the possible reasons, as potential hypotheses for future research.

Rumbaut (1997) lays a theoretical foundation for treating various generations of immigrants, which may be of use here. To the conventional categories of first and second generations, Rumbaut (1997: 951) adds the intermediary categories of "1.25,"

TABLE 54.3: Poverty Rates of Cohorts of Immigrants, 1996*

Age at Immigration	Period of Immigration							Average (All Immigrants)	Average*
	Before 1946*	1946–50*	1951–60*	1961–70*	1971–80*	1981–90*	1991–96*		
0–4	17.1	10.9	10.8	12.7	21.9	23.0	—	23.9	15.7
5–12	18.3	10.5	10.5	12.7	18.9	34.0	50.0	27.2	19.0
13–19	28.8	13.5	14.6	13.2	18.8	31.7	54.9	26.6	25.9
20–24	27.5	12.8	16.4	10.4	16.6	29.4	44.9	21.6	21.6
25–29	27.6	17.6	15.7	12.9	14.9	29.6	43.1	23.4	23.4
30–34	33.3	18.6	17.4	17.3	15.6	25.6	48.7	26.6	26.6
35–39	37.5	29.9	19.5	19.7	18.8	27.9	53.4	31.7	31.7
40–44	100.0	34.6	28.3	19.1	22.6	28.9	53.5	34.5	34.5
45–49	—	31.3	27.7	21.7	24.9	29.2	51.0	34.5	34.5
50–54	—	33.3	38.7	33.7	28.2	30.1	44.4	34.7	34.7
55–59	—	—	14.3	30.8	31.3	35.4	43.7	36.9	36.9
60 +	—	—	—	27.3	31.1	36.2	40.5	37.1	37.1
Average	21.3	15.1	15.2	14.2	18.8	30.1	48.3	26.6	24.9

*Only those aged 16 years and older in 1996 included.

"1.5," and "1.75" generations, in reference to those who migrated at ages 13–17 (adolescence and secondary school), 6–12 (after primary socialization and the beginning of elementary school), and 0–5 (preschool), respectively. Using this categorization, it is clear that the age group with an unusually high rate of poverty is the "1.25" generation. Adolescence is often a time of enormous psychological and emotional unrest. Adolescents have to deal with a range of difficulties, from generational conflict to peer pressures. Such pressures are confounded for immigrant adolescents, as they have also to deal with the burdens of learning a new language and functioning in a new cultural environment. Immigrant adolescents are also more likely to experience what Igoa (1995) calls "fragmented formal education" owing to their families' frequent mobility and high instability during the immediate years after arrival. Rumbaut points out that to overcome these difficulties, they need strong support by, and the collaboration of, parents and teachers. In most cases, however, immigrant parents are too busy securing their economic foothold, particularly in the early years of arrival, and have little time to spend with their children. The possibility of discrimination at school also deprives adolescent immigrants of the potential support of their teachers. The "1.25" generation immigrants find themselves alone in the face of these difficulties. Everything is left to their individual capacities and motivation. But, as Gordon (1995: 530) has remarked, the individual motivation for educational attainment and economic success may also be suppressed against "a background of environmental disadvantages, institutional racism, and doubts about the likely rewards for qualifications." The most likely outcome to which such circumstances are conducive is failure.

Another possible explanation of the poor economic performance of the "1.25" generation immigrants may be their lower level of social capital, as suggested by Portes (1995). The main thrust of Portes's thesis is that second-generation immigrants become assimilated, but not necessarily into the mainstream culture. Depending on factors such as their neighbourhoods, he argues, they may be assimilated into the underclass:

[the] overconcentration in the inner cities, which is a direct consequence of the lower economic resources of recent immigrants, has an unexpected consequence, namely to bring the offspring of these immigrants into close contact with downtrodden domestic minorities.... The confrontation with inner-city values places the second generation in a serious dilemma (Portes, 1995: 252).

Although this issue has not been systematically addressed in the Canadian context, the available studies allude to its relevance to Canada as well. In a study of neighbourhood poverty in Canada, Kazemipur and Halli (1997), for instance, have shown the overconcentration of certain ethnic groups, mostly visible minorities, in neighbourhoods with more than 40% poverty rates. In another attempt, Kazemipur and Halli (2000) have found that the visible minority immigrants, who are overrepresented in ghetto neighbourhoods, also tend to show a lower level of intergenerational mobility in terms of education and occupation. Further and more sophisticated research on this issue is seriously hampered by the lack of specific data sets combining the neighbourhood variables and individual characteristics.

CONCLUSION AND IMPLICATIONS

Some have argued that recent immigrants show a lower-than-expected economic performance, and have alluded to their lower "quality" (e.g., education, work experience) as the cause (Borjas, 1994). Our study of the experiences of low-income immigrants in Canada supports the first part of this argument—that is, that recent immigrants have a poorer economic record as compared to the previous cohorts—but it seriously questions the validity of the second part pertaining to the causes of such trends. Rather, we found that the odds of poverty among immigrants increased due to lower levels of returns to "quality" variables such as education, language skills, and type of employment, along with the penalizing effects of factors such as their racial origin and immigrant status.

Such findings, if sustained through more rigorous studies using more comprehensive data, have far-reaching implications for both public policy and future research. Over the past few years, Canadian studies have increasingly highlighted the significance of the lower returns to human capital endowments of immigrants, manifested in things such as the mismatch between their educational qualifications and occupations, or between their professional qualifications before and after migration (Basran and Zong, 1998); the lower returns to the educational investment of those immigrants with credentials earned abroad (Wanner, 1998); and the adoption of self-employment by immigrants as a result of their blocked mobility in salaried jobs typically dependent on education (Li, 2000). The problem is cited too frequently, and its existence and prevalence shown in too many different ways, to be disregarded as a passing phenomenon. It calls for a thorough revision of the procedures currently in effect for evaluation of the foreign credentials of immigrants.

Racial discrimination is another problem that deserves more attention. Although the findings of this study on the effect of racial discrimination are far from definitive (due to the inherent measurement limitations in the data used here), they are consistent with the findings of many previous studies and also with the trends observed in other immigrant-receiving countries. If left unchecked, the problem of race is only going to intensify. As Reitz (1998) has legitimately argued, the current flows of immigrants from Asia, Africa, and Latin America is going to make racial diversity a central feature of all industrial nations, and more so for immigrant-intensive countries such as Canada. Against this background, prevalence of racial discrimination in Canada would imply underutilization of human resources at present, and the potential for social conflicts in the future. None of these is a small enough problem to ignore.

The present study also implies two particular directions for future research, one more of a technical nature, the other conceptual. Despite their richness, the census data do not provide adequate information on language skills. Given the centrality of language acquisition in the later social and economic experiences of immigrants, this inadequacy renders census data of limited use for the study of immigrants. Ironically, there is enough emphasis on measuring language skills in procedures related to immigrants—including the processing of the applications for landed immigrant status, or the decisions regarding the costs of language training of family-class immigrants—but these emphases evaporate in the later data-collection practices.

The conceptual problem involves the gender aspect of the issue of poverty examined above. In the recent surge of poverty in Canada, women have suffered more severely compared to men, a notion captured in the use of the term "feminization of poverty" in recent sociological literature (see Duffy and Mandell, 1994; Duffy and Pupo, 1992; Kazemipur and Halli, 2000). So, a study of poverty in the general population without regard to gender runs the risk of masking the peculiar situation of low-income women. For immigrant women, the problem has an additional dimension, as their experiences are different from both native-born women and also immigrant men. At the heart of these differential experiences lies the fact that, according to Pendakur and Pendakur (1998), the heads of prospective immigrant families are likely to be men, screened for occupational suitability and job readiness, and therefore more likely to enter Canada with recognized and rewarded credentials and jobs ready for them. As a result, female immigrants are more susceptible to losing their human capital or not getting its full return. Several studies have persuasively shown that the findings based on the study of male immigrants are not readily generalizable to female immigrants (Satzewich, 1995; Reitz, 1998; Pendakur and Pendakur, 1998), so much so that Ng (1986) has argued that "immigrant women" have come to be constituted as a distinct social category in the Canadian labour market. The findings of this study need to be furthered by including the gender dimension of poverty among immigrants.

CRITICAL THINKING QUESTIONS

1. With reference to the article, review your choice of three reasons why immigrants are more likely to suffer from poverty than non-immigrants. As a sociologist, do you think poverty among Canadian immigrant populations will get better or worse over the next twenty years? Defend your answer.
2. Compare and contrast two theories introduced by the authors that attempt to explain the economic performance of immigrants.
3. Review and discuss the unique challenges faced by the "1.25" generation.

REFERENCES

Abu-Laban, Y. 1998. "Welcome/STAY OUT: The contradictions of Canadian integration and immigration policies at the millennium." *Canadian Ethnic Studies,* Vol. 30, No. 3, pp. 190–211.

Basran, G. S., and L. Zong. 1998. Devaluation of foreign credentials as perceived by nonwhite professional immigrants. *Canadian Ethnic Studies,* Vol. 30, No. 3, pp. 6–23.

Borjas, G. J. 1994. The economics of immigration. *Journal of Economic Literature,* Vol. 32, pp. 1667–1717.

Duffy, A., and N. Mandell. 1994. Poverty in Canada. In *Society in question.* R. Brym (ed.). Toronto: Harcourt Brace & Company, pp. 96–104.

Duffy, A., and N. Pupo. 1992. *Part-time paradox: Connecting gender, work, and family.* Toronto: McClelland & Stewart.

Dunk, P. 1999. Racism, ethnic prejudice, whiteness and the working class. In *Racism and social inequality in Canada.*

V Satzewich (ed.). Toronto: Thompson Educational Publishing, Inc., pp. 201–22.

Economic Council of Canada. 1991. *New faces in the crowd: Economic and social impacts of immigration.* Ottawa: Minister of Supply and Services.

Fellegi, I. P. 1997. On poverty and low income. <http://www.statcan.ca/english/concepts/poverty/pauv.htm>, viewed Jan 27, 1998.

Gans, H. J. 1992. Second-generation decline: Scenarios for the economic and ethnic futures of the post-1965 American immigrants. *Ethnic and Racial Studies,* Vol. 15, No. 2, pp. 173–92.

Gordon, I. 1995. "The impact of economic change on minorities and migrants in western Europe." In *Poverty, inequality, and the future of social policy.* K. McFate, R. Lawson, and W. Wilson (eds.). New York: Russell Sage Foundation, pp. 521–42.

Gordon, M. M. 1964. *Assimilation in American life.* New York: Oxford UP.

Grant, H. M., and R. R. Oertel. 1998. "Diminishing returns to immigration? Interpreting the economic experience of Canadian immigrants." *Canadian Ethnic Studies,* Vol. 30, No. 3, pp. 56–76.

Igoa, C. 1995. *The Inner world of the immigrant child.* New York: St. Martin's Press.

Kazemipur, A., and S. S. Halli. 1997. Plight of immigrants: The spatial concentration of poverty in Canada. *Canadian Journal of Regional Science,* Vol. 20, Nos. 1–2, pp. 11–28.

———2000. *The new poverty in Canada: Ethnic groups and ghetto neighbourhoods.* Toronto: Thompson Educational Publishing, Inc.

Lautard, E. H., and D. J. Loree. 1984. Ethnic stratification in Canada, 1931–1971. *Canadian Journal of Sociology,* Vol. 9, No. 3, pp. 333–44.

Li, P. 1999. The market value and social value of race. In *Racism and social inequality in Canada.* V. Satzewich (ed.). Toronto: Thompson Educational Publishing, Inc., pp. 115–30.

Li, P. 2000. Economic returns of immigrants' self-employment. *Canadian Journal of Sociology,* Vol. 25, No. 1, pp. 1–34.

Marchak, M. P. 1991. *The integrated circus.* Montreal and Kingston: McGill-Queen's University Press.

Massey et al., 1994. An evaluation of international migration theory: The North American case. *Population and development review,* Vol. 20, No. 4, pp. 699–751.

Ng, R. 1986. The social construction of immigrant women in Canada. In *The politics of diversity: Feminism, Marxism and nationalism.* R. Hamilton and M. Barrett (eds.). Montreal: Bookcentre, pp. 269–86.

Park, R. E., and E. W. Burgess. 1924. *Introduction to the science of sociology.* Chicago: U of Chicago P.

Pendakur, K., and R. Pendakur. 1998. The colour of money: Earnings differentials among ethnic groups in Canada. *Canadian Journal of Economics,* Vol. 31, No. 3, pp. 518–48.

Porter, J. 1965. *The vertical mosaic.* Toronto: U of Toronto P.

Portes, A. 1995. Children of immigrants: Segmented assimilation and its determinants. In *The economic sociology of immigration.* A. Portes (ed.). New York: Russell Sage Foundation.

Portes, A., and R.G. Rumbaut. 1996. *Immigrant America: A portrait.* 2nd ed. Berkeley: U of California P.

Reitz, J. G. 1998. *Warmth of the welcome: The social causes of economic success for immigrants in different nations and cities.* Boulder, Colo.: Westview Press.

Reitz, J. G., and R. Breton. 1994. *The illusion of difference: Realities of ethnicity in Canada and the United* States. Toronto: C.D. Howe Institute.

Rifkin, J. 1995. *The end of work.* New York: G.E. Putnam's Sons.

Ruggles, P. 1990. *Drawing the line: Alternative poverty measures and their implications for public policy.* Washington, D.C.: The Urban Institute Press.

Rumbaut, R. G. 1997. Assimilation and its discontents: Between rhetoric and reality. *International Migration Review,* Vol. 31, No. 4, pp. 923–60.

Sarlo, C. A. 1992. *Poverty in Canada.* Vancouver: The Fraser Institute.

——1994. *Poverty in Canada.* 2nd ed. Vancouver: The Fraser Institute.

Satzewich, V. 1995. Social stratification: Class and racial inequality. In *Social issues and contradictions in Canadian society,* 2nd ed. B. S. Bolaria (ed.). Toronto: Harcourt Brace Canada, pp. 98–121.

Statistics Canada, 1998. Low Income Cut-offs. Cat. No. 13-551-X1B.

Teeple, G. 1995. *Globalization and the decline of social reform.* Toronto: Garamond Press.

Wanner, R. A. 1998. Prejudice, profit, or productivity: Explaining returns to human capital among male immigrants to Canada. *Canadian Ethnic Studies,* Vol. 30, No. 3, pp. 24–55.

Population
and
Urbanization

CLASSIC

CONTEMPORARY

CROSS-CULTURAL

55

The Metropolis
and Mental Life

Georg Simmel

In this, one of his best-known essays, Simmel examines what might be called the "spiritual condition" of the modern world. His focus is the city, in which forces of modernity—including anonymity, a detached sophistication, and a preoccupation with commercial matters—are most clearly evident. Note that Simmel finds reason both to praise this new world and to warn of its ability to destroy our humanity.

The deepest problems of modern life derive from the claim of the individual to preserve the autonomy and individuality of his existence in the face of overwhelming social forces, of historical heritage, of external culture, and of the technique of life. The fight with nature which primitive man has to wage for his *bodily* existence attains in this modern form its latest transformation. The eighteenth century called upon man to free himself of all the historical bonds in the state and in religion, in morals and in economics. Man's nature, originally good and common

Source: Reprinted and abridged with the permission of The Free Press, a Division of Simon & Schuster from *The Sociology of Georg Simmel*, translated and edited by Kurt H. Wolff. Copyright © 1950, copyright renewed 1978 by The Free Press.

to all, should develop unhampered. In addition to more liberty, the nineteenth century demanded the functional specialization of man and his work; this specialization makes one individual incomparable to another, and each of them indispensable to the highest possible extent. However, this specialization makes each man the more directly dependent upon the supplementary activities of all others.

Nietzsche sees the full development of the individual conditioned by the most ruthless struggle of individuals; socialism believes in the suppression of all competition for the same reason. Be that as it may, in all these positions the same basic motive is at work: The person resists to being leveled down and worn out by a social-technological mechanism.

An inquiry into the inner meaning of specifically modern life and its products, into the soul of the cultural body, so to speak, must seek to solve the equation which structures like the metropolis set up between the individual and the superindividual contents of life. Such an inquiry must answer the question of how the personality accommodates itself in the adjustments to external forces. This will be my task today.

The psychological basis of the metropolitan type of individuality consists in the *intensification of nervous stimulation* which results from the swift and uninterrupted change of outer and inner stimuli. Man is a differentiating creature. His mind is stimulated by the difference between a momentary impression and the one which preceded it. Lasting impressions, impressions which differ only slightly from one another, impressions which take a regular and habitual course and show regular and habitual contrasts—all these use up, so to speak, less consciousness than does the rapid crowding of changing images, the sharp discontinuity in the grasp of a single glance, and the unexpectedness of onrushing impressions. These are the psychological conditions which the metropolis creates. With each crossing of the street, with the tempo and multiplicity of economic, occupational and social life, the city sets up a deep contrast with small town and rural life with reference to the sensory foundations of psychic life. The metropolis exacts from man as a discriminating creature a different amount of consciousness than does rural life. Here the rhythm of life and sensory mental imagery flows more slowly, more habitually, and more evenly. Precisely in this connection the sophisticated character of metropolitan psychic life becomes understandable—as over against small town life, which rests more upon deeply felt and emotional relationships. These latter are rooted in the more unconscious layers of the psyche and grow most readily in the steady rhythm of uninterrupted habituations. The intellect, however, has its locus in the transparent, conscious, higher layers of the psyche; it is the most adaptable of our inner forces. In order to accommodate to change and to the contrast of phenomena, the intellect does not require any shocks and inner upheavals; it is only through such upheavals that the more conservative mind could accommodate to the metropolitan rhythm of events. Thus the metropolitan type of man—which, of course, exists in a thousand individual variants—develops an organ protecting him against the threatening currents and discrepancies of his external environment which would uproot him. He reacts with his head instead of his heart. In this an increased awareness assumes the psychic prerogative. Metropolitan life, thus, underlies a heightened awareness and a predominance of intelligence in metropolitan man. The reaction to metropolitan phenomena is shifted to that organ which is least sensitive and quite remote from the depth of the personality. Intellectuality is thus seen to preserve subjective life against the overwhelming power of metropolitan life, and intellectuality branches out in many directions and is integrated with numerous discrete phenomena.

The metropolis has always been the seat of the money economy. Here the multiplicity and concentration of economic exchange gives an importance to the means of exchange which the scantiness of rural commerce would not have allowed. Money economy and the dominance of the intellect are intrinsically connected. They share a matter-of-fact attitude in dealing with men and with things; and, in this attitude, a formal justice is often coupled with an inconsiderate hardness. The intellectually sophisticated person is indifferent to all genuine individuality, because relationships and reactions result from it which cannot be exhausted with logical operations. In the same manner, the individuality of phenomena is not commensurate with the pecuniary principle. Money is concerned only with what is common to all: It asks for the exchange value, it reduces all quality and individuality to the question: How much? All intimate emotional relations between persons are founded in their individuality, whereas in rational relations man is reckoned with like a number, like an element which is in itself indifferent. Only the objective measurable achievement is of interest. Thus metropolitan man reckons with his merchants and customers, his domestic servants and often even with persons with whom he is obliged to have social intercourse. These features of intellectuality contrast with the nature of the small circle in which the inevitable knowledge of individuality as inevitably produces a warmer tone of behavior, a behavior which is beyond a mere objective balancing of service and return. In the sphere of the economic psychology of the small group it is of importance that under primitive conditions production serves the customer who orders the goods, so that the producer and the consumer are acquainted. The modern metropolis, however, is supplied almost entirely by production for the market, that is, for entirely unknown purchasers who never personally enter the producer's actual field of vision. Through this anonymity the interests of each party acquire an unmerciful matter-of-factness; and the intellectually calculating economic egoisms of both parties need not fear any deflection because of the imponderables of personal relationships. The money economy dominates the metropolis; it has displaced the last survivals of domestic production and the direct barter of goods; it minimizes, from day to day, the amount of work ordered by customers. The matter-of-fact attitude is obviously so intimately interrelated with the money economy, which is dominant in the metropolis, that nobody can say whether the intellectualistic mentality first promoted the money economy or whether the latter determined the former. The metropolitan way of life is certainly the most fertile soil for this reciprocity, a point which I shall document merely by citing the dictum of the most eminent English constitutional historian: Throughout the whole course of English history, London has never acted as England's heart but often as England's intellect and always as her moneybag!

In certain seemingly insignificant traits, which lie upon the surface of life, the same psychic currents characteristically unite. Modern mind has become more and more calculating. The calculative exactness of practical life which the money economy has brought about corresponds to the ideal of natural science: to transform the world into an arithmetic problem, to fix every part of the world by mathematical formulas. Only money economy has filled the days of so many people with weighing, calculating, with numerical determinations, with a reduction of qualitative values to quantitative ones. Through the calculative nature of money a new precision, a certainty in the definition of identities and differences, an unambiguousness in agreements and arrangements has been brought about in the relations of life-elements—just as externally this precision has been effected by the universal diffusion of pocket watches. However, the conditions of metropolitan life are at once cause and effect of this trait. The relationships and affairs of the typical metropolitan usually are so varied and complex that without the strictest punctuality in promises and services the whole structure would break down into an inextricable chaos. Above all, this necessity is brought about by the aggregation of so many people with such differentiated interests, who must integrate their relations and activities into a highly complex organism. If all clocks and watches in Berlin would suddenly go wrong in different ways, even if only by one hour, all economic life and communication of the city would be disrupted for a long time. In addition an apparently mere external factor, long distances, would make all waiting and broken appointments result in an ill-afforded waste of time. Thus, the technique of metropolitan life is unimaginable without the most punctual integration of all activities and mutual relations into a stable and impersonal time schedule. Here again the general conclusions of this entire task of reflection become obvious, namely, that from each point on the surface of existence—however closely attached to the surface alone—one may drop a sounding into the depth of the psyche so that all the most banal externalities of life finally are connected with the ultimate decisions concerning the meaning and style of life. Punctuality, calculability, exactness are forced upon life by the complexity and extension of metropolitan existence and are not only most intimately connected with its money economy and intellectualistic character. These traits must also color the contents of life and favor the exclusion of those irrational, instinctive, sovereign traits and impulses which aim at determining the mode of life from within, instead of receiving the general and precisely schematized form of life from without.…

The same factors which have thus coalesced into the exactness and minute precision of the form of life have coalesced into a structure of the highest impersonality; on the other hand, they have promoted a highly personal subjectivity. There is perhaps no psychic phenomenon which has been so unconditionally reserved to the metropolis as has the blasé attitude. The blasé attitude results first from the rapidly changing and closely compressed contrasting stimulations of the nerves. From this, the enhancement of metropolitan intellectuality, also, seems originally to stem. Therefore, stupid people who are not intellectually alive in the first place usually are not exactly blasé. A life in boundless pursuit of pleasure makes one blasé because it agitates the nerves to their strongest reactivity for such a long time that they finally cease to react at all. In the same way, through the rapidity and contradictoriness of their changes, more harmless impressions force such violent responses, tearing the nerves so brutally hither and thither that their last reserves of strength are spent; and if one remains in the same milieu they have no time to gather new strength. An incapacity thus emerges to react to new sensations with the appropriate energy. This constitutes that blasé attitude which, in fact, every metropolitan child shows when compared with children of quieter and less changeable milieus.

This physiological source of the metropolitan blasé attitude is joined by another source which flows from the money economy. The essence of the blasé attitude consists in the blunting of discrimination. This does not mean that the objects are not perceived, as is the case with the half-wit, but rather that the meaning and differing values of things, and thereby the things themselves, are experienced as insubstantial. They appear to the blasé person in an evenly flat and gray tone; no one object deserves preference over any other. This mood is the faithful subjective reflection of the completely internalized money economy. By being the equivalent to all the manifold things in one and the same way, money becomes the most frightful leveler. For money expresses all qualitative differences of things in terms of "how much?" Money, with all its colorlessness and indifference, becomes the common denominator of all values; irreparably it hollows out the core of things, their individuality, their specific value, and their incomparability. All things float with equal specific gravity in the constantly moving stream of money. All things lie on the same level and differ from one another only in the size of the area which they cover. In the individual case this coloration, or rather discoloration, of things through their money equivalence may be unnoticeably minute. However, through the relations of the rich to the objects to be had for money, perhaps even through the total character which the mentality of the contemporary public everywhere imparts to these objects, the exclusively pecuniary evaluation of objects has become quite considerable. The large cities, the main seats of the money exchange, bring the purchasability of things to the fore much more impressively than do smaller localities. That is why cities are also the genuine locale of the blasé attitude. In the blasé attitude the concentration of men and things stimulate the nervous system of the individual to its highest achievement so that it attains its peak. Through the mere quantitative intensification of the same conditioning factors this achievement is transformed into its opposite and appears in the peculiar adjustment of the blasé attitude. In this phenomenon the nerves find in the refusal to react to their stimulation the last possibility of accommodating to the contents and forms of metropolitan life. The self-preservation of certain personalities is brought at the price of devaluating the whole objective world, a devaluation which in the end unavoidably drags one's own personality down into a feeling of the same worthlessness.

Whereas the subject of this form of existence has to come to terms with it entirely for himself, his self-preservation in the face of the large city demands from him a no less negative behavior of a social nature. This mental attitude of metropolitans toward one another we may designate, from a formal point of view, as reserve. If so many inner reactions were responses to the continuous external contacts with innumerable people as are those in the small town, where one knows almost everybody one meets and where one has a positive relation to almost everyone, one would be completely atomized internally and come to an unimaginable psychic state. Partly this psychological fact, partly the right to distrust which men have in the face of the touch-and-go elements of metropolitan life, necessitates our reserve. As a result of this reserve we frequently do not even know by sight those who have been our neighbors for years. And it is this reserve which in the eyes of the small-town people makes us appear to be cold and heartless. Indeed, if I do not deceive myself, the inner aspect of this outer reserve is not only indifference but, more often than we are aware, it is a slight aversion, a mutual strangeness and repulsion, which will break into hatred and fight at the moment of a closer contact, however caused. The whole inner organization of such an extensive communicative life rests upon an extremely varied hierarchy of sympathies, indifferences, and aversions of the briefest as well as of the most permanent nature. The sphere of indifference in this hierarchy is not as large as might appear on the surface. Our psychic activity still responds to almost every impression of somebody else with a somewhat distinct feeling. The unconscious, fluid, and changing character of this impression seems to result in a state of indifference. Actually this indifference would be just as unnatural as the diffusion of indiscriminate

mutual suggestion would be unbearable. From both these typical dangers of the metropolis, indifference and indiscriminate suggestibility, antipathy protects us. A latent antipathy and the preparatory stage of practical antagonism affect the distances and aversions without which this mode of life could not at all be led. The extent and the mixture of this style of life, the rhythm of its emergence and disappearance, the forms in which it is satisfied—all these, with the unifying motives in the narrower sense, form the inseparable whole of the metropolitan style of life. What appears in the metropolitan style of life directly as dissociation is in reality only one of its elemental forms of socialization.

This reserve with its overtone of hidden aversion appears in turn as the form or the cloak of a more general mental phenomenon of the metropolis: It grants to the individual a kind and an amount of personal freedom which has no analogy whatsoever under other conditions. The metropolis goes back to one of the large developmental tendencies of social life as such, to one of the few tendencies for which an approximately universal formula can be discovered. The earliest phase of social formations found in historical as well as in contemporary social structures is this: a relatively small circle firmly closed against neighboring, strange, or in some way antagonistic circles. However, this circle is closely coherent and allows its individual members only a narrow field for the development of unique qualities and free, self-responsible movements. Political and kinship groups, parties and religious associations begin in this way. The self-preservation of very young associations requires the establishment of strict boundaries and a centripetal unity. Therefore they cannot allow the individual freedom and unique inner and outer development. From this stage social development proceeds at once in two different, yet corresponding, directions. To the extent to which the group grows—numerically, spatially, in significance and in content of life—to the same degree the group's direct, inner unity loosens, and the rigidity of the original demarcation against others is softened through mutual relations and connections. At the same time, the individual gains freedom of movement, far beyond the first jealous delimitation. The individual also gains a specific individuality to which the division of labor in the enlarged group gives both occasion and necessity....

It is not only the immediate size of the area and the number of persons which, because of the universal historical correlation between the enlargement of the circle and the personal inner and outer freedom, has made the metropolis the locale of freedom. It is rather in transcending this visible expanse that any given city becomes the seat of cosmopolitanism. The horizon of the city expands in a manner comparable to the way in which wealth develops; a certain amount of property increases in a quasi-automatical way in ever more rapid progression. As soon as a certain limit has been passed, the economic, personal, and intellectual relations of the citizenry, the sphere of intellectual predominance of the city over its hinterland, grow as in geometrical progression. Every gain in dynamic extension becomes a step, not for an equal, but for a new and larger extension. From every thread spinning out of the city, ever new threads grow as if by themselves, just as within the city the unearned increment of ground rent, through the mere increase in communication, brings the owner automatically increasing profits. At this point, the quantitative aspect of life is transformed directly into qualitative traits of character. The sphere of life of the small town is, in the main, self-contained and autarchic. For it is the decisive nature of the metropolis that its inner life overflows by waves into a far-flung national or international area....

The most profound reason, however, why the metropolis conduces to the urge for the most individual personal existence—no matter whether justified and successful—appears to me to be the following: The development of modern culture is characterized by the preponderance of what one may call the "objective spirit" over the "subjective spirit." This is to say, in language as well as in law, in the technique of production as well as in art, in science as well as in the objects of the domestic environment, there is embodied a sum of spirit. The individual in his intellectual development follows the growth of this spirit very imperfectly and at an ever increasing distance. If, for instance, we view the immense culture which for the last hundred years has been embodied in things and in knowledge, in institutions and in comforts, and if we compare all this with the cultural progress of the individual during the same period—at least in high status groups—a frightful disproportion in growth between the two becomes evident. Indeed, at some points we notice a retrogression in the culture of the individual with reference to spirituality, delicacy, and idealism. This discrepancy results essentially from the growing division of labor. For the division of labor demands from the individual an ever more one-sided accomplishment, and the greatest advance in a one-sided pursuit only too frequently means dearth to the personality of the individual. In any case, he can cope less and less with the overgrowth of objective culture. The individual is reduced to a negligible quantity, perhaps less in his consciousness than in his practice and in the totality of his obscure emotional states that are derived from this practice. The individual has become a mere cog in an enormous organization of things and powers which tear from his hands all progress, spirituality, and value in order to transform them from their subjective form into the form of a purely objective life. It needs merely to be pointed out that the metropolis is the genuine arena of this culture which outgrows all personal life. Here in buildings and educational institutions, in the wonders and comforts of space-conquering technology, in the formations of community life, and in the visible institutions of the state, is offered such an overwhelming fullness of crystallized and impersonalized spirit that the personality, so to speak, cannot maintain itself under its impact. On the one hand, life is made infinitely easy for the personality in that stimulations, interests, uses of time, and consciousness are offered to it from all sides. They carry the person as if in a stream, and one needs hardly to swim for oneself. On the other hand, however, life is composed more and more of these impersonal contents and offerings which tend to displace the genuine personal colorations and incomparabilities. This results in the individual's summoning the utmost in uniqueness and particularization, in order to preserve his most personal core. He has to exaggerate this personal element in order to remain audible even to himself....

CRITICAL THINKING QUESTIONS

1. In what respects does the metropolis symbolize modern society?
2. What does Simmel mean by suggesting that in modern cities, people experience an "intensification of nervous stimulation"? How do we react "with our heads instead of with our hearts"?
3. What does Simmel see as the achievements of modern urban life? What does he think has been lost in the process?

56

Population
and
Urbanization

Africville: The Life and Death of a Canadian Black Community

CLASSIC

CONTEMPORARY

CROSS-CULTURAL

Donald H. Clairmont
and Dennis William Magill

Clairmont and Magill review the effects of an urban redevelopment program that relocated 80 black families in Halifax during the 1960s. The program was intended to promote humanitarian motives but the experience of Africville demonstrates the many problems associated with forced relocation programs.

To seek social change, without due recognition of the manifest and latent functions performed by the social organization undergoing change, is to indulge in social ritual rather than social engineering.[1]

— *Robert K. Merton*

Halifax, the foundation city of English-speaking Canada, experienced much change during its first two hundred years of existence. Yet the facelift and redevelopment it has undergone since the late 1950s have effected a change as dramatic as the 1917 explosion that levelled much of the city. Stimulated by the Stephenson Report of 1957,[2] urban renewal and redevelopment have resulted in the relocation of thousands of people, the demolition of hundreds of buildings, and the construction

Source: From Donald H. Clairmont and Dennis W. Magill. 1999. *Africville: The Life and Death of a Canadian Black Community*, Third Edition (pp. 1–19). Toronto: Canadian Scholars' Press. Reprinted by permission of Canadian Scholars' Press Inc.

of impressive business and governmental complexes. The Africville relocation was part of the larger redevelopment pattern; Africville residents constituted some eight to ten percent of the people affected by approved urban renewal schemes in the city of Halifax during the relocation years.

Africville was a black community within the city of Halifax, inhabited by approximately four hundred people, comprising eighty families, many of whom were descended from settlers who had moved there over a century ago. Tucked away in a corner of the city, relatively invisible, and thought of as a "shack town," Africville was a depressed community both in physical and in socioeconomic terms. Its dwellings were located beside the city dump, and railroad tracks cut across the one dirt road leading into the area. Sewerage, lighting, and other public services were conspicuously absent. The people had little education, very low incomes, and many were underemployed. Property claims were in chaos. Only a handful of families could establish legal title; others claimed squatter rights; and still others rented. Africville, long a black mark against society, had been designated for future industrial and harbour development. Many observers reported that despite these liabilities there was a strong sense of community and that some residents expressed satisfaction with living in Africville.

In 1964 the small black ghetto of Africville began to be phased out of existence. By that time most residents of Halifax, black and white, had come to think of Africville as "the slum by the dump." Most Haligonians, including some Africville residents, did not regard the community as viable and recognized a need for planned social change. The relocation plan announced by the city of Halifax, which purported to be more than simply a real estate operation, appeared to be a response to this need. The plan emphasized humanitarian concern, included employment and education programs, and referred to the creation of new opportunities for the people of Africville. To the general public, the proposed relocation was a progressive step.

In addition to official pronouncements, there were other indications that the Africville program would be more humane and progressive than the typical North American urban relocation. Halifax city council had adopted recommendations contained in a report submitted by a noted Canadian welfare specialist experienced in urban renewal. There was much preliminary discussion of the relocation by city officials among themselves, with Africville residents, and with a "caretaker" group of black and white professionals associated with the Halifax Human Rights Advisory Committee. Relocation plans were not *ad hoc* and haphazard. City officials were required to articulate their policies well and in detail; many implications and alternatives were considered.

There were also indications in the relocation decision-making structure that the Africville program might realize its official rhetoric. A social worker was appointed by the city to take front-line responsibility for the varied aspects of the relocation and to act as liaison between the city administration and the relocatees. The social worker, who was on loan from the Nova Scotia Department of Public Welfare, had a measure of autonomy vis-à-vis the city and an independent contingency fund to meet day-to-day emergencies and opportunities with a minimum of bureaucratic delay. In negotiating the real estate aspects of relocation, the social worker brought proposed agreements before a special advisory committee consisting of aldermen and several members of the Halifax Human Rights Advisory Committee.

In terms of its rationale, public rhetoric, and organizational structure, the Africville relocation seemed worthy of study. The plan was *liberal-oriented* (that is, aimed at ending segregation and providing improved opportunities for the disadvantaged), *welfare-oriented* (that is, it hoped to coordinate employment, educational, and rehabilitative programs with the rehousing of people), and run by experts (that is, the planning, execution, and advise were provided by professionals). An examination of the Africville relocation could be expected to yield greater fundamental insight into planned social change than would a study of typical relocation programs that were accomplished by administrative fiat and stressed primarily the physical removal of persons. It seemed important to study and evaluate the Africville relocation both in its particularity and against the background of general relocation issues.

There were additional reasons for studying the Africville relocation. First, Africville was part of a trend in the 1960s for governmental initiative in relocation programs, and there was reason to expect that other tentative relocations in Nova Scotia and elsewhere would be patterned after the Africville experience. Second, Africville had attracted national and even international notice, and there was broad public interest in the relocation. Third, accounts of pre-relocation social conditions and attitudes were available. Two surveys had been conducted[3] and other material was available in city records. Finally, in 1968 the Africville relocation had already been acclaimed locally as a success. One city alderman noted:

The social significance of the Africville program is already beginning to show positive results as far as individual families are concerned. The children are performing more satisfactorily in school and they seem to take more of an interest in their new surroundings. This report is not intended to indicate that the program has been 100 percent successful; however I believe it can be said that it has been at least 75 percent, judging by the comments of the relocated families.[4]

Private communication with city officials and relocation officials in the United States and Canada brought forth praise for the organization and rhetoric of the Africville relocation.

Was the Africville relocation a success? If so, from whose perspective? To what extent? What accounted for the success or lack of it? It is hoped that answers to these and related questions will contribute to an appreciation of the Africville relocation and of relocation generally.

THE RELOCATION PHENOMENON

Relocation must be seen in the context of a general North American mobility pattern, and certain distinctive features should be noted. The most important distinction is that relocation is part of planned social change carried out, or at least approved, by public agency. The initiation of relocation, as seen by the relocatees, is usually involuntary and an immediate function of the political process. Our present concern is with relocation as it pertains to private residences, involves neighbourhoods or communities, and is a function of comprehensive programs of social change. This kind of relocation accounts for but a small measure of the mobility noted in Canada and the United States, but it was significant because it was distinctive. It was noted earlier that the Africville relocation was itself part of a much larger redevelopment project in the city of Halifax. In terms of the sweep of lifestyle change, even such large urban projects have been dwarfed by post–Second World War Canadian relocation projects in the Arctic and in Newfoundland. In 1953, Newfoundland, with 6000 miles of coastline and

approximately 1150 settlements, undertook a program to move people from the small outposts to larger viable communities which could be serviced efficiently. Between 1965 and 1970 over 3250 households were moved.[5]

As many low-income Americans and Canadians can testify, urban renewal is a prime example of forced relocation. Urban renewal legislation began in the 1940s in both countries. By 1968 approximately forty-five Canadian urban redevelopments had been initiated at a cost of 270 million dollars for 1500 cleared acres.[6] While the scope of urban renewal in Canada was quite small in the light of American experience, the Canadian program was significant enough that one can complain that there were too few Canadian studies looking into the politics, issues, and human consequences of renewal programs. To overcome this lack of knowledge and to place the Africville relocation in perspective, more comprehensive themes will be discussed in this [selection].

From a political-administrative perspective there are four relocation models: the traditional, development, liberal-welfare, and political. The Africville project is the best Canadian example of the liberal-welfare type of relocation.... [T]hese models vary along six dimensions: (1) ideological premises; (2) formulation of policy; (3) implementation of policy; (4) intended beneficiaries; (5) central actors and organizational units; and (6) key problems. These models are ideal types to which actual relocation programs correspond to a greater or lesser degree.

THE DEVELOPMENT MODEL

The development model was the most prevalent political-administrative approach to relocation in North America. This type of relocation was usually justified in terms of supposed benefits for the system as a whole, whether the system is society, the city, etc. It was usually initiated by order of political authorities and administered by bureaucrats; it was not anticipated that relocatees would benefit other than indirectly. The underlying ideology of the development model was system-oriented and neo-capitalist; an accurate statement of its premise in urban renewal has been offered by Wallace: "[it considers] renewal, as a public activity, to be intervention in a market and competitive system and to be justified by the need to make up for imperfections in the market mechanism that impede the adjustment process, to eliminate conditions which are economic or social liabilities."[7] In the context of contemporary urban renewal, the development model incorporated the usual city-design approach, focusing on questions of beautification, zoning, and structure,[8] and was usually intended to increase the city tax base and achieve civic pride or attract industry.

The development model can be illustrated by past urban renewal programs in Toronto. Ignoring relocatees as viable interest groups the programs operated implicitly on the basis of certain ideological premises: to correct imperfections in the social system (removal of so-called slums) and overall system development (economic growth), or both. As is the case in many Canadian cities, Toronto's past development policy was closely linked to the businesses and commercial-property industry which provided homes, apartment buildings, shopping centres, and industrial complexes. Thus the elimination of "blight areas" and construction of highrise apartment and office buildings generated an important source of urban revenue. Referring to this policy of "dollar planning," Fraser observed:

As long as Toronto, [in 1972] like all other municipalities in Canada has to depend upon property taxes as its sole source of income, the overwhelming power of development interests in determining the direction and quality of Toronto's growth will remain unchallenged.

...[T]he key to a municipality's prosperity remains its rate of growth; Toronto planners have been consistently ignored by city councils that have been over the years almost exclusively uninterested in any discussions about the quality of that development.[9]

A non-urban example of the development model of relocation has been described by John Matthiasson, in his study of the forced relocation of a band of Cree Indians in Northern Manitoba. The Cree were relocated to make way for a gigantic power project; they were not involved in the project planning and despite their displeasure "they accepted in a fatalistic manner the announcement of the relocation. They believed that the decision had been made by higher authorities, and that they had neither the right nor power to question it."[10]

The development model of relocation had its limitations. In particular, its econocentric and "undemocratic" features were criticized. The assumption that relocatees benefit indirectly from relocation was challenged, as was the premise that the system as a whole somehow redistributed fairly the benefits accruing from forcing people to move and facilitating the development of private industry. Some critics argued that if one included social-psychological factors in one's conception of costs, the relocatees could be seen as subsidizing the rest of the system. The criticism had some effect, and the liberal-welfare model became increasingly common.[11] One official explained:

In the fifteen years since [urban renewal's] inception, we have seen a progressive broadening of the concept and a strengthening of tools. We have seen, increasingly, both the need for, and realization of, rapprochement between physical and social planning, between renewal and social action. But the fully effective liaison of the two approaches has almost everywhere been frustrated by the absence of the tools to deal as effectively with the problems of human beings as with the problems of physical decay and blight.[12]

Another writer has observed,

social welfare can no longer be treated as the responsibility of private and more or less bountiful ladies and gentlemen or as the less respected branch of the social welfare community and the city government. Tied as it is to the concerns as dear to the heart of the country as economic prosperity it merits a place in the inner sanctum, particularly of planning commissions.[13]

THE LIBERAL-WELFARE MODEL

The "rediscovery" of poverty,[14] the war on poverty, the increasing pressure "from below" upon the development model, and the broadening definition of urban renewal led to the widespread emergence of the liberal-welfare-oriented approach. The liberal-welfare model, like the development model, emphasized expertise and technical knowledge in its operation and administration, and invariably was initiated by public authority. The principal difference is that the liberal-welfare model purported to benefit the relocatees primarily and directly. Under this model, welfare officials often saw themselves as "caretakers" for the relocatees; one relocation official has said, "the department of relocation is the tenants' advocate."[15] The liberal-welfare model of relocation was characterized by a host of social welfare programs supplemental to housing policies and was regarded as an opportunity for a multifaceted attack on poverty and other problems. It was this liberal-welfare model and its assumptions that shaped the rhetoric underlying the 1963–64 decision to relocate Africville.

Ideologically, the liberal-welfare model was much like the development model in that it tended to operate with a consensus model of society and posited a basic congruency between the interests of relocatees and those of society as a whole, it was "undemocratic" in the same sense as the development model; the low-status relocatees were accorded little attention, either as participants in the implicit political process or as contributions to specific policies or plans of action. There was an effort, however, to persuade rather than to ignore the relocatees. Criticism of the liberal-welfare model of relocation was related primarily to the ideological level. Some writers noted that liberal welfarism had become part of the establishment of contemporary North American society.[16] Its proponents were presumed to be handmaidens of strong vested interests, reconciling the disadvantaged and patching up the symptoms of social malaise. Critics pointed out that the special

programs associated with the liberal-welfare model of relocation tended to be short-term and unsuccessful. The welfare rhetoric often diverted attention from the gains and benefits accruing to the middle-income and elite groups in society. The critics attacked the liberal-welfare model on the premise that the social problems to which it is ostensibly directed could be solved only through profound structural change effecting a redistribution of resources, and by providing relocatees with the consciousness and resources to restructure their own lives.

The liberal-welfare model is best illustrated by the Africville relocation…. The community of Africville was defined as a social problem, and relocation was regarded as an intervention strategy designed to help solve the "social and economic problems of Africville residents." The central actors in the formation and implementation of relocation policy were politicians, bureaucrats, experts, and middle-class caretakers; there was no meaningful *collective* participation by Africville residents. The relocatees were to be major beneficiaries through compensation, welfare payments, and rehabilitative retraining programs. The major problem with the relocation was that, although rooted in liberal-welfare rhetoric, it failed to achieve its manifest goals.

THE POLITICAL MODEL

The liberal-welfare model of relocation was revised and developed both as a response to criticism at the ideological level and in reaction to its lack of operational success. There was a growing interest in citizen participation in all phases of relocation; in the firmer acceptance, structurally and culturally, of the advocacy function of relocation officials; in the coordination of relocation services; and in the provision of resources. It is difficult to assess how far this interest has been translated into fact. There appeared to be a shift in the 1970s, at least conceptually, to the political model of relocation and a frank recognition that relocation usually entailed a conflict of interest, for example, between the relocatees and the city. There was an attempt to structure the conflict by providing relocatees with resources to develop a parallel structure to that of the government. Although society and the relocatee were considered to benefit equally, this political perspective assumed that relocatees benefited both directly and indirectly; directly in terms of, say, housing and other welfare services, and indirectly by participating in the basic decision-making and the determination of their life situation. The political model of relocation was based on the premise that social problems were political problems and emphasized solutions through political action; relocation was approached primarily as a situation in which problems were solved not by the application of expertise but by the resolution of conflicting interests.

Beyond the considerable costs (the dollar cost is less hidden than in the other relocation model) and administrative difficulties entailed, there were other grounds for criticism of the political model. There was a tendency to overemphasize the solidarity and common interests of relocatees, to exaggerate the multiplying effects of political participation in relocation,[17] and to raise serious questions about how far government could proceed or would proceed in fostering extra-parliamentary political action.

Citizen participation, a core element in the political model, was institutionalized in the United States by the community action programs of the 1964 Economic Opportunity Act. Numerous books and articles, far too many to cite, have discussed the reasons, operations, and failures of "maximum feasible participation" of the poor in the war on poverty.[18] Citizen participation was also part of the United States model city programs, which required that local residents be involved in the planning process and implementation of changes in their neighbourhoods. Contrasted with the United States, Canada has relatively few examples of related social-animation projects. The rise

of "militant" citizen groups was a phenomenon which developed later in Canada. The public outcry against the community work of the Company of Young Canadians and the subsequent governmental intervention to close this organization may be an indication of the limits of this perspective. The only Canadian publication illustrating the political model of a relocation is Fraser's study of Toronto's Trefann Court. Trefann Court residents successfully fought off a development-type relocation project; subsequently, the conflict arising from different interests was recognized as an integral part of the city's social organization. Despite internal community conflict between homeowners and tenants, a number of community residents, leaning heavily on outside: "resource people," developed a cohesive organization and set up a working committee (a parallel structure) to establish a conceptual scheme for community change in conjunction with the existing city bureaucracy. The Trefann Court case also pointed to a key problem in the political model, that of assessing the representativeness of any one group of citizens to speak, argue, or vote for an entire community. With the establishment of "parallel structures," many citizens grow frustrated with the tedious detail involved in committee work. In Fraser's words:

> The fact that the Working Committee operated under formal rules of order, dominated by minutes, reports, rules of procedure and legislative decorum widened the gap between the committee and the community. As debates became more lengthy, detailed and technical, the meetings became harder to follow for the ordinary Trefann resident who might drop in.[19]

THE TRADITIONAL MODEL

Finally, there is the traditional model of relocation in North American society. This is a limiting type of relocation carried out under governmental auspices, for it is a form of planned social change characterized by self-help and self-direction. It is the neighbourhood or community leaders, often indigenous minority-group leaders working through indigenous social organizations, who plan and carry out the relocation, generally with official support and some resource commitment by government agencies. The traditional model entails a largely laissez-faire strategy whereby the relocatees benefit directly and technical expertise is used to advise rather than to direct. Criticism of this approach contends that, without political action, neither the available resources nor the generation of initiative can be effective in the case of low-status groups.

There are numerous examples of the traditional model of relocation. Group settlement and resettlement in various parts of Canada have been common. The relocation of Beechville, a black community on the outskirts of Halifax, is an example within the Halifax metropolitan area. Community leaders, anticipating a government attempt to relocate the residents, organized themselves into a co-operative housing association, received funds from Central Mortgage and Housing Corporation, and reorganized their community partly on their own terms. The scope available for traditional relocation models lessens as society becomes more technocratic and centralized.

CONCEPTUAL FRAMEWORK

…[O]ur emphasis will be on the liberal-welfare model of planned social change and its implementation during the Africville relocation. During the analysis we focus on questions of power and exchange among the various participants of the relocation. Thus, from the perspective of power and exchange,[20] we can examine the power resources and relationships among the individual persons and groups involved in the relocation, the historical evolution of these social facts, the goals held by the different parties, and the strategies and tactics employed in establishing the terms of the relocation "contract." We can also analyse the role of outsiders, experts, and community "leaders" and focus on questions such as the mobilization of advocacy, relocation resistances and alternatives, and the relation of

rhetoric to action. It is vital in the Africville case to have a larger historical view, observing the historical exchange patterns between the city and the Africville people and tracing the implications of these patterns in making Africville "ripe for relocation" and in influencing the relocation decision-making and mechanics.

An aspect of this perspective concerns the context of negotiations and the bargaining strategies developed by the parties involved. Accordingly, attention was devoted to probing the relocatees' knowledge about the relocation; their strategies (use of lawyers, co-operation with fellow relocatees, and development of special arguments in dealing with city officials), and their perceptions of the city's goals, strategies, and resources. The relocation social worker completed a questionnaire concerning each relocated family which paid considerable attention to his negotiations with relocatees and his perception of their goals, strategies, and resources. This perspective included the concepts of rewards, costs, profits, and distributive justice. It would appear, for instance, that relocatees would have been satisfied with the relocation if rewards exceeded costs and if they thought that the city and other relocatees would not "get a better deal." Information concerning rewards, costs, sense of distributive justice, and satisfaction was obtained through the questionnaires, the interviews, and the case studies.

Despite problems in measuring each relocatee's perception of the relative profit accruing to himself or herself, other relocatees, and the city of Halifax, and problems occasioned by differences between long-term and short-term effects, this power and exchange approach is significant for the relocation literature which often appears to keep aloof from the "blood and guts" of relocation transaction. Equally important, by placing the Africville relocation within a typology of relocation models, it is possible to explore the domain consensus (that is, the basic terms of reference held in common and prerequisite to any exchange) associated with the liberal-welfare approach, and especially how such *domain* consensus (for example, "disadvantaged communities or people have few intrinsically valuable resources and need to be guided by sympathetic experts") develops and how it sets the limits and context of bargaining and reciprocity.

RESEARCH STRATEGIES

The methods employed in this study were varied: questionnaires, in-depth interviews, historical documents, newspapers, case studies, and "bull sessions" with relocatees. A useful baseline source of data was the survey of Halifax blacks, including Africville [residents], conducted in 1959 by the Institute of Public Affairs, Dalhousie University. The original questionnaires were available for re-analysis, an important consideration since many of the data were not published and the published material contained several significant inaccuracies.[21] The 1959 survey questionnaire provided basic demographic data as well as information concerning mobility aspirations, employment, education, and social life.

The collection of data for this study began in 1968. The researchers arranged for two students from the Maritime School of Social Work to prepare twenty case studies.[22] A review of the students' case studies and field notes, guided by the perspective developed by the researchers, aided the drafting of a questionnaire. In 1968 current addresses of the relocatees were also traced and brief acquaintance interviews were conducted.

The most intensive data collection period was June to December 1969. One of the researchers (D.W.M.) conducted in-depth, tape-recorded interviews with individual people associated with the relocation decision-making and implementation: politicians, city officials, middle-class caretakers, the relocation social worker, consultants, and Africville relocatees involved in the decision-making. During these interviews an open-ended interview guide[23] was used to explore knowledge of Africville and awareness of pre-1964 relocation attempts and also the actual relocation decision-making and mechanics. Each of the approximately two-hour interviews was transcribed and

analysed for patterns. Many quotations used in this book are taken from these tape-recorded interviews.

Concurrently, the other researcher (D.H.C.), with two assistants, was meeting informally with the relocatees, individually and in "bull sessions." On the basis of these experiences and the case studies, we all drafted and pre-tested an extensive questionnaire. From September to December, 1969, the questionnaire was employed by interviewers hired and trained by the researchers. The lengthy questionnaire[24] asked about the relocatee's background characteristics: life in Africville, personal knowledge of relocation decision-making processes, relocation strategies, negotiations, costs, rewards, and post-relocation conditions. The questionnaire was given to all household heads and spouses who had lived in Africville and had received a relocation settlement of any kind. Approximately 140 persons were interviewed, several in places as far distant as Winnipeg and Toronto.

In June, 1969, the relocation social worker spent eight days answering a questionnaire[25] on the relocatees' background characteristics, his relocation bargaining with each relocatee, and his perception of the latter's rewards, costs, and strategies. Such data enabled us to analyse more precisely the relationships among parties to the relocation, for similar data from the relocatees and their perception of the relocation social worker were obtained from the relocatee questionnaire.

Two other research tactics were employed at the same time as the interviews were conducted. One of our assistants was conducting in-depth, tape-recorded interviews with black leaders in the Halifax area concerning their assessment of Africville and the implications of relocation. Another assistant was gathering historical data and interviewing selected Africville relocatees concerning the historical development of the community. Important sources of historical data were the minutes of Halifax City Council (read from 1852 to 1969), reports of the Board of Halifax School Commissioners, the Nova Scotia

Public Archives, files in the Registry of Deeds, the Halifax *Mail-Star* library, and the minutes of the Halifax Human Rights Advisory Committee. In all phases of research, the Africville files in the Social Planning Department, City of Halifax were of especial value.

PHASES OF THE AFRICVILLE STUDY

The Africville Relocation Report, in addition to being an examination of relocation and planned social change and a contribution to the sparse literature on blacks in Nova Scotia, represents a fusion of research and action. The researchers did not begin the study until virtually all the Africville people had been relocated, and the research strategy resulted in the study being more than an evaluation.[26] The process of obtaining collective as well as individual responses, and of establishing a meaningful exchange with relocatees, fostered collective action from former Africville residents. Some local government officials objected to what they have referred to as the researchers' "activist" bias. The researchers maintain, however, that exchanges had to be worked out with the subjects of research as well as with the funding agencies. The liberal ethic posits informed voluntary consent as fundamental to adult social interaction; informed voluntary consent requires, in turn, meaningful exchange among the participants.

The study began in October, 1968 with a meeting of relocated Africville people. This was the first time since relocation that former residents of Africville had met collectively. This stormy meeting, called by the researchers, was a public airing of relocatee grievances and led to relocatee support of the proposed study. Subsequent talk of forming committees to press grievances with the city of Halifax was an important result of the meeting. The researchers encouraged this tendency, for the expressed grievances appeared legitimate, and the researchers considered that it would be both possible and important to tap a collective or group dimension in the relocation process as well

as to study the usual social-psychological considerations.

Later in the same week, at a meeting that the researchers had arranged with city officials, relocation caretakers, and civic leaders, the researchers related the expressed grievances of the relocatees and urged remedial action. General support for the proposed study was obtained at this second meeting, and the pending reconsideration of relocation by the city's newly created Social Planning Department was crystallized.

During the winter and spring of 1969, as the present study was being planned in detail, the action-stimulus of the researchers' early efforts was bearing fruit. Social Planning Department officials were meeting with the relocatees and, as it were, planning the second phase (not initially called for) of the Africville relocation. With provincial and municipal grants totalling seventy thousand dollars, the Seaview Credit Union was organized to assist relocatees experiencing financial crises; in addition, plans were formulated to meet housing and employment needs, and special consideration was to be given to former Africville residents whose needs could be met within the city's existing welfare system. A relocatee was hired to manage the credit union and to assist with other anticipated programs.

During the main data-gathering period, the summer of 1969, and in line with a decision to obtain collective as well as individual responses, the researchers met with informed groups of Africville relocatees to discuss current and future remedial action, it became apparent that the so-called second phase of the relocation would be inadequate to meet the people's needs. There was little identification with the credit union and it was floundering, for many relocatees who became members were either unable or unwilling to repay loans. Other anticipated programs and action promised by the city were delayed or forgotten due to bureaucratic entanglements and to lack of organization and pressure on the part of the relocatees.

The relocatees still had legitimate grievances related to unkept promises made at the time of relocation and later. With the formation of the Africville Action Committee, a third phase of the relocation began in the fall of 1969 and winter of 1970. The task of this new committee, developed from group discussions held between the researchers and relocatees, was to effect governmental redress through organized pressure. Several position papers were developed by the Africville Action Committee and negotiations were reopened with the city of Halifax. Although numerous meetings of relocatees were held during the first half of 1970, problems within the Africville Action Committee and the absence of resource people until the fall of 1970 hindered progress. With the committee stumbling along, and the credit union and other city-sponsored projects either ineffectual or nonexistent, the relocation process appeared to have petered out. The action committee was reactivated when one of the authors (D.H.C.) returned to Halifax permanently in the fall of 1970 and groups of relocatees were subsequently reinvolved in reading and criticizing a draft of the present study and in evaluating the relocation and the remedial action taken. Since the fall of 1970, the Africville Action Committee was active. Widespread support for its claims was obtained from community organizations, subcommittees were established to deal with questions of employment, housing, and financial compensation; and city council authorized the establishment of a city negotiating team to meet with representatives of the action committee.

In 1974, at the time of publication of the first edition of this book, the Africville Action Committee, to all intents and purposes, had ceased to function. Although it could claim some credit for a special employment training program through which a number of unemployed Africville relocatees had found jobs, the action committee fell far short of its goals.

The city's lack of a positive imaginative response and the internal organizational problems of the action committee hindered other proposals. What remained in 1974 was a reorganized credit union, a modest base for further redress and group action. However, by 1999 the Seaview Credit Union was no longer in existence; it had collapsed over two decades ago. However, the community is not dead.... Africville still thrives in the hearts and minds of many of the relocatees. In addition, Africville still has rich symbolic value for fostering black consciousness in Nova Scotia.

POSTSCRIPT

Throughout the study, we consciously and deliberately attempted to achieve a viable fusion of research and social responsibility. The research focussed on the collective responses of the group as well as on individual responses. At each stage in the study (conception, data gathering, data analysis, and preparation for publication) the collective and individual inputs that gave the study an action potential were obtained from relocatees. Drafts of appropriate chapters were sent for critical comment to officials and others involved in the relocation. The study became a stimulus to action because the normal researcher-subject exchanges could be worked out in concrete, actual terms. This was preferable to the usual research situation where, in effecting exchanges with the people being studied, the researcher typically makes vague references to the possible benefit of the study and does little or nothing to follow up implied promises of action.[27] But of course, our research strategy has its weakness too. It is difficult to feel satisfied that the kind of exchange relations that we established had productive consequences. Despite our involvement (in the early 1970s) with petitions, committee work, and attempts at rational problem solving, little redress of the inadequacies of the relocation program was achieved and the manifest goals of the liberal-welfare rhetoric of the relocation remain, in large measure, unrealized.

CRITICAL THINKING QUESTIONS

1. Review the key characteristics of the *development* and *liberal-welfare* relocation models. What are the strengths and weaknesses of each?
2. Have there been any relocation or revitalization programs in your community? If so, which relocation model appears to have provided the justification for the move? Are the people who were relocated still in the community today?
3. In your opinion, can we effectively revitalize our communities without forcing people to move? How?

NOTES

1. *Social Theory and Social Structure* (Glencoe, Ill.: The Free Press, 1949), p. 80.

2. Gordon Stephenson, *A Redevelopment Study of Halifax, Nova Scotia* (Halifax, N.S.: City of Halifax, 1957).

3. *The Condition of the Negroes of Halifax City, Nova Scotia* (Halifax: Institute of Public Affairs, Dalhousie University, 1962); and G. Brand, *Interdepartmental Committee* on *Human Rights: Survey Reports* (Halifax, N.S.: Nova Scotia Department of Welfare, Social Development Division, 1963).

4. Minutes of the Halifax City Council, Halifax, N.S., September 14, 1967.

5. The Government of Newfoundland initiated the program in 1953. In 1965 a joint federal-provincial program was initiated under a resettlement act. In 1970 the program was placed under the direction of the Federal Department of Regional Economic Expansion. For an overview of the resettlement program, see Noel Iverson and D. Ralph Matthews, *Communities in Decline: An Examination of Household Resettlement in Newfoundland,* Newfoundland Social and Economic Studies, No. 6, (St. John's, Nfld.: Memorial University of Newfoundland, Institute of Social and Economic Research, 1968). For a critical assessment of studies of the resettlement program, see Jim Lotz, "Resettlement and Social Change in Newfoundland," *Canadian Review of Sociology and Anthropology 8* (February, 1971): 48–59.

6. See Table 4, "Completed Redevelopment Projects" in *Urban Renewal* (Toronto: Centre for Urban and Community Studies, University of Toronto, 1968). Reprinted from *University of Toronto Law Journal,* 18. No. 3 (1968): 243.

7. David A. Wallace, "The Conceptualizing of Urban Renewal," *Urban Renewal* (Toronto: Centre for Urban and Community Studies, University of Toronto, 1968), 251.

8. An example of such a project is one reported by Thurz in southwest Washington, D.C. Little was done for the relocatees, but the relocation was widely acclaimed for its futuristic redevelopment design. For a critique of this approach, see Daniel Thurz, *Where Are They Now?* Washington, D.C.: Health and Welfare Council of the National Capital Area, 1966). See also, Jane Jacobs, *The Death and Life of Great American Cities* (New York: Random House, 1961).

9. Graham Fraser, *Fighting Back: Urban Renewal in Trefann Court* (Toronto: Hakkert, 1972), p. 55.

10. John Matthiasson, "Forced Relocation: An Evaluative Case Study," paper presented at the annual meeting of the Canadian Sociology and Anthropology Association, Winnipeg, 1970.

11. In recent years some minor progressive modifications have been introduced with reference to the development model; these deal with advance notice and public hearings, relocation compensation, and the availability of housing stock. See, Robert P. Groberg, *Centralized Relocation* (Washington, D.C.: National Association of Housing and Redevelopment Officials, 1969).

12. William L. Slayton, "Poverty and Urban Renewal," quoted in Hans B. C. Spiegel, "Human Considerations in Urban Renewal," *Urban Renewal,* op. cit., 311.

13. Elizabeth Wood, "Social Welfare Planning," quoted in Spiegel, op. cit., 315.

14. For a discussion of this, see Kenneth Craig, "Sociologists and Motivating Strategies," M.A. thesis, University of Guelph, Department of Sociology, 1971.

15. Groberg, op. cit., p. 172.

16. See Alvin W. Gouldner, *The Coming Crisis of Western Sociology* (New York: Basic Books, 1970), pp. 500–02.

17. Relocation is a short-term consideration, for most services brought to bear on relocatee problems rarely extend beyond rehousing. A more general critique of the multiplying effect of citizens' involvement in relocation is given by S. M. Miller and Frank Riessman, *Social Class and Social Policy* (New York: Basic Books Inc., 1968).

18. The historical antecedents and reasons for the legislation are discussed in Daniel Moynihan, *Maximum Feasible Misunderstanding* (New York: Free Press, 1970). For an alternative interpretation, see Francis Fox Piven and Richard A. Cloward, *Regulating the Poor: The Functions of Public Welfare* (New York: Random Vintage Books, 1972), pp. 248–84. The operation of the program is discussed by Ralph M. Kramer, *Participation of the Poor: Comparative Community Case Studies* in *the War on Poverty* (Englewood Cliffs, N.J.: Prentice Hall, 1969).

19. Fraser, op. cit., p. 262.

20. For a discussion of this theoretical perspective, see Peter M. Blau, *Exchange and Power in Social Life* (New York: Wiley, 1964); and George Caspar Homans, *Social Behavior: Its Elementary Forms* (New York: Harcourt, Brace and World, 1961).

21. *The Condition of the Negroes of Halifax City,* Nova Scotia, op. cit.

22. Sarah M. Beaton, "Effects of Relocation: A Study of Ten Families Relocated from Africville, Halifax, Nova Scotia," Master of Social Work Thesis, Maritime School of Social Work, Halifax, N.S., 1969; and Bernard MacDougall, "Urban Relocation of Africville Residents," Master of Social Work Thesis, Maritime School of Social Work, Halifax, N.S., 1969.

23. The interview guide is published in Donald H. Clairmont and Dennis W. Magill, *Africville Relocation Report* (Halifax, N.S.: Institute of Public Affairs, Dalhousie University, 1971), pp. A131–A135.

24. Ibid., pp. A97–A128.

25. Ibid., pp. A83–A96.

26. Some relocation studies have been carried out as part of the relocation decision-making, see William H. Key, *When People Are Forced to Move* (Topeka, Kansas: Menninger Foundation, 1967), mimeographed, others have been concurrent with the relocating of people, see Herbert J. Gans, *The Urban Villagers: Group and Class in The Life of Italian Americans* (New York: The Free Press, 1962). The present study is unique in that it fostered collective action carried out after the relocation.

27. See Craig, op. cit.

57

Let's *Reduce* Global Population!

J. Kenneth Smail

Population
and
Urbanization

CLASSIC

CONTEMPORARY

CROSS-CULTURAL

A familiar concern is holding the line on world population increase. But, some people are asking, has population growth already gone too far? In this selection, Ken Smail argues that the long-term "carrying capacity" of the planet may only be half the number of people we have now. And the time left to begin reducing population is running out fast.

The main point of this essay is simply stated. Within the next half-century, it is essential for the human species to have in place a flexible voluntary, equitable, and internationally coordinated plan to dramatically reduce world population by at least two-thirds. This process of voluntary consensus building—local, national, and global— must begin now.

The mathematical inevitability that human numbers will continue their dramatic increase over the next two generations (to perhaps 9 billion or more by the year 2050), the high probability that this numerical increase will worsen the problems that already plague humanity (economic, political, environmental, social, moral, etc.), and the growing realization that the Earth may only be able to support a global human population in

Source: This is a revised version of an essay published as a pamphlet by Negative Population Growth (Smail, 1995) and then—after revision and expansion—as a journal article in *Population and Environment* (Smail, 1997) and *Politics and the Life Sciences* (Smail, 1997). Reprinted with permission of the author (e-mail address: Smail@kenyon.edu).

the 2 to 3 billion range at an "adequate to comfortable" standard of living, only reinforce this sense of urgency.

There are, however, hopeful signs. In recent years, we have finally begun to come to terms with the fact that the consequences of the twentieth century's rapid and seemingly uncontrolled population growth will soon place us—if it has not done so already—in the greatest crisis our species has yet encountered.

TEN INESCAPABLE REALITIES

In order better to appreciate the scope and ramifications of this still partly hidden crisis, I shall briefly call attention to ten essential and inescapable realities that must be fully understood and soon confronted.

First, during the present century world population will have grown from somewhere around 1.6 billion in 1900 to slightly more than 6 billion by the year 2000, an almost fourfold increase in but 100 years. This is an unprecedented numerical

415

expansion. Throughout human history, world population growth measured over similar 100-year intervals has been virtually nonexistent or, at most, modestly incremental; it has only become markedly exponential within the last few hundred years. To illustrate this on a more easily comprehensible scale, based on the recent rate of increase of nearly 90 million per year, human population growth during the 1990s alone amounted to nearly 1 billion, an astonishing 20 increase in but little more than a single decade. Just by itself, this increase is equivalent to the total global population in the year 1800 and is approximately triple the estimated world population (ca. 300 million) at the height of the Roman Empire. It is a chastening thought that even moderate demographic projections suggest that this billion-per-decade rate of increase will continue well into the century, and that the current global total of 6 billion (late 1999 estimate) could easily reach 9 to 10 billion by mid-twenty-first century.

Second, even if a fully effective program of zero population growth (ZPG) were implemented immediately, by limiting human fertility to what demographers term the *replacement rate* (roughly 2.1 children per female), global population would nevertheless continue its rapid rate of expansion. In fact, demographers estimate that it would take at least two to three generations (fifty to seventy-five years) at ZPG fertility levels just to reach a point of population stability, unfortunately at numbers considerably higher than at present. This powerful *population momentum* results from the fact that an unusually high proportion (nearly one-third) of the current world population is under the age of fifteen and has not yet reproduced. Even more broad-based population profiles may be found throughout the developing world, where the under-fifteen age cohort often exceeds 40 percent and where birth rates have remained high even as mortality rates have fallen. While there are some recent indications that fertility rates are beginning to decline, the current composite for the less-developed world—excluding China—is still nearly double (ca. 3.8) that needed for ZPG.

Third, in addition to fertility levels, it is essential to understand that population growth is also significantly affected by changes in mortality rates. In fact, demographic transition theory suggests that the earlier stages of rapid population expansion are typically fueled more by significant reductions in death rates (i.e., decreased childhood mortality and/or enhanced adult longevity) than by changes in birth rates. Nor does recent empirical data suggest that average human life expectancy has reached anywhere near its theoretical upper limit, in either the developing or developed worlds. Consequently, unless there appears a deadly pandemic, a devastating world war or a massive breakdown in public health (or a combination of all three), it is obvious that ongoing global gains in human longevity will continue to make a major contribution to world population expansion over the next half-century, regardless of whatever progress might be made in reducing fertility.

Fourth, all previous examples of significant human population expansion—and subsequent (occasionally rapid) decline—have been primarily local or, at most, regional phenomena. At the present time, given the current global rate of increase of some 220,000 people per day (more than 9,000 per hour), it is ludicrous to speak of significant empty spaces left on Earth to colonize, certainly when compared with but a century ago. And it is ridiculous to suggest that "off Earth" (extraterrestrial) migration will somehow be sufficient to siphon away excess human population, in either the near or more distant future.

Fifth, given the data and observations presented thus far, it becomes increasingly apparent that the time span available for implementing an effective program of population "control" may be quite limited, with a window of opportunity—even in the more optimistic scenarios—that may not extend much beyond the middle of the next century. As mentioned previously, most middle-of-the-road demographic projections for the year 2050 two generations from now—are in the 8 to 9 billion range. Several observations might help to bring these demographic estimates and the above-mentioned "limited" time span into somewhat better perspective:

- the year 2050 is closer to the present than the year 1950
- an infant born in 2000 will be only 50 years old in the year 2050
- a young person entering the job market in the early twenty-first century will have reached retirement age in the year 2050

These observations also make it quite clear that *those already born*—ourselves, our children, and our grandchildren—will have to confront the overwhelming impact of an additional 3–4 billion people.

Sixth, the Earth's long-term carrying capacity, in terms of resources, is indeed finite, despite the continuing use of economic models predicated on seemingly unlimited growth, and notwithstanding the high probability of continued scientific/technological progress. Some further terminological clarification may be useful. "Long-term" is most reasonably defined on the order of several hundred years, at least; it emphatically does not mean the five to fifteen year horizon typical of much economic forecasting or political prognostication. Over this much longer time span, it thus becomes much more appropriate—perhaps even essential to civilizational survival—to define a sustainable human population size in terms of optimums rather than maximums. Further, *what "could" be supported in the short term is not necessary what "should" be humanity's goal over the longer term.*

As far as resources are concerned, whether these be characterized as renewable or nonrenewable, it is becoming increasingly apparent that the era of inexpensive energy (derived from fossil fuels), adequate food supplies (whether plant or animal), readily available or easily extractable raw materials (from wood to minerals), plentiful fresh water, and readily accessible "open space" is rapidly coming to a close, almost certainly within the next half-century. And finally, the consequences of future scientific/technological advances—whether in terms of energy production, technological efficiency, agricultural productivity, or creation of alternative materials—are much more likely to be incremental than revolutionary, notwithstanding frequent and grandiose claims for the latter.

Seventh, rhetoric about "sustainable growth" is at best a continuing exercise in economic self-deception and at worst a politically pernicious oxymoron. Almost certainly, working toward some sort of *steady-state sustainability* is much more realistic scientifically, (probably) more attainable economically, and (perhaps) more prudent politically. Assertions that the Earth might be able to support a population of 10, 15, or even 20 billion people for an indefinite period of time at a standard of living superior to the present are not only cruelly misleading but almost certainly false. Rather, extrapolations from the work of a growing number of ecologists, demographers, and numerous others suggest the distinct possibility that *the Earth's true carrying capacity—defined simply as humans in long-term adaptive balance with their ecological setting, resource base, and each other—may already have been exceeded by a factor of two or more.*

To the best of my knowledge, no evidence contradicts this sobering—perhaps even frightening—assessment. Consequently, since at some point in the not-too-distant future the negative consequences and ecological damage stemming from the mutually reinforcing effects of excessive human reproduction and overconsumption of resources could well become irreversible, and because there is only one Earth with which to experiment, it is undoubtedly better for our species to err on the side of prudence, exercising wherever possible a cautious and careful stewardship.

Eighth, only about 20 percent of the current world population (ca. 1.2 billion people) could be said to have a *generally adequate* standard of living, defined here as a level of affluence roughly approximating that of the so-called "developed" world (Western Europe, Japan, and North America). The other 80 percent (ca. 4.8 billion), incorporating most of the inhabitants of what have been termed the "developing nations," live in conditions ranging from mild deprivation to severe deficiency. Despite well-intentioned efforts to the contrary, there is little evidence that this imbalance is going to decrease in any significant way, and a strong likelihood that it may get worse, particularly in view of the fact that more than 90 percent of all future population expansion is projected to occur in these less-developed regions of the world. In fact, there is growing concern that when this burgeoning population growth in the developing world is combined with excessive or wasteful per capita energy and resource consumption in much of the developed world, widespread environmental deterioration (systemic breakdown?) in a number of the Earth's more heavily stressed ecosystems will become increasingly likely. This is especially worrisome in regions already beset by short-sighted or counterproductive economic policies, chronic political instability, and growing social unrest, particularly when one considers that nearly all nations in the less-developed world currently have an understandable desire—not surprisingly expressed as a fundamental right—to increase their standard of living (per capita energy and resource consumption) to something approximating "first world" levels.

Ninth, to follow up on the point just made, the total impact of human numbers on the global environment is often described as the product of three basic multipliers: (1) population size; (2) per capita energy and resource consumption (affluence); and (3) technological efficiency in the production, utilization, and conservation of such energy and resources. This relationship is usually expressed by some variant of the now well-known $I = PAT$ equation: Impact = Population × Affluence × Technology. This simple formula enables one to demonstrate much more clearly the quantitative scope of humanity's dilemma over the next fifty to seventy-five years, particularly if the following projections are anywhere near accurate:

- human population could well *double* by the end of the twenty-first century, from our current 6 billion to perhaps 12 billion or more
- global energy and resource consumption could easily *quadruple* or more during the same period, particularly if (as just indicated in item 8) the less-developed nations are successful in their current efforts to significantly improve their citizens' standard of living to something approaching developed-world norms
- new technologies applied to current energy and resource inefficiencies might be successful in reducing per capita waste or effluence *by half*, or even *two-thirds,* in both the developed and developing worlds

Given these reasonable estimates, the conclusion seems inescapable that the human species' total impact on the Earth's already stressed ecosystem could easily *triple to quadruple* by the middle of the twenty-first century. This impact could be even greater if current (and future) efforts at energy and resource conservation turn out to be less successful than hoped for, or if (as seems likely) the mathematical relationship between these several multipliers is something more than simply linear. It is therefore very important to keep a close watch—for harbingers of future trends and/or problems—on current events in the growing group of nations now experiencing rapid economic development and modernization, with particular attention being given to ongoing changes in India and China, two states whose combined size represents nearly half the population of the less-developed world.

Tenth, and finally, there are two additional considerations—matters not usually factored into the $I = PAT$ equation—that must also be taken into account in any attempt to coordinate appropriate responses to the rapidly increasing global environmental impact described in points 6 through 9. First, given current and likely ongoing scientific uncertainties about environmental limits and ecosystem resilience, not to mention the potential dangers of irreversible damage if such limits are stretched too far (i.e., a permanently reduced carrying capacity), it is extremely important to design into any future planning an adequate safety factor (or sufficient margin for error). In other words, any attempt at "guided social engineering" on the massive scale that will clearly be necessary over the next century will require at least as much attention to safety margins, internal coordination, and systems redundancy as may be found in other major engineering accomplishments—from designing airplanes to building the Channel Tunnel to landing astronauts on the moon.

In addition, such planning must consider yet another seemingly intractable problem. Because the human species not only shares the Earth—but has also co-evolved—with literally millions of other life forms, the closely related issues of wilderness conservation and biodiversity preservation must also be taken fully into account, on several different levels (pragmatic, aesthetic, and moral). In simplest terms, it has now become a matter of critical importance to ask some very basic questions about what proportion of the Earth's surface the human species has the right to exploit or transform—or, conversely, how much of the Earth's surface should be reserved for the protection and preservation of all other life forms. As many have argued, often in eloquent terms, our species will likely be more successful in confronting and resolving these questions—not to mention the other complex problems that are now crowding in upon us—*if we can collectively come to regard ourselves more as the Earth's long-term stewards than its absolute masters.*

To sum up, if the above "inescapable realities" are indeed valid, it is obvious that rational, equitable, and attainable population goals will have to be established in the very near future. It is also obvious that these goals will have to address—and in some fashion resolve—a powerful internal conflict: how to create and sustain an adequate standard of living for *all* the world's peoples, minimizing as much as possible the growing inequities between rich and poor, while simultaneously neither overstressing nor exceeding the Earth's longer-term carrying capacity. *I submit that these goals cannot be reached, or this conflict resolved, unless and until world population is dramatically reduced—to somewhere around 2 to 3 billion people—within the next two centuries.*

CRITICAL THINKING QUESTIONS

1. Why, according to this reading, is simply holding the line on population increase not enough?
2. What about the fact that humans share the earth with millions of other life forms? In facing up to the problem of population increase, what responsibility do we have for other species?
3. All in all, do you agree with Smail that we must find a way to reduce global population? Why or why not?

REFERENCES

Smail, J. Kenneth. 1995. Confronting the 21st century's hidden crisis: Reducing human numbers by 80%. *NPG Forum.* Teaneck, N.J.: Negative Population Growth.

———. 1997. Averting the 21st century's demographic crisis: Can human numbers be reduced by 75%? *Population and Environment,* 18 (6): 565–80.

———. Beyond population stabilization: The case for dramatically reducing global human numbers. Roundtable: World Population Policy commentary and responses. *Politics and the Life Sciences,* 16, 2 (September, 1997): 183–236.

58

Why Humanity Faces Ultimate Catastrophe

Thomas Robert Malthus

In this selection, from "An Essay on the Principle of Population," Thomas Robert Malthus foretells human calamity. His dire prediction is based on a single assertion: Human beings will overwhelm the earth's capacity to provide for us. Many of today's environmentalists (sometimes termed "neo-Malthusians") accept this principle and echo his early warning.

STATEMENT OF THE SUBJECT: RATIOS OF THE INCREASE OF POPULATION AND FOOD

In an inquiry concerning the improvement of society, the mode of conducting the subject which naturally presents itself is

1. To investigate the causes that have hitherto impeded the progress of mankind towards happiness
2. To examine the probability of the total or partial removal of the causes in [the] future

To enter fully into this question, and to enumerate all the causes that have hitherto influenced human improvement, would be

much beyond the power of an individual. The principal object of the present essay is to examine the effects of one great cause intimately united with the very nature of man; which, though it has been constantly and powerfully operating since the commencement of society, has been little noticed by the writers who have treated this subject. The facts which establish the existence of this cause have, indeed, been repeatedly stated and acknowledged; but its natural and necessary effects have been almost totally overlooked; though probably among these effects may be reckoned a very considerable portion of that vice and misery, and of that unequal distribution of the bounties of nature, which it has been the unceasing object of the enlightened philanthropist in all ages to correct.

*Source:*From *On the Principle of Population,* Vol. I, by T. R. Malthus (New York: E. P. Dutton & Co., Inc., 1914; orig. 1798).

The cause to which I allude is the constant tendency in all animated life to increase beyond the nourishment prepared for it.

It is observed by Dr. Franklin that there is no bound to the prolific nature of plants or animals but what is made by their crowding and interfering with each other's means of subsistence. Were the face of the earth, he says, vacant of other plants, it might be gradually sowed and overspread with one kind only, as for instance with fennel: and were it empty of other inhabitants, it might in a few ages be replenished from one nation only, as for instance with Englishmen.[1]

This is incontrovertibly true. Through the animal and vegetable kingdoms Nature has scattered the seeds of life abroad with the most profuse and liberal hand; but has been comparatively sparing in the room and the nourishment necessary to rear them. The germs of existence contained in this earth, if they could freely develop themselves, would fill millions of worlds in the course of a few thousand years. Necessity, that imperious, all pervading law of nature, restrains them within the prescribed bounds. The race of plants and the race of animals shrink under this great restrictive law; and man cannot by any efforts of reason escape from it.

In plants and irrational animals, the view of the subject is simple. They are all impelled by a powerful instinct to the increase of their species; and this instinct is interrupted by no doubts about providing for their offspring. Wherever therefore there is liberty, the power of increase is exerted; and the super-abundant effects are repressed afterwards by want of room and nourishment.

The effects of this check on man are more complicated. Impelled to the increase of his species by an equally powerful instinct, reason interrupts his career, and asks him whether he may not bring beings into the world for whom he cannot provide the means of support. If he attends to this natural suggestion, the restriction too frequently produces vice. If he hear it not, the human race will be constantly endeavouring to increase beyond the mean of subsistence. But as,

by the law of our nature which makes food necessary to the life of man, population can never actually increase beyond the lowest nourishment capable of supporting it, a strong check on population, from the difficulty of acquiring food, must be constantly in operation. This difficulty must fall somewhere, and must necessarily be severely felt in some or other of the various forms of misery, or the fear of misery, by a large portion of mankind.

That population has this constant tendency to increase beyond the means of subsistence, and that it is kept to its necessary level by these causes, will sufficiently appear from a review of the different states of society in which man has existed. But, before we proceed to this review, the subject will, perhaps, be seen in a clearer light if we endeavour to ascertain what would be the natural increase of population if left to exert itself with perfect freedom; and what might be expected to be the rate of increase in the production of the earth under the most favourable circumstances of human industry.

It will be allowed that no country has hitherto been known where the manners were so pure and simple, and the means of subsistence so abundant, that no check whatever has existed to early marriages from the difficulty of providing for a family, and that no waste of the human species has been occasioned by vicious customs, by towns, by unhealthy occupations, or too severe labour. Consequently in no state that we have yet known has the power of population been left to exert itself with perfect freedom.

Whether the law of marriage be instituted, or not, the dictate of nature and virtue seems to be an early attachment to one woman; and where there were no impediments of any kind in the way of a union to which such an attachment would lead, and no causes of depopulation afterwards, the increase of the human species would be evidently much greater than any increase which has been hitherto known....

It may safely be pronounced,...that population, when unchecked, goes on doubling itself every twenty-five years, or increases in a geometrical ratio.

The rate according to which the productions of the earth may be supposed to increase, it will not be so easy to determine. Of this, however, we may be perfectly certain, that the ratio of their increase in a limited territory must be of a totally different nature from the ratio of the increase of population. A thousand millions are just as easily doubled every twenty-five years by the power of population as a thousand. But the food to support the increase from the greater number will by no means be obtained with the same facility. Man is necessarily confined in room. When acre has been added to acre till all the fertile land is occupied, the yearly increase of food must depend upon the melioration of the land already in possession. This is a fund, which, from the nature of all soils, instead of increasing, must be gradually diminishing. But population, could it be supplied with food, would go on with unexhausted vigour; and the increase of one period would furnish the power of a greater increase the next, and this without any limit....

Europe is by no means so fully peopled as it might be. In Europe there is the fairest chance that human industry may receive its best direction. The science of agriculture has been much studied in England and Scotland; and there is still a great portion of uncultivated land in these countries. Let us consider at what rate the produce of this island might be supposed to increase under circumstances the most favourable to improvement.

If it be allowed that by the best possible policy, and great encouragements to agriculture, the average produce of the island could be doubled in the first twenty-five years, it will be allowing, probably, a greater increase than could with reason be expected.

In the next twenty-five years, it is impossible to suppose that the produce could be quadrupled. It would be contrary to all our knowledge of the properties of land. The improvement of the barren parts would be a work of time and labour; and it must be evident to those who have the slightest acquaintance with agricultural subjects that, in proportion as cultivation extended, the additions that could yearly be made to the former average produce must be gradually and regularly diminishing. That we may be the better able to compare the increase of population and food, let us make a supposition, which, without pretending to accuracy, is clearly more favourable to the power of production in the earth than any experience we have had of its qualities will warrant.

Let us suppose that the yearly additions which might be made to the former average produce, instead of decreasing, which they certainly would do, were to remain the same; and that the produce of this island might be increased every twenty-five years by a quantity equal to what it at present produces. The most enthusiastic speculator cannot suppose a greater increase than this. In a few centuries it would make every acre of land in the island like a garden.

If this supposition be applied to the whole earth, and if it be allowed that the subsistence for man which the earth affords might be increased every twenty-five years by a quantity equal to what it at present produces, this will be supposing a rate of increase much greater than we can imagine that any possible exertions of mankind could make it.

It may be fairly pronounced, therefore, that, considering the present average state of the earth, the means of subsistence, under circumstances the most favourable to human industry, could not possibly be made to increase faster than in an arithmetical ratio.

The necessary effects of these two different rates of increase, when brought together, will be very striking. Let us call the population of this island eleven millions; and suppose the present produce equal to the easy support of such a number. In the first twenty-five years the population would be twenty-two millions, and the food being also doubled, the means of subsistence would be equal to this increase. In the next twenty-five years, the population would be forty-four millions, and the means of subsistence only equal to the support of thirty-three millions. In the next period the population would be eighty-eight millions, and the means of subsistence just equal to the support of half that number. And, at the conclusion of the first century, the population would be a hundred and seventy-six millions, and the means of subsistence only equal to the support of fifty-five millions, leaving a population of a hundred and twenty-one millions totally unprovided for.

Taking the whole earth, instead of this island, emigration would of course be excluded; and, supposing the present population equal to a thousand millions, the human species would increase as the numbers, 1, 2, 4, 8, 16, 32, 64, 128, 256, and subsistence as 1, 2, 3, 4, 5, 6, 7, 8, 9. In two centuries the population would be to the means of subsistence as 256 to 9; in three centuries as 4096 to 13, and in two thousand years the difference would be almost incalculable....

CRITICAL THINKING QUESTIONS

1. According to Malthus, at what rate does human population increase? At what rate can the earth's food supplies be increased?
2. Malthus published his essay in 1798; in the two centuries since then, has his dire prediction come to pass? Why or why not?
3. Following Malthus's thinking, what should be the cornerstone of the world's program to protect the environment? Do you agree with his position or not?

NOTE

1. Franklin's Miscell, p. 9.

Environment
and
Society

CONTEMPORARY

CLASSIC

CROSS-CULTURAL

59

Intensive Hog Farming in Manitoba: Transnational Treadmills and Local Conflicts

Joel Novek

Factory-based hog farming has grown quickly in Western Canada. In this article, Novek investigates the environmental impacts of this growth and also reviews the approval process for such developments. Novek finds that hog-farm developments are inspiring fierce political debate on both community and provincial levels.

The tragedy in Walkerton, Ontario, and growing fears of water contamination in other parts of rural Canada, have added to the debate about intensive livestock operations (ILOs) designed for the large-scale factory farming of animals (Edwards and Ladd, 2000; Thu, 1996; Thu and Durrenberger, 1994; Durning and Brough, 1991). The expansion of ILOs is part of the transition to a new food regime characterized by large concentrated units, technologically sophisticated supply chains, vertical integration and production of a specialized commodity for global markets (Friedman, 1991, 1998; Hamilton, 1994; Goodman and Redclift, 1991). Critics of industrialized agribusiness (Berry, 1991; Kenney, 1991) have raised concerns about the environmental sustainability of this food regime in regards to air, water and soil quality, as well as threats to human health. ILOs produce an added challenge to sustainability with their requirements for the

Source: Excerpted from J. Noveck. 2003. "Intensive Hog Farming in Manitoba: Transnational Treadmills and Local Conflicts." *Canadian Review of Sociology and Anthropology,* 40(1), 3–26.

assimilation of vast quantities of animal waste (Durning and Brough, 1991).

Factory farming and corporate concentration in agriculture pose the question of which governance strategies may best be employed to ensure that these operations are regulated in the public interest. Canadian provinces and rural municipalities, similar to other localities faced with homogenizing market pressures (Sachs, 1999), have been placed in a political quandary—internally divided on the issue of ILOs and lacking sufficient information or jurisdictional authority to practise effective environmental democracy.

This paper will examine the problem of ILO pollution and its regulation with a focus on the province of Manitoba, the site over the past decade of Canada's fastest growing intensive hog industry. It will be analysed as a case study of the "treadmill of production" (Schnaiberg and Gould, 1994; Gould, Schnaiberg and Weinberg, 1996) in livestock agriculture, which is characterized by the expansion of large and highly concentrated production units. The tendency toward economic concentration, vertical integration and corporate ownership (Edwards and Ladd, 2000; Thu, 1996; Goodman and Redclift, 1991) has been underway at the expense of smaller-scale, less specialized operations. This expansion has resulted in growing environmental impact—the "negative externalities of a production treadmill" (Bell, 1998: 78)—from intensive hog farming. Hog wastes may be responsible for nitrate leaching and phosphorus runoff in water, as well as the release of harmful pathogens and offensive odours (Mussel and Martin, 2000). The environment acts as a sewer (Redclift, 1996; Yearley, 1996) for the waste products of industrialized food production, and the effects are differentially distributed. The increasing visibility of environmental concerns poses the question of state action. Deregulation and neo-liberal agricultural policies (De Lind, 1995; Thu, 1995) instituted to accelerate the treadmill have led to the downloading of much of the responsibility for ILO governance onto rural municipalities. The resulting conflicts over hog barns at the local level have underlined the state's contradictory role as development promoter and environmental regulator (Schnaiberg and Gould, 1994; Cable and Cable, 1995). Thus, this paper will also be concerned with the state's problematic efforts to construct legitimation frameworks (Hall, 1998) to manage this contradiction.

METHODOLOGY

Information for this paper has been collected from heterogeneous sources, which is necessary because there is no central source of information on the hog industry in Manitoba. Documentation on the pork industry has been obtained from government documents by means of the extensive network of provincial libraries. The public registry file of Manitoba Conservation has been the most important source of documentation. Much information has been obtained from newspapers and magazines, especially the rural and agricultural press.

Many of these articles are accessible on-line. Interviews were conducted with 30 persons connected with the pork industry either as developers, regulators or environmental opponents. This includes officials from the provincial departments of Agriculture, Conservation and Intergovernmental Affairs. These interviews were conducted in person or on the telephone. All interviews were conducted in a semi-structured format in which standardized questions were combined with ample opportunities for subjects to express their own opinions about the matters under discussion. Detailed notes were taken during each interview. Finally, I attended hearings on Manitoba's Livestock Stewardship Initiative, municipal council meetings, and environmental gatherings dealing with the hog industry in various parts of the province.

MANITOBA'S HOG INDUSTRY

Manitoba has been an important part of the "wheat economy" (Fowke, 1957) that dominated economic life in the Canadian prairies throughout much of the last century. During the final quarter of the twentieth century, Western Canada's grain economy has undergone a secular decline from which there is little prospect of recovery (Qualman, 2000). Between 1971 and 1996, the number of Manitobans who lived on farms declined from over 131,000 to less than 80,000, while the proportion of Manitobans employed on farms dropped from 13% to 7% (Livestock Stewardship Panel, 2000). A key factor behind this decline has been depressed prices and the crisis of profitability (Hall, 1998; Goodman and Redclift, 1991) in world grain markets. Also, railway deregulation has led to much higher grain shipping costs. Faced with low prices and high freight rates, producers were encouraged to transform comparative weakness into comparative advantage by converting cheap grain into feed inputs for the burgeoning hog sector. The provincial government and agribusiness interests began to stress the "Manitoba advantage," based on calculations that showed the Canadian prairies to be among the most advantageous places in the world to raise hogs (Martin et al., 1999). The ingredients were low costs for feed grain, a vast acreage (13.3 million acres in Manitoba) under cultivation and available for waste assimilation, and pro-business attitudes (Manitoba Agriculture and Food, n.d.). Pork producers from Northern Europe to North Carolina facing environmental and regulatory constraints were welcomed to Manitoba's greener pastures. Pork industry advocates claimed that Manitoba would benefit from value-added production and globalized export markets (Manitoba Agriculture and Food, n.d.). Shipping meat would be more economically advantageous than merely shipping grain, and manure would replace chemical fertilizer with a natural alternative, producing a self-sustaining industry.

The expansion of Manitoba's hog industry only makes sense in the context of the globalization of agricultural organization and trade. World pork imports tripled between 1981 and 1999, while Canada's small domestic market stagnated (Martin et al, 1999.). Canadian producers are counting on rising incomes and the adoption of a meat-saturated diet (Agriculture and Agrifood Canada, 1997), especially in Asia, the world's largest pork importer, to underpin their growth. There is a window of opportunity because some of the world's leading pork-producing areas—notably Denmark, the Netherlands, North Carolina and Taiwan—are now facing severe environmental limits on production (Martin et al., 1999). Western Canada's new role in the global food regime is to specialize in the feed grain/livestock production/waste assimilation end of the food chain. This represents an acceleration of the "treadmill of production" (Schnaiberg and Gould, 1994) for prairie agriculture, one that is characterized by a diminishing number of producers engaged in much larger-scale and more intensive farming practices. Food production is maintained in Western Canada, but at the cost of subjecting

the land and water to risk from widespread live-stock-manure application. The concept of the "treadmill of production" has been extended up to the global and down to the local level in its most recent formulation as a "transnational treadmill" (Gould, Schnaiberg and Weinberg, 1996) in which nations and regions compete for jobs and investment in the context of global capital mobility. This could provide some perspective on the willingness of many communities in Western Canada and elsewhere to court investment from the international livestock industry by taking on the waste-assimilation risks.

Dining the 1990s, the Manitoba advantage appeared to be on track as Manitoba had the fastest-growing hog industry in Canada (Livestock Stewardship Panel, 2000). It surpassed Alberta as Canada's third-largest producer, after Quebec and Ontario. Market hog production in Manitoba has been increasing by 12% annually and exceeded 5 million hogs by 2000. Indeed, hogs surpassed both wheat and canola to become the leading source of revenue for Manitoba farmers (Rampton, 2000). Maple Leaf Foods, an offshoot of the McCain's agrifood empire, completed construction of Canada's biggest packing plant in Brandon, which has the capacity to slaughter 90,000 hogs per week. Maple Leaf also took a giant step towards vertical integration of the supply chain with the acquisition of Landmark Feeds, Western Canada's largest livestock-feed manufacturer, and Elite Swine, Canada's second largest corporate hog-producer. U.S.-based Smithfield, the world's largest pork producer, bought Schneiders, a Canadian meat packer with substantial slaughter-capacity in Manitoba. Hog-industry boosters predicted a further doubling of production to 10 million hogs annually (Fallding, 2000). Alarmed, hog-industry opponents, grouped in a loose coalition called Hogwatch Manitoba, invoked fears of a flood-prone province awash in a sea of manure[1] and called for a moratorium on new barns.[2]

TABLE 59.1: Number of Pig Farms and Average Number of Pigs per Farm,
Manitoba and Canada, 1981–2000

Year	Number of Pig Farms, Manitoba	Average Number of Pigs per Farm, Manitoba	Average Number of Pigs per Farm, Canada
1981	5098	172	177
1986	3563	301	268
1991	2969	434	345
1996	2064	861	523
2000	1430	1354	884

Source: Statistics Canada, 2001

Although many hog barns are directly owned by large corporations, "vertical co-ordination," rather than vertical integration, is probably the dominant trend (Manitoba Pork Study Committee, 1994). In this model, corporations contract with farm proprietors to supply an array of goods and services, including hogs, feed, antibiotics, veterinary services and even the climate-controlled structures in which the hogs spend their short lives. The farmer is heavily dependent on the management company to provide the inputs necessary for the supply chain and to market the finished product. The farmer provides the site and labour and, most importantly, the land on which the liquid waste must be spread. Three of the ten largest hog-production companies in Canada are now based in Manitoba (Freese, 2000), while a fourth has major operations there.[3]

The hog industry has become disembedded from normative structures which were established to regulate Western Canadian agriculture during the last century, and has pursued more explicitly market-based strategies. The new mode of organization based on concentrated factory farming and globalized markets can be conceptualized, following the work of Lipietz (1987; 1992), as part of the transition from Fordist to post-Fordist food regimes (Kenney et al., 1991; Friedman, 1998). In the Fordist regime, government regulation of supply and pooling of output allow a relatively large number of agricultural producers some protection from market uncertainties. The

post-Fordist regime, on the other hand, privileges deregulated markets, concentrated production and industrial methods such as ILOs and biotechnology. The Canadian regulatory model was established along Fordist lines by the middle of the last century with the Canadian Wheat Board, a federal agency, monopolizing international grain sales, while the giant prairie agricultural co-operatives dominated grain handling. The model was extended from grain to other commodities, including pork, which in Manitoba came under an exclusive, provincial marketing monopoly, Manitoba Pork, which engaged in "single-desk selling."

This arrangement was seen as beneficial for the smaller producers, since it provided them with a collective marketing channel (Rampton, 1999). The larger producers, increasingly influential in the industry, lobbied against it, arguing that they could carry out more effective marketing on their own. A provincial government commission (Manitoba Pork Study Committee, 1994) that studied the issue found that Manitoba Pork was blocking the growth of an industry characterized by concentrated production and transnational marketing. The provincial government agreed and, in a series of restructuring moves in the 1990s, ended Manitoba Pork's marketing monopoly (Rampton, 1999). Manitoba Pork was transformed into the Manitoba Pork Council, an industry-lobbying group that represented the largest producers and would play a major role in the industry's public-relations battles with environmental opponents. Deregulation was seen as a victory for the big producers, processors and corporate investors, who were now free to carry out their business unrestrained by any need to "co-operate" with their smaller counterparts (Rampton, 1999). However, deregulation was bitterly opposed by many of the smaller producers, who became vulnerable to the pressures exerted by the big corporate supply and processing networks (Bell, 1999). Dwindling in numbers and influence, they could be ignored. The neo-liberal approach to farm policy complemented the treadmill of production in the prairie livestock sector and permitted the hog industry, dominated by the largest producers, to expand rapidly.

COMMUNITY POLARIZATION

In 1982, at the start of Manitoba's hog boom, few of the province's towns, villages and rural municipalities practised development planning. In that year, 33 of 201 municipalities reported full or partial development plans, while only eight reported zoning by-laws, the most powerful tool for regulating land use (Manitoba Intergovernmental Affairs, 2001). Today, reflecting in large part the imperatives of ILO expansion, over 80% of municipalities are involved in some form of development planning, while 122 now report zoning by-laws (Manitoba Intergovernmental Affairs, 2001). Not only were Manitoba's rural communities lacking the legal authority to control the hog industry, they also lacked the cultural authority. There is virtually no history of local regulation of agricultural land-use in Manitoba. Producers were expected to engage in good stewardship. The Manitoba Clean Environment Commission (1979: 3) commented, "In the past the intensity of livestock production operations was usually limited by the ability of the land to produce feed and forage." Few normative mechanisms existed to control the behaviour of factory farms, which

not only produced huge concentrations of manure but which also reaped an economic benefit from spreading it as close as possible to its point of origin (Innis, 1999). In the absence of strong legal and cultural mechanisms to control producer behaviour, the logic of local treadmills (Gould, Schnaiberg and Weinberg, 1996) took over in many rural communities. With the decline of traditional mixed farming, ILOs became the major investment opportunity in the local economy. Allied industries such as feed mills, construction and trucking all hoped to benefit. Local governments saw a means of reversing declines in population, employment and tax revenues.

The logic of treadmills and the limitations of community regulation of hog barns converged in a section of Manitoba known as the Interlake. Located north of Winnipeg between two huge bodies of freshwater, Lake Winnipeg and Lake Manitoba, the region was smoothed out by glaciers and is low-lying, flat and flood-prone. Water tables are high and the land surface is varied, ranging from hard clay to sand to marshland. The population is largely rural, and fishing, mixed farming and tourism remain important pillars of the regional economy. The wetlands are of prime ecological significance. Although hogs and cattle have long been raised in the Interlake, intensive factory farming played little role in the region's economy until the early 1990s. The bulk of Manitoba's hog industry was (and largely remains) concentrated in the southeast and south-central sections of the province (Statistics Canada, 1997). Intensive livestock operations require extensive amounts of land that can adequately absorb the nutrients from manure. Residential developments, restrictive municipal bylaws and environmental opposition eventually led to a scarcity of land available for manure spreading in the ILO-saturated areas (Sanders, 2001), and hog barn promoters looked elsewhere. The Interlake beckoned with its supply of relatively inexpensive land and fresh water.

In 1993, Puratone, one of Manitoba's largest corporate hog-producers, proposed a 2000-sow barn expandable to a 4000-sow, three-site operation in the Interlake municipality of Armstrong. The site was adjacent to two other municipalities, Bifrost and Gimli. Furthermore, the site was beside a creek that flowed through Bifrost and Gimli to drain into Lake Winnipeg, six miles away. Interviews with provincial government officials and community activists involved in assessing the proposal revealed significant concerns. Since the storage system would have the capacity to hold 4 million gallons of untreated hog waste, water quality was the primary issue. Although three jurisdictions were affected, only one, Armstrong, had the authority to decide, thus effectively splitting the opposition. Armstrong had (and still has) no by-laws to control land use and treadmill politics were paramount. No by-laws means no requirement for a public meeting for a conditional land-use application. Instead, "informational" meetings were conducted by representatives of the company and provincial government officials to convince local people that they would benefit. Higher prices for feed grain, loads of "organic" fertilizer and higher municipal revenues were promised as rewards. Local influentials such as the reeve (mayor), members of town council and the Chamber of Commerce threw their support behind hog barn development. Rumours circulated (and were denied) that town notables had become investors.

Town council approved the proposal. However, grass-roots opposition quickly mobilized. Opposition groups, such as the Bifrost Ratepayers Association and Interlake Citizens for a Clean Environment, were formed and picketing got underway outside the municipal office. The media started to cover the protests. Tempers flared during one protest and the RCMP was called in to restore calm. Under public pressure, the council reversed itself and rejected the hog barn's application. The company wrote to the municipality and threatened to sue, arguing that without by-laws they had no legal basis to deny the permit. Construction commenced but the controversy was not ended. The partially completed structure mysteriously burned to the ground. Another time the barn site was shot up and a security guard beaten. It was eventually completed, but problems continued. The irrigation gun equipment, touted as state of the art, jammed and flooded fields with manure. One local resident commented that "the sewage looked like lakes from the air." Gimli, which has a large lakefront and recreational industry, imposed restrictions on livestock operations and manure spreading, but Bifrost and Armstrong continued to encourage hog barns.

Controversy spread to other regions of the province as the industry grew. In 2000 a record 52 proposals for new or expanded ILOs totalling 35,642 AU and worth over $200 million were put forward (Manitoba Agriculture and Food, 2000). The previous record was 40 proposals of 21,596 AU in 1998. Since most hogs are produced in southeastern and southcentral Manitoba, where land-use and water-quality concerns are slowing further growth, much of the expansion has now shifted to southwestern Manitoba, a heavily agricultural area (Statistics Canada, 1996) where grain and cattle, rather than hog farming, are dominant. In 2000, for example, the southwest region received 20 of the 52 proposals, totalling 8692 AU. In 1995, it received only one proposal for 112 AU. Many of these proposals, especially those by corporate operators, are being vigorously contested. Plans by Premium Pork, an Ontario-based corporate producer and one of Canada's largest, to build up to 10 big farrowing and feeder barns in the southwestern communities of Hamiota, Shoal Lake and Strathclair have aroused strong opposition from local cattle and grain farmers. Perhaps the bitterest divisions have occurred over the company's proposal for two 2500 sow barns in the municipality of Rossburn. The approval was granted, and then rescinded, in a series of raucous meetings in which the RCMP and, later, private security guards provided public safety. Afterwards, local clergy appealed for calm.

The delegation of responsibility for decisions on siting hog barns to the rural municipalities has polarized the local decision-making process. Not only was there a treadmill logic in favour of development but, equally important, grass-roots opposition quickly mobilized. Grass-roots activism has grown rapidly in the regulatory vacuum in which ILOs have multiplied, seemingly unconstrained by existing legal and political institutions. The intensity of hog barn disputes is indicative of the uncertain and often contradictory outcomes of a major environmental issue, which is fought out community by community. The salience (Cable and Cable, 1995) of such disputes is augmented by the interaction of socio-economic factors—notably the introduction of corporate operations into rural communities—along with fears of significant environmental damage. These conflicts are often constructed as zero sum, directly pitting economic beneficiaries against environmental victims and polarizing rural communities into "environmental classes" (Murphy, 1994: 188). According to interviews conducted for this project, many producers believe that hog barns offer the only reasonable chance of surviving economically under highly competitive conditions. Opponents, on the other hand, believe that they will suffer the environmental impact of other people's success. Salience is further intensified by the new focus on water quality—and, by implication, human health—rather than odour, as the greatest perceived environmental impact of ILOs. This is confirmed in a recent Environics national poll (Miller; 1998) in which hog barns are viewed as the most environmentally damaging form of agriculture and water quality as the greatest public concern.

A woman from southeastern Manitoba where hog barns are numerous stated, "I have nothing against pig farms in general but remember—our children have to drink the water." An activist from Western Manitoba reflected the view common among hog barn opponents that provincial environmental standards are weak: "Who cares if a hog factory meets so-called provincial standards—I still don't want them in our community." Hogwatch Manitoba, the umbrella organization for a loose coalition of sixteen environmental, community, family-farm and animal-welfare groups fighting hog-industry expansion, has grown in membership and in tactical sophistication. It now routinely dispatches activists to rural land-use hearings across the province to counter hog barn proposals and to organize local opponents. Despite some successes, the Hogwatch leadership has grown frustrated with a municipal approval process it perceives as dominated by local politicians lacking the expertise to evaluate technically complex proposals and open to industry pressures (Hogwatch Manitoba, 2001). A leading Hogwatch organizer has urged the provincial government to take more responsibility to set environmental standards: "Rural municipalities shouldn't be left on their own to okay hog operations as they often don't have the resources to analyse complicated environmental and technical data."

Ironically, the hog industry has also grown disillusioned with a process that it views as uncertain, conflict-ridden and subject to the vagaries of municipal politics. Conditional land-use hearings require public meetings where industry representatives are often subject to criticism, sometimes strident and angry, when environmental or public health issues are in dispute. Many proposals have been defeated or delayed. A representative from Elite Swine, a dominant player in the supply chain, asserted that municipal land-use hearings should "stick to facts... and guarantee that if proponents meet all guidelines then their permit should be issued." The chairman of the Manitoba Pork Council, the leading industry lobby group, has complained, "Local politics sometimes ignores the merits of an application and pays more attention to public pressure."

The industry also wants the province to impose uniform standards, just not as high as those advocated by their environmental opponents. The desire for greater provincial involvement is echoed by many municipal councillors themselves. "It's just too complex, we need more help," stated the mayor of one municipality that has experienced significant controversy over hog barn proposals. New concerns about water quality have increased the complexity, as well as the intensity, of many of the discussions, further straining the effectiveness of the municipal approval process.

DISCUSSION

The expansion of the hog industry in Manitoba presents a useful case study of the global treadmill of production in agriculture. It has been characterized by the ascendancy of large-scale, specialized producers allied with meat processors, suppliers and other corporate interests. Smaller hog producers and more traditional mixed farmers have found themselves at a disadvantage compared to factory farms. Investment has flowed in from Europe and the U.S., as well as central Canada, and export markets have been targeted in the U.S., Europe and Asia. Manitoba has promoted this development as a positive response to the crisis in prairie agriculture. Pork is a value-added answer to low grain prices and profits, as well as competitive global markets. The provincial government has supported acceleration of the treadmill and allied itself with corporate interests seeking to grow the hog industry. Economic deregulation and neo-liberal policies have accompanied these developments. The hog industry has become disembedded from the key components of the Canadian system of agricultural regulation developed in the last century—notably marketing boards, co-operatives and orderly marketing arrangements. The policy of deregulation represents an important disjunction with the past agricultural policy that much more reflected the political power of the smaller producers.

Treadmills may operate on a global scale but environmental externalities are likely to be differentially distributed (Gould, Schnaiberg and Weinberg, 1996; Yearley, 1996) and local in their impact. This has been the case in Manitoba, where certain communities, notably in the southeastern part of the province where the industry is concentrated, have become sewers for livestock wastes. The rural municipalities have also borne the brunt of polarized debates about hog barn sitings. Municipal governments often lack the expertise to evaluate complex environmental issues, while local economic forces make hog barn projects difficult to resist. In recent years, the explosive issue of water contamination and the threat to public health have changed the terms of the debate. Environmental concerns about ILOs have become more visible and more politically potent. Pressure has grown on the Manitoba government to take a much more prominent role in ILO regulation.

This pressure has been exerted from both sides of the debate. Environmentalists have demanded that the province impose higher minimum standards for hog barns and greatly step up the policing of manure-management practices. The hog industry, too, has demanded uniform—though lower—provincial standards to replace the current patchwork of municipal by-laws and variances and, presumably, to facilitate the hog-barn approval process. The provincial government has set standards for manure management through the Manure and Mortalities Regulation and plans to step up monitoring by increasing the number of inspectors to 16 by 2002.

CONCLUSIONS

The hog industry has played a leading role in the transition to a more intense and specialized form of industrialized agriculture in Manitoba, as well as other parts of North America. It has become disembedded from the major regulatory institutions established to organize the marketing of agricultural products in Western Canada during the past century. Agriculture maintains its position on the transnational treadmill of production, but at increased risk to the resources that sustain its life-support base. The Canadian prairies are a major recipient of investment in the international livestock industry, but also a sewer for its animal wastes. The negative externalities from this industry's expansion have now become politically visible and a powerful issue in many rural communities. The state has been challenged to manage this contentious problem while preserving its basic commitment to treadmill expansion.

Environmental opposition to the unregulated expansion of livestock production through factory farms has grown too strong to ignore, especially, post-Walkerton, as the threat to water quality becomes the focal point of public concern. Conflicts in the rural municipalities that were given the primary responsibility for approving hog barn proposals have been intense and highly polarizing. The level of conflict, plus the inadequacy of local environmental expertise, suggest the limitations of local government in coping with the negative externalities of transnational treadmills. The hog industry itself has begun to demand at least a limited form of re-regulation. This may seem counterintuitive, but it is not uncommon for industry lobby groups to support state environmental standards under certain circumstances (Yearley, 1996). To the proponents of the Manitoba hog industry, expanded provincial regulation may be preferable to the conflict situation in many rural municipalities, where it is far from certain that all hog barn proposals will be approved. Equally important, regulation is a form of legitimation; it is harder to argue against a proposal that is compliant with legally established standards.

The new approach preserves treadmill expansion of ILOs, but adds stepped-up provincial environmental management combined with a legitimation discourse derived from the rhetoric of sustainable development. The environmental regulation of ILOs implies a recognition that a landscape of factory farms will require a level of state control similar to that established to control pollution in the manufacturing sector decades ago. This raises some questions that cannot be answered in this paper, but that might be instructive for further research. These questions revolve around the use of environmental regulations as perhaps the dominant societal tool to assert some collective control over ILOs, especially since neo-liberal agricultural policies have largely freed ILOs from the vestiges of economic regulation. What would be the distributional consequences? Would higher environmental standards privilege the bigger, richer and more industrialized operations and establish barriers to entry against smaller producers? Or, would smaller producers, mixed farmers and "organic" operations find an opening to improve their market share? Furthermore, would state environmental management combined with the rhetoric of sustainable development succeed as a legitimation discourse supporting ILO expansion? It remains to be seen whether this approach will prove successful in managing the contradictions among the various actors and interests that were unleashed by the acceleration of this powerful treadmill.

CRITICAL THINKING QUESTIONS

1. Review and discuss an industrial development (completed or proposed) in your community or region. Review some similarities and differences between Novek's findings and the development in your area.
2. Besides the obvious environmental challenges presented by intensive hog production, speculate on the social and cultural costs imposed by the global expansion of the "treadmill of production."

3. As a sociologist, do you see any resolution to the apparent contradiction between people's resistance to large industrial food-production operations on the one hand, and, on the other, their driving twenty miles to an American "big box" retail chain in search of low-priced food?

NOTES

1. The debate on "hog density" has to do with how many hogs—and potentially how much manure—are produced in a given area. While Manitoba has about 13 million acres under cultivation, more than half the hogs are produced in three agricultural zones in southeastern and southcentral Manitoba comprising about three million acres (Statistics Canada, 1997). Some estimates suggest that the municipalities with the mast concentrated production, such as Hanover in southeastern Manitoba, have a "hog density" equivalent to the highest levels found in Europe or the U.S. (Fallding, 2000).
2. Quebec, Canada's largest pork producer, announced curbs on hog-industry expansion in 165 rural municipalities. The moratorium is in response to widespread odour and water-quality problems.
3. Elite Swine (a subsidiary of Maple Leaf Foods) of Landmark, Manitoba, with 58,600 sows, is the second largest corporate hog-producer in Canada after Quebec-based Cooperative fédérée; other Manitoba companies on the top-ten list are Puratone of Niverville with 23,000 sows and Hytek of La Broquerie with 20,000 sows. Premium Pork, with 21,000 sows, is based in Lucan, Ontario, but has substantial operations in Manitoba (Freese, 2000).

REFERENCES

Agriculture and Agrifood Canada. 1997. Investing in Canada's hog and pork industry. www.aeis.agr.ca/mish/aisd/redmeat.

Bell, I. 1999. Manitoba hog producer exits with chagrin. *Western Producer.* 11 March

Bell, M. 1998. *An invitation to environmental sociology.* Thousand Oaks, Calif.: Pine Forge Press.

Berry, W. 1991. Living with the land. *Journal of Soil and Water Conservation,* Nov.–Dec., 390–93.

Cable, S. and C. Cable. 1995. *Environmental problems, grassroots solutions.* New York: St. Martin's Press.

De Lind, L. 1995. The state, hog hotels and the right to farm: A curious relationship. *Agriculture and Human Values,* Vol. 12, No 3, 34–44.

Durning, A., and H. Brough.1991. *Taking stock: Animal farming and the environment.* Worldwatch Paper 103. Washington, D.C.: Worldwatch Institute.

Edwards, B., and A. Ladd. 2000. Environmental justice, swine production and farm loss in North Carolina. *Sociological Spectrum,* No. 20, 263–90.

Fallding, H. 2000. A look at pigs in a poke. *Winnipeg Free Press.* 15 August.

Freese, B. 2000. Pork powerhouses 2000. *Successful Farming Online.* www.agriculture.com.sfonline/archive.

Friedman, H. 1991. Changes in the international division of labour: Agrifood complexes and export agriculture. In *Towards a new political economy of agriculture.* W. Friedland et al. (eds.). Boulder, Colo.: Westview Press, 65–93.

Friedman, H. 1998. A sustainable world food economy. In *Political ecology: Global and local.* R. Kell et al. (eds.). London: Routledge, 87–101.

Goodman, D., and M. Redclift. 1991. *Refashioning nature: Food, ecology and culture.* London: Routledge.

Gould, K., A. Schnaiberg and A. Weinberg. 1996. *Local environmental struggles.* Cambridge: Cambridge University Press.

Hall, A. 1998. Sustainable agriculture and conservation tillage: Managing the contradictions. *Canadian Review of Sociology and Anthropology,* Vol. 35, No. 2, 221–51.

Hamilton, N. 1994. Agriculture without farmers? Is industrialization restructuring American food production and threatening the future of sustainable agriculture? *Northern Illinois University Law Review,* No. 14, 613–37.

Hogwatch Manitoba. 2001. *Brief to the Canadian Environmental Defence Fund.*

Innis, N. 1999. Regulating livestock waste. *Choices: The Magazine of Food Farm and Resource Issues,* Vol. 14, No. 2, 14–20.

Kenney, M., et al. 1991. Agriculture in US Fordism: The integration of the productive consumer. In *Toward a new political economy of agriculture.* W. Friedland et. al. (eds.). Boulder, Colo.: Westview Press, 173–88.

Lipietz, A. 1987. *Mirages and miracles.* London: Verso.

——1992. *Toward a new economic order.* New York: Oxford.

Livestock Stewardship Panel. 2000. *Sustainable livestock development in Manitoba: Finding common ground.* Winnipeg: Government of Manitoba.

Manitoba Agriculture and Food. n.d. *Pork in Manitoba.* www.gov.mb.ca/agriculture/livestock.

——2000. *Technical review reports.* Communications from Eastern/Interlake and Southwestern Regions.

Manitoba Clean Environment Commission. 1979. *Report on an investigation of intensive livestock operations in Manitoba.* Winnipeg: Government of Manitoba.

Manitoba Intergovernmental Affairs. 2001. *Status of planning programs.* Winnipeg: Government of Manitoba.

Manitoba Pork Study Committee. 1994. *Manitoba's pork industry: Building for the 21st century.* Winnipeg: Government of Manitoba.

Martin, L., et al. 1999. *Prospects for hog production and processing in Canada: Update.* Guelph, Ont.: The George Morris Centre. www.geogemorris.org/publications.

Miller, D. 1998. *Canadians and the environmental impacts of the hog industry.* Environics International. http: //res2.agr.ca/initiatives/fumiernet/en/hems/miller.

Murphy, R. 1994. *Rationality and nature: A sociological inquiry into a changing relationship.* San Francisco: Westview Press.

Mussel, A., and L. Martin. 2000. *Manure as a public health issue: What accountability and direction for livestock agriculture?* Special Report. Guelph, Ont.: The George Morris Centre.

Qualman, D. 2000. The fight for the family farm. *Quarterly Review: Economic and Social Trends in Manitoba.* Winnipeg: Canadian Centre for Policy Alternatives. Winter, 8.

Rampton, R. 1999. Pork top earner in Manitoba. *Western Producer.* 3 February.

Redclift, M. 1996. *Wasted: Counting the costs of global consumption.* London: Earthscan.

Sachs, W. 1999. *Planet dialectics.* London: Zed Books.

Sanders, C. 2001. Mitchell residents fighting hog barn. *Winnipeg Free Press.* 2 February.

Schnaiberg, A., and K. Gould. 1994. *Environment and society: The enduring conflict.* New York: St. Martin's Press.

Statistics Canada. 1996. *Census of population 1996: Manitoba census divisions and subdivisions.* estat.statcan.ca/cgi-win.

——1997. *Agricultural Profile of Manitoba.* Catalogue 95-178-XPB. Ottawa: Minister of Supply and Services.

——2001. *Livestock Statistics.* Catalogue 23-603-XPE. Ottawa: Minister of Supply and Services.

Thu, K. Piggeries and politics: Rural development and Iowa's multibillion dollar swine industry. *Culture and Agriculture,* No. 53, 19–23.

Thu, K., and P. Durrenberger. 1994. North Carolina's hog industry: The rest of the story. *Culture and Agriculture,* No. 49, 20–23.

Yearley, S. 1996. *Sociology, environmentalism, globalization.* London: Sage Publications.

60

Supporting Indigenous Peoples

Alan Thein Durning

A particular concern of many environmentalists (and social scientists) is the steady loss of this planet's cultural diversity as thousands of small societies are pushed aside by the relentless march of economic development. This selection describes the problem and points out that protecting indigenous peoples is not just a matter of justice—the well-being of everyone in the world depends on it.

In July of 1992, an aged chief of the Lumad people in the Philippines—a man with a price on his head for his opposition to local energy development—sat at the base of the cloud-covered volcano Mount Apo and made a simple plea.

"Our Christian brothers are enjoying their life here in the plains," said eighty-six-year-old Chief Tulalang Maway, sweeping his arm toward the provincial town of Kidapawan and the agricultural lands beyond, lands his tribe long ago ceded to immigrants from afar. Turning toward the mountain—a Lumad sacred site that he has vowed to defend "to the last drop of blood"— Maway slowly finished his thought, "We only ask them to leave us our last sanctuary."

Source: "Supporting Indigenous Peoples," by Alan Thein Durning, in *State of the World 1993: A Worldwatch Institute Report on Progress Toward a Sustainable Society,* edited by Lester R. Brown et al. Copyright © 1993 by Worldwatch Institute. Reprinted by permission of W. W. Norton & Company, Inc.

Chief Maway's words could have been spoken by almost any tribal Filipino, or, for that matter, any Native American, Australian aborigine, African pygmy, or member of one of the world's thousands of other distinct indigenous cultures. All have ancient ties to the land, water, and wildlife of their ancestral domains, and all are endangered by onrushing forces of the outside world. They have been decimated by violence and plagues. Their cultures have been eroded by missionaries and exploited by wily entrepreneurs. Their subsistence economies have been dismantled in the pursuit of national development. And their homelands have been invaded by commercial resource extractors and overrun by landless peasants.

Chief Maway's entreaty, in its essence, is the call of indigenous peoples everywhere: the plea that their lands be spared further abuse, that their birthright be returned to them. It is a petition that the world's dominant cultures have long ignored, believing the passing of native peoples and their antiquated ways was an inevitable, if lamentable, cost of progress. That view, never morally defensible, is now demonstrably untenable.

Indigenous peoples are the sole guardians of vast, little-disturbed habitats in remote parts of every continent. These territories, which together encompass an area larger than Australia, provide important ecological services: They regulate hydrological cycles, maintain local and global climatic stability, and harbor a wealth of biological and genetic diversity. Indeed, indigenous homelands may provide safe haven for more endangered plant and animal species than all the world's nature reserves. Native peoples, moreover, often hold the key to these vaults of biological diversity. They possess a body of ecological knowledge—encoded in their languages, customs, and subsistence practices—that rivals the libraries of modern science.

The human rights enshrined in international law have long demanded that states shield indigenous cultures, but instead these cultures have been dismembered. A more self-interested appeal appears to be in order: Supporting indigenous survival is an objective necessity, even for those callous to the justice of the cause. As a practical matter, the world's dominant cultures cannot sustain the earth's ecological health—a requisite of human advancement—without the aid of the world's endangered cultures. Biological diversity is inextricably linked to cultural diversity.

Around the globe, indigenous peoples are fighting for their ancestral territories. They are struggling in courts and national parliaments, gaining power through new mass movements and international campaigns, and—as on the slopes of Mount Apo—defending their inheritance with their lives. The question is, Who will stand with them?

STATE OF THE NATIONS

Indigenous peoples (or "native" or "tribal" peoples) are found on every continent and in most countries. [See Table 60.1] The extreme variations in their ways of life and current circumstances defy ready definition. Indeed, many anthropologists insist that indigenous peoples are defined only by the way they define themselves: They think of themselves as members of a distinct people. Still, many indigenous cultures share a number of characteristics that help describe, if not define, them.

They are typically descendants of the original inhabitants of an area taken over by more powerful outsiders. They are distinct from their country's dominant group in language, culture, or religion. Most have a custodial concept of land and other resources, in part defining themselves in relation to the habitat from which they draw their livelihood. They commonly live in or maintain strong ties to a subsistence economy; many are, or are descendants of, hunter-gatherers, fishers, nomadic or seasonal herders, shifting forest farmers, or subsistence peasant cultivators. And their social relations are often tribal, involving collective management of natural resources, thick networks of bonds between individuals, and group decision making, often by consensus among elders.

Measured by spoken languages, the single best indicator of a distinct culture, all the world's people belong to 6,000 cultures; 4,000–5,000 of these are indigenous ones. Of the 5.5 billion humans on the planet, some 190 million to 625 million are indigenous people. (These ranges are wide because of varying definitions of "indigenous." The higher figures include ethnic nations that lack political autonomy, such as Tibetans, Kurds, and Zulus, while the lower figures count only smaller, subnational societies.) In some countries, especially those settled by Europeans in the past five centuries, indigenous populations are fairly easy to count. [See Table 60.2] By contrast, lines between indigenous peoples and ethnic minorities are difficult to draw in Asia and Africa, where cultural diversity remains greatest.

Regardless of where lines are drawn, however, human cultures are disappearing at unprecedented rates. Worldwide, the loss of cultural diversity is keeping pace with the global loss of biological

TABLE 60.1: Indigenous Peoples of the World, 1992

Region	Indigenous Peoples
Africa and Middle East	Great cultural diversity throughout continent; "indigenous" share hotly contested lands. Some 25–30 million nomadic herders or pastoralists in East Africa, Sahel, and Arabian peninsula include Bedouin, Dinka, Masai, Turkana. San (Bushmen) of Namibia and Botswana and pygmies of central African rain forest, both traditionally hunter-gatherers, have occupied present home lands for at least 20,000 years. (25–350 million indigenous people overall, depending on definitions; 2,000 languages)
Americas	Native Americans concentrated near centers of ancient civilizations: Aztec in Mexico, Mayan in Central America, and Incan in Andes of Bolivia, Ecuador, and Peru. In Latin America, most Indians farm small plots; in North America, 2 million Indians live in cities and on reservations. (42 million; 900 languages)
Arctic	Inuit (Eskimo) and other Arctic peoples of North America, Greenland, and Siberia traditionally fishers, whalers, and hunters. Sami (Lapp) of northern Scandinavia are traditionally reindeer herders. (2 million; 50 languages)
East Asia	Chinese indigenous peoples, numbering up to 82 million, mostly subsistence farmers such as Bulang of south China or former pastoralists such as ethnic Mongolians of north and west China. Ainu of Japan and aboriginal Taiwanese now largely industrial laborers. (12–84 million; 150 languages)
Oceania	Aborigines of Australia and Maoris of New Zealand, traditionally farmers, fishers, hunters, and gatherers. Many now raise livestock. Islanders of South Pacific continue to fish and harvest marine resources. (3 million; 500 languages)
South Asia	Gond, Bhil, and other adivasis, or tribal peoples, inhabit forest belt of central India. In Bangladesh, adivasis concentrated in Chittagong hills on Burmese border, several million tribal farmers and pastoralists in Afghanistan, Pakistan, Nepal, Iran, and central Asian republics of former Soviet Union. (74–91 million; 700 languages)
Southeast Asia	Tribal Hmong, Karen, and other forest-farming peoples form Asia ethnic mosaic covering up lands. Indigenous population follows distribution of forest: Laos has more forest and tribal peoples, Myanmar and Vietnam have less forest and fewer people, and Thailand and mainland Malaysia have the least. Tribal peoples are concentrated at the extreme ends of the Philippine and Indonesian archipelagos. Island of New Guinea—split politically between Indonesia and Papua New Guinea—populated by indigenous tribes. (32–55 million; 1,950 languages)

Source: Worldwatch Institute.

diversity. Anthropologist Jason Clay of Cultural Survival in Cambridge, Massachusetts, writes, "there have been more...extinctions of tribal peoples in this century than in any other in history." Brazil alone lost eighty-seven tribes in the first half of the century. One-third of North American languages and two-thirds of Australian languages have disappeared since 1800—the overwhelming share of them since 1900.

Cultures are dying out even faster than the peoples who belong to them. University of Alaska linguist Michael Krauss projects that half the world's languages—the storehouses of peoples' intellectual heritages—will disappear within a century. These languages, and arguably the cultures they embody, are no longer passed on to

sufficient numbers of children to ensure their survival. Krauss likens such cultures to animal species doomed to extinction because their populations are below the threshold needed for adequate reproduction. Only 5 percent of all languages, moreover, enjoy the relative safety of having at least a half-million speakers.

To trace the history of indigenous peoples' subjugation is simply to recast the story of the rise of the world's dominant cultures: the spread of Han Chinese into Central and Southeast Asia, the ascent of Aryan empires on the Indian subcontinent, the southward advance of Bantu cultures across Africa, and the creation of a world economy first through European colonialism and then through industrial development. Surviving

TABLE 60.2: Estimated Populations of Indigenous
Peoples, Selected Countries, 1992

Country	Population[a]	Share of National Population
	(million)	*(percent)*
Papua New Guinea	3.0	77
Bolivia	5.6	70
Guatemala	4.6	47
Peru	9.0	40
Ecuador	3.8	38
Myanmar	14.0	33
Laos	1.3	30
Mexico	10.9	12
New Zealand	0.4	12
Chile	1.2	9
Philippines	6.0	9
India	63.0	7
Malaysia	0.8	4
Canada	0.9	4
Australia	0.4	2
Brazil	1.5	1
Bangladesh	1.2	1
Thailand	0.5	1
United States	2.0	1
Former Soviet Union	1.4	>1

[a] Generally excludes those of mixed ancestry.

Source: Worldwatch Institute

indigenous cultures are often but tattered remnants of their predecessors' societies.

When Christopher Columbus reached the New World in 1492, there were perhaps 54 million people in the Americas, almost as many as in Europe at the time; their numbers plummeted, however, as plagues radiated from the landfalls of the conquistadors. Five centuries later, the indigenous peoples of the Americas, numbering some 42 million, have yet to match their earlier population. Similar contractions followed the arrival of Europeans in Australia, New Zealand, and Siberia.

Worldwide, virtually no indigenous peoples remain entirely isolated from national societies. By indoctrination or brute force, nations have assimilated native groups into the cultural mainstream. As a consequence, few follow the ways of their ancestors unchanged. Just one tenth of the Penan hunter-gatherers continue to hunt in the rain forests of Malaysian Borneo. A similar share of the Sami (Lapp) reindeer-herders of northern Scandinavia accompany their herds on the Arctic ranges. Half of North American Indians and many New Zealand Maori dwell in cities.

Tragically, indigenous peoples whose cultures are besieged frequently end up on the bottom of the national economy. They are often the first sent to war for the state, as in Namibia and the Philippines, and the last to go to work: Unemployment in Canadian Indian communities averages 50 percent. They are overrepresented among migrant laborers in India, beggars in Mexico, and uranium miners in the United States. They are often drawn into the shadow economy: They grow drug crops in northern Thailand, run gambling casinos in the United States, and sell their daughters into prostitution in Taiwan. Everywhere, racism against them is rampant. India's adivasis, or tribal people, endure hardships comparable to the "untouchables," the most downtrodden caste.

Native peoples' inferior social status is sometimes codified in national law and perpetuated by institutionalized abuse. Many members of the hill tribes in Thailand are denied citizenship, and until 1988 the Brazilian constitution legally classified Indians as minors and wards of the state. In the extreme, nation-states are simply genocidal: Burmese soldiers systemically raped, murdered, and enslaved thousands of Arakanese villagers in early 1992. Guatemala has exterminated perhaps 100,000 Mayans in its three-decade counterinsurgency. Similar numbers of indigenous people have died in East Timor and Irian Jaya since 1970 at the hands of Indonesian forces intent on solidifying their power.

In much of the world, the oppression that indigenous peoples suffer has indelibly marked their own psyches, manifesting itself in depression and social disintegration. Says Tamara Gliminova of the Khant people of Siberia, "When they spit into your soul for this long, there is little left."

HOMELANDS

Indigenous peoples not yet engulfed in modern societies live mostly in what Mexican anthropologist Gonzalo Aguirre Beltran called "regions of refuge," places so rugged, desolate, or remote that they have been little disturbed by the industrial economy. They remain in these areas for tragic reasons. Peoples in more fertile lands were eradicated outright to make way for settlers and plantations, or they retreated—sometimes at gun point—into these natural havens. Whereas indigenous peoples exercised de facto control over most of the earth's ecosystems as recently as two centuries ago, the territory they now occupy is reduced to an estimated 12–19 percent of the earth's land area—depending, again, on where the line between indigenous peoples and ethnic nations is drawn. And governments recognize their ownership of but a fraction of that area.

Gaining legal protection for the remainder of their subsistence base is most indigenous peoples' highest political priority. If they lose this struggle, their cultures stand little chance of surviving. As the World Council of Indigenous Peoples, a global federation based in Canada, wrote in 1985, "Next to shooting Indigenous Peoples, the surest way to kill us is to separate us from our part of the Earth." Most native peoples are bound to their land through relationships both practical and spiritual, routine and historical. Tribal Filipino Edtami Mansayagan, attempting to communicate the pain he feels at the destruction of the rivers, valleys, meadows, and hillsides of his people's mountain domain, exclaims, "these are the living pages of our unwritten history." The question of who shall control resources in the regions of refuge is the crux of indigenous survival.

Indigenous homelands are important not only to endangered cultures; they are also of exceptional ecological value. Intact indigenous communities and little-disturbed ecosystems overlap with singular regularity, from the coastal swamps of South America to the shifting sands of the Sahara, from the ice floes of the circumpolar north to the coral reefs of the South Pacific. When, for example, a National Geographic Society team in Washington, D.C., compiled a map of Indian lands and remaining forest cover in Central America in 1992, they confirmed the personal observation of Geodisio Castillo, a Kuna Indian from Panama: "Where there are forests there are indigenous people, and where there are indigenous people there are forests."

Because populations of both indigenous peoples and unique plant and animal species are numerically concentrated in remnant habitats in the tropics—precisely the regions of refuge that Beltran was referring to—the biosphere's most diverse habitats are usually homes to endangered cultures. The persistence of biological diversity in these regions is no accident. In the Philippines and Thailand, both representative cases, little more than a third of the land officially zoned as forest remains forest-covered; the tracts that do still stand are largely those protected by tribal people.

The relationship between cultural diversity and biological diversity stands out even in global statistics. Just nine countries together account for 60 percent of human languages. Of these nine centers of cultural diversity, six are also on the roster of biological "megadiversity" countries—nations with exceptional numbers of unique plant and animal species…. By the same token, two-thirds of all megadiversity countries also rank at the top of the cultural diversity league, with more than 100 languages spoken in each.

Everywhere, the world economy now intrudes on what is left of native lands, as it has for centuries. Writes World Bank anthropologist Shelton Davis: "The creation of a…global economy…has meant the pillage of native peoples' lands, labor and resources and their enforced acculturation and spiritual conquest. Each cycle of global economic expansion—the search for gold and spices in the sixteenth century, the fur trade and sugar estate economics of the seventeenth and eighteenth centuries, the rise of the great coffee, copra and…tropical fruit plantations in the late nineteenth and early twentieth centuries, the modern search for petroleum, strategic minerals, and tropical hardwoods—was based upon the exploitation of natural resources or primary commodities and led to the displacement of indigenous peoples and the undermining of traditional cultures."

The juggernaut of the money economy has not slowed in the late twentieth century; if anything, it has accelerated. Soaring consumer demand among the world's fortunate and burgeoning populations among the unfortunate fuel the economy's drive into native peoples' territories. Loggers, miners, commercial fishers, small farmers, plantation growers, dam builders, oil drillers— all come to seek their fortunes. Governments that equate progress with export earnings aid them, and military establishments bent on controlling far-flung territories back them.

Logging, in particular, is a menace because so many indigenous peoples dwell in woodlands. Japanese builders, for example, are devouring the ancient hardwood forests of tropical Borneo, home of the Penan and other Dayak peoples for disposable concrete molds. Most mahogany exported from Latin America is now logged illegally on Indian reserves and most nonplantation teak cut in Asia currently comes from tribal lands in the war-torn hills of Myanmar.

The consequences of mining on native lands are also ruinous. In the late eighties, for instance, tens of thousands of gold prospectors infiltrated the remote northern Brazilian haven of the Yanomami, the last large, isolated group of indigenous peoples in the Americas. The miners turned streams into sewers, contaminated the environment with the 1,000 tons of toxic mercury they used to purify gold, and precipitated an epidemic of malaria that killed more than a thousand children and elders. Just in time, the Brazilian government recognized and began defending the Yanomami

homeland in early 1992, a rare and hopeful precedent in the annals of indigenous history. Still, in Brazil overall, mining concessions overlap 34 percent of Indian lands….

Other energy projects, especially large dams, also take their toll on native habitats. In the north of Canada, the provincial electric utility Hydro Quebec completed a massive project called James Bay I in 1985, inundating vast areas of Cree Indian hunting grounds and unexpectedly contaminating fisheries with naturally occurring heavy metals that had previously been locked away in the soil. The Cree and neighboring Inuit tribes have organized against the project's next gigantic phase, James Bay II. The $60-billion project would tame eleven wild rivers, altering a France-sized area to generate 27,000 megawatts of exportable power. As Matthew Coon-Come, Grand Chief of the Cree, says, "The only people who have the right to build dams on our territory are the beavers."…

Commercial producers have also taken over indigenous lands for large-scale agriculture. The Barabaig herders of Tanzania have lost more than 400 square kilometers of dry-season range to a mechanized wheat farm. Private ranchers in Botswana have enclosed grazing lands for their own use, and Australian ranchers have usurped aboriginal lands. In peninsular Malaysia, palm and rubber plantations have left the Orang Asli (Original People) with tiny fractions of their ancient tropical forests.

Less dramatic but more pervasive is the ubiquitous invasion of small farmers onto indigenous lands. Sometimes sponsored by the state but ultimately driven by population growth and maldistribution of farmland, poor settlers encroach on native lands everywhere. In Indonesia during the eighties, for example, the government shifted 2 million people from densely populated islands such as Java to 800,000 hectares of newly cleared plots in sparsely populated indigenous provinces such as Irian Jaya, Kalimantan, and Sumatra. Half the area settled was virgin forest— much of it indigenous territory….

Few states recognize indigenous peoples' rights over homelands, and where they do, those rights are often partial, qualified, or of ambiguous legal force. Countries may recognize customary rights in theory, but enforce common or statutory law against those rights whenever there is a conflict; or they may sanction indigenous rights but refuse to enforce them. Through this cloud of legal contradictions a few countries stand out as exceptional. Papua New Guinea and Ecuador acknowledge indigenous title to large shares of national territory, and Canada and Australia recognize rights over extensive areas.... Still, across all the earth's climatic and ecological zones—from the Arctic tundra to the temperate and nontropical forests to the savannahs and deserts—native peoples control slim shares of their ancestral domains....

STEWARDS

Sustainable use of local resources is simple self-preservation for people whose way of life is tied to the fertility and natural abundance of the land. Any community that knows its children and grandchildren will live exactly where it does is more apt to take a longer view than a community without attachments to local places.

Moreover, native peoples frequently aim to preserve not just a standard of living but a way of life rooted in the uniqueness of a local place. Colombian anthropologist Martin von Hildebrand notes, "The Indians often tell me that the difference between a colonist [a non-Indian settler] and an Indian is that the colonist wants to leave money for his children and that the Indians want to leave forests for their children."

Indigenous peoples' unmediated dependence on natural abundance has its parallel in their peerless ecological knowledge. Most forest-dwelling tribes display an utter mastery of botany. One typical group, the Shuar people of Ecuador's Amazonian lowlands, uses 800 species of plants for medicine, food, animal fodder, fuel, construction, fishing, and hunting supplies.

Native peoples commonly know as much about ecological processes that affect the availability of natural resources as they do about those resources' diverse uses. South Pacific islanders can predict to the day and hour the beginning of the annual spawning runs of many fish. Whaling peoples of northern Canada have proved to skeptical western marine biologists that bowhead whales migrate under pack ice. Coastal aborigines in Australia distinguish between eighty different tidal conditions.

Specialists trained in western science often fail to recognize indigenous ecological knowledge because of the cultural and religious ways in which indigenous peoples record and transmit that learning. Ways of life that developed over scores of generations could only thrive by encoding ecological sustainability into the body of practice, myth, and taboo that passes from parent to child....

What are the conditions in which traditional systems of ecological management can persist in the modern world? First, indigenous peoples must have secure rights to their subsistence base—rights that are not only recognized but enforced by the state and, ideally, backed by international law. Latin American tribes such as the Shuar of Ecuador, when threatened with losing their land, have cleared their own forests and taken up cattle ranching, because these actions prove ownership in Latin America. Had Ecuador backed up the Shuar's land rights, the ranching would have been unnecessary.

Second, for indigenous ecological stewardship to survive the onslaught of the outside world, indigenous peoples must be organized politically and the state in which they reside must allow democratic initiatives. The Khant and Mansi peoples of Siberia, just as most indigenous people in the former Soviet Union, were nominally autonomous in their customary territories under Soviet law, but political repression precluded the organized defense of that terrain until the end of the eighties. Since then, the peoples of Siberia have begun organizing themselves to turn paper rights into real local control. In neighboring China, in contrast, indigenous homelands remain pure legal fictions because the state crushes all representative organizations.

Third, indigenous communities must have access to information, support, and advice from friendly sources if they are to surmount the obstacles of the outside world. The tribal people of Papua New Guinea know much about their local environments, for example, but they know little about the impacts of large-scale logging and mining. Foreign and domestic investors have often played on this ignorance, assuring remote groups that no lasting harm would result from leasing parts of their land to resource extractors. If the forest peoples of Papua New Guinea could learn from the experience of indigenous peoples elsewhere—through supportive organizations and indigenous peoples' federations—they might be more careful.

A handful of peoples around the world have succeeded in satisfying all three of these conditions....

RISING FROM THE FRONTIER

From the smallest tribal settlements to the U.N. General Assembly, indigenous peoples' organizations are making themselves felt. Their grassroots movements have spread rapidly since 1970, gaining strength in numbers and through improvement of their political skills. They have pooled their talents in regional, national, and global federations to broaden their influence. This uprising, which like any movement has its share of internal rivalries, may eventually bring fundamental advances in the status of all endangered cultures....

In a world where almost all nations have publicly committed themselves to the goal of sustainable development and most have signed a global treaty for the protection of biological diversity, the questions of cultural survival and indigenous homelands cannot be avoided much longer. As guardians and stewards of remote and fragile ecosystems, indigenous cultures could play a crucial role in safeguarding humanity's planetary home. But they cannot do it alone. They need the support of international law and national policy, and they need the understanding and aid of the world's more numerous peoples.

Giving native peoples power over their own lives raises issues for the world's dominant culture as well—a consumerist and individualist culture born in Europe and bred in the United States. Indeed, indigenous peoples may offer more than a best-bet alternative for preserving the outlying areas where they live. They may offer living examples of cultural patterns that can help revive ancient values within everyone: devotion to future generations, ethical regard for nature, and commitment to community among people. The question may be, then, Are indigenous peoples the past, or are they the future?

CRITICAL THINKING QUESTIONS

1. How many indigenous cultures are there on this planet? What general traits do they have in common?
2. Why are the world's tribal peoples disappearing?
3. The author asserts that sustaining the world's natural environment depends on assuring the future of indigenous peoples. Why is this so?

61

On the Origins of Social Movements

Jo Freeman

According to Jo Freeman, a "spark of life" sometimes transforms a group of like-minded people into a social movement. In this excerpt from her work, Freeman analyzes this process, illustrating her ideas with account of the civil rights movement and the women's movement in the United States.

Most movements have inconspicuous beginnings. The significant elements of their origins are usually forgotten or distorted by the time a trained observer seeks to trace them out. Perhaps this is why the theoretical literature on social movements usually concentrates on causes (Gurr, 1970; Davies, 1962; Oberschall, 1973) and motivations (Toch, 1965; Cantril, 1941; Hoffer, 1951; Adorno et al., 1950), while the "spark of life" by which the "mass is to cross the threshold of organizational life" (Lowi, 1971: 41) has received scant attention....

From where do the people come who make up the initial, organizing cadre

Source: From *Social Movements of the Sixties and Seventies,* ed. Jo Freeman, pp. 8–13, 17–30, copyright © 1983 by Jo Freeman. Reprinted by permission.

of a movement? How do they come together, and how do they come to share a similar view of the world in circumstances that compel them to political action? In what ways does the nature of the original center affect the future development of the movement?

Before answering these questions, let us first look at data on the origins of [two] social movements prominent in the sixties and seventies: civil rights...and women's liberation.

These data identify recurrent elements involved in movement formation. The ways in which these elements interact, given a sufficient level of strain, would support the following propositions:

Proposition 1. The need for a *preexisting communications network* or infra-structure within the social base of a movement is a primary prerequisite for "spontaneous" activity. Masses alone do not form movements, however discontented they may be. Groups of previously unorganized individuals may spontaneously form into small local associations— usually along the lines of informal social networks—in response to a specific strain or crisis. If they are not linked in some manner, however, the protest does not become generalized but remains a local irritant or dissolves completely. If a movement is to spread rapidly, the communications network must already exist. If only the rudiments of a network exist, movement formation requires a high input of "organizing" activity.

Proposition 2. Not just any communications network will do. It must be a network that is *co-optable* to the new ideas of the incipient movement.[1] To be co-optable, it must be composed of like-minded people whose backgrounds, experiences, or location in the social structure make them receptive to the ideas of a specific new movement.

Proposition 3. Given the existence of a co-optable communications network, or at least the rudimentary development of a potential one, and a situation of strain, one or more precipitants are required. Here, two distinct patterns emerge that often overlap. In one, a *crisis* galvanizes the network into spontaneous action in a new direction. In the other, one or more persons begin *organizing* a new organization or disseminating a new idea. For spontaneous action to occur, the communications network must be well formed or the initial protest will not survive the incipient stage. If it is not well formed, organizing efforts must occur; that is, one or more persons must specifically attempt to construct a movement. To be successful, organizers must be skilled and must have a fertile field in which to work. If no communications network already exists, there must at least be emerging spontaneous groups that are acutely attuned to the issue, albeit uncoordinated. To sum up, if a co-optable communications network is already established, a crisis is

all that is necessary to galvanize it. If it is rudimentary, an organizing cadre of one or more persons is necessary. Such a cadre is superfluous if the former conditions fully exist, but it is essential if they do not.

THE CIVIL RIGHTS MOVEMENT

The civil rights movement has two origins, although one contributed significantly to the other. The first can be dated from December 7, 1955, when the arrest of Rosa Parks for occupying a "white" seat on a bus stimulated both the Montgomery Bus Boycott and the formation of the Montgomery Improvement Association. The second can be dated either from February 1, 1960, when four freshmen at A & T College in Greensboro, North Carolina, sat in at a white lunch counter, or from April 15–17, when a conference at Shaw University in Raleigh, North Carolina, resulted in the formation of the Student Non-Violent Co-ordinating Committee. To understand why there were two origins one has to understand the social structure of the southern black community, as an incipient generation gap alone is inadequate to explain it.

Within this community the two most important institutions, often the only institutions, were the church and the black college. They provided the primary networks through which most southern blacks interacted and communicated with one another on a regular basis. In turn, the colleges and churches were linked in a regional communications network. These institutions were also the source of black leadership, for being a "preacher or a teacher" were the main status positions in black society. Of the two, the church was by far the more important; it touched on more people's lives and was the largest and oldest institution in the black community. Even during slavery there had been an "invisible church." After emancipation, "organized religious life became the chief means by which a structured or organized social life came into existence among the Negro masses" (Frazier, 1963: 17). Furthermore, preachers were more economically independent of white society than were teachers.

Neither of these institutions represented all the segments of black society, but the segments they did represent eventually formed the main social base for supplying civil rights activists. The church was composed of a male leadership and a largely middle-aged, lower-class female followership. The black colleges were the homes of black intellectuals and middle-class youth, male and female.

Both origins of the civil rights movement resulted in the formation of new organizations, despite the fact that at least three seemingly potential social movement organizations already existed. The wealthiest of these was the Urban League, founded in 1910. It, however, was not only largely restricted to a small portion of the black and white bourgeoisie but, until 1961, felt itself to be "essentially a social service agency" (Clark, 1966: 245).

Founded in 1909, the National Association for the Advancement of Colored People (NAACP) pursued channels of legal change until it finally persuaded the Supreme Court to abolish educational segregation in *Brown* v. *Board of Education.* More than any other single event, this decision created the atmosphere of rising expectations that helped precipitate the movement. The NAACP suffered from its own success, however. Having organized itself primarily to support court cases and utilize other "respectable" means, it "either was not able or did not desire to modify its program in response to new demands. It believed it should continue its important work by using those techniques it had already perfected" (Blumer, 1951: 199).

The Congress of Racial Equality, like the other two organizations, was founded in the North. It began "in 1942 as the Chicago Committee of Racial Equality, which was composed primarily of students at the University of Chicago. An offshoot of the pacifist Fellowship of Reconciliation, its leaders were middle-class intellectual reformers, less prominent and more alienated from the mainstream of American society than the founders of the NAACP. They regarded the NAACP's legalism

as too gradualist and ineffective, and aimed to apply Gandhian techniques of non-violent direct action to the problem of race relations in the United States. A year later, the Chicago Committee joined with a half dozen other groups that had emerged across the country, mostly under the encouragement of the F. O. R. to form a federation known as the Congress of Racial Equality" (Rudwick & Meier, 1970: 10).

CORE's activities anticipated many of the main forms of protest of the civil rights movement, and its attitudes certainly seemed to fit CORE for the role of a major civil rights organization. But though it became quite influential, at the time the movement actually began, CORE had declined almost to the point of extinction. Its failure reflects the historical reality that organizations are less likely to create social movements than be created by them. More important, CORE was poorly situated to lead a movement of southern blacks. Northern-based and composed primarily of pacifist intellectuals, it had no roots in any of the existing structures of the black community, and in the North these structures were themselves weak. CORE could be a source of ideas, but not of coordination.

The coordination of a new movement required the creation of a new organization. But that was not apparent until after the Montgomery bus boycott began. That boycott was organized through institutions already existing in the black community of Montgomery.

Rosa Parks's refusal to give up her seat on the bus to a white man was not the first time such defiance of segregation laws had occurred. There had been talk of a boycott the previous time, but after local black leaders had a congenial meeting with the city commissioners, nothing happened—on either side (King, 1958: 37–41). When Parks, a former secretary of the local NAACP, was arrested, she immediately called E. D. Nixon, at that time the president of the local chapter. He not only bailed her out but informed a few influential women in the city, most of whom were members of the Women's Political Council. After numerous phone calls between their members, it was the

WPC that actually suggested the boycott, and E. D. Nixon who initially organized it (ibid.: 44–5).

The Montgomery Improvement Association (MIA) was formed at a meeting of eighteen ministers and civic leaders the Monday after Parks's conviction and a day of successful boycotting, to provide ongoing coordination. No one then suspected that coordination would be necessary for over a year, with car pools organized to provide alternative transportation for seventeen thousand riders a day. During this time the MIA grew slowly to a staff of ten in order to handle the voluminous correspondence, as well as to provide rides and keep the movement's momentum going. The organization, and the car pools, were financed by $250,000 in donations that poured in from all over the world in response to heavy press publicity about the boycott. But the organizational framework for the boycott and the MIA was the church. Most, although not all, of the officers were ministers, and Sunday meetings with congregations continued to be the main means of communicating with members of the black community and encouraging them to continue the protest.

The boycott did not end until the federal courts ruled Alabama's bus segregation laws unconstitutional late in 1956—at the same time that state courts ruled the boycott illegal. In the meantime, black leaders throughout the South had visited Montgomery, and out of the discussions came agreement to continue antisegregation protests regularly and systematically under the aegis of a new organization, the Southern Christian Leadership Conference. The NAACP could not lead the protests because, according to an SCLC pamphlet, "during the late fifties, the NAACP had been driven out of some Southern states. Its branches were outlawed as foreign corporations and its lawyers were charged with barratry, that is, persistently inciting litigation."

On January 10, 1957, over one hundred people gathered in Atlanta at a meeting called by four ministers, including Martin Luther King. Bayard Rustin drew up the "working papers." Initially called the Southern Leadership Conference on Transportation and Nonviolent Integration, the SCLC never developed a mass base even when it changed its name. It established numerous "affiliates" but did most of its work through the churches in the communities to which it sent its fieldworkers.

The church was not just the only institution available for a movement to work through; in many ways it was ideal. It performed "the central organizing function in the Negro community" (Holloway, 1969: 22), providing both access to large masses of people on a regular basis and a natural leadership. As Wyatt Tee Walker, former executive director of SCLC, commented, "The Church today is central to the movement. If a Negro's going to have a meeting, where's he going to have it? Mostly he doesn't have a Masonic lodge, and he's not going to get the public schools. And the church is the primary means of communication" (Brink & Harris, 1964: 103). Thus the church eventually came to be the center of the voter registration drives as well as many of the other activities of the civil rights movement.

Even the young men and women of SNCC had to use the church, though they had trouble doing so because, unlike most of the officers of SCLC, they were not themselves ministers and thus did not have a "fraternal" connection. Instead they tended to draw many of their resources and people from outside the particular town in which they were working by utilizing their natural organizational base, the college.

SNCC did not begin the sit-ins, but came out of them. Once begun, the idea of the sit-in spread initially by means of the mass media. But such sit-ins almost always took place in towns where there were Negro colleges, and groups on these campuses essentially organized the sit-in activities of their communities. Nonetheless, "CORE, with its long emphasis of nonviolent direct action, played an important part, once the sit-ins began, as an educational and organizing agent" (Zinn, 1964: 23). CORE had very few staff in the South, but there were enough to at least hold classes and practice sessions in nonviolence.

It was SCLC, however, that was actually responsible for the formation of SNCC; though it might well have organized itself eventually. Ella Baker, then executive secretary of SCLC, thought something should be done to coordinate the rapidly spreading sit-ins in 1960, and many members of SCLC thought it might be appropriate to organize a youth group. With SCLC money, Baker persuaded her alma mater, Shaw University, to provide facilities to contact the groups at centers of sit-in activity. Some two hundred people showed up for the meeting, decided to have no official connection with SCLC beyond a "friendly relationship," and formed the Student Non-Violent Co-ordinating Committee (Zinn, 1964: 32–4). It had no members, and its fieldworkers numbered two hundred at their highest point, but it was from the campuses, especially the southern black colleges, that it drew its sustenance and upon which its organizational base rested.…

THE WOMEN'S LIBERATION MOVEMENT[2]

Women are not well organized. Historically tied to the family and isolated from their own kind, only in the nineteenth century did women in this country have the opportunity to develop independent associations of their own. These associations took years and years of careful organizational work to build. Eventually they formed the basis for the suffrage movement of the early twentieth century. The associations took less time to die. Today the Women's Trade Union League, the General Federation of Women's Clubs, the Women's Christian Temperance Union, not to mention the powerful National Women's Suffrage Association, are all either dead or a pale shadow of their former selves.

As of 1960, not one organization of women had the potential to become a social movement organization, nor was there any form of "neutral" structure of interaction to provide the base for such an organization. The closest exception to the former was the National Women's Party, which has remained dedicated to feminist concerns since its inception in 1916. However, the NWP has been essentially a lobbying group for the Equal Rights Amendment since 1923. From the beginning, the NWP believed that a small group of women concentrating their efforts in the right places was more effective than a mass appeal, and so was not appalled by the fact that as late as 1969 even the majority of avowed feminists in this country had never heard of the ERA or the NWP.

The one large women's organization that might have provided a base for a social movement was the 180,000-member Federation of Business and Professional Women's Clubs. Yet, while it has steadily lobbied for legislation of importance to women, as late as "1966 BPW rejected a number of suggestions that it redefine…goals and tactics and become a kind of 'NAACP for women'…out of fear of being labeled 'feminist'" (Hole & Levine, 1971: 89).

Before any social movement could develop among women, there had to be created a structure to bring potential feminist sympathizers together. To be sure, groups such as the BPW, and institutions such as the women's colleges, might be a good source of adherents for such a movement. But they were determined not to be the source of leadership.

What happened in the 1960s was the development of two new communications networks in which women played prominent roles that allowed, even forced, an awakened interest in the old feminist ideas. As a result, the movement actually has two origins, from two different strata of society, with two different styles, orientations, values, and forms of organization. The first of these will be referred to as the "older branch" of the movement, partially because it began first and partially because it was on the older side of the "generation gap" that pervaded the sixties. Its most prominent organization is the National Organization for Women (NOW), which was also the first to be formed. The style of its movement organizations tends to be traditional with elected officers, boards of directors, bylaws, and the other trappings of democratic procedure. Conversely, the "younger branch" consisted of innumerable small groups engaged in a variety of activities whose contact with one another was always tenuous (Freeman, 1975: 50).

The forces that led to NOW's formation were set in motion in 1961 when President Kennedy established the President's Commission on the Status of Women at the behest of Esther Petersen, then director of the Women's Bureau. Its 1963 report, *American Women,* and subsequent committee publications documented just how thoroughly women were denied many rights and opportunities. The most significant response to the activity of the President's commission was the establishment of some fifty state commissions to do similar research on a state level. The Presidential and State Commission activity laid the groundwork for the future movement in two significant ways: (1) It unearthed ample evidence of women's unequal status and in the process convinced many previously uninterested women that something should be done; (2) It created a climate of expectations that something would be done. The women of the Presidential and State Commissions who were exposed to these influences exchanged visits, correspondence, and staff, and met with one another at an annual commission convention. They were in a position to share and mutually reinforce their growing awareness and concern over women's issues. These commissions thus provided an embryonic communications network.

During this time, two other events of significance occurred. The first was the publication of Betty Friedan's *The Feminine Mystique* in 1963. A quick best seller, the book stimulated many women to question the *status quo* and some women to suggest to Friedan that an organization be formed to do something about it. The second event was the addition of "sex" to the 1964 Civil Rights Act.

Many thought the "sex" provision was a joke, and the Equal Employment Opportunity Commission treated it as one, refusing to enforce it seriously. But a rapidly growing feminist coterie within the EEOC argued that "sex" would be taken more seriously if there were

"some sort of NAACP for women" to put pressure on the government.

On June 30, 1966, these three strands of incipient feminism came together, and NOW was tied from the knot. At that time, government officials running the Third National Conference of Commissions on the Status of Women, ironically titled "Targets for Action," forbade the presentation of a suggested resolution calling for the EEOC to treat sex discrimination with the same consideration as race discrimination. The officials said one government agency could not be allowed to pressure another, despite the fact that the state commissions were not federal agencies. The small group of women who desired such a resolution had met the night before in Friedan's hotel room to discuss the possibility of a civil rights organization for women. Not convinced of its need, they chose instead to propose the resolution. When conference officials vetoed it, they held a whispered conversation over lunch and agreed to form an action organization "to bring women into full participation in the mainstream of American society now, assuming all the privileges and responsibilities thereof in truly equal partnership with men." The name NOW was coined by Friedan who was at the conference doing research on a book. When word leaked out, twenty-eight women paid five dollars each to join before the day was over (Friedan, 1967: 4).

By the time the organizing conference was held the following October 29 through 30, over three hundred men and women had become charter members. It is impossible to do a breakdown on the composition of the charter membership, but one of the officers and board is possible. Such a breakdown accurately reflected NOW's origins. Friedan was president, two former EEOC commissioners were vice presidents, a representative of the United Auto Workers Women's Committee was secretary-treasurer, and there were seven past and present members of the State Commissions on the Status of Women on the twenty member board. One hundred twenty-six of the charter members were Wisconsin residents—and Wisconsin had the most active state Commission. Occupationally, the board and officers were primarily from the professions, labor, government, and communications fields. Of these, only those from labor had any experience in organizing, and they resigned a year later in a dispute over support of the Equal Rights Amendment. Instead of organizational experience, what the early NOW members had was experience in working with and in the media, and it was here that their early efforts were aimed.

As a result, NOW often gave the impression of being larger than it was. It was highly successful in getting in the press; much less successful in either bringing about concrete changes or forming an organization. Thus it was not until 1970, when the national press simultaneously did major stories on the women's liberation movement, that NOW's membership increased significantly.

In the meantime, unaware of and unknown to NOW, the EEOC, or the State Commissions, younger women began forming their own movement. Here, too, the groundwork had been laid some years before. The different social action projects of the sixties had attracted many women, who were quickly shunted into traditional roles and faced with the self-evident contradiction of working in a "freedom movement" but not being very free. No single "youth movement" activity or organization is responsible for forming the younger branch of the women's liberation movement, but together they created a "radical community" in which like-minded people continually interacted or were made aware of one another. This community provided the necessary network of communication and its radical ideas the framework of analysis that "explained" the dismal situation in which radical women found themselves.

Papers had been circulated on women and individual temporary women's caucuses had been held as early as 1964 (see Hayden & King, 1966). But it was not until 1967 and 1968 that the groups developed a determined, if cautious, continuity and began to consciously expand themselves. At least five groups in five different cities (Chicago, Toronto, Detroit, Seattle, and Gainesville, Florida)

formed spontaneously, independently of one another. They came at an auspicious moment, for 1967 was the year in which the blacks kicked the whites out of the civil rights movement, student power was discredited by SDS, and the New Left was on the wane. Only draft resistance activities were on the increase, and this movement more than any other exemplified the social inequities of the sexes. Men could resist the draft. Women could only counsel resistance.

At this point, there were few opportunities available for political work. Some women fit well into the secondary role of draft counseling. Many didn't. For years their complaints of unfair treatment had been forestalled by movement men with the dictum that those things could wait until after the Revolution. Now these political women found time on their hands, but still the men would not listen.

A typical example was the event that precipitated the formation of the Chicago group, the first independent group in this country. At the August 1967 National Conference for New Politics convention a women's caucus met for days, but was told its resolution wasn't significant enough to merit a floor discussion. By threatening to tie up the convention with procedural motions the women succeeded in having their statement tacked to the end of the agenda. It was never discussed. The chair refused to recognize any of the many women standing by the microphone, their hands straining upwards. When he instead called on someone to speak on "the forgotten American, the American Indian," five women rushed the podium to demand an explanation. But the chairman just patted one of them on the head (literally) and told her, "Cool down, little girl. We have more important things to talk about than women's problems."

The "little girl" was Shulamith Firestone, future author of *The Dialectic of Sex,* and she didn't cool down. Instead she joined with another Chicago woman she met there who had unsuccessfully tried to organize a women's group that summer, to call a meeting of the women who had halfheartedly attended those summer meetings. Telling their stories to those women, they stimulated sufficient rage to carry the group for three months, and by that time it was a permanent institution.

Another somewhat similar event occurred in Seattle the following winter. At the University of Washington an SDS organizer was explaining to a large meeting how white college youth established rapport with the poor whites with whom they were working. "He noted that sometimes after analyzing societal ills, the men shared leisure time by 'balling a chick together.' He pointed out that such activities did much to enhance the political consciousness of the poor white youth. A woman in the audience asked, 'And what did it do for the consciousness of the chick?'" (Hole & Levine, 1971: 120). After the meeting, a handful of enraged women formed Seattle's first group.

Subsequent groups to the initial five were largely organized rather than formed spontaneously out of recent events. In particular, the Chicago group was responsible for the formation of many new groups in Chicago and in other cities. Unlike NOW, the women in the first groups had had years of experience as trained organizers. They knew how to utilize the infrastructure of the radical community, the underground press, and the free universities to disseminate women's liberation ideas. Chicago, as a center of New Left activity, had the largest number of politically conscious organizers. Many traveled widely to leftist conferences and demonstrations, and most used the opportunity to talk with other women about the new movement. In spite of public derision by radical men, or perhaps because of it, young women steadily formed new groups around the country.

ANALYSIS

From these data there appear to be four essential elements involved in movement formation: (1) the growth of a preexisting communications network that is (2) co-optable to the ideas of the new movement; (3) a series of crises that

galvanize into action people involved in a co-optable network, and/or (4) subsequent organizing effort to weld the spontaneous groups together into a movement. Each of these elements needs to be examined in detail.

COMMUNICATIONS NETWORK

…The women's liberation movement…illustrates the importance of a network precisely because the conditions for a movement existed *before* a network came into being, but the movement didn't exist until afterward. Analysts of socioeconomic causes have concluded that the movement could have started anytime within a twenty-year period. Strain for women was as great in 1955 as in 1965 (Ferriss, 1971). What changed was the organizational situation. It was not until new networks emerged among women aware of inequities beyond local boundaries that a movement could grow past the point of occasional, spontaneous uprisings. The fact that two distinct movements, with two separate origins, developed from two networks unaware of each other is further evidence of the key role of preexisting communications networks as the fertile soil in which new movements can sprout.

References to the importance of a preexisting communications network appear frequently in case studies of social movements, though the theoretical writers were much slower to recognize their salience. According to Buck (1920: 43–4), the Grange established a degree of organization among American farmers in the nineteenth century that greatly facilitated the spread of future farmers' protests. Lipset has reported that in Saskatchewan, "the rapid acceptance of new ideas and movements…can be attributed mainly to the high degree of organization.… The role of the social structure of the western wheat belt in facilitating the rise of new movements has never been sufficiently appreciated by historians and sociologists. Repeated challenges and crises forced the western farmers to create many more community institutions (especially cooperatives and economic pressure groups) than are necessary in a more stable area. These groups in turn provided a structural basis for immediate action in critical situations. [Therefore] though it was a new radical party, the C. C. F. did not have to build up an organization from scratch" (1959: 206).

Similarly, Heberle (1951: 232) reports several findings that Nazism was most successful in small, well-integrated communities. As Lipset put it, these findings "sharply challenge the various interpretations of Nazism as the product of the growth of anomie and the general rootlessness of modern urban industrial society" (1959: 146).

Indirect evidence attesting to the essential role of formal and informal communications networks is found in diffusion theory, which emphasizes the importance of personal interaction rather than impersonal media communication in the spread of ideas (Rogers, 1962; Lionberger, 1960). This personal influence occurs through the organizational patterns of a community (Lionberger, 1960: 73). It does not occur through the mass media. The mass media may be a source of information, but they are not a key source of influence.

Their lesser importance in relation to preexisting communications networks was examined in one study on "The Failure of an Incipient Social Movement" (Jackson, Peterson, Bull, Monsen, & Richmond, 1960). In 1957 a potential tax protest movement in Los Angeles generated considerable interest and publicity for a little over a month but was dead within a year. According to the authors, this did not reflect a lack of public notice. They concluded that "mass communication alone is probably insufficient without a network of communication specifically linking those interested in the matter.... If a movement is to grow rapidly, it cannot rely upon its own network of communication, but must capitalize on networks already in existence" (p. 37).

A major reason it took social scientists so long to acknowledge the importance of communications networks was because the prevailing theories of the post–World War II era emphasized increasing social dislocation and anomie. Mass society theorists, as they were called, hypothesized that

significant community institutions that linked individuals to governing elites were breaking down, that society was becoming a mass of isolated individuals. These individuals were seen as increasingly irresponsible and ungovernable, prone to irrational protests because they had no mediating institutions through which to pursue grievances (Kornhauser, 1959).

In emphasizing disintegrating vertical connections, mass society theorists passed lightly over the role of horizontal ones, only occasionally acknowledging that "the combination of internal contact and external isolation facilitates the work of the mass agitator" (Kornhauser, 1959: 218). This focus changed in the early seventies. Pinard's study of the Social Credit Party of Quebec (1971) severely criticized mass society theory, arguing instead that "when strains are severe and widespread a new movement is more likely to meet its early success among the more strongly integrated citizens" (Pinard, 1971: 192).

This insight was expanded by Oberschall (1973), who created a six-cell table to predict both the occurrence and type of protest. As did the mass society theorists, Oberschall said that even when there are grievances, protest will not occur outside institutional channels by those who are connected, through their own leadership or patron/client relationships, with governing elites. Among those who are segmented from such elites, the type of protest will be determined by whether there is communal, associational, or little organization. In the latter case, discontent is expressed through riots or other short-lived violent uprisings. "It is under conditions of strong...ties and segmentation that the possibility of the rapid spread of opposition movements on a continuous basis exists" (p. 123).

The movements we have studied would confirm Oberschall's conclusions, but not as strongly as he makes them. In all these cases a preexisting communications network was a necessary but insufficient condition for movement formation. Yet the newly formed networks among student radicals, welfare recipients, and women can hardly compare with the longstanding ties provided by the southern black churches and colleges. Their ties were tenuous and may not have survived the demise of their movements.

The importance of segmentation, or lack of connection with relevant elites, is less obvious in the sixties' movements. The higher socioeconomic status of incipient feminists and Movement leaders would imply greater access to elites than is true for blacks or welfare recipients. If Oberschall were correct, these closer connections should either have permitted easier and more rapid grievance solutions or more effective social control. They did neither. Indeed, it was the group most closely connected to decision-making elites—women of the Presidential and State Commission—who were among the earliest to see the need of a protest organization. Women of the younger branch of the movement did have their grievances against the men of the New Left effectively suppressed for several years, but even they eventually rejected this kind of elite control, even when it meant rejecting the men.

Conversely, Piven and Cloward show that the establishment of closer ties between leaders of local welfare rights groups and welfare workers through advisory councils and community coordinators led to a curtailment of militance and the institutionalization of grievances (1977: 326–31). They also argue that the development of government-funded community programs effectively co-opted many local black movement leaders in the North and that federal channeling of black protest in the South into voter registration projects focused the movement there into traditional electoral politics (ibid.: 253). In short, the evidence about the role of segmentation in movement formation is ambiguous. The effect may be varied considerably by the nature of the political system.

CO-OPTABILITY

A recurrent theme in our studies is that not just any communications network will do. It must be one that is co-optable to the ideas of the new movement. The Business and Professional Women's (BPW) clubs were a network among women, but having rejected feminism, they could not overcome the ideological barrier to new political action until after feminism became established.…

On the other hand, the women on the Presidential and State Commissions and the feminist coterie of the EEOC were co-optable largely because their immersion in the facts of female status and the details of sex discrimination cases made them very conscious of the need for change. Likewise, the young women of the "radical community" lived in an atmosphere of questioning, confrontation, and change. They absorbed an ideology of "freedom" and "liberation" far more potent than any latent "antifeminism" might have been.…

Exactly what makes a network co-optable is harder to elucidate. Pinard (1971: 186) noted the necessity for groups to *"possess* or *develop* an ideology or simply subjective interests congruent with that of a new movement" for them to "act as mobilizing rather than restraining agents toward that movement," but did not further explore what affected the "primary group climate." More illumination is provided by the diffusion of innovation studies that point out the necessity for new ideas to fit in with already established norms for changes to happen easily. Furthermore, a social system that has as a value "innovativeness" (as the radical community did) will more rapidly adopt ideas than one that looks upon the habitual performance of traditional practices as the ideal (as most organized women's groups did in the fifties). Usually, as Lionberger (1960: 91) points out, "people act in terms of past experience and knowledge." People who have had similar experiences are likely to share similar perceptions of a situation and to mutually reinforce those perceptions as well as their subsequent interpretation. A co-optable network, then, is one whose members have had common experiences that predispose them to be receptive to the particular new ideas of the incipient movement and who are not faced with structural or ideological barriers to action. If the new movement as an "innovation" can interpret these experiences and perceptions in ways that point out channels for social action, then participation in a social movement becomes the logical thing to do.

THE ROLE OF CRISES

As our examples have illustrated, similar perceptions must be translated into action. This is often done by a crisis. For blacks in Montgomery, this was generated by Rosa Parks's refusal to give up her seat on a bus to a white man. For women who formed the older branch of the women's movement, the impetus to organize was the refusal of the EEOC to enforce the sex provision of Title VII, precipitated by the concomitant refusal of federal officials at the conference to allow a supportive resolution. For younger women there were a series of minor crises.

While not all movements are formed by such precipitating events, they are quite common as they serve to crystallize and focus discontent. From their own experiences, directly and concretely, people feel the need for change in a situation that allows for an exchange of feelings with others, mutual validation, and a subsequent reinforcement of innovative interpretation. Perception of an immediate need for change is a major factor in predisposing people to accept new ideas (Rogers, 1962: 280). Nothing makes desire for change more acute than a crisis. Such a crisis need not be a major one; it need only embody collective discontent.

ORGANIZING EFFORTS

A crisis will only catalyze a well-formed communications network. If such networks are embryonically developed or only partially co-optable, the potentially active individuals in them must be linked together by someone…. As Jackson et al. (1960: 37) stated, "Some protest may persist where the source of trouble is constantly present.

But interest ordinarily cannot be maintained unless there is a welding of spontaneous groups into some stable organization." In other words, people must be organized. Social movements do not simply occur.

The role of the organizer in movement formation is another neglected aspect of the theoretical literature. There has been great concern with leadership, but the two roles are distinct and not always performed by the same individual. In the early stages of a movement, it is the organizer much more than any leader who is important, and such an individual or cadre must often operate behind the scenes. The nature and function of these two roles was most clearly evident in the Townsend old-age movement of the thirties. Townsend was the "charismatic" leader, but the movement was organized by his partner, real estate promoter Robert Clements. Townsend himself acknowledges that without Clements's help, the movement would never have gone beyond the idea stage (Holzman, 1963).

The importance of organizers is pervasive in the sixties' movements. Dr. King may have been the public spokesperson of the Montgomery Bus Boycott who caught the eye of the media, but it was E. D. Nixon who organized it. Certainly the "organizing cadre" that young women in the radical community came to be was key to the growth of that branch of the women's liberation movement, despite the fact that no "leaders" were produced (and were actively discouraged). The existence of many leaders but no organizers in the older branch of the women's liberation movement readily explains its subsequent slow development….

The function of the organizer has been explored indirectly by other analysts. Rogers (1962) devotes many pages to the "change agent" who, while he does not necessarily weld a group together or "construct" a movement, does many of the same things for agricultural innovation that an organizer does for political change. Mass society theory makes frequent reference to the "agitator," though not in a truly informative way. Interest groups are often organized by single individuals and some of them evolve into social movements. Salisbury's study of farmers' organizations finds this a recurrent theme. He also discovered that "a considerable number of farm groups were subsidized by other, older, groups.... The Farm Bureau was organized and long sustained by subsidies, some from federal and state governments, and some by local businessmen" (Salisbury, 1959: 13).

These patterns are similar to ones we have found in the formation of social movements. Other organizations, even the government, often serve as training centers for organizers and sources of material support to aid the formation of groups and/or movements. The civil rights movement was the training ground for many an organizer of other movements.... The role of the government in the formation of the National Welfare Rights Organization was so significant that it would lead one to wonder if this association should be considered more of an interest group in the traditional sense than a movement "core" organization.

From all this it would appear that training as an organizer or at least as a proselytizer or entrepreneur of some kind is a necessary background for those individuals who act as movement innovators. Even in something as seemingly spontaneous as a social movement, the professional is more valuable than the amateur.

CRITICAL THINKING QUESTIONS

1. Why has the role of communications networks in the formation of social movements only recently received the attention of researchers?
2. How do leadership roles emerge in social movements? Are "leaders" the same as "organizers"?
3. Cite some similarities and differences between the development of the civil rights movement and the women's movement.

NOTES

1. The only use of this significant word appears rather incidentally in Turner (1964): 123.
2. Data for this section are based on my observations while a founder and participant in the younger branch of the Chicago women's liberation movement from 1967 through 1969 and editor of the first (at that time, only) national newsletter. I was able, through extensive correspondence and interviews, to keep a record of how each group around the country started, where the organizers got the idea from, who they had talked to, what conferences were held and who attended, the political affiliations (or lack of them) of the first members, and so forth. Although I was a member of Chicago NOW, information on the origins of it and the other older branch organizations comes entirely through ex post facto interviews of the principals and examination of early papers in preparation for my dissertation on the women's liberation movement. Most of my informants requested that their contribution remain confidential.

REFERENCES

Adorno, L. W., et al. 1950. *The authoritarian personality.* New York: Harper & Row.

Blumer, H. 1951. Social movements. In *New outline of the principles of sociology,* ed. A. M. Lee. New York: Barnes and Noble.

Brink, W., and L. Harris. 1964. *The Negro revolution in America.* New York: Simon & Schuster.

Buck, S. J. 1920. *The agrarian crusade.* New Haven, Conn.: Yale University Press.

Cantril, H. 1941. *The psychology of social movements.* New York: Wiley.

Clark, K. B. 1966. The civil rights movement: Momentum and organization. *Daedalus,* Winter.

Davies, J. C. 1962. Toward a theory of revolution. *American Sociological Review,* 27(1): 5–19.

Ferriss, A. L. 1971. *Indicators of trends in the status of American women.* New York: Russell Sage Foundation.

Firestone, S. 1971. *Dialectics of sex.* New York: Morrow.

Frazier, E. F. 1963. *The Negro church in America.* New York: Schocken.

Freeman, J. 1975. *The politics of women's liberation.* New York: Longman.

Friedan, B. 1963. *The feminine mystique.* New York: Dell.

———. 1967. NOW: How it began. *Women Speaking,* April.

Gurr, T. 1970. *Why men rebel.* Princeton, N.J.: Princeton University Press.

Hayden, C., and M. King. 1966. A kind of memo. *Liberation,* April.

Heberle, R. 1951. *Social movements.* New York: Appleton-Century-Crofts.

Hoffer, E. 1951. *The true believer.* New York: Harper & Row.

Hole, J., and E. Levine. 1971. *Rebirth of feminism.* New York: Quadrangle.A

Holloway, H. 1969. *The politics of the Southern Negro.* New York: Random House.

Holzman, A. 1963. *The Townsend movement: A political study.* New York: Bookman.

Jackson, M., et al. 1960. The failure of an incipient social movement. *Pacific Sociological Review,* 3(1): 40.

King, M. L., Jr. 1958. *Stride toward freedom.* New York: Harper & Row.

Kornhauser, W. 1959. *The politics of mass society.* Glencoe, Ill.: Free Press.

Lionberger, H. F. 1960. *Adoption of new ideas and practices.* Ames: Iowa State University Press.

Lipset, S. M. 1959. *Agrarian socialism.* Berkeley: University of California Press.

Lowi, T. J. 1971. *The politics of discord.* New York: Basic Books.

Oberschall, A. 1973. *Social conflict and social movements.* Englewood Cliffs, N.J.: Prentice-Hall.

Pinard, M. 1971. *The rise of a third party: A study in crisis politics.* Englewood Cliffs, N.J.: Prentice-Hall.

Piven, F. F., and R. Cloward. 1977. *Poor people's movements: Why they succeed, how they fail.* New York: Pantheon.

Rogers, E. M. 1962. *Diffusion of innovations.* New York: Free Press.

Rudwick, E., and A. Meier. 1970. Organizational structure and goal succession: A comparative analysis of the NAACP and CORE, 1964–1968. *Social Science Quarterly,* 51 (June).

Salisbury, R. H. 1969. An exchange theory of interest groups. *Midwest Journal of Political Science,* 13(1), (February).

Toch, H. 1965. *The social psychology of social movements.* Indianapolis, Ind.: Bobbs-Merrill.

Zinn, H. 1964. *SNCC: The new abolitionists.* Boston: Beacon Press.

Collective Behaviour
and
Social Movements

CLASSIC

CONTEMPORARY

CROSS-CULTURAL

62

Are Labour Unions Obsolete in the New Global Economy?

Don Wells

In this article Wells questions the contemporary significance of labour unions. Wells's examination investigates the role of unions in today's hypercompetitive economy—is it possible that unions are becoming obsolete?

Around the world unions are in decline. For the first time since the 1960s the proportion of Canadians who belong to unions has fallen below 30 per cent. In the private sector, once the main bastion of organized labour, the proportion of union workers is down to 14 per cent. Those employees whose numbers are growing the fastest in Canada—the young, immigrants, private service-sector workers—are the least unionized.

About union decline there is no doubt, and many theories have been advanced to explain it. One theory is that these trends reflect the irrelevance of unions in the new global economy. Thanks to new technologies and management systems, workers in "post-hierarchical" organizations are now "empowered" on the job. Old antagonisms are said to be dissolving in a new spirit of cooperation. We're all bosses now. Academics talk about liberated, fulfilling work not as a radical goal but as capitalism's own project. From a pragmatic

Source: D. Wells. 2003. "Are Labour Unions Obsolete in the New Global Economy?" *Inroads,* 13, 46–53.

perspective, it is argued, this new cooperation reflects the realism of our times. In today's hypercompetitive economy, labour–management conflicts are luxuries we can't afford. Who needs unions?

However, despite all the talk about "post-hierarchical" work, it is extraordinary how little evidence supports this view. When studies are done of workplaces where this kind of liberating work is supposed to exist, few find appreciable increases in workers' control. Typically, management control is stronger. Except in some categories of highly skilled workers (a minority) and some marginal accommodations to worker preferences, the old divide between those who design work and those who do it, between those who order and those who obey, has not changed much at all.

Perhaps this is why, outside human resource management textbooks, the language of workplace "empowerment" is heard less often these days. In its place, the more pragmatic language of "competitiveness" and "survival" has emerged as the dominant argument for union decline in the new global economy. "Free markets," a set of abstract forces out there, have their own in-built imperatives, we are warned. Non-unionism is at the top of the list.

This seems plausible on the surface. After all, the Canadian economy is highly dependent on international trade, especially with the United States. The United States has a far lower rate of unionization than Canada. Indeed, it has long had one of the lowest rates of unionization in the industrialized world. If low rates of unionization determine trade competitiveness, the United States should be close to the top. But it's not. While Canada has a healthy trade surplus, the United States has a huge trade deficit. Other highly unionized countries are also highly trade-competitive. For example, like Canada, Sweden in one of the most open economies in the world. Its rate of unionization is now more than 95 per cent of its labour force. And Sweden is highly competitive.

Contrary to popular perception, there is considerable evidence that unionized workplaces are often *more* competitive, more innovative and more productive. Unions also tend to produce other good effects. After controlling for the influence of education, experience and other factors, unionized workers in the United States enjoy an average 10 to 15 per cent higher level of wages than non-union workers. The union wage premium in Canada has been calculated to be even higher. Unions are also a major force for greater social equality. It's almost impossible to have decent health care, public pensions, public education and a host of other beneficial social policies without a strong labour movement. This is a key reason why the United Stares has consistently produced the highest level of economic inequality—including the highest poverty rate—among advanced industrial countries.

If union decline can't be explained on the grounds that work has been liberated or that unionized workplaces aren't competitive, let us look at another frequently heard explanation: people don't

want to join unions. Survey after survey has shown that many workers want to join unions. Despite widespread propaganda by the corporate mass media, a recent survey found that 44 per cent of private sector workers in the United States said they would join a union if offered the choice. If this happened, U.S. private sector union membership would immediately triple.

ANTI-UNION STRATEGIES

So why don't more people join unions? Employer and government anti-unionism is a big part of the answer. Noting a significant increase in anti-union discrimination around the world, the UN-affiliated International Labour Organization (ILO) cites Canada for denying workers the right to strike by abusing its use of compulsory binding arbitration. The ILO also cites Canada for denying collective bargaining rights to many public sector workers. In addition, provincial governments now deny 10 to 15 per cent of their employees the right to strike on the grounds that they provide "essential services." Provincial governments have also weakened "unfair labour practice" laws and eliminated provisions that certify unions when enough workers have signed union cards. And provinces have scrapped anti-scab laws and given employers more freedom to hire and fire as they see fit. Furthermore, in the last decade, the proportion of government jobs in the economy has fallen by almost a third. Most of the jobs lost have been union jobs.

Many private sector employers have been even more aggressive. In addition to using court injunctions and "replacement" (scab) labour, employers are resorting to sophisticated union-busting tactics. It is common practice to use rigorous hiring procedures to eliminate applicants with union sympathies. When employers commit unfair labour practices, they frequently pay no penalties, and when they do pay penalties, the fine can be less than those for jaywalking.

Governments have facilitated private sector anti-unionism by abandoning the priorities they once gave to low-unemployment policies, public health care and other social programs that gave workers a measure of protection. Ottawa has made huge cuts in social welfare and in employment insurance coverage and payments, thus undermining economic security. Whereas nine of ten unemployed workers were once eligible for unemployment insurance, today fewer than four in ten qualify. In most provinces the minimum wage has fallen below poverty levels. These and other policies are promoting a flood of precarious, part-time, short-term "bad jobs" with little job security, low wages and few if any fringe benefits. For an increasing number of Canadians, stable jobs and careers have been replaced by a sequence of employment "episodes," making it rarer to maintain a fixed relationship with any employer, or with fellow workers and one's community. In this context, union organizing is much more difficult.

On top of these kinds of attacks on unions, in many countries workers' rights to joint unions are specifically denied. This is frequently the case in export processing zones (EPZs) which have been created to attract foreign investment in the global South. Investors' workplaces in EPZs are often exempted from a country's labour laws, and their employees are barred from joining unions. Even where unions are not illegal, union rights are often denied through mass firings, blacklists and other forms of repression. In addition, many countries, including the United States and Canada, deny domestic workers and migrant workers the right to join unions. Agricultural workers are another category often excluded from unions. Given that half the world's workforce is rural, this has enormous significance.

New management strategies are another reason for union decline. In Canada, the United States and other industrial economies, modern industrial unionism was born in large factories. Today, big factory capitalism is declining. Employers are decentralizing, outsourcing and subcontracting work. In part this reflects the fact that workplaces in growing sectors of the economy, such as restaurants, retail stores and financial

services, tend to be small. The trend to smaller workplaces also reflects management's use of new information technologies to coordinate production and distribution around the world. These smaller workplaces are easier for management to control. They are also harder and more costly for unions to organize and administer.

Similarly, new information technologies, together with declining transportation costs and the decline of tariffs and other trade barriers, make it easier for firms to locate in low-wage, high-repression, largely non-union jurisdictions. In the United States, for example, firms have been moving to southern states where "right to work" laws make it illegal to require workers to join unions. In such labour-intensive industries as clothing, toys, electronics and footwear, transnational corporations (TNCs) have been moving to China, Vietnam and other countries where manufacturing wages are 20 to 30 cents an hour. Typically these TNCs are part of complex global production chains in which subcontractors subcontract to other subcontractors and a host of small firms and home workshops diffuse and disguise responsibility for labour rights. Many of these TNCs now "regime shop" for even lower labour standards, pressuring governments and workers to compete for investment and jobs by reducing wages, accepting worse working conditions and restricting labour rights, including the right to join unions.

It is in this context that we are witnessing the rise of global sweatshops. In one recent case, a well-known firm in Canada, which advertises itself as a socially responsible company, has been accused of forcing 16-year-olds in China to work up to 98 hours per week and exposing them to toxic chemicals while paying them 22 cents an hour. In another case, a Chinese manufacturer of McDonald's Happy Meal toys has been charged with employing 13-year-olds to work 16-hour days for $3 a day. A U. S. court recently convicted the owner of a factory in American Samoa of "modern-day slavery." A study of Nike has concluded that it is "still the norm" for the 500,000 overseas workers employed in Nike contract factories to face "excessive work hours, poverty wages, harass- ment, and restrictions on organizing." In countries such as China and Vietnam, where most of the world's imports of clothing and many other labour- intensive goods come from, it is illegal to join independent unions, and workers who try to exer- cise these rights are liable to find themselves in jail or an insane asylum. This anti-labour "race to the bottom" is also causing a return of sweatshops in industrialized countries such as Canada and the United States. In Los Angeles and New York, for example, two thirds of the clothing firms have been found to violate minimum-wage, health and safety, overtime and other basic labour standards.

THE INFORMAL ECONOMY

More fundamental to explaining the decline of unions is the rapid growth of the informal econ- omy in almost every corner of the world. Varying from country to country and region to region, the informal economy is highly diverse. It includes workers in survival activities such as street vendors, shoe shiners, garbage scav- engers, scrap and rag pickers, and domestic workers employed by households, home workers and workers in sweatshops, and self-employed people operating on their own or with family members. International economic organizations such as the World Bank and the International Monetary Fund promote this informalization of employment through "structural adjustment programs" that pressure governments to privatize public sectors and expand exports through anti- labour policies. TNCs are increasingly taking advantage of these pressures. Many of their suppli- ers are based in informal economies. For example, Unilever sells soap through street vendors and Coca-Cola is sold through kiosks. Furthermore, as international trade-liberalization destroys the market niches of domestic firms in the global South, more workers are being forced into the informal economy.

Indeed, it is in the informal economy that most jobs are being created. In Africa more than

90 per cent of new jobs in the past decade have been created in the informal economy. In Latin America the informal economy accounts for 60 per cent of urban employment, according to ILO data. In Russia estimates of secondary employ- ment (usually casual, unregistered employment) range from 35 to 90 per cent of the employed population. In Asia informal employment ranges from 45 to 85 per cent of nonagricultural employment. Informal employment is also grow- ing in industrialized economies. In the European Union it is now estimated that "undeclared work" amounts to between 10 and 28 million jobs. Around the globe an estimated 211 million children between 5 and 14 years old wash cars, shine shoes, hawk, deliver goods, weave, make fireworks, matches, clothing, furniture and bricks, and do hard physical work such as scav- enging, construction and commercial agricul- ture. Many of these children perform the most dangerous and degrading forms of work, includ- ing prostitution and drug trafficking, to survive.

These kinds of workers are least likely to have the right to join unions. Most have been left completely outside the labour laws, with little or no protection against arbitrary dismissal, work- place health and safety hazards, excessive over- time and other violations of basic labour rights and standards. All these "decent work deficits," as the ILO calls them, could be corrected if work- ers were able to form strong, independent unions. However, even when workers do have an official right to join unions, employers rarely allow it. According to the ILO, "informal" workers "repre- sent the largest concentration of needs without voice, the silent majority of the world's economy."

THE CRISIS OF LEGITIMACY

When the decline of unions around the world is put in these contexts of changing power relations between employers and workers and between government and workers, it is hard not to conclude that good unions are needed more than ever. Together with the visibility of the crimes of Enron, Worldcom and other giant TNCs, the "might is right" exercise of corporate power is generating a crisis of legitimacy. This crisis is reflected in opinion polls and in the "global justice" demonstrations in Seattle, Vancouver, Quebec City, Prague, Genoa, Washington and elsewhere. It is reflected as well in the unprecedented rise of the global "anti-sweat" movement. It may have contributed to the even more massive, and equally unprecedented, global movement against the war in Iraq.

In Canada we saw a turning point earlier, in 1988, when the majority of Canadians voted against "free trade" and got it anyway. For Canadians, this experience politicized the new global economy in a way it had never been politicized before. This new politicization of "free markets" underlies popular opposition to NAFTA, the Multilateral Agreement on Investment, the Free Trade Area of the Americas, the World Trade Organization, the World Bank, the International Monetary Fund and the ideology of neoliberal regionalization and globalization. It signifies a growing visibility of antagonisms between, on the one hand, the interests of political and corporate elites and, on the other, growing segments of the Canadian population, including many youth, immigrants, faith groups, consumers, unionists, environmentalists, feminists and activists of all sorts.

In key respects this new politics represents a contest for democracy itself. The new global economy is contributing not only to a "representation deficit" when in comes to union rights, but also to a "democratic deficit" when it comes to citizen rights. Union rights are core democratic rights; labour rights and democratic rights are inseparable. Increasingly in the new global economy, labour is becoming an unregulated commodity. Where markets are sovereign, the labour of citizens and of society is narrowed down to mere economic exchange instead of being the heart of democratic politics. While property rights have been constitutionalized in international economic agreements, labour and other human rights have been left outside, in the realm of the voluntary and private. Democratic trade unions are more representative of society than the plutocratic

command structures of private corporations. If the main point of government becomes aligning society with these private "market forces," where lies democracy?

REVITALIZED UNIONS

As part of this new contest for democracy, there are signs that labour movements are taking new forms. In Canada, these include "flying squads" of workers, retirees, students and other activists who support striking and locked-out workers in other workplaces, as well as solidarity actions between unions and the homeless and links between unions and a host of other social movements, including the environmental, anti-racist, feminist, student and peace movements. Particularly prominent is the growing participation of unionists in solidarity with workers in the global South, in the global justice movement and in the anti-war movement. There are also signs of a re-emergence of grassroots participation in some unions and of the development of alliances with non-union workers, including those who define themselves primarily in non-class terms: immigrants, ethnic and "racial" groups, women, youth and others.

Another indication of revitalization is the shift toward new organizing. In Canada, several unions are devoting dramatically increased resources to organizing growing numbers of private sector workers, including hotel workers, restaurant workers, retail workers and security guards, many in part-time and temporary jobs. Many medical, teaching and other professionals are also joining unions as part of their resistance to public sector budget cuts. Professional unionization is also often a response to administrators' challenges to professional autonomy. Thus, in the United States, doctors are increasingly at loggerheads with powerful managed-care companies. Many university teachers are unionizing because they face similar challenges. The spectre haunting universities is electronic education delivered by low-paid academic nomads on short-term contracts, with excessive teaching loads and little or no time for their research.

"Community unionism" centred on alliances between unions and community groups in pursuit of common goals is another indication of union revitalization. In the communities in which they live, union members are working with minority-rights groups, religious groups, women's groups, training agencies and other organizations. These union–community partnerships help with organizing drives, promote improved community services, fight against cuts in social programs, campaign against racial and gender discrimination, improve schools, build social housing and pursue a host of other community goals. In the United States, for example, community unionism has been effective in helping to organize home workers, home-care providers, sweatshop workers and other marginalized, often invisible workers, including undocumented immigrants. Recently, a broad coalition of labour, religious and community groups worked with Latino and Chinese American workers to pass an Unpaid Wages Prohibition Act. As a result, New York State now has the strongest wage-enforcement law in the United States.

In other parts of the world unions are active in promoting democratic worker co-operatives to organize workers. In Singapore, the labour movement helped create a workers' co-op among self-employed taxi and minibus drivers. In Benin, unions helped build a producer co-op spanning 33 villages. In the Philippines, the labour movement organized a cooperative for poor families by providing loans, training and a social security program and by helping members market their products.

All these are signs not of the demise of unions but of the labour movement's growing adaptation to the new global economy. The history of unions is a history of workers organizing themselves on the basis of solidarity with one another and with their allies. Management strategies change. State policies change. And so do labour movements. We are seeing the decline of certain forms of unionism, particularly the more bureaucratic ones. At the same time, we are also witnessing a new wave of politicization and the mobilization of broader, more participatory forms of unionism. What has not changed is the need for workers to organize themselves.

CRITICAL THINKING QUESTIONS

1. With reference to the article, discuss the following quote: "It's almost impossible to have decent health care, public pensions, public education and a host of other beneficial social policies without a strong labour movement."
2. As a sociologist, and with reference to your course material, do you see a role for unions in today's society? Justify your answer.
3. Are there any examples of the "informal economy" in your own community, and if so, are they consistent with Wells's findings? If not, how would you explain their absence?

Collective Behaviour
and
Social Movements

CLASSIC

CONTEMPORARY

CROSS-CULTURAL

63

Abortion Movements
in Poland, Great Britain,
and the United States

Janet Hadley

Perhaps one of the best-known feminist slogans during the early 1970s was that "a woman has a right to choose" whether to terminate a pregnancy. About 38 percent of the world's population lives in countries where abortion is available on request. Although abortion has been legal in the United States and most of Europe for at least twenty-five years, it remains an explosive issue in many countries and has spawned "for" and "against" social movements and collective behaviour. In this reading, Janet Hadley examines some of the controversies and campaigns of abortion rights movements in Poland, the United States, and Great Britain.

In recent years in the United States, in Poland, and in Ireland, too, national politics has at times been convulsed by the issue of abortion. In Germany the historic reunification of East and West almost foundered amid wrangling about conflicting abortion laws. How can abortion, hardly an issue comparable to the great affairs of state, such as the economy or national security, have an impact such as this?

This is an account, first, of how post-Communist Poland found itself in the grip of the abortion debate and secondly how the issue came to be such a seemingly permanent shadow on the political landscape in the United States, in the wake of the Supreme Court's 1973 landmark decision on abortion in the case of *Roe* v. *Wade*. It offers some ideas about why.

The account focuses on abortion, primarily as a method of birth control, which women have always sought out, legally when they can, illegally when they must. The controversies and campaigns recorded and the ideas offered here concentrate on women's access to affordable, safe and legal abortion—an essential part of women's reproductive freedom in a world where five hundred women die every day from the complications of unsafe abortion (World Health Organization, 1993).

The way abortion has at times dominated public debate in both Poland and the United States can hardly be exaggerated, but the contexts are very different. At times, during the 1992 American presidential election campaign, it seemed as if the fate of the United States for the next four years hung solely on the thread of the abortion issue. Economic issues, national security, even political scandals were all pushed into the background. But no one was too surprised to encounter this wild card in the United States' electoral politics. It had been thus, on and off, for around twenty years, since the 1973 Supreme Court judgement

Source: Janet Hadley, "God's Bullies: Attacks on Abortion," *Feminist Review*, Vol. 48 (Fall 1994), pp. 94–113. Reprinted with permission of Taylor & Francis Ltd., Oxford, U.K.

which had sanctioned abortion as a woman's constitutional right.

It was, however, probably a lot harder for anyone to have predicted events in Poland where, for more than four years, well before the forty-year-old Communist regime was finally sloughed off, abortion took centre stage. The renascent right in Poland selected abortion as the first block of the social welfare system for demolition. The battle over it highlights the new relationship between the Roman Catholic Church—once the main element of opposition alongside Solidarity—and the state. As the democratization of Eastern Europe got under way, abortion was one of the first laws to come under fire (Einhorn, 1993).

In some ways the abortion debate in Poland, which of all the former Soviet bloc countries has undergone by far the most draconian reversal of its abortion law, is quite straightforward: The opponents of abortion are solidly Roman Catholic and perceive their efforts as part of the task of rescuing Poland from its years of godlessness. The debate in Poland harks back to the relatively straightforward arguments which took place in Britain at the time of the passing of the Abortion Act in 1967.

In the United States, on the other hand, the issue has been linked to a much more extensive catalogue of perceived "social degeneracy." Opposition to abortion in the United States involves a curious alliance of religious and secular New Right groupings and much of the driving force has been provided, not by the Roman Catholic Church, but by evangelical Christians....

POLAND: NO PLACE TO BE A WOMAN

...What we have been witnessing in Poland since 1989, according to one observer, is the "Church's colossal efforts to replace a totalitarian state with a theocracy" (Kissling, 1992). Weekly Masses from Rome are broadcast on Polish TV these days. Scientific conferences open with High Mass, blessings and so on, and military personnel

are sent on pilgrimages. Classes in religion (i.e., Roman Catholicism) are mandatory for children in state schools. There is little doubt that the bishops of Poland, who behave more like leaders of a political party than as simple guardians of moral values, have their sights set not only on banning abortion but also divorce, provision of contraception, and other hallmarks of a secular society. One commentator wrote in 1991:

> From the very beginning until its unexpected culmination in June [1991—when a draft anti-abortion bill was rejected by parliament in the face of huge pro-choice demonstrations] the Polish controversy on abortion was a classic example of political conflict. Nobody cared any more about subtle moral or political arguments. It was clear that who wins the abortion debate will control the political situation in Poland. (Szawarski, 1991)

The irony is that not only was June 1991 far from being the "culmination," but also that nobody today could be said to have won. (Women, of course, lost.)

The final law, signed by President Lech Walesa in February 1993, was seen by opponents of abortion as a compromise. It is much weaker than they would have liked. The original anti-abortion bill, first published in 1989, promised three years' imprisonment for a woman who induced her own abortion, as well for any doctor caught performing an illegal operation. Under the new law, two years' imprisonment awaits an abortionist, but a woman inducing her own abortion will not face gaol [jail].

The new law allows abortion when a woman's life or health is in danger, after rape or incest, or if there is suspected fetal abnormality. But prenatal testing is only permissible if there is a family history of genetic disorder. There are token provisions urging local authorities to provide contraceptive services.

The Church's Power and Influence

The religious context of the abortion row in Poland goes a long way to explaining how it came to be such a passionate, extreme and dominating issue. Around 95 percent of its 39 million people consider themselves Catholic and there is a very strong family tradition of Catholicism, which during the Communist era greatly strengthened the Church as a focus of national identity and a shelter for opposition. Having a Polish Pope helps too; when John Paul II visited in 1991, he urged his fellow Poles to free themselves from a law permitting abortion, which he called a tragic inheritance of Communism.

Even when the Communist grip seemed at its most unyielding, the Church consistently harried the authorities on issues of sexual control. In a recent survey, conducted since the fall of the Communists, and reported in the *Guardian* (9/14/93), 95 percent of Polish women said they rely on personal experience for their sex education and 73 percent said they had had an unplanned pregnancy.

The only sex-education manual ever produced in Poland had to be withdrawn because of Church protest. Roman Catholic opposition to contraception has been effective—76 percent of the urban population and 87 percent of the rural population use only Church-approved 'natural' methods of fertility control (Mrugala, 1991). (Priests often determine what is sold in local pharmacies.) Poland's 1956 abortion law contained no conscience clause, but the Church's success in pressuring doctors can be judged from the fact that in some state hospitals, staff refusal made it impossible to get an abortion. As early as 1973, Church protests over the rising abortion rate and the behaviour of "callous young women" forced the government to set up a commission to consider whether the law needed amending (Okolski, 1988).

But the pressures on women to have abortions were very strong. Even for those who wanted it, contraception has never been easily available, and was of notoriously poor quality. Abortion—which was free in state hospitals after 1959, and easy to obtain—was therefore the main method of birth control. Women only had to report that they were "in a difficult life situation." "Poland's hard life finds more and more women choosing abortions," reported *The New York Times* in 1983, citing families in some cities waiting eighteen years to obtain a small apartment. Despite the Church's denunciations, there were an estimated 600,000 abortions a year, compared to just 700,000 live births.

Times may have been hard in 1983, but the economic "shock therapy" of post-Communist Poland has brought unimaginable hardship in its wake. Unemployment is now 2.8 million and will be one-fifth of the workforce in three years' time. The bishops have deplored this, by urging *women* to leave the labour market, to ease unemployment and ensure that men's wages increase. They have made no adverse comment on the virtual shutdown of state-financed child care.

The Bishops, the State, and the Medical Profession

The episcopate first floated the idea of outlawing abortion in 1988, deeming it to be a mortal threat to the "biological substance of the nation." In the spring of 1989 an Unborn Child Protection Bill was published and the Pope hurried to send his congratulations.

In 1990, however, long before the legislative battle had got into its stride, the Ministry of Health took its own initiative, saying that women wanting abortion would now need the permission of three physicians and of a psychologist, whose appointment had been approved by the local bishop, and that an abortion for social reasons must be requested in writing (*The New York Times*, 4/21/92). The psychologist's job is to dissuade women, mainly by putting the frighteners on them. Sterilization and the in-vitro fertilization programme were suspended.

As Poland created its first parliament, abortion became the bellwether for fitness to serve. Anyone supporting abortion rights was traduced as a surreptitious advocate for Communism. Throughout 1990 and 1991 the battle raged, overshadowing the upheavals of the new market economy. Huge demonstrations in favour of abortion took place in Warsaw and women's groups began to get organized to defend abortion rights. Solidarity was split on the issue. Bills were proposed and defeated in dizzying succession. Parish priests threatened to withhold sacraments from anyone who did not sign the petitions against "killing innocent children."

The anti-abortion movement targeted not only abortion but family planning provision, too, blocking the launch of an information campaign in the textile city of Lodz, where there has been an unusually high rate of congenital abnormalities among babies born to women working in the textile factories (Rich, 1991). Their activity was partly financed by pro-life organizations from the United States, such as Human Life International. This evangelical group, fired by a vision of "re-Christianized united Europe stretching from the Atlantic to the Urals," vowed to "flood Eastern Europe" with films, videos (such as *The Silent Scream* which has been shown in Polish schools), fetal models and other propaganda. In 1992, Operation Rescue blockaded a clinic in the Baltic port of Gdynia, with protesters from the United States, Canada and the U.K.

Although one smear in circulation was that "only communists and Jews favor abortion," there is little direct evidence that the antiabortion campaign was fuelled by a nationalist pro-natalism—a desire to demographically overwhelm Poland's minorities. There was, however, a definite bid to appeal to a repressive notion of proper and traditional Polish "womanhood." The term "emancipation for women" is laden with Communist overtones and has often in reality meant the notorious "double burden" or overloading of women, in Poland and Eastern Europe in general, in which they have been expected to shoulder full-time jobs as well as forty hours a week shopping, cooking, cleaning, laundry, with only the aid of very poor-quality pre-school child care and medical care (Jankowska, 1993). Against such a reality, a misty vision of womanhood may have a definite allure.

May 1992 brought another turn of the screw. A new code of medical ethics made it professionally unethical for doctors to perform abortions except in cases of rape or incest or when the woman's life was in danger. Violations would lead to suspension of the doctor's license. The code effectively ended hospital abortions and prenatal testing: Some institutions put up signs, "No Abortions."

The issue continued to rock the government, which twice postponed a final vote on abortion. By the end of 1992, the conflict was extreme enough to threaten the fragile coalition government, an improbable seven-party affair. A million people signed a petition for a referendum. Meanwhile, 61 percent of Poles said they favoured the provisions of the 1956 law.

Turning the Clock Back

Nevertheless, when the government could postpone a vote no longer, a law was finally passed early in 1993. Under the new law, only 3 percent of the abortions previously performed in Poland are now deemed legal. Two years in gaol awaits an illegal abortionist, but there is no punishment for a woman who obtains an illegal operation. Although it is the most restrictive abortion law in Europe, apart from Ireland's, pro-choice campaigners comforted themselves with the rueful thought that things could easily have been much worse.

The legislation satisfies no one. Both sides have vowed to fight on. Even before President Lech Walesa signed the new law, the 1992 doctors' code—a *de facto* ban on abortions in Poland—was having its effect. The Warsaw police morgue has begun receiving bodies of women bearing witness to botched abortions. For the last three years, cases of infanticide have steadily increased.

Deaths will be outnumbered by injuries. Romania, where abortion was illegal until the fall of Ceausescu in 1989, shows the way. Staff at a clinic for women in Bucharest, set up by Marie Stopes International, found that 80 percent of patients were suffering from past incompetent abortions.

A helpline set up in Warsaw by pro-abortion campaigners is receiving calls from men seeking advice because their wives are refusing to have sex any more. Women are phoning for help, reporting that even in circumstances which comply with the new law, they are being refused operations. In Poland's deep Catholic south, a pregnant Cracow woman, furnished with a police report confirming that she had been raped, was refused help at the hospital (Hoell, 1993).

All the desolately familiar symptoms of outlawed abortion are there: police raids on clinics, small ads appearing in the newspapers: "Gynaecologist: Interventions." The price is $350–1,000: The average monthly wage is $200. For professional women "medical tours" can be arranged—to the Ukraine, to Kaliningrad, even to Holland. (But not to the Czech Republic, which in the wake of Poland's new law, moved swiftly to outlaw abortions for foreign visitors.)

Paradoxically, the last few years have seen a burgeoning of women's organizations, formed to defend abortion and women's rights. It is an irony, comments Hanna Jankowska, "when the word 'feminist' sounds in this country like an insult" (1993). But sustaining the momentum of such organizations is uphill work. People are consumed by the effort to cope with the effects of 38 percent inflation.

There are signs that the Church may have overplayed its hand in its attempt to introduce a legislative version of "absolute morality" as part of a plan to create a theocratic Poland. There was strong public support for a referendum on abortion, which the Church opposed, and its popularity has dropped by half since Communism collapsed, according to opinion polls (*Catholic Herald*, 9/9/93). The Irish Church found itself in similar trouble after the referendum on abortion in Ireland in 1992, an event which was much reported in the Polish media.

But it is hard to draw sound parallels with Ireland: The Republic is certainly behind the times, but there are signs that slowly things are creeping forward for women in Ireland. Nothing compares with the crudeness with which the clock hands have been wrenched *back* in Poland.

In September 1993, the political coalition which fostered the anti-abortion legislation suffered a crushing defeat in national elections. The pace of reform was thought to be the main culprit, but the unpopularity of the anti-abortion law was also held to blame. Proabortion campaigners are preparing a new bill to reverse the law, scarcely before the ink is dry. In January 1994, Polish doctors amended their medical code, somewhat relaxing the abortion guidelines and increasing scope for prenatal diagnosis of fetal abnormalities.

The bishops and their allies intend to press on towards a theocratic state. They have stated: "We must reject the false and harmful belief—which unfortunately is grounded in social consciousness —that a secular state is perceived as the only and fundamental guarantee of freedom and equality of citizens" (Szawarski, 1991). If they succeed in creating a model Roman Catholic state, it will be women who suffer most directly. That is why no one in Poland, on whichever side of the abortion divide, underestimates the importance of the struggle around abortion as a stalking horse for what may yet come.

It is not possible to yoke together the national experience of abortion politics in Poland with that of the United States, only to offer them as two distinct examples of how abortion seemed at times to be the tail that wagged the dog of national politics. It has been quite remarkable to find abortion ricocheting around the political arena in Poland and other Eastern European countries. But the issue has played a crucial part in the politics of the United States for almost twenty years: in itself an astonishing phenomenon.

USA, 1973—THE SUPREME COURT LIGHTS THE FUSE

Until the historic U.S. Supreme Court judgment of 1973, in the case of *Roe* v. *Wade* (which I shall call plain *Roe*), abortion was not a major issue in the United States. In the late 1960s, when campaigners for abortion reform in California asked people to sign petitions, it took so long for people to think and talk before deciding where they stood that no more than four or five signatures could be gathered in an afternoon's work (Luker, 1984).

But the spark of *Roe* caught dry tinder at once and is still burning. Today, everyone has an opinion on abortion: After thousands of opinion polls, hours of TV debating, radio phone-ins and miles of newsprint, people know with certainty whether they are "pro-choice" or "pro-life."

In the late nineteenth century it was doctors who pressed for anti-abortion legislation in the United States, partly to strengthen the delineation of medicine as a regulated, elite profession. Making abortion illegal, unless performed by a doctor, was an effective way of cutting the ground from under the "quacks." The laws granted doctors alone the discretion to decide when a woman's life was sufficiently endangered to justify the loss of fetal life.

For almost seventy years legal abortion was a matter for medical judgement. Its prevalence and the criteria used varied enormously. Women who could not get legal abortions resorted to illegal practitioners and practices. But in the 1950s and 1960s exclusive medical control over abortion began to crumble.

Briefly, women's lives were changing as they entered the labour market in increasing numbers—for a married woman an unintended pregnancy became much more of a disaster than in the past; secondly, the improvements of medicine and obstetrics made pregnancy and childbirth much safer and made it harder for doctors to cloak a decision to perform an abortion for a wealthy patient behind the excuse that continuing the pregnancy would gravely endanger her health. Doctors' work became much more hospital-based and could be more easily scrutinized and regulated than when they worked in private consulting rooms.

Thirdly, women began to question the right of doctors and lawyers, or anyone, to decide whether or not they should have to continue an unintended pregnancy. Finally, the effects of the Thalidomide cases and the advent of effective contraception all played a part in dragging decisions and policies on abortion into the harsh public light of politics.

Some states began to permit abortion. Between 1967 and 1973, seventeen states rescinded their restrictions on abortion. Thousands of women crossed state boundaries to obtain abortions (Gold, 1990). Abortion was happening, despite its continuing prohibition under federal law.

Several decades of Supreme Court decisions—for instance, acknowledging it was no business of the state (or states) to seek to outlaw the use and purchase of contraceptives—had smoothed the path towards the *Roe* judgment, but nonetheless, when it eventually came, it was quite dramatic. The court said that a woman's right to obtain an abortion, like her right to use contraception without government interference is constitutionally protected, as part of her fundamental right to privacy. And that because the right to privacy is fundamental (rights under the American constitution are ranked, and *fundamental* trumps every other kind of right) states must show a "compelling interest" before they can intervene.

The court stressed that, of course, the decision to abort must be made together with a doctor. But it devised a sliding scale of maternal/fetal rights, practically sanctioning "abortion on demand" in the first trimester and gradually increasing the amount of protection afforded to the fetus as the weeks of pregnancy progressed.

No Room for Compromise

The significance of the Supreme Court ruling in 1973 was that it turned abortion into a constitutional issue, declaring it a fundamental right of the female citizen, and sweeping away all the various state restrictions. In doing so it called into question the deeply held beliefs of people accustomed to thinking that *theirs* was the majority opinion and set the state on a collision course with an indefatigable group of its citizens. As long as abortion had been purely a medical issue, as it is in Britain (see below) it had been much more difficult to challenge, and far less in the public domain.

The absolute divide between right-to-life/pro-life/anti-choice/anti-abortion people, and the rest is the embryo or fetus. If you believe that the embryo or later the fetus is a person, a human being in the fullest sense, the moral equivalent of a woman, everything else falls into place. The Supreme Court questioned this notion and opened the door to the years of court challenge, endless legislative pressure and single-issue pressure-group politics. For those who believe that abortion is the equivalent of homicide there can hardly be a compromise.

The impact of the *Roe* judgement was enormous. Overnight literally, the opposition mobilized.[1] Its attack has had two aims: to upset and overturn the judicial applecart and at the same time to erect as many obstacles as possible between a woman and a legal abortion. It's been a busy twenty years: *Roe* has been harried almost to extinction by state regulations, such as imposed waiting periods, demands for "informed consent," such as making the woman look at images of fetal development—at all stages, no matter how early her own pregnancy. As pro-choice campaigner Lawrence Lader said, after *Roe,* "We thought we had won. We were wrong" (*Family Planning World*, Jan/Feb, 1992).

At first, state attempts to regulate abortion after Roe received a cool response in the Supreme Court, but as the New Right has gained power and judges appointed to the court became more conservative, so the judgements have hardened against abortion rights.

Wide-ranging Success for Abortion's Opponents

The cultural and political climate today is of course very different from that surrounding *Roe* in 1973. On the day of the Supreme Court's ruling on *Roe*, newspapers reported an agreement which might bring an end to the war in Vietnam and carried obituaries of former President Lyndon B. Johnson, whose presidency was marked domestically by the civil rights movement, Black Power and the movement against the war in Vietnam. This is not the place to rehearse the cultural "backlash" of the years since then except to highlight how wide-ranging it has been.

Susan Faludi, for instance, recounts the fate of a script for the TV show *Cagney and Lacey*. In "Choices," as the early 1980s' episode was to be called, Cagney—the single woman in the feisty female cop duo—became pregnant. CBS programming executives went beserk at the mere idea of abortion (even as an option to be rejected). They demanded numerous rewrites until in the final version, Cagney only mistakenly thinks she is pregnant. "Lacey…tells her that if she had been pregnant she should have got married. Abortion is never offered as a choice" (Faludi, 1992: 186).

The anti-abortion lobby drew comfort not only from *Cagney and Lacey* but also from the White House. As the violence against clinics increased in 1984 after Ronald Reagan's election to a second term as president, he refused to condemn the actions and their perpetrators (Blanchard & Prewitt, 1993).[2]

Opinion polls show that Americans' attitude to abortion was and generally remains "permit but discourage." It was not very hard to convert such ambivalence into support for restrictions on government funding and so on. The most significant curtailment of rights for low-income women was the Hyde Amendment of 1979 which denied Medicaid funding for abortion, except where a woman's life is in danger. There have also been severe and wide-ranging restrictions on the use of public facilities for abortion: It is illegal, for instance, to perform a private abortion in a private building standing on publicly owned land. By 1979 no federal funds could be used to provide abortion or abortion-related services (Petchesky, 1984).

Today, only half the United States' medical schools even offer the option of training in abortion procedures, and fewer and fewer young doctors are willing to perform abortions. Many gynaecologists still performing abortions are reaching retirement, and in a 1985 study, two-thirds of the gynaecologists in the United States stated that they would not terminate pregnancy. Who would choose to conduct their professional working life in a bullet-proof vest, with an armed guard at the clinic door? In 1988, 83 percent of all United States counties lacked any facilities for abortion, and those counties contain 31 percent of U.S. women aged between fifteen and forty-four (Alan Guttmacher Institute, 1993).

A shadowy world of unlicensed, unregulated abortion facilities in private doctors' offices is beginning to emerge. There are estimated to be several dozen in New York City alone, and a doctor there was recently prosecuted for a botched abortion on a twenty-one-year-old immigrant woman, who subsequently gave birth to a severely mutilated infant (*Family Planning World*, May/June, 1993).

And yet, despite all the legislative obstacles and the physical harassment, the anti-abortion movement has made no dent in the number of abortions taking place in the United States. The overall figure has hovered steadily around 1.6 million a year.

Who Opposes Abortion Rights?

The intimidation of anti-abortion activists, such as Operation Rescue, or the Lambs of Christ, and the violence and terrorism against abortion clinics is what immediately comes to mind when thinking about abortion's opponents, but it is not the only face of the opposition.

After the *Roe* judgment, the Catholic Church was the first into action, with plangent denunciation and millions of dollars poured into new anti-abortion organizations. But as the New Right in the Republican party set out deliberately to woo the anti-abortion voters, as part of its efforts to shift the party itself to the right, the anti-abortion alliance became a curious blend—from Catholics to born-again Christian evangelicals, to more secular "New Right" types. It was ultimately to prove a volatile coalition.

Abortion has been and still is the kernel of a protracted campaign against the social trends of the second half of the twentieth century, and for a reinstatement of "traditional family values." The Reagan presidency boosted the legitimacy, power and influence of "God's bullies" as they have been aptly called. Although the specific goal of the antiabortionists is to outlaw abortions, it is important to see this in a wider context of conservatism, attacks on welfare and so on.

The movement has two faces—first, the lobbyists and court challengers, as well as the image-makers, whose ideological offensive has sought to control the public perception of abortion and the women who seek it (Petchesky, 1984). In 1990 alone there were 465 abortion-related bills presented to state legislatures (McKeegan, 1992). The anti-abortion lobby has used its muscle in the ballot box with considerable effect. Single-issue voting can tip the scales when results are close and election turnouts are low. Packing state legislatures and other elected bodies has been a systematic strategy and for twenty years abortion has wracked the United States, from school boards to Congress.

Secondly, there is the face of direct action, some of it peaceful, but nevertheless extremely intimidating, some of it violent and explicitly women-hating. In 1991 in Wichita, south Kansas, there were more than 2,600 arrests as 30,000 anti-abortion protesters blockaded an abortion clinic. In the last fifteen years around a hundred clinics have been bombed or set on fire. Others have had medical equipment wrecked. Clinic staff and their families have been harassed; doctors have been shot at; in March 1993, one was even killed. Pregnant women arriving at abortion clinics have had to run a gauntlet of screaming demonstrators, some hurling plastic fetal models, some videotaping their faces and noting the numbers on their car license plates for subsequent tracing and personal harassment.

A study of men convicted of anti-abortion violence concluded that they are "clearly acting out of a desire to maintain the dependent status of women." Many also favour policies such as capital and corporal punishment (Blanchard & Prewitt, 1993). Somewhat in a grey area of legality lie the fake abortion clinics which have been set up and are listed in the Yellow Pages, which harangue women who turn up hoping to arrange an abortion, and force them to look at often gruesome pictures of fetuses....

WHY HAS BRITAIN'S ABORTION DEBATE BEEN DIFFERENT?

It seems worth briefly comparing the struggle in the United States with that in Britain, whose political process has never been gripped by the throat as it has in the United States. Pro-choice Republican Senator Robert Packwood explained what the attentions of a single-minded group such as the U.S. anti-abortion lobby mean to his daily political life:

[The pro-lifers] are a frightening force. They are people who are with you 99 percent of the time, but if you vote against them on this issue it doesn't matter what else you stand for. (Tribe, 1992)

That's hard to imagine in Britain. Of course, there have been times when abortion has been a hot issue in the U.K., swelling MPs' mailbags and prompting heated exchanges on *Question Time,* but it has at no time been such dynamite, compelling British MPs to refer their every political step to its impact on those of their supporters who oppose abortion. Part of the reason is that Britain is relatively indifferent to religion and has no comparably powerful, organized fundamentalist or Roman Catholic population. Also, laws made in the United States Supreme Court positively invite legal challenge and counter-challenge. Laws made by Parliament are more resilient in general.

What's more, part of the reason is in the abortion law itself. It is for doctors, says Britain's 1967 Abortion Act—two doctors—to decide whether a woman needs an abortion, under the terms specified by the law. The rights of women do not remotely enter into it. Many campaigners who

have defended the provisions of the 1967 Act, from no less than sixteen parliamentary attempts to curtail its scope, believe that it is the Act's reliance on doctors that has allowed it to escape relatively unscathed after twenty-five years.

When opponents of abortion in Britain have attacked the Act, its defenders have quite legitimately and cogently been able to point out that it is not *women* who make the final decision, but (respectable) professionals. (Funding cuts in the National Health Service and excessive Department of Health regulations have more stealthily debilitated abortion provision in Britain—that is another story.) Although the inherent paternalism in the framing of the Act is not only demeaning but has also led to unfair geographical differences in women's access to a sympathetic, prompt abortion service, the pragmatic, defensive value of investing the responsibility in the medical profession is worth noting.

CRITICAL THINKING QUESTIONS

1. Numerous physicians who provide abortion services have been murdered and Planned Parenthood clinics bombed in the United States. Why, in contrast, has Poland not experienced such violent attacks on the medical profession and on women who seek abortions?
2. In contrast to the United States and Poland, why has there been little debate about abortion in Great Britain?
3. Opponents of abortion in Europe and the United States often describe abortion as a breakdown of "social values" and the "traditional family." In contrast, proponents of abortion emphasize a woman's reproductive rights. According to Hadley, how do politics, religion, and economics ultimately shape policy and many women's destiny in abortion debates?

NOTES

1. Kristin Luker (Luker, 1984) describes how would-be activists phoned around frantically in the days after the court decision, trying to find an organization to join.

Many of them—women, married, housewives with small children, had never joined anything before—not even the school parent-teacher association.

2. Ronald Reagan not only refused to condemn the violence, in 1984 he wrote a bizarre call-to-arms against abortion, with help from Malcolm Muggeridge *(Abortion and the Conscience of the Nation.* Thomas Nelson, Nashville, 1984).

REFERENCES

Alan Guttmacher Institute. 1993. *Abortion in the United States: Facts in brief.* New York.

Blanchard, D., and T. J. Prewitt. 1993. *Religious violence and abortion.* University Press of Florida.

Einhorn, B. 1993. Polish backlash. *Everywoman*, April, 1993.

Faludi, S. 1992. *Backlash.* London: Vintage.

Gold, R. B. 1990. *Abortion and women's health: The turning point for America.* New York: Alan Guttmacher Institute.

Hoell, S. 1993. Strict new law drives abortion underground in Poland. *Reuters*, 14 December.

Jankowska, H. 1993. The reproductive rights campaign in Poland. *Women's Studies International Forum*, 16, 3: 291–96.

Kissling, F. 1992. The Church's heavy hand in Poland. *Planned Parenthood in Europe* 21, 2 (May): 18–9.

Luker, K. 1984. *Abortion and the politics of motherhood.* Berkeley: University of California Press.

McKeegan, M. 1992. *Mutiny in the ranks of the right.* New York: The Free Press, Maxwell Macmillan International.

Mrugala, G. 1991. Polish family planning in crisis: The Roman Catholic influence. *Planned Parenthood in Europe* 20, 2, (September): 4–5.

Okolski, M. 1988. 'Poland' in Sachdev, P., *International handbook on abortion.* New York: Greenwood Press.

Petchesky, R. 1984. *Abortion and woman's choice.* New York, Longman.

Rich, V. 1991. Poland: Abortion and contraception. *Lancet*, 338, 875, (13 July): 108–9.

Szawarski, Z. 1991. Abortion in Poland. *British Journal of Obstetrics and Gynaecology*, 98 (December): 1202–4.

Tribe, L. 1992. *Abortion: The clash of absolutes.* New York, Norton.

World Health Organization. 1993. *Progress in human reproductive research*, No. 25. Geneva.

Social Change,
Media,
and Modernity

CLASSIC

CONTEMPORARY

CROSS-CULTURAL

64

The Disenchantment of Modern Life

Max Weber

In this excerpt from the speech "Science as a Vocation," delivered at Munich University in 1918, Weber claims that the rise of science has changed our way of thinking about the world. Where, in the past, humans confronted a world of mystical forces beyond comprehension, we now assume that all things yield to human comprehension. Thus, Weber concludes, the world has become "disenchanted." Notice, however, that something is lost in the process for, unlike the churches of the past, science can provide no answer to questions of ultimate meaning in life.

Scientific progress is a fraction, the most important fraction, of the process of intellectualization which we have been undergoing for thousands of years and which nowadays is usually judged in such an extremely negative way. Let us first clarify what this intellectualist rationalization, created by science and by scientifically oriented technology, means practically.

Does it mean that we, today, for instance, everyone sitting in this hall, have a greater knowledge of the conditions of life under which we exist than has an American Indian or a Hottentot? Hardly. Unless he is a physicist, one who rides on the streetcar has no idea how the car happened to get into motion. And he does not need to know. He is satisfied that he may "count" on the behavior of the streetcar, and he orients his conduct according to this expectation; but he knows nothing about

what it takes to produce such a car so that it can move. The savage knows incomparably more about his tools. When we spend money today I bet that even if there are colleagues of political economy here in the hall, almost every one of them will hold a different answer in readiness to the question: How does it happen that one can buy something for money—sometimes more and sometimes less? The savage knows what he does in order to get his daily food and which institutions serve him in this pursuit. The increasing intellectualization and rationalization do *not,* therefore, indicate an increased and general knowledge of the conditions under which one lives.

It means something else, namely, the knowledge or belief that if one but wished one *could* learn it at any time. Hence, it means that principally there are no mysterious incalculable forces that come into play, but rather that one can, in principle, master all things by calculation. This means that the world is disenchanted. One need no longer have recourse to magical means in order to master or implore the spirits, as did the savage, for whom such mysterious powers existed. Technical means and calculations perform the service. This above all is what intellectualization means.…

Science today is a "vocation" organized in special disciplines in the service of selfclarification and knowledge of interrelated facts. It is not the gift of grace of seers and prophets dispensing sacred values and revelations, nor does it partake of the contemplation of sages and philosophers about the meaning of the universe. This, to be sure, is the inescapable condition of our historical situation. We cannot evade it so long as we remain true to ourselves. And if Tolstoi's question recurs to you: As science does not, who is to answer the question: "What shall we do, and, how shall we arrange our lives?" or, in the words used here tonight: "Which of the warring gods should we serve? Or should we serve perhaps an entirely different god, and who is he?" then one can say that only a prophet or a savior can give the answers.…

To the person who cannot bear the fate of the times like a man, one must say: May he rather return silently, without the usual publicity build-up of renegades, but simply and plainly. The arms of the old churches are opened widely and compassionately for him. After all, they do not make it hard for him. One way or another he has to bring his "intellectual sacrifice"—that is inevitable. If he can really do it, we shall not rebuke him. For such an intellectual sacrifice in favor of an unconditional religious devotion is ethically quite a different matter than the evasion of the plain duty of intellectual integrity, which sets in if one lacks the courage to clarify one's own ultimate standpoint and rather facilitates this duty by feeble relative judgments. In my eyes, such religious return stands higher than the academic prophecy, which does not clearly realize that in the lecture-rooms of the university no other virtue holds but plain intellectual integrity: Integrity, however, compels us to state that for the many who today tarry for new prophets and saviors, the situation is the same as resounds in the beautiful Edomite watchman's song of the period of exile that has been included among Isaiah's oracles:

He calleth to me out of Seir, Watchman, what of the night? The watchman said, The morning cometh, and also the night: if ye will enquire, enquire ye: return, come.

The people to whom this was said has enquired and tarried for more than two millennia, and we are shaken when we realize its fate. From this we want to draw the lesson that nothing is gained by yearning and tarrying alone, and we shall act differently. We shall set to work and meet the "demands of the day," in human relations as well as in our vocation. This, however, is plain and simple, if each finds and obeys the demon who holds the fibers of his very life.

CRITICAL THINKING QUESTIONS

1. In what sense do members of a traditional society know more about their world than we do? In what sense do we know more?
2. What is "Tolstoi's question"? Why can science not answer it?
3. What does Weber see as the great burden of living in a modern society? In other words, what comforts of the past are less available to modern people?

Social Change,
Media,
and Modernity

CLASSIC

CONTEMPORARY

CROSS-CULTURAL

65

Internet Censorship as "Cybriety": Freud, McLuhan, and Media Pleasures

Tony Tremblay

In this article, Tremblay suggests that our social concern over questionable media content is nothing new. Long before the Internet there were many media expressions that challenged social convention. Tremblay's analysis of Internet censorship draws much insight from an historical review of media content and social change.

In November 1995, the sleepy Canadian town of Sackville, New Brunswick, was witness to what Freud and Foucault might have called an age-old autoerotic drama, one characterized by a predictable latency—a discrepancy between action and reaction, performance and reception. The event to which I am referring took place at Mount Allison University's Owens Art Gallery, where performance art and theater are regularly staged. Student Chris Yorke and a female actor, clad only in smashed eggs and silver tree tinsel, performed simulated oral sex on one another in front of an audience of almost fifty people. Although no one in the audience complained, and no one walked out, the viewers' acceptance, even appreciation, of the performance did little to sanction it. Very little. When the performance was subsequently reviewed in the local newspaper, the public's moral outrage was silently and decisively

marshaled. A few days later, Chris Yorke was charged with public indecency. In finding Yorke guilty of indecency in the performance of his art, New Brunswick Judge Irwin Lampert declared that "community standards are the best measure of what is obscene and what is not." Yorke's only comment was as historically encoded as the judge's: "Human sexuality has been the subject of art for centuries; I feel violated by this decision" *(Telegraph Journal* E5). Indeed, Yorke had been subject to the same social forces that violated the turn-of-the-century performance artists of *Serpentine Dance* (1895) and *Pull Down the Curtains, Suzie* (1904), two early peepshows made for Edison's Kinetscope. If the Mount Allison situation teaches us anything, it is how fundamentally sexuality is inscribed with cultural sanction, and how that sanction recurs as regular historical performance.

With increasing frequency over the last few years, the Internet has become a flash point for the debate between free speech and censorship. Various Netscape sites have been removed from the

Source: The complete contents of this article originally appeared in *Mosaic, a journal for the interdisciplinary study of literature,* Vol. 32.1, Spring 1999, pp. 167–182. Reprinted with permission of the publisher.

Web, and others have been blackened by Internet Providers to protest social sanction. Two years ago in the United States, Congress hurriedly passed the Communication Decency Act, only to see it ruled unconstitutional a short time later. In Canada, a January 1999 British Columbia judgment challenged the legality of restricting access to child pornography on the Web. Since that ruling, public opinion has been galvanized for censure: the call for Internet censorship—what I am terming "cybriety" (cyber-sobriety)—has been mobilized. The Internet, that vast mystical panacea that holds, we are told, so much of our hope for the future, is under threat. What are we to make of this, we non-cybrarians, occasional-surfers of the virtual world? In the early days of this debate, we can be certain of only one thing: left to the pundits, censorship becomes obscured. As Sallie Tisdale writes, "Censorship...makes it impossible not only to talk about the censored object, but about censorship" (13). "Pornography," concurs Walter Kendrick, "names an argument, not a thing" (31). And so censorship debates, regardless of what is being censored, are ideologically laden. These debates therefore require some historio-cultural archaeology to make sense of them.

The novel, photography/film, and now the Internet are good sites with which to ground an exploration of the social psychology of censorship, as these are not only our most popular media, but those which perhaps best illustrate the action of all new media in the self-satisfying ("autoerotic") and unregulated ("offensive") stage of infancy. I do not mean to suggest any kind of structural evolution across these media, but to point simply to a historical recurrence that is observable in each medium's infancy, the time when each thrives in the unreflexive rapture of its own autoeroticism, independent of the sanction of the censor. Hybridizing McLuhan and Freud, I will argue that because all media are extensions of the body—speech extends the ear, print extends the eye—any new medium is inherently pleasurable; and, being pleasurable, any new

medium invites the infantile game of daring, a pushing of the limits of what is "socially" acceptable in order to fulfill desire. Just as Freud's infant, outside social sanction, fetishizes its own body, fondling itself in the most embarrassing of public/(*private*) places, so will I show that the human body is fetishized vicariously through all new media. Being bodily, all new media are therefore dangerous, as are all *new* technologies, a condition that further invites embargo. In "outering" the Central Nervous System, the Internet, as McLuhan predicted, is likewise bodily, given to an age-old autoerotic drama that is rife with the inevitability of social sanction. My essay will illustrate how a recourse to literary history and to diegetic (or narrative) pattern is particularly instructive in the exploration of censorship as a cultural phenomenon.

Sixteenth-century readers of the novel, the new narrative form of the time, were much less prudish than we are today, their openness reflected in a heady engagement with the lower-class anthropomorphism of sin, sex, the grotesque, and other bodily subversions. That a Benedictine monk was one of the most accomplished at presenting this orgiastic carnival of delights is simply a condition of pre-Reformation Christianity. Rabelais knew, as did the Roman Church fathers, that the otherwise respectable citizens of court and abbey were spectators, and, as spectators, they were voyeurs, always seeking an uncensored vista from which to watch the lower classes in the frenzy of their physicality. Rabelais's advance was to use the new narrative medium, the novel, to create a space and conditions (privacy and anonymity) within which learned spectators could discreetly exercise their fetish.

The significance of the new medium of the novel in this consideration of media lies in its formal and thematic generosity in meeting and satisfying an audience, as all new forms do. In extending us outward, all new media and technology *inevitably* satisfy, holding us, at least in their infancy, in the spell of Freud's autoerotic "mirror stage." The provenance of the new medium of the novel was significant too, for not only was it populist in terms of autoerotic content, but in structural ancestry as well. Rising from "the rich soil" of verse narratives (Church 19), those oral forms that could *not* be sanctioned, the new genre paralleled the unlegislated folktale, which was "full of blunt, amused, and salacious stories...of castration and masturbation and incest, necrophilia and zoophilia, the mysterious power of the vagina and the clitoris" (Tisdale 13).

In his work on scribal culture, McLuhan referred to this "becoming" as a spontaneous "outering" of the full sensibility of the people. So rare was this full flowering, McLuhan wrote, that it has found expression only in medieval, Restoration, and modern renewals. If McLuhan and Walter Ong are correct in suggesting that the Gutenberg press changed the medieval psyche from an ear to an eye reliance, then 16th-century readers were also "seeing" the world vicariously (and phenomenologically) for the first time, much as we are experiencing the world today for the first time through virtual and in some cases synchronous multi-media. In the span of less than one hundred years, then, the body was celebrated both in "becoming" (the late-Medieval carnivalesque) and in sensory recombination (the early-Renaissance carnality that swapped an ear for an eye). The sensory stimulus must have been unimaginably emancipating, wildly titillating, and, therefore, terribly threatening.

The autoeroticism of the new medium of the novel, when considered in the light of the onanistic eroticism of silent reading, suggests a medieval psyche that was fully invested in its own program of channeling desire. In its infancy, the novel was a representation of the body that lay below the surface of a coercive culture; reading was therefore a sensual delight, evident in Alberto Manguel's playful evocation of Colette's early reading fantasies:

It is summer. Sunk deep in the soft bed among feather pillows, with the inconstant rumble of carts on the cobble-stones outside the window in the Rue de l'Hospice in the grey village of Saint-Sauveur-en-Puisaye, an eight-year-old girl is silently reading Victor Hugo's *Les Misérables*. She doesn't read many books; she reads the same ones over and over again. She loves *Les Misérables* with what she'll later call "a reasoning passion"; she feels she can nestle in its pages "like a dog in its kennel." Every night she longs to follow Jean Valjean on his agonizing peregrinations, meet Cosette again, meet Marius, even the dreaded Javert.... Her mother does not believe in fiction: "so many complications, so much passionate love in those novels." (140)

The emergence and coercion of the 16th-century novel reveals that the "producerly" delight that Manguel attributes to Colette must exist covertly, otherwise risk being sanctioned in the "Name of the Father."

With the advent of photography at the height of the Victorian era, the diegetic cycle of corporeal form and censorship was repeated yet again, this time in response to the "zoögyroscopes" and wet-plate photographs of "the human figure in motion" (Muybridge viii). Knowing that the body, as opposed to the word, is defined in movement, photography pioneers Eadweard Muybridge and Thomas Eakins produced stills of nude bodies in motion—women washing clothes, men jumping, etc. By the time of the "kinematograph" at the turn of the century (*kinema* from the Greek, meaning "motion"), early film opportunists began producing "loops," known today as "skinflicks," which presented versions of porn and erotica to both male and female viewers alike, many of whom gathered to watch these celluloid vaudevilles in polite company and respectable surroundings (Czitrom 46). The more recent history of film also reveals that film producers not only understood, but were willing to monopolize on, the autoerotic tactility of their medium. Anthony Crabbe's research found that it was almost solely producers and corporate shareholders who challenged censors when the "traditional film industry [of the early 1970s] was in sharp decline" (48). The resulting "decensorship of the time" not only produced our modern culture's classic *blue nuits* (*Au Pair Girls, Behind the Green Door, Deep Throat,* and *Emmanuelle*), but more fundamentally brought people back to the theater, renewing again the people's desire for a marketplace carnality, and renewing again the cycle of prudish outcry and embargo. That film chose vaudeville as its first "popular" spectacle and rescue, just as the 16th-century novel chose the carnivalesque, is a curious and instructive recurrence indeed, establishing populist precedents for the inundation of "Adult" Cyber Malls on the Internet.

This short analysis of our most popular narrative media illustrates that, in terms of the evolution of their forms, the novel and photography/film are similar in fundamental ways: they begin, in infancy, in an unreflexive drama of autoeroticism; they suffer through the mediating and coercive ideologies of corporate sanction; and they emerge as mature forms when they begin to foreground and problematize their own discursives, as if their greatest fears were their own "base" tendencies. To maintain corporeal sovereignty (the authority of the body), both forms then go underground, where "'specialist' sex" and other expressions of the body, regardless of whether in film or book form, are available to those who want them.

Today, cyber theorists reiterate the by now familiar insights of Rabelais, Muybridge, and Mulvey. Cameron Bailey's work is one such reiteration, suggesting that with the Internet "the suburban ideal of postwar North America returns in virtual form: communication at a safe distance, community without contact. Is it any wonder that when movies visualize the Net's matrix of communication, it so often resembles the cool, aerial patterns of a suburb at night?" (22). Claudia Springer concurs with Bailey, noting that "at a time when paranoia over human contact in response to the AIDS virus is common, human interaction should occur through computerized communication, with the participants far apart and unable to touch each other" (71). Much of the efficacy and the enticement of the Internet, then, is that it is so anonymous; "browsers," "lurkers," "hyperqueens," and those in "MUDs" and "cyberdrag" can be whomever or whatever they choose without anyone ever knowing who they really are—or can

they? This is the key question that always attends the constructed private spaces of autoeroticism. Are those spaces secure enough? In the case of the computer, the electronic footprints left in cyberspace in secret files like "NETSCAPE.HST" are often enough, when discovered, to wrest the subject from his illusory symbiosis with the imaginary.

Once again, a reversion to narrative dreamwork is instructive. In Irwin Winkler's 1995 cyber-thriller *The Net,* Sandra Bullock's computer wizardry complements her reclusiveness, affording her a rich, anonymous identity. So vivifying is this private-world onanism that one of her computer's screen-saver messages reads, "The computer is the ultimate condom." Wrapped in cyber-shield, her psyche lives in abandon, pleasuring itself at will. She exists as a kind of etherized libido without any incarnate identity. When her scant "real" identity is stolen, she is hard-pressed to locate another fleshy being who can corroborate the materiality of her existence. The film's sexual metaphor was wisely chosen, as this historio-diegetic exploration of media has demonstrated; for, while condoms protect the innocent in the high-risk application of their primal business, they also sometimes don't, a breaking that foregrounds identity as nothing else does, with paternity being the ultimate exposure. So, yes, condoms and the Net do license risky behavior—both mask identity to free the libido—but both can also rupture, an imprimatur of risk that is the exact opposite of what the reclusive identity, Mulvey's already "alienated subject," seeks.

This paradox, evident also in De Palma's *Body Double,* is a result of our historical mind/body schizophrenia, which in the late 20th century is manifest as our culture's simultaneous technofetish and technophobia. We seek vicarious gratification through our extended sensoria, of which virtual technologies and the Internet are the newest extensions, but at the same time fear that bodily abandon is either dangerous or unworthy of our high rationalism—hence the censure. In fear of reprisal, sanction, or worse, fulfillment, we construct taboos, like the contemporary cybermyth that computers will themselves become sensate and, like a teacher, parent, or omniscient God, will exact great revenge for our masturbatory inclinations. The Internet may very well be our most advanced technology today, but the deep grammar of its formal apparatus is not new. In opening private spaces within which humans can cross dress, don multiple personalities, and explore their repressed sexualities, the Internet is but the latest anthropomorphic envelope. Its targeting by censors should not be read as specific to its own nature, but as specific to the nature of all new media. The furor over Internet censorship is tantamount to a recurrence of the psychoanalytic morality play that has gone on since the Church fathers censored the Bacchanalia and since social forces mollified, sanitized, and "coerced" the autoeroticism of various other extensions of the body.

It should be no surprise that another censorship movement is forming in Germany today, this time in response to the Internet. And while, at least on the surface, a good deal of Germany's lead in the Internet censorship area appears to be rooted in the suppression of hate, the definition of hate is easily expandable beyond race and religion to include other ideological texts, such as the body. This malleability of application lends itself to what Tzvetan Todorov referred to as a "contagion" of ideology. And while it is foolish to argue against the suppression of hate, it should not follow that the body is part of that which is suppressed, for, as this essay illustrates, hate is not part of the spontaneous action of new media in vivifying the body. Actually, just the opposite. As Todorov understood, hate, like sexuality, has become discourse; and so it is left to the critic, finally, to perform the delicate surgery that separates one ideology from another—in the case of this essay, the body and its technological extensions (the book, photography/film, and the Internet).

As McLuhan counseled, "The essence of education" should provide "civil defense against media fallout (i.e., against 'the subliminal operation of our own technologies')" (*Gutenberg Galaxy* 246). Will we forever ignore history, will we be led in deference again, looking to television and other politically motivated interests to form our opinions? If we allow ourselves to become embroiled in a cleverly orchestrated debate that speaks to gender and other ideologically charged "blind spots;" as Walter Kendrick calls them, then the answer is surely YES. The lesson offered by McLuhan lies in his own reversion to history and narrative to seek that which recurs in human behavior when humans embrace new media and technologies. That lesson imparts a simple but demanding humanism: that we must not release anyone from the responsibility of clear statement, historical precedent, and vital particulars. The Internet can be as complex as its current industrial "discourse;" or as simple as a recurring historical moment, one which again extends human desire into the expressive realms of the autoerotic. Given the evidence thus far, I hold for the latter. Internet censorship, or cybriety, is not new; it is a re-run of our favorite drama, the psychoanalytic morality play that teeters between our desires and our fear of their fulfillment.

CRITICAL THINKING QUESTIONS

1. Do you agree with Tremblay's assertion that efforts to censor the Internet are a reflection of nothing new but rather represent a continuation of social responses that have occurred in the past? Discuss.
2. With reference to the article, discuss the pros and cons of censoring content on the Internet.
3. Which medium, the Internet or television, do you see as having a greater influence on social change? Do you think your answer might be different in ten years? Why?

REFERENCES

Bailey, Cameron. 1995. Virtual skin: Articulating race in cyberspace: *Border/Lines*. No. 38/39 (December): 19–24.

Church, Richard. 1957. *The growth of the English novel.* London: Methuen.

Crabbe, Anthony. 1988. Feature-length sex films. *Perspectives on pornography: Sexuality in film and* *literature, e*d. Gary Day and Clive Bloom, 44–66. New York: St. Martin's.

Czitrom, Daniel. 1982. *Media and the American mind: From Morse to McLuhan.* Chapel Hill: U of North Carolina P.

Kendrick, Walter. 1987. *The secret museum: Pornography in modern culture.* New York: Penguin.

Manguel, Alberto. 1996. *A history of reading.* Toronto: Knopf.

McLuhan, Marshall. 1962. *The Gutenberg galaxy: The making of typographic man.* Toronto: U of Toronto P.

——1964. *Understanding media: The extensions of man.* New York: McGraw-Hill.

Mulvey, Laura. 1989. Visual pleasure and narrative cinema and Afterthoughts on "visual pleasure and narrative cinema" inspired by King Vidor's *Duel in the Sun* (1946). *Visual and other pleasures.* 14–26; 29–38. Bloomington: Indiana UP.

Muybridge, Eadweard. 1955. *The human figure in motion.* New York: Dover.

The Net. Dir. Irwin Winkler. Written by John Brancato and Michael Ferris. With Sandra Bullock, Jeremy Northam, and Dennis Miller. Columbia Pictures. 1995.

Springer, Claudia. 1996. *Electronic eros: Bodies and desire in the postindustrial age.* Austin: U of Texas.

Telegraph Journal. [Saint John, NB]. Community shouldn't define obscenity. 22 February 1997: E5.

Tisdale, Sallie. 1994. *Talk Dirty to Me: An Intimate Philosophy of Sex.* New York: Anchor.

Todorov, Tzvetan. 1977. *The poetics of prose,* trans. Richard Howard. Ithaca: Cornell UP.

Social Change,
Media,
and Modernity

CLASSIC

CONTEMPORARY

CROSS-CULTURAL

66

Running Out of Control: Understanding Globalization

R. Alan Hedley

Hedley offers an introduction to globalization and its many technological, social, economic, and political ramifications. His analysis requires us to reflect on our own situation from a global perspective and from a sociological perspective.

Albert Einstein (1936) once observed that the categories are not inherent in the phenomena. In other words, concepts such as "globalization" and "information and communications technology revolution" are human constructs we have developed in order to understand better the complexities of what we believe is happening in the world. Theories are simplified models of reality, and the first step in theory construction is categorization or classification. Over the past few decades, researchers and social commentators have coined the term "globalization" in order to focus on what they believe are interrelated processes which are having tremendous impacts on our lives in the late twentieth and early twenty-first centuries. Consequently, there is no

one correct definition of globalization; it has many different meanings and interpretations, depending upon who is discussing it and in what context. However, there are elements of agreement as to what globalization means.

The derivation of the term "globalization" implies that it involves worldwide processes that are relatively novel and still unfolding. These multidimensional processes are being experienced unevenly throughout the world and in different sectors of social life. *Globalization is a complex set of human forces involving the production, distribution/transmission, and consumption of technical, economic, political, and sociocultural goods and services which are administratively and technologically integrated on a worldwide basis.* This definition highlights the point that globalization comprises technological, economic, political (including military), and sociocultural dimensions. Together these interrelated dimensions make up the (human) global system which operates within the broader global ecological environment.

Source: Abridged from "Understanding Globalization" in *Running Out of Control: Dilemmas of Globalization*, by R. Alan Hedley, pp. 5–37. Bloomfield, Conn.: Kumarian Press, 2002. Reprinted with permission of the publisher.

Concerning the four dimensions of globalization,...innovations in transportation, communication, and information processing within the past three or four decades have permitted the creation of a technological infrastructure that facilitates the other dimensions of globalization. While technology may be seen as the facilitating means to modern globalization, the primary motivation has been economic—the harnessing of natural and human resources and the establishing of markets and investments worldwide by capitalist enterprise to achieve greater corporate control. In part, to counter the forces of technologically enhanced global capitalism, and to represent civic interests, governments and nongovernmental organizations have also globalized through the formation of international alliances. However, these coalitions have been insufficient to moderate the effects of another important dimension of globalization—the worldwide cultural overlay of Western values, norms, institutions, and practices. Because globalization was initiated predominately by corporations and countries in the Western world, inevitably, what is produced, transmitted, and consumed is monocultural. Thus, globalization as a multidimensional concept involves a worldwide technological infrastructure in which Western-style capitalism predominates.

Finally, if technology facilitates globalization, the ecological biosphere within which we all live represents its outside limits. Certainly during the past few decades, mounting evidence on a variety of fronts such as climate change, pollution, ozone depletion, cumulative environmental degradation, and population growth indicates we are nearing these limits. Consequently, globalization also involves a critical tension between our technological ability to modify the natural environment and the ultimate ecological constraints beyond which human existence is impossible.

In the following section, I describe the various forces instrumental in producing our globalized world.

FORCES OF GLOBALIZATION

The world has always been a large place, but in some sense it has become much smaller than it was. It measures 25,000 miles in circumference (*Britannica,* 1999). As recently as the late nineteenth century, the great science fiction writer Jules Verne wrote the then unbelievable novel, *Around the World in Eighty Days.* Today, not only can we physically circumnavigate the world in one day, we can electronically orbit the planet in just eight seconds (Phillips, 1996)—three hundred times faster than Shakespeare's magical Puck. Globalization is both feasible and viable now because of technological innovations in transportation, communication, and information processing during the latter part of the twentieth century. In fact, many experts claim that these interrelated innovations constitute the basis for a new technological revolution every bit as significant as the industrial revolution some 250 years earlier.

A major impetus for this recent revolution was World War II, itself a global phenomenon. Government-sponsored research centers produced myriad inventions and discoveries that were applied to the war effort. Some of these, most notably the work in nuclear fission, rocketry, and jet engines, contributed directly to the arsenal of the warring nations, whereas others such as materials development (plastic, superalloys, aluminum, and synthetics) made more indirect contributions. A third area of concentration involved the development of reliable, high-speed support systems, and it was in this context that the computer and telecommunications industries were created and set the stage for the information and communications technology (ICT) revolution that was to follow.

The fact that these technological innovations were organizationally sponsored highlights a second underlying force of globalization. In the years following World War II, organizations in the private, public, and civil sectors all harnessed these innovations to suit their purposes. In the private sector, corporations employed these innovations to secure competitive advantage by becoming transnational in their operations. In the public sector, governments entered into international alliances in attempts to create a stable world order out of the chaos produced by the War. And in reaction to these moves on the part of organizations in the private and public sectors, ordinary citizens—civil society—formed international nongovernmental [NGOs] organizations of their own in order to achieve what they believed were important development objectives. Consequently, technologically enhanced organizations of all types were also instrumental in ushering in the global age.

Finally, on an individual basis, people all over the world also helped to bring about globalization. They enthusiastically adopted the numerous technological innovations in transportation, communication, and information processing to reach out and touch others, both physically and electronically, all around the globe.

Following is a discussion of each of these three main forces of globalization.

Technological Forces

Transportation Notable innovations in transportation during the past fifty years include the launching of container ships for shipping raw materials and finished manufactured goods worldwide, the introduction of commercial jets, and the debut of space travel. With regard to container ships, Herman (1983: 135) states that "the impact of containerization on the shipping industry can rightly be compared to the impact which steamships had on the field when they were first introduced over a hundred years ago." A container ship has specially designed holds, hatches, and cranes which enable it to take whole truck trailers on board without loading or unloading their contents. This reduces ship time in port (from 65 [percent] to 25 percent annually), cuts stevedoring costs, and virtually eliminates pilferage. It also permits the construction of larger, faster (from fifteen [knots] to twenty-five knots), more

fuel-efficient vessels which reduces total operating expenses. For example, Herman (1983: 135) cites comparative statistics on the North Atlantic route for 1970: "fifty containerships provide a tonnage greater by approximately one-third than the one hundred and seventy vessels which operated there only one-half decade before." And given that "over 80 percent of world trade by volume is carried by ship" (Herman, 1983: 3), the inducements offered by containerization are substantial.

The idea of container ships emerged in 1951 when a shipping company "took a converted truck body as deck cargo from Miami to Puerto Rico" (Gilman, 1983: 8). Pearson and Fossey (1982: 220) report that only 106 container ships were built worldwide prior to the 1960s; however, in the 1960s, 478 were constructed, and in the following decade, 1,931 more container ships were launched.

While container ships are important for the efficient and speedy transportation of goods, jet aircraft are invaluable for transporting people and time-sensitive cargo quickly around the globe. The first commercial jet airline service was introduced in Britain in 1952 (Woytinsky & Woytinski, 1955: 500). By 1962, "the difference in speed between the fastest piston-engined transport and a jet was 240 miles an hour, a differential almost as great as all the speed increases made by commercial airplanes between 1918 and 1953" (Serling, 1982: 100). In effect, the world became smaller and more accessible. Recent figures on worldwide air traffic demonstrate this point. According to the International Civil Aviation Organization (ICAO, 2001), in 1999 world airlines carried some 1.6 billion people and 28.2 million metric tons of air cargo (see Box 66.1).

The concept of globalization received a major boost on October 4, 1957, when the Soviet Union successfully launched Sputnik I, the first-ever space satellite. About the size of a basketball and weighing 183 pounds, it took just ninety-eight minutes to orbit the planet (NASA, 2000). Subsequent space flights provided the first photographs of the Earth as a globe. No longer was it necessary only to conceptualize it in this

BOX 66.1
FEDEX: A GLOBAL CORPORATION

At 11:45 a.m. on June 11, 2000, I shipped a paper by FedEx from my office in Victoria, Canada, to a colleague in Madras, India. From Victoria, the paper went to Vancouver (4:16 p.m.) and Memphis, Tennessee (6:14 p.m.), FedEx headquarters and central routing hub. My paper left Memphis on 06/12/00 at 2:46 a.m. bound for the European hub city of Paris (8:18 p.m.), and then on to Dubai in the Persian Gulf (2:17 p.m., 06/13/00), and Bombay, India (3:00 a.m., 06/14/00), where it had to wait for commercial customs release (11:00 a.m.). My paper arrived in Madras (9:08 a.m., 06/15/00) and was finally delivered to my Indian colleague (11:30 a.m.).

All of this information I obtained from entering my FedEx tracking number at the FedEx Web site (**www.fedex.com**). My paper was merely one of millions of shipments that FedEx handles and tracks every day.

According to a July 11, 2000, FedEx Corporation press release posted on its Web site:

FedEx Express, a $15 billion subsidiary of FedEx Corp., connects areas that generate 90% of the world's gross domestic product in 24–48 hours with door-to-door, customs cleared service and a money back guarantee. The company's unmatched air route authorities and infrastructure make it the world's largest express transportation company, providing fast, reliable and time-definite transportation of more than 3.3 million items to 210 countries each working day. FedEx employs approximately 145,000 employees and has more than 43,000 drop-off locations, 663 aircraft and 44,500 vehicles in its integrated global network. The company maintains electronic connections with more than 2.5 million customers via FedEx Powership®, FedEx Ship®, and FedEx InternetShip®.

fashion; now we could actually *see* it as a spherical whole. Space flight literally produced a new world view of planet Earth. Our world definitely became smaller.

Communication and Information Processing
While technological innovations in transportation reduced the constraints of time and space, advances in communications and information processing technology have virtually eliminated these formerly circumscribing barriers, thus accounting for the claims of a new ICT revolution.

Naisbitt (1982) discusses how developments in information and communications technology have collapsed what he calls the "information float"—the time it takes for a sender of information first to collect and process information, and then to transmit it through some communication channel to a receiver, who also must process it. Whereas the information float was a factor that could not be ignored before the 1970s, today it is trivial. Naisbitt (1982: 23) explains:

One way to think about the foreshortening of the information float is to think about when the world changed from trading goods and services to standardized currencies. Just imagine how that speeded up transactions. Now, with the use of electrons to send money around the world at the speed of light, we have almost completely collapsed the…information float. The shift from money to electronics is as basic as when we first went from barter to money.

At the very core of this transformation was the creation of the electronic microchip:

In the microchip, combining millions of components operating in billionths of seconds in a space the size of the wing of a fly, human beings built a machine that overcame all the conventional limits of mechanical time and space. Made essentially of the silicon in sand—one of the most common substances in earth—microchips find their value not in their substance but in their intellectual content: their design or software. (Gilder, 1989: 12)

Business applications of the microchip took place between 1969 and 1971 at Intel Corporation, which "developed all the key components of the personal computer—the working memory, the software memory, and the microprocessor CPU" (Gilder, 1989: 92). Thus was born the first stage of the ICT microelectronic revolution.

Another stage came into being in 1970 when scientists at Corning Glass Works announced that they had "created a medium [optical fiber] that could transport unprecedented amounts of information on laser beams for commercially viable distances" (Diebold, 1990: 132), thus providing the first revolutionary medium for what is now known as the information highway—the Internet. In parallel with this discovery, work was also proceeding on wireless and satellite connectivity (Bell Labs, 1999).

Coincident with these developments, another momentous event in the creation of the ICT revolution occurred in 1969. In order to withstand the possibility of a nuclear military attack, the U.S. Department of Defense's Advanced Research Projects Agency created a centerless network of supercomputers at major universities and research centers, such that if one computer was struck, the others could still function independently (Flower, 1997; Kahn, 1999). Called ARPNET, this electronic network was the forerunner of the Internet which was formally established in 1989. "Widespread development of LANS [local area networks], PCs [personal computers] and workstations in the 1980s, [as well as the growing use of e-mail], allowed the nascent Internet to flourish" (Leiner et al., 2000).

All of these developments, taking place at approximately the same time, together formed the foundation for a globalized world little constrained by time and space. And, given recent leading edge developments in transportation, communication, and information processing, there is every reason to expect this trajectory of innovation to continue. In fact, as a result of these innovations the distinction among these terms is becoming blurred. Consider, for example, the relatively new practice of telecommuting—the partial or complete substitution of telecommunications services for transportation to a conventional workplace. In reality, it is a creative and innovative blend of all three of these processes. According to a 2001 survey of the U.S. labor force, 28.8 million workers were transporting themselves both physically and electronically to work (International Telework Association, 2001); worldwide, the number of teleworkers is projected to rise to 137 million by 2003 (Edwards, 2001). Other creative blends of transportation, communication, and information processing include teleconferencing, teleshopping, virtual education, virtual surgery, and space satellites.

Although I have provided specific dates when these various technological innovations were recorded in history, in actual fact they took years to come to fruition. The years following World War II (particularly given the breakup of European colonial empires and the Cold War tensions between capitalism and communism) represented an era of economic reconstruction and scientific enterprise and application. However, as Table 66.1 indicates, a global ICT infrastructure is by no means in place for the vast majority of the world. Most people living in low and middle income countries (85 percent of the world's population) are on the other side of what has been termed the digital divide. Substantial proportions of people have yet even to acquire electricity or access a telephone. The World Resources Institute (2000) contends "as much as 80 percent of the world's population has never made a phone call." In addition, it estimates that there are more telephones in New York City than in all of rural Asia, and more Internet accounts in the city of London than in the continent of Africa. Although the Internet connected approximately 513 million people in 2001 (Nua Internet Surveys, 2001), that represents only 8.4 percent of the world's population. In other words, while many significant technological innovations have indeed been achieved since World War II, they have yet to be diffused globally.

TABLE 66.1: Transportation, Communication, and Information Indicators

Indicators	Income of Countries			
	Low	*Middle*	*High*	*World*
Population (millions, 1999)	2417	2667	891	5975
Percent population	40.5	44.6	15	100
Kilograms of oil equivalent consumption per capita (1997)	563	1368	5369	1692
Air passengers carried (millions, 1998)	54	292	1121	1467
Percent air passengers	3.7	19.9	76.4	100
Radios per 1000 people (1997)	157	359	1286	418
TV sets per 1000 people (1998)	76	257	661	247
Telephone main lines/1000 (1998)	23	109	567	146
Mobile telephones/1000 (1998)	2	31	265	55
Personal computers/1000 (1998)	3	23	311	71
Internet hosts/10,000 (Jan./00)	0.4	10	777	120

Source: Adapted from World Bank, 2001: 275, 293, 309, 311.

Note: According to the World Bank (2001: 271): "Economies are classified into three categories according to income.... The GNP per capita cutoff levels are as follows: low-income, $755 or less in 1999; middle-income, $756–9,265; and high income, $9,266 or more."

Organizational Forces

Transnational Corporations A transnational corporation (TNC) is "any enterprise that undertakes foreign direct investment, owns or controls income-gathering assets in more than one country, produces goods or services outside its country of origin, or engages in international production" (Biersteker, 1978: xii). Variously termed multinational corporations or multinational enterprises, transnational corporations are formal business organizations that have spatially dispersed operations in at least two countries. One of the most transnational of all major TNCs (see Table 66.2) is Nestlé, the Swiss food giant: 84 percent of its total assets, 99 percent of its sales, and 97 percent of its workforce are foreign-based (UNCTAD, 1999: 78).

Although TNCs were in existence prior to the twentieth century (colonial trading companies such as the East India Company, Hudson Bay Company, and the Virginia Company of London were precursors of the modern TNC), it is only since the 1960s that they have become a major force on the world scene (World Bank, 1987: 45). Table 66.3 corroborates this fact by listing the foreign direct investment (FDI) stock of corporations at various intervals during the twentieth century. In 1900, only European corporations were major transnational players, but by 1930 American TNCs had begun to make their presence felt. The year 1960 is pivotal because it marks the new global era in corporate transnationalization. For each of the decades from 1960 to the present, world FDI stock has more than tripled, whereas it only doubled during the entire first half of the twentieth century.

TABLE 66.2: Annual Revenues of Leading
Corporations and Gross National
Products of Selected Countries 1998–99
(billions of US$)

Nation/Corporation	GNP/Revenues
United States (1)	$7,921.3
Japan (2)	4,089.9
Germany (3)	2,122.7
France (4)	1,466.2
United Kingdom (5)	1,263.8
General Motors (1)	176.6
Denmark (23)	176.4
Wal-Mart Stores (2)	166.8
Exxon Mobil (3)	163.9
Ford Motor (4)	162.6
DaimlerChrysler (5)	160.0
Norway (25)	152.1
Greece (31)	122.9
South Africa (32)	119.0
Mitsui (6)	118.6
Mitsubishi (7)	117.8
Toyota Motor (8)	115.7
General Electric (9)	111.6
Iran (33)	109.6
Royal Dutch/Shell Group (11)	105.4
Israel (36)	95.2
Nippon Telegraph and Telephone (13)	93.6
International Business Machines (16)	87.5
BP Amoco (17)	83.4
Volkswagen (19)	80.1
Malaysia (39)	79.8
Hitachi (23)	71.9
Chile (42)	71.3
Matsushita (24)	65.6
Philip Morris (29)	61.8
Sony (30)	60.1
Boeing (32)	58.0
New Zealand (46)	55.8
Honda Motor (34)	54.8
Nissan Motor (36)	53.7
Czech Republic (48)	51.8
Toshiba (38)	51.6
Bank of America (39)	51.4
Nestlé (41)	50.0
Hungary (51)	45.6

Sources: For annual revenues of corporations, *Fortune*,
2000: F1–F2; for GNP, World Bank, 2000: 230–31.

Notes: Gross national product (GNP) measures the total
value of goods and services produced by citizens (resident
and nonresident) of a particular nation. The numbers in
parentheses refer to the overall rank of a nation or corporation in terms of either GNP or revenues.

The phenomenal increase in transnational
corporate activity during the last four decades
may be accounted for in large part by the technological innovations in transportation, communication, and information processing I have just
discussed. They permitted corporations to establish profitable worldwide operations and still
maintain effective and timely control. Not since
before World War II and the Great Depression
which preceded it had the corporate sector much
opportunity to demonstrate its economic clout. It
was in this mood that it eagerly embraced all
technological innovations that would give it
competitive advantage. Consequently the three-
fold increase in foreign direct investment between
1960 and 1971 by technologically enhanced,
transnationalizing corporations reveals another
manifestation of the new global age. Table 66.3
indicates that TNCs from just eleven countries
accounted for 82 percent of all foreign direct
investment in 1999. American TNCs comprised
almost one-quarter of the total foreign investment, and corporations in the Triad (United
States, European Union, and Japan) were responsible for nearly 80 percent of world FDI stock
(UNCTAD, 2000: 300). Clearly, TNCs mainly
operate out of and invest in the developed countries of the global economy.

The magnitude of foreign investment flow in
the world is illustrated by the fact that worldwide
sales of foreign affiliates in 1999 were $13.6 tril-
lion. This figure is almost twice as high as world
exports of goods and services valued at $6.9 tril-
lion (UNCTAD, 2000: 4). This means that global
networks of transnational corporations have
replaced in importance traditional import-export
practices of the past in terms of delivering goods
and services to markets worldwide. In 1999,
some 63,000 TNCs controlled 690,000 foreign
affiliates around the globe (UNCTAD, 2000: 9).
These two sets of facts underline the central and
growing importance of TNCs in structuring
international economic relations.

The rise of modern transnational corporations
and the power they hold are reflected in Table 66.2

TABLE 66.3: Foreign Direct Investment Stock by Country (billions of US$)

Country	1900[a]	1930[a]	1960[a]	1971	1980	1990	1999[b]
United States	0.5	14.7	31.8	82.8	220.2	430.5	1131.5
United Kingdom	12.1	18.2	13.2	23.1	80.4	229.2	664.1
Germany	4.8	1.1	0.6	7.0	43.1	151.6	420.9
Netherlands	1.1	2.3	1.7	3.5	42.1	109.0	306.4
France	5.2	3.5	2.2	9.2	23.6	110.1	298.0
Japan	neg[c]	neg	neg	4.3	19.6	201.4	292.8
Switzerland	neg	neg	neg	6.5	21.5	66.1	199.5
Canada	neg	1.3	3.0	5.7	23.8	84.8	178.3
Italy	neg	neg	neg	NA[d]	7.3	57.3	168.4
Belgium & Luxembourg	neg	neg	neg	NA	6.0	40.6	159.5
Sweden	neg	0.5	0.5	3.3	3.7	49.5	105.0
Others	neg	neg	neg	13.5	31.9	186.2	834.9
Total[e]	23.8	41.6	53.8	159.2	523.2	1716.4	4759.3

Sources: Data for 1970–71 adapted from Buckley, 1985: 200. Data for 1980–1999 from UNCTAD, 2000: 300–5.

Notes:
a. Includes foreign portfolio (individual) investment and foreign direct (TNC) investment.
b. Estimates.
c. Negligible.
d. Not available.
e. World total, excluding Comecon countries, except for 1998.

which compares the annual revenues of some of the world's largest global companies with the gross national products (the annual total value of goods and services produced by resident and nonresident citizens of a particular country) of selected countries. For example, General Motors, the leading corporation in revenues in 1999, had the twenty-third largest economy in the world ($176.7 billion), edging out Denmark at $176.4 billion, and surpassing by far the combined national output of New Zealand, Hungary, and the Czech Republic. These statistics would appear to give some truth to the old saying that "what's good for General Motors is good for the country" (Wilson, 1952). Of the one hundred largest economies in the world, nearly half (forty-nine) are transnational corporations (*Fortune,* 2000: F1–F2; World Bank, 2000: 230–31).

Of the five hundred largest corporations in the world, more than one-quarter (128) are in the financial sector (banks, insurance, and securities) (*Fortune,* 2000: F15–F21). A major reason for this is that most of the services and products financial firms provided can be traded electronically, and consequently these organizations have taken great advantage of the new global ICT infrastructure. As the editors of *Fortune* (2000: F15) state: "Money went global long before 'globalization' became a buzzword. That's why banks have the most entries on the [Global 500] list, as well as the highest revenues and profits." Other firms well represented in the Global 500 are those instrumental in the move toward globalization: modern transportation (aerospace, airlines, and courier services), communication (telecommunications, network communications, and mass media), and information processing (computers, computer services, and electronics). Of these corporations, those in the mass media have been extremely influential in promoting a global perspective in that they transmit content as well as providing infrastructure....

Environmental Movement The environmental movement is comprised of many grass-roots and international NGOs, as well as scientific organizations, all over the world. What makes it unique in establishing the case for globalization is the growing realization that our planet and everything on it comprise a very complex, interdependent, living whole. This means that when humans modify their environment in certain ways—such as urbanization, agriculture, forestry, mining and so forth—other consequences, both foreseen and unforeseen, are bound to follow. Approximately thirty years ago, the concept of biological diversity or biodiversity—"the total variability of life on Earth"—was coined, largely in an attempt to focus research on the extent to which human beings are contributing toward environmental degradation, and whether some of the evident trends are reversible (Heywood & Baste, 1995). It was also at this time that the concept of sustainable development originated (Fisher, 1993).

Why is biodiversity important? Aside from being important for the particular natural systems under siege and for providing needed resources such as food, water, shelter, and medicine for human survival, there is a more comprehensive set of reasons relating to globalization as a worldview.

The sheer diversity of life is of inestimable value. It provides a foundation for the continued existence of a healthy planet and our own well-being. Many biologists now believe that ecosystems rich in diversity gain greater resilience and are therefore able to recover more readily from stresses such as drought or human-induced degradation. When ecosystems are diverse, there is a range of pathways for primary production and ecological processes such as nutrient cycling, so that if one is damaged or destroyed, an alternative pathway may be used and the ecosystem can continue functioning at its normal level. If biological diversity is greatly diminished, the functioning of ecosystems is put at risk. (Biodiversity Unit, 1993)

Contributing to the concept of Earth as an interconnected organism, the American National Aeronautics and Space Administration (NASA), in conjunction with Japan and the European Space Agency, has launched a series of satellites that have established "an international Earth-observing capability" involving "a global-scale examination of the Earth to study the interaction

of all the environmental factors—air, water, land, biota—that make up the Earth system" (NASA, 1996). NASA reports that "scientists have been observing the Earth from space for more than 30 years, making measurements of the atmosphere, the oceans, the polar regions and land masses" (NASA, 1996).

Consequently, the environmental movement has been instrumental in altering people's perceptions of the world in which they live. Instead of focusing only on the particular geographical location in which they live, human beings are now coming to realize that their actions may have consequences for the world at large and for the quality of life they and subsequent generations will enjoy.

Individual Forces

Physical Migration As well as technological innovations and transnational organizations and alliances, individual people also comprise a globalizing force in that the human population, aided largely by improvements in transportation, has become increasingly mobile in a variety of ways.

Mass movements of people around the globe is a post-war phenomenon. During World War II, international travel was restricted, and during the Great Depression before it, the world economy rarely permitted it. With respect to emigration, the most permanent form of human migration, it is only since the war that vast numbers of people have emigrated, mostly from poor to rich countries. The major receiving countries have been the United States, Germany, Canada, and Australia (World Bank, 2000: 38), such that their populations have become increasingly diverse. The World Bank (2000: 37–40) reports that in recent years between two and three million people emigrate annually, with the consequence that now more than 130 million are living outside the countries in which they were born. To these figures must be added international refugees, and as conflicts and natural disasters have risen, so has forced migration. In 1975, the world's international refugees numbered 2.5 million, but just twenty years later, that total had multiplied almost ten times to 23 million (World Bank, 2000: 38).

Less permanent forms of migration include international guest workers (mostly to Europe and the United States), exchange students, and tourists. The demand for guest workers, mainly from North Africa, South Asia, and Mexico, is partly a function of the global economy, but increasingly it is tied to the demographic profile of the industrially developed countries. As a whole, the total fertility rate in the high income countries is below replacement level (1.7 births per woman), and the population is aging (World Bank, 2000: 243), which could lead to eventual labor shortages. To the extent that these trends continue, demand for foreign labor could increase substantially during the twenty-first century.

Study abroad and foreign exchange are also relatively recent occurrences in terms of the numbers involved and variety of programs offered. For example, at my own mid-sized university, there are currently 118 student and faculty exchange agreements with other universities in 27 different countries (UVic International, 2000). In 1998–99 in the United States, almost half a million foreign students enrolled in colleges and universities, three times more than in the mid-1970s (Open Doors, 1999a). In turn, nearly 114,000 American students studied abroad during 1997–98, a 15 percent increase over the previous year (Open Doors, 1999b). Worldwide, Switzerland has the greatest percentage (15.9 percent) of foreign students at the tertiary level, followed by Australia (12.6 percent), Austria (11.5 percent), and the United Kingdom (10.8 percent) (OECD, 2000c). Clearly, the option to complete at least part of a degree program in another country has become increasingly viable.

International tourism has also expanded enormously during the past fifty years. According to the World Tourism Organization (2000), "Between 1950 and 1999 the number of international arrivals has shown an evolution from a mere 25 million

international arrivals to the current 664 million, corresponding to an average annual growth rate of 7 percent." Not only has the number of tourists increased, so too have their destinations. In 1950, almost all of the 25 million tourists went to just fifteen countries; however, in 1999, more than seventy countries hosted at least one million international visitors. Air transport was the most common means of travel (43.7 percent), followed by road (41.4 percent), sea (7.8 percent), and rail (7.0 percent), and France, Spain, the United States, Italy, and China were the most popular destinations. (See Box 66.2 to find out who accompanies these international travelers.)

Not only is international tourism a significant force of globalization, it also contributes in a huge way to the global economy:

In 1998, international tourism and international fare receipts (receipts related to passenger transport of residents of other countries) accounted for roughly 8 percent of total export earnings on goods and services worldwide. Total international tourism receipts, including those generated by international fares, amounted to an estimated US\$532 billion, surpassing all other international trade categories. (World Tourism Organization, 2000)

In other words, international tourism generates more revenue than international trade in either automotive products (\$525 billion), chemicals (\$503 billion), food (\$443 billion), computer and office equipment (\$399 billion), fuels (\$344 billion), textiles and clothing (\$331 billion), or telecommunications equipment (\$283 billion). And considering that international tourism is on an annual growth trajectory of 7 percent, it will only become a more important contributor to the world gross domestic product.

Electronic Migration Not only are people physically traversing the globe in increasing numbers, they are also orbiting it electronically at a skyrocketing rate. The International Telecommunication Union (ITU, 2000) reports that international telephone calls in 1999 reached a new high of 100 billion minutes, climbing an average of 10 billion

---

BOX 66.2
MICROBES FLY THE GLOBAL SKIES

A report in my local newspaper (*Times Colonist,* 10/13/00: A1) warned of "a big year for flu" because so many people from all over the world attended the Olympics in Australia, which "had an especially prolonged flu season this year." A check at FluNet, maintained by the World Health Organization (WHO) **(http:// oms2.b3e.jussie.fr/FluNet/f_recent_activity. htm)** confirmed that there had been a "regional outbreak" of influenza in Australia between September 10 and October 14, 2000.

A search at the WHO site led me to the *WHO Report on Global Surveillance of Epidemic-prone Infectious Diseases* **(www. who.int/emc-documents/surveillance/ whocdscsrisr2001c.html)** which states: "In the modern world, with increased globalization, and rapid air travel, there is a need for international coordination and collaboration. Everyone has a stake in preventing epidemics." The *Report* focuses on nine infectious diseases (including influenza) all of which have "high epidemic potential."

More recently, with outbreaks of hoof and mouth and mad cow diseases in Europe, especially Britain, customs officers and disease control experts in all countries are taking special precautions to prevent the global spread of these highly infectious diseases via international travelers. These measures include prohibiting passengers from carrying any agricultural products with them, mandatory notification of any farm contact, requiring antibiotic foot baths for the shoe soles of all deplaning passengers, placing additional inspectors and dog teams at airports,and public education programs **(www.naturalhealthyliving.com/ article1007. html)**.

The Centers for Disease Control and Prevention headquartered in Atlanta in the United States maintain a comprehensive "Travelers' Health" Web site **(www.cdc.gov/ travel)**.

---

minutes per year since 1995. According to the ITU, "the world market for telecommunications (services and equipment) doubled between 1990 and 1999," and is being driven now by the burgeoning mobile cellular communications market. "At the end of 1999, there were more than 450 million subscribers around the world, up from just 11 million in 1990,…a compound annual growth rate of more than 50 percent per year" (ITU, 2000). The ITU estimates that mobile cellular subscribers will actually exceed conventional fixed-line users during this decade.

Also contributing to the rapid growth of electronic migration is the use of the Internet in general and for e-mail in particular. As I have already reported, Nua Internet Surveys (2001)

estimated that 513 million people had accessed the Internet at least once during the three months before August 2001, and this figure is projected to rise to more than 765 million by 2005 (CommerceNet, 2000). In January 2002, the Internet Software Consortium counted more than 147 million host sites on the Internet, almost 38 million more than it enumerated twelve months earlier. Quite clearly, all forms of electronic communication are growing exponentially.

COUNTERFORCES TO GLOBALIZATION

On at least three levels, huge proportions of humanity are put at risk by the forces of globalization, and consequently, there are growing signs that many people are actively resisting the global age. On the most general level, examine how the world is divided by region. In describing various regions of the world, certain terms come to be adopted, first by official agencies such as the United Nations and national governments, and then more generally by scholars, journalists, and others interested in making sense out of international relations and development. For example, in 1980 Willy Brandt coined the terms "North" and "South" in his *Report of the Independent Commission on International Development Issues* (Brandt Report, 1980). In this report is a map of the world with a bold line dividing it into two parts— North and South.… I have used the terms "developed" and "developing" countries which are categories created by the United Nations to classify all countries in the world. This classification scheme mirrors the North–South dichotomy. These terms are often used as convenient labels to divide the world into two camps—rich and poor. The fact that the global ICT revolution is presently taking place largely in the rich, developed North is generating backlash in the poor, developing South. Many fear that it could broaden the already enormous development gap between North and South (South Commission, 1990).

Paralleling and exacerbating this development gap is a cultural gap which has widened as a result of globalization. On the one side are predominant Western cultural perspectives and values, including Christianity and the global use of English. On the other side are non-Western cultural perspectives and values, including religions other than Christianity and non-European languages. Individual countries and cultural groups within the South are voicing concerns that the forces of globalization could threaten their ethnic, religious, and linguistic heritage and ways of living (Hedley, 2000: 595–97).

Finally, within the developed countries, there is what might be termed a growing class disparity. Studies of the distribution of income and wealth over the last three decades of the twentieth century reveal increasing inequality and polarity (Morris & Western, 1999; Keister & Moller, 2000). It is claimed that global restructuring has caused at least part of this disparity. Consequently, workers and citizens who are not part of the vanguard of the global era, although they are the overwhelming majority, are increasingly disaffected by the promises of globalization.

On each of these three levels of analysis— regional, cultural, and class—it is the larger of the two categories that is at risk from the forces of globalization. Thus, from the perspective of the South, or the non-Western, or the masses, globalization is not viewed with enthusiasm, and consequently active opposition to it could result. These constitute the counterforces to globalization.

…The global technological and organizational infrastructure has been established primarily by corporations, governments, and individuals in rich developed countries for their own benefit. As I mentioned, the overwhelming majority of the world's population has yet to be connected to this infrastructure.… To date, globalization is an exclusionary force, denying active participation to particular regions, cultures, and classes. In turn, this is causing backlash. For many nations, cultures, institutions, organizations and individuals in the world, modern globalism constitutes and elitist, Northern-based, Western-focused, technologically supported form of economic and cultural imperialism. In order to turn this vicious circle into a virtuous circle, the President of the World Bank (Wolfensohn, 1997: 6) has issued a *Challenge of Inclusion* "to reduce… disparities across and within countries, to bring more people into the economic mainstream, [and] to promote equitable access to the benefits of development regardless of nationality, race, or gender." Whether this challenge becomes reality remains to be seen; however, until it does, the world as a whole cannot truly be characterized as globalized.

CRITICAL THINKING QUESTIONS

1. Review the innovations in transportation and communication discussed in this article and how they have fuelled globalization. Do you feel that these two areas will continue to influence global change? Why or why not?
2. What are the positive aspects of transnational corporations (TNCs)? What are the negative aspects?
3. Discuss why biodiversity is important when discussing globalization. Do you feel that environmental movements are becoming more or less influential? Use examples to support your position.
4. Compare and contrast physical and electronic migration. Which do you feel will be a more important source of migration over the next 50 years? Why?

REFERENCES

Bell Labs. 1999. Wireless Milestones. [Online}. Available: **http://www.lucent.com/minds/trends/trends_v4n1/timeline.html**. Accessed 08/23/00.

Biersteker, T. J. 1978. *Distortion of development? Contending perspectives on the multinational corporation.* Cambridge, Mass.: MIT Press.

Biodiversity Unit, Commonwealth of Australia. 1993. Biodiversity Series, Paper No. 1. [Online]. Available: **http://kaos.erin.gov.au/life/general_info/op1.html**. Accessed 05/29/00.

Brandt Report. 1980. *North-South: A program for survival. Report of the Independent Commission on International Development Issues.* Cambridge, Mass.: MIT Press.

Britannica. 1999. Earth. [Online]. Available: **http://www.britannica.com/bcom/eb.arti.../0,5716,32267+1+31726,00.html**. Accessed 10/02/00.

Buckley, P. J. 1985. Testing theories of the multinational enterprise. In *The economic theory of the multinational enterprise,* eds. P. J. Buckley, and M. Casson. London: Macmillan.

CommerceNet. 2000. Worldwide Internet Population. [Online]. Available: **http://www.commerce.net/research/stats/wwstats.html**. Accessed 10/05/00.

Diebold, J. 1990. *The innovators: The discoveries, inventions, and breakthroughs of our time.* New York: Truman Talley Books/Plume.

Edwards, J. 2001. Government—help or hindrance to deployment of teleworking? [Online]. Available:

http://www.cefrio.qc.ca/allocutions/presentations/johnedwards.ppt. Accessed 01/18/02.

Einstein, A. 1936. Physics and reality. Journal of the Franklin Institute 221(3). Reprinted in *Ideas and opinions by Albert Einstein,.* ed. C. Seelig, 1954, 290–323. New York: Wings Books.

Fisher, J. 1993. *The road from Rio: Sustainable development and the non-governmental movement in the third world.* Wesport, Conn.: Praeger.

Flower, J. 1997. The future of the Internet: an overview. In *The future of the Internet,* eds. D. Bender et al., 10–7. San Diego, Calif.: Greenhaven.

Form, W. 1979. Comparative industrial sociology and the convergence hypothesis. *Annual Review of Sociology,* 5: 1–25.

Fortune. 2000. The Fortune Global 500. *Fortune,* 142(3): 227–F24.

Gilder, G. 1989. *Microcosm: The quantum revolution in economics and technology.* New York: Simon & Schuster.

Gilman, S. 1983. *The competitive dynamics of container shipping.* Aldershot, U.K.: Gower.

Hedley, R. A. 2000. Convergence in natural, social, and technical systems: A critique. *Current Science,* 79(5): 592–601.

Herman, A. 1983. *Shipping conferences.* Deventer, Neth.: Kluwer, Law and Taxation.

Heywood, V. H., and I. Baste. 1995. In *Global biodiversity assessment,* eds. V. H. Heywood, and R. T. Watson, 1–9. Cambridge: Cambridge University Press.

ICAO. 2001. Growth in air traffic projected to continue. [Online]. Available: **http://www.icao.org/icao/en/pio200106.htm**. Accessed 06/24/01.

International Telework Association. 2001. Telework American 2001. [Online]. Available: **http://www.telecommute.org/twa/twa2001/newsrelease.htm**. Accessed 01/18/02.

ITU. 2000. ITU Telecommunication Indicators Update. [Online]. Available: **http://www.itu.int/journal/200006/E/html/indicat.htm**. Accessed 10/10/00.

Kahn, R. E. 1999. Evolution of the Internet. In *World communication and information report 1999–2000,* 157–64. Paris: UNESCO.

Keister, L. A., and S. Moller. 2000. Wealth inequality in the United States. *Annual Review of Sociology,* 26: 63–81.

Leiner, B. M. et al. 2000. A brief history of the Internet. [Online]. Available: **http://www.isoc.org/internet/history/brief.shtml**. Accessed 05/11/02.

Morris, M., and B. Western. 1999. Inequality in earnings at the close of the twentieth century. *Annual Review of Sociology,* 25: 623–57.

Naisbitt, J. 1982. *Megatrends: Ten new directions transforming our lives.* New York: Warner.

NASA. 1996. The Earth Observing System: Understanding planet Earth. [Online]. Available: **http://pao.gsfc.nasa.gov/ gsfc/service/gallery/fact_sheets/earthsci/fs-96(06)-009.htm**. Accessed 09/27/00.

NASA. 2000. Sputnik and the dawn of the space age. [Online]. Available: **http://www.hq.nasa.gov/office/pao/ History/sputnik/**. Accessed 09/27/00.

Nua Internet Surveys. 2001. How many online? [Online]. Available: **http://www.nua.ie/surveys/how_many_online/ index.html**. Accessed 01/18/02.

OECD. 2000c. *OECD in figures*. Paris: Author.

Open Doors. 1999a. Fast facts. [Online]. Available: **http://www.opendoorsweb.org/Press/fast_facts.htm**. Accessed 10/05/00.

———. 1999b. 113,959 U.S. students have studied abroad this year. [Online]. Available: **http://www.opendoorsweb.org/Lead%20Stories/ stab1.htm**. Accessed 10/05/00.

Pearson, R., and J. Fossey. 1983. *World deep-sea container shipping: A geographical, economic and statistical analysis*. Aldershot, U.K.: Gower.

Phillips, P. 1996. *Jules Verne, around the world in eighty days*. [Online]. Available: **http://www.people.virginia.edu/ ~mtp0f/flips/review3.html**. Accessed 09/26/00.

Serling, R. J. 1982. *The jet age*. Alexandria, Va.: Time-Life.

South Commission. 1990. *The Challenge to the South: The report of the South Commission*. New York: Oxford University Press.

UNCTAD. 1999. *World investment report 1999*. New York: United Nations Conference on Trade and Development.

———. 2000. *World investment report 2000*. New York: United Nations Conference on Trade and Development.

UVic International. 2000. [Online]. Available: **http://www.uvic.ca/international.html**. Accessed 09/26/00.

Wilson, C. E. 1952. Statement to the Senate Armed Forces Committee. In *Familiar quotations,* ed., John Bartlett (1980), 817. Boston: Little, Brown.

Wolfensohn, J. D. 1997. *The challenge of inclusion*. Address to the board of governors of the World Bank Group, Hong Kong, China.

World Bank. 1987. *World development report 1987*. New York: Oxford University Press.

———. 2000. *World development report 1999/2000*. Oxford: Oxford University Press.

———. 2001. *World development report 2000/2001*. Oxford: Oxford University Press.

World Resources Institute. 2000. WRI conference explores new businesses to transform global digital divide into dividends. [Online]. Available: **http://www.igc.org/ wri/press/dd_transform.html**. Accessed 10/17/00.

World Tourism Organization. 2000. Tourism highlights 2000. [Online]. Available: **http://www.world-tourism.org/ esta/monograf/highligh/HL_MK.htm.** Accessed 10/05/00.

Woytinsky, W. S., and E. S. Woytinski. 1955. *World commerce and governments: Trends and outlook*. New York: Twentieth Century Fund.

Social Change,
Media,
and Modernity

CLASSIC

CONTEMPORARY

CROSS-CULTURAL

67

The Price of Modernization: The Case of Brazil's Kaiapo Indians

Marlise Simons

Among the billions of poor people throughout the developing world, few have a chance for a better life. But the Kaiapo, people who live deep in Brazil's rain forest, have found a way to improve their lives. Has affluence been the blessing that the Kaiapo imagined it would be? To some, the modernization of the Kaiapo amounts to little more than the systematic destruction of their traditional way of life.

It is getting dark when Chief Kanhonk sits down in the yard outside his home, ready for a long evening of conversation. Night birds are calling from the bush that sparkles with fireflies. Whooping frogs make a racket by the river. No one seems worried by the squadron of bats sweeping low overhead.

It is that important moment of the day when Indians of the Amazon, who use no written language, meet to talk, pass on information, and tell stories. The night is when they recall ancestral customs, interpret dreams, and comment on changes in nature and other events of the day. But from a nearby home come the sounds of a powerful rival: A television set is screeching cartoons at a group of children. I understand now why, that morning, by way of saying hello, these naked children of the rain forest had shouted things like "He-Man" and "Flintstones."

Three years ago, when money from the sale of gold nuggets and mahogany trees was pouring into Gorotire, Chief Kanhonk agreed to bring in television, or the "big ghost," as it is called here. A shiny satellite dish now stands on the earthen plaza like an alien sculpture, signaling that Gorotire—a small settlement of some 800 people on the Fresco River, a tributary of the Amazon—has become one of the wealthiest Indian villages in Brazil.

Yet Chief Kanhonk appears to regret his decision. "I have been saying that people must buy useful things like knives or fishing hooks," he says darkly. "Television does not fill the stomach. It only shows our children and grandchildren white people's things."

The "big ghost" is just one of the changes that have been sweeping over Gorotire, but it seems to be worrying the elders the most. Some believe it is powerful enough to rob them of their culture. Bebtopup, the oldest medicine man in the village, explains his misgivings: "The night is the time the old people teach the young people. Television has stolen the night."

Source: "The Amazon's Savvy Indians," by Marlise Simons, *The New York Times Magazine,* February 26, 1989, pp. 36–37, 48–52. Copyright © 1989 by The New York Times Company. Reprinted with permission.

When I discuss this with Eduardo Viveiros, a Brazilian anthropologist who works with a more isolated Amazonian tribe, he seems less worried. "At least they quickly understood the consequences of watching television," he says. "Many people never discover. Now Gorotire can make a choice."

It was the issue of choice that first drew me to the Kaiapo Indians of the lower Amazon Basin. They seemed to be challenging the widely held notion that forest Indians are defenseless in face of the pressures of the competitive and predatory Western world around them. Unlike most of Brazil's 230,000 Indians, they go out into the white world to defend their interests, and it is no longer unusual to see Kaiapo men—in their stunning body paint and feathered headdresses—showing up in Congress in Brasilia, the nation's capital, or lobbying by doing a war dance outside a government office. They have even bought Western gadgets to record and film their festivals.

Once the masters of immense stretches of forest and savannas, the Kaiapo were for hundreds of years among the most skillful farmers and hunters and fiercest warriors of central Brazil. They terrified other tribes with their raids. From the seventeenth to the nineteenth centuries, they not only resisted the slaving raids of the Portuguese invaders but they also attacked white traders and gold prospectors with such a vengeance that royal orders came from Portugal to destroy the Kaiapo. The white man's wrath and his diseases killed many, yet there are still close to 3,600 Kaiapo in more than a dozen different villages near the Xingu River. They have quarreled and regrouped, but their lands, several vast reservations, are more secure than those of many other tribes.

After many years of isolation in the forest, the Kaiapo now have to deal with the growing encroachments of white society. "They are going through a great transition," says Darrell Posey, an American anthropologist who has worked in Gorotire for more than a decade. "Their survival is a miracle in itself. But I worry whether they can go on making the changes on their own terms."

Colombia, Ecuador, Peru, and Venezuela—four of nine nations in the Amazon Basin, which harbors some 800,000 Indians—each have large numbers of tropical-forest Indians. But nowhere are pressures on Indian land as great as they are in Brazil. As the Amazon is opened up, developers bring in highways, settlers, cattle ranchers, mines, and hydroelectric dams. In Brazil alone, more than ninety tribes have disappeared since the beginning of this century.

The clearing of large areas of the rain forest and the fate of the Indians are also rapidly becoming an issue of international concern. Interest in the region has risen as ecological concerns, such as ozone depletion, the greenhouse effect, and other changes in the global environment become political issues. More attention is paid to scientists who are alarmed at the destruction of the rain forest—a vital flywheel in the world's climate and the nursery of at least half of the world's plant and animal species.

This has also prompted an increasing interest in the highly structured world of the forest Indians and their ancient and intricate knowledge of nature that permits them to survive in the tropical jungle without destroying it. (The Hall of South American Peoples, which includes a life-size model of a Kaiapo warrior, recently opened at the Museum of Natural History in New York City.)

As Indians find greater support among environmentalists, they also get more organized in their fight to protect their habitat. The Kaiapo held their first international congress last week in Altamira, in central Brazil, protesting government plans to build several massive dams that would flood Indian land.

In Brazil, Indian tribes occupy 10 percent of the nation's territory, although much of their land has not been demarcated. Brazil's past military regimes elevated Indian affairs to a national-security issue, because many tribes live in large areas of border land. It is official policy to integrate Indians into the larger society, and the National Indian Foundation, with its 4900 employees, is in charge of implementing this.

In my eighteen years in Latin America, I have heard many politicians and anthropologists discuss what is usually called "the Indian problem," what to "do" about cultures that have changed little in thousands of years. One school of thought holds that the remote tribes should be kept isolated and protected until they can slowly make their own choices. Another school accepts that the Indian world is on the wane, and talks about "guiding" the Indians toward inevitable change—a process that should take several generations.

But some anthropologists and politicians, including the Brazilian government, believe in still more rapid integration. When Romeo Jucá was head of the Indian Foundation, he said that it was only right for Indians to exploit their wealth, even if it meant acculturation. "We have to be careful how fast we go," he said, "but being Indian does not mean you have to be poor."

Gerardo Reichel-Dolmatoff is one of Latin America's most respected anthropologists. He insists that the Indians are their own best guides into Western society. An Austrian-born Colombian, Reichel-Dolmatoff has worked in Colombia's forests, at the Amazon's headwaters, for almost fifty years. "We cannot choose for them," he insists. "And we cannot put them into reserves, ghettos, ashokas. They are not museum exhibits.... If Indians choose the negative aspects of our civilization, we cannot control that. If there is one basic truth in anthropology, it is that cultures change. Static cultures do not exist."

The Indians themselves are pleading for more protection and respect for their cultures. Conrad Gorinsky, son of a Guyana Indian mother and himself a chemist in London, recently said: "We don't want the Indians to change because we have them comfortably in the back of our mind like a kind of Shangri-La, something we can turn to even if we work ourselves to death in New York. But we are hounding and maligning them instead of recognizing them as the guardians of the forests, of the world's genetic banks, of our germ plasma and lifelines."

The aboriginal peoples we call Indians are as different from one another as, say, Europeans are. Even the most isolated groups remain separate fiefdoms with widely varying experiences, beliefs, and histories. The degree of contact they have with the outside world is just as varied.

I first met Kaiapo tribesmen three years ago in Belém, a large city at the mouth of the Amazon. I saw them again in Brasilia, the capital. In both places, they demonstrated their political skills and capacity to mobilize, showing up in large numbers to protest measures by the government. They seemed particularly adept at commanding the attention of the press. Their body paint, feathers, and other paraphernalia made them appear warlike, exotic, and photogenic.

Back in Gorotire, as it turns out, they are more "ordinary." Wearing feathers and beads, explains Kubei, a chief's son, is for special occasions. "It's our suit and tie." Besides the satellite dish, the Kaiapo also have their own small airplane. Their new wealth has also given them the luxury of hiring non-Indians to help plant new fields. But they remain ready to attack white intruders; some of the adult men have markings on their chests that record the number of outsiders they have killed.

Two roads fan out from the center of Gorotire. A new sand track leads east on a five-hour drive to the town of Redenção. The other road goes south and, in a sense, it leads into the past. Dipping into the forest, it becomes a path that meanders through open patches where the Kaiapo women grow corn, sweet potatoes, bananas, manioc. On the plain ahead, it joins an ancient trail system that once reached for hundreds of miles into northern and western Brazil.

One morning, Beptopup (medicine man, shaman, connoisseur of nature), the anthropologist Darrell Posey (who speaks the Kaiapo language), and I wander into the bush. Beptopup walks past the plants the way you go down a street where you know everyone. Stopping, nodding, his face lighting up with happy recognition, he sometimes goes into a song—a soft, high-pitch chant for a particular plant.

He picks leaves, each one familiar, each one useful. One serves to remove body hair. Another, he says, can prevent pregnancy. The underside of one leaf is so rough it is used to sandpaper wood and file fingernails. Beptopup collects his plants in the morning, he says, because "that is when they have the most strength."

Stopping at a shrub, we look at the large circle around its stem, where nothing grows. "This and other plants have been sent to a laboratory for analysis," says Posey. "We think this one has a natural weedkiller."

Beptopup holds up a branch of what he calls the "eye of the jaguar." "This was our flashlight," he says, showing how to set it afire and swing it gently so its strong glow will light one's path.

One afternoon, when the heat has crept into everything, the women and children come back from the fields to their village. They stop and sit in a creek to escape the swirling gnats and buzzing bees. Others sit outside their homes, going about their age-old business. One woman plucks the radiant feathers of a dead macaw. Another removes her eyebrows and eyelashes, because the Kaiapo women think they are ugly. (A nurse once told me that this custom might have a hygienic origin—to ward off parasites, for instance.) Kaiapo women also deepen their foreheads by shaving the top of their head in a triangle that reaches the crown—a fearsome sight to the unaccustomed eye.

I envy a mother who is clearly enjoying herself fingerpainting her three children. She draws black designs with genipap juice. On the face and the feet she puts red dye from the "urucu," or annatto, plant; Indians say it keeps away chiggers and ticks.

Change has come to Gorotire along the other road, the one leading east to Redenção. Recent Kaiapo history is full of "firsts," but a notable turning point came when prospectors struck gold on Gorotire land in 1980. The Kaiapo raided the camp, twenty miles from the village, but failed to drive away the trespassers. Then they made a deal.

Last fall, when I was visiting Gorotire, about 2,000 gold diggers were stripping the land to the

bone farther upstream, and the River Fresco passed the village the color of mud, its water contaminated with oil and mercury. I heard no one complain about that. Gorotire gets 7 percent of the mine's profits—several pounds of gold a week.

In 1984, a lumber company completed the first road. It signed a contract with the Indian Foundation for Gorotire's mahogany (the Indians are wards of the Brazilian government). Most of the mahogany is gone now, and the government agency split the profits with the Kaiapo. Gorotire chose to spend its gold and timber profits on new water and electricity lines and rows of brick houses. Only about half of the inhabitants now live in traditional palm-frond huts.

The young Kaiapo who earn a salary as supervisors at the gold camp have bought their own gas stoves, radios, sofas, and mattresses. For the community, the four tribal chiefs ordered several boats, trucks, and a small plane that ferries people and goods among nearby Kaiapo villages.

One evening, a truck arriving from Redenção—bringing rice, sugar, bottled gas, oil for the generator—is another reminder of how fast Gorotire is adapting to a Western economy. From being a largely self-sufficient community of hunters and farmers, it is now increasingly dependent on outside goods. In Gorotire, it is clearly money, no longer disease or violence, that has become the greatest catalyst for change. Money has given the Kaiapo the means and the confidence to travel and lobby for their rights. At the same time, it is making them more vulnerable.

I have seen other villages where Indians have received large sums of money—for the passage of a railroad or a powerline, or from a mining company. Such money is usually released in installments, through banks, but its arrival has put new strains on the role of the chiefs. Money and goods have introduced a new, materialistic expression of power in societies that have been egalitarian. Among most Indians, a man's prestige has always depended not on what he acquires but on what he gives away.

In Gorotire, some of the young men complain that the chiefs are not distributing community money and goods equally, that the chiefs' relatives and favorites are getting a bigger share and more privileges.

Darrell Posey, the anthropologist, believes the greatest political change came with the road. With it, he says, "the Kaiapo chiefs lost control of which people and what goods would come in." Previously, the chiefs had been the sole distributors. They had also played the vital roles of keeping the peace and leading the ceremonies. Now, the chiefs hardly know the liturgy of the ceremonies; their main task seems to be to deal with the outside world.

The transition is also changing the role of the medicine man. Bebtopup, for example, has an arsenal of remedies for the common ailments—fevers, diarrheas, snake bites, wounds. But he and his colleagues have lost prestige because they do not know how to deal with the diseases brought to Gorotire by white men, such as the pneumonia that strikes the children and the malaria spreading from the gold miners' camp.

Anthropologists sometimes say that when outsiders visit the Indian world, they often focus on themes central not to Indians but to themselves. This might explain why I was so bothered by the garbage, the flotsam of Western civilization.

Gorotire's setting is Arcadian. It lies on a bluff overlooking the River Fresco, with views of the forests across and the mountains behind. Spring rains bring waterfalls and blossoms. But these days the village is awash with rusting cans, plastic wrappers, tapes sprung from their cassettes, discarded mattresses, and clothes. New domestic animals such as dogs, pigs, and ducks have left a carpet of droppings. And giant rats, which suddenly appeared some years ago, seem to be everywhere; some have bitten small children.

"Indians have never had garbage that was not biodegradable," says Sandra Machado, a Brazilian researching Kaiapo farming techniques here. "No one wants to take care of it."

It is a mild moonlit evening, and in the men's house many Kaiapo are watching soccer on television. The bank of the river is a quieter place to talk. "If you look beyond the garbage and the stone houses, this is still a strong and coherent indigenous culture," says Darrell Posey, speaking of the mixed feelings he has about a decade of developments in Gorotire. "Despite everything, the language is alive, the festivals and initiation rights are observed."

Posey says that the Kaiapo in Gorotire and in other villages continue with their age-old natural farming techniques, using plants to fix nitrogen in the soil, chunks of termite nests instead of chemical fertilizers, plant infusions to kill pests, the nests of ferocious ants to protect fruit trees from other ant predators.

Biologists often complain that there have been many studies of exotic rituals, paraphernalia, and kinships of Indians, but that Western science has paid scant attention to the Indians' use of animals and plants.

Like others working in the Amazon region, Posey worries about the gap between the old and the young. "The old chiefs are turning over decisions to the young because they can drive a truck or operate a video machine or go to the bank," he says. "But the young people don't see the relevance of learning the tribal knowledge and it's being lost."

"You can afford to lose one generation," he adds, "because grandparents do the teaching of their grandchildren. But you cannot afford to lose two generations."

Gorotire has a small Government school, designed to help Indians integrate into the national society. The teacher, who speaks only Portuguese, has started organizing annual Independence Day parades. On the blackboard is a list of patriotic holidays, including Independence Day and the Day of the Soldier. I ask the children later what a soldier is. "Something of white people," one of them says.

Chief Poropot agrees that everyone must learn Portuguese. "The language of the Kaiapo is very ancient and it will never end," he says. "But the women and the children need to learn Portuguese to defend themselves."

Defend themselves? "If they go to shop in Redenção, they have to talk," he says. "If they get sick, they cannot tell the doctor what they have."

Thirty miles from Gorotire, in the village of Aukre, another Kaiapo tribe is choosing a different strategy for change. Its best-known member is Paiakan, thirty-seven years old, the son of Chief Tikiri.

Calm and articulate, Paiakan has been named to "keep an eye on the whites" in the state capital of Belém. He acts as a kind of roving ambassador for the Kaiapo, even though each village is autonomous. When Kaiapo interests are threatened, he sends out warnings to the communities.

Paiakan's contacts with the outside world and the many pitfalls it holds for Indians have made him more conservative, he says, more so than in the early days, in the 1970s, when he first left home to work on the Trans-Amazonian Highway. As his father's main adviser, he has insisted that Aukre remain a traditional village.

It is built in the age-old circle of mud-and-thatch huts. There is no television, running water, pigs, or piles of garbage. Paiakan and his father have also banned logging and gold digging. This appears to have saved Aukre from the consumerism—and widespread influenza and malaria—of Gorotire.

"The lumber men have come to us with their bags of money," he says. "And we know we have a lot of gold. But we do not want to bring a lot of money in. The Indian still does not know the value of white man's objects or how to treat them." Paiakan cites clothing as an example. "The Indian wears something until it is stiff with dirt, then he throws it out."

But people now want things from the "world of the whites," he continues. "Pressure from the white society is so strong, there is no wall that can stop it." It is the task of the chief to measure the change, provide explanations, he says. "If someone wants to get a radio or a tape recorder, the chiefs cannot stop it."

In Aukre, where two aging chiefs are still in charge of buying goods for the community, they say that they will not buy gadgets. "We explain

we cannot buy this thing for you because we do not have the batteries you need and we cannot repair it," Paiakan says.

Of late, Paiakan has been invited abroad to campaign for the protection of the rain forest. He knows the problem only too well. Ranchers have moved almost to the reservation's doorstep, felled trees, and set massive forest fires. Because of deforestation, there have been unusual changes in the water level of the Fresco River.

"Our people are getting very disoriented," says Paiakan. "It would be as if people from another planet came to your cities and started to tear down your houses. The forest is our home." With all the destruction going on, he continues, "the breath of life is drifting up and away from us."

At the age of seventy-eight and retired from teaching at the University of California at Los Angeles, the anthropologist Gerardo Reichel-Dolmatoff lives in Bogotá, Colombia, and is still writing. After studying changes in the Amazon for five decades, he is not optimistic about the prospects for the Indians.

"In Colombia, I don't know of a single case where an aboriginal culture has found a strong adaptive mechanism," he says. "Physical survival is possible. But I have not seen the ancient values replaced by a workable value system. I wish I could be more positive. But in fifty years I have seen too many traditions being lost, too many tribes disappear.

"For 500 years we have witnessed the destruction of the Indians. Now we are witnessing the destruction of the habitat. I suggest more field work, and immediate field work, because soon it will be too late."

At a conference on ethnobiology last fall, Reichel-Dolmatoff urged scientists to insist on spreading the message that Western science has much to learn from Indians, from their well-adapted lives and deeply felt beliefs, their view that whatever man subtracts he must restore by other means.

What suggestions has he made to Indians?

"Indians have to stay in touch with their language—that is absolutely essential," he says. "It embodies their thought patterns, their values, their philosophy." Moreover, he says, talented young Indians should be given a modern academic education, but also the chance to keep in touch with their people. "They come from cultures based on extraordinary realism and imagery. They should not be forced to enter at the lowest level of our society."

One night, I ask the chiefs in Gorotire: What happens if the gold runs out? After all, most of the mahogany is already gone. Young tribesmen have wanted to invest some of the income, and the chiefs have accepted the idea. Gorotire has bought a home in Belém for Kaiapo who travel there, as well as three houses in Redenção. There is talk of buying a farm, a curious thought, perhaps, for a community that lives on 8 million acres of land. But the Kaiapo, so they say, want it so that white farmers can grow rice for them.

And there is talk of planting new mahogany trees. Soon the conversation turns to a bird that a tribesman explains is very important. It is the bird, he says, that spreads the mahogany seeds.

CRITICAL THINKING QUESTIONS

1. What have been the short-term consequences of the Kaiapo's new wealth? What are the Kaiapo's long-term prospects?
2. What arguments can be made for the continued effort by the Kaiapo to economically develop their resources? What arguments can be made against doing so?
3. In what ways are other countries involved in the changes taking place in the Amazon Basin?

PHOTO CREDITS